W9-AZR-776

History Alive! The UNITED STATES

Teachers' Curriculum Institute

Bert Bower   Jim Lobdell

Managing Editor: Jeri Hayes
Project Editor: Joyce Bartky
Developmental Editor: John Bergez
Editorial Assistant: Anna Embree
Art Director: Tim Stephenson
Production Coordinator: Lynn Sanchez
Graphic Designer: Christy Uyeno
Illustrator: Richard Boles
Photo Editor: Margee Robinson
Operations Manager: Ellen Mapstone

This book is published by Teachers' Curriculum Institute.

Teachers' Curriculum Institute
PO Box 50996
1170 East Meadow Drive
Palo Alto, CA 94303

Customer Service: (800) 497-6138
www.historyalive.com

Copyright © 2002 by Teachers' Curriculum Institute.

Permission is granted to reproduce student materials only. No other parts of this publication may be reproduced without written permission from the publisher. Printed in the United States of America.

ISBN 1-58371-187-2

4 5 6 7 8 9 10   05 04 03

Diane Hart is a writer and consultant specializing in history and social studies. She is the author of several social studies textbooks as well as resources for teachers, including *Authentic Assessment: A Handbook for Educators*. She has written texts for special needs and limited English students that are used not only in schools, but also in prisons, adult literacy, and citizenship classes. Recently she has been developing materials for video, multimedia, and the Internet.

A former teacher and Woodrow Wilson Fellow, with a master's degree in history from Stanford University, Diane remains deeply involved in social studies education. She is an active participant in the National and California Councils for the Social Studies.

In both her professional and volunteer activities, Diane has served as a bridge between social studies teachers and students on the one hand, and textbook publishers and media developers on the other. Her goal is always to help the latter better meet the needs and goals of the former.

Program Directors
Bert Bower
Jim Lobdell

Author
Diane Hart

Contributing Writers
Laura Alavosus
Christine Freeman
Tedd Levy

Senior Curriculum Developers
Joyce Bartky
Vern Cleary
Terry Coburn
Steve Seely
Kelly Shafsky

Contributing Curriculum Developers
Melissa Aubuchon, City of Ladue School District, St. Louis, Missouri
Connie Davidson, San Leandro Unified School District, San Leandro, California
Nicolle Hutchinson, Broward County Public Schools, Miramar, Florida
Julie Peters, Woodstock Community Union School District #200, Woodstock, Illinois
Debra Schneider, Tracy Unified School District, Tracy, California

Consultants
Jeanne Barry
Readability Consultant
Jeanne Barry and Associates, Inc.
Incline Village, Nevada
Kate Kinsella, Ed.D
Reading and TESOL Specialist
Department of Secondary Education
College of Education
San Francisco State University
San Francisco, California
David Knipfer
Mapping Specialists, Ltd.
Madison, Wisconsin
Chuck Taft
Internet Content Consultant
University School of Milwaukee
Milwaukee, Wisconsin

Scholars
Maureen Booth
Constitutional Law Consultant
Maynard, Massachusetts
Stanley J. Underdal, Ph.D
Scholar of Native American Studies, Ethnicity, and Race in U.S. History and History of the West
San Jose State University
San Jose, California

"... government of the people, by the people, for the people, shall not perish from the earth."

Abraham Lincoln
Gettysburg Address, November 19, 1863

Contents

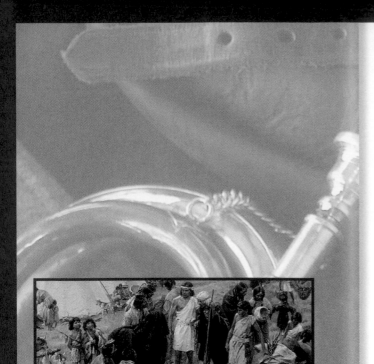

From the Art Collection of The Abell-Hanger Foundation of Midland, Texas. Exhibited at The Petroleum Museum, Midland, Texas

The Granger Collection, New York

The Granger Collection, New York

The Granger Collection, New York

The Granger Collection, New York

The Granger Collection, New York

The Granger Collection, New York

The Granger Collection, New York

The Granger Collection, New York

The Granger Collection, New York

The Granger Collection, New York

The Granger Collection, New York

From the Art Collection of The Abell-Hanger Foundation of Midland, Texas. Exhibited at The Petroleum Museum, Midland, Texas

What materials were used to make these houses?

What materials were used to make these people's clothes?

What are these people trading?

The Native Americans

1.1 Introduction

As a cold winter wind howls outside, the children huddle under thick fur blankets. They listen to their grandmother's soothing voice. "In the beginning there was the Great Spirit," Grandmother begins, "who ruled over a world of sky and water." Then the Great Spirit, says Grandmother, created land, plants, and animals. Finally, from living wood, the Great Spirit carved people for the new world.

These Abenaki children of New England are learning how their people began. Most groups have beliefs about where they came from. You may have heard stories about how your own relatives first arrived in America. But do you know where your ancestors were living 10,000 years ago?

Only if you are Native American did you have relatives in America that long ago. Europeans and other groups did not start arriving until a little more than 500 years ago. For thousands of years, these First People had the American continents to themselves. In this chapter, you will learn about these resourceful people and the creative ways they developed to live in tune with the natural world.

Even today, scientists are trying to find out more about the first Americans. These early people left few written records to tell us what their lives were like, so researchers study other items they left behind. What has survived? Not much. A few animal and human bones, some stone and metal tools, bits of pottery. Like detectives, scientists sift through these clues, trying to imagine how these people lived and how their lives changed over time. When scientists find a new object, they try to figure out whether it supports their current ideas or suggests new ones.

In your lifetime, scientists will probably learn much more about the first Americans and may revise many of their conclusions. This chapter tells these people's stories as we know them today.

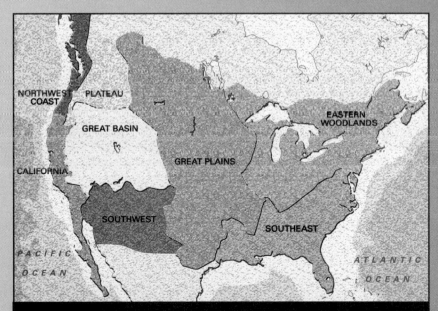

Graphic Organizer: Map of Cultural Regions
You will use this map to learn about the adaptations made by Native Americans living in eight cultural regions.

migrate: To move from one place and establish a home in a new place. A move of a large number of people is called a *migration,* and the people who move are called *migrants.* Some animals also migrate, usually with the seasons.

Scientists believe that the first Americans migrated from Siberia to Alaska across a land bridge called Beringia. These people were following mammoths and other prey that moved east in search of grazing land.

1.2 Migration Routes of the First Americans

The first Americans probably migrated on foot from Siberia, in Asia, to present-day Alaska. Today, Alaska and Asia are separated by a strip of ocean called the Bering Strait. But there was a time when a land bridge connected them.

Across a Land Bridge   About 30,000 years ago, the most recent Ice Age began. As temperatures fell, much of the earth was covered by glaciers, sheets of ice up to a mile thick. With water locked up in the glaciers, the level of the oceans dropped 200 feet. This exposed a wide bridge of land between Asia and North America that scientists call Beringia.

In the summer, Beringia's grasslands attracted large Asian mammals, such as mammoths, long-haired cousins of the elephant. Over thousands of years, the animals slowly spread eastward. Generations of Siberian hunter families followed. Armed with only stone-tipped spears, they killed these huge, powerful animals for food. Eventually, perhaps between 10,000 and 20,000 years ago, some of them reached America. Other migrants may have traveled along the coast of Beringia by boat to catch fish, seals, and other marine mammals.

Migrating East and South   Once in America, hunters followed the animals south, where spring brought fresh grasses. Then, about 10,000 years ago, the earth warmed up again. As the glaciers melted and the oceans rose, the land bridge disappeared. Mammoths and other traditional prey began to die off, perhaps from disease, overhunting, or the change in the climate.

Native Americans now had to find new sources of food and new materials for clothing and shelter. So they became hunter-gatherers, catching smaller animals, fishing more, and collecting edible plants and seeds. Over thousands of years, they spread across the two American continents, from the Pacific to the Atlantic, and from Alaska all the way to the tip of South America.

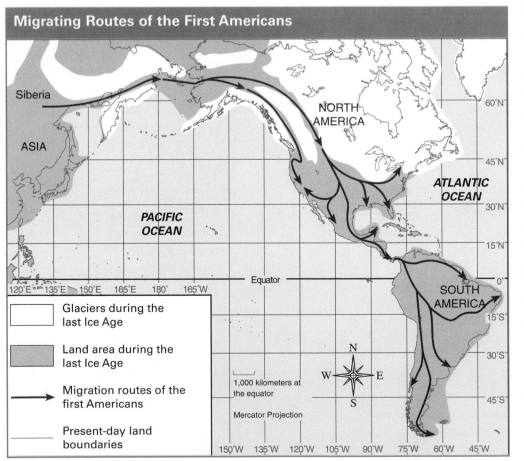

Migrating Routes of the First Americans

Siberia
ASIA
PACIFIC OCEAN
NORTH AMERICA
ATLANTIC OCEAN
SOUTH AMERICA
Equator

60°N
45°N
30°N
15°N
0°
15°S
30°S
45°S

120°E 135°E 150°E 165°E 180° 165°W
150°W 135°W 120°W 105°W 90°W 75°W 60°W 45°W

1,000 kilometers at the equator
Mercator Projection

N W E S

- Glaciers during the last Ice Age
- Land area during the last Ice Age
- Migration routes of the first Americans
- Present-day land boundaries

1.3 Native Americans Adapt to the Environment

The tents in this Inuit camp in Northern Alaska were made from seal and caribou skins. The Inuit used the inflated seal skins, hanging from the poles, as floats.

Native Americans lived in a variety of places, from snowy forests to dry deserts and vast grasslands. Each of these kinds of places is an **environment**. An environment includes everything that surrounds us—land, water, animals, and plants. Each environment also has a climate, or long-term weather pattern. Groups of Native Americans survived by adapting, or changing, their style of living to suit each environment, its climate, and its **natural resources**.

Using Natural Resources   Native Americans learned to use the natural resources in their environments for food, clothing, and shelter. In the frigid regions of the far north, early Americans survived by hunting caribou in the summer and sea mammals in the winter. They fashioned warm, hooded clothing from animal skins. To avoid being blinded by the glare of the sun shining on snow, they made goggles out of bone with slits to see through.

The people of the north lived most of the year in houses made from driftwood and animal skins. In winter, hunters built temporary shelters called *iglus* out of blocks of snow.

In warmer climates, early Americans gathered wild plants. Then, about 7,000 years ago, they learned to raise crops such as squash, chili peppers, beans, and corn. Growing their own food enabled them to settle in one place instead of following animals or searching for edible plants in the wild. These early farmers built the first villages and towns in America.

Native American Cultural Regions   Over generations, groups of Native Americans developed their own **cultures,** or ways of life. Many became part of larger groupings that were loosely organized under common leaders.

Groups living in the same type of environment often adapted in similar ways. Forest dwellers often lived in houses covered with tree bark, while many desert peoples made shelters out of branches covered with brush.

Using such artifacts (items made by people), historians have grouped Native American peoples into **cultural regions**. A cultural region is made up of people who share a similar language and way of life.

By the 1400s, between one and two million Native Americans lived in ten major cultural regions north of Mexico. Later in this chapter, you will take a close-up look at eight of these regions. They include the Northwest Coast, California, the Great Basin, the Plateau, the Southwest, the Great Plains, the Eastern Woodlands, and the Southeast.

environment: all of the physical surroundings in a place, including land, water, animals, plants, and climate

natural resources: useful materials found in nature, including water, vegetation, animals, and minerals

culture: a people's way of life, including beliefs, customs, food, dwellings, and clothing

cultural region: an area in which a group of people share a similar culture and language

Native American Cultural Regions

Native American Clothing

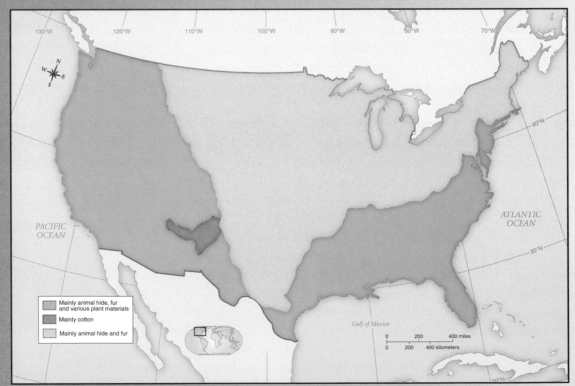

Mainly animal hide, fur and various plant materials

Mainly cotton

Mainly animal hide and fur

Native American Housing

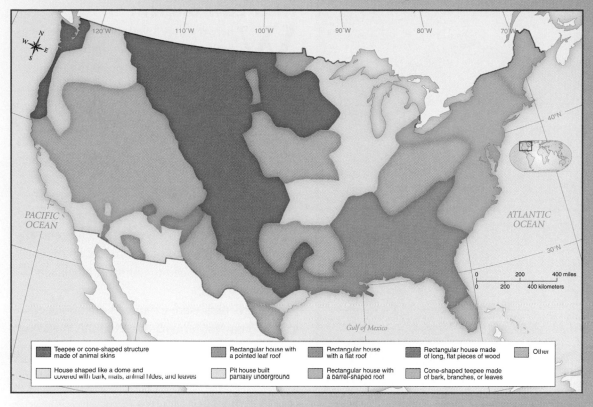

Legend:
- Teepee or cone-shaped structure made of animal skins
- House shaped like a dome and covered with bark, mats, animal hides, and leaves
- Rectangular house with a pointed leaf roof
- Pit house built partially underground
- Rectangular house with a flat roof
- Rectangular house with a barrel-shaped roof
- Rectangular house made of long, flat pieces of wood
- Cone-shaped teepee made of bark, branches, or leaves
- Other

Native American Food

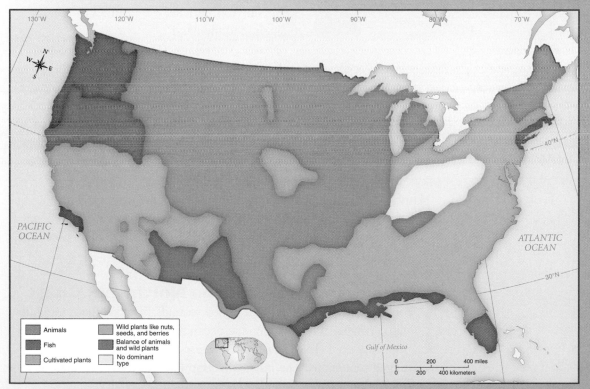

Legend:
- Animals
- Fish
- Cultivated plants
- Wild plants like nuts, seeds, and berries
- Balance of animals and wild plants
- No dominant type

Native Americans believed humans, animals, plants, and even inanimate objects had their own spirits. Because of this belief, Native Americans felt related to all parts of nature.

1.4 First Americans' View of Their Environment

Wherever they lived, Native Americans had a strong connection to their surroundings. They viewed themselves as a part of the community of plants, animals, and other natural objects. As a Sioux said, "From Wakan Tanka, the Great Spirit, there came a great unifying life force that flowed in and through all things—the flowers of the plains, blowing winds, rocks, trees, birds, animals—and was the same force that had been breathed into the first man."

Nature's Spirits   Native Americans generally believed that each part of nature had its own spirit. Each person had to maintain a balance with these spirits.

These beliefs were expressed in various customs. Southwest farmers, for example, made corn a part of every ceremony. Hunters gave thanks to the animals they killed.

Using the Land   Unlike Europeans, Native Americans did not believe that land could be owned as private property. But each group was deeply connected to its homeland—the area where its people lived most of the year. If necessary, Native Americans would fight to protect their right to this land.

Native Americans adapted the land to suit their needs. Woodlands people set fires to clear heavy forest growth, so deer could browse and berries could grow. Southwest farmers built ditches to carry water to dry fields.

These practices had seldom harmed the environment. As one Native American historian explains, "We dug our clams here, caught our salmon over there, got…seagull eggs on another island…. By the time we came back here, this place had replenished itself."

Native Americans tried not to waste anything taken from nature. A California woman recalled, "When we…kill meat, we eat it all up. When we dig roots we make little holes…. We shake down acorns and pine nuts. We don't chop down the trees."

1.5 Native Americans of the Northwest Coast

The Northwest Coast cultural region extends from southern Oregon into Canada. Winters along the ocean are cold but not icy, and summers are cool. To the east, thick forests of fir, spruce, and cedar cover rugged mountains. The mountains trap Pacific storms, so there is heavy rainfall much of the year.

Abundant Food   Northwest people found food plentiful, particularly from the sea. They built their villages along the narrow beaches and bays of the coastline, and on nearby islands. They gathered clams, other shell-fish, and seaweed from shallow waters. They ventured onto the sea in canoes to hunt seals, sea lions, and whales, as well as halibut and other fish. The forests provided deer, moose, bear, elk, beaver, and mountain goat.

For each kind of creature, hunters developed special weapons. To catch seals, for example, they made long wooden harpoons, or spears. The har-poon had a barbed tip made of bone that held firmly in the seal's hide once it was struck. At the other end, hunters fastened a long rope so that they would not lose either the weapon or their prey.

In early summer, masses of salmon swam from the ocean up the rivers to lay their eggs. Men built wooden fences across the rivers to block the fish, making them easier to net. Women dried salmon meat so that it could be eaten all year long.

Builders and Carvers   The forests of the Northwest provided materials for houses and many useful objects. Using wedges and stone-headed sledgehammers, men cut long, thin boards from logs or living trees. They joined these planks to build large, sturdy houses. To keep out the rain, they made roof shingles out of large sheets of cedar bark.

Women cut strips from the soft inner bark and used them to make baskets, mats, rope, and blankets. They even wove the strips of bark into waterproof capes.

With abundant food nearby, the Northwest people had time to practice crafts. Women made decorative shell buttons and sewed them onto their clothing with ivory needles. Men used tools such as wooden wedges, bone drills, stone chisels, and stone knives to carve detailed animal masks and wooden bowls.

Native Americans of the Northwest relied on the thick forests, abundant seafood, and plentiful game to meet their needs.

1.6 Native Americans of California

The California cultural region stretches from southern Oregon through Baja California. Ocean storms bring winter rains to this region. But summers are hot and dry, particularly inland.

The California region includes not only the coast, but also the coastal foothills, an inland valley, deserts, and the western side of the Sierra Nevada mountain range. Over 100 small groups made their homes in these diverse environments, more than in any other cultural region.

Many Sources of Food

Groups living along the coast of Northern California depended on salmon for much of their food. Farther south, coastal people relied more on shellfish. Away from the coast, groups hunted deer with bows and arrows. They set snares to trap rabbits and used nets to capture ducks. California people also gathered roots, berries, and pine nuts.

Most people in the region relied on acorns from oak trees as a basic food. In the fall, women harvested the acorns, shelled them, and pounded the nuts into meal. Water was rinsed through the meal to remove its bitterness. Women cooked the meal by mixing it with water in tightly woven baskets and then dropping hot cooking stones into the mixture.

Clothing, Houses, and Baskets   As they worked, the women wore simple aprons or skirts made from grasses or other plants, or sometimes from leather strips. In colder months, they wrapped themselves in animal hides.

Because the climate was mild, California people built simple homes. In forested areas, men used tools made from the antlers of deer and elk to strip large slabs of bark from redwood trees. They draped these into a cone shape to form a house. In marshy areas, people wove thick mats of reeds to drape over a cone-shaped framework of poles.

California people wove plant materials into many useful items. They made cooking baskets, storage baskets, sifters, and fish traps. Women used fine weaving and elegant patterns to make beautiful baskets, decorating their work with clamshells and bird feathers.

The California cultural region contains many different environments. Along the coast, huge redwood trees cover coastal mountains. In the inland areas, oaks and berries grow on rolling hills.

1.7 Native Americans of the Great Basin

To the east of California lies the Great Basin, a low area between the Sierra Nevada and the Rocky Mountains. The mountains on either side of this region block the rain, making this land mostly desert.

The plants that grow in this area are those that need little water, such as low grasses, sagebrush, and craggy piñon trees. Only small animals, such as rabbits and lizards, live in this harsh region.

With limited food and water, only a few families could live in a place at one time. For this reason, people of the Great Basin traveled in small groups and spent much of their time looking for food.

Extreme Heat and Cold   Wherever people camped, they made temporary shelters of willow poles shaped into a cone and covered with brush or reeds. Almost all year, they carried water in baskets coated with sap from pine trees.

When winter came, temperatures dropped below freezing. To keep warm, people made robes out of rabbit hides. First they twisted long strips of hide so that only the fur showed. Then they wove these strips on a willow loom. Each adult robe required about 100 rabbit skins.

Life was difficult for Native Americans who lived in the Great Basin. Because of extreme temperatures and sparse rainfall, few plants and animals survive there.

Searching for Food   In this arid (dry) environment, people followed food sources from season to season. In spring, they camped by valley lakes and streams swollen with melted snow. Men attracted migrating ducks with floating decoys made from reeds. When birds landed, the men chased them into nets. Meanwhile, women gathered duck eggs and the tender shoots of cattail plants.

When the streams dried up in summer, Great Basin people enjoyed snakes and grasshoppers as treats. But mostly they ate plants, almost 100 kinds. Women used sharp sticks to dig up roots. To knock seeds loose from plants, they wove flat baskets called *seed beaters*. From the mountain slopes they gathered ripe berries.

In autumn, bands harvested pine nuts and hunted fat jackrabbits. As winter arrived, the Great Basin people bundled into their rabbit robes in the warmer hills. In huts and caves, they lived off food they had dried earlier, waiting for the ducks to return in spring.

1.8 Native Americans of the Plateau

North of the Great Basin lies the Plateau cultural region. This region is bounded by the Cascade Range to the west, the Rockies to the east, and the Fraser River, in present-day Canada, to the north.

The mountains in this area have dense forests. The flatter, central part is drier and covered with grass and sagebrush. Winters are long and cold, while summers remain gentle.

The Plateau people hunted and gathered with the seasons. The cool, wet climate made it fairly easy to find enough to eat. So, too, did the Plateau's two mighty river systems, the Columbia and the Fraser.

Sturdy Houses and Clothing   Plateau people built their villages along major rivers. The rivers provided drinking water, fish, and driftwood to use for houses and firewood.

Food was so plentiful that some groups were able to live in their villages year-round. To stay cool in summer and warm in winter, they built their homes partly underground. They dug a pit, lined it with a frame of logs, and covered everything with saplings, reeds, and mud.

Plateau people used their weaving skills to create many kinds of baskets, as well as elaborate hats. As the cold months approached, they spent more time making clothes. In the fall, men hunted antelope and deer. Then women scraped and softened the hides for dresses, leggings, and shirts. They decorated their work with designs of seeds and shells.

Camas and Salmon   Although hunting usually provided plenty of meat in the fall, most of the time Plateau people relied on fish and plants for food. In spring, they gathered sprouts of wild onions and carrots from the low grasslands. Their particular favorite was camas, a starchy root related to lilies. Women uprooted it with willow digging sticks for eating raw, for roasting, and for grinding into flour.

The food most important to Plateau people was salmon. When the salmon migrated upstream, men stood on wooden platforms built over the water. From there, they could spear or net fish easily.

The Plateau cultural region features flatlands, rolling hills, and steep gorges. Large rivers provide water.

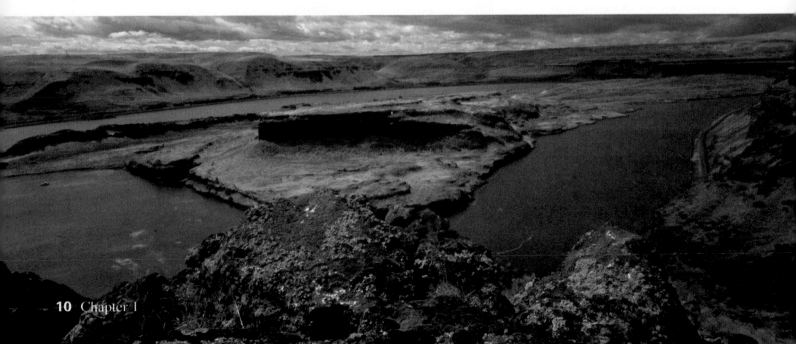

1.9 Native Americans of the Southwest

The Southwest cultural region includes present-day Arizona, New Mexico, southern Utah and Colorado, and portions of Texas, Oklahoma, and California. This region has many environments—canyons, mountains, deserts, and flat-topped mesas. It even has two major rivers, the Colorado and the Rio Grande. But rain seldom falls anywhere.

The heat and lack of water made living in the Southwest a challenge. Yet some Native Americans learned to love this arid land. "The whole Southwest was a House Made of Dawn," goes an old Indian song. "There were many colors on the hills and on the plain, and there was a dark wilderness on the mountains beyond."

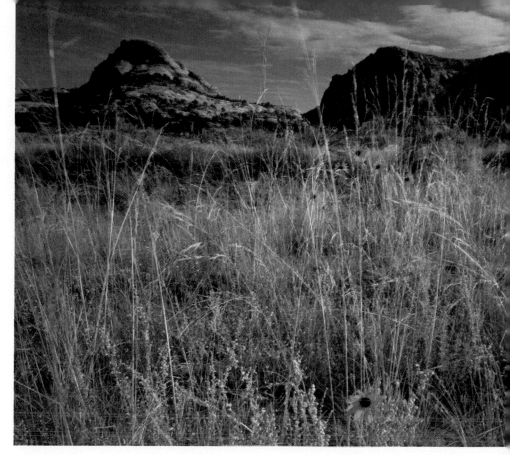

Survival in the Southwest was a challenge. The area contains mountains, flat-topped mesas, canyons, and deserts. Sparse rainfall prevents the growth of many trees and plants.

Mesa People   Different groups found different ways of surviving in the Southwest. Some lived as nomadic (wandering) desert hunters. Along the Colorado River, small groups hunted, gathered, and farmed. Others planted fields of corn, beans, and squash on the tops of high, flat areas called *mesas*.

The mesa people lacked trees for building homes. Instead, they made homes from the earth itself. Using bricks of *adobe* (sun-baked clay), they built thick-walled houses that protected them from summer heat and winter cold. Their villages looked like apartment houses that reached up to four stories high and had hundreds of rooms. A single village, called a *pueblo*, might house 1,000 people.

To protect their bodies from the sun, mesa people wore clothes made of cotton that they grew, spun, and wove into cloth. Using plants and minerals, they dyed fabrics with bright colors.

Corn Culture   Despite living in a desert, the early mesa people learned to grow corn, beans, and squash. Corn was by far their most important crop.

To make the most of infrequent rain, farmers planted near naturally flooded areas like the mouths of large streambeds or the bases of mesas, where rain runoff flowed. Men dug irrigation ditches from the streams to the fields, and built small dams to hold summer rain.

Girls spent many hours a day grinding corn kernels into cornmeal. The women cooked the cornmeal into bread in clay ovens. In clay pots, they cooked stews of corn, rabbit meat, and chili peppers.

1.10 Native Americans of the Great Plains

The Great Plains cultural region is a vast area of treeless grasslands. The Great Plains stretch for 2,000 miles from the Rockies to the Mississippi Valley, and from Canada to the Gulf of Mexico. The eastern part of this region has more water and softer soil than the western part. In the drier west, short, dense grasses provided perfect grazing for millions of buffalo.

The Great Plains region is mostly tree-less grassland with cold winters and hot summers. Buffalo and other animals grazed freely over a vast territory.

Buffalo Hunters   On the Eastern Plains, various groups took up farming, going on buffalo-hunting trips only a few months each year. On the Western Plains, Native Americans followed buffalo herds much of the year.

In the spring and early summer, small groups lay in ambush where buffalo came to drink. The hunters gripped hardwood bows reinforced with strips of buffalo tendon. Taking aim, each man let loose a wooden arrow tipped with a sharp stone and arrayed with feathers to help it fly straight.

In the fall, huge buffalo herds gathered, and Plains people traveled in larger bands. The men sometimes made a trap for the buffalo by heaping stones into two short walls to form a V-shaped passage. The walls forced the buffalo closer together as they approached a cliff. Behind the herd, peo-ple set a grass fire or made loud noises to panic the buffalo. The animals stampeded between the walls and over the cliff edge. Below, waiting hunters finished them off with spears or bows and arrows.

Using the Buffalo   Buffalo provided the main food for Plains people. Women and children cut up the buffalo with bone knives. Extra meat was dried and kept for winter.

Plains Indians used every part of the buffalo. Buffalo hides were turned into shields, waterproof containers, warm robes, and bedding. For clothing and bags, women softened the hides with bone scrapers and rubbed in buf-falo brains and fat.

Buffalo hair and sinew were twined into bowstrings and ropes. Horns and hooves became spoons and bowls, or were boiled down to make glue. Dried buffalo dung provided fuel for fires.

Buffalo provided materials for housing as well. Using tendons as thread, women sewed 8 to 20 buffalo skins together. The skins were then fastened around a tall cone of poles to make a *tipi,* a Plains word for "dwelling."

Plains people became even more successful when Spanish explorers introduced horses to the region. With horses, hunters could bring down more buffalo and move faster and more comfortably to new hunting grounds.

1.11 Native Americans of the Eastern Woodlands

The Eastern Woodlands cultural region reaches from the Mississippi River eastward to the Atlantic Ocean, and from Canada to North Carolina. Here, winter snows and summer rains produce endless forests, lakes, and streams.

Two language groups emerged in this region. In most of the territory, people spoke Algonquian languages. In New York and around the southern Great Lakes lived the Iroquois-speaking groups described in this section.

Plentiful Woods   The forests provided most of what Iroquois people needed to live. For food, hunters prowled through the forests to track deer. Men also hunted bears, trapped beavers, caught birds in nets, and speared fish. Women gathered fresh greens, nuts, and berries. They made syrup by boiling down sap from maple trees.

Instead of walking through the thick forests, Iroquois often paddled log and bark canoes along lakes and rivers. Because waterways also provided fish and drinking water, the Iroquois built their villages nearby.

Each village had dozens of sturdy log-frame houses covered with elm bark. Such longhouses were usually about 20 feet wide and over 100 feet long. Several related families lived in sections of the longhouse.

Women Farmers   To clear a space for farming, Iroquois men burned away trees and underbrush. Women did the rest. After hoeing the soil, they planted corn, sometimes several varieties. Around the cornstalks, they let beans twine. Squash stayed near the ground, keeping down weeds and holding moisture in the soil.

When the planting was done, women tanned deerskin to make skirts, capes, and moccasins (soft shoes). They ground corn with wooden sticks in hollowed-out tree trunks or between two stones. In the fall, they stored the harvest, often in large bark bins in the longhouses. Iroquois crops included sunflowers, tobacco, and many vegetables that are still planted in American gardens today.

Dense forests are home to deer, beavers, and other wildlife, and provided food, clothing, and shelter for the Native Americans of the Eastern Woodlands.

1.12 Native Americans of the Southeast

The Southeast cultural region stretches from the southern part of the Ohio Valley to the Gulf of Mexico, and from Texas to the Atlantic Ocean. This region's fertile coastal plains, river valleys, mountains, and swamps all have long, warm, humid summers and mild winters. In this green countryside, the people of the Southeast found growing crops fairly easy.

Towns Built around Mounds

Some Southeastern peoples built towns dominated by large earthen mounds. The first mounds were burial sites. Centuries later, people made mounds several stories high as platforms for temples.

Building these mounds took months, even years, because people had to move the dirt one basketful at a time. Workers building mounds had no time to help grow or find food. But Southeastern groups had developed a type of corn that grew so fast, they could harvest two crops a year. Farmers raised enough food to feed the people building the mounds.

A single Southeastern town might have had 2 to 12 mounds arrayed around a central town plaza. Around these mounds, people clustered their houses. They built their homes from strips of young trees woven into a rectangular frame and plastered with clay. Roofs were pointed and made of leaves.

A Fertile Region Beyond their homes, fields lay in all directions. With the region's long growing season, Southeastern people relied on corn, beans, squash, pumpkins, and sunflowers for most of their food.

Women worked the fields with hoes made of stone, shell, or animal shoulder blades fastened to wooden handles. Men sometimes hunted, using blowguns for squirrels, rabbits, and turkeys, and bows and arrows for large animals like deer. They even brought home alligators and turtles.

To complete their varied diet, women gathered edible plants like sweet potatoes, wild rice, and persimmons. Because they wore simple, short deerskin skirts, they didn't spend much time making clothing. Instead, they used stones, shells, feathers, pearls, bones, and clay to fashion rings, earrings, arm rings, and hairpins.

The Southeast cultural region includes river valleys, mountains, coastal plains, and swamps. The mild climate allowed Native Americans of the Southeast to grow corn, beans, squash, and other crops.

1.13 Chapter Summary

In this chapter, you read about the first people to settle in North America. You used a map to study the adaptations made by Native Americans living in eight cultural regions.

The ancestors of Native Americans migrated to America from Asia across a land bridge during the last Ice Age. As their descendants traveled east and south, they had to adapt to the challenges of living in many different environments.

Wherever they settled, Native Americans had a special relationship with the world around them. They believed they were part of nature, and they treated the environment with respect.

Native Americans were a diverse group who spoke many languages. People living in different cultural regions developed distinctive ways of life that were suited to their environment's climate and natural resources. Scientists study these ways of life by examining the artifacts America's first people left behind.

Depending on where they lived, Native Americans ate different food, built different kinds of houses, and clothed themselves in different ways. They also practiced many kinds of crafts, making such things as jewelry, fine baskets, and animal masks. Native Americans built the first towns and villages in North America, and they were the continent's first farmers.

For thousands of years, these First People had the Americas to themselves. That would change when Europeans learned of the existence of the American continents. In the next chapter, you will read about the first explorers and settlers to arrive in America from European countries.

This drawing by John White, one of the first English colonists in North America, shows the village life of the Secotan people who lived in North Carolina.

When do you think ships like this sailed the oceans?
Judging from this illustration, what do you think some sailors feared?
What other fears do you think sailors had?

2

European Exploration and Settlement

2.1 Introduction

Half a world away from where Native Americans made their homes, Europeans had no knowledge of these peoples or the land where they lived. When Europeans looked west, they saw only a vast ocean.

Europeans were far more interested in the lands that lay to the east. In the late 1200s, a young man named Marco Polo traveled through Asia with his father, a merchant and trader from Venice, Italy. Marco Polo spent 17 years in China. When he returned to Venice, people flocked to hear his stories of "the Indies," as India and East Asia were then known. He was called "the man of a million tales."

Eventually, a writer helped Marco Polo put his adventures into a book. The book described the wonders Polo had seen in China. It told of rich silks and rare spices, gold and jewels, and luxurious palaces.

When Marco Polo's book was published, only a few people in Europe could read. Those who did read it were fascinated by its description of riches to the east. Merchants and traders were eager to find the fastest way to get there. The land route that Polo had traveled was long and dangerous. His tales inspired explorers to find a route by sea.

Some explorers would seek a route to China by going around the southern tip of Africa. But a few brave souls looked to the west for another route. This took courage, because no one knew how far west sailors would have to sail to reach Asia or what monsters and terrors might await them far from Europe's shore.

In this chapter, you will learn how Christopher Columbus defied these dangers and sailed west to find a route to China. As you will see, his unexpected discovery of America led to competition among European nations to explore and profit from the land they called the New World.

Graphic Organizer: Illustration
You will use this illustration to learn about European exploration and settlement of the Americas.

2.2 Spain Starts an Empire

Marco Polo's book continued to be read over the next two centuries. This was a time of great change in Europe. The rediscovered writings of ancient Greeks and Romans inspired a new interest in learning and art. This period of lively new thinking has become known as the Renaissance, a word that means "rebirth."

During this time, the invention of the printing press made books, including Marco Polo's, more available. As Europeans learned about the world beyond Europe, they became eager to explore these far-off lands.

On October 12, 1492, Columbus stepped on land and claimed for Spain an island he named San Salvador. The people he encountered were peaceful, their only weapons being small wooden spears.

Columbus's Discoveries   One of the people who was inspired by Marco Polo's writings was an Italian seaman named Christopher Columbus. After studying maps of the world, Columbus became convinced that the shortest route to the Indies lay to the west, across the Atlantic Ocean.

Columbus looked for someone who could pay for the ships and men he needed to test his idea. Eventually, he was able to convince King Ferdinand and Queen Isabella of Spain to sponsor a voyage.

In August 1492, Columbus sailed west with three small ships. After more than a month at sea, his sailors raised the cry of "Land!" The land turned out to be a small island in what we now call the Caribbean Sea.

Columbus was thrilled. In a later letter, he wrote, "I write this to tell you how in thirty-three days I sailed to the Indies with the fleet that the illustrious King and Queen…gave me, where I discovered a great many islands, inhabited by numberless people." Mistakenly believing that he had reached the Indies, Columbus called these people Indians.

In reality, the islanders were Native Americans who spoke a language called Taino. The Taino lived in a peaceful fishing community. Never had they seen people like the ones who had suddenly appeared on their shores. Yet they were friendly and welcoming. Columbus wrote, "They are so unsuspicious and so generous with what they possess, that no one who had not seen it would believe it."

Columbus promptly claimed the island for Spain and named it San Salvador, which means "Holy Savior." From there he sailed on to other islands. Convinced that China lay nearby, Columbus sailed back to Spain for more ships and men.

Columbus made four trips to the Caribbean, finding more islands, as well as the continent of South America. Each time he discovered a new place, he claimed it for Spain. Columbus died still believing he had found Asia, but later explorers quickly realized that he had actually stumbled on a "New World" unknown to Europe—the continents of North and South America.

The Columbian Exchange   The voyages of Columbus triggered a great transfer of people, plants, animals, and diseases back and forth across the Atlantic Ocean. This transfer, which still continues today, is called the Columbian Exchange. The Columbian Exchange brought valuable new crops such as corn and potatoes to Europe. These foods greatly improved the diet of the average European. Many Europeans also found new opportunities by crossing the Atlantic to settle in the Americas.

For Native Americans, however, the exchange began badly. The Europeans who came to America brought with them germs that caused smallpox and other diseases deadly to Native Americans. Historians estimate that in some areas, 90 percent of the native population was wiped out by European diseases.

Slavery Comes to America   This high death rate contributed to the introduction of African slaves to the Americas. Some of the Spanish settlers in the Caribbean had started gold mines. Others raised sugar, a crop of great value in Europe. At first the settlers forced Indians to work for them.

At first, Spanish settlers relied on the forced labor of Native Americans to work their sugar plantations. When disease wiped out this labor force, the Spanish turned to African slaves to perform the backbreaking task of harvesting and refining sugar cane.

The Granger Collection, New York

The Granger Collection, New York

But as native people began dying in great numbers from European diseases, the settlers looked for a new work force. Before long, enslaved Africans were replacing Indians.

Slavery had existed around the world since ancient times. Often people who lost wars were enslaved, or treated as the property of their conquerors. By the late 1400s, European explorers in West Africa were trading guns and other goods for slaves captured by Africans.

In the 1500s, European slave traders began shipping slaves to the Caribbean for sale. Over the next three centuries, millions of Africans would be carried across the Atlantic in crowded, disease-infested ships. The terrible voyage lasted anywhere from weeks to months. Many died before it was over.

When the Africans arrived in the Americas, they were sold to their new masters at auctions. Many perished from disease and overwork. Those who survived faced a lifetime of forced labor as slaves.

Cortés, shown here with his translator, is trying to convince a group of Native Americans to help him conquer the Aztecs. With the help of Aztec enemies and smallpox, Cortés captured the Aztec capital of Tenochtitlán.

slavery: The treatment of people as property for the purpose of forcing them to do labor. People who are denied freedom in this way are called *slaves* and are said to be *enslaved.*

conquistadors: Spanish soldier-explorers, especially those who conquered the native peoples of Mexico and Peru

Cortés Conquers Mexico After Columbus's voyages, Spain began sending soldiers called **conquistadors** across the Atlantic. Their mission was to conquer a vast empire for Spain. Along the way, the conquistadors hoped to get rich.

In 1519, Hernán Cortés arrived in Mexico with horses and 500 soldiers. There he heard about the powerful Aztecs who ruled much of Mexico. When Cortés and his men reached the Aztec capital of Tenochtitlán, they could not believe their eyes. A beautiful city seemed to rise out of a sparkling lake. One Spaniard wrote, "Some of our soldiers asked whether the things that we saw were not a dream."

The Aztecs were not sure what to make of the strangers. They had never seen men dressed in metal armor and riding horses. Some mistook Cortés for the great Aztec god Quetzalcoatl and welcomed him as a hero. They would soon change their minds.

With the help of Indians who hated their Aztec rulers, and smallpox—which killed large numbers of Aztec warriors—Cortés conquered Tenochtitlán. The Spaniards pulled the city down and used its stones to build Mexico City, the capital of a new Spanish empire called New Spain.

Pizarro Conquers Peru Smallpox also helped another Spanish conquistador, Francisco Pizarro, conquer an empire in South America. In 1532, Pizarro led an attack on the powerful Inca empire in present-day Peru. Luckily for Pizarro, smallpox reached Peru many months before him, killing thousands of Incas and leaving their empire badly divided.

Pizarro captured the Inca ruler, Atahualpa, but promised to release him in exchange for gold. To save their ruler, the Incas filled three rooms with gold and silver treasures. Pizarro killed Atahualpa anyway and took over the leaderless Inca empire. From there, Spanish conquistadors conquered most of South America.

Exploring the Americas

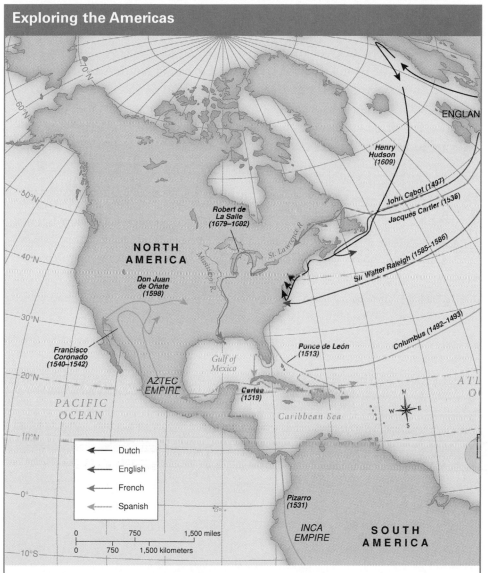

- Identify at least four details about this map.
- What do the different arrows represent?
- Which sections of the Western Hemisphere were explored by the Spanish? By the French? By the English? By the Dutch?
- Which country explored the most territory in the Western Hemisphere?
- Why do you think this country explored the most territory?

colony: a new settlement or territory established and governed by a country in another land

2.3 The Spanish Borderlands

In both Mexico and Peru, conquistadors found gold and silver riches beyond their wildest dreams. Hoping for still more, they pushed north into lands that are now part of the United States. Because these lands were located on the far edges of Spain's North American empire, they were known as the Spanish borderlands.

Florida   One of the first Spanish expeditions into North America was led by a man named Juan Ponce de León. He had sailed with Columbus to the Caribbean and made his fortune by discovering gold on the island of Puerto Rico. Despite his wealth, Ponce de León couldn't stop thinking about Indian rumors of a "fountain of youth" that made old people young again. Restless for more adventure, he set off to find the truth about these tales of everlasting youth.

Ponce de León landed on a sunny peninsula of North America in April 1513. Because he had sighted this lush new land on Easter Sunday, he called it La Florida, meaning "flowery." (The name is short for "flowery Easter.") Eight years later, he returned to Florida with 200 men to establish a Spanish settlement, or **colony**. Native Americans in the area used poisoned arrows to drive off the invaders. Instead of finding a fountain of youth, Ponce de León died from a poisoned arrow in his stomach.

Although Coronado never found the Seven Cities of Cíbola, his explorations opened a new area for Spanish settlement.

The "Seven Cities of Cíbola"   Another legend sparked new Spanish expeditions into North America. An old European tale told of the "Seven Cities of Cíbola." These cities were said to be so fabulously rich that the

The Granger Collection, New York

streets and houses were decorated with gold and jewels. When the Spanish heard Indians tell similar tales, they became convinced that the Seven Cities of Cíbola were somewhere in North America.

Spanish explorers first looked for the seven cities in Florida and in present-day Texas. They found plenty of adventure, but no golden cities. Then a Spanish priest named Marcos de Niza claimed to have seen a shimmering golden city in what is now New Mexico. He raced back to Mexico City with the news.

The Coronado Expedition In 1540, a famed conquistador named Francisco Vásquez de Coronado set out from Mexico City with a large expedition and de Niza as his guide. Their goal was to find the legendary golden cities.

After traveling north more than 7,000 miles, the expedition found a Native American *pueblo* (a village of apartment-like buildings made of stone and adobe rising four and five stories high). To de Niza, this might have looked like a golden city. But to Coronado, it was a "little, crowded village…all crumpled up together." The enraged expedition leader sent the priest home.

The Coronado expedition continued north onto the Great Plains before giving up the search for golden cities. Disappointed, Coronado reported to Spain, "Everything is the opposite of [what] was related, except the name of the cities and the large stone houses…. The Seven Cities are seven little villages."

St. Augustine was originally a presidio, or fort, built by the Spanish to protect their claim to Florida. It is the oldest permanent European settlement in the United States.

Settling the Borderlands As conquistadors explored new territories, they claimed the areas for Spain. By 1600, the Spanish borderlands extended west from Florida across present-day Texas, New Mexico, Arizona, and California.

At first, Spain did little to encourage settlement in these far-flung areas. But when rival European nations also began to show an interest in the land, small bands of soldiers were sent to these regions to protect the claims. The soldiers lived in walled forts called *presidios*.

In 1565, for example, a Spanish naval officer named Pedro Menéndez de Avilés was sent to Florida to protect the area from French explorers. Menéndez successfully drove the French out of their Florida base and built a fort on the peninsula's Atlantic coast. Menéndez named the fort Saint Augustine. Over the years, Spanish soldiers based at St. Augustine successful defended the fort, and Spanish claims to Florida, from both French and English rivals. Today, St. Augustine is the oldest permanent settlement founded by Europeans in the United States.

Missions were established to convert Native Americans to Christianity and increase Spanish control over the land. Missions included a church and the farmland on which missionaries produced almost all of what they needed to survive.

Catholic **missionaries** accompanied the soldiers to the borderlands. Missionaries are priests who try to persuade people to convert to their religion. The priests built settlements called *missions* where they taught local Indians new skills and the Christian faith. Each mission grew its own food and produced most of what the missionaries needed to survive far from towns and trading centers.

Hardy bands of settlers also moved into the borderlands. There they established towns and farms. Juan de Oñate, who had made a fortune mining silver in Mexico, led the settlement of New Mexico. In 1598, Oñate brought 400 settlers and 7,000 animals from Mexico to New Mexico. The long overland journey took a year and a half to complete.

At first, the Pueblo Indians of New Mexico welcomed the newcomers. Unfortunately, the Spanish repaid the Indians' kindness with cruelty. Indians were made to work for the settlers as slaves. Catholic priests ordered Pueblo religious leaders who continued to practice their traditional rituals to be whipped. Such treatment led the Pueblo people to rise up in revolt and drive the Spanish out. Twelve years would pass before Spanish settlers returned to New Mexico.

During the 1600s and 1700s, settlement of the Spanish borderlands proceeded slowly. But in time, the language, religion, and culture of Spain spread across much of the American Southwest.

Impact on Native Americans The arrival of Spanish settlers had a great impact on the native peoples of the borderlands. The Pueblo people, for example, learned from the Spanish how to use new tools, grow new foods, and raise sheep for wool. In turn, the Indians introduced the Spanish to new techniques for growing crops in the desert soil.

From Florida to California, some Native Americans converted to the Catholic faith. The converts often lived and worked in and around the missions, growing crops and helping to maintain the churches and other buildings. However, even converts often continued to practice their traditional religious rituals as well.

Unfortunately, wherever the Spanish settled, they brought with them diseases to which native peoples had no resistance. Smallpox, measles, and influenza often wiped out entire villages. Before Coronado's expedition, there had been more than 100 Indian pueblos in New Mexico. By 1700, only 18 remained.

missionaries: people who travel to a territory or community in order to make converts to their religion

2.4 New France

As Spanish colonies sent ships loaded with gold and silver home to Spain, all of Europe watched with envy. Every year, Spain seemed to become more wealthy and more powerful. Other nations wanted their share of riches from the New World. But none was strong enough to challenge Spain's American empire. Instead, they would have to seek their fortunes in areas not yet claimed by Spain.

trappers: adventurers who capture and kill animals, such as beavers, for their fur

Claiming New France   In 1534, France sent Jacques Cartier to explore the Atlantic coastline of North America. His goal was to find a Northwest Passage, an all-water route through the North American continent to the Pacific Ocean. Such a passage would provide a shortcut for ships sailing west to Asia.

Cartier failed to find such a passage. But he did claim the land we know today as Canada for France. He later named this land New France. Cartier also discovered something almost as valuable as Spanish gold—beaver fur. Beaver hats were a hot fashion item in Europe, and French hatmakers were willing to pay high prices for beaver pelts.

Settling New France   The first settlement in New France was founded by Samuel de Champlain. In 1608, Champlain sailed up the St. Lawrence River and built a trading post he called Quebec. For the next 150 years, Quebec would be a base for French explorers, soldiers, missionaries, traders, and fur **trappers**.

From Quebec, fur trappers pushed west in search of beaver. They called themselves *coureurs de bois,* which means "wood rangers" in French. Catholic missionaries followed the trappers, seeking converts among the native peoples.

Like the Spanish borderlands, New France failed to attract large numbers of settlers. The harsh climate of New France discouraged French farmers from crossing the Atlantic. So did the colony's policy of granting the best land along the St. Lawrence River to French nobles who then planned to rent it out to farmers. The few settlers who did come soon got tired of renting and left their farms to search for furs.

The image below shows two *coureurs de bois,* which means "wood rangers" in French. These fur trappers, who roamed New France in search of beaver pelts, learned trapping skills from the Native Americans.

Native American Business Partners Because the French were more interested in furs than farming, they did not try to conquer the Indians and put them to work as the Spanish had done. Instead, the French made Native Americans their business partners.

After founding Quebec, Champlain made friends with the nearby Indians, especially the Huron. Fur trappers lived in Huron villages, learned the Huron language, and married Huron women. From the Huron they learned how to survive for months in the wilderness. Unfortunately, the friendship between the French and Huron exposed the Huron to European diseases, which swept through their villages and killed many of them.

Champlain even joined the Huron in an attack on their enemies the Iroquois. He later wrote:

The French made friends with the Native Americans in New France, and often assisted them in battles with their enemies. Here, Samuel de Champlain, in the center, helps the Huron Indians defeat the Iroquois.

"I marched some 20 paces ahead of the rest, until I was about 30 paces from the enemy…. When I saw them making a move to fire at us, I rested my musket against my cheek and aimed directly at one of their three chiefs. With the same shot, two fell to the ground, and one of their men was wounded…. When our side saw this shot…they began to raise such loud cries that one could not have heard it thunder. Meanwhile, the arrows flew on both sides."

The astonished Iroquois, who had never seen or heard gunfire before, fled in terror. From that day on, the Iroquois would be the bitter enemies of the French.

Claiming Louisiana The search for furs led the French far inland from Quebec. In 1673, two explorers, Father Marquette and Louis Joliet, explored the great Mississippi River. They hoped that this waterway would be the long-sought Northwest Passage. But they discovered that, instead of flowing west to the Pacific Ocean, the river flowed south toward the Gulf of Mexico. Disappointed, they returned to New France.

Nine years later, Robert de La Salle explored the entire length of the Mississippi River. On April 9, 1682, he planted a French flag at the mouth of the river and claimed everything west of the Mississippi River for France. La Salle named this vast area Louisiana for the French monarch, King Louis XIV.

2.5 Jamestown: The First English Colony

Columbus's voyages inspired John Cabot, an Italian living in England, to seek his own western route to Asia. In 1497, Cabot, who had moved to England from Venice, sailed west across the Atlantic. He landed in Newfoundland, an island off the coast of Canada. A fellow Venetian living in London wrote of Cabot's brief landing:

He coasted for three hundred leagues and landed; saw no human beings, but he has brought here to the king certain snares which had been set to catch game, and a needle for making nets; he also found some felled trees, by which he judged there were inhabitants, and he returned to his ship in alarm…. The discoverer…planted on this newly-found land a large cross, with one flag of England and another of St. Mark [the patron saint of Venice] on account of his being a Venetian.

John Cabot, an Italian exploring for England, sailed to Newfoundland and Nova Scotia, off the coast of present-day Canada. He believed he had reached Asia, and claimed the land for England. Two years later, he was lost at sea when he set out on an expedition to find Japan.

Like Columbus, Cabot mistakenly believed that he had landed in Asia. Later, however, England would claim all of North America because of the flag planted by Cabot in 1497.

The Lost Colony of Roanoke

Nearly a century later, an English noble named Sir Walter Raleigh tried to start a colony on Roanoke Island off the coast of present-day North Carolina. Indians on the island welcomed the settlers and gave them traps for catching fish. The newcomers, however, were more interested in looking for gold than fishing. When their supplies ran low, they returned to England.

In 1587, Raleigh sent a second group of colonists to Roanoke. Unfortunately, they arrived too late in the season to plant crops. Their leader, John White, sailed back to England for more supplies. While White was in England, however, fighting broke out between England and Spain. As a result, his return to Roanoke was delayed for three years.

When White finally reached the island, the colonists had disappeared. Carved on a doorpost was the word CROATOAN. To this day, both the meaning of this word and what happened to the lost colony of Roanoke remain a mystery.

The Granger Collection, New York

The Granger Collection, New York

The first colonists at Jamestown settled in an area they believed would be easy to defend against Native Americans and the Spanish. However, the land was marshy and infested with malaria-carrying mosquitoes.

Settling Jamestown Twenty years went by before a permanent English colony was established in America. In 1607, a group of merchants formed the London Company to start a money-making colony in Virginia. The company crammed 144 settlers into three tiny ships and sent them across the Atlantic. The settlers were to ship back valuable goods such as furs and timber.

When they reached Virginia, the colonists settled on a swampy peninsula they believed could be easily defended against Native Americans or Spanish ships. They called their new home Jamestown after King James I. What the settlers didn't know was that the spot they chose to settle would soon be swarming with disease-carrying mosquitoes. It was also surrounded by a large and powerful Native American group.

To make matters worse, the Jamestown settlers were a mix of gentlemen and craftsmen. None of them knew much about farming. Nor were they willing to work very hard at it. They thought they were in Virginia to look for gold, not to provide for themselves.

As the food the settlers had brought with them disappeared, they began to trade with the Indians, bartering glass beads and iron hatchets for corn and meat. But barter wasn't easy. Many Indians decided they would sooner kill the English—or just let them starve—than trade. Hunger and disease soon took their toll. Every few days, another body was carried off to the graveyard.

In 1608, a natural leader named Captain John Smith took control of Jamestown. "If any would not work," announced Smith, "neither should he eat." The men were hungry, so they worked.

While scouting for food, Smith was captured by the Indians and brought to a smoky longhouse. Seated at one end, he saw Powhatan, the Indians' powerful chief. The Indians greeted Smith with a loud shout and a great feast. But when the meal ended, the mood changed. Smith was about to be clubbed to death when a young girl leapt out of the shadows. "She took my head in her arms and laid her own upon mine to save me from death," Smith later wrote.

Smith's savior was Pocahontas, Chief Powhatan's favorite daughter. From that moment on, she would think of Smith as her brother. Pocahontas helped Smith save Jamestown by bringing food and keeping peace with her people. "She, next under God," Smith wrote, "was…the instrument to preserve this colony from death, famine, and utter confusion."

The Starving Time   Jamestown's troubles, however, were far from over. In the fall of 1609, after being injured in a gunpowder explosion, Smith returned to England. The following winter was the worst ever—so bad that it came to be known as the "Starving Time."

Without Smith and Pocahontas to act as go-betweens, the Indians refused to trade with the settlers. The English ate dogs, rats, and even human corpses to survive. By spring, only 60 of the 500 people Smith had left in the fall remained alive.

When supply ships arrived the following spring, the survivors were ordered to abandon their failed colony. Then three more English ships arrived with food, 150 new colonists, and 100 soldiers. Jamestown was saved again.

Jamestown Survives   Even with more settlers, the people of Jamestown lived in constant danger of Indian attacks. To end that threat, the English kidnapped Pocahontas and held her hostage. For a year, Pocahontas remained a prisoner—but a willing and curious one. During that time she learned English, adopted the Christian faith, and made new friends.

Among those new friends was a widower named John Rolfe. Rolfe had already helped the colony survive by finding a crop that could be raised in Virginia and sold for good prices in England—tobacco. The happy settlers went tobacco mad, planting the crop everywhere, even in Jamestown's streets.

Now Rolfe helped again by making a proposal of marriage to Pocahontas. Both the governor of Jamestown and Chief Powhatan gave their consent to this unusual match. Maybe they hoped that the marriage would help end the conflict between their peoples.

The union of Pocahontas and John Rolfe did bring peace to Jamestown. In 1616, Rolfe wrote, "Our people yearly plant and reap quietly, and travel in the woods…as freely and securely from danger…as in England."

Pocahontas, the daughter of a powerful Indian leader, brought food to the Jamestown settlers and helped them survive. Pocahontas later married John Rolfe and visited England with him. This portrait of her in European dress is the only authentic painting of her.

Ætatis suæ 21. A°. 1616.

Peter Minuit is shown offering Native Americans knives, beads, blankets, and trinkets worth about $24 in exchange for Manhattan Island.

2.6 New Netherland: The Short-Lived Dutch Settlement

While John Smith was struggling to save the colony of Jamestown, an English sailor named Henry Hudson was exploring the coastline farther north for the Netherlands. Henry Hudson's voyage was sponsored by Dutch merchants who hoped to find the Northwest Passage. (The people of the Netherlands are called the Dutch.)

In 1609, Hudson discovered a deep river full of fish, and thought it might just take him all the way across the continent. It didn't, of course, but he claimed the land along its banks for the Netherlands. The river was later named the Hudson in his honor, and the territory he claimed became known as New Netherland.

In 1621, Dutch merchants formed the Dutch West India Company to start a colony in America. The first Dutch colonists settled along the upper Hudson where they built Fort Orange, near present-day Albany, New York. The new colonists quickly found that there were good profits to be made in the fur trade. They established trading posts along the Hudson River. The largest was on Manhattan Island at the river's mouth.

Relations with Native Americans In 1626, the Dutch West India Company sent Peter Minuit to New Netherland as the colony's governor. Wanting peaceful relations with the Indians, the company told Minuit that any native peoples on Manhattan Island "must not be expelled with violence or threats but be persuaded with kind words…or should be given something."

Following orders, Minuit offered the island's Indians iron pots, beads, and blankets worth about $24 in exchange for their land. The Native Americans didn't believe that anyone could own land. Laughing at the foolishness of the white men, they made the trade.

The Granger Collection, New York

Dutch traders also made deals with members of the powerful Iroquois Confederacy, an alliance of five Indian groups who lived across the northern portion of New Netherland. The French had long supplied the Huron, the Iroquois' great rivals, with guns in exchange for furs. It made sense for the Iroquois to become partners with the Dutch, who supplied them with the weapons they needed to stand up to the Huron.

This partnership also made sense for the Dutch. The French were their main rivals in the fur trade. For most of the 1600s, the Iroquois kept the French from moving into the fur-rich Ohio Valley.

New Amsterdam   As the fur trade expanded, the Dutch settlement on Manhattan swelled to over 1,000 people. In 1647, the Dutch West India Company hired Peter Stuyvesant as the colony's new governor. When he arrived at Manhattan, Stuyvesant declared that the settlement would be called New Amsterdam, after the capital city of the Netherlands.

Stuyvesant had lost his right leg in battle, and he stomped around on a wooden leg that was decorated with silver nails. People called him "Old Silvernails" or "Peg Leg Pete." Although he was a strong leader, "Old Silvernails" was generally disliked. When Dutchmen who had been elected as city councilors disagreed with him, he called them "ignorant subjects" and threatened to ship them back to the Netherlands in pieces if they gave him trouble.

Despite his reputation as a grouch, Stuyvesant governed New Amsterdam for 17 years. During this time, he captured a nearby Swedish colony and invited its settlers to live in New Amsterdam. By 1660, the colony had nearly 8,000 people, including Europeans from many nations as well as enslaved Africans. New Amsterdam also provided refuge for Jews who were seeking freedom to follow their religion in peace.

Peter Stuyvesant, the Dutch governor of New Amsterdam, surrendered the settlement to the British without a shot being fired. Outnumbered and out-gunned, Stuyvesant bowed to the pleas of his people to avoid bloodshed and destruction.

The Granger Collection, New York

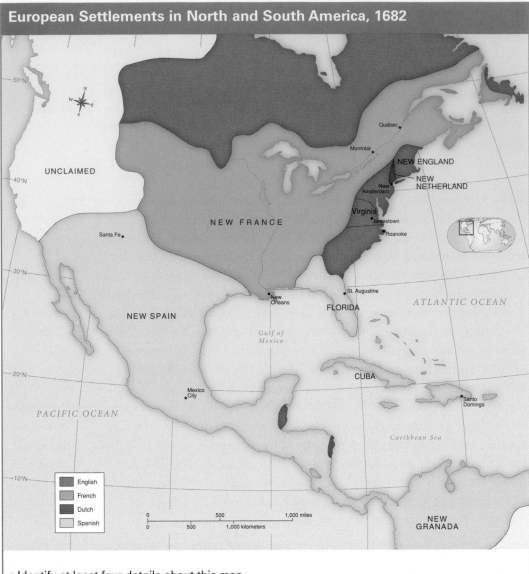

European Settlements in North and South America, 1682

- Identify at least four details about this map.
- What do the different colors on the map represent?
- Which country settled the largest area? Which country settled the smallest area?
- What connections do you see between this map and the map "Exploring the Americas"?
- Which European country first settled the area in which you live?

New Netherland Becomes New York Stuyvesant's biggest problem was that the English wanted to drive the Dutch out of North America. England's king, Charles II, refused to recognize Dutch claims to New Netherland. In 1664, Charles gave his brother, James, the Duke of York, ownership of all Dutch lands in America—if he could conquer them.

James promptly organized a small invasion fleet to take the colony. When the English arrived, they sent Stuyvesant a letter demanding his surrender. Stuyvesant tore up the note and refused to consider giving up until New Amsterdam's chief gunner reported that the city's supply of gunpowder was damp and useless. Without firing a shot, the English took over New Netherland and renamed the colony New York.

2.7 Chapter Summary

In this chapter, you read about the first European settlements in the "New World." You used an illustration to learn about the European exploration and settlement of the Americas.

Europeans called the Americas the "New World" because their discovery came as a surprise to them. Explorers like Christopher Columbus were actually looking for a westward route to Asia when they stumbled onto these continents.

European nations competed to claim these new lands and the riches they might contain. Spain claimed vast territories, including Mexico and the southwestern portion of the future United States. In their search for gold and other treasures, Spanish conquistadors conquered the Aztecs of Mexico and the Incas of Peru. The Spanish also brought enslaved Africans to the Americas to plant and harvest crops. In the American Southwest, Spanish missionaries worked to convert Native Americans to Christianity.

The French, meanwhile, staked a claim to much of present-day Canada, as well as Louisiana, the territory west of the Mississippi River. Most French settlers were more interested in trapping and trading furs than in farming or establishing large settlements.

The English based their claim to North America on John Cabot's voyage in 1497. After several attempts, the English established their first permanent colony at Jamestown in Virginia.

The Dutch established their own foothold in North America by founding the colony of New Amsterdam. The English, however, drove the Dutch out and renamed the colony New York.

For Native Americans, the arrival of Europeans brought many changes. The newcomers brought new technology and ideas to the native people. But they also brought deadly diseases that killed great numbers of the first Americans.

The Granger Collection, New York

The exploration and settlement of the Americas brought amazing changes both to Europe and to the New World.

How do you think these people make a living?

What occupations would need boats like these?

What do you think is the occupation of people living here?

The Granger Collection, New York

The Granger Collection, New York

The Granger Collection, New York

The English Colonies in America

3.1 Introduction

In the mid-1700s, a German schoolteacher named Gottlieb Mittelberger boarded a ship bound for the colony of Pennsylvania, in far-off America. Mittelberger had borrowed the cost of his passage by signing on as an **indentured servant**. When he arrived in the colonies, he would have to settle his debt by working for several years for the master who bought his services.

As Mittelberger discovered, the voyage across the Atlantic was horrible. Most passengers suffered greatly from illness and hunger. "The people are packed densely," Mittelberger wrote, "like herrings so to say, in the large sea vessels. One person receives a place of scarcely 2 feet width and 6 feet length.... There is on board these ships terrible misery, stench, fumes, horror, vomiting, many kinds of seasickness, fever, dysentery, headache, heat, constipation, boils, scurvy, cancer, mouth-rot, and the like, all of which come from old and sharply salted food and meat, also from very bad and foul water."

When the nightmarish voyage ended, Mittelberger had to stay on board the ship until his service was bought. Depending on their age and strength, most indentured servants were obliged to work for their masters for three to six years. But, as Mittelberger noted, "young people, from 10 to 15 years, must serve till they are 21 years old."

Why were people willing to go through such hardships to come to the colonies? Many colonists came to America for the chance to own land and start a new life. Others were seeking freedom to practice their religion.

There were some who did not have a choice. A number of convicts (people in jail) were forced to go to America to work off their debts as indentured servants. And millions of Africans were kidnapped from their homelands and brought to the colonies as slaves.

In this chapter, you'll read about the people who settled the English colonies, and why they came. You'll also read in detail about 8 of the 13 colonies. As you do, try to find out what made each one unique.

Graphic Organizer: Spoke Diagram
You will use a spoke diagram to record important features of 8 of the original 13 colonies

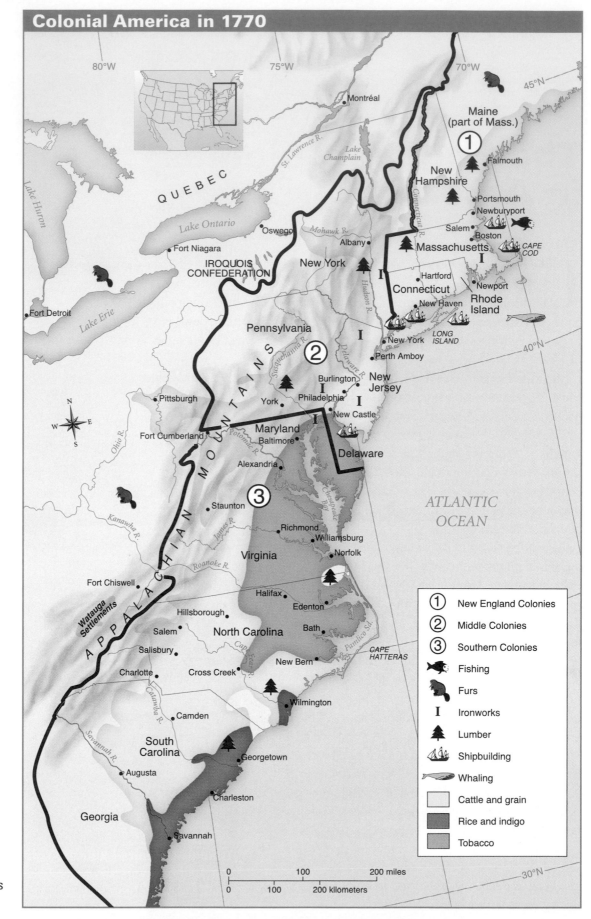

Colonial America in 1770

Maine (part of Mass.)

New Hampshire

Massachusetts

Connecticut

Rhode Island

New York

Pennsylvania

New Jersey

Maryland

Delaware

Virginia

North Carolina

South Carolina

Georgia

QUEBEC

IROQUOIS CONFEDERATION

APPALACHIAN MOUNTAINS

ATLANTIC OCEAN

Montréal
Oswego
Fort Niagara
Fort Detroit
Albany
Falmouth
Portsmouth
Newburyport
Salem
Boston
Newport
Hartford
New Haven
New York
Perth Amboy
Burlington
Philadelphia
York
Pittsburgh
New Castle
Baltimore
Alexandria
Fort Cumberland
Staunton
Richmond
Williamsburg
Norfolk
Fort Chiswell
Halifax
Edenton
Hillsborough
Bath
Salem
New Bern
Salisbury
Cross Creek
Charlotte
Wilmington
Camden
Augusta
Georgetown
Charleston
Savannah

Lake Huron
Lake Ontario
Lake Erie
Lake Champlain
St. Lawrence R.
Mohawk R.
Hudson R.
Connecticut R.
Susquehanna R.
Delaware R.
Potomac R.
Ohio R.
Kanawha R.
James R.
Roanoke R.
Catawba R.
Savannah R.
Cape Fear R.

Wauauga Settlements

LONG ISLAND
CAPE COD
CAPE HATTERAS
Chesapeake Bay
Pamlico Sd.

80°W 75°W 70°W 45°N 40°N 30°N

Legend

1. New England Colonies
2. Middle Colonies
3. Southern Colonies
- Fishing
- Furs
- Ironworks (I)
- Lumber
- Shipbuilding
- Whaling
- Cattle and grain
- Rice and indigo
- Tobacco

0 100 200 miles
0 100 200 kilometers

By 1770, the 13 American colonies had developed distinctive ways of life that would affect the development of America for years to come.

3.2 The New England, Middle, and Southern Colonial Regions

English settlers established colonies in North America for many reasons. Some colonies were set up by groups of businessmen who hoped to profit from resources found in the "New World." Several colonies were settled by people looking for a place to practice their religion freely. One colony was established as a refuge for debtors (people who owe money). The debtors would otherwise have been tossed into prison. The English government supported all these efforts in part because it was competing for land in the New World with such nations as France and Spain.

By 1733, there were 13 British colonies strung along the Atlantic coastline. They can be grouped into three distinct regions: the New England, Middle, and Southern Colonies. These regions had different climates and resources that encouraged settlers to develop different ways of life.

The New England Colonies   The New England region included the colonies of Massachusetts, Rhode Island, Connecticut, and New Hampshire. As you will read in the next section, the first settlers of these colonies came to America seeking religious freedom.

In New England, farming was difficult because of the long, cold winters and the region's rocky, hilly wilderness. But the forests and the sea provided useful resources and ways to make a living. New Englanders built their economy on small farms, lumbering, fishing, shipbuilding, and trade.

The Middle Colonies   The four Middle Colonies were New York, Pennsylvania, New Jersey, and Delaware. The landscape of this region ranged from the rich soil of coastal New Jersey and Delaware to the valleys and wooded mountains of New York and Pennsylvania. Farmers in the Middle Colonies raised a wide variety of crops and livestock. Lumbering, shipbuilding, and other occupations added to the variety of opportunities in these colonies.

By the 1700s, Philadelphia, in the Middle Colony of Pennsylania, had become a bustling trading center and one of the most important cities in the English colonies. It was the first city in America to establish a public school or a newspaper. It was also the first to use a grid or checkerboard pattern to set up its streets.

A DESCRIPTION OF THE SITUATION, HARBOUR &c. OF THE CITY AND PORT OF PHILADELPHIA.

cash crops: crops, such as tobacco, sugar, and cotton, raised in large quantities in order to be sold for profit

assembly: an elected group of lawmakers

democratic: Ruled by the people. In a democracy, citizens elect representatives to make and carry out laws.

The people who settled the Middle Colonies represented many cultures and religions. One important group, the Quakers, started the colony of Pennsylvania. Like the early settlers of New England, the Quakers were looking for freedom to practice their religion. Others seeking religious freedom soon followed. Settlements of French, Dutch, Germans, Swedes, Danes, Finns, Scots, Irish, and English spread throughout the Middle Colonies.

The Southern Colonies   The five Southern Colonies were Maryland, Virginia, North Carolina, South Carolina, and Georgia. This region featured broad rivers and vast wetlands that gradually merged with the sea. Here, the soil and the hot, wet climate were ideal for growing tobacco, rice, and other **cash crops**.

Wealthy colonists took advantage of these conditions by establishing large farms called *plantations*. Plantation owners relied on indentured servants and enslaved Africans to sow and harvest their fields. After being harvested, the crops could be brought by river to the coast and loaded on ships for transport to other colonies and to Europe.

In New England, the church was at the center of both religious and political life. This church's pews could be removed to make room for tables used in town meetings.

Government in the Colonies   All the colonies were settled with the permission of the king of England. For each colony, the king issued a charter, a formal document that outlined the colony's geographic boundaries and specified how it would be governed.

Because the colonies were so far away from England, however, they needed to be able to make their own laws and keep peace and order.

The colonies developed different forms of government, depending on the purpose of the settlement. Most of the colonies were self-governing. Colonists elected members of their community to a general **assembly**, which made their laws.

Many colonies also had a governor appointed by the king. As the king's representative, the governor could overrule the elected assembly. Some colonies also had councils, groups of men who represented the English businessmen involved in starting the colony.

In Massachusetts, religious-minded colonists established a theocracy, a government whose leaders ruled in the name of God. In time, however, a system of town meetings evolved in which colonists voted for representatives to govern them.

In many ways, the colonies were more **democratic** than England. Still, not all colonists had a voice in the government. Usually, only free, white, land-owning men were allowed to vote. In some colonies, voters also had to belong to the preferred church. Other colonists—including women, servants, slaves, and skilled tradesmen who were not landowners—had no voting rights.

3.3 Massachusetts: New England Colony

In the early 1600s, religion was very important in England. The king ruled the official Church of England, also called the Anglican Church. However, not everyone agreed with the Church's ideas and practices.

One group, called **Puritans** by their opponents, wanted to "purify" the Church by making services simpler and doing away with ranks of authority. Some of the Puritans, called Separatists, wanted to separate from the English church and form their own congregations. When Separatists were put in jail for not going to Anglican services, some of them moved to Holland, where they could practice their religion freely.

But Holland wasn't home, and the Separatists wanted their children to grow up in an English culture. In 1620, about 50 Separatists set sail for America aboard the *Mayflower*. The Separatists had become Pilgrims, people who travel for religious reasons. The Pilgrims hoped to build their idea of a perfect society in America. During their voyage, they signed an agreement called the Mayflower Compact that described the way they would govern themselves in the new world.

After a long, uncomfortable journey across the Atlantic, the Pilgrims landed at Plymouth, near Cape Cod. Luckily for them, the local Indians welcomed them. Without the help of these Native Americans, the Pilgrims might not have survived their first winter. The Indians taught them how to plant crops, trap animals, and catch fish. In 1621, the Pilgrims invited the Indians to share their first harvest in a three-day feast of thanksgiving. Americans still celebrate this holiday.

Ten years later, a large group of Puritans decided to follow the Pilgrims to America. The king was relieved to see them go and sent them off with a charter for the colony of Massachusetts Bay. The charter said that the Massachusetts colonists would govern themselves. The Puritans were pleased with the charter, because they wanted to build a community governed by the rules of the Bible. They hoped to set an example for the rest of the world. Their governor, John Winthrop, said, "We must consider that we shall be as a city upon a hill. The eyes of all people are upon us."

Puritans: People who wanted to "purify" the English Church. Puritans wanted to simplify the Church's ceremonies and its ranks of authority.

**Massachusetts
New England Colony**

Founders
Pilgrims led by William Bradford (1620); Puritans led by John Winthrop (1630)

Settlers
Puritans seeking escape from religious persecution

Climate
Harsh winters and warm summers

Geography
Sandy coast with good ports, rich pastures, forests

Economy/Occupations
Crop and livestock farming, lumber, shops, shipping

Religion
Puritan

Government
Self-governing with strong religious influence

John Winthrop was a founder and later the governor of Massachusetts. Here, we see him giving a blessing to soldiers in the colony.

slave trade: the business of capturing, transporting, and selling people as slaves

Rhode Island:
New England Colony

Founders
Roger Williams
and Anne Hutchinson

Settlers
People seeking religious freedom

Climate
Hot, humid summers and
cold, snowy winters

Geography
Coastal lowlands;
flat, rocky woodlands

Economy/Occupations
Farming (large cattle and dairy farms,
small independent farms), lumber,
shipbuilding, fishing, whaling, trade

Religion
Various faiths

Government
Self-governing

3.4 Rhode Island: New England Colony

The Puritans of Massachusetts gained religious freedom, but it was a liberty they kept to themselves. They set up a government that required everyone in the colony to worship in the same way.

When a young minister named Roger Williams began preaching different ideas, the Puritans put him on trial. Williams believed that all people should be able to worship in any way they chose. "Forced worship," he declared, "stinks in God's nostrils."

The Puritans ordered Williams sent back to England. Instead, on a cold winter day in 1636, he left his wife and children and fled south. After trudging through snow for days, he met a group of Indians near Narragansett Bay. The Indians cared for him until spring. When his family and a few followers joined him, Williams bought land from the Indians for a settlement. He called it Providence, a word meaning "the guidance and care of God."

Roger Williams welcomed people with different religious beliefs. Two years after he and his followers settled Providence, a colonist named Anne Hutchinson was also forced to leave Massachusetts for preaching against the Puritans. She and her family followed Williams and established a settlement called Portsmouth. In 1647, these and other settlements became the colony of Rhode Island.

The ideal of freedom in Rhode Island did not extend to enslaved Africans. Sea merchants soon discovered the riches that could be made in the **slave trade**. As a result, Rhode Island became one of the largest slave-trading centers in the world. Slave trading helped make the fortunes of some of the wealthiest families in New England. At the same time, the isolated coves along the Rhode Island coast provided perfect hiding places for pirates and their stolen goods.

Puritans in other colonies were disgusted by these activities. Reverend Cotton Mather of Boston called Rhode Island "the sewer of New England." To these Puritans, Rhode Island represented people and ideas that they rejected from their own communities. Using a word that implied "criminals," they invented their own name for the colony: "Rogues' Island."

This woodcut shows Roger Williams building a crude cabin after he fled Massachusetts in the bitter cold of winter.

3.5 Connecticut: New England Colony

Even in Massachusetts, not all Puritans shared exactly the same ideas. Thomas Hooker was a Puritan clergyman who lived in New Towne, a fast-growing community next to Boston. Hooker didn't always agree with the laws and leadership in Massachusetts. When he heard about a fertile valley along a river to the west, he convinced his family and about 100 other people to move there with him.

It took Hooker and his followers two weeks to travel to the Connecticut Valley with all their animals and belongings. There they established a settlement on the site of an old Dutch fort where an earlier group of English colonists had settled. They called their new community Hartford. In 1639, Hartford joined with two other settlements to form the colony of Connecticut.

Hooker believed that government should be based on the "free consent of the people, to whom belongs the choice of public magistrates [officials], by God's own allowance." He helped draw up the first written plan of government for any of the colonies. This document was called the Fundamental Orders. The Fundamental Orders guaranteed the right to vote to all men who were members of the Puritan church.

Meanwhile, other Puritans formed a separate colony nearby called New Haven. The Puritans of New Haven agreed to live by the "Word of God." Their laws were more strict than those in Hooker's Connecticut colony.

Neither of these colonies, however, was legally authorized by the king. Then, in 1662, King Charles II granted a charter for a new Connecticut Colony that included New Haven. This charter gave the colonists of Connecticut more rights than those enjoyed by any other colonists except in Rhode Island. Legend says that when King James II sent Governor Andros to Hartford 15 years later to take back the colonists' charter, someone stole it and hid it in the trunk of a huge white oak tree. The "Charter Oak" became a symbol of Connecticut's freedom.

Connecticut: New England Colony

Founders
Thomas Hooker

Settlers
Puritans seeking a new settlement

Climate
Cold winters, mild summers

Geography
Forested hills, seacoast

Economy/Occupations
Farming (crops and livestock), shipbuilding, fishing, whaling

Religion
Puritan

Government
Written constitution (the Fundamental Orders), self-governing

Thomas Hooker and about 100 others established the community of Hartford in the fertile Connecticut Valley. It later became a part of the colony of Connecticut.

3.6 New York: Middle Colony

In Chapter 2, you read about how the English took control of the settlement of New Netherland in 1664. The English renamed the colony New York in honor of its new proprietor (owner), James, the Duke of York. The duke gave huge chunks of his colony to two friends, Sir George Carteret and Lord John Berkeley. These men then established the colony of New Jersey to the south of New York.

The duke also awarded large estates along the Hudson River to wealthy Englishmen. The new landowners charged high rents to farmers working their land. This practice created a great difference in wealth between the landowners and their poor tenants. It also discouraged people from settling in New York.

The duke of York expected his colony to be a money-making business. As its owner, he appointed the people who ran the colony. He also issued his own laws and decided what New Yorkers should pay in taxes.

New York's rich landlords approved of the duke's approach to governing his colony. But farmers, fishermen, and tradespeople did not. They demanded the right to elect an assembly to make laws for New York. The duke refused, saying that elected assemblies had a habit of "disturbing the peace of the government."

After years of protest, the duke finally allowed New Yorkers to elect an assembly in 1683. This first assembly passed 15 laws. The most important was a charter listing a number of rights that most colonists thought they should have as English citizens. Among them were the right to elect their own lawmakers, the right to trial by jury, and the right to worship as they pleased.

When the duke saw what the assembly had done, he abolished it. New Yorkers did not get a new assembly until, under the leadership of Jacob Leisler, they rebelled in 1689. Leisler was elected commander in chief of a democratic council that governed until 1691. That year, New York was finally granted the right to elect an assembly with the power to pass laws and set taxes for the colony.

Ships navigate the harbor of New Amsterdam in the 1660s. The city was later renamed New York and became one of the busiest and most important ports in the world.

3.7 Pennsylvania: Middle Colony

The Granger Collection, New York

When William Penn asked King Charles II to let him establish a colony in America, the king had two very good reasons for granting his request. First, he could repay a large debt that he owed to Penn's father, Admiral Penn. Second, he could get rid of William. The younger Penn had been a thorn in the king's side for a long time.

William Penn was a member of the Society of Friends, or Quakers. The Quakers believed in a simple lifestyle and in treating all people as equal. They refused to bow before the king, fight in wars, or pay taxes to the Church of England.

In 1668, the king threw Penn in jail, hoping to stop him from preaching the Quakers' ideas. To the king's dismay, Penn continued preaching after his release.

This picture shows William Penn making a treaty with Indians about 1770. Penn insisted that the Delaware Indians be treated fairly and paid for their land.

With the Quakers unwelcome in England, Penn wanted to establish a colony in America where they would be safe. In 1681, the king granted Penn a huge area of land between the Puritan colonies of New England and the Anglican colonies of the South. In honor of Penn's father, the colony was called Pennsylvania.

Penn advertised his colony all over Europe. In his Great Law of 1682, he promised that people of all faiths would be treated equally.

Penn's appeal attracted settlers from several countries. An early colonist in Pennsylvania marveled at the prosperity and peace in the colony. He wrote, "Poor people (both Men and Women) of all kinds, can here get three times the Wages for their Labour they can in England or Wales…. Here are no Beggars to be seen…. Jealousie among Men is here very rare…. nor are old Maids to be met with; for all commonly Marry before they are Twenty Years of Age."

Penn named his capital city Philadelphia (Greek for "City of Brotherly Love"). From there, he wrote great documents of government that made Pennsylvania the first democracy in America.

Pennsylvania: Middle Colony

Founders
William Penn

Settlers
English Quakers and other Europeans seeking freedom and equality

Climate
Cold winters and hot, humid summers

Geography
Rolling hills, trees, and fertile soil

Economy/Occupations
Farming (crops and dairy), merchants and tradesmen, lumber, shipbuilding

Religion
Various faiths

Government
Self-governing

The Granger Collection, New York

Sir Cecilius Calvert, or Second Lord Baltimore, the founder of Maryland. Calvert established laws to protect Catholics from persecution in the colony.

ANNO Dni 1647
Ætatis 41

3.8 Maryland: Southern Colony

The founding of Maryland was a family enterprise. Sir George Calvert, named Lord Baltimore by King James I, was an English gentleman who became a Roman Catholic. In England, with its official Anglican Church, Catholics were treated harshly. Calvert wanted to start a colony "founded on religious freedom where there would not only be a good life, but also a prosperous one for those bold enough to take the risk." As a businessman, he also hoped the colony would make his own family more prosperous (wealthy).

Unfortunately, Calvert died while he was still bargaining with the king. The new king, King Charles I, granted a charter for the colony to Calvert's son Cecil, the new Lord Baltimore. The charter gave the Calverts complete control of the colony, which was called Maryland.

Armed with these powers, Cecil named his brother Leonard to be governor. In order to make money from the colony, Cecil needed to attract both Protestant and Catholic settlers. He told Leonard to be "very careful to preserve unity and peace…and treat the Protestants with as much mildness and favor as justice will permit."

Leonard's expedition arrived in Maryland in 1634. There, he and his followers built St. Mary's City on a high, dry bluff they purchased from Native Americans. The following year, Leonard agreed to let Maryland elect an assembly.

As more and more settlers arrived, Leonard could see that Catholics would always be outnumbered in the colony. To protect their rights, in 1649 he helped pass America's first law guaranteeing religious liberty, the Act Concerning Religion. This law, however, applied only to Christians. Jews and atheists (people who deny the existence of God) were not included.

Despite the Calverts' efforts, Protestants and Catholics remained suspicious of one another and waged a tug-of-war in Maryland for more than a century. During this time, the colony's founding family lost and regained power several times. Still, George Calvert's dream was fulfilled. Catholics in Maryland worshipped freely and took part in the colony's government alongside Protestants.

Maryland: Southern Colony

Founders
Cecil Calvert (Lord Baltimore)

Settlers
Catholics and Protestants seeking religious and political freedom

Climate
Cold, rainy winters and hot, humid summers

Geography
Low, fertile land surrounding the Chesapeake Bay

Economy/Occupations
Farming, (crops, beef, dairy), lumber, shipping, fishing, iron mining

Religion
Various faiths, particularly Catholic

Government
Self-governing

3.9 Virginia: Southern Colony

In Chapter 2, you read about Jamestown, Virginia, the first successful English settlement in America. After a shaky start, Virginia began to grow and prosper. By 1700, the descendants of those early settlers were wealthy landowners and the most important people in Virginia.

The economy of Virginia was based on tobacco. Tobacco planters needed vast areas of land to be successful. They also needed a large number of workers to grow their crop.

At first, planters tried putting Indians to work. But Indians in this area were not used to farming. Worse, many of them died of diseases they caught from the colonists. The others faded into the forests and disappeared.

Next, tobacco planters tried bringing poor people from England to work their land. In exchange for free passage to Virginia, the workers agreed to become indentured servants for a period of five to seven years. Many men, women, and children came to Virginia as indentured servants. After completing their service, they were given their freedom along with a small plot of land, some clothing, tools, and seeds.

The first Africans brought to Virginia were also treated as indentured servants. At first they had the same rights and freedoms as white servants. Once their service ended, they could buy land and servants of their own.

Gradually, however, planters turned to slaves to solve their labor problem. Slaves brought from Africa cost twice as much as servants, but they did not leave after a few years.

For the planters, enslaving Africans had other advantages as well. Most Africans were hard workers who were used to farming. And because of their dark skin, it was hard for them to escape from their owners and blend into the rest of the population.

In 1661, the Virginia House of Burgesses passed a law making African workers slaves for life. By 1700, Virginia had more than 16,000 enslaved Africans—more than one fourth of the colony's population. For Virginia, slavery had become a way of life.

The first African slaves were brought to Jamestown, Virginia, in 1619, the year before the Pilgrims landed at Plymouth Rock.

Virginia: Southern Colony

Founders
Sir Walter Raleigh and the Virginia Company

Settlers
English landowners, skilled laborers (shoemakers, bricklayers, tailors, etc.), people seeking profits

Climate
Mild winters and hot, humid summers

Geography
Coastal lowlands; wooded mountains

Economy/Occupations
Farming (plantations and small independent farms)

Religion
Church of England

Government
Self-governing

The Granger Collection, New York

Founders
George II and
James Edward Oglethorpe

Settlers
Debtors from English prisons, Europeans
seeking religious freedom and cheap land

Climate
Short, mild winters and
long, hot, humid summers

Geography
Wetlands and red-clay plains;
forested mountains

Economy/Occupations
Farming (plantations and independent
farms), trade, skilled labor

Religion
Various faiths

Government
Self-governing

3.10 Georgia: Southern Colony

Georgia, the 13th and last colony, was founded by a group of Englishmen whose business plan was based on a grand and noble idea. They wanted to help poor people in England stay out of debtor's prison. In England at this time, people who couldn't pay their bills went to jail. James Oglethorpe inspired wealthy Englishmen to give money to help establish a colony where the poor could build better lives instead of going to jail.

King George II and his government liked this plan because the Georgia colony would help keep the Spanish from moving north out of Florida. Georgia would stand between Spanish Florida and the rest of the British colonies to the north.

The Englishmen's plan depended upon getting the cooperation of settlers. But there weren't many poor debtors who wanted to start new lives in the wilderness of North America. Some thought prison would be a safer place.

Instead of an army of poor people, the colonists who went with Oglethorpe to Georgia in 1732 were adventurers much like the settlers in the other colonies. In addition, many Protestants, Catholics, and Jews came to Georgia in search of religious freedom.

As many had feared, life was not easy in Georgia. The Spaniards in Florida wanted to control Georgia, and they continually attacked the new settlements. The Georgians fought them off without any help from the other British colonies. To make matters worse, Oglethorpe had specific ideas about how the colonists should live. He established laws against drinking alcohol and owning slaves. He thought the settlers should live on small farms and learn to farm their land themselves.

The settlers weren't about to go along. They wanted to farm large plantations and own slaves like the wealthy planters in neighboring colonies. They disliked some of Oglethorpe's other rules as well.

Trying to mold Georgia into his idea of a perfect society, Oglethorpe lost all his money. For its settlers, however, Georgia became as successful as the other Southern Colonies.

The Granger Collection, New York

James Oglethorpe, the founder of Georgia, is pictured here in Scottish dress.

3.11 Chapter Summary

In this chapter, you read about the settlement of the 13 English colonies in the future United States. You used a spoke diagram to record important features of eight of these colonies.

Settlers had many reasons to come to America in the 1600s and 1700s. Two important reasons were freedom of religion and the chance to start a new life. However, even though colonists treasured freedom for themselves, enslaved Africans were taken to America by force.

The New England, Middle, and Southern Colonies all had distinctive geographies and natural resources. As a result, different ways of life developed in each of these regions. Colonies also varied in their form of government. All, however, were democratic to some degree.

In the New England Colonies, religion and geography were key influences. Although Puritans sometimes disagreed with one another, they hoped to establish model communities based on their religious faith. New England's forests and coastline made lumbering, shipbuilding, and trade very important to the region's economy.

The Middle Colonies were geographically, culturally, and religiously diverse. Catholics, Quakers, Anglicans, and members of other Protestant faiths all found homes in this region.

In the Southern Colonies, climate and geography encouraged the planting of cash crops and the development of large plantations. In time, slave labor would become a major part of the economy of this region.

What was daily life like for the settlers, servants, and slaves who came to America? You'll find out in the next chapter.

Handbills like this one lured colonists from Europe to the American colonies.

NOVA BRITANNIA.
OFFERING MOST
Excellent fruites by Planting in VIRGINIA.
Exciting all such as be well affected to further the same.

Printed for SAMVEL MACHAM, and are to be sold at his Shop in Pauls Church-yard, at the Signe of the Bul-head.
LONDON
1609.

What different classes of people can you see?

What do these men have in their cart and where might they be going?

Life in the Colonies

4.1 Introduction

In 1723, a tired teenager stepped off a boat onto Philadelphia's Market Street wharf. He was an odd-looking sight. Not having luggage, he had stuffed his pockets with extra clothes. The young man followed a group of "clean dressed people" into a Quaker meeting house, where he soon fell asleep.

The sleeping teenager with the lumpy clothes was Benjamin Franklin. Recently, he had run away from his brother James's print shop in Boston. When he was 12, Franklin had signed a contract to work for his brother for nine years. But after enduring James's nasty temper for five years, Franklin packed his pockets and left.

In Philadelphia, Franklin quickly found work as a printer's assistant. Within a few years, he had saved enough money to open his own print shop. His first success was a newspaper called the *Pennsylvania Gazette*.

In 1732, readers of the *Gazette* saw an advertisement for *Poor Richard's Almanac.* An *almanac* is a book, published annually, that contains information about weather predictions, the times of sunrises and sunsets, planting advice for farmers, and other useful subjects. According to the advertisement, *Poor Richard's Almanac* was written by "Richard Saunders" and printed by "B. Franklin." Nobody knew then that the author and printer were actually the same person.

In addition to the usual information contained in almanacs, Franklin mixed in some proverbs, or wise sayings. Several of them are still remembered today. Three of the best-known are:

"A penny saved is a penny earned."

"Early to bed, early to rise, makes a man healthy, wealthy, and wise."

"Fish and visitors smell in three days."

Poor Richard's Almanac sold so well that Franklin was able to retire at age 42. A man of many talents, he spent the rest of his long life as a scientist, inventor, political leader, diplomat, and national postmaster.

Franklin's rise from penniless runaway to wealthy printer was one of many colonial success stories. In this chapter, you will learn what life was like for people throughout the colonies in the early 1700s.

Journal On Colonial Life

Home Life
- Farm
- City

Society
- Rights of Colonists
- Crime and Punishment
- Class Differences
- African Americans

Mind and Spirit
- Religion
- Education

Life Style
- Families
- Leisure
- Food

Graphic Organizer: Journal
You will use a journal to organize information about various aspects of colonial life.

Although most farmers lived in one-room farmhouses, they held out hope that they would achieve wealth like that pictured above.

4.2 Life on a Farm

Nine out of ten people in the colonies lived on small family farms. Most farm families either raised or made nearly everything they needed. One farmer wrote with pride that, in a single year, "I never laid out (besides my taxes) more than ten dollars.... Nothing to wear, eat, or drink was purchased, as my farm provided all."

The first and hardest task facing farm families was to clear the land of trees. The colonists had only simple, basic tools. They cut down trees with axes and saws. Then they used the same tools to cut square timbers and flat planks for building houses, barns, and fences.

Imagine living on a colonial farm. Your home is a single large room with a chimney at one end. In this room, your family cooks, eats, and sleeps. Your parents sleep in a large bed built into one corner. Your younger brothers and sisters sleep in a smaller "trundle" bed, a bed that can slide under the big bed during the day. At bedtime, you climb a ladder next to the chimney to sleep in an attic or a loft. As your family grows, you help to build another room on the other side of the chimney.

The fireplace is the only source of heat for warmth and cooking. So, keeping a supply of firewood is important. The fire is kept burning all the time because, without matches, it is very difficult to light a new one.

Cooking is one of the most dangerous jobs on your farm. Food is cooked in heavy iron pots hung over an open fire. While lifting or stirring these pots, your mother might burn her hands, scorch her clothes, or strain her back.

Life on your farm starts before sunrise. Everyone wakes up early to share the work. Chores include cutting wood, feeding animals, clearing land, tending crops, building fences, making furniture and tools, gathering eggs, spinning thread, weaving cloth, sewing clothes, making candles and soap, cooking, cleaning, and caring for babies.

How does this compare with life in your home today?

4.3 Life in Cities

In 1750, one colonist out of 20 lived in a city. Compared to the quiet farm life, cities were exciting places.

The heart of the city was the waterfront. There, ships brought news from England as well as eagerly awaited items such as paint, carpets, furniture, and books.

Just beyond the docks, a marketplace bustled with fishermen selling their catch and farmers selling fresh eggs, milk, and cheese. Close by were taverns, where food and drink were served. People gathered there to exchange gossip and news from other colonies.

The nearby streets were lined with shops. Sparks flew from the blacksmith's block as he hammered iron into tools. Shoemakers, clockmakers, silversmiths, tailors, and other craftspeople turned out goods based on the latest designs from England. There were barbers to cut colonists' hair and wigmakers to make it look long again.

Cities were noisy, smelly places. Church bells rang out daily. Carts clattered loudly over streets paved with round cobblestones. The air was filled with the stench of rotting garbage and open sewers, but the colonists were used to it. Animals ran loose in the street. During hot weather, clouds of flies and mosquitoes swarmed about.

Colonial cities were very small by today's standards. Boston and Philadelphia, the two largest, had fewer than 20,000 people in 1700.

City homes were close together on winding streets. Most were built of wood with thatched roofs, like the houses the colonists had left behind in Europe. Their windows were small, because glass was costly.

For lighting, colonists used torches made of pine that burned brightly when they were wedged between hearthstones in the fireplace. Colonists also burned grease in metal containers called "betty lamps" and made candles scented with bayberries.

With torches and candles lighting homes, fire was a constant danger. Colonists kept fire buckets hanging by their front doors. When a fire broke out, the whole town helped to put it out. Grabbing their buckets, colonists formed a double line from the fire to a river, pond, or well. They passed the buckets full of water from hand to hand up one line to the fire. Then the empty buckets went hand over hand back down the opposite line to be filled again.

4.4 Rights of Colonists

Colonists in America saw themselves as English citizens. They expected the same **rights** that citizens enjoyed in England. The most important of these was the right to have a voice in their government.

rights: powers or privileges that belong to people as citizens and that cannot or should not be taken away by the government

Parliament: the lawmaking body of England, consisting of representatives from throughout the kingdom

petition (verb): to make a formal demand or request

The Magna Carta The English people had won the right to participate in their government only after a long struggle. A key victory in this struggle came in 1215, when King John agreed to sign the Magna Carta, or "Great Charter." This agreement established the idea that the power of the monarch (ruler) was limited. Not even the king was above the law.

The next major victory was the founding of **Parliament** in 1265. Parliament was made up of representatives from across England. Over time, it became a lawmaking body with the power to approve laws and taxes proposed by the king or queen.

The Granger Collection, New York

Colonists established assemblies to promote citizen rights. The English tradition of self-government thrived in all 13 colonies. Here we see a depiction of the first colonial assembly of Virginia in 1619.

In 1685, James, the Duke of York, became King James II. As you read in Chapter 3, King James did not want to share power with an elected assembly in New York. Nor did he want to share power with an elected Parliament in England. When he tried to rule without Parliament, James was forced off his throne. This event, which took place without bloodshed, is known as the Glorious Revolution.

The English Bill of Rights
In 1689, Parliament offered the crown to Prince William of Orange and his wife, Mary. In exchange, they had to agree to an act, or law, known as the English Bill of Rights. This act said that the power to make laws and impose taxes belonged to the people's elected representatives in Parliament and to no one else. It also included a bill, or list, of rights that belonged to the people. Among these were the right to **petition** the king and the right to trial by jury.

English colonists saw the Glorious Revolution as a victory not only for Parliament, but for their colonial assemblies as well. They wanted to choose the people who made their laws and set their taxes. After all, this was a cherished right of all English citizens.

The Granger Collection, New York

4.5 Crime and Punishment

Each colonial assembly passed its own laws defining crimes and punishments. However, most crimes were treated similarly in all the colonies.

Certain very serious crimes could be punished by death. These included murder, treason (acts of disloyalty toward the government), and piracy (robbery at sea). Puritans in New England added other crimes to this list based on their understanding of God's law in the Bible. In New England, colonists could be put to death for "denying the true God" or for striking or cursing their parents.

Crimes such as theft, forgery, and highway robbery carried harsh punishments in every colony. For these crimes, people might be jailed, whipped, or branded with hot irons.

Lesser crimes, such as drunkenness and breaking the Sabbath (working or traveling on Sunday), were punished with fines, short jail terms, or public humiliation. A colonist caught breaking the Sabbath, for example, might be locked in the town stocks. Stocks were a heavy wooden frame with holes for a person's neck, wrists, and ankles. Lawbreakers were locked for hours in this device in a public place where others might make fun of them.

No group had firmer ideas about right and wrong than New England's Puritans. The Puritans required everyone to attend church on Sundays. They also forbade anyone to work or play on that day. The Puritans wrote their Sunday laws in books with blue paper bindings. For this reason, these rules came to be known as *blue laws.* Some blue laws persist to this day. In Massachusetts, for example, it is still illegal to sell liquor on Sundays.

The Puritans were constantly on the watch for signs of Satan (an evil angel who rebelled against God). Satan was thought to work through witches. In 1691, fear of witchcraft exploded in Salem, Massachusetts, when several young girls were seen acting strangely in church. When they were questioned, the girls accused their neighbors of being witches and putting spells on them. Twenty accused witches were put to death in the Salem Witch Trials before calm was restored and the townspeople realized that the girls' accusations were not true.

Courts, like the one pictured above, were important to social life in the colonies. This painting depicts a woman being tried for witchcraft in Salem, Massachusetts, in 1692.

4.6 Class Differences

Like many people today, those living in colonial times were eager to "move up in the world." In England, "moving up" was difficult. A person's **class**, or place in society, was determined largely by family, inherited titles (such as "duke" or "baron"), and wealth.

In colonial America, however, titles and family background meant little. Most colonists started out poor. Those with ambition could use their brains and talents to climb the social ladder. A poor boy, for example, might turn into an upper-class gentleman by becoming a successful planter, merchant, or lawyer. A poor girl could move up by marrying a man of a higher social class. In America, what set the classes apart was not family background, but money.

"Clothing makes the man!" This old saying aptly describes colonial society. In the colonies, people's clothes showed their social position. Only the gentry, or wealthy class, wore gold or silver, colored lace, buttons, boots, and wigs. Some colonies forbade ordinary citizens from wearing such "excess apparel" (clothing) and even fined those who disobeyed.

The middle class was made up of farmers and artisans (skilled crafts-people). These were people who owned their own land or businesses. Many had enough property to qualify to vote. During the week, people of the middle class wore plain but brightly colored clothes. On Sundays, they wore dark, somber clothing.

The lower class was mostly made up of farmhands and other workers. Members of this class depended on others for their wages. With little or no property of their own, they were not allowed to vote. Some were able to save enough money to buy land or start a business and rise to the middle class. Others remained wage earners their entire lives.

At the bottom of colonial society were indentured servants and slaves. Indentured servants made up a third of New England's settlers, and almost half of those who settled the Middle Colonies. Some eventually saved enough money to buy land and rise to the middle class. Others became wage earners. But even the poorest white laborers were better off than most African Americans.

Class divisions are apparent in this painting. The wealthy sit high on a wagon, surrounded by stacks of trunks carrying their many possessions. The children of the farmhands and servants bid the travelers farewell.

4.7 Life for African Americans

You read in Chapter 3 how slavery first came to Virginia. From there, it spread both north and south. By the early 1700s, enslaved Africans were living in every colony. Even Benjamin Franklin owned slaves for a time. But like most people in the northern colonies, Franklin found that hiring workers when he needed them cost less than owning slaves.

In the Southern Colonies, however, slavery expanded rapidly. From Virginia to Georgia, slaves helped raise tobacco, rice, indigo, and other cash crops.

The Atlantic Slave Trade   Most of the slaves who were brought to the colonies came from West Africa. Year after year, slave ships filled with cloth, guns, and rum sailed from the colonies to the coast of West Africa. There, these goods were traded for Africans. The ships then returned to the Americas carrying their human cargoes.

For the Africans packed onto slave ships, the ocean crossing—known as the Middle Passage—was a nightmare. Olaudah Equiano was just ten years old when he was put onto a slave ship. He never forgot "the closeness of the place…which was so crowded that each had scarcely room to turn himself." Nor did he forget "the shrieks of the women, and groans of the dying." The terrified boy refused to eat, hoping "for the last friend, Death, to relieve me."

Although Equiano survived the voyage, many Africans died of sickness or despair. Even so, the Atlantic slave trade was very profitable. Many colonial merchants built fortunes trading in human beings.

Work without Hope   The slaves' masters in America demanded hard work. Most enslaved Africans were put to work in the fields raising crops. Others worked as nurses, carpenters, blacksmiths, drivers, servants, gardeners, and midwives (people who assist women giving birth). Unlike other colonists, slaves had little hope of making a better life. Their position was fixed at the bottom of colonial society.

Some Africans rebelled against slavery by refusing to work or running away. But most adapted to their unhappy condition as best they could. Slowly and painfully, they began to create a new African American way of life.

The Granger Collection, New York

The first slaves were brought to the United States in 1619 to help produce tobacco in the Virginia colony. Above, we see slaves tending tobacco while their owner relaxes, feet up, smoking his pipe.

4.8 Religion

First Great Awakening: a revival of religious feeling and belief in the American colonies that began in the 1730s

Religion was an important part of colonial life. Most colonists tried to lead good lives based on their faith. Children grew up reading the Bible from cover to cover several times over.

Puritan Church Services In New England, the sound of a drum or horn called Puritans to worship on Sunday morning. "Captains of the Watch" made sure everyone was a "Sabbath-keeper." Sometimes, houses were searched to ensure that everyone was at church.

Church services were held in the town meetinghouse. This was the most important building in the community and was used for all public meetings. Inside were rows of wooden benches called *pews,* and a pulpit (a platform where the preacher stood). A "Seating Committee" carefully assigned seats, with the best ones going to older, wealthy people.

Services could last as long as five hours. At midday, villagers would go to "noon-houses" near the church to warm themselves by a fire, eat, and socialize. Then they returned to church for the long afternoon sermon.

The First Great Awakening

Beginning in the 1730s, a religious movement known as the **First Great Awakening** swept through the colonies. This movement was spurred by a feeling that people had lost their religious faith. "The forms of religion were kept up," a Puritan observed, but the "power of Godliness" was missing.

To revive people's religious spirit, preachers traveled from town to town holding outdoor "revival" meetings. There they delivered fiery sermons to huge crowds. Their words touched the hearts and souls of many colonists. Benjamin Franklin wrote about the change he observed in Philadelphia:

Colonial society had a strong religious flavor. Above, we see colonial citizens gathered around a church on Sunday.

From being thoughtless or indifferent about religion, it seemed as if all the world were growing religious, so that one could not walk through the town in an evening without hearing psalms [Bible songs] sung in different families of every street.

The Great Awakening had a powerful effect on the colonies. It helped spread the idea that all people are equal in the eyes of God. Ordinary people did not need long sermons or years of education to understand God's will. All they needed was an open heart and a desire to know God's truth.

4.9 Education

Except in New England, most children in the colonies received little formal education. Neither the Middle nor the Southern Colonies had public schools.

In the Southern Colonies, most families were spread out along rivers. A few neighbors might get together to hire a teacher for their children. Often, wealthy planters hired tutors to educate younger children at home. Older children were sent to schools in distant cities, or even England, to complete their education.

In the Middle Colonies, religious differences among Quakers, Catholics, Jews, Baptists, and other religious groups slowed the growth of public education. Each religious group or family had to decide for itself how to educate its children. Some groups built church schools. Others were content to have parents teach their children at home.

Only in New England were towns required to provide public schools. The Puritans' support for education was inspired by their faith. They wanted their children to be able to read God's word in the Bible.

To encourage education, Massachusetts passed a law in 1647 that required every town with 50 families or more to hire an instructor to teach their children to read and write. Towns with more than 100 families were required to build a school. Similar laws were passed in other New England colonies.

Parents were asked to contribute whatever they could to the village school. This might mean money, vegetables, firewood, or anything else the school needed. Often, land was set aside as "school-meadows" or "school-fields." This land was then rented out to raise money for teachers' salaries.

Schools were one-room buildings with a chimney and fireplace in the center. There were no maps, or boards to write on. Pencils and paper were scarce. Students shouted out spelling words and wrote sums in ink on pieces of bark. There was usually one book, the *New England Primer,* which was used to teach the alphabet, syllables, and prayers.

Most colonists believed that boys needed more education than girls. "Female education, in the best families," wrote Abigail Adams, "went no further than writing and arithmetic; in some few and rare instances, music, and dancing."

The Granger Collection, New York

Children gather with their teacher in a colonial school. These children were among a minority of children who received formal education. Most children did not go to school beyond the elementary level.

Family life was at the center of colonial society. Here, a family is gathered around a fire on a cold, wintry evening. A mother and grandmother work while the father relaxes and the children play.

4.10 Colonial Families

The concept of family has changed many times throughout history. Today, most people think of a family as being made up of parents and their children. In colonial times, however, families might include grandparents, aunts and uncles, cousins, and stepchildren.

Marriage   Colonial men and women generally married in their early to mid-20s. Those who arrived in America as indentured servants were not allowed to marry until they had gained their freedom.

Men outnumbered women throughout the colonies. As a result, almost every woman was assured of receiving a marriage proposal. "Maid servants of good honest stock [family]," wrote a colonist, could "choose their husbands out of the better sort of people." For a young woman, though, life as a wife and mother often proved to be even harder than life as an indentured servant.

Large Families   Colonial families were generally large. Most families had between seven and ten children. (Benjamin Franklin had 17 brothers and sisters!) Farm families, in particular, needed all the hands they could get to help with the chores.

Religious and cultural backgrounds influenced colonists' ideas about raising children. But almost everywhere in the colonies, children were expected to be productive members of the family.

Married women gave birth many times, but nearly half of all children died before they reached adulthood. Childhood deaths were especially high in the Middle and Southern Colonies, where the deadly disease of malaria raged. Adults often died young as well. After the death of a wife or husband, men and women usually remarried quickly. Thus, households often swelled with stepchildren as well as adopted orphans (children whose parents had died).

Whether colonists lived in cities, in villages, or on isolated farms, their lives focused on their families. Family members took care of one another because there was no one else to do so. Young families often welcomed elderly grandparents, aunts, uncles, and cousins into their homes when they could no longer care for themselves. It didn't matter if there was barely enough room for everyone. No one would turn away a needy relative.

4.11 Leisure

While most colonists worked hard, they enjoyed their periods of leisure (time away from work). They also took advantage of gatherings, such as town meetings and Sunday services, to talk with neighbors and make friends.

Bees and Frolics   When possible, colonists combined work and play by organizing "bees" and "frolics." New settlers might hold a "chopping bee" in which all the neighbors helped clear the trees off their land. Other frolics included corn-husking bees for men and quilting bees for women. Sharing the work made it faster and a lot more fun.

The Germans introduced house and barn raisings to the colonies. At these events, neighbors joined together to build the frame of a house or barn in one day. The men assembled the four walls flat on the ground and then raised them into place. Meanwhile, the women prepared a huge feast. At the end of the day, everyone danced on the barn's new floor.

Here, we see Dutch settlers in a spirited game of bowls in New Amsterdam. Below, colonists enjoy a form of billiards called "trock."

The Granger Collection, New York

Toys and Sports   Colonial children had a few simple toys, such as dolls, marbles, and tops. They played games of tag, blindman's bluff, and stoolball, which was related to the English game of cricket (a game like baseball). Children in New England also enjoyed "coasting" downhill on sleds. Adults must have thought coasting was dangerous, because several communities forbade it.

Adults enjoyed several sports. Almost every village had a bowling green. Here men rolled egg-shaped balls down a lane of grass toward a white ball called a "jack." Colonists also played a game similar to backgammon called "tick-tack" and a form of billiards (pool) called "trock."

In the south, fox hunting with horses and hounds was a popular sport. Card playing was another favorite pastime, one that New England Puritans disapproved of strongly. Horse racing, cockfighting, and bull baiting were also popular.

Fairs were held throughout the colonies. At these events, colonists competed in contests of skill and artistry. There were footraces, wrestling matches, dance contests, and wild scrambles to see who could win a prize by catching a greased pig or climbing a greased pole.

Life in the Colonies   **59**

The Granger Collection, New York

Food preparation occupied a great deal of time in the colonies. Here, we see one woman rolling corn meal while another cooks on the stove. The woman in the doorway is using a butter churn.

4.12 Food

The first colonists in North America traded with Indians for their food. The Indians taught them how to grow and cook corn, which became a major part of the colonists' diet. Colonial children knew that morning and evening meals would probably consist of something made from corn.

Most colonists ate ground corn-meal cooked into a mush or a cake every day. Women pounded corn for hours in wooden bowls called *mortars*. It is said that fishermen lost in a fog would know they were close to land when they heard the pounding sound.

Meat was a favorite food for many colonists. Colonists hunted wild deer, rabbits, and birds. They also raised pigs, cattle, and chickens. Their biggest problem with meat was how to keep it from going bad. Without refrigerators, meat had to be salted, smoked, or pickled to keep it from rotting. Colonists often used pepper and other spices to disguise the bad taste of old meat.

Fruit was another major food. Apple trees grew well in the New England and Middle Colonies. "Apple pie is used through the whole year," wrote a visitor to Delaware in 1758. "And when fresh apples are no longer to be had, dried ones are used. It is the evening meal of children." In spring and summer, children picked wild huckleberries, blackberries, blueberries, grapes, and strawberries. In the Southern Colonies, colonists had more peaches than they could eat.

Many colonists thought vegetables were unhealthy, particularly if eaten raw. Still, they learned to be thankful for native pumpkins, squash, beans, peas, and sweet potatoes. They also planted root vegetables, such as parsnips, turnips, carrots, and onions. In the English tradition, they cooked these vegetables into mushy stews seasoned with meat and herbs from their gardens.

Great iron pots of stew simmered 24 hours a day in colonial fireplaces. Keeping food hot reduced the chances that it would spoil. Each day, bowls of stew were served at the main meal, which was eaten between noon and three o'clock. For breakfast and dinner, colonists ate mostly some form of corn mush sweetened with milk, fruit, honey, molasses, or maple syrup.

4.13 Chapter Summary

In this chapter, you read about life in the American colonies during the early 1700s. You used a journal to organize information about various aspects of colonial life.

Whether they lived on farms, in villages, or in cities, colonists worked hard. Farm families produced most of what they needed for themselves. In the cities, many trades and crafts developed.

American colonists expected to enjoy all the rights of English citizens, especially the right to have a voice in their own government. Crimes and punishments were defined by colonial assemblies. Often, punishments were harsh.

Class differences in the colonies were based mostly on wealth. Most people in lower classes could hope to move up through hard work. Enslaved African Americans had almost no such hope. After being brought to America in chains, they faced a life of forced obedience and toil.

Religion was very important to the colonists. The First Great Awakening revived religious feeling and helped spread the idea that all people are equal.

Except in New England, most colonial children received little education. Instead, they were expected to contribute to the work of the farm or home. Most colonial families were large. Often they included many relatives besides the parents and their children.

Much of colonial life was hard work, even preparing food. But colonists found ways to mix work with play. They also enjoyed sports and games.

For most of the 1700s, the colonists were content to be ruled by English laws. In the next chapter, however, you'll learn how tensions grew between the colonists and the government in far-off England.

This panorama of Philadelphia in 1702 reveals a number of aspects of colonial life. Church steeples, government buildings, colonial homes, ships, and citizens on unpaved colonial roads are all evident in the painting.

PHILADELPHIA IN THE OLDEN TIME

The Granger Collection, New York

What is happening here? Who is the man on horseback?

Why might this man be happy? Is he a Loyalist or a Patriot?

What might these Loyalists be thinking?

Toward Independence

5.1 Introduction

An almost full moon cast a pale light over Boston on April 18, 1775. But the night was anything but quiet. Mounted on Brown Beauty, one of the fastest horses in Massachusetts, Paul Revere woke up the countryside with alarming news. British troops stationed in Boston were on the move! They had orders to march to the nearby town of Concord and seize weapons that the colonists had stored there.

This was news that local Patriots had been waiting for. **Patriots** were Americans who believed that the colonies had the right to govern themselves. On hearing Revere's warning, Patriots around Concord grabbed their muskets and prepared to meet the British troops.

The same news filled Loyalists with dread. **Loyalists** were Americans who felt a deep loyalty to Great Britain. They saw themselves as faithful subjects of the king. They were horrified by the idea of taking up arms against British troops. How did colonists become so divided in their feelings about the British? As you read in the last chapter, most Americans were content with British rule in the early 1700s. In this chapter, you will learn what happened to change the relationship between Britain and the colonies.

The story begins in the 1750s, when Britain and the colonies fought a war against the French and their Indian **allies**. The French and Indian War left Britain with huge debts and a vast new empire to protect. To solve its problems, the British government passed new laws that tightened its control of the colonies. Some of these laws also placed new taxes on the colonists.

Americans were stunned. They had always had the right to make their own laws and taxes. Suddenly, Britain was changing the rules. It wasn't right, the colonists protested. It wasn't fair!

You probably know just how they felt. In this chapter, you will see how these feelings led the colonists to the brink of war.

Graphic Organizer: Metaphor
You will use a metaphor to compare the tensions between Britain and the colonies to the strained relationship between a principal and students.

Before 1763, the colonies enjoyed life free from British control.

militia: a small army made up of ordinary citizens who are available to fight in an emergency

5.2 Before 1763

By 1750, the American colonies were bursting with growth. In just a century, the population of the colonies had grown from 50,000 to more than a million people. What brought about this rapid growth? Cheap land? Religious tolerance? Economic opportunity? All of these were important in attracting people to the colonies. But there was another reason.

For more than a century, the British government had mostly left the colonies alone to solve their own problems. During this time, Americans had learned to govern themselves. Each colony elected its own assembly. Like the British Parliament, the assemblies had the power to pass laws and create taxes. Each assembly also decided how the colony's tax money should be spent. Americans had more freedom to run their own affairs than ordinary people in any country in Europe.

Conflict in the Ohio Valley   As the colonies grew, settlers began to dream of moving across the Appalachian Mountains and into the Ohio Valley—the region between the Ohio and Mississippi Rivers. Both Britain and France claimed this area. In 1754, the French made good on their claim by building a fort where the city of Pittsburgh stands today. They called it Fort Duquesne (doo-KANE).

News of the fort alarmed the governor of Virginia. He ordered a small force of Virginia **militia** to drive the French out of the Ohio Valley. Militias are small armies of citizens who are trained to fight in an emergency. To head the militia, the governor chose a 22-year-old volunteer named George Washington.

Today, Americans remember George Washington as a great Patriot, a military hero, and the first president of the United States. In 1754, however, he was just an ambitious young man with no land or money. Washington believed that his best chance of getting ahead was to become an officer in the British army. There was only one problem with his plan. Most British officers believed that colonists made lousy soldiers.

The expedition into the Ohio Valley gave Washington a chance to prove them wrong. Near Fort Duquesne, he came across a French scouting party that was camped in the woods. Washington ordered his men to open fire. It was an easy victory. "I heard the bullets whistle," he wrote afterward. "And, believe me, there is something charming in the sound."

The French and Indian War   Washington's whistling bullets were the first shots in a conflict known as the French and Indian War. This war was part of a long struggle between France and Britain for territory and power. Because many Native Americans fought with France in this latest conflict, the colonists called it the French and Indian War.

In 1755, Britain sent 1,400 British soldiers to Virginia to finish the job that Washington had begun. They were led by a bumbling general named Edward Braddock. The soldiers' job was to clear the French out of the Ohio Valley. Washington joined the army as a volunteer, hoping to make a good impression on General Braddock.

The British army's march into the Ohio Valley was a disaster. The troops' bright red uniforms made them perfect targets for French sharp-shooters and their Indian allies. Two-thirds of the soldiers were killed.

Washington himself narrowly escaped death. "I had four Bullets through my Coat and two horses shot under me," he wrote in his journal. Showing great courage, Washington led the survivors back to Virginia. There, he was greeted as a hero.

The French and Indian War raged for seven long years. The turning point came in 1759, when British troops captured Canada. In 1763, Britain and France signed a peace treaty ending the war. In this treaty, France ceded, or gave, Canada to Great Britain.

Americans were thrilled with this victory. Great Britain now controlled a vastly expanded American empire. Never before had the colonists felt so proud of being British. And never before had the future of the colonies looked so bright.

Here, we see George Washington tipping his hat to the British flag at Fort Duquesne. The British captured the badly damaged fort in 1758. It was rebuilt and called Fort Pitt. The city of Pittsburg was later built here.

The Granger Collection, New York

5.3 Early British Actions

Changes that were taking place in Britain soon clouded the colonists' bright future. A new king, George III, had been crowned in 1760. He was not a bright man. One historian wrote that "he was very stupid, really stupid." He was also proud and stubborn. Worse yet, he was determined to be a "take-charge" kind of ruler, especially in the colonies.

Unfortunately, the people George III chose to help him were not much brighter than he was. And they knew very little about conditions in America. Before long, they were taking actions that enraged the colonists.

The Proclamation of 1763 The British government faced a number of problems after the French and Indian War. One was how to keep colonists and Native Americans from killing each other as settlers pushed westward. No problem, said George III. Simply draw a line down the crest of the Appalachian Mountains. Tell settlers to stay east of that line and Indians to stay west of it.

This was what the king ordered in his Proclamation of 1763. To Americans, the king's order suggested **tyranny,** or the unjust use of government power. They argued that the lands east of the Appalachians were already mostly settled. The only place that farmers could find new land was west of the mountains. Besides, the Proclamation was too late. Settlers were already crossing the mountains.

The British government ignored these arguments. To keep peace on the frontier, it decided to expand the British army in America to 7,500 men.

tyranny: The unjust use of government power. A ruler who uses power in this way is called a *tyrant.*

North America in 1763

The Proclamation of 1763 prohibited settlers from moving west of the Appalachian Mountains. King George hoped this would prevent conflict between the colonists and Native Americans.

The Stamp Act angered the colonists, who felt that taxation without representation was unfair. Protests, such as the one shown here, forced Parliament to repeal the act.

The Stamp Act   The British government had other problems besides keeping colonists and Native Americans from killing each other. One was how to pay off the large debt left over from the French and Indian War.

The solution seemed obvious to Prime Minister George Grenville, the leader of the British government. People in Britain were already paying taxes on everything from windows to salt. In contrast, Americans were probably the most lightly taxed people in the British Empire. It was time, said Grenville, for the colonists to pay their fair share of the cost of protecting them.

In 1765, Grenville proposed a new act, or law, called the Stamp Act. This law required colonists to buy a stamp for every piece of paper they used. Newspapers had to be printed on stamped paper. Wills, licenses, and even playing cards had to have stamps.

Once again, the colonists sensed tyranny. One newspaper, *The Pennsylvania Journal*, said that as soon as "this shocking Act was known, it filled all British America from one End to the other, with Astonishment and Grief."

It wasn't just the idea of higher taxes that upset the colonists. They were willing to pay taxes passed by their own assemblies, where their representatives could vote on them. But the colonists had no representatives in Parliament. For this reason, they argued, Parliament had no right to tax them. They saw the Stamp Act as a violation of their rights as British subjects. "No taxation without representation!" they cried.

Some colonists protested the Stamp Act by sending messages to Parliament. Loyalists simply refused to buy stamps. Patriots, however, took more violent action. Mobs calling themselves "Sons of Liberty" attacked tax collectors' homes. Protesters in Connecticut even started to bury one tax collector alive. Only when he heard dirt being shoveled onto his coffin did the terrified tax collector agree to resign from his post.

After months of protest, Parliament **repealed,** or canceled, the Stamp Act. Americans greeted the news with great celebration. Church bells rang, bands played, and everyone hoped the troubles with Britain were over.

According to the Stamp Act, colonists had to buy stamps like this and place them on all paper products, such as newspapers, wills, and playing cards.

repeal: to take back, or to cancel, a law

The Quartering Act   As anger over the Stamp Act began to fade, Americans noticed another law passed by Parliament in 1765. Called the Quartering Act, this law ordered colonial assemblies to provide British troops with quarters, or housing. The colonists were also told to furnish the soldiers with "candles, firing, bedding, cooking utensils, salt, vinegar, and…beer or cider."

Of course, providing for the soldiers cost money. New Jersey protested that the new law was "as much an Act for laying taxes" on the colonists as the Stamp Act. New Yorkers asked why they should pay to keep troops in their colony. After all, they said, the soldiers just took up space and did nothing.

In 1767, the New York assembly decided not to vote any funds for "salt, vinegar and liquor." The British government reacted by refusing to let the assembly meet until it agreed to obey the Quartering Act. Once again, tempers began to rise on both sides of the Atlantic.

In 1768, the British government sent soldiers to Boston to enforce the Townshend Acts. This Paul Revere engraving shows the troops landing.

5.4 The Townshend Acts

The next British leader to face the challenge of taxing the colonies was Charles Townshend. He was also known as "Champagne Charlie" because of his habit of making speeches in Parliament after drinking champagne. Townshend believed that the colonists' bad behavior made it even more important to keep an army in America. Once he was asked in Parliament if he would dare to make the colonists pay for that army. Stamping his foot, Townshend shouted, "I will, I will."

And he did. In 1767, Townshend persuaded Parliament to pass the Townshend Acts. The new laws placed a duty, or tax, on certain goods the colonies imported from Britain. These goods included such popular items as glass, paint, paper, and tea.

Having kept his promise, Townshend caught the flu and died. But his new laws increased the unhappiness of the colonists.

A Boycott of British Goods   To many colonists, the Townshend duties were simply taxes in disguise. Once again, they were determined not to pay taxes that their assemblies had not voted on.

A Boston Patriot named Samuel Adams led the opposition to the Townshend Acts. Adams was not much to look at, and he was a failure at business. But he was gifted at stirring up protests through his speeches and writing. The governor of Massachusetts once complained, "Every dip of his pen stung like a horned snake."

Adams wrote a letter protesting the Townshend Acts that was sent to every colony. The letter argued that the new duties violated the colonists' rights as British citizens. To protect those rights, the colonies decided to **boycott** British goods. This was a peaceful form of protest that even Loyalists could support. One by one, all of the colonies agreed to support the boycott.

Women were very important in making the boycott work, since they did most of the shopping. The *Virginia Gazette* wrote that one woman could "do more for the good of her country than five hundred noisy sons of liberty, with all their mobs and riots." Women found many ways to avoid buying British imports. They sewed dresses out of homespun cloth, brewed tea from pine needles, and bought only American-made goods.

Repeal of the Townshend Acts   Meanwhile, a new leader named Lord North became head of the British government. Described as a "great, heavy, booby-looking man," Lord North embarrassed his supporters by taking naps in Parliament. But he was good with numbers, and he could see that the Townshend duties were a big money-loser. The duties didn't begin to make up for all the money British merchants were losing because of the boycott.

Early in 1770, North persuaded Parliament to repeal all of the Townshend duties, except for one—the tax on tea. Some members of Parliament argued that keeping the duty on tea was asking for more trouble. But stubborn King George wasn't ready to give up on the idea of taxing Americans.

"I am clear that there must always be one tax to keep up the right," the king said. "And, as such, I approve the tea duty."

5.5 The Boston Massacre

On the same day that Parliament repealed most of the Townshend duties, a brawl broke out between soldiers and colonists in Boston. When the dust cleared, five Bostonians were dead and ten were injured.

Patriots called this incident the "Boston Massacre." A massacre is the killing of defenseless people. What really happened was a small riot.

Trouble had been brewing in Boston for months before the riot. To the British, Boston Patriots were the worst troublemakers in the colonies. In 1768, the government had sent four regiments of troops to keep order in Boston.

Bostonians resented the British soldiers. They made fun of their red uniforms by calling them "lobsterbacks." Sam Adams even taught his dog to nip at soldiers' heels.

Despite such insults, the troops were forbidden to fire on citizens. Knowing this only made Bostonians bolder in their attacks. General Thomas Gage, the commander of the British army in America, wrote that "the people were as Lawless…after the Troops arrived, as they were before."

boycott: To refuse to buy one or more goods from a certain source. An organized refusal by many people is also called a boycott.

Paul Revere's famous engraving of the Boston Massacre stirred up deep colonial resentment.

Mob Violence Breaks Out   On March 5, 1770, a noisy mob began throwing rocks and ice balls at troops guarding the Boston Customs House. "Come on you Rascals, you bloody-backs," they shouted. "Fire if you dare." Some Patriot leaders tried to persuade the crowd to go home. So did Captain Thomas Preston, the commander of the soldiers. But their pleas had no effect.

As the mob pressed forward, someone knocked a soldier to the ground. The troops panicked and opened fire. Two bullets struck Crispus Attucks, a large black man at the front of the crowd. He was the first to die, but not the last. The enraged crowd went home only after receiving a promise that the troops would be tried for murder.

Paul Revere's engraving of five coffins showing the victims of the Boston Massacre appeared on flyers to remind colonists of British brutality.

Massacre or Self-Defense?   Sam Adams saw this event as a perfect opportunity to whip up anti-British feeling. He called the riot a "horrid massacre" and had Paul Revere, a local silversmith, engrave a picture of it. Revere's engraving shows soldiers firing at peaceful, unarmed citizens.

Prints of Revere's engraving were distributed throughout the colonies. Patriots saw the Boston Massacre as proof that the British should pull out all of their troops from the colonies. Loyalists saw the tragedy as proof that troops were needed more than ever, if only to control Patriot hotheads.

One hero came out of this sad event. He was a Boston lawyer named John Adams. Like his cousin Sam, John Adams was a Patriot. But he also believed that every person had the right to a fair trial, even the hated redcoats (British soldiers). Adams agreed to defend the soldiers, even though he knew that his action would cost him friends and clients.

At the murder trial, Adams argued that the troops had acted in self-defense. The jury found six of the soldiers not guilty. Two of them were found guilty only of manslaughter, or causing death without meaning to.

Throughout his long life, John Adams remained proud of his defense of the British soldiers. He said that upholding the law in this case was "one of the best pieces of service I ever rendered to my country."

5.6 The Boston Tea Party

Despite the hopes of Patriots like Sam Adams, the Boston Massacre did not spark new protests against British rule. Instead, the repeal of the Townshend duties led to a period of calm. True, there was still a small duty on tea. But the tax didn't seem to bother Loyalists very much. And Patriots could always drink Dutch tea that had been smuggled into the colonies without paying duties.

Things did not stay peaceful, however. In 1773, a new law called the Tea Act prompted more protests. One of them was the incident that became known as the Boston Tea Party.

The Tea Act The Tea Act was Lord North's attempt to rescue the British East India Company. This large trading company controlled all the trade between Britain and Asia. For years it had been a moneymaker for Britain. But the American boycott of British tea hurt the company badly. By 1773, it was in danger of going broke unless it could sell off the 17 million pounds of tea that was sitting in its London warehouses.

The Tea Act lowered the cost of tea that was sold by the British East Indian Company in the colonies. As a result, even taxed British tea became cheaper than smuggled Dutch tea. The Tea Act also gave the British East India Company a monopoly, or complete control, over tea sales in the colonies. From now on, the only merchants who could sell the bargain-priced tea were those chosen by the company.

Lord North may have thought he could trick Americans into buying taxed tea by making it so cheap, but colonists weren't fooled. They saw the Tea Act as still another attempt to tax them without their consent.

In addition, many merchants were alarmed by the East India Company's monopoly over the tea trade. They wondered what the British government might try to control next. Would there be a monopoly on cloth? On sugar? Nervous merchants wondered what would happen to their businesses if other goods were also restricted. The thought of more monopolies made them shudder.

The Granger Collection, New York

Tea Ships Arrive When the British East India Company's tea ships sailed into American ports, angry protesters kept them from unloading their cargoes. More than one ship turned back for England, still filled with tea. In Boston, however, the governor ordered the British navy to block the exit from Boston Harbor. He insisted that the three tea ships would not leave until all their tea was unloaded.

On December 16, 1773, the Sons of Liberty decided to unload the tea, but not in the way the governor had in mind. That night, about 50 men dressed as Mohawk Indians boarded the three ships. One of them, George Hewes, described what happened:

To protest the tax on tea, Patriots disguised as Native Americans threw 342 chests of tea overboard from three British ships. Colonists later called this the Boston Tea Party.

"We then were ordered by our commander to open the hatches and take out all the chests of tea and throw them overboard...and we immediately proceeded to execute his orders, first cutting and splitting the chests with our tomahawks.... In about three hours from the time we went on board, we had thus broken and thrown overboard every tea chest to be found on the ship.... We were surrounded by British armed ships, but no attempt was made to resist us."

Toward Independence **71**

About 90,000 pounds of tea was dumped into the sea that night. Nothing else on the ships was touched.

News of the Boston Tea Party excited Patriots throughout the colonies. "This is the most magnificent moment of all," wrote John Adams in his journal the next day. "This Destruction of the Tea is so bold, so daring, so firm…it must have…important Consequences." He was right.

5.7 The Intolerable Acts

Lord North was stunned by news of the Boston Tea Party. As he saw it, he had tried to help the colonists by sending them cheap tea. And what did they do? They threw it in the sea! This time they had gone too far!

King George agreed. To him, the issue was no longer about taxes. It was about Britain's control over the colonies. "We must master them totally," he declared, "or leave them to themselves." And the king wasn't about to leave the colonies to themselves.

Britain's anger led Parliament to pass a new series of laws in 1774. These laws were so harsh that many colonists called them "intolerable," or unacceptable. Throughout the colonies, they became known as the Intolerable Acts.

The British considered those who protested the Tea Act to be lawless troublemakers. In this cartoon, the tax collector, who has been tarred and feathered, is being forced to drink tea.

Parliament Punishes Massachusetts The Intolerable Acts were designed to punish Massachusetts for the Boston Tea Party. The first law closed Boston Harbor to all shipping until the ruined tea was paid for. The second law placed the government of Massachusetts firmly under British control. Colonists in Massachusetts could not even hold a town meeting without the governor's permission. The third law said that British soldiers who were accused of murder would be tried in England, not in the colonies. Finally, more troops were sent to Boston to enforce the new laws.

A few British leaders worried that the Intolerable Acts might push the colonies into rebellion. But George III was sure they would force the colonists to give in to British authority.

The Colonies Begin to Unite   In fact, the Intolerable Acts did not force the colonists to give in. Boston Patriots declared they would "abandon their city to flames" before paying a penny for the lost tea. Merchants in other cities showed their support by closing their shops. Many colonies sent food and money to Boston so that its citizens would not starve.

In Virginia, lawmakers drafted a resolution in support of Massachusetts. The Virginians said that everyone's rights were at stake. "An attack made on one of our sister colonies," they declared, "is an attack made on all British America."

The Virginians also called for a congress, or meeting, of delegates from all the colonies. The purpose of the congress would be to find a peaceful solution to the conflicts with Great Britain.

Not all Americans agreed with this plan. In every colony, there were Loyalists who thought that Bostonians had gone too far and should pay for the tea. If they were forced to choose, they would side with the king against Sam Adams and his Sons of Liberty. To them, it was the misguided Patriots who were causing all the trouble.

The First Continental Congress   In September 1774, some 50 leaders from 12 colonies met in Philadelphia. The meeting brought together delegates from most of the British colonies on the North American continent. For this reason, it was called the First Continental Congress.

The delegates were used to thinking of themselves as citizens of their own colonies. Patrick Henry, a leader from Virginia, urged them to come together as one people. "I am not a Virginian," he declared, "but an American." But only strong Patriots like Sam and John Adams were ready to think of themselves this way. Many delegates were strong Loyalists who still thought of themselves as British. Still others, like George Washington, were somewhere in between. Only one thing united the delegates—their love of liberty and hatred of tyranny.

In spite of their differences, the delegates agreed to send a respectful message to King George. The message urged the king to consider their complaints and to recognize their rights.

The delegates also called for a new boycott of British goods until Parliament repealed the Intolerable Acts. Finally, they agreed to meet again the following May if the boycott didn't work.

The Colonies Form Militias   In towns and cities throughout the colonies, Patriots appointed committees to enforce the boycott. In case the boycott didn't work, they also began organizing local militias. In New England, the volunteers called themselves Minutemen because they could be ready to fight in just 60 seconds.

Across the colonies, militias marched and drilled. In New Hampshire, unknown persons stole 100 barrels of gunpowder and 16 cannons from a British fort. Similar thefts occurred in other colonies. Rather than forcing the colonies to give in, the Intolerable Acts had brought the two sides to the brink of war.

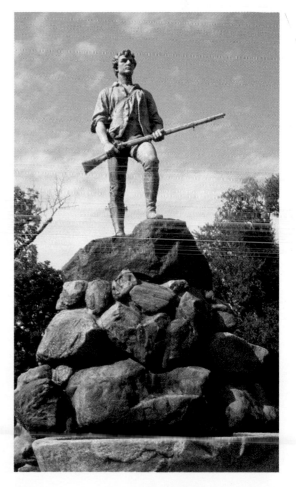

Colonies began forming militias after the Intolerable Acts to enforce a boycott of British goods. Shown here is a statue of a member of the New England militia known as the Minutemen.

5.8 Lexington and Concord

King George had made many mistakes in his decisions about the colonies. The Continental Congress listed all these mistakes in its message to the king. Now he made another one.

Rather than consider the colonists' complaints, King George refused even to answer their message. "The New England governments are in a state of rebellion," he said. "Blows must decide whether they are to be subject to this country or independent." In Boston, General Gage, the king's commander of British troops in America, got ready to deliver those blows.

This hand-colored engraving by Amos Doolittle shows the British firing upon the Minutemen who are gathered at Lexington. This was the first battle in what would be a seven-year war.

The First Blow at Lexington   In April 1775, a spy told General Gage that the colonists were hiding a large supply of gunpowder and weapons in the nearby village of Concord. Gage decided to strike at once.

The general ordered 700 of his best troops to march to Concord and seize the weapons. To keep the colonists from moving the weapons, the attack had to be a surprise. And so Gage had his troops march the 20 miles to Concord at night.

The colonists had their own spies. When Gage's troops slipped out of Boston on April 18, 1775, Patriots were watching their every move. Soon

Paul Revere and William Dawes were galloping through the countryside, warning colonists that the British were coming.

At Lexington, a village on the road to Concord, a small band of Minutemen gathered nervously in the chilly night air. "Stand your ground," ordered Captain John Parker. "Don't fire unless fired upon! But if they mean to have a war, let it begin here."

Suddenly, British troops appeared in the early morning mist. A shot rang out—from where, no one knew for certain. Without orders, the soldiers rushed forward, shooting wildly.

When the firing stopped, eight colonists lay dead or dying. Another ten were limping to safety with painful wounds. The British gave three cheers for victory and marched on to Concord.

The Second Blow at Concord
By breakfast time, the British were in Concord, looking for gunpowder and weapons. But colonists had moved the gunpowder and hidden the weapons. In frustration, the soldiers piled up a few wooden tools, tents, and gun carriages and set them on fire.

On a ridge outside the city, militiamen from the surrounding countryside watched the smoke rise. "Are you going to let them burn the town down?" shouted one man.

At the North Bridge in Concord, the Minutemen fired upon British troops who had occupied the town. Surprised by the fury of the colonial attack, the British fled in panic. The Amos Doolittle engraving on the left shows the bridge at the time of the battle. The photo on the right shows the bridge today.

"No!" replied Captain Isaac Davis. "I haven't a man that's afraid to go."

Captain Davis marched his volunteers down the hill. As they approached Concord's North Bridge, British troops opened fire. Davis fell dead, a bullet through his heart.

The British expected the Americans to break and run. To their surprise, the Minutemen stood their ground and fired back. Two minutes later, it was the redcoats who were running away in panic.

The retreat back to Boston was a nightmare for the British. More than 4,000 armed and angry Minutemen lined their route, shooting at every red-coat they saw. By the end of the day, 74 British soldiers were dead, and another 200 were wounded or missing. The colonists counted their own losses as 49 dead and 41 wounded.

A British officer described what it was like to face the colonists' fury that day. "Whoever looks upon them as an irregular mob," the officer said, "will find himself much mistaken."

Indeed, since the French and Indian War, the British had been mistaken about Americans again and again. Their biggest mistake, however, was in thinking that ordinary people—farmers, merchants, workers, and house-wives—would not fight for rights that they held dear. At Lexington and Concord, Americans proved they were not only willing to fight for their rights. They were even willing to die for them.

5.9 Chapter Summary

In this chapter, you read about tensions between the colonies and Britain between 1763 and 1775. You used the metaphor of a principal and students to describe that relationship. American colonists had grown used to governing themselves, and they felt strongly about their right to do so. This belief in self-government created tensions after the French and Indian War. The war left Britain with huge debts and a much larger empire to govern. Parliament tried to deal with these challenges by imposing new taxes and passing new laws.

Colonists resisted "taxation without representation" through protests, boycotts, and riots. In 1774, delegates at the First Continental Congress sent a formal complaint to the king. Meanwhile, Patriots began forming militias to defend themselves against British troops.

King George III was determined to teach the colonists a lesson. But at Lexington and Concord, Patriots showed they would rather fight than give up their rights. The bloodshed there was a turning point in the colonies' relationship with Britain. In the next chapter, you will see how these clashes triggered an all-out war and the birth of a new nation.

Sons of Liberty raise a Liberty Pole in 1776. Liberty Poles were used to promote patriotism.

The Granger Collection, New York

The Granger Collection, New York

Thomas Jefferson

Benjamin Franklin

John Adams

What role did each of these three men play in drafting the Declaration of Independence?

The Declaration of Independence

6.1 Introduction

As you read in Chapter 5, the bloodshed at Lexington and Concord marked a turning point for the colonies. The day after the clashes, horseback riders galloped through the colonies with news of Britain's "barbarous murders" of innocent militiamen. Most Americans were deeply shocked by the news. More urgently than ever before, they debated what the colonies should do about the trouble with Great Britain.

The choices were clear enough. The colonies could declare their independence—a course that would surely lead to war. Or they could continue with protests and petitions. This choice would keep the colonies at peace, but at what cost to the colonists' freedom?

No one was more outspoken in his support for independence than Patrick Henry of Virginia. After the passage of the Intolerable Acts, Henry delivered to the Virginia House of Burgesses one of the most famous speeches in American history.

"There is no room for hope," Henry began. "If we wish to be free… we must fight! Our chains are forged. Their clanking can be heard on the plains of Boston. The war is inevitable—and let it come!"

Then Henry spoke to those who treasured peace above freedom:

"Gentlemen may cry, peace, peace—but there is no peace. The war is actually begun. The next gale that sweeps from the north will bring to our ears the clash of resounding arms!… What is it that gentlemen wish?…Is life so dear, or peace so sweet, as to be purchased at the price of chains and slavery? Forbid it, Almighty God! I know not what course others may take; but as for me, give me liberty, or give me death!"

Despite the passionate words of Patriots like Patrick Henry, most colonists remained reluctant (hesitant) rebels. As you will read in this chapter, only after war had already started did the colonies decide to declare their independence.

Graphic Organizer: Visual Metaphor
You will use this visual metaphor of an unraveling rope to understand the historical events that led the colonists to declare independence.

The Granger Collection, New York

Orderly rows of British soldiers marched up Breed's Hill and eventually defeated American forces when the rebels ran out of gunpowder. The fierce fighting proved the British would not easily defeat the colonists.

6.2 The War Begins

On May 10, 1775, the Second Continental Congress met in Philadelphia. By then, New England militia had massed around Boston. The first question facing Congress was who should command this "New England Army." The obvious answer was a New Englander.

George Washington and the Continental Army   John Adams of Massachusetts had another idea. He proposed that Congress create a "continental army" made up of troops from all the colonies. To lead this army, Adams nominated "a gentleman whose skill as an officer, whose…great talents and universal character would…unite…the colonies better than any other person alive." That man was George Washington of Virginia.

The delegates agreed. They unanimously elected Washington to be commander-in-chief of the new Continental Army.

The Battle of Bunker Hill   Meanwhile, militiamen near Boston made plans to fortify two hills that overlooked the city—Bunker Hill and Breed's Hill. On the night of June 16, Israel Putnam led a few hundred men up Breed's Hill. In four hours of furious digging, they erected a crude fort on the top of the hill.

The fort worried British general William Howe, who had just arrived from England with fresh troops. Howe ordered an immediate attack. Under a hot June sun, some 2,000 redcoated troops formed two long lines at the base of Breed's Hill. At Howe's order, they marched up the slope.

As the lines moved ever closer, Putnam ordered his men, "Don't fire until you see the whites of their eyes." Only when the British were almost on top of them did the militiamen pull their triggers. The red lines broke and fell back in confusion.

The British regrouped and attacked again. Once more the Americans stopped their advance. On their third attack, the redcoats finally took the hill—but only because the Americans had used up all their gunpowder and pulled back.

This clash, which was misnamed the Battle of Bunker Hill, was short but very bloody. More than 1,000 British troops were killed or wounded, and nearly half that many Americans. British and Americans alike knew that this was no small skirmish on a village green. A war had begun.

6.3 The Siege of Boston

A week later, George Washington took command of his new army. He found "a mixed multitude of people…under very little discipline, order, or government." Washington worked hard to impose order. One man wrote, "Everyone is made to know his place and keep in it.… . It is surprising how much work has been done."

Ticonderoga A month later, a dismayed Washington learned that the army had only 36 barrels of gunpowder—enough for each soldier to fire just nine shots. To deceive the British, Washington started a rumor in Boston that he had 1,800 barrels of gunpowder—more than he knew what to do with! Luckily, the British swallowed this tall tale. Meanwhile, Washington sent desperate letters to the colonies begging for gunpowder.

Washington got his powder. But he still did not dare attack the British forces in Boston. To do that he needed artillery—heavy guns, such as cannons—to bombard their defenses. In desperation, Washington sent a Boston bookseller named Henry Knox to Fort Ticonderoga to round up some big guns.

Ticonderoga was an old British fort located at the southern end of Lake Champlain in New York. A few months earlier, militiamen led by Ethan Allen and Benjamin Arnold had seized the fort. The Americans had little use for the run-down fort, but its guns would prove priceless.

As winter set in, Knox loaded 59 cannons onto huge sleds and dragged them 300 miles to Boston. Knox's 42 sleds also carried 2,300 pounds of lead for future bullets. Boston was about to be put under siege.

George Washington turned an undisciplined army, composed of troops from all the colonies, into an effective fighting force.

The British Abandon Boston

On March 4, 1776, the British soldiers in Boston awoke to a frightening sight. The night before, the ridges of nearby Dorchester Heights had been bare. Now they bristled with cannons, all aimed on the city.

Rather than risk another bloodbath, General Howe abandoned the city. Within days, more than a hundred ships left Boston Harbor for Canada. The ships carried 9,000 British troops as well as 1,100 Loyalists who preferred to leave their homes behind rather than live with rebels.

Some Americans hoped the war was over. Washington, however, knew that it was only beginning.

traitor: a person guilty of the crime of treason, or disloyalty to the government

Nearly a year passed between the skirmishes at Lexington and Concord and the British retreat from Boston. During that time, there was little talk of independence. Most colonists still considered themselves loyal British subjects. Their quarrel was not with Great Britain itself, but with its policies toward the colonies.

The Olive Branch Petition Many Americans pinned their hopes for peace on King George. In July 1775, Congress sent a petition to George III asking him to end the quarrel. John Adams called the petition an "olive branch," because olive tree branches are an ancient symbol of peace.

By the time the petition reached London, however, the king had declared the colonies to be in "open and avowed rebellion." He ordered his ministers "to bring the **traitors** to justice."

Being called a traitor was enough to change the mind of one of Washington's generals. The general confessed that he had long "looked with some degree of horror on the scheme of separation." Now he agreed with Patrick Henry that "we must be independent or slaves."

Common Sense Many colonists, however, still looked with "horror" at the idea of independence. Then, early in 1776, a Patriot named Thomas Paine published a fiery pamphlet entitled *Common Sense*. Paine scoffed at the idea that Americans owed any loyalty to King George. "Of more worth is one honest man to society," he wrote, "than all the crowned ruffians who ever lived."

Paine also attacked the argument that the colonies' ties to Britain had benefited Americans. Just the opposite was true, he said. American trade had suffered under British control. Americans had also been hurt by being dragged into Britain's European wars.

Paine ended with a vision of an independent America as a homeland of liberty. "Ye that love mankind!" he urged. "Ye that dare oppose not only the tyranny, but the tyrant, stand forth!… The sun never shined on a cause of greater worth."

Within a few months, more than 120,000 copies of *Common Sense* were printed. Paine's arguments helped persuade thousands of colonists that independence was not only sensible, but the key to a brighter future.

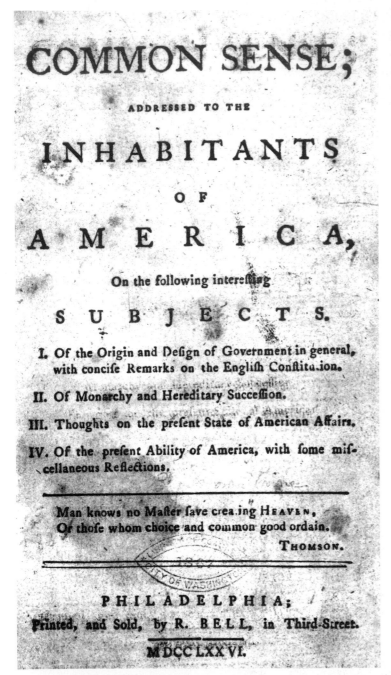

Thomas Paine's pamphlet *Common Sense* persuaded many colonists to support independence.

6.5 Thomas Jefferson Drafts a Declaration

A few weeks after the British left Boston, the Continental Congress appointed a committee to write a declaration, or formal statement, of independence. The task of drafting the declaration went to the committee's youngest member, 33-year-old Thomas Jefferson of Virginia. A shy man, Jefferson said little in Congress. But he spoke brilliantly with his pen.

Jefferson's job was to explain to the world why the colonies were choosing to separate from Britain. "When in the course of human events," he began, if one people finds it necessary to break its ties with another, "a decent respect to the opinions of mankind" requires that they explain their actions.

Natural Rights Jefferson's explanation was simple, but revolutionary. Loyalists had argued that colonists had a duty to obey the king, whose authority came from God. Jefferson reasoned quite differently. All people are born equal in God's sight, he began, and all are entitled to the same basic rights. In Jefferson's eloquent words:

"We hold these truths to be self-evident, that all men are created equal, that they are endowed by their Creator with certain unalienable rights, that among these are life, liberty, and the pursuit of happiness."

After Thomas Jefferson wrote the first draft of the Declaration of Independence, Benjamin Franklin and John Adams suggested changes.

Governments are formed, Jefferson said, "to secure these rights." Their power to rule comes from "the consent of the governed." If a government fails to protect people's rights, "it is the right of the people to alter or abolish it." The people can then create a new government that will protect "their safety and happiness."

The King's Crimes King George, Jefferson continued, had shown no concern for the rights of colonists. Instead, the king's policies had been aimed at establishing "an absolute tyranny over these states [the colonies]."

As proof, Jefferson included a long list of the king's abuses. In all these actions, Jefferson claimed, George III had shown that he was "unfit to be the ruler of a free people."

The time had come, Jefferson concluded, for the colonies' ties to Britain to be broken. "These United Colonies are," he declared, "and of right ought to be, free and independent states."

6.6 The Final Break

On July 1, 1776, the Second Continental Congress met in Philadelphia's State House to debate independence. By noon, the temperature outside had soared into the nineties, and a thunderstorm was gathering. Inside the State House, emotions were equally hot and stormy. By the end of the day, the issue was still undecided.

The next day was cooler and calmer. On July 2, 12 colonies voted for independence. New York cast no vote.

No delegate was more excited about the colonies' decision than John Adams. He wrote to his wife Abigail, "The second of July…will be celebrated by succeeding generations…with pomp and parade, with shows, games, sports, guns, bells, bonfires and illuminations, from one end of the continent to the other, from this time forward forevermore."

Debate over Slavery Adams was wrong about the date that would be celebrated as America's birthday, but only because Congress decided to revise Jefferson's declaration. Most of the delegates liked what they read, except for a passage on slavery. Jefferson had charged King George with violating the "sacred rights of life and liberty…of a distant people [by] carrying them into slavery."

Almost no one liked this passage. Southerners feared that it might lead to demands to free the slaves. Northerners worried that New England merchants, who profited from the slave trade, might be offended. Even delegates who opposed slavery felt that it was unfair to blame the king for enslaving Africans. The passage was struck out.

Independence Day On July 4, the delegates approved a final version of the Declaration of Independence. One by one, they stepped forward to sign it. In doing so, they pledged to support independence with "our lives, our fortunes, and our sacred honor."

This was a serious pledge. Every signer knew that he was committing an act of treason against Great Britain. If the new "United States of America" failed to win its freedom, each of them could end up swinging from a hangman's rope. Knowing this, Benjamin Franklin told the delegates, "We must all hang together. Or most assuredly we shall all hang separately."

Slavery was not mentioned in the Declaration of Independence because the slave trade was important to the economy of many of the colonies. In the triangular trade shown on this map, rum and iron were shipped from New England to West Africa. In West Africa, these products were exchanged for slaves. Then the slaves were taken to the West Indies (Caribbean), where they were traded for molasses and sugar. Finally, the molasses and sugar were brought back to New England.

Triangular Trade and the Enslavement of Africans

6.7 Chapter Summary

In this chapter, you read how the American colonies took the dramatic step of declaring their independence. You used a visual metaphor to describe the key historic events that led up to the Declaration of Independence. Soon after the skirmishes at Lexington and Concord, the struggle with Great Britain turned into all-out war. The Second Continental Congress elected George Washington as the head of the Continental Army. After the bloody Battle of Bunker Hill, American troops threatened the city of Boston with heavy guns. The British decided to abandon the city.

The failure of the Olive Branch Petition, and Thomas Paine's eloquent pamphlet, *Common Sense,* moved the colonies closer to a declaration of independence. Thomas Jefferson, a delegate to the Second Continental Congress, was selected to write a draft of the declaration.

On July 4, 1776, the delegates took their lives in their hands by signing the Declaration of Independence. For the first time in history, a government was being established on the basis of the natural rights of people and the duty of government to honor those rights.

But independence could not be won with words alone. As you will read in the next chapter, the colonies now faced the challenge of winning a war against the most powerful nation in the world.

This poster shows the delegates leaving Independence Hall to announce the signing of the Declaration of Independence.

The Signers of the Declaration of Independence

Fifty-six men signed the Declaration of Independence. Who were they, and what happened to them?

As a group, the signers were wealthy and well educated. Twenty-four were lawyers or judges. Eleven were merchants. Nine were farmers or plantation owners.

The signers pledged their lives to defend the Declaration. Many paid dearly for that promise.

Carter Braxton, a wealthy planter and trader from Virginia, lost his ships to the British navy during the war. After selling his home and property to pay his debts, he died in rags.

Late in the war, Thomas Nelson, Jr. saw his home taken over by the British as a headquarters before a major battle. He told General Washington to open fire on the house. Nelson's home was destroyed, and he died a poor man.

Francis Lewis and John Hart lost more than their homes and property. The British put Lewis's wife in jail, and she died shortly after. Hart lived in forests and caves for more than a year after fleeing the British. When he returned, his wife was dead and his 13 children were nowhere to be found. Saddened and exhausted, he died a few weeks later.

Twelve of the signers had their homes burned. Five were captured by the British and tortured before they died. Nine died from wounds or hardships suffered during the war. The sons of two signers were killed while serving in the army.

Thousands of other women and men, both famous and forgotten, suffered terrible losses during the war with Britain. Like the signers of the Declaration of Independence, they pledged all they cared about to the cause that united them.

What differences can you see between the soldiers in these two armies?

The Granger Collection, New York

7

The American Revolution

7.1 Introduction

When the **Revolutionary War** began in 1775, 15-year-old Joseph Martin was too young to join the Continental Army. But when recruiters returned to his Connecticut village a year later, he was ready to go.

The recruiters were looking for volunteers to go to New York, where the British were rumored to have landed 15,000 troops. "I did not care if there were fifteen times fifteen thousand," Martin said later. "I never gave a thought about numbers. The Americans were invincible [unbeatable] in my opinion."

Just two days after the Declaration of Independence was signed, Martin traded his plow for a musket (an early type of rifle). A week later he arrived in New York City, where he hoped to "sniff a little gunpowder." As he recalled, "I was now what I had long wished to be, a soldier. I had obtained my heart's desire; it was now my business to prove myself equal to my new profession."

If Martin had known what lay ahead, he might not have been so pleased about his new profession. The army in New York was ill trained, ill equipped, and just plain ill. "Almost the whole regiment are sick," reported a Massachusetts officer of his unit.

The British army, in contrast, was well trained, well equipped, and well supported by the Royal Navy. Rather than the 15,000 troops Martin had heard about, the British had assembled a force of 25,000 men in New York. More than 400 British ships bobbed in New York Harbor. This was the biggest army and the largest fleet the British had ever sent overseas.

In the face of such overwhelming force, the Americans should have been easily defeated. But they were not. In this chapter, you will read how soldiers like Joseph Martin stood up to mighty Britain to win a revolution and a new nation.

Graphic Organizer: Metaphor
You will use this metaphor of a game of Capture the Flag to understand the factors that helped decide the outcome of the Revolutionary War.

7.2 American Strengths and Weaknesses

At first, the Continental soldier was poorly trained and poorly equipped. He suffered a lack of gunpowder, rifles, food, and clothing. Some men had only spears or axes for weapons.

The Patriots began their revolution in a weak position. They had a hastily organized, untrained army and a tiny navy. Their weaknesses were far more obvious than their strengths.

American Weaknesses   The Continental Army was always short of men. General Washington never had more than 20,000 troops at one time and place. Many soldiers enlisted for six months or a year. Just when they were learning how to fight, they would pick up their muskets and go home to tend to their farms and families.

Few Americans were trained for battle. Some could shoot well enough from behind a tree. But when facing a mass of well-disciplined redcoats, they were likely to turn and run.

The army was plagued by shortages. Guns and gunpowder were so scarce that Benjamin Franklin suggested arming the troops with bows and arrows. Food shortages forced soldiers to beg for handouts. Uniforms were scarce as well. In winter, one could track shoeless soldiers by their bloody footprints in the snow.

Such shortages outraged Washington. But when he complained to the Continental Congress, nothing changed. Congress, the new nation's only government, lacked the power to raise money for supplies by taxing the states (the former colonies).

In desperation, Congress printed paper money to pay for the war. But the value of this money dropped so low that merchants demanded to be paid in gold instead. And like everything else, gold was scarce.

American Strengths   Still, the Americans had strengths. One was the patriotism of people like Joseph Martin, who willingly gave their lives to defend their liberty and their homes. Without them, the war would have been quickly lost.

The Americans also received help from overseas. Motivated by their old hatred of the English, the French secretly aided the rebels. During the first two years of the war, 90 percent of the Americans' gunpowder came from Europe, mostly from France.

The Americans' other great strength was their commander. George Washington was more than an experienced military leader. He was also a man who inspired courage and confidence. In the dark days to come, it was Washington who would keep the army together.

7.3 British Strengths and Weaknesses

Britain, in contrast to the American colonies, entered the war with many advantages. But looks can be deceiving, and the British encountered many problems as well.

mercenaries: professional soldiers who fight for anyone who will pay them

British Strengths   With a professional army of 50,000 troops, British forces greatly outnumbered the Continental Army. In addition, George III hired 30,000 **mercenaries**. These hired soldiers were known as Hessians because they came from a part of Germany called Hesse-Cassel. The British were also able to recruit many Loyalists, African Americans, and Native Americans into their forces.

British and Hessian troops were well trained in European military tactics. They excelled in large battles fought by a mass of troops on open ground. They also had far more experience than Americans at firing artillery.

The British forces were also well supplied. Compared to the pitifully equipped Continental Army, they seldom lacked for food, uniforms, weapons, or ammunition.

British Weaknesses   Even so, the war presented Britain with huge problems. One was the distance between Britain and America. Sending troops and supplies across the Atlantic was slow and costly. News of battles arrived in England long after they had occurred, making planning difficult.

A second problem was that King George and his ministers were never able to convince the British people that defeating the rebels was vital to Britain's future. There were no Joseph Martins in England volunteering to fight the Americans. The longer the war dragged on, the less happy British taxpayers were about paying its heavy costs.

A third problem was poor leadership. Lord George Germain, the man chosen to run the war, had no real sense of how to defeat the rebels. How could he? He had never set foot in America. Nor did it occur to him to go see for himself what his army was up against. If he had, Germain might have realized that this was not a war that could be won by conquering a city or two. To end the revolution, his forces would have to crush the Patriots' will to fight, state by state. Instead, Germain kept changing plans and generals, hoping that some combination of the two would bring him an easy victory.

The Granger Collection, New York

The British soldier was a trained professional. He was well equipped with ammunition, a good musket, adequate food, and uniforms.

7.4 Britain Almost Wins the War

After abandoning Boston in the spring of 1776, Germain came up with his first plan for winning the war. British forces, led by General William Howe, were ordered to capture New York City. From that base, British troops would then move north to destroy the rebellion at its heart—Massachusetts.

To block the British invasion, Washington hurried with his army from Boston to New York. It was there that he heard good news: Congress had finally declared the colonies to be "free and independent states."

Washington had the Declaration of Independence read aloud to his troops. The time had come, he said, to "show our enemies, and the whole world, that free men, contending for their own land, are superior to any mercenaries on Earth." Most of his men agreed that independence was a prize worth fighting for.

African Americans faced a difficult decision during the Revolution. Would the Americans or the British give them freedom at the end of the war? At the Battle of Cowpens in South Carolina, pictured above, the Continental Army, which included African Americans, soundly defeated the British.

African Americans and the War

For African Americans, however, the Declaration of Independence raised both hopes and questions. Did Jefferson's words, "all men are created equal," apply to them? Would independence bring an end to slavery? Should they join the Revolution?

Even before independence was declared, a number of African Americans had joined the Patriot cause. Black militiamen fought at Lexington, Concord, and Bunker Hill. Early in the war, however, blacks were banned from the Continental Army. Washington did not want the army to become a haven for runaway slaves.

In contrast, the British promised freedom to all slaves who took up arms for the king. As a result, thousands of runaways became Loyalists and fought for Britain.

A shortage of volunteers soon forced Washington to change his mind. By 1779, about 15 percent of the soldiers in the Continental Army were African Americans. Large numbers of black sailors also served in the Continental Navy.

As black Americans joined the war effort, whites began to question their own beliefs. How could they accept slavery if they truly believed that all people are created equal, with the same rights to life, liberty, and happiness? By the time the war ended, Vermont, Connecticut, Massachusetts, New Hampshire, Rhode Island, and Pennsylvania had all taken steps to end slavery.

The Granger Collection, New York

While chasing the retreating Continental Army, British soldiers looted homes of Americans, both Patriots and Loyalists. Such actions turned many former supporters into enemies.

Defeat in New York On August 27, 1776, the American and British armies met in Brooklyn, New York, for what promised to be a decisive battle. The Americans began their defense of the city "in high spirits." But the inexperienced Americans were no match for the British, with their greater numbers and superior training. In two days of fighting, the British lost only 377 men, while the Americans lost 1,407.

Satisfied that the war was nearly won, Howe ordered a halt to the British attack. Washington, he assumed, would do what any self-respecting European general would do in a hopeless situation. He would surrender honorably. And so Howe waited.

Washington had no intention of giving up. But for his army to survive, he would have to retreat. Even though Washington knew this, he could not bring himself to utter the shameful word "retreat."

An officer named Thomas Mifflin rescued him from his pride. "What is your strength?" Mifflin asked. "Nine thousand," Washington replied. "Not enough," said Mifflin bluntly, "We must retreat."

Fading Hopes The battle for New York City was the first of many defeats for the Americans. In the weeks that followed, British forces chased the Americans out of New York, through New Jersey, and finally across the Delaware River into Pennsylvania.

For Joseph Martin and his comrades, this was a trying time. There was little food to eat, and the soldiers grew weak from hunger. As the weather turned cold, muddy roads and icy streams added to their misery. With their terms of enlistment nearly up, many soldiers headed for home. Along the way they spread the word that anyone who volunteered to risk his life in the Continental Army had to be crazy.

By the time Washington reached Pennsylvania, he had only a few thousand men. Many of his remaining troops, he reported, were "entirely naked and most so thinly clad [clothed] as to be unfit for service." More troops had to be found, and found quickly, he wrote his brother. Otherwise, "I think the game will be pretty well up."

7.5 A Pep Talk and Surprise Victories

By the end of 1776, the British also thought the war was just about won. General Howe offered to pardon all rebels who signed a statement promising to "remain in peaceful obedience" to the king. Thousands took him up on his offer.

The Crisis Washington knew that he had to do something, and quickly. Gathering his last troops together, he read to them from Thomas Paine's new pamphlet, *The Crisis:*

These are the times that try men's souls. The summer soldier and the sunshine patriot will, in this crisis, shrink from the service of their country; but he that stands it NOW, deserves the love and thanks of man and woman.

Next, Washington outlined a daring plan to attack Hessian troops who were camped for the winter in Trenton, New Jersey. Heartened by Paine's words, his men did not "shrink from the service of their country."

With morale low and his soldiers threatening to return home, George Washington planned a daring attack on the Hessians at Trenton. Crossing the ice-choked Delaware River, he surprised the enemy, overwhelming them completely.

Victory in Trenton Late on December 25, 1776, Washington's army crossed the ice-choked Delaware River in small boats. On the New Jersey shore, Washington gave his men the password for the long night march ahead: "Victory or Death."

As the Americans made their way toward Trenton, a driving snow chilled them to the bone. Ice and rocks cut through their worn-out shoes. One officer reported to Washington that the troops' guns were too wet to fire. "Use the bayonets," the general replied. "The town must be taken."

When the Americans reached Trenton, they found the Hessians happily sleeping off their Christmas feasts. Caught completely by surprise, the mercenaries surrendered. Washington took 868 prisoners without losing a single man. A week later, the Americans captured another 300 British troops at Princeton, New Jersey. These defeats told Howe that it would take more than capturing New York City and issuing pardons to win the war.

News of Washington's victories electrified Patriots. "A few days ago they had given up their cause for lost," wrote an unhappy Loyalist. "Their late successes have turned the scale and they are all liberty mad again." The game was not yet up.

7.6 The Tide Begins to Turn

When the Revolution began, both sides adopted the same military **strategy,** or overall plan for winning the war. That strategy was to defeat the enemy in one big battle.

After barely escaping from New York, Washington revised his strategy. In the future, he wrote Congress, he would avoid large battles that might put his army at risk. Instead, the war would be "defensive." Rather than defeating the British, Washington hoped to tire them out.

A New British Strategy Germain revised the British strategy as well. His new plan was to divide the rebels by taking control of New York's Hudson River Valley. Control of this waterway would allow the British to cut New England off from the rest of the states. Without men and supplies from New England, the Continental Army would surely collapse.

To carry out this plan, General John Burgoyne left Canada in June 1777, with about 8,000 British soldiers and Indian warriors. He planned to move this army south to Albany, New York. There he would meet up with General Howe, who was supposed to march his army north from New York City.

Problems with Burgoyne's Plan There were two big problems with Burgoyne's plan. The first was that what looked like an easy invasion route on a map was anything but easy. The route Burgoyne chose from Canada to Albany took his army through more than 20 miles of tangled wilderness. His army had to build bridges, chop down countless trees, and lay out miles of log roads through swamps as it crept toward Albany.

To make matters worse, Burgoyne didn't travel light. His army was slowed by more than 600 wagons, 30 of them filled with his personal baggage. Even in the wilderness, "Gentleman Johnny" Burgoyne sipped champagne with his supper.

The second problem with Burgoyne's plan was that General Howe had his own ideas about how to win the war. Instead of marching to Albany, Howe headed for Philadelphia, the rebels' capital. There he hoped to lure Washington into another major battle. Howe hoped it would be the last one.

> **strategy:** An overall plan (for example, for winning a war). Specific ways of carrying out a strategy are called *tactics.*

The wife, children, and slave of General Philip Schulyer burned the family wheat fields, so as to leave nothing useful for British forces advancing toward Saratoga.

The Granger Collection, New York

The American Revolution **93**

ally: a nation that joins another nation in some common effort, such as winning a war

Washington, however, refused to risk his army in another big battle. He would not fight for Philadelphia. Instead, he played hide and seek with Howe, attacking here and there and then disappearing into the countryside.

A Turning Point   By the time the slow-moving Burgoyne finally reached Saratoga Springs on the Hudson River, the area was swarming with militia. Although the rebels outnumbered his army, Burgoyne ordered an attack. Again and again the rebels beat back Burgoyne's troops. On October 17, 1777, Gentleman Johnny accepted defeat.

Burgoyne's surrender marked a turning point in the war. Before the victory at Saratoga, the American cause had looked hopeless to most of the world. Now the Americans had shown they could stand up to a British army and win.

Not long after this victory, France came into the war as an **ally** of the United States. The French government sent money, weapons, troops, and warships to the Americans. Spain also entered the war against Britain. The American cause no longer looked quite so hopeless.

The Granger Collection, New York

George Washington is shown with the Marquis de Lafayette at Valley Forge. Lafayette, a Frenchman who aided the Americans, described the American soldiers there as "in want of everything; they had neither coats, nor hats, nor shirts nor shoes; their feet and their legs froze until they grew black."

Winter at Valley Forge

Saratoga was a stunning victory, but the war was far from over. While General Washington's army roamed the countryside, Howe's forces still occupied Philadelphia.

Late in 1777, Congress declared a day of thanksgiving. By this time, Washington and his army were on their way to Valley Forge, Pennsylvania, to make camp for the winter. Joseph Martin described the army's "celebration":

"We had nothing to eat for two or three days previous.... But we must now have what Congress said, a sumptuous [lavish] Thanksgiving.... It gave each and every man a gill [a few ounces] of rice and a tablespoon of vinegar! The army was now not only starved but naked. The greatest part were not only shirtless and barefoot, but destitute of [without] all other clothing, especially blankets."

Washington's troops were hungry because many farmers preferred to sell food to the British. The British paid them in gold, while Congress paid them in paper money. As for uniforms and blankets, merchants had raised the prices for these items sky-high. This desire for profits at the army's expense outraged Washington. "No punishment," he fumed, "is too great for the man who can build his greatness upon his country's ruin."

To distract his men from their misery, Washington put Baron Friedrich von Steuben, a volunteer from Prussia, in charge of training. The Prussian's method, wrote Martin, was "continual drill." It worked wonders. "The army grows stronger every day," wrote one officer. "There is a spirit of discipline among the troops that is better than numbers."

Another foreign volunteer, the Marquis de Lafayette, also helped raise the troops' spirits. Although he was one of the richest men in France, Lafayette chose to share the hardships of Valley Forge. He even used his own money to buy the men warm clothing. "The patient fortitude [courage] of the officers and soldiers," Lafayette wrote, "was a continual miracle."

When at last spring arrived, Washington received news that the British were about to abandon Philadelphia. The time had come to put his newly trained army to the test.

The Battle of Monmouth

By this time, Sir Henry Clinton had replaced General Howe as commander of the British forces in America. In Clinton's view, taking over Philadelphia had gained the British nothing. He ordered his army to retreat to New York City, where the Royal Navy could keep it supplied by sea.

Now it was Washington's turn to chase an army across New Jersey. On June 28, 1778, he caught up with the retreating British near Monmouth, New Jersey. In the battle that followed, Washington was everywhere, constantly rallying his men to stand and fight. "Cheering them by his voice and example," wrote Lafayette, "never had I beheld [seen] so superb a man."

Late that night, the British slipped across the Hudson River to safety in New York City. Washington camped with his army nearby. It was pleasing, he wrote, "that after two years maneuvering…both armies are brought back to the very point they set out from." Neither army knew it yet, but the war in the North was over.

At the Battle of Monmouth in New Jersey, George Washington led his troops in an attack on retreating British forces. Although the Americans won, the British were able to slip away during the night and sail safely to New York.

The Granger Collection, New York

The Granger Collection, New York

This engraving shows Francis Marion crossing the Pee Dee River in South Carolina. Marion, known as the Swamp Fox because of his tactic of ambushing the British from the marshes of the South, never led a force of more than 70 men.

guerrillas: soldiers who operate on their own and are not part of a regular army

7.7 The War Goes South

After failing to conquer any state in the North, the British changed strategies yet again. Their new plan was to move the war to the South. There, they believed, thousands of Loyalists were just waiting to join the king's cause.

Clinton began his "southern campaign" with a successful attack on Savannah, Georgia. From Georgia, he moved on to take control of North and South Carolina. At that point, Clinton returned to New York City, leaving Lord Charles Cornwallis to run the war in the South.

Saving the South   Cornwallis soon learned that he did not really control the Carolinas after all. **Guerrillas**—soldiers who are not part of a regular army—kept the American cause alive. One of them was Francis Marion, who was also known as the "Swamp Fox." Marion's band of rebels harassed the British with hit-and-run raids. Then they faded into the swamps and forests like foxes.

Late in 1780, Washington sent General Nathaniel Greene to slow the British advance through the South. Greene's army was too small to meet Cornwallis in a major battle. Instead, Greene led Cornwallis's troops on an exhausting chase through the southern backcountry. He wrote of his strategy, "We fight, get beat, rise, and fight again."

Greene's strategy worked wonderfully. In April 1781, Cornwallis wrote that he was "quite tired of marching about the country." He moved his army to Yorktown, a sleepy tobacco port on Chesapeake Bay in Virginia, for a good rest.

A Trap at Yorktown   By the time Cornwallis was settling into Yorktown, France had sent nearly 5,000 troops to join Washington's army in New York. In August, Washington learned that another 3,000 troops were scheduled to arrive soon in 29 French warships.

Washington used this information to set a trap for Cornwallis. Secretly, he moved his army south to Virginia. When they arrived, they joined the French and surrounded Yorktown on land with more than 16,000 troops.

Meanwhile, the French warships showed up just in time to seal off the entrance to Chesapeake Bay. Their appearance was a crucial help to the Americans. Now Cornwallis was cut off from the British navy and any hope of rescue by sea.

The trap was sprung on October 6, 1781. Joseph Martin watched as a flag was raised to signal American and French gunners to open fire on Yorktown. "I confess I felt a secret pride swell in my heart," he wrote, "when I saw the 'star-spangled banner' waving majestically." The shelling went on for days, until "most of the guns in the enemy's works were silenced."

Cornwallis Surrenders   With Yorktown exploding around him, at first Cornwallis clung to the hope that the British navy would come to his rescue. When no ships arrived, he finally agreed to surrender.

On October 19, 1781, American and French troops formed two long lines that stretched for more than a mile along the road to Yorktown—the French on one side, the Americans on the other. The two lines could not have looked more different. The French were dressed in elegant uniforms that gleamed with gold and silver braid in the afternoon sun. The Americans' uniforms—and not everyone even had uniforms—were patched and faded. Behind the lines stood civilians who had traveled for miles to witness this glorious event.

After hours of waiting, the crowd watched as 8,000 British troops left Yorktown to lay down their arms. The defeated troops moved "with slow and solemn step." They were accompanied by a slow tune known as "The World Turned Upside Down." This same sad tune had been played at Saratoga after the British surrender.

Cornwallis did not take part in this ceremony, saying that he was ill. In reality, the British commander could not bear to surrender publicly to an army that he looked down on as "a contemptible and undisciplined rabble [mob]." While Cornwallis sulked in his tent, his men surrendered their arms. Many of them wept bitter tears.

To the watching Americans, there was nothing sad about that day. "It was a noble sight to us," wrote Martin, "and the more so, as it seemed to promise a speedy conclusion to the contest."

This painting by John Trumbull shows the British surrender at Yorktown on October 19, 1781. At the center is General Benjamin Lincoln leading the British. On the right is General Washington in front of the American flag. On the left are French, Polish, and Prussian soldiers.

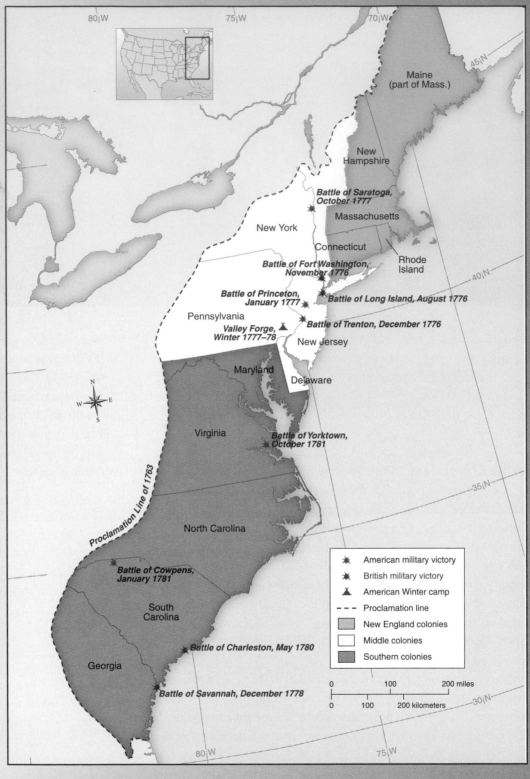

Map: Key Battles of the American Revolution

- Battle of Saratoga, October 1777
- Battle of Fort Washington, November 1776
- Battle of Princeton, January 1777
- Battle of Long Island, August 1776
- Battle of Trenton, December 1776
- Valley Forge, Winter 1777–78
- Battle of Yorktown, October 1781
- Battle of Cowpens, January 1781
- Battle of Charleston, May 1780
- Battle of Savannah, December 1778

Maine (part of Mass.), New Hampshire, Massachusetts, New York, Connecticut, Rhode Island, Pennsylvania, New Jersey, Maryland, Delaware, Virginia, North Carolina, South Carolina, Georgia

Proclamation Line of 1763

Legend:
- ✹ American military victory
- ✴ British military victory
- ▲ American Winter camp
- - - - Proclamation line
- New England colonies
- Middle colonies
- Southern colonies

Scale: 0 — 100 — 200 miles / 0 — 100 — 200 kilometers

1. Identify at least four interesting details on this map.

2. What do the blue, white, and red sections of the map represent?

3. In which region(s)—New England Colonies, Middle Colonies or Southern Colonies—did the key battles of the American Revolution take place?

4. How does this map show why the British were not able to defeat the Americans in the American Revolution?

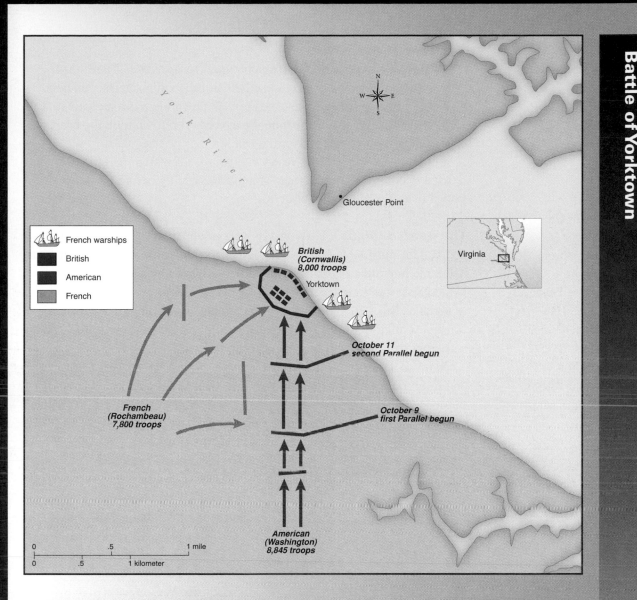

1. Identify at least four interesting details on this map.

2. Which three countries were involved in this battle?

3. According to the map, what did American and French forces do to defeat the British at the Battle of Yorktown?

4. How do you think Americans responded to the outcome of the Battle of Yorktown? The British? The French? Explain.

treaty: a formal agreement between nations

7.8 The War Ends

The conclusion of the war was not quite as speedy as Martin had hoped. When Lord North, the British prime minister, heard about Cornwallis's defeat, he paced up and down the room repeating, "Oh God! It is all over!" The British public agreed. Yorktown took the heart out of whatever support was left for the war.

But King George was not ready to give up. Even after Yorktown, he refused to consider surrendering. Months dragged by before he was finally forced to accept the reality of defeat.

The Treaty of Paris Early in 1783, representatives of the United States and Britain signed a peace **treaty** (agreement) in Paris. The Treaty of Paris had three important parts. First, Great Britain agreed to recognize the United States as an independent nation. Second, Britain gave up its claims to all lands between the Atlantic Coast and the Mississippi River, from Canada south to Florida. Third, the United States agreed to return all rights and property taken from Loyalists during the war.

Many Loyalists did not trust the treaty's promise of fair treatment—and for good reason. During the war, Loyalists had been badly treated by Patriots. More than 80,000 black and white Loyalists left the United States to settle in British Canada.

This painting of the Paris Peace Convention, which ended the Revolutionary War, is unfinished. The British delegates refused to pose. The Americans, from left to right, are John Jay, John Adams, Benjamin Franklin, Henry Laurens, and Franklin's grandson.

The Cost of Freedom For most Americans, the end of the war was a time for joy and celebration. They had won more than a great revolution. They had also gained the freedom to govern themselves and to create their own future.

But liberty came at a high price. During the long conflict, at least 6,200 Americans were killed in combat. An estimated 10,000 died in camp of diseases, and another 8,500 as British prisoners. As a proportion of the total population, more Americans died fighting the Revolutionary War than in any other conflict except the Civil War, in which Americans fought one another.

George Washington knew better than most just how costly and precious Americans' freedom was. He also understood the great responsibility that came with that freedom. "With our fate," he wrote at war's end, "will the destiny of unborn millions be involved."

7.9 Chapter Summary

In this chapter, you read how the American colonies won their independence from Great Britain. You used a visual metaphor to record factors that helped to decide the outcome of the Revolutionary War.

At the start of the war, the Americans seemed sure to lose the fight with Britain. The poorly trained and poorly equipped American forces were no match for Britain's professional army and huge navy. But patriotic feeling, help from overseas, and a magnificent commander helped to overcome British strengths. In addition, fighting a war in far-off America posed major problems for the British.

Still, the British enjoyed a string of victories in the early part of the war. After the loss of New York, only Washington's leadership kept the Americans going. Then, beginning with the victory at Saratoga, the tide began to turn. When France and Spain joined in the conflict, the Americans had the help they needed to outlast the British.

The war's climax came when the Americans, with the help of the French, trapped Cornwallis's army at Yorktown. After Cornwallis surrendered, it was only a matter of time until Britain gave up the fight.

The conflict ended officially with the signing of the Treaty of Paris. In this agreement, Britain recognized the United States as an independent country.

At great cost in lives and property, the Americans had won their freedom. Now they faced the enormous task of organizing a government for their new nation.

The Granger Collection, New York

The Revolutionary War officially ended with the signing of the Treaty of Paris in 1783. British troops agreed to leave American soil "with all convenient speed."

The Granger Collection, New York

Why would the delegates want George Washington to lead the Constitutional Convention?

Why would Benjamin Franklin be a good delegate to the Constitutional Convention?

What might these men be thinking?

Creating the Constitution

8.1 Introduction

When the Revolutionary War ended, no one was happier than a small, bookish Virginia Patriot named James Madison. And no one was more worried about the future of the United States. While serving in Congress during the war, Madison had tried and failed to get the states to work easily together. He doubted that things would improve now that the war was over.

After declaring independence in 1776, Congress had tried to unite the states under one national government. This proved to be a difficult task. Most members of Congress were nervous about creating a strong central government. They feared that such a government would trample the very rights they were fighting to preserve.

Their solution was a plan of government known as the **Articles of Confederation**. The Articles created "a firm league of friendship" in which "each state retains its sovereignty, freedom, and independence." This "league of friendship" was a loose union in which the thirteen states cooperated for common purposes. It was run by Congress, in which each state had one vote.

On paper, the Articles of Confederation gave Congress several important powers. It could make war and peace, raise an army and a navy, print money, and set up a postal system.

In reality, however, these powers were limited by the inability of Congress to impose taxes. Instead, Congress had to ask the states for funds to do anything. All too often, the states ignored Congress's "humble requests." The result, said Madison, was that the Articles were no more effective at binding the states into a nation than "a rope of sand."

In this chapter, you will read about the new nation's shaky start under the Articles of Confederation. You will also learn how Madison and other leaders came together in Philadelphia's Independence Hall in 1787 in the hope of forming "a more perfect union."

Graphic Organizer: Illustration
You will annotate this drawing of the Assembly Room at Independence Hall to organize information about the Constitutional Convention.

territory: A region designated by Congress and organized under a governor. A territory may apply to become a state when it has a large enough population.

8.2 Early Quarrels and Accomplishments

Even before the Revolutionary War ended, the states began quarreling among themselves. Many of their quarrels were about taxes on goods that crossed state borders. New York, for example, taxed firewood from Connecticut and cabbages from New Jersey. The states also quarreled over boundaries. The inability of Congress to end such disagreements was one of the key weaknesses of the Articles of Confederation.

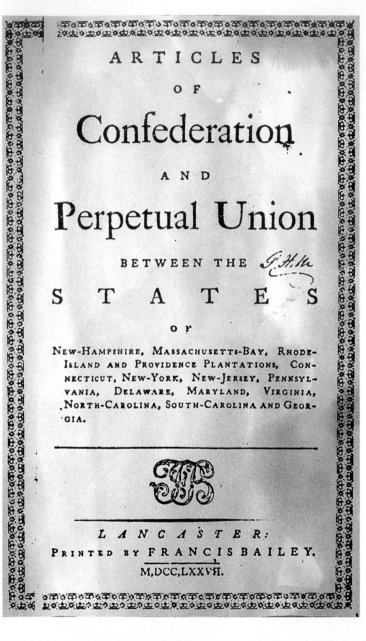

ARTICLES

OF

Confederation

AND

Perpetual Union

BETWEEN THE *G. H. M.*

S T A T E S

OF

NEW-HAMPSHIRE, MASSACHUSETTS-BAY, RHODE-ISLAND AND PROVIDENCE PLANTATIONS, CONNECTICUT, NEW-YORK, NEW-JERSEY, PENNSYLVANIA, DELAWARE, MARYLAND, VIRGINIA, NORTH-CAROLINA, SOUTH-CAROLINA AND GEORGIA.

LANCASTER:
PRINTED BY FRANCIS BAILEY.
M,DCC,LXXVII.

The Granger Collection, New York

This is the title page from the Articles of Confederation, the first constitution of the United States. Under the Articles, the states held the most power. The national government could not collect taxes or settle disputes between states.

Developing Western Lands Congress did get the states to agree on one important issue: how to develop the western lands acquired by the United States in the Treaty of Paris.

At that time, there was no orderly way of dividing up and selling these lands. Settlers walked into the wilderness and claimed the land they liked. Disputes over who owned what land clogged the courts.

To end this confusion, Congress passed the Land Ordinance of 1785. Under this law, western lands were divided into six-mile squares called *townships*. Each township was then divided into 36 sections of 640 acres each. One section of each square was set aside to support the township's public schools. The other sections were to be sold to settlers.

Surveyors proceeded to lay out townships in the Ohio Valley, then known as the Northwest **Territory**. By 1787, the government was ready to sell sections to settlers. This raised the question of how these areas should be governed. Were they to be colonies of the United States or new states?

The Northwest Ordinance Congress answered this question in the Northwest Ordinance of 1787. This law divided the Northwest Territory into smaller territories, each governed by a territorial governor. As soon as a territory had 5,000 free adult males, it could elect its own legislature, or lawmaking body. When the population reached 60,000, a territory could apply to Congress to become a state.

The Northwest Ordinance included a list of rights that gave settlers the same privileges as other citizens, except for one. Slavery was banned in the Northwest Territory.

This system of settlement served the nation well. Over time, the United States would continue to establish territories as it spread to the Pacific Ocean and beyond.

8.3 Shays's Rebellion and the Need for Change

Under the Articles of Confederation, the new nation also had serious money problems. The paper money printed by Congress during the war was worthless. Congress had the power to make coins that would not lose their value. But it lacked gold or silver to mint into coins.

The states reacted to the money shortage by printing their own paper currency (money). Before long, bills of different sizes and colors were floating from state to state. No one knew what any of these currencies were worth, but most agreed that they were not worth much.

arsenal: a place where weapons and ammunition are stored

Massachusetts Farmers Rebel

The money shortage was particularly hard on farmers who could not earn enough to pay their debts and taxes. In Massachusetts, judges ordered farmers to sell their land and livestock to pay off their debts. Led by Daniel Shays, a hero of Bunker Hill, Massachusetts farmers rebelled.

First, Shays and his followers closed down courthouses to keep judges from taking their farms. Then they marched on the national **arsenal** at Springfield to seize the weapons stored there. Having disbanded the Continental Army, Congress was unable to stop them.

Massachusetts ended Shays's Rebellion by sending militia troops to Springfield to restore order. To many Americans, however, the uprising was a disturbing sign that the nation they had fought so hard to create was falling apart. "No respect is paid to the federal [national] authority," Madison wrote to a friend. "It is not possible that a government can last long under these circumstances."

The Granger Collection, New York

Daniel Shays, shown at the top right, and his followers closed down court-houses to prevent judges from seizing their land when they could not pay their debts. Many American leaders saw the rebellion as a sign that the government under the Articles of Confederation was not working.

A Call for a Convention

Shays's Rebellion shocked Congress into calling for a convention to consider "the situation of the United States." Each state was invited to send delegates to Philadelphia in May 1787, "for the sole and express purpose of revising the Articles of Confederation."

Madison was ready. For the past year he had devoted himself to the study of governments, both ancient and modern. The lesson of the past was always the same. A nation that was made up of many groups needed a strong central government, or it was soon torn apart by quarrels. The question was, would Americans heed this lesson?

8.4 Opening the Constitutional Convention

Philadelphia was already hot and sticky when delegates began drifting into the city. On May 25, the Constitutional Convention met for the first time in the east room of the Pennsylvania State House (later known as Independence Hall). The Declaration of Independence had been debated in this very room just 11 years earlier. The delegates would meet in the east room all summer on days so steamy that, as one visitor wrote, "the slightest movement is painful."

The delegates' first action was to elect George Washington president of the convention. No man was more admired and respected than the former commander in chief of the Continental Army. When the war ended, Washington could have used his power and popularity to make himself a king. Instead, he went home to Virginia to resume his life as an ordinary citizen. But despite his reluctance to return to public life, Washington would play a key role by presiding over the convention and lending it his prestige.

The Delegates   Fifty-five delegates from 12 states attended the convention. Rhode Island, which prided itself as "the home of the otherwise minded" and feared a strong national government, boycotted the meeting.

Some leaders of the revolution were missing. John Adams and Thomas Jefferson were representing the United States in Great Britain and France. Others who did not attend included Sam Adams, John Hancock, and Patrick Henry. They feared a strong national government would endanger the rights of states.

The delegates to the Constitutional Convention met on May 25, 1787, in the same hall where the Declaration of Independence was signed. Today, the building is called Independence Hall.

The Granger Collection, New York

As a group, the delegates were, in the words of a modern historian, "the well-bred, the well-fed, the well-read, and the well-wed." Their average age was 42. At 81, Benjamin Franklin of Pennsylvania was the oldest. He arrived at the convention each day in a sedan chair carried by four good-natured prisoners from a nearby jail.

Most of the delegates brought extensive political experience to the meeting. More than two thirds were lawyers. More than one in three owned slaves. Thomas Jefferson was so impressed by the ability and experience of these men that he called the convention "an assembly of demi-gods."

The Father of the Constitution   The best prepared of these "godlike" figures was James Madison of Virginia. His influence was so great that later he would be called the "Father of the Constitution." Georgia delegate William Pierce wrote this sketch of Madison:

In the management of every great question he evidently took the lead in the Convention.... He always comes forward the best informed Man of any point in debate. The affairs of the United States, he perhaps, has the most correct knowledge of, of any man in the Union.... Mr. Madison is about 37 years of age, a Gentleman of great modesty, with a remarkably sweet temper.

Madison addressed the convention more than 200 times. When he was not speaking, he took notes. Sitting near the front of the room so that he could hear everything that was said, Madison wrote down nearly every word. When collected together, his notes covered more than 600 printed pages. From this remarkable record, we know what went on inside the convention day by day.

The Rule of Secrecy   At the time, however, no one outside the convention knew what was happening. After choosing a president, the delegates voted on rules for the convention. The most important was the rule of secrecy. The delegates wanted to feel free to speak their minds without causing alarm or opposition among the general public. They agreed to keep whatever was said in the meeting room a secret until their work was done.

One day Washington was handed some notes that had been dropped in the hall outside the east room. Washington pocketed the paper until the end of debate the next day. Then, in his sternest voice, he lectured the delegates on the importance of secrecy. "I know not whose paper it is," Washington said as he flung the notes on his desk. "But here it is, let him who owns it take it." The notes were never claimed. Instead, they lay on Washington's desk for days.

Like Washington, the delegates took the rule of secrecy very seriously. During that long summer, not a single word about the convention debates appeared in any newspaper.

Benjamin Franklin, the oldest delegate to the Constitutional Convention, had doubts about the final Constitution. However, he said, "The older I grow, the more apt I am to doubt my own judgment and pay more respect to the judgment of others."

Delegates to the Constitutional Convention, 1787

New Hampshire
John Langdon
Nicholas Gilman

Massachusetts
Caleb Strong
Elbridge Gerry
Nathanial Gorham
Rufus King

Connecticut
Oliver Ellsworth
Roger Sherman
William Samuel Johnson

New York
Alexander Hamilton
John Lansing, Jr.
Robert Yates

New Jersey
David Brearley
Jonathan Dayton
William Churchill
  Houston
William Livingston
William Paterson

Pennsylvania
Benjamin Franklin
George Clymer
Gouverneur Morris
James Wilson
Jarod Ingersoll
Robet Morris
Thomas Fitzsimons
Thomas Mifflin

Delaware
George Read
Gunning Bedford, Jr.
Jacob Broom

John Dickinson
Richard Bassett

Maryland
Daniel Carroll
Daniel of St. Thomas
  Jenifer
James McHenry
John Francis Mercer
Luther Martin

Virginia
Edmund Randolph
George Mason
George Washington
George Wythe
James Madison
James McClurg
John Blair

North Carolina
Alexander Martin
Hugh Williamson
Richard Dobbs Spaight, Sr.
William Blount
William Richard Davie

South Carolina
Charles Cotesworth
  Pinckney
Charles Pinckney
John Rutledge
Pierce Butler

Georgia
Abraham Baldwin
William Few
William Houston
William Pierce

James Wilson

William Paterson

George Mason

8.5 Issue: How Should States Be Represented in the New Government?

constitution: a written plan that provides the basic framework of a government

Once the convention was organized, the delegates got down to business. In most of their minds, that business was to revise the Articles of Confederation. To their surprise, the Virginia delegation presented them with a completely new plan of government. After a lengthy debate, the delegates agreed to throw out the Articles of Confederation and write a new **constitution**.

While the delegates—later known as the *framers*—agreed to design a new framework of government, they were divided on a key issue. Where should the government's power to rule come from? The states? Or the people? Under the Articles of Confederation, the answer was the states. Madison's answer in the Virginia Plan was that the government's power should come directly from the people.

The Virginia Plan The Virginia Plan called for a strong national government with three branches or parts. A legislative branch, or congress, would make laws. An executive branch would carry out ("execute") the laws. A judicial branch, or system of courts, would apply and interpret the laws.

Under the Virginia Plan, Congress was to be made up of two houses, the House of Representatives and the Senate. The number of lawmakers that a state could send to Congress depended on its population. States with a large number of people would have more representatives than smaller states.

Delegates from Virginia, Pennsylvania, and other large states liked the Virginia Plan. Having the new government represent people, not states, would give them more representatives and more power in both houses of Congress.

The New Jersey Plan Not surprisingly, delegates from the small states disliked the Virginia Plan. Just as the convention was about to vote on it, William Paterson of New Jersey introduced a rival proposal.

Like the Virginia Plan, the New Jersey Plan called for a government with three branches. However, the legislative branch would have just one house, not two. And each state would have an equal vote in Congress, no matter how big or small. This plan, Paterson argued, would keep the small states from being "swallowed up" by their more populous neighbors.

Population of States, 1790

A major issue that confronted the Constitutional Convention was how to determine representation in the new government. Should each state have the same number of representatives, or should representation be based on population? Looking at this chart, which states would want equal representation for each state?

8.6 Resolution: The Great Compromise

The New Jersey Plan was warmly received by delegates from small states. The majority of delegates, however, saw Paterson's plan as little improvement over the Articles of Confederation and rejected it. But they could not agree on what should replace it.

Roger Sherman, a signer of the Declaration of Independence, helped construct the Great Compromise that called for a Congress of two houses. Each state had equal representation in one house and representation based on population in the other house.

Tempers Rise   The debate over who Congress should represent continued into July, with tempers rising day by day.

To most delegates from large states, representation based on population seemed both logical and fair. "Can we forget for whom we are forming a Government?" asked James Wilson of Pennsylvania. "Is it for men, or for the imaginary beings called States?"

To Wilson, the answer was obvious. But his logic could not overcome the fears of small-state delegates. One hot Saturday afternoon, Gunning Bedford of Delaware tore into the delegates from large states. "They insist," he said, "they will never hurt or injure the lesser states." His reply was, "I do not, gentlemen, trust you!" If the large states continued trying to "crush the smaller states," Bedford warned, "the small ones will find some foreign ally of more honor and good faith who will take them by the hand and do them justice."

Rufus King of Massachusetts was shocked at this reference to foreign powers. He shot back that he was "grieved, that such a thought had entered into the heart." Still, every delegate knew that Britain, France, and Spain were just waiting for the United States to fall apart so that they could pick up the pieces.

compromise: an agreement in which both sides in a dispute agree to give up something they want in order to achieve a settlement

A Compromise Is Reached   Finally, a **compromise** was proposed based on a plan put forward earlier by Roger Sherman of Connecticut.

The compromise plan kept a two-house Congress. The first house, the House of Representatives, would represent the people. In this house, the number of representatives from each state would be based on the state's population. The second house, the Senate, would represent the states. Each state would have two senators, to be elected by their state legislatures.

The vote was very close, but the compromise plan was approved. This plan saved the convention and became known as the Great Compromise.

8.7 Issue: How Should Slaves Be Counted?

The Great Compromise kept the framers working together. But having agreed to base representation in one house of Congress on state population, they faced a new and difficult question. As Gouverneur Morris of Pennsylvania put it, "Upon what principle shall the slaves be computed in the representation?"

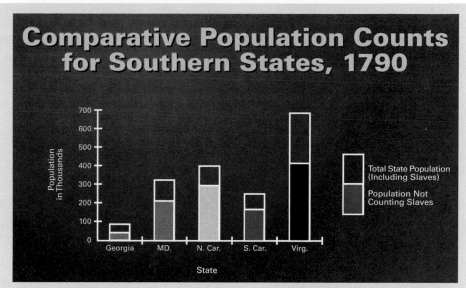

Comparative Population Counts for Southern States, 1790

How would representatives from the states shown in this chart want slaves to be counted? Would they want slaves to be counted as population for determining representation in Congress, or would they want slaves to be counted as property that could be taxed?

People or Property? Like everyone else, southerners naturally wanted as many representatives in the House as possible. To them, the answer was clear. Slaves should be counted the same as any other people in determining representation.

To northerners, however, the answer was not so clear. Were slaves to be considered people with a right to be represented in Congress? Or were they property?

"Blacks are property and are used to the southward as horses and cattle to the northward," argued Elbridge Gerry of Massachusetts. Most northern delegates agreed. Slaves should be counted, all right, but as property that could be taxed like any other property. If slaves were to be counted as people in determining representation in Congress, said Morris, "then make them citizens and let them vote."

New Thinking on Slavery This argument signaled an important change in white Americans' thinking about slavery. During the colonial period, most whites had simply accepted slavery as part of the human condition.

As you read in Chapter 7, the Declaration of Independence and the Revolutionary War forced many whites to reexamine their views on slavery. As they did so, more and more came to the conclusion that slavery was wrong. After the war, anti-slavery groups were organized in many states.

In the North, this new thinking led one state after another to pass laws ending slavery. Although many southerners were uneasy about slavery, they were not yet ready to abolish it. The South's economy was still too dependent on the labor of enslaved African Americans. But some southern states did pass laws making it easier for owners to free their slaves.

The question facing the framers was how far they could take this new thinking in a nation that was becoming half-slave and half-free.

8.8 Resolution: The Three-Fifths Compromise

After a bitter debate, Madison proposed a compromise. Count each slave as three fifths of a person, he suggested, when determining a state's population. The delegates approved this idea, known as the *three-fifths compromise*.

Declaring a slave to be three fifths of a person made a mockery of the statement in the Declaration of Independence that "all men are created equal." Still, the delegates adopted the compromise because it seemed the only way to keep the convention moving forward.

Control of Trade   Another question about slavery was raised by a dispute over trade. Northern delegates favored giving Congress broad power to control trade between the states and other countries. They believed that this power would be used to help business in the North.

This proposal made southern delegates nervous. They worried that Congress might try to tax southern export crops such as rice and tobacco. "We almost shuddered," wrote James McHenry of Maryland, "at the fate of the commerce [trade] of Maryland, should we be unable to make a change in this extraordinary power." Southerners also worried that Congress would use its power over trade to outlaw the slave trade—the importing of slaves from Africa.

Northern and southern delegates agreed to a compromise regarding the slave trade. Congress could control trade but could not tax exports or interfere with the slave trade for 20 years.

Miss Fillis and child, and Bill, Sold at publick Sale in May 12th Christiansburg, montgomery County.

Ending the Slave Trade

Southerners had reason to fear this. By 1787, several states had already outlawed the slave trade within their boundaries. And a majority of the convention's delegates, including many southerners, favored ending the slave trade completely.

Two states, however, objected that their economies would collapse without a constant supply of fresh slaves. "South Carolina and Georgia cannot do without slaves," said Charles Pinckney of South Carolina. Neither state would agree to any constitution that threatened the slave trade.

Again, the delegates settled on a compromise. The southern delegates agreed to give Congress power to control trade, but with two limitations. First, Congress could not place any tax on exports going to other countries. Second, Congress could not interfere with the slave trade for 20 years, or until 1808. After that time, the importing of slaves into the United States could be forbidden.

8.9 Issue: How Should the Chief Executive Be Elected?

Another major question facing the delegates concerned who would head the new government's executive branch. Early in the convention, Charles Pinckney urged the creation of a "vigorous executive." James Wilson followed with a proposal that a single person serve as the chief executive.

A sudden silence fell over the convention. A single executive? Just the words brought to mind unhappy memories of King George III.

Wilson broke the silence by explaining that good government

depends on clear, timely, and responsible leadership. Such leadership, he said, is most likely to be found in a single person.

One Executive or Three?   Edmund Randolph of Virginia disliked this proposal. He preferred a three-member executive drawn from different parts of the country. Three people, he argued, could lead the country better than one.

Benjamin Franklin opposed a single executive for different reasons. "The first man put at the helm will be a good one," said Franklin, thinking of George Washington. "Nobody knows what sort may come afterwards." The next chief executive, he warned, might be overly ambitious or too "fond of war."

In spite of these objections, the framers agreed to a single executive, to be called the *president*. To keep this leader from becoming too kinglike, they limited the president's term to four years. A vice president was also to be elected to fill that term if the president died in office.

Choosing the Chief Executive   Equally troubling was the issue of how to choose the chief executive. Some delegates wanted Congress to appoint the president. Gouverneur Morris objected. The president "must not be made a flunky of the Congress," he argued. "It must not be able to say to him: 'You owe your appointment to us.'"

Several delegates thought that the people should elect the president. Madison, however, argued that voters would naturally vote for someone from their own state. As a result, this method would not be fair to candidates from small states.

Still others suggested that the president be elected by a specially chosen group of "electors" from each state. Such a group, they felt, would be able look beyond state interests to make a wise choice for the entire country.

Many delegates felt that ordinary citizens, such as those pictured above, were not suited to elect the president. Roger Sherman stated, "The people should have as little to do as may be about the government. They want information, and are constantly liable to be misled."

8.10 Resolution: The Electoral College

After some 60 votes on the issue of how to elect the president, the framers reached another compromise. Neither Congress nor the people, they decided, should choose the president and vice president. Instead, a special body called the **Electoral College** would elect them.

Electoral College: The group established by the Constitution to elect the president and vice president. Voters in each state choose their electors.

The Electoral College System The Electoral College is made up of electors who cast votes to elect the president and vice president every four years. Each state has as many electors in the Electoral College as the number of senators and representatives it sends to Congress.

The delegates left the method of choosing electors up to each state. Before 1820, state legislatures chose electors in most states. Today, the people choose their state's electors when they vote in presidential elections. The electors then cast their ballots for president and vice president on a date chosen by Congress.

Originally, the electors voted for two candidates without saying which one they preferred for president or vice president. The candidate receiving the most votes became president. The runner-up became vice president. As you will read in Chapter 11, this system caused great confusion in the election of 1800 and was later changed.

Political Parties and Elections The Electoral College system looks very odd to most Americans today. In our age of instant communication, it is hard to appreciate the framers' concern that voters would not know enough about candidates outside their own state to choose a president wisely.

The delegates could not have predicted how quickly communications would improve in the United States. Nor could they foresee the rise of national political parties. Within a few years of the convention, political parties were nominating candidates for president and educating voters in every state about those candidates.

The Electoral College system still affects presidential elections today. In most states, the candidate who gets the most votes—even if less than a majority—gets all of that state's electoral votes. As a result, a candidate can win a majority in the Electoral College without necessarily winning a majority of the votes cast across the country. Naturally enough, presidential candidates do their heaviest campaigning in the states with the most electoral votes.

This is a copy of the Electoral College vote for the election of 1789. At that time, which states had the most electoral votes?

8.11 The Convention Ends

By the end of summer, the hard work of designing the Constitution was finished. But the new plan still had to be accepted by the states.

ratify: To formally approve a plan or an agreement. The process of approval is called *ratification*.

Approving the Constitution   The first question was how many states would have to **ratify,** or approve, the Constitution before it could go into effect. Should ratification require approval by all 13 states? By a majority of seven? The framers compromised on nine states.

The second question was who should ratify the Constitution—the people, or state legislatures? Ratification by state legislatures would be faster and easier. Madison, however, argued strongly that the people were "the fountain of all power" and should decide. The majority of delegates agreed. The Constitution would be ratified at special conventions by delegates elected by the people in each state.

Signing the Constitution

On September 17, 1787, the delegates declared the Constitution complete. As this last meeting began, Franklin shared his final thoughts, which would be printed in more than 50 newspapers.

"I confess that I do not entirely approve of this Constitution," he began. But no convention could produce a perfect plan. "It therefore astonishes me," he continued, "to find this system approaching so near to perfect… and I think it will astonish our enemies." Franklin added that he approved the final plan "because I expect no better, and because I am not sure that it is not the best." He urged "every member of the convention" to "put his name to this instrument."

Only 38 of the original 55 delegates signed the Constitution on September 17, 1787. Fourteen delegates had returned home before the conclusion of the convention, and three others also refused to sign.

Not everyone was won over by Franklin's words. Fourteen delegates left the convention before it ended, and three other doubters—Edmund Randolph and George Mason of Virginia, and Elbridge Gerry of Massachusetts—did not sign the Constitution either. Mason felt it gave too much power to the national government. Gerry refused to sign because he believed the new plan did not protect the rights of the people.

When the signing was over, Franklin confessed that he had often looked at the sun carved on the back of George Washington's chair and wondered whether it was about to rise or set. "But now," he said, "I have the happiness to know that it is a rising and not a setting sun." A new day was dawning for the United States.

8.12 The Constitution Goes to the Nation

republic: a country governed by elected representatives

Newspapers in every state printed the Constitution as soon as they could get it. What readers found was a plan that would create a "federal" system of government, in which a strong national government shared power with the states. Before long, the entire country was debating the same issues that had kept the convention in session for four long months.

The Federalists Supporters of the Constitution called themselves Federalists. The Federalists argued that the Constitution would create a national government that was strong enough to unite the quarreling states into a single **republic**.

James Madison, Alexander Hamilton, and John Jay led the Federalist campaign for ratification. In a series of newspaper articles, they recalled the weaknesses of the government under the Articles of Confederation. They showed how the Constitution would remedy those weaknesses by creating a stronger, more effective Union of the states.

The Federalist leaders also addressed the fears of many Americans that a strong government would threaten their freedom or take away their rights. The powers given to the government, they pointed out, were strictly limited. In addition, those powers were divided among three branches so that no one branch could become too powerful. The influential articles written by Madison, Hamilton, and Jay were later collected and published as *The Federalist Papers*.

The Constitution had to be approved by nine states. This political cartoon shows 11 states, pictured as columns, supporting the Constitution, while two states are hesitating.

The Anti-Federalists Opponents of the Constitution were known as Anti-Federalists. They found much to dislike about the new plan. Congress, they feared, would ruin the country with taxes. The president had power enough to rule like a king. And the judicial branch would swallow up state courts.

The Anti-Federalists also complained about what was missing from the plan. Their main complaint was that the plan listed the powers of the government but not the rights of the people. Most of all, the Anti-Federalists feared change. The idea of giving up any state power to form a stronger Union made them uneasy.

After listening to the arguments, Madison wrote that the question facing the nation was "whether the Union shall or shall not be continued. There is, in my opinion, no middle ground to be taken."

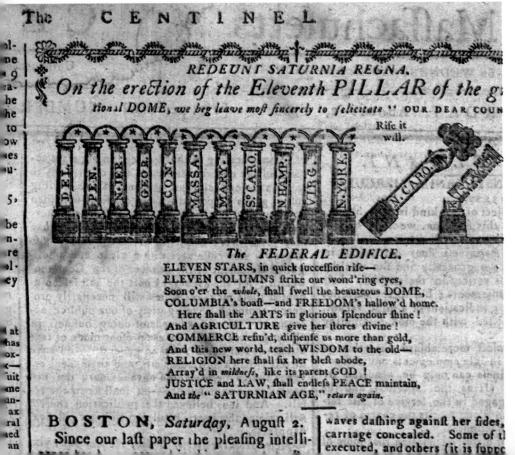

8.13 Chapter Summary

In this chapter, you read about the Constitutional Convention, the historic meeting that replaced the Articles of Confederation with a new plan of government for the United States. You used an annotated drawing of the Assembly Room at Independence Hall to organize information about the Convention.

The Articles of Confederation, which were America's first attempt at self-government, created a loose union of states under a weak central government. This government saw the new nation through the Revolutionary War. It also established a procedure for settling western territories. But, as Shays's Rebellion showed, it was too weak in peacetime to keep order or protect its own property.

Delegates to the Constitutional Convention quickly agreed to create a new constitution. For four long months, they argued in secret over a number of issues that often threatened to destroy the meeting. In the end, the framework they created included a series of compromises.

One of these agreements, the Great Compromise, established how the states were to be represented in the legislative branch of government. The three-fifths compromise settled how slaves were to be counted in determining a state's population. A third set of compromises created a single chief executive, to be chosen by the Electoral College.

The labors of the framers were only the beginning. Their new Constitution had to be ratified by the people through special state conventions. Federalists, who supported the Constitution, were opposed by Anti-Federalists, who feared the power of the proposed national government. Now it was up to the people to decide.

During the convention, Benjamin Franklin wondered if the sun painted on the back of George Washington's chair was rising or setting. At the conclusion of the convention, Franklin optimistically concluded it was a rising sun.

What are these buildings?

The Constitution: A More Perfect Union

9.1 Introduction

When the delegates left Independence Hall in September 1787, they each carried a copy of the Constitution. Their task now was to convince their states to approve the document that they had worked so hard to write.

As you read in the last chapter, writing the Constitution involved many compromises. Most of all, the framers, or writers, wanted a central government that would be strong and lasting, but not so strong that it endangered people's freedoms. In this chapter, you will see how the Constitution meets these goals.

The delegates wanted ordinary citizens to understand and support the Constitution. For this reason, they organized its contents very clearly. After a short introduction, they divided the Constitution into parts called *articles*. Then they split each article into numbered sections that present topics in a careful order.

This structure can help you find information in the Constitution. For instance, the first section in the article on the president describes how the president is chosen. The second section lists the president's powers. The third section lists presidential duties, and the fourth explains how the president can be removed from office. If you wanted to find out whether the president can sign treaties, where would you look?

One of the marvels of the Constitution is the way it combines a strong framework for the government with flexibility. In general, the delegates allow Congress, the president, and the courts to add details to the basic framework. They also included procedures for changing the Constitution.

This combination of strength and flexibility makes the Constitution a "living document." Like a plant or an animal, the Constitution keeps its basic nature, yet it also changes with the times. The "living" quality of the Constitution helps to explain why it has survived for so long.

The delegates did their work well. More than 200 years after the Constitution was created for a new nation, a vastly different United States is still governed by this ingenious document.

Graphic Organizer: An Annotated Illustration
You will use an illustration of newspapers in government offices to understand the organization and powers of the federal government.

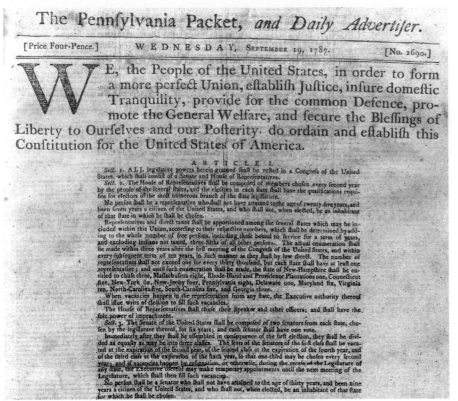

The Pennfylvania Packet, and Daily Advertifer.

[Price Four-Pence.] WEDNESDAY, September 19, 1787. [No. 2690.]

WE, the People of the United States, in order to form a more perfect Union, eftablifh Juftice, infure domeftic Tranquility, provide for the common Defence, promote the General Welfare, and fecure the Bleffings of Liberty to Ourfelves and our Pofterity, do ordain and eftablifh this Conftitution for the United States of America.

Library Company of Philadelphia

9.2 The Preamble Tells the Goals of Government

The delegates who crafted the Constitution chose each word carefully. Some of their best-known words come in the introduction, called the *Preamble*. The Preamble explains the reasons for the new government.

The Constitution begins with the memorable phrase "We the People." With these words, the delegates announced that the Constitution based its authority on the people themselves. The power to form the government did not come from the states or from the existing government. It did not come from a sovereign (ruler) appointed by God. Instead, the power came from ordinary Americans. This concept is known as **popular sovereignty**.

The Preamble then lists the goals of the new government. First, the delegates wanted to "form a more perfect Union." This meant building a country that could take advantage of the strengths the states gained from working together.

The Constitution also aims to "establish Justice." Americans wanted to be ruled by laws, not by the might of soldiers or the decisions of kings. The same laws would apply to all people.

The delegates hoped that the new government would "insure domestic Tranquility." By "tranquility," they meant peace and order. If the new system worked well, people would not fight the government or each other.

The new government would "provide for the common defense." In other words, the national government would be responsible for protecting Americans from foreign invaders. This would allow for stronger protection than if each state had its own army and navy.

The delegates wanted the new government to "promote the general Welfare." This means that it could support an economy and society in which people could prosper.

Finally, the delegates hoped to "secure the Blessings of Liberty to ourselves and our Posterity." By "posterity," the delegates meant the generations that would come after them. They wanted Americans to enjoy freedom then and in the future. We are their future, their posterity.

The delegates knew that these goals required a national government, but many people were suspicious of a strong central government. For this reason, the delegates tried to create a balanced framework that people could trust.

The delegates to the Constitutional Convention met in secret at Independence Hall in Philadelphia in 1787. Ordinary citizens got their first look at the Constitution in newspapers like the *Pennsylvania Packet,* pictured above.

popular sovereignty: the idea that the authority of government comes from the people

9.3 The Legislative Branch Makes Laws

For the framers of the Constitution, the first step in building a trusted government was to create a fair way to make laws. Article I of the Constitution gives the power to make laws to the **legislative branch** of government.

The Structure of Congress The Constitution creates a **bicameral** (two part) national legislature, called Congress. The two parts, or "houses," of Congress are the House of Representatives and the Senate.

Members of the Senate serve six-year terms so that they can enjoy some independence from the day-to-day opinions of voters. In contrast, members of the House serve two-year terms. As a result, they have to face the voters much more often. In this way, the framers tried to balance the independence and thoughtfulness of the Senate with the House's responsiveness to the changing wishes of the voters.

The framers also designed Congress to balance the rights of large and small states. Thus, while every state gets two senators, representation in the House is based on population. States with more people have more House representatives. To determine the number of representatives for each state, the Constitution calls for a census (a count of the population) every ten years. In time, the number of representatives in the House was set at 435.

The framers considered the Senate to be the "upper house" of the legislature. Its members are supposed to be wiser and more experienced than members of the "lower house." Senators must be at least 30 years old, while House members must be 25. Senators must have been citizens for nine years, House members for just seven years.

Originally, the Constitution allowed state legislatures to choose the two senators to represent their state. Today, however, senators are elected by popular vote (direct vote by the people).

How Congress Passes Laws The primary job of Congress is to make laws. Any member of the House or Senate can submit a proposal for a new law, called a **bill**. However, only the House can propose new taxes.

legislative branch: The law-making part of government, called the *legislature*. To *legislate* is to make a law.

bicameral: Having two law-making parts. *Bicameral* comes from Latin words meaning "two rooms."

bill: a proposed law

Senators and members of Congress listen to a speech given by the president in the chambers of the House of Representatives. The president must get congressional approval for his ideas before they can become law.

veto: To reject a proposed law or a bill. Only the president can veto bills.

If a majority in one house votes in favor of the bill, it is sent to the other house for debate. If both houses approve the bill, it goes to the president. The bill becomes a law if the president signs it.

If the president doesn't approve of a proposed law, he can **veto** (reject) it. Congress can override the president's veto, which means passing the bill over the president's objections. But to do so requires a two-thirds majority in both houses.

The Powers of Congress

Article I spells out other powers of Congress. For example, only Congress can decide how to spend the money raised through taxes. Other congressional powers include the power to raise an army and navy, to declare war, to pay government debts, and to grant citizenship.

In addition, Congress may "make all laws which shall be necessary and proper" to carry out its other powers. This power, known as the "elastic clause," gives Congress the flexibility needed to do its job. Over the years, the elastic clause has been stretched to allow Congress to do many things that were never listed among its powers in the Constitution.

How a Bill Becomes Law

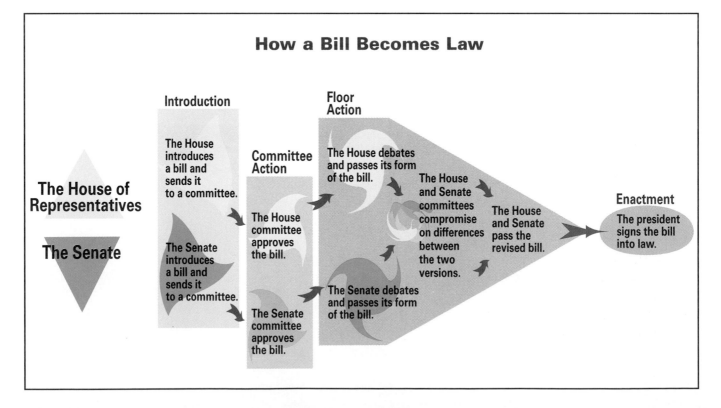

The House of Representatives

The Senate

Introduction

The House introduces a bill and sends it to a committee.

The Senate introduces a bill and sends it to a committee.

Committee Action

The House committee approves the bill.

The Senate committee approves the bill.

Floor Action

The House debates and passes its form of the bill.

The Senate debates and passes its form of the bill.

The House and Senate committees compromise on differences between the two versions.

The House and Senate pass the revised bill.

Enactment

The president signs the bill into law.

9.4 The Executive Branch Carries Out the Laws

A government needs people to carry out, or execute, the laws passed by the legislature. For instance, when Congress approves a tax, someone must collect the money. When Congress appropriates, or sets aside, money for low-cost housing, someone must build and manage the housing.

Article II of the Constitution describes the branch of government that fills this role, the **executive branch**. The head of the executive branch is the president. The president is often called the Chief Executive.

Electing the President   As you read in Chapter 8, delegates at the Constitutional Congress were not prepared to let the people elect the president directly. Instead, they decided that the president would be selected by a group of "electors." Each state would have the same number of electors as it had representatives and senators. To win the presidency, a candidate needs a majority of the "electoral vote."

The president serves a four-year term and may run for reelection. A new president makes a solemn promise called the *oath of office*. The Constitution gives the exact words of the oath. Notice that the president promises to "defend the Constitution." These words reinforce the importance of the Constitution as the basic law of the land.

The Constitution always refers to the president as "he." All the delegates to the Constitutional Convention were men, and they probably assumed that only men would ever vote or hold office. In fact, women were not guaranteed the right to vote in national elections until 1920. But nothing in the Constitution prevents a woman from being elected president.

Presidents are at the center of the American political stage. Here we see President Clinton meeting with his cabinet and other close advisors.

executive branch: the part of government that "executes" (carries out) the laws

impeach: to formally accuse an official of a crime related to official duties

judicial branch: the part of government, consisting of the Supreme Court and lower federal courts, that interprets the laws

The Powers of the President   The president does more than carry out laws passed by Congress. The president is Commander in Chief of the nation's military forces. He or she can, with the consent of the Senate, make treaties, or formal agreements, with other nations. The president nominates, or recommends, ambassadors (official representatives to other countries) and Supreme Court justices (judges). Finally, the president can grant pardons to people convicted of violating federal (national) laws.

The framers expected that the executive branch would need organizations called "departments" to carry out its duties. For example, the State Department handles relations with other nations. The Justice Department is involved in law enforcement as well as in court actions. The heads of executive departments are members of the president's cabinet, a formal group of advisors.

Today, the executive branch has over a dozen departments. Each department contains smaller, specialized agencies. For instance, the Department of Health and Human Services contains the Food and Drug Administration. This agency works to ensure that foods and medicines meet safety standards that have been set by Congress.

Removing the President   The Constitution gives Congress the power to remove a president or other officials from office if they commit certain crimes related to their duties. The House of Representatives can vote to impeach the president. To *impeach* means to formally accuse the president of the crimes specified in the Constitution. These include "Bribery, or other high Crimes and Misdemeanors." If the House votes to **impeach,** the Senate puts the president on trial, with the senators serving as the jury. If found guilty, the president is removed from office.

9.5 The Judicial Branch Interprets the Law

The framers intended the Constitution to be the "supreme Law of the Land." That means no other laws or actions by the government can conflict with the Constitution. Protecting the Constitution is one of the principal responsibilities of the third branch of government, the **judicial branch**. The judicial branch consists of the system of federal courts and judges.

Article III of the Constitution gives the basic framework of the judicial branch. It establishes the country's highest court, the Supreme Court. It also gives Congress the power to create "inferior" (lower) courts to meet the nation's needs.

In addition to protecting the Constitution, federal courts have the power to resolve disputes that involve national laws, the federal government, or the states. People accused of breaking national laws can be tried in federal courts.

The Federal Court System   Congress has authorized two main sets of inferior federal courts. These lower courts are called *district courts* and *appellate courts*.

Most cases involving federal laws are first heard in district court. The United States is divided into large geographic districts. Each district covers several states. Citizens can "appeal" decisions given in district court, which means asking a higher court to review the case. Courts that review cases are called *courts of appeal* or *appellate courts*. An appellate court only considers whether the original trial was fair and legal. A decision by an appellate court can be appealed to the Supreme Court.

The Powers of the Supreme Court The Supreme Court is the last stop in the judicial system. Its decisions are final, and they are binding on all lower courts. The Constitution does not specify the size of the Supreme Court. Congress has set it at nine members, who are called *justices*. The Constitution says that all federal judges, including Supreme Court justices, serve for "good behavior." Once they are appointed, the justices usually serve on the Court for life.

A dispute goes directly to the Supreme Court only if it involves a state or an ambassador from another country. Any other case comes to the Supreme Court after a trial and an appeal in lower courts. Participants in either national or state courts may eventually appeal cases to the Supreme Court.

The nine members of the United States Supreme Court hold very important positions in American government. Their legal opinions on everything from gun control, the death penalty, and abortion rights to prayer in schools are enforced.

Every year, lawyers ask the Supreme Court to review thousands of cases, but they agree to consider only about a hundred. The Supreme Court usually reviews a case only if the justices think that the decision made by a lower court might conflict with the Constitution or a federal law. After hearing statements from both sides, the justices debate among themselves and vote. Supreme Court decisions are announced and explained in writing. These decisions then guide later decisions in lower courts.

Early in its history, the Supreme Court defined the power of "judicial review." This is the power to decide whether laws and actions by the legislative and executive branches conflict with the Constitution. Courts all over the country rely on the Supreme Court for guidance about what is constitutional. Judicial review gives the Supreme Court great power in its role of protecting the "supreme Law of the Land."

checks and balances: the system that allows each branch of government to limit the powers of the other branches

9.6 Checks and Balances between the Branches

The framers of the Constitution were very concerned about achieving a balance between a strong national government and protection for American freedoms. Dividing the federal government into three branches was one way they hoped to limit the government's power. But what would keep one branch from dominating the others? As one delegate to the Constitutional Convention pointed out, "From the nature of man, we may be sure that those who have power in their hands…will always, when they can…increase it."

Because of this concern, the framers developed a system that would enable each branch of the government to limit the power of the other branches. This system is called **checks and balances**.

Checking the Power of Other Branches   "Checks" allow one branch to block the actions of another branch. For instance, Congress has the power to pass laws. But the president can check this power by vetoing a bill before it becomes law. In turn, Congress can check the president's power by overriding the veto.

Similarly, the judicial branch can check the actions of the other two branches. Through its power of judicial review, the Supreme Court can declare that a law, a treaty, or an executive action is unconstitutional.

This diagram illustrates the concept of checks and balances, one of the most significant features of the Constitution. Checks and balances prevent one branch of government from gaining too much power.

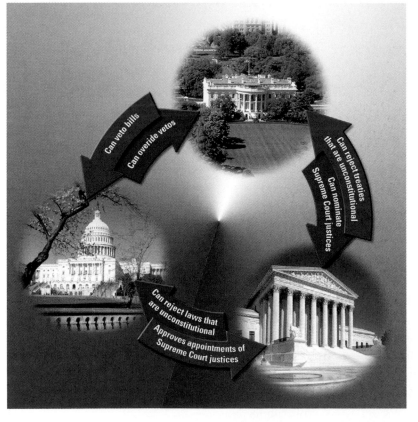

Can veto bills
Can override vetos
Can reject treaties that are unconstitutional
Can nominate Supreme Court justices
Can reject laws that are unconstitutional
Approves appointments of Supreme Court justices

Balancing the Power of Other Branches   "Balances" allow each branch of the government to have some role in the actions and power of the other branches. For instance, judges are appointed to the Supreme Court only if the president nominates them and the Senate approves the nomination. Similarly, the president has the power to sign treaties, but they take effect only if the Senate approves them.

The powers of the judicial branch are also balanced against the powers of the other branches. Even though the Supreme Court can declare laws unconstitutional, it is the president who chooses federal judges—and the Senate must approve these appointments. In addition, Congress can impeach federal judges. In these ways, the legislative and executive branches have some role in the actions of the judicial branch.

These checks and balances keep any one branch of the federal government from being too strong. This balance of powers is one of the most important features of the American system of government.

9.7 The Amendment Process Changes the Constitution

amendment: a change to the Constitution

The framers knew that the Constitution would need to be changed over time. As Thomas Jefferson said, the Constitution "belongs to the living and not to the dead." At the same time, they wanted the Constitution to provide a lasting and stable framework for the government. To maintain that stability, the framers made changing the Constitution possible, but difficult.

Changing the Constitution

Article V describes how changes, called **amendments,** can be made to the Constitution. Proposing an amendment requires a vote of two thirds of both houses of Congress, or a national convention called by Congress at the request of two thirds of the legislatures of all the states. Thus, either Congress or the states can start the process of amending the Constitution.

Proposing an amendment is only the first step. Before an amendment can become part of the Constitution, it must be approved by the legislatures (or by special conventions) in three quarters of the states. Once an amendment is approved, it becomes part of the supreme law of the land.

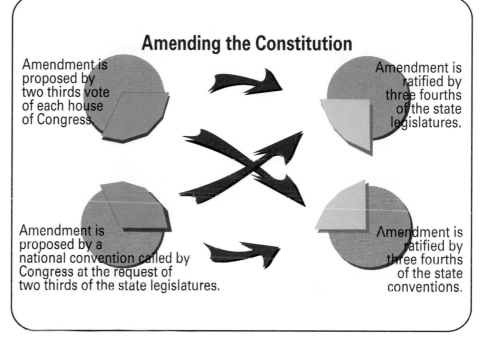

Amending the Constitution

Amendment is proposed by two thirds vote of each house of Congress.

Amendment is ratified by three fourths of the state legislatures.

Amendment is proposed by a national convention called by Congress at the request of two thirds of the state legislatures.

Amendment is ratified by three fourths of the state conventions.

This chart shows the different ways that amendments to the Constitution can be proposed and approved. Amendments are proposed in Congress on a regular basis. The vast majority of the proposals fail.

Amendments So Far   Over the years, people have suggested more than 10,000 amendments to the Constitution. Only 27 of these have been approved.

The first ten amendments were added almost immediately after the Constitution was ratified (approved by the states). These amendments were demanded by many Americans in exchange for their support for the Constitution. Called the Bill of Rights, these ten amendments primarily guarantee specific rights to citizens. The Bill of Rights is so important in American history that the next chapter is devoted to it.

The other 17 amendments became part of the Constitution one at a time. Some of them changed the way certain public officials are elected. Others guaranteed the rights of certain groups of Americans. For instance, the Thirteenth Amendment made slavery illegal. The Nineteenth Amendment guaranteed women the right to vote. And the Twenty-sixth Amendment gave the right to vote to all citizens over the age of 18. Ideas for other amendments are proposed from time to time, but chances are that very few of them will become part of the Constitution.

The Constitution divides power between the federal and state governments. The idea behind the separation of powers is to create a unified nation while also protecting local control.

federalism: the constitutional system that divides power between the national and state governments

9.8 The Federal System Connects the Nation and the States

The framers of the Constitution wanted a strong national government, but they also wanted the states to keep significant powers. They accomplished both goals by creating a federal system of government in which power is shared between the national and state governments.

Powers Belonging to the National Government Some powers are given solely to the national government. In general, these are powers best exercised by one central authority. For example, only the national government can print and coin money. The framers had learned from bitter experience that having separate state currencies made no sense. The national government also controls relations with foreign nations.

In addition, Article VI states that the Constitution and the laws flowing from it are the "supreme Law of the Land." A state's constitution, laws, and judicial decisions must agree with the Constitution. They must also not conflict with any other federal laws or treaties. Everyone who holds a state or federal office must promise to support the Constitution.

Powers Belonging to the States Powers not given to the national government by the Constitution are retained by the states. For instance, the Constitution does not say anything about schools, marriage, establishing local governments, owning property, licensing doctors and lawyers, or most crimes. The states make the laws that guide these areas of American life.

The Constitution does, however, outline the responsibilities of states to each other in a federal system of government. Article IV says that each state must give "full Faith and Credit" to the laws and court decisions of other states. This means accepting other states' laws and decisions as legal. For example, a marriage or divorce legalized in one state is legal in every state.

The Constitution does not allow one state to discriminate unreasonably against a citizen of another state. A state may not, for example, refuse to let a child who was born in another state attend its public schools. States are also required to help each other track down fleeing criminals and (before the Thirteenth Amendment ended slavery) runaway slaves. Criminals cannot escape justice by fleeing to another state. Nor could slaves become free simply by escaping to another state.

Shared Powers Federal and state governments also share some powers. Both can raise taxes, build roads, and borrow money, for example.

If you think **federalism,** or sharing power, sounds complicated, you're right. Consider presidential elections. Congress sets the date for national elections, but the states register voters and run the elections. States count the ballots, but the national government organizes the Electoral College vote, which officially determines who will be president.

Americans have struggled to maintain the proper balance between the powers of the national and state governments since the Revolution. Debates over that balance will surely continue far into the future.

The Granger Collection, New York

Americans have good reason to celebrate the Constitution. It has worked effectively for more than 200 years, ensuring that the American system of government remains strong today.

9.9 Chapter Summary

In this chapter, you used an illustration of newspapers in a government office to learn about the organization and powers of the federal government as described in the Constitution.

The Constitution created in 1787 is both strong and flexible. As the first words of the Preamble tell us, its authority comes directly from the people, not the states. Power is divided among three branches of government. The legislative branch makes the laws, the executive branch carries out the laws, and the judicial branch makes sure that the actions of the other two branches agree with the Constitution and federal laws. A system of checks and balances keeps any branch from gaining too much power. The Constitution also ensures that power is shared between the states and the national government in a system known as *federalism*.

For all its strength, the Constitution has been flexible enough to adapt to changing times. The framers purposely made the process of amending the Constitution difficult. Still, 27 amendments have been added since it was written. The first ten amendments, called the Bill of Rights, guarantee the most cherished rights of Americans citizens. You will read about these amendments in the next chapter.

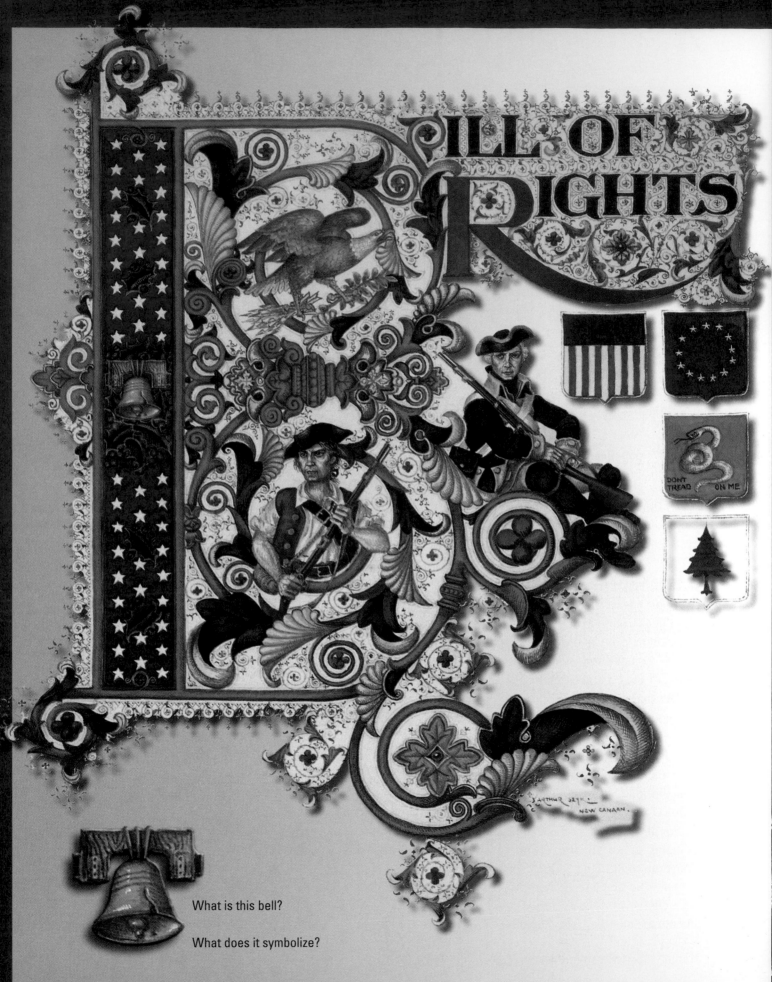

BILL OF RIGHTS

What is this bell?

What does it symbolize?

130

The Bill of Rights

10.1 Introduction

To James Madison, the creation of the Constitution seemed nothing less than "a miracle." By 1788, however, it seemed that it would take another miracle to get it adopted.

The adoption of the Constitution depended upon ratification, or approval, by 9 of the 13 states. Ratification started off smoothy, with Delaware, Pennsylvania, New Jersey, Georgia, and Connecticut all saying yes. Then came Massachusetts, where opposition ran strong.

When the Massachusetts ratification convention met early in 1788, defeat seemed certain. Opponents objected that the Constitution did not list the rights of the people. Many delegates said that they would not vote in favor of ratification unless such a list were added at once.

In desperation, the Constitution's supporters, the Federalists, looked to John Hancock, the state's governor. Hancock had stayed away from the convention, pleading a painful attack of gout. In fact, he was waiting to make an appearance until he could be sure to be on the winning side.

The Federalists tried to take advantage of Hancock's vanity. Virginia, they hinted, might not ratify the Constitution. If it did not, then George Washington, a Virginian, could not run for president. And if Washington didn't run, who was the best choice for the honor? Why, none other than the great governor of Massachusetts!

Hancock swallowed the bait. The governor was carried into the convention, his feet swathed in bandages. In a dramatic speech, he urged the delegates to approve the Constitution as it was. At the same time, he promised that the first task of the new Congress would be to amend the Constitution by adding a **bill of rights**.

The vote was close, but Massachusetts chose to ratify. The Federalists' strategy, "Ratify now, amend later," also worked well in other states. By the end of 1788, the Constitution was the law of the land.

In this chapter, you will learn how Federalists made good on their promise to add a list of rights to the Constitution. You will also learn how these rights work to protect Americans from abuses of government power.

Graphic Organizer: Visual Metaphor
You will use this visual metaphor of a protective wall to learn about the rights protected by the Bill of Rights.

10.2 Creating the Bill of Rights

For all his hopes, John Hancock never got to be president. By a narrow vote, Virginia did ratify the Constitution. In the first presidential election, held in 1789, George Washington became the nation's first president. John Adams of Massachusetts was chosen to be vice president.

When the first Congress met that year, no one seemed in much of a hurry to amend the Constitution. Representative James Madison, however, did not forget the promises made during the ratification debate. Originally, he had opposed adding a bill of rights to the Constitution. Such a listing seemed unnecessary to him. Thomas Jefferson helped change his mind. In a letter to Madison, Jefferson argued that "a bill of rights is what the people are entitled to against every government on Earth…and what no just government should refuse."

While Congress debated other issues, Madison sifted through nearly 100 proposed amendments. He chose those that seemed least controversial (likely to cause conflict) and presented them to Congress on June 8, 1789.

Critics jumped on Madison's proposals as meaningless "milk and water" cures for imaginary problems. The debate that followed was, in Madison's words, "extremely difficult." As months dragged on with no agreement, he wrote to a friend that the Bill of Rights had become a "nauseous project." Still, he persevered until Congress finally approved 12 amendments.

A young James Madison is pictured here. Often called "the Father of the Constitution," Madison also crafted the Bill of Rights that was debated and approved in 1791.

Ratification by the States   Under the Constitution, three quarters of the states must ratify an amendment before it can become law. The states rejected the first two amendments, which dealt with the size of congressional districts and congressional pay raises. Both amendments were considered unnecessary. By 1791, the required number of states (nine) had approved the other ten amendments. Together, these ten amendments form the Bill of Rights.

When Madison first proposed the Bill of Rights, some people saw his amendments as useless "paper barriers" against abuses of government power. For more than 200 years, however, his "paper barriers" have proven far stronger than even Madison might have hoped.

10.3 First Amendment Rights

Madison combined five basic freedoms into the First Amendment. These are freedom of religion, of speech, of the press, and of assembly, and the right to petition the government. Many people consider these basic freedoms to be the most important part of the Bill of Rights.

These First Amendment rights would have been meaningless, however, without some way to protect them. When a person believes that the government has violated these rights, he or she may challenge the government's action in court. The same is true of all other rights protected in the Constitution.

If the case reaches the Supreme Court, the nine Supreme Court justices decide how the Constitution applies to the situation. After hearing both sides, the justices vote on their decision. One of the justices from the majority side then writes a majority opinion. This document explains how the Court interpreted the Constitution to reach its decision. Any justices who disagree with the majority decision may write minority opinions explaining their reasoning.

As you read about First Amendment rights, you will see how the Supreme Court has applied these rights to real-life situations.

The Right to Worship Freely   The First Amendment has two guarantees of religious freedom. The first says, "Congress shall make no law respecting an establishment of religion." This means that Congress cannot make any faith the official religion of the United States. Nor can it make laws that favor any religion over another. The purpose of this guarantee, in Jefferson's words, was to build "a wall of separation between church and state."

How high should that wall be? The Supreme Court considered this question in a 1971 case known as *Lemon v. Kurtzman*. This case challenged a Pennsylvania law that used public tax money to pay for books and teachers' salaries at private religious schools. The Court ruled that the law was unconstitutional because it allowed too close a connection between government and religion.

The second religious guarantee in the First Amendment says "Congress shall make no law... prohibiting the free exercise" of religion. This means that people can believe, or not believe, whatever they want about religion, without fear of punishment.

However, they can't necessarily *do* whatever they want in the name

The beliefs of minority religious groups, like the Hare Khrishnas in this image, are protected by the Bill of Rights.

of religious freedom. For instance, the Supreme Court has ruled that parents are not free to deny their children medical treatment or vaccinations because of their religious beliefs.

The Right to Free Speech and Press   The First Amendment protects freedom of speech and freedom of the press. The Supreme Court often treats these rights together as the right of free expression. Thomas Jefferson considered this right to be extremely important. He once said, "If it were left to me to decide whether we should have a government without a free press or a free press without a government, I would prefer the latter."

Americans had learned in colonial days that free expression was their best protection against abuse of government power. In 1735, John Peter Zenger was arrested for printing reports that the governor of New York had taken bribes. The prosecutors said that it was illegal to damage the governor's good name, even if Zenger had published the truth. Zenger's lawyer argued that no one should be jailed for "exposing and opposing arbitrary power by speaking and writing the truth." Fortunately, the jury agreed, and Zenger was freed.

Although the First Amendment protects the right to speak freely in public places, like streets and parks, that right is not unlimited. The Supreme Court has allowed limits on some kinds of speech, such as speech that endangers public safety. As one justice said, "The most stringent [strongest] protection of free speech would not protect a man in falsely shouting, 'Fire!' in a theater and causing a panic."

Freedom of speech and the press are two of the most cherished rights held by Americans. Rallies, such as the one you see here, have been an important part of the American tradition since colonial times.

The Supreme Court has ruled that "speech" means more than just words. Free expression includes "symbolic speech," or actions people take to express their opinions.

Protection of symbolic speech was an issue in the case of *Texas v. Johnson*. This case involved a man who had been convicted in Texas of burning an American flag as a form of protest. When he appealed his case to the Supreme Court, the justices overturned his conviction. No form of expression can be banned, the Court ruled, just because "society finds the idea itself offensive or disagreeable."

The Court has also ruled that freedom of the press applies to more than just newspapers and magazines. It also applies to other communication media, such as books, television, movies, and the Internet. Freedom of expression is protected in all media, even when what people say offends others. As one justice explained, the purpose of freedom of speech isn't to protect "free thought for those who agree with us but freedom for the thought that we hate."

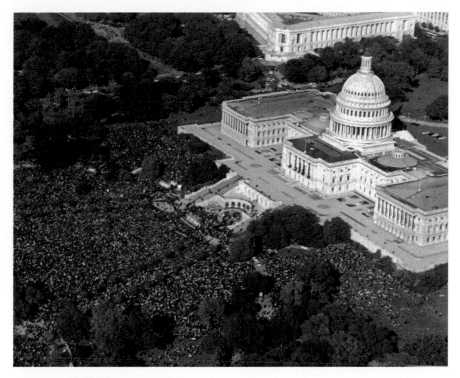

On October 16, 1995, hundreds of thousands of black men marched and assembled at a rally on the steps of the United States capitol. The demonstration was called the "Million Man March," and it illustrates the importance of the First Amendment.

The Right to Assemble and Petition The final two rights protected in the First Amendment are the right to peaceably assemble (meet together with others) and to petition (appeal to) the government.

Americans had come to value both of these rights in their conflict with the British government over taxation without representation. You read in Chapter 5 how colonial leaders assembled in the Continental Congress and petitioned King George to change his policies.

The right to assembly means that citizens can use public property for meetings and demonstrations. Parades, protest marches, and political rallies are all forms of peaceful assembly protected by the First Amendment.

While the First Amendment protects peaceful meetings, it does not give people the right to close streets or buildings, or to protest violently. Police can arrest a speaker who urges listeners to riot or to break the law.

What if an assembly is peaceful, but the people watching it are not? This question came up in the case of *Gregory v. Chicago*. The case began when comedian Dick Gregory led a protest march to the home of Chicago's mayor. Residents in the neighborhood began throwing eggs and shouting insults at the marchers. Fearful of a riot, the police asked the marchers to leave. When the marchers refused, the police arrested them.

The marchers challenged their arrests in court, claiming that their protest was protected under the First Amendment's right of assembly. The Supreme Court agreed that the marchers had assembled peacefully. If anyone should have been arrested, it was the mayor's neighbors.

10.4 Citizen Protections

The next three amendments protect citizens from different kinds of government abuse. All three reflect the unhappy experience of American colonists under British rule.

Second Amendment: The Right to Bear Arms During colonial times, Britain had used a standing (permanent) army to keep the colonists in line. After winning their independence, Americans remained suspicious of standing armies. They preferred to rely on volunteer state militias to protect their new nation. The Second Amendment states that "A well-regulated militia, being necessary to the security of a free state, the right of the people to keep and bear arms shall not be infringed [limited]."

The meaning of this amendment has been much debated. Some argue that it protects the right of people to own guns *only* if they are part of an organized militia. (An example is today's National Guard.) Others believe that the Second Amendment protects the right of individuals to own weapons for their own self-defense.

Third Amendment: Quartering Troops in Homes Before the Revolution, Britain had forced colonists to open their homes to British soldiers. The Third Amendment gave Americans the right to refuse such requests. "No soldier," it says, "shall…be quartered [housed] in any house, without the consent of the owner."

Today, soldiers are not quartered in homes. The Third Amendment remains important, however, as a warning to the government to respect the privacy of people's homes. As Justice Joseph Story said, "A man's house shall be his own castle, privileged against all civil and military intrusion."

In colonial America, guns were an important part of everyday life. They were used for hunting and for protection in a time when the police were often very distant. Also, militias protected colonists against outside invasion and Indian attacks.

The Granger Collection, New York

Fourth Amendment: Searches and Seizures The Fourth Amendment protects people and their belongings from "unreasonable searches and seizures." (A *seizure* is the act of forcibly taking control of a person or property.) Before arresting a person or searching someone's home, the police must show a judge that there is good reason for allowing the action. The judge then issues a **warrant** that says exactly who will be arrested or what will be searched.

The purpose of protections such as this one, wrote Justice Louis Brandeis, is to guarantee "the right to be left alone—the most comprehensive of rights and the right most valued by civilized men."

The police must follow careful guidelines in searches and seizures of private property.

10.5 Legal Rights and Protections

The next four amendments lay out the rights and protections that apply to people who are accused of crimes or are involved in other legal disputes.

Fifth Amendment: Legal Rights The Fifth Amendment is the longest amendment in the Bill of Rights. It lists five important rights of citizens involved with the justice system.

First, this amendment gives people who are accused of serious crimes the right to a grand jury hearing. A *grand jury* is a group of citizens who hear the government's evidence and decide whether it justifies a trial. If so, the grand jury issues an indictment, or formal charge. If not, the accused person is released.

Second, the amendment protects citizens from "double jeopardy." (*Jeopardy* means risk.) This means that a person who is tried for a crime and found not guilty cannot be tried again for that same crime.

Third, the amendment prohibits **self-incrimination**. This means that the police cannot force people to say things that might be used against them in a trial.

Today, police are required to remind people of their right to remain silent before they start to question them. They must also warn people that anything they do say can be used against them at a trial. This reminder is known as the "Miranda warning," after the case in which the Supreme Court defined this requirement.

The protection against self-incrimination also applies to **defendants** testifying in court. They may refuse to answer questions that might damage their case. This refusal is called "taking the Fifth."

warrant: an order from a judge that authorizes police or other officials to take a certain action, such as searching someone's property

self-incrimination: the act of giving testimony that can be used against oneself

defendants: people who are required to defend themselves in a legal action; an example is an accused person who is put on trial for a crime

Next, the amendment says that a person cannot be "deprived of life, liberty, or property, without due process of law." The term *due process* means that the government must follow clear rules and act reasonably as it carries out the law. For example, the Supreme Court has ruled that every person should be presumed innocent until proven guilty. In addition, the government must prove its case against a defendant "beyond a reasonable doubt."

Finally, the Fifth Amendment says that the government cannot take someone's private property for public use "without just compensation." This means that the government must pay a fair price when it takes over a person's property for purposes such as building roads or parks.

Sixth Amendment: Criminal Trial Rights   The Sixth Amendment lists a number of rights that are designed to provide accused persons with fair trials. It begins with the right to "a speedy and public trial, by an impartial jury."

The right to a speedy trial means that people cannot be kept in jail for long periods before being judged at a trial. Speedy trials also ensure that witnesses testify while their memories of events are still fresh.

"Public" means that trials may not be held in secret. Citizens have a right to attend trials to make sure that justice is being done.

An accused person also has the right to be judged by a jury of people who live in his or her area. The jury must be "impartial," which means that jurors are not prejudiced (influenced) against the defendant. Courts have also said that prosecutors cannot exclude potential jurors just because of their race or gender.

Before a trial, the prosecutor must tell the accused person not only the charge, but the time and place of the supposed crime. This information is essential to the accused person in preparing his or her defense.

A defendant also has the right to hear and question all witnesses who testify at the trial. In addition, the defendant can ask the court to order reluctant (unwilling) witnesses to testify against their wishes.

Lastly, a defendant has the right to an attorney to assist in his or her defense. The Supreme Court has called this the most important of all the rights of accused persons. Without legal help, an innocent person may all too easily be convicted of a crime. In the past, only people with money to hire lawyers enjoyed this important right. Today, people accused of crimes are provided with a lawyer if they cannot afford to pay for one.

Seventh Amendment: Civil Trial Rights   Not all trials involve criminal actions. Some trials decide civil cases, or disputes between people or businesses. Civil cases typically involve money,

Lieutenant Colonel Oliver North testified before Congress in 1987. He took the Fifth Amendment to avoid giving evidence regarding his involvement in a government arms deal.

property, or family matters, such as divorce. The Seventh Amendment says that in all but the most minor cases, people involved in a civil case have a right to a jury trial.

The Seventh Amendment also says that "no fact tried by a jury shall be otherwise reexamined." This means that after a jury decides the facts of a case, no judge can overrule the jury's decision.

Eighth Amendment: Bail and Punishments   The Eighth Amendment protects an accused person's rights both before and after trial. Before a trial, it forbids a judge from demanding "excessive" bail. *Bail* is money or property given to the court to hold until an accused person shows up at trial. If a defendant cannot pay bail, he or she stays in jail until trial. The Eighth Amendment prevents judges from using unreasonably high bail to keep someone in jail before his or her day in court.

After trial, if the person is found guilty, the Eighth Amendment forbids "excessive fines" and "cruel and unusual punishments." It does not say what such punishments are. In 1791, physical punishments like whipping and branding were common. Today, they are considered cruel. As Justice Thurgood Marshall has written, "A penalty that was permissible at one time in our nation's history is not necessarily permissible today."

The Supreme Court has interpreted this amendment to mean that punishments must be "proportionate" to the crime. Judges cannot, for example, impose long prison terms on people convicted of minor crimes. The Court has also ruled that the amendment prohibits inhumane prison conditions, such as depriving prisoners of food.

Today, Americans continue to debate whether the death penalty should be banned under the Eighth Amendment. Opponents of the death penalty have argued that executing anyone is a cruel and unusual punishment, no matter how horrible their crime. The Supreme Court has disagreed. In a 1976 case known as *Gregg v. Georgia,* the Court ruled that "the punishment of death for the crime of murder does not under all circumstances, violate the Eighth Amendment."

A lawyer tries to convince the jury to decide in his client's favor during a trial. The right to a jury trial is one of a number of citizen protections found in the Sixth Amendment.

Your Legal Rights and Protections

Before being charged with a crime, you are protected from	After an arrest, you have the right to	Once indicted, you have the right to
• a search of your property without a search warrant. • arrest by the police without a warrant or good reason.	• remain silent when questioned. • talk to a lawyer. • have a grand jury hearing to weigh the evidence against you.	• know the charges against you. • reasonable bail. • a speedy trial. • a jury trial.
At your trial, you have the right to • question witnesses against you. • call witnesses in your defense. • refuse to answer questions that could harm you. • be defended by a lawyer.	If found innocent, you are protected from • double jeopardy.	If found guilty, you are protected from • excessive fines. • cruel or unusual punishments.

10.6 Other Rights and Powers

The last two amendments were included to help keep a proper balance of rights and power among the federal government, the people, and the states.

Amendment Nine: Rights Retained by the People   One argument raised against putting a bill of rights in the Constitution was that no list could be complete. If some rights were listed and others were not, did this mean that people had only the listed rights?

The Ninth Amendment says that even though "certain rights" are listed in the Constitution, other rights not listed there are also "retained [kept] by the people." An example of this is the right to privacy.

Amendment Ten: Powers Reserved to the States   The Tenth Amendment was included to protect the states from excessive federal power. It says that powers not given to the national government by the Constitution are "reserved to the states…or to the people."

This amendment was tested in *McCulloch v. Maryland*. The case began in 1816 when Congress chartered a national bank. Many states protested that the Tenth Amendment prohibited Congress from creating a bank because this power is not listed in the Constitution. In 1818, Maryland expressed its disapproval by levying a tax on the national bank.

James McCulloch, an officer of the Baltimore branch of the bank, refused to pay the tax. If the tax were set high enough, he protested, the state could drive the bank out of business. The effect would be the same as letting Maryland veto an act of Congress.

Maryland took McCulloch to court for failing to pay the tax. The state argued that not only was the bank unconstitutional, but under the Tenth Amendment, Maryland had the power to tax it.

The Supreme Court sided with McCulloch. It ruled that the Tenth Amendment did not forbid the chartering of a federal bank. The "necessary and proper clause" of the Constitution gave Congress the power to do so. The Court also ruled that when state and national power conflict, national power is supreme. Since Congress's power to create a bank was superior to Maryland's power to tax, the tax was unconstitutional.

This cartoon illustrates how passionate Americans are about their rights, even those that don't exist.

Calvin and Hobbes

by Bill Watterson

CALVIN AND HOBBES © 1990 Watterson. Reprinted with permission of UNIVERSAL PRESS SYNDICATE. All rights reserved.

10.7 Chapter Summary

In this chapter, you read about the Bill of Rights, the first ten amendments to the Constitution. You used a visual metaphor to organize information about the amendments.

The promise of a bill of rights was key to getting the Constitution ratified by the states. As a member of the first Congress, James Madison proposed the amendments that guarantee the rights of citizens of the United States.

The First Amendment spells out five basic freedoms enjoyed by all Americans, from freedom of speech to the right to petition the government. The Second, Third, and Fourth Amendments specify protections for ordinary citizens against the abuse of government power.

The Fifth through Eighth Amendments are intended to guarantee fair treatment for people who are involved in legal actions.

The Ninth and Tenth Amendments concern the relationships among the federal government, the states, and the people.

As with other parts of the Constitution, the Supreme Court has interpreted the provisions of the Bill of Rights over time and applied them to new situations. But the spirit of these amendments remains much the same as when James Madison drafted them more than 200 years ago. His "unnecessary" addition to the Constitution has become the foundation of the rights and liberties Americans have learned to cherish.

The Bill of Rights contains many of the rights that we think of as American freedoms.

141

Thomas Jefferson was the first secretary of state. What were his responsibilities?

Alexander Hamilton was the first secretary of the treasury. What were his responsibilities?

The Granger Collection, New York

Political Developments in the Early Republic

11.1 Introduction

The painting to the left shows four leaders in the first government formed under the Constitution. On the far right stands George Washington, who had been lured out of retirement to serve as the nation's first president. Seldom has a leader seemed more reluctant (hesitant) to take power. "My movements to the chair of government," he wrote on leaving home, "will be accompanied by feelings not unlike those of a culprit [criminal] who is going to the place of his execution."

Henry Knox sits opposite Washington. During the Revolutionary War, this Boston bookseller became a general and Washington's close friend and advisor. When Washington became president in 1789, he made Knox his secretary of war.

Take a close look at the two men in the middle of the picture. Alexander Hamilton, who stands beside the president, served as Washington's secretary of the treasury. Thomas Jefferson, who stands behind Knox, served as secretary of state. It was his job to manage relations between the United States and other countries.

Washington chose Hamilton and Jefferson for these positions because of all they had in common. Both were strong patriots. Both had served their country during the Revolutionary War—Hamilton in the Continental Army and Jefferson in the Continental Congress. Both had brilliant minds.

For all they had in common, the two men were opposites in many ways. Hamilton dressed with great care. Jefferson was sloppy with clothes. Hamilton moved with precision. Jefferson slouched. Hamilton was a doer who moved briskly from task to task. Jefferson was a thinker who took time to explore ideas.

The expression "opposites attract" may be true in love, but not in politics. As you will discover in this chapter, Hamilton and Jefferson soon became political rivals. Their rivalry eventually gave rise to the nation's first political parties and a new way of electing the nation's president.

Graphic Organizer: Character Collage
You will use this character collage to understand the political differences between the Federalist and the Democratic-Republican Parties.

inauguration: a formal ceremony to mark the beginning of something, such as a president's term of office

11.2 Launching the New Government

On April 30, 1789, George Washington took the oath of office as the first president of the United States. After his **inauguration,** Washington addressed both houses of Congress. He asked Congress to work with him to put into place "the wise measures on which the success of this government must depend." At times his hands shook so much that he had trouble reading his speech.

The Title Debate   Washington had reason to be nervous. The first Congress was deeply divided. Some members were eager to build a strong national government. Others were just as eager to limit the power of the new government. These differences showed up immediately in a debate over what title to use when addressing the president.

Vice President John Adams pointed out that European heads of government had titles like "Your Excellency" that showed respect for their office. The president, he argued, should have a similar title. Supporters of a strong national government agreed.

Others argued that such titles smelled of royalty and had no place in a democracy. A few members of Congress joked that the rather plump Adams should be given the title "His Rotundity" (His Roundness). The debate finally ended when Washington let it be known that he preferred the simple title "Mr. President."

Setting Up the Executive Branch   Next, Congress turned to the task of creating executive departments. As Washington had feared, arguments broke out at once over what those departments should be and what powers they should have.

Congress eventually approved three departments. A Department of State was set up to handle relations with other countries. A Department of War was established to defend the nation. A Treasury Department was set up to oversee the nation's finances. Congress also created an attorney general to serve as the president's legal advisor, and a postmaster general to head the postal system.

Washington chose men he trusted—such as Jefferson, Hamilton, and Knox—to fill these positions. He often met with them to ask for their ideas and advice. As you learned in Chapter 9, the heads of the executive departments became known as the president's *cabinet.*

Martha Washington, shown on the left, held tea parties on Friday evenings at the presidential mansion in New York City. At these parties, political leaders and their wives could discuss important issues with President Washington, shown near the center.

11.3 Washington as President

The most critical problem facing the new government was money. The national treasury was empty. Congress had the power to raise funds through taxes. But its members argued endlessly about what to tax and by how much. In 1791, Congress finally agreed to place an excise tax on whiskey and other "luxury" goods, such as carriages. An *excise tax* is a tax on the production or sale of a product.

The Whiskey Rebellion Settlers living west of the Appalachian Mountains howled in protest. Western farmers found it too costly to haul their grain across the mountains to sell in eastern cities. Instead, they distilled their bulky wheat into whiskey, which could be shipped more cheaply. Many farmers complained that the tax made their whisky too expensive, and refused to pay it.

The Granger Collection, New York

The Whiskey Rebellion was a serious challenge to the new nation's ability to enforce its laws. When several hundred Whiskey Boys refused to pay a federal whiskey tax, President Washington personally led 13,000 state militia troops to put down the rebellion.

To end these protests, Congress lowered the excise tax in 1793. Most farmers began to pay up, but not the tax rebels of western Pennsylvania. These "Whiskey Boys" tarred and feathered tax collectors who tried to enforce the law.

Hamilton and Washington saw the Whiskey Rebellion as a threat to the authority of the national government. At Hamilton's urging, Washington led 13,000 state militia troops across the mountains to crush the rebels. Faced with overwhelming force, the rebellion melted away.

Jefferson thought that the idea of sending an army to catch a few tax rebels was foolish. Even worse, he believed, Hamilton was prepared to violate people's liberties by using armed force to put down opposition to government policies.

The French Revolution Meanwhile, the nation was caught up in a debate over events in France. In 1789, the French people rebelled against their king. The leaders of the French Revolution dreamed of building a nation based on "Liberty, Equality, and Fraternity," or brotherhood. Three years later, France became a republic and declared "a war of all peoples against all kings."

Many Americans were thrilled by the French Revolution. This was especially true of Jefferson and his followers, who began calling themselves Democratic-Republicans, or simply Republicans. The Republicans saw the French Revolution as part of a great crusade for democracy.

Political Developments in the Early Republic **145**

party: an organized political group

In time, news from France caused supporters of the revolution to think again. Cheered on by angry mobs, France's revolutionary government began lopping off the heads of wealthy nobles. Some 20,000 men, women, and children were killed.

Hamilton and his followers, who called themselves Federalists, were appalled by the bloodshed. Many Federalists were themselves well-off. After hearing about the fate of wealthy families in France, they began to finger their own necks, wondering whether such terrors could happen in the United States. "Behold France," warned one Federalist, "an open hell…in which we see…perhaps our own future."

When the French Revolution turned violent, and an endless stream of nobles was beheaded on the guillotine, many Americans withdrew their support for the revolution.

Washington's Farewell Address The growing division between Republicans and Federalists so disturbed Washington that he agreed to run for a second term as president in 1792. He was the only person, Hamilton and Jefferson told him, who could keep the nation from pulling apart.

Near the end of his second term, Washington announced that he would not run again. Before leaving office, the president prepared a farewell address, or message. In it he reminded Americans of all that bound them together as a people. "With slight shades of difference," he said, "you have the same religion, manners, habits, and political principles. You have in a common cause fought and triumphed together."

Next, Washington warned of two threats to the nation's future. You will read about one of those threats—problems with other countries—in the next chapter. The other threat was "the spirit of **party**." (A *party* is a political group.) It was natural for people to hold different opinions, Washington said. But he warned against the dangers of passionate loyalty to parties. If fighting between parties was not controlled, it could tear the young nation apart.

Despite his worries for the future, Washington had much to be proud of as he left office. The new government was up and running. The nation was growing so fast that it had added three new states—Kentucky, Tennessee, and Vermont. Most of all, Washington had steered his government safely through quarrelsome times. He left the nation united and at peace.

The Granger Collection, New York

11.4 Alexander Hamilton and the Federalist Party

Washington's warnings did not stop the rise of political parties in the young nation. The Federalist Party appeared first during the debates over the ratification of the Constitution. Its most influential leader was Washington's energetic treasury secretary, Alexander Hamilton.

Personal Background   Hamilton was born in the West Indies and raised on the Caribbean island of St. Croix. When Hamilton was 13, a devastating hurricane struck the island. Hamilton wrote a vivid description of the storm that impressed all who read it. A few St. Croix leaders arranged to send the talented teenager to New York, where he could get the education he deserved. Once in America, Hamilton never looked back.

Hamilton grew up to be a small, slim, handsome man. His blue eyes were said to turn black when he was angry. But most of the time they sparkled with intelligence and energy. With no money or family connections to help him rise in the world, he made his way on ability, ambition, and charm.

George Washington spotted Hamilton's talents early in the Revolutionary War. Washington made the young man his aide-de-camp, or personal assistant. Near the end of the war, Hamilton improved his fortunes by marrying Elizabeth Schuyler. His new wife came from one of New York's richest and most powerful families. With her family's political backing, Hamilton was elected to represent New York in Congress after the war. Later, he served as a delegate from New York to the Constitutional Convention.

View of Human Nature   Hamilton's view of human nature was shaped by his wartime experiences. All too often, he had seen people put their own interests and personal profit above patriotism and the needs of the country. "Every man ought to be supposed a knave [scoundrel]," he concluded, "and to have no other end [goal] in all his actions, but private interests."

Most Federalists shared Hamilton's view that people were basically selfish and out for themselves. For this reason, they distrusted any system of government that gave too much power to the "the mob," or the common people. Such a system, said Hamilton, could only lead to "error, confusion, and instability."

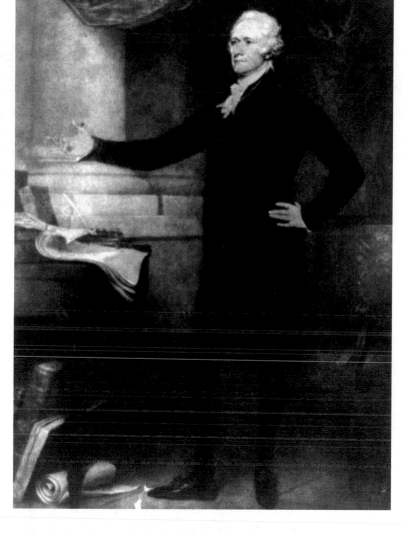

This portrait of Alexander Hamilton was painted by John Trumbull, a famous American artist. Hamilton rose from poverty to become a leader of the Federalist Party. His brilliant career was cut short when he was killed in a duel with Vice President Aaron Burr, whom he had accused of being a traitor.

Best Form of Government   Federalists believed that the country should be ruled by "the best people"—educated, wealthy, public-spirited men like themselves. Such people had the time, education, and background to run the country wisely. They could also be trusted to make decisions for the general good, not just for themselves. "Those who own the country," said Federalist John Jay bluntly, "ought to govern it."

Federalists favored a strong national government. They hoped to use the new government's powers under the Constitution to unite the quarreling states and keep order among the people. In their view, the rights of states were not nearly as important as national power and unity.

Hamilton agreed. Having grown up in the Caribbean, Hamilton had no deep loyalty to any state. His country was not New York, but the United States of America. And he hoped to see his adopted country become a great and powerful nation.

Ideal Economy   Hamilton's dream of national greatness depended on the United States developing a strong economy. In 1790, the nation's economy was still based mainly on agriculture. Hamilton wanted to expand the economy and increase the nation's wealth by using the power of the federal government to promote business, manufacturing, and trade.

Before this could happen, the new nation needed to begin paying off the huge debts that Congress and the states had piled up during the Revolutionary War. In 1790, Hamilton presented Congress with a plan to pay off all war debts as quickly as possible. If the debts were not promptly paid, he warned, the government would lose respect both at home and abroad.

Hamilton's plan for repaying the debts was opposed by many Americans, especially in the South. Most southern states had already paid their war debts. They saw little reason to help states in the North pay off what they still owed.

To save his plan, Hamilton linked it to another issue—the location of the nation's permanent capital. Both northerners and southerners wanted the capital to be located in their section of the country. Hamilton promised to support a location in the South if southerners would support his debt plan. The

Alexander Hamilton believed that to become strong, the United States needed to develop businesses such as this foundry (factory for melting and shaping metal) in Connecticut.

debt plan was passed, and the nation's new capital—called the District of Columbia—was located in the South on the Potomac River between Maryland and Virginia.

Next, Hamilton asked Congress to establish a national bank. Such a bank, Hamilton said, would help the government by collecting taxes and keeping those funds safe. It would print paper money backed by the government, giving the nation a stable currency. Most important, the bank would make loans to businesspeople to build new factories and ships. As business and trade expanded, Hamilton argued, all Americans would be better off.

Once again, Hamilton's proposal ran into a storm of opposition. Where in the Constitution, his opponents asked, was Congress given the power to establish a bank? In their view, Congress could exercise only those powers specifically listed in the Constitution.

Hamilton established the first national bank, pictured here in 1933. The bank collected taxes, printed money, and made loans to businesses.

Hamilton, in contrast, supported a loose construction (broad interpretation) of the Constitution. He pointed out that the "elastic clause" allowed Congress to "make all laws which shall be necessary and proper" for carrying out its listed powers. Since collecting taxes was one of those powers, Congress could set up a bank to help the government with tax collection.

After much debate, Hamilton was able get his bank approved by Congress. Once established, the Bank of the United States helped the nation's economy grow and prosper.

Relations with Britain and France   When the French Revolution began, Hamilton hoped that it would lead to the "establishment of free and good government." But as he watched it lead instead to chaos and bloodshed, his enthusiasm for the revolution cooled.

When war broke out between France and England in 1793, most Federalists sided with Britain. Some were merchants and shippers whose business depended on trade with America's former enemy. Others simply felt more comfortable supporting orderly Britain against revolutionary France.

Hamilton leaned toward Britain for yet another reason. Great Britain was all that he hoped the United States would become one day: a powerful and respected nation that could defend itself against any enemy.

Thomas Jefferson was one of America's greatest patriots. His strongest support came from the middle class: farmers, laborers, artisans, and shopkeepers.

11.5 Thomas Jefferson and the Republican Party

Hamilton's success in getting his plans through Congress alarmed Thomas Jefferson and his fellow Republicans. In Jefferson's view, almost everything Hamilton did to put the United States on the path to greatness was instead a step down the road to ruin. The two men held very different views on almost everything.

Personal Background   Jefferson was born in Virginia to an old and respected family. One of ten children, he was gifted with many talents. As a boy, he learned to ride, hunt, sing, dance, and play the violin. Later, he carried a violin with him in all his travels.

Jefferson was also a gifted student. When he entered college at age 16, he already knew Greek and Latin. He seemed to know something about almost everything. He once wrote that "not a sprig of grass [is] uninteresting to me." This boundless curiosity would remain with him all his life.

Jefferson grew up to be a tall, lanky man with reddish brown hair. Abigail Adams, the wife of John Adams, wrote that his appearance was "not unworthy of a God." With land inherited from his father, Jefferson set himself up as a Virginia tobacco planter. Like other planters, he used slaves to work his land.

Once he was established as a planter, Jefferson entered Virginia politics. As a politician, he lacked the ability to make stirring speeches. Instead, Jefferson spoke eloquently with his pen. His words in the Declaration of Independence and other writings are still read and admired today.

View of Human Nature   Jefferson's view of human nature was much more hopeful than Hamilton's. He assumed that informed citizens could make good decisions for themselves and their country. "I have so much confidence in the good sense of men," Jefferson wrote when revolution broke out in France, "that I am never afraid of the issue [outcome] where reason is left free to exert her force."

Jefferson had great faith in the goodness and wisdom of people who worked the soil—farmers and planters like himself. "State a problem to a ploughman [farmer] and a professor," he said, and "the former will decide it often better than the latter."

Best Form of Government   Republicans favored democracy over any other form of government. They had no patience with the Federalists' view that only the "best people" should rule. To Republicans, this view came dangerously close to monarchy, or rule by a king.

Republicans believed that the best government was the one that governed the least. A small government with limited powers was most likely to leave the people alone to enjoy the blessings of liberty. To keep the national government small, they insisted on a strict construction, or interpretation, of the Constitution. The Constitution, they insisted, meant exactly what it said, no more and no less. Any addition to the powers listed there, such as the creation of a national bank, was unconstitutional and dangerous.

Along with a weak national government, Republicans favored strong state governments. State governments, they argued, were closer to the people, and the people could control them more easily. Strong state governments could also keep the national government from growing too powerful.

Ideal Economy   Like most Americans in the 1790s, Jefferson was a country man. He believed that the nation's future lay not with Federalist bankers and merchants, but with plain, Republican farm folk. "Those who labor in the earth," he wrote, "are the chosen people of God, if ever He had a chosen people."

Republicans favored an economy based on agriculture. They opposed any measures, such as the national bank, designed to encourage the growth of business and manufacturing. In their view, the national bank was not only unconstitutional, but anti-farmer. While the bank was happy to loan money to businesspeople to build factories and ships, it did not make loans to farmers to buy land.

The Granger Collection, New York

Agriculture, according to Jefferson, was the most important part of the economy. He believed farming was the best occupation because it kept people out of corrupt cities.

Relations with Britain and France   Another issue that sparked heated arguments between Republicans and Federalists was the French Revolution. Most Americans favored the revolution until it turned violent and led to war. As you have read, most Federalists then turned against the new French republic and sided with Great Britain. For this change of heart, a Republican newspaper branded the Federalists "British bootlickers."

Despite the violence of the revolution, most Republicans continued to support France. While regretting the bloodshed, they argued that a few

Political Developments in the Early Republic   **151**

The Granger Collection, New York

Edmond Genet, who called himself Citizen Genet, was the French representative to the United States. During his stay, he attempted to convince Americans to join the French in their war with Britain. After Genet insulted President Washington, he was ordered to leave the country.

thousand noble heads was a small price to pay for freedom. For their loyalty to France, Republicans were scorned in a Federalist newspaper as "frog-eating, man-eating, blood-drinking cannibals."

In 1793, the French government sent Edmond Genet to the United States as its new official representative. Genet preferred to be called "Citizen," using the title adopted by French revolutionaries to emphasize the equality of all people. His mission was to convince Americans that they should join France in its war against Great Britain.

Citizen Genet was welcomed by Republicans as a conquering hero. As he traveled about the country preaching against kings and nobles, he was cheered by large crowds. In Philadelphia, the nation's temporary capital, a great banquet was held in his honor. Throughout the city, people drank toasts to Citizen Genet and to France.

The cheering crowds quickly went to Genet's head. When he formally presented himself to President Washington, he expected another warm and enthusiastic reception. Washington, however, did not want to be drawn into war with Britain. His response to Genet was cool and dignified.

Genet began making speeches attacking the president. "I live in the midst of continual parties," he crowed. "Old man Washington is jealous of my success, and of the enthusiasm with which the whole town flocks to my house." These attacks on Washington brought thousands of Genet's supporters into the streets of Philadelphia. "Day after day," recalled Vice President Adams, the protesters "threatened to drag Washington out of his house, and effect [bring about] a revolution in the government, or compel it to declare war in favor of the French revolution."

This was too much, even for Jefferson. Washington's cabinet agreed that Genet had to go. Calling him "hotheaded…disrespectful, and even indecent toward the President," Secretary of State Jefferson asked the French government to recall its troublesome representative.

11.6 The Presidency of John Adams

When the framers of the Constitution created the Electoral College, they imagined that the electors would simply choose the two best leaders for president and vice president. That was how the nation's first two presidential elections worked. By the third election in 1796, however, it was clear that political parties had become part of the election process.

The Republicans backed Thomas Jefferson for president that year. His support came mainly from farmers in the South and the West. The Federalists supported John Adams, who appealed to lawyers, merchants, shipowners, and businesspeople in the North. When the electoral votes were counted, John Adams was elected president by just three votes. Jefferson came in second, making him vice president. The nation's new top two leaders were political enemies from opposing parties.

The Alien and Sedition Acts   At first, President Adams tried to work closely with Jefferson. "Party violence," he found, made such efforts "useless." Meanwhile, Federalists in Congress passed four controversial laws known as the Alien and Sedition Acts. They argued that these laws were needed to protect the country from troublemakers like Citizen Genet. In fact, the real purpose of the Alien and Sedition Acts was to make life difficult for the Federalists' rivals, the Republicans.

Three of the laws, the Alien Acts, were aimed at **aliens** (noncitizens). The first lengthened the time it took for an immigrant to become a citizen with the right to vote from 5 to 14 years. Since most immigrants voted Republican, Jefferson saw this law as an attack on his party. The other two Alien Acts allowed the president to either jail or deport (expel) aliens who were suspected of stirring up trouble. Although these laws were never enforced, they did frighten a number of French spies and rabble-rousers into leaving the country.

The Sedition Act made **sedition**—encouraging rebellion against the government—a crime. Its definition of *sedition* included "printing, writing, or speaking in a scandalous or malicious [hateful] way against the government… Congress…or the President." Hamilton approved of this law, believing that it would punish only those who published vicious lies intended to destroy the government.

aliens: people who have come from other countries and are not yet citizens

sedition: the crime of encouraging rebellion against the government

John Adams, a Federalist, was elected the second president of the United States by the slim margin of 71 votes to 68 votes in the Electoral College. Thomas Jefferson, a Democratic-Republican, became the vice president.

The Granger Collection, New York

nullify: To refuse to recognize a federal law. This action by a state is called *nullification*.

states' rights: All rights kept by the states under the Constitution. Supporters of states' rights sometimes argued that states were not obliged to honor federal laws that they believed violated the Constitution.

In this cartoon, the devil and the British lion encourage a Federalist editor, represented by the hedgehog, to cross out important phrases from America's great documents. Liberty weeps at Benjamin Franklin's tomb.

Instead, the Sedition Act was used to punish Republican newspaper editors who delighted in insulting Adams. One, for example, called him "old, querulous [whiny], bald, blind, crippled, toothless Adams." Twenty-five people were arrested under the new law. Ten of them were convicted of printing seditious opinions.

The Virginia and Kentucky Resolutions Republicans viewed the Sedition Act as an attack on the rights of free speech and free press. Since the federal government was enforcing the act, they looked to the states to protect these precious freedoms.

Jefferson and Madison drew up a set of resolutions, or statements, opposing the Alien and Sedition Acts and sent them to state legislatures for approval. They argued that Congress had gone beyond the Constitution in passing these acts. States, therefore, had a duty to **nullify** the laws—that is, to declare them to be without legal force.

Only two states, Virginia and Kentucky, adopted the resolutions.

The arguments put forward in the Virginia and Kentucky Resolutions were based on the **states' rights** theory of the Constitution. This theory holds that the states created the Constitution. In doing so, they gave up certain rights. Rights not specifically given to the federal government remained with the states. Of these, one of the most important is the right to judge whether the federal government is using its powers properly.

When no other states approved the Virginia and Kentucky Resolutions, the protest died. The states' rights theory, however, was not forgotten. It would be raised and tested again in the years ahead.

The New National Capital
In the fall of 1800, the federal government moved to the city of Washington in the District of Columbia. Most of the government's buildings were still under construction. President Adams' wife, Abigail, described the new "President's House" as a "castle" in which "not one room or chamber is finished." She used the large East Room for hanging laundry, as it was not fit for anything else.

After years of wandering from city to city, the national government finally had a permanent home.

The Granger Collection, New York

11.7 The Election of 1800

The move to Washington, D.C., came in the middle of the 1800 presidential election. Once again, Republican leaders backed Jefferson for president. Hoping to avoid the strange outcome of the last election, they chose a New York politician named Aaron Burr to run as his vice president.

The Federalists chose John Adams to run for reelection as president. Charles Pinckney of South Carolina was selected to run for vice president. Some Federalists would have preferred Hamilton as their presidential candidate, including Hamilton himself. But Hamilton was not eligible to run, because the Constitution requires the president to be an American-born citizen.

The Granger Collection, New York

The Campaign   The candidates outlined their campaign issues early. Jefferson supported the Constitution and states' rights. He promised to run a "frugal and simple" government. Adams ran on his record of peace and prosperity.

The campaign, however, was run more on insults than on issues. Republican newspapers attacked Adams as a tyrant. They even accused him of wanting to turn the nation into a monarchy so that his children could follow him on the presidential throne.

Federalist newspapers called Jefferson a "howling atheist" (someone who denies the existence of God). Jefferson, they charged, would "destroy religion, introduce immorality, and loosen the bonds of all society." Frightened by these charges, some elderly Federalists buried their Bibles to keep them safe from the "godless" Republicans.

Charles Pinckney, above, and Aaron Burr, below, were vice presidential candidates in the election of 1800.

The Divided Federalists   Meanwhile, Hamilton and his followers refused to support Adams because of disagreements over the president's foreign policy. You will read more about this split in the next chapter. "We shall never find ourselves in the straight line of Federalism while Mr. Adams is President," moaned Oliver Wolcott, one of Hamilton's close allies.

As the campaign heated up, Hamilton worked feverishly behind the scenes to convince the men chosen for the Electoral College to cast their presidential ballots for Pinckney over Adams. Pinckney seemed more likely than Adams to value Hamilton's advice and his firm Federalist principles. With Pinckney as president, Hamilton believed that he would be able to personally guide the United States into the new century.

The Granger Collection, New York

The Granger Collection, New York

Here, Republican women help Thomas Jefferson win the election in New Jersey in 1800. Women were allowed to vote in New Jersey until 1808.

11.8 A Deadlock and a New Amendment

When the Electoral College voted early in 1801, it was clear that Adams had lost the election. But to whom? Under the Constitution, each elector cast two votes, with the idea that the candidate finishing second would be vice president. All of the Republican electors voted for Jefferson and Burr. The result was a tie between them.

Breaking the Tie In the case of a tie, the Constitution sends the election to the House of Representatives. There, each state has one vote. Burr should have told his supporters in the House to elect Jefferson president, as his party wanted. Instead, he remained silent, hoping the election might go his way. When the House voted, the vote was another tie.

After 6 days and 35 ballots, it was Federalist Alexander Hamilton who broke the deadlock. He asked his supporters in the House to vote for Jefferson. Of the two Republicans, he said, "Jefferson is to be preferred. He is by far not so dangerous a man." The tie was broken, and Jefferson was elected president.

In 1804, the Twelfth Amendment was added to the Constitution to prevent such ties. The amendment calls for the Electoral College to cast separate ballots for president and vice president. If no presidential candidate receives a majority of electoral votes, the House of Representatives chooses a president from the top three candidates. If no candidate for vice president receives a majority, the Senate chooses the vice president.

A Peaceful Revolution The election of 1800 was a victory for Jefferson and his Republican Party. But it was also a victory for the new system of government established by the Constitution. In other countries, power changed hands by means of a war or revolution. In the United States, power had passed from one group to another without a single shot being fired.

No one was more pleased by this outcome than the nation's third president. "The Revolution of 1800," Jefferson wrote with pride, was not brought about "by the sword." Americans had learned that it was better to fight for power with parties and ballots than with armies and bullets.

11.9 Chapter Summary

In this chapter, you read about the beginnings of political parties in the United States. You used character collages of Alexander Hamilton and Thomas Jefferson to learn about the political differences of the Federalist and Democratic-Republican Parties during the 1790s.

Both Alexander Hamilton and Thomas Jefferson served in President Washington's cabinet. Their responses to the Whiskey Rebellion and the French Revolution revealed the sharp differences between these talented men, and between their supporters.

Hamilton and the Federalists believed in a strong national government run by wealthy and well-educated men. Hamilton also favored using the national government's power to support business, manufacturing, and trade. Alarmed by the violence of the French Revolution, he and other Federalists favored Great Britain in its war with France.

In contrast, Jefferson and the Republicans looked to the mass of informed citizens to safeguard democracy. They championed the rights of states and the interests of farmers and planters. Republicans saw the French Revolution as a step toward democracy, and they attacked the Federalists' support for Great Britain.

During the presidency of John Adams, Federalists used the Alien and Sedition Acts to attack the Republicans. In response, Republicans urged states to nullify these laws.

The emergence of political parties revealed a need to change the Constitution. The election of 1800 resulted in a tie between the Republican candidates for president and vice president. To prevent such a tie from happening again, the Twelfth Amendment calls for electors to cast separate ballots for president and vice president.

While the young nation worked to strengthen its political institutions, it also faced threats from other countries. In the next chapter, you will read about how the United States responded to these threats.

Thomas Jefferson, left, and Alexander Hamilton, right, led the first political parties of the new nation. Sharp differences existed between these two parties.

The Granger Collection, New York

What does each of these symbols stand for?

12

Foreign Affairs in the Young Nation

12.1 Introduction

Did you know that you are carrying a history lesson in your pocket or purse? You'll find it on any $1 bill. Take out a dollar and see for yourself!

Look first at the portrait of George Washington. Americans still honor this leader as "First in war, first in peace, and first in the hearts of his countrymen." But few remember that Washington defined our nation's first **foreign policy**. During his presidency, Washington set principles that would guide the United States in its future dealings with other nations.

Turn the dollar bill over. You will see two circles showing the Great Seal of the United States. For thousands of years, governments have used seals like this one to mark their approval of important documents. Our nation's founders thought that a national seal was so important that they began work on it the same day that they declared independence—July 4, 1776. In 1782, Congress approved the design we see today on our money.

The elements on the Great Seal represent the founders' hopes and dreams for the United States. For example, the unfinished pyramid on one side of the seal signifies strength and endurance. The bald eagle on the other side is a symbol of national power. In one talon, it grasps the arrows of war. In the other, it holds an olive branch of peace.

The arrows and olive branch are perfect symbols of two foreign policy choices. The United States could be actively involved in world affairs, risking war. Or it could avoid involvement in other nations' conflicts in the hope of staying at peace. Arrows or olive branch? Which choice would you have made for the new nation? In this chapter, you will read about four dilemmas faced by early presidents of the United States. Their decisions influenced the future of U.S. foreign policy.

Isolationism   Involvement

Graphic Organizer: Spectrum
You will use a spectrum to chart the range of U.S. foreign policy from isolationism to involvement.

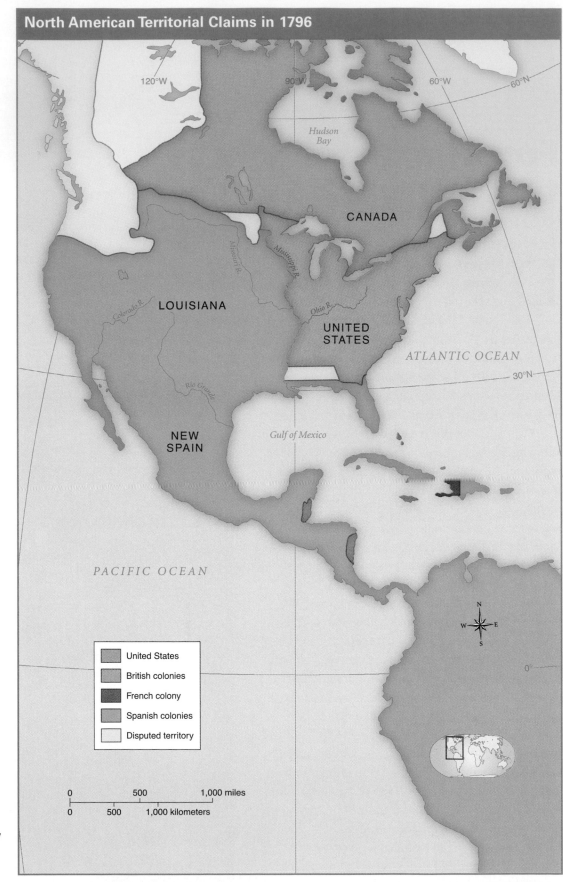

North American Territorial Claims in 1796

120°W 90°W 60°W 60°N

Hudson Bay

CANADA

Missouri R. *Mississippi R.*

LOUISIANA *Ohio R.*

UNITED STATES

Colorado R.

ATLANTIC OCEAN

30°N

Rio Grande

NEW SPAIN

Gulf of Mexico

PACIFIC OCEAN

0°

Legend:
- United States
- British colonies
- French colony
- Spanish colonies
- Disputed territory

0   500   1,000 miles
0   500 1,000 kilometers

In 1796, the United States was surrounded by colonies that belonged to European countries. What problems might this have caused for the newly independent United States?

12.2 President Washington Creates a Foreign Policy

neutrality: a policy of not choosing sides in a war or dispute between other countries

isolationism: a policy of avoiding political or military agreements with other countries; first established by George Washington

When George Washington took office as the nation's first president in 1789, America was looking weak. The army that Washington had commanded during the Revolutionary War had gone home. It had not been replaced for two reasons. First, an army would cost money that the government did not have. Second, Americans had learned that a standing army could be used to take away their liberty. State militia troops, they believed, could handle any threats the country might face.

And there were threats. The new nation was surrounded by unfriendly powers. To the north, Britain still controlled Canada. The British also refused to abandon their forts in the Ohio Valley, even though this region now belonged to the United States. To the south and west, Spain controlled Florida and Louisiana.

Events in Europe also threatened the new nation. As you read in Chapter 11, in 1789, the French people rose up against their king and declared France a republic. Most Americans were thrilled by the French Revolution. However, when France went to war with Britain in 1793, President Washington faced a difficult decision. During its own revolution, the United States had signed a treaty of alliance with France. (*Alliances* are agreements made with other nations to aid and support each other.) In that treaty, the United States had promised to aid France in time of war. Many Americans were eager to honor that pledge, even if it meant going to war with Britain.

Washington knew that the United States was not prepared for war. Instead, he announced a policy of **neutrality**. Under this policy, the United States would do nothing to aid either France or Britain in their war against each other.

Before leaving office, Washington summed up his foreign policy in his famous farewell address. The United States, he said, could gain nothing by becoming involved in other nations' affairs. "It is our true policy," he declared, "to steer clear of permanent alliances with any portion of the foreign world." Washington's policy of avoiding alliances with other countries became known as **isolationism**. For the next century, isolationism would be the foundation of American foreign policy.

George Washington was considered a hero even in his own time. Here we see Lady Liberty crowning a bust of Washington. The inscription on the bust reads "First in War, First in Peace, First in the Hearts of His Countrymen."

12.3 Dilemma 1: What Should President Adams Do to Protect American Ships?

Isolationism sounded good in theory. But it was often hard to stay out of other countries' conflicts. No one knew this better than John Adams, the nation's second president. Adams tried to follow Washington's policy of neutrality. With France, however, staying neutral proved difficult.

The Jay Treaty   French leaders hoped that Britain's refusal to leave the Ohio Valley would lead to war between England and the United States. Those hopes were dashed when Washington sent Chief Justice John Jay to London to settle things with the British. In the Jay Treaty, the British finally agreed to pull their troops from the Ohio Valley. French officials viewed the Jay Treaty as a betrayal by the United States. In July 1796, the French navy began attacking American merchant ships bound for Britain. Over the next year, French warships seized 316 American ships.

The XYZ Affair   President Adams sent three envoys, or representatives, to France to end the attacks. French Foreign Minister Talleyrand refused to receive the Americans. Instead, they were met by secret agents, later identified only as X, Y, and Z. The agents said that no peace talks would be held unless Talleyrand received a large sum of money as a tribute. (A *tribute* is a payment of money as the price of protection.) "No! No! Not a sixpence!" responded the shocked envoys.

The XYZ Affair outraged Americans. At the president's urging, Congress voted to recruit an army of 10,000 men. It also voted to build 12 new ships for the nation's tiny navy. The slogan "Millions for defense, but not one cent for tribute!" was heard everywhere as Americans prepared for war.

Meanwhile, Congress authorized American warships and privately owned ships, called *privateers,* to launch a "half-war" on the seas. During this undeclared war, American ships captured more than 80 armed French vessels.

As war fever mounted, John Adams—never a lovable leader—found himself unexpectedly popular. His Federalist Party also gained support in all parts of the country. The question facing Adams was whether doing the popular thing by unleashing the arrows of war on France was also the best thing for the country.

In this cartoon, American envoys meet with a French diplomat, depicted as a multiheaded monster holding a dagger. The cartoonist shared the very negative view of French diplomacy held by most Americans in the 1790s.

The Granger Collection, New York

12.4 What Happened: Adams Pursues Peace

Adams knew that no matter how good war might be for the Federalist Party, it would not be good for the country. In February 1799, the president announced that he was sending a peace mission to France. Federalist leaders were furious. They pleaded with the president to change his mind, but Adams would not budge.

By the time the peace mission reached France, Napoleon Bonaparte had taken over the French government. The Americans found that Napoleon was eager to make peace with both Britain and the United States. He had already ordered an end to the seizure of American ships and the release of captured American sailors.

More importantly, Napoleon agreed to end France's 1778 alliance with the United States. While the alliance with France had been essential to the United States during the Revolutionary War, it had brought nothing but trouble since then. In exchange, the Americans agreed not to ask France to pay for all the ships it had seized. This meant that the U.S. government would have to pay American ship owners for their lost property. To Adams, this seemed a small price to pay for peace.

Choosing the olive branch cost Adams political popularity. His pursuit of peace caused strong disagreements within the Federalist Party. These disagreements cost Adams and the Federalists votes when he ran for reelection in 1800. As you read in Chapter 11, Jefferson defeated Adams, and the Federalist Party lost much of its support. Over the next few years, Adams would watch his Federalist Party slowly fade away.

Still, Adams had no regrets. He wrote:

> "I will defend my missions to France, as long as I have an eye to direct my hand, or a finger to hold my pen.... I desire no other inscription over my gravestone than: 'Here lies John Adams, who took upon himself the responsibility of the peace with France in the year 1800.'"

Adams left the nation at peace and with no permanent alliances that might drag it into war. He had a right to feel proud.

The Granger Collection, New York

President Adams believed the United States needed a strong navy. Congress approved the construction of 12 warships, including the *Philadelphia*, which is shown under construction in the image above.

Foreign Affairs in the Young Nation **163**

12.5 Dilemma 2: How Should President Jefferson Deal with Pirates?

Peace with France did not last long. By 1803, France and Britain were again at war. As the conflict heated up, both nations began seizing American ships that were trading with their enemy. President Thomas Jefferson, who took office in 1801, complained bitterly that "England has become a den of pirates and France has become a den of thieves." Still, like Washington and Adams before him, Jefferson tried to follow a policy of neutrality.

Impressment Remaining neutral when ships were being seized was hard enough. It became even harder when Britain began impressing, or kidnapping, American sailors to serve in the British navy. The British claimed that the men they impressed were British deserters. This may have been true in some cases, as some sailors may well have fled the terrible conditions on British ships. Yet thousands of unlucky Americans were also impressed and forced to toil on Britain's "floating hells."

American anger over impressment peaked in 1807 after a British warship, the *Leopard,* stopped an American warship, the *Chesapeake,* to search for deserters. When the *Chesapeake*'s captain refused to allow a search, the *Leopard* opened fire. Twenty-one American sailors were killed or wounded. This attack triggered another case of war fever, this time against Britain.

In the late 1700s and early 1800s, the Mediterranean Sea was filled with pirates who attacked American merchant ships. The United States paid tribute to leaders of the Barbary Coast states to prevent these attacks.

Piracy American ships faced a different threat from the Barbary States of North Africa: piracy, or robbery at sea. For years, pirates from Morocco, Algiers, Tunis, and Tripoli had preyed on merchant ships entering the Mediterranean Sea. The pirates seized the ships and held their crews for ransom.

Presidents Washington and Adams both paid tribute to Barbary State rulers in exchange for the safety of American ships. While Americans were shouting "millions for defense, but not one cent for tribute" during the XYZ Affair, the United States was quietly sending money to the Barbary States.

By the time Jefferson became president, the United States had paid the Barbary States almost $2 million. The ruler of Tripoli, however, demanded still more tribute. To show that he was serious, he declared war on the United States. Jefferson hated war. But he also hated paying tribute. The question was, which was worse?

The Barbary Coast

Collection of The New-York Historical Society, Negative number 7278

12.6 What Happened: Jefferson Solves Half the Problem

As much as Jefferson hated war, he hated paying tribute more. In 1802, he sent a small fleet of warships to the Mediterranean to protect American shipping. The war plodded along until 1804, when American ships began bombarding Tripoli with their cannons. One of the ships, the *Philadelphia,* ran aground on a hidden reef in the harbor. The captain and crew were captured and held for ransom.

Rather than let pirates have the *Philadelphia,* a young naval officer named Stephen Decatur led a raiding party into

the heavily guarded Tripoli harbor and set the ship afire. A year later, Tripoli signed a peace treaty with the United States. Tripoli agreed to stop demanding tribute payments. In return, the United States paid a $60,000 ransom for the crew of the *Philadelphia*. This was a bargain compared to the $3 million first demanded.

Pirates from other Barbary States continued to plunder ships in the Mediterranean. In 1815, American and European naval forces finally destroyed the pirate bases.

Meanwhile, Jefferson tried desperately to convince both France and Britain to leave American ships alone. All of his efforts failed. Between 1803 and 1807, Britain seized at least a thousand American ships. France captured about half that many.

When diplomacy failed, Jefferson proposed an **embargo**—a complete halt in trade with other nations. Under the Embargo Act of 1807, no foreign ships could enter U.S. ports, and no American ships could leave, except to trade at other U.S. ports. Jefferson hoped that stopping trade would prove so painful to France and Britain that they would agree to leave American ships alone.

The embargo, however, proved far more painful to Americans than to anyone in Europe. Some 55,000 seamen lost their jobs while their ships rotted at deserted docks. In New England, newspapers cursed Jefferson's "Dambargo." They also pointed out that *embargo* spelled backward reads "O-grab-me," which made sense to all who were feeling its pinch.

Congress repealed the unpopular Embargo Act in 1809. American ships returned to the seas, and French and British warships continued to attack them.

President Jefferson ordered an embargo—a halt of trade with foreign countries—to force Britain and France to leave American ships alone. This political cartoon pictures the embargo (Ograbme) as a snapping turtle hurting U.S. merchants more than Britain or France.

embargo: a government order that stops merchant ships from leaving or entering a country's ports

12.7 Dilemma 3: What Should President Madison Do to Protect Sailors and Settlers?

President James Madison, who took office in 1809, tried a new approach to protecting Americans at sea. He offered France and Britain the following deal: If you agree to stop attacking American ships, the United States will stop trading with your enemy.

This was an opportunity that Napoleon could not resist. He announced that France agreed to Madison's deal. At the same time, he gave his navy secret orders to continue seizing American ships headed for British ports. Madison, who desperately wanted to believe Napoleon's false promise, cut off all trade with Britain.

Meanwhile, the British refused Madison's offer and continued seizing ships and impressing American sailors. To Madison, there seemed only one way to force Britain to respect the rights of American ships and sailors. He began to think about abandoning Washington's policy of isolationism. He wondered if the country would stand behind a war with Britain.

Support for war came mostly from the South and the West. New England merchants knew that war would mean a blockade (ships blocking the way in or out) of their ports by the British navy. They preferred to take their chances with the troubles at sea.

Southerners and westerners had two reasons for favoring war. Like all Americans, they deeply resented Britain's policy of impressing American sailors. They also saw war as an opportunity to make the lands west of the

This lithograph shows William Harrison, on the far left, encouraging his troops during the battle of Tippecanoe Creek. After the battle, Harrison's men discovered that the Indians were armed with British guns, which added to Americans' anger at the British.

The Granger Collection, New York

Appalachian Mountains safer for settlers. By getting rid of the British forces in Canada, they could cut off supplies to raiding Indians.

As settlers moved into the Ohio and Mississippi River Valleys, they pushed many of the Indians in those regions off their lands. Two Shawnee Indians—a chief named Tecumseh and his brother, the Prophet—decided that the only way to stop the settlers was to unite Native Americans up and down the Mississippi River into one great Indian nation. Only by working together, they said, could the Indians defend their land against the settlers' westward march.

Tecumseh built a center for his Indian nation, called Prophetstown, on Tippecanoe Creek in Indiana Territory. The strength of Tecumseh's following alarmed settlers. Rather than wait for the Indians to attack, Indiana governor William Henry Harrison organized an army of militia troops and marched to Prophetstown.

As dawn broke on November 7, 1811, Harrison's troops were shaken from their sleep by Indian war cries. By the end of the day, both sides had lost many men, and Prophetstown was a smoking ruin. Among the ashes, Harrison's men found British guns. This was proof of what many settlers had long suspected: British military forces in Canada were providing weapons to Chief Tecumseh.

Several new congressmen from the South and the West shared this suspicion. Henry Clay of Kentucky, John C. Calhoun of South Carolina, and others were so eager for war that they were nicknamed "War Hawks." The War Hawks argued that driving the British out of Canada would help to end the Indian threat. And once the British were gone, Canada could be added to the United States.

Madison hesitated. Was the nation strong enough to launch the arrows of war? Or should he hold tightly to the olive branch of peace?

The Shawnee leader Tecumseh, pictured above, united Native Americans in an attempt to halt the advance of white settlers onto Indian lands.

12.8 What Happened: Madison Launches the War of 1812

Madison chose to abandon isolationism. At his request, Congress declared war on Britain on July 17, 1812. This was a very bold step for a nation with an army of 7,000 poorly trained men and a navy of only 16 ships.

Invading Canada   The fact that the United States was completely unprepared for the War of 1812 did not discourage the War Hawks. To them the conquest of Canada was "a mere matter of marching." Once American troops crossed the border, they said, Canadians would welcome them as liberators. Just the opposite was true. Each time Americans invaded Canada, they were driven back as unwelcome intruders.

Despite their failure to conquer Canada, American forces did make the lands west of the Appalachians safer for settlers. In 1813, Tecumseh was killed during a major battle in Canada. With him died his dream of creating a powerful Indian nation. Over time, most of the Native Americans who fought with Tecumseh would be driven out of the Ohio Valley.

The Granger Collection, New York

The United States gained control of Lake Erie during the War of 1812 as a result of the victory of naval forces under the leadership of Oliver Hazard Perry at Put-in-Bay in 1813.

Washington and Baltimore

In August 1814, the British brought the war deep into American territory by invading Washington, D.C., and burning the city. On returning to the capital, Margaret Bayard Smith wrote that nothing remained of the president's house "but its cracked and blacken'd walls…. Who would have thought that this mass so solid, so magnificent, so grand which seemed built for the generations to come, should by the hands of a few men and in the space of a few hours, be thus irreparably destroy'd."

After Washington, the British turned to the port city of Baltimore. Fort McHenry guarded the entrance to Baltimore's harbor. On September 13, 1814, British warships began shelling the fort. As night fell, the exploding bombs cast a red glow over the harbor.

An American lawyer named Francis Scott Key watched the bombardment through the long night. When dawn broke, he was thrilled to see that the American flag still waved over Fort McHenry. Key captured his feelings in a poem that was later put to music as "The Star-Spangled Banner."

The Battle of New Orleans   A few months later, the British launched another invasion, this time of New Orleans. The city was defended by General Andrew Jackson and a rag-tag army of 7,000 militia troops, free African Americans, Indians, and pirates.

On January 8, 1815, 7,500 British troops marched confidently into battle. Jackson's troops met them with deadly fire, turning the field of battle into a "sea of blood." Some 2,000 British troops were killed or wounded, compared with only about 20 Americans.

The Battle of New Orleans was the greatest American victory in the War of 1812. It made Andrew Jackson a national hero. It was also totally unnecessary. Two weeks before the battle, American and British diplomats meeting at Ghent, in Belgium, had signed a peace treaty ending the war. The news did not reach the city of New Orleans or the British troops until after the battle was fought. The Treaty of Ghent settled none of the issues that had led to the war. Still, Americans were pleased to have peace.

12.9 Dilemma 4: What Should President Monroe Do to Support the New Latin American Nations?

James Monroe became president in 1817. After the excitement of the War of 1812, he was happy to return the nation to its policy of isolationism. Americans began to turn their attention away from Europe to events happening in their own back yard. From Mexico to the tip of South America, colonial peoples were rising up in revolt against Spain.

Latin America's Revolutions In Mexico, the revolt against Spanish rule was inspired by a priest named Miguel Hidalgo. On September 16, 1810, Hidalgo spoke to a crowd of poor Indians in the town of Dolores. "My children," Hidalgo cried, "when will you recover lands stolen from your ancestors three hundred years ago by the hated Spaniards? Down with bad government! Death to the Spaniards!" Hidalgo's speech, remembered today as the "Cry of Dolores," inspired a revolution that lasted ten years. In 1821, Mexico finally won its independence from Spain.

Two other leaders liberated South America. In 1810, a Venezuelan named Simón Bolívar launched a revolution in the north with the cry: "Spaniards! You will receive death at our hands! Americans! You will receive life!" José de San Martín, a revolutionary from Argentina, led the struggle for independence in the south. By the end of 1825, the last Spanish troops had been driven out of South America.

The New Latin American Nations
Many Americans were excited by what Congressman Clay described as the "glorious spectacle of eighteen millions of people stuggling to burst their chains and be free." The British also supported the revolutions, for their own reasons. Spain had not allowed other nations to trade with its colonies. Once freed from Spanish rule, the new Latin American nations were able to open their doors to foreign trade.

Other European leaders were not so pleased. Some even began to talk of helping Spain recover its lost colonies. In 1823, Britain asked the United States to join it in sending a message to these leaders, telling them to leave Latin America alone.

President James Monroe asked former presidents Thomas Jefferson and James Madison for advice. Should the United States do something to support the new Latin American nations? If so, what?

A Catholic priest, Miguel Hidalgo (lower center) inspired an independence movement in Mexico. In his upraised hand, Hidalgo holds the flames of revolution that spread throughout Latin America in the early 1800s.

Foreign Affairs in the Young Nation **169**

secretary of state: The head of the State Department, who oversees matters relating to foreign countries. The secretary of state is an important member of the president's cabinet.

doctrine: a statement of official government policy, especially in foreign affairs

With the Monroe Doctrine by his side, Uncle Sam puts out his hands in warning to foreign powers to keep their "hands off" the Americas. Even though the Monroe Doctrine is over 180 years old, it still guides American presidents as they make foreign policy decisions.

12.10 What Happened: The U.S. Issues the Monroe Doctrine

Both Thomas Jefferson and James Madison liked the idea of joining with Britain to send a warning to the nations of Europe. Jefferson wrote to Monroe, "Our first and fundamental maxim [principle] should be, never entangle ourselves in the broils [fights] of Europe. Our second, never to suffer Europe to meddle with…America, North and South."

President Monroe's **secretary of state,** John Quincy Adams, agreed with Jefferson's principles. But he insisted that "it would be more candid [honest], as well as more dignified," for the United States to speak boldly for itself. Though never a bold man himself, Monroe agreed.

In 1823, President Monroe made a speech to Congress announcing a policy that became known as the Monroe **Doctrine**. Monroe stated that the nations of North and South America were "not to be considered as subjects for future colonization by any European powers." The United States, he said, would view efforts by Europeans to take over "any portion of this hemisphere as dangerous to our peace and safety."

Europeans denounced Monroe's message as arrogant. "By what right," asked a French newspaper, did the United States presume to tell other nations what they could do in "the two Americas"?

Americans, however, cheered Monroe's message. It made them proud to see the United States stand up for the freedom-loving people of Latin America. If Europeans "attempt to control the destinies of South America," boasted a Boston newspaper, "they will find…an eagle in their way."

In the years ahead, the Monroe Doctrine joined isolationism as a basic principle of U.S. foreign policy. The doctrine asserted that the United States would not accept European interference in American affairs. It also contained another, hidden message. By its very boldness, the Monroe Doctrine told the world that the United States was no longer a weak collection of quarreling states. It had become a strong and confident nation, a nation to be respected by the world.

The Granger Collection, New York

12.11 Chapter Summary

In this chapter, you learned about the birth of foreign policy in the United States. You used a spectrum to chart the range of U.S. foreign policy from isolationism to involvement.

Our first president, George Washington, knew that the young United States was not prepared for war. He established a policy of isolationism that stated America would avoid alliances with other countries. Each president following Washington faced new dilemmas that required decisions about what was best for America.

During the presidency of John Adams, the dilemma involved French attacks on American ships. Adams followed Washington's policy of isolationism and kept America at peace.

President Thomas Jefferson also faced threats at sea. When peace talks failed, he declared an embargo on American ports. It, too, was unsuccessful. President James Madison then tried offering a trade deal to both France and Britain. But the attacks at sea continued. Madison finally abandoned isolationism and declared war on Britain in 1812. The War of 1812 resulted in a peace treaty with Britain.

President Monroe's dilemma was whether or not to support the new Latin American states against European nations. Monroe issued a policy called the Monroe Doctrine. In it, he warned the nations of Europe to leave the Americas alone. The Monroe Doctrine established the United States as a strong and confident nation, willing to stand up for its own freedom and that of others. In the next chapter, you will learn how the United States continued to develop its resources and strengths.

The American eagle holds the olive branch of peace in one talon and the arrows of war in the other. Both are necessary to protect the "liberty" (at the top) that Americans hold so dear.

In what ways was life different for people
living in these two sections of the country?

The Granger Collection, New York

13

The Worlds of North and South

13.1 Introduction

Eli Whitney, a young man from Massachusetts, listened politely to the Georgia planters' complaints. Tobacco prices were low, and rice and indigo prices weren't much better. Cotton grew well, but cleaning the seeds out of cotton fibers was a big problem. A slave picking out seeds by hand could clean only a few pounds a day. At that rate, even using cheap slave labor, there was no profit in raising cotton. Unless something changed, the future of farming in the South looked bleak.

As the planters talked, a solution to their problem began to take shape in Whitney's head. While growing up in Massachusetts, Whitney had revealed a gift for invention. As a boy, he had found a way to manufacture nails more quickly than by hand. From nails, he had gone on to hat pins and men's canes. After graduating from college in 1792, Whitney went to Georgia to work as a tutor. Instead of tutoring, however, he became intrigued by the problem of cotton cleaning and, he wrote, "struck out a plan of a machine in my mind."

The result, as you will read, was a simple but brilliant invention that changed life in both the North and the South—but in very different ways. This probably did not surprise Whitney. As a northerner living in the South, he had already noticed many differences between the two sections of the country.

Northerners and southerners shared the same language and worshipped in the same kinds of churches. They shared a fierce pride in their country and a faith in democracy. Yet their outlooks and attitudes about many things were quite different. The two sections also differed in other ways, including their economies, transportation systems, and societies. During the early 1800s, these differences led to sharply conflicting views on many national issues—so much so that, at times, northerners and southerners seemed to be living in two separate worlds.

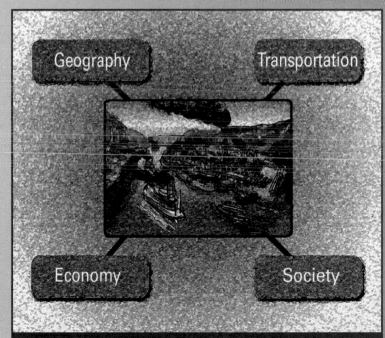

Graphic Organizer: Spoke Diagram
You will use spoke diagrams to learn about the worlds of the North and the South.

13.2 Geography of the North

From the rocky shores of Maine to the gently rolling plains of Iowa, the North included a variety of climates and natural features. Northerners adapted to these geographical differences by creating different industries and ways of making a living.

Climate All the northern states experienced four very distinct seasons, from frozen winters to hot, humid summers. But the most northerly states, such as Maine and Minnesota, had colder winters and shorter summer growing seasons than states farther south, such as Pennsylvania and Ohio.

To a visitor from the South, the season that seemed most foreign was winter. Southerners weren't used to the fierce cold that froze lakes and kept snow on the ground for months at a time.

Natural Features Different areas of the North had distinctive natural features. Along the jagged New England coast, for example, there were hundreds of bays and inlets that were perfect for use as harbors. Shipbuilders, fishermen, and merchants flourished in this area, while towns such as Boston became busy seaports.

Inland from the sea lay a narrow, flat plain. During the ice age, glaciers had scraped across this plain, leaving behind a thin covering of rocky soil. Farming was never easy here. Instead, many people turned to trade and crafts. Others moved west in search of better farmland.

New England's hills rose sharply above V-shaped valleys carved by steep streams. The hillsides offered barely enough land for a small farm, but they were covered with thick forests of spruce and fir. New Englanders found that they could make money by harvesting timber. The wood was used for shipbuilding and in trade with other countries.

Farther south in New York, Pennsylvania, and New Jersey, broad rivers like the Hudson and the Delaware had deposited rich soil over wide plains. People living in these areas supported themselves by farming.

Across the Appalachians lay the Central Plains, a large, forested region drained by the Ohio River and the "father of waters," the mighty Mississippi. The Central Plains boast some of the best agricultural soil on Earth. From Ohio to Illinois, settlers cleared the forests to make way for farms.

This photograph shows a section of New England coastline. Which geographic features can you identify?

13.3 Geography of the South

The South extended from Maryland south to the tip of Florida, and from the Atlantic Coast west to Louisiana and Texas. This section's climate and natural features encouraged southerners to base their way of life on agriculture.

Climate   Compared to the North, the southern states enjoyed mild winters and long, hot, humid summers. Plentiful rainfall and long growing seasons made this a perfect place for raising warm-weather crops that would have withered and died farther north.

Natural Features   Wide coastal plains edged the southern shoreline from Chesapeake Bay to the Gulf of Mexico. These fertile lowlands stretched inland for as much as 300 miles in parts of the South.

Along the coast, the plains were dotted with swamps and marshes. These damp lowlands were ideal for growing rice and sugar cane, which thrived in warm, soggy soil. Indigo was grown on the dry land above the swamps, and tobacco and corn were farmed farther inland. A visitor to this section noted that "the planters, by the richness of the soil, live [in] the most easy and pleasant manner of any people I have met with."

Above the plains rose the Appalachian Mountains. Settlers who ventured into this rugged backcountry carved farms and orchards out of rolling hills and mountain hollows. Some backcountry farmers were said to "work on land so steep that they keep falling out of their cornfields."

Although most people in the South were farmers, southerners used natural resources in other ways as well. In North Carolina, they harvested thick pine forests for lumber. From Chesapeake Bay in Virginia and Maryland, they gathered fish, oysters, and crabs.

An especially important feature of the South was its broad, flat rivers. Many of the South's earliest towns were built at the mouths of rivers. As people moved away from the coast, they followed the rivers inland, building their homes and farms alongside these water highways. Oceangoing ships could even sail up southern rivers to conduct business right at a planter's private dock. Here, the ships were loaded with tobacco or other cash crops for sale in the Caribbean or Europe.

This photograph shows a southern waterway. What geographic features can you identify?

13.4 Economy of the South

plantation: a large area of privately owned land where crops were grown through the labor of workers, usually slaves, who lived on the land

cotton gin: a hand-operated machine that cleans seeds and other unwanted material from cotton

The South's economy was based on agriculture, and southerners were proud of it. Said one Alabama politician, "We want no manufactures; we desire no trading, no mechanical or manufacturing classes. As long as we have our rice, our tobacco, and our cotton, we can command wealth to purchase all we want."

Although most white southerners worked their own small farms, **plantation** owners used slaves to grow such cash crops as tobacco, rice, sugar cane, and indigo. By the early 1790s, however, the use of slaves had begun to decline. Europeans were unwilling to pay high prices for tobacco and rice, which they could purchase more cheaply from other British colonies. Cotton was a promising crop, but growers who experimented with it had a hard time making a profit. Until some way was found to clean the seeds out of its fiber easily, cotton was of little value. Discouraged planters were buying fewer slaves, and even letting some go free.

In 1793, a young Yale graduate named Eli Whitney took a job tutoring children on a Georgia plantation. There he saw his first cotton boll. Observing the way cotton was cleaned by hand, Whitney had an idea. "If a machine could be invented that would clean the cotton with expedition [speed]," he wrote his father, "it would be a great thing...to the country."

Whitney set to work. Six months later, he had a working machine that would change the face of the South.

The Granger Collection, New York

The economy of the South was based on agriculture. After the invention of the cotton gin in 1793, cotton quickly became the most important crop in the South.

King Cotton Whitney's "cotton engine," called the **cotton gin** for short, was a simple machine that used rotating combs to separate cotton fiber from its seeds. Using a cotton gin, a single worker could clean as much cotton as 50 laborers working by hand.

Across the South, planters began growing cotton. Within ten years, cotton was the section's most important crop. By 1860, sales of cotton overseas earned more money than all other U.S. exports combined. It was little wonder that many southerners liked to boast, "Cotton is King."

Expanding Demand for Land and Slaves Raising cotton in the same fields year after year soon wore out the soil. In search of fresh, fertile soil, cotton planters pushed west. By 1850, cotton plantations stretched from the Atlantic Coast to Texas.

Whitney had hoped that his invention would lighten the work of slaves. Instead, it made slavery more important than ever to the South. As cotton spread westward, slavery followed. Between 1790 and 1850, the number of slaves in the South rose from 500,000 to more than 3 million.

With white southerners putting all their money into land and slaves, they had little interest in building factories. As a result, wrote an Alabama newspaper, "We purchase all our luxuries and necessities from the North… the slaveholder dresses in Northern goods, rides in a Northern saddle, sports his Northern carriage, reads Northern books. In Northern vessels his products are carried to market."

One successful southern factory was the Tredegar Iron Works in Richmond, Virginia. Using mostly slave labor, the factory made ammunition and weapons for the U.S. army, as well as steam engines, rails, and locomotives. But the vast majority of white southerners made their living off the land.

13.5 Economy of the North

If cotton was king in the South, inventiveness seemed to rule the North. One French visitor commented, "In Massachusetts and Connecticut, there is not a laborer who has not invented a machine or a tool."

In colonial times, Americans created everything they needed—every shirt or gun—by hand. Beginning in the late 1700s, however, inventors started to devise machines to make products more quickly and cheaply. This shift from hand manufacturing to machines is called the **Industrial Revolution**.

Industrial Revolution: The dramatic change in economies brought about by the use of machines to do work formerly done by hand. The Industrial Revolution began in England in the late 1700s and spread to America and the rest of Europe.

The fast-flowing rivers found in the North provided the power source for early textile mills such as the one in the background of this painting.

Factories, such as the one shown above, produced more goods and made them more affordable. However, they also put many skilled craftspeople out of work.

The Growth of Industry In 1810, Francis Cabot Lowell, a failing businessman from Boston, visited England. There he saw how mill owners were using machines to spin cotton into thread and weave the threads into cloth. To power these devices, they used fast-moving streams to turn a wheel, which in turn supplied energy to the machinery.

Lowell memorized the design of the British machines. When he returned to Massachusetts, he built even better ones. By 1815, he and his partners had built the first American textile factory, along the Merrimack River. This factory combined spinning and weaving machinery in the same building. One observer marveled that Lowell's mill "took your bale of cotton in at one end and gave out yards of cloth at the other, after goodness knows what digestive process."

To run his machinery, Lowell hired young farmwomen, who jumped at the chance to earn cash wages. The "Lowell girls" toiled 12 to 15 hours each day, with only Sundays off. Soon textile mills were springing up all along other northern rivers.

By the 1830s, inventors had learned to use steam engines to power machinery. With steam engines, businesspeople could build factories anywhere, not just along rivers. Meanwhile, the inventive Eli Whitney showed manufacturers how they could assemble products even more cheaply by making them from identical, interchangeable parts.

New inventions and manufacturing methods made goods cheaper and more plentiful. But they also shifted work from skilled craftspeople to less skilled laborers. When Elias Howe developed the sewing machine, for example, skilled seamstresses could not compete. Some took jobs in garment factories, but they earned much less money working the sewing machines than they had sewing by hand.

Although factory workers were free to quit their jobs, they had little say in their working conditions. One mill manager said, "I regard people just as I regard my machinery. So long as they can do my work for what I choose to pay them, I keep them, getting out of them all I can." To some southerners, working under such conditions seemed worse than slavery.

Machines Make Agriculture More Efficient The Industrial Revolution changed northern agriculture as well. In 1831, Virginia farmer Cyrus McCormick built a working model of "a right smart" machine called a *reaper*. A reaper could cut 28 times more grain than a single man using a scythe (a hand tool with a long, curved blade).

In 1847, McCormick built a reaper factory in Chicago. Using interchangeable parts, he was soon producing several thousand reapers a year. By making it easier to harvest large quantities of wheat, inventions like the reaper helped transform the Central Plains into America's "bread basket."

Thanks to the Industrial Revolution, the northern economy grew rapidly after 1800. By 1860, the value of manufacturing in the North was ten times greater than in the South.

13.6 Transportation in the North

Factory owners needed fast, inexpensive ways to deliver their goods to distant customers. South Carolina congressman John C. Calhoun had a solution. "Let us bind the republic together," he said, "with a perfect system of roads and canals." Calhoun called such projects "internal improvements."

Building Better Roads In the early 1800s, most American roads were rutted boneshakers. In 1806, Congress funded the construction of a National Road across the Appalachian Mountains. The purpose of this highway was to tie the new western states with the East. With its smooth gravel surface, the National Road was a joy to travel.

As popular as the National Road was, in 1816 President James Monroe vetoed a bill that would have given states money to build more roads. Monroe argued that spending federal money for internal improvements within a state was unconstitutional.

Fast Ships and Canals   Even with better roads, river travel was still faster and cheaper than travel by land. But moving upstream, against a river's current, was hard work. To solve this problem, inventors experimented with boats powered by steam engines.

In 1807, Robert Fulton showed that steamboats were practical by racing the steamboat *Clermont* upstream on New York's Hudson River. Said Fulton, "I overtook many boats and passed them as if they had been at anchor." A Dutchman watching the strange craft from the shore shouted, "The devil is on his way up-river with a sawmill on a boat!" By the 1820s, smoke-belching steamboats were chugging up and down major rivers and across the Great Lakes.

Of course, rivers weren't always located where people needed them. In 1817, the state of New York hired engineers and workers to build a 363-mile canal from the Hudson River to Lake Erie. The Erie Canal provided the first all-water link between farms on the Central Plains and East Coast cities. It was so successful that other states built canals as well.

Overseas traders also needed faster ways to travel. Sailing ships sometimes took so long to cross the Pacific Ocean that the goods they carried spoiled. In the 1840s, sleek clipper ships were introduced that cut ocean travel time in half. The clipper ships spurred northern trade with foreign ports around the world.

Traveling by Rail   The future of transportation, however, lay not on water, but on rails. Inspired by the success of steamboats, inventors developed steam-powered locomotives. Steam-powered trains traveled faster than steamboats, and they could go wherever tracks could be laid—even across mountains.

So many railroad companies were laying tracks by the 1840s that railroads had become the North's biggest business. By 1860, more than 20,000 miles of rail linked northern factories to cities hundreds of miles away.

Many new and faster forms of transportation were put to use in the North. How many of them can you identify in the image below?

Museum of Art, Rhode Island School of Design/Mary B. Jackson Fund

PROVIDENCE.NORFOLK AND   BALTIMORE STEAMSHIP LINE.

13.7 Transportation in the South

Most rail lines were in the North. In the South, people and goods continued to move on rivers. The slow current and broad channels of southern rivers made water travel easy and relatively cheap.

The most important southern product shipped by water was cotton. On plantation docks, slaves loaded cotton bales directly onto steam powered riverboats. The riverboats then traveled hundreds of miles downstream to such port cities as Savannah, Georgia, or Mobile, Alabama. West of the Appalachians, most cotton moved down the Mississippi River, the mightiest of all the southern waterways. The cotton boom made New Orleans, the port at the mouth of the Mississippi, one of the South's few big cities. Once the cotton reached the sea, it was loaded onto sailing ships headed for ports in England or the North.

Because river travel was the South's main form of transportation, most southern towns and cities sprang up along waterways. With little need for roads or canals to connect these settlements, southerners opposed bills in Congress that would use federal funds to built internal improvements. Such bills, they believed, would benefit the North far more than the South.

Some railroads were built in the South, including lines that helped southern farmers ship their products to the North. Southerners were proud of the fact that the iron rails for many of their section's railroads came from Virginia's Tredegar Iron Works. Still, in 1860 the South had just 10,000 miles of rail, compared with over 20,000 miles in the North.

This photograph shows products being loaded onto steam-powered riverboats. What geographic feature of the South made riverboats the most practical way to transport goods?

The Worlds of North and South **181**

Geography Challenge
Comparing the Worlds of North and South

Agriculture, 1860

Legend:
- Corn
- Cotton
- Rice
- Tobacco
- Wheat
- Northern states
- Southern states
- Border states
- * West Virginia, state 1863

Railroads, 1860

Legend:
- -- Railroads
- Northern states
- Southern states
- Border states
- * West Virginia, state 1863

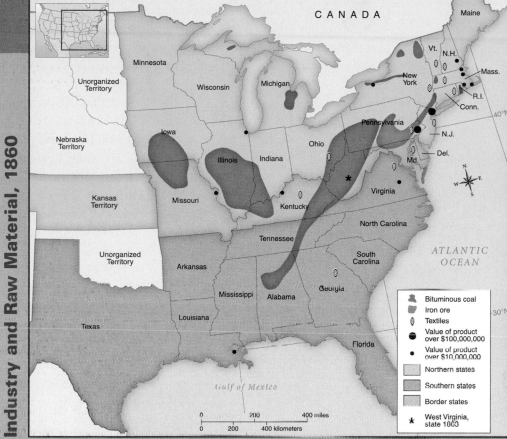

Industry and Raw Material, 1860

Legend:
- Bituminous coal
- Iron ore
- Textiles
- ● Value of product over $100,000,000
- • Value of product over $10,000,000
- Northern states
- Southern states
- Border states
- ✷ West Virginia, state 1863

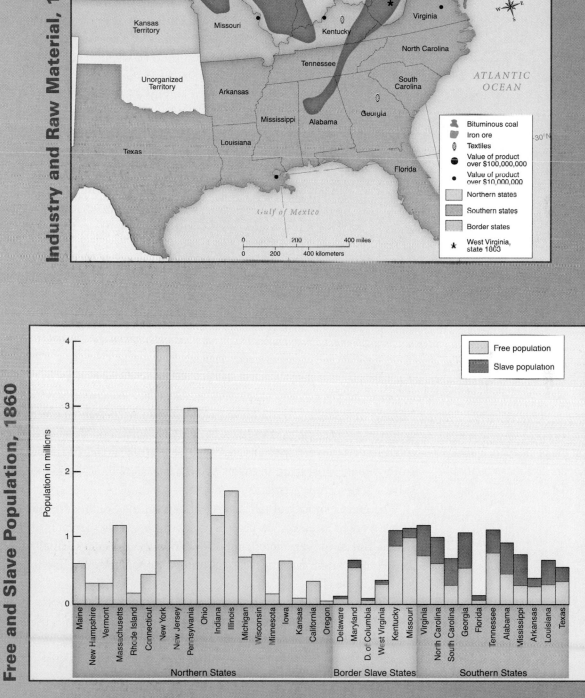

Free and Slave Population, 1860

Population in millions

- Free population
- Slave population

Northern States: Maine, New Hampshire, Vermont, Massachusetts, Rhode Island, Connecticut, New York, New Jersey, Pennsylvania, Ohio, Indiana, Illinois, Michigan, Wisconsin, Minnesota, Iowa, Kansas, California, Oregon

Border Slave States: Delaware, Maryland, D. of Columbia, West Virginia, Kentucky, Missouri

Southern States: Virginia, North Carolina, South Carolina, Georgia, Florida, Tennessee, Alabama, Mississippi, Arkansas, Louisiana, Texas

13.8 Society of the South

Southerners measured wealth in terms of land and slaves. The few whites who owned vast plantations held the highest rank in southern society. The lowest-ranking southerners were enslaved African Americans. Between these two groups stood white farmers and workers, and free blacks, each with a distinct way of life.

The Granger Collection, New York

Even though they made up only a small percentage of the population, wealthy plantation owners, like those pictured above, dominated the economy and politics of the South.

White Southerners Wealthy planters modeled their homes and lives on European nobility. Their big mansions featured tall columns and fancy gardens. They treasured a leisurely way of life, filled with parties and social visits. This small group of wealthy planters were considered the South's natural leaders, and they held most of the important political offices in their states.

Most white southerners owned some land, but only about one in four owned even one slave. These families worked their own fields and made most of what they needed themselves. About 10 percent of whites were too poor to own any land. They rented rugged mountain or forest land and paid the rent with the crops they raised. Even with hunting and trapping, these families often had barely enough to eat.

African Americans in the South A small minority of the African Americans living in the South were free blacks. Resented by white southerners, free blacks were often forced to wear special badges, pay extra taxes, and live separately from whites. Most lived in towns and cities, where they found jobs as skilled craftspeople, servants, or laborers.

The great majority of African Americans in the South were slaves. Some worked as cooks, carpenters, blacksmiths, house servants, or nurse-maids. But most were field hands who labored "in the cotton field as soon as it is light in the morning…not permitted to be a moment idle until it is too dark to see."

Almost all southerners, rich and poor, black and white, lived a rural life, closer to nature than those who toiled in the crowded factories up north. Their daily lives still were governed by the rising and setting of the sun and the changing of the seasons, rather than by the railroad schedule or the factory clock.

The Granger Collection, New York

13.9 Society of the North

As in the South, most people in the North were neither wealthy nor powerful. But northerners believed that by hard work, ordinary people could acquire wealth and influence.

Despite the rise of industry, about seven in ten northerners still lived on farms by 1860. Children were expected to help with the planting and harvesting. Sometimes, when they weren't needed on the farm, they attended school. On Sundays, the whole family met their neighbors at church.

A growing number of northerners, however, lived in the new towns and cities that were sprouting up around factories and alongside railroad lines. New or old, northern cities often lacked sewers and paved streets. In dirty and crowded neighborhoods, diseases spread rapidly. "The streets are filthy," wrote one observer about New York City, "and the stranger is not a little surprised to meet the hogs walking about in them, for the purpose of devouring the vegetables and trash thrown into the gutter."

African Americans in the North   After the American Revolution, all of the northern states had taken steps to end slavery. Although African Americans in the North were free, they were not treated as equal to whites. In most states they could not vote, hold office, serve on juries, or attend white churches and schools.

In 1860, most people in the North still lived on farms, but more and more people were moving to towns and cities like the one shown below. These cities often sprang up near factories and railroad hubs.

African Americans responded by forming their own churches and starting their own businesses. Because few employers would give them skilled jobs, African Americans often worked as laborers or servants.

Immigrants Arrive in the North Between 1845 and 1860, four million **immigrants**—most of them from Ireland and Germany—swelled the North's growing population. In Ireland, a potato famine drove thousands of families to America. In Germany, a failed revolution sent people fleeing overseas. Some immigrants had enough money to buy land and farm. But most settled in cities, where they found jobs in mills and factories.

Some northerners resented the newcomers. Occasionally, anti-immigrant feeling exploded into riots. More often it was expressed in everyday discrimination, such as help-wanted signs with the words, "No Irish need apply." Still the immigrants came, attracted, said one German newcomer, by "a new society with almost limitless opportunities open to all."

13.10 Chapter Summary

In this chapter, you learned how the North and the South developed differently from each other in the first half of the 1800s. You used spoke diagrams to describe the geography, economy, transportation, and society of the two sections.

> **immigrant:** A person who moves from one country to another. Such a movement is called *immigration*.

Look at the two images of the South (left) and the North (right). How many features of geography, economy, transportation, and society can you identify?

The Granger Collection, New York

Geography was a principal reason why northerners and southerners developed different ways of life. In contrast to the variety of trades and businesses in the North, the South depended primarily on agriculture. Although only a minority of white southerners owned slaves, much of the South's economy depended on slave labor.

In the North, the new inventions of the Industrial Revolution led to the development of mills and factories. Increasing numbers of people went to work as wage earners. New machines such as Cyrus McCormick's reaper revolutionized agriculture.

Dramatic improvements in transportation made it easier for northerners to travel and to ship goods over long distances. In the South, however, people continued to travel by river, and rail lines were fewer.

Southern society was divided into ranks. The wealthy few enjoyed great influence and power. But even the poorest whites ranked above African Americans, whether free or slave.

The North, too, had its wealthy class. But farmers and laborers alike believed they could create comfortable lives for their families through hard work.

The different worlds of the North and South led to conflicting points of view on many issues such as slavery, internal improvements, and trade. In the next chapter, you will see how these different viewpoints began to affect national politics.

The Granger Collection, New York

The Granger Collection, New York

What do you think these voters are talking about?

What type of candidate might these voters vote for?

What type of candidate might these voters vote for?

14

Andrew Jackson and the Growth of American Democracy

14.1 Introduction

The presidential campaign of 1828 was one of the dirtiest in American history. The election pitted John Quincy Adams, the nation's sixth president, against Andrew Jackson, the popular hero of the Battle of New Orleans.

During the campaign, both sides hurled reckless accusations at each other, a practice called *mudslinging*. Adams was called a "Sabbath-breaker" for traveling on Sunday. He was falsely accused of being an alcoholic. He was accused of using "public money" to purchase "gambling furniture" for the White House. In reality, he had used his own money to purchase a billiard table. Strangely, his opponents missed the one truth that might have shocked most Americans of the day. The very formal and proper Adams had a habit of swimming naked in the Potomac River.

The president's supporters lashed back. They called Jackson a crude and ignorant man who was not fit to be president. They also raked up old scandals about his wife, Rachel. She was accused of marrying Jackson while she was still knowingly wed to her first husband (not true). One newspaper even charged Jackson's mother with immoral behavior (not true). Jackson was called "Old Hickory" by his troops because he was as tough as "the hardest wood in creation." But when he read these lies, he broke down and cried.

When the votes were counted, Jackson was clearly the people's choice. But he was not the choice of the rich and **well-born** people who were used to running the country—the planters, merchants, bankers, and lawyers. "Nobody knows what he will do," wrote Senator Daniel Webster gloomily. "My fear is stronger than my hope."

Jackson proved to be a controversial president. In this chapter, you will discover how he was viewed by several groups of Americans, including not only the rich and well-born, but also the common people, Native Americans, and supporters of states' rights.

Graphic Organizer: Character Portraits
You will draw facial expressions on the figures to record various groups' reactions to Andrew Jackson's presidency.

People of every color, age, and class mobbed the White House to see Andrew Jackson take his oath of office. One observer claimed that the scene was like the invasion of barbarians into Rome.

14.2 The Inauguration of Andrew Jackson

On March 4, 1829, more than 10,000 people from every state crowded into Washington, D.C., to witness the inauguration of their hero. The visitors overwhelmed local hotels, sleeping five to a bed and drinking the city dry of whiskey. "I have never seen such a crowd here before," observed Senator Webster. "Persons have come 500 miles to see General Jackson, and they really seem to think the country has been rescued from some…disaster."

Many of the people flocking into the capital were first-time voters. Until the 1820s, the right to vote had been limited to the rich and well-born. Only white men with property, it was said, had the education and experience to vote wisely.

The new states forming west of the Appalachians challenged this argument. Along the frontier, all men—rich or poor, educated or not— shared the same opportunities and dangers. They believed they should also share the same rights, including the right to vote.

With the western states leading the way, voting laws were changed to give the "common man" the right to vote. This expansion of democracy did not yet include African Americans, Native Americans, or women. Still, over one million Americans voted in 1828, more than three times as many as voted in 1824.

Many of these new voters did believe that they had rescued the country from disaster. In their view, the national government had been taken over by corrupt "monied interests"— that is, the rich. During his campaign, Jackson had promised to throw these rascals out and return the government to "the people."

According to eyewitness Margaret Bayard Smith, Jackson's inauguration was "an imposing and majestic spectacle." Afterward, a huge crowd followed Jackson to the White House to celebrate. As the crowd surged in, the celebration turned into a near riot.

"Ladies fainted, men were seen with bloody noses, and such a scene of confusion took place as is impossible to describe," wrote Smith. Jackson was nearly "pressed to death and suffocated by the people" before escaping out a back door. "But it was the people's day, and the people's president," Smith concluded. "And the people would rule."

14.3 From the Frontier to the White House

The "people's president" was the first "**self-made**" man" to occupy the White House. Jackson was born in 1767, on the South Carolina frontier. His father died before he was born, leaving Jackson, his mother, and two brothers in poverty. Young Andrew loved sports more than schoolwork. He also had a hot temper. He would pick a fight at the drop of a hat, a friend recalled, and "he'd drop the hat himself."

The American Revolution ended Jackson's childhood. When he was just 13, Jackson joined the local militia and was captured by the British. One day, a British officer ordered Jackson to polish his boots. "Sir," he replied boldly, "I am a prisoner of war and demand to be treated as such." The outraged officer lashed out with his sword, slicing the boy's head and hand. Jackson carried the scars to his grave.

self-made: achieving wealth or influence through one's own effort rather than being born to a privileged family

The Frontier Lawyer After the war, Jackson decided to become a lawyer. He went to work in a law office in Salisbury, North Carolina. He quickly became known as "the most roaring, rollicking, game-cocking, horse-racing, card-playing, mischievous fellow" in town. The wonder is that he learned any law at all.

In 1788, Jackson headed west to Nashville, Tennessee, to practice law. At that time, Nashville was a tiny clump of rough cabins and tents beside the Cumberland River. But the town grew quickly, and Jackson's practice grew with it. He soon earned enough money to buy land and slaves and set himself up as a gentleman planter.

Despite his success, Jackson never outgrew his hot temper. A slave trader named Charles Dickinson found this out when he called Jackson

Andrew Jackson was born in this cabin in a small, rural South Carolina town. He received little formal education, but in his teens he studied law to become a lawyer.

Jackson is shown here at the Battle of New Orleans, where he became a national hero after defeating the British.

Collection of the New-York Historical Society, Negative number 8838

Jackson Forever!
The Hero of Two Wars and of Orleans!
The Man of the People!
HE WHO COULD NOT BARTER NOR BARGAIN FOR THE
PRESIDENCY!
Who, although " *A Military Chieftain*," valued the purity of Elections and of the Electors, MORE than the Office of PRESIDENT itself! Although the greatest in the gift of his countrymen, and the highest in point of dignity of any in the world,
BECAUSE
It should be derived from the
PEOPLE!
No Gag Laws! No Black Cockades! No Reign of Terror! No Standing Army or Navy Officers, when under the pay of Government, to browbeat, or
KNOCK DOWN
Old Revolutionary Characters, or our Representatives while in the discharge of their duty. To the Polls then, and vote for those who will support
OLD HICKORY
AND THE ELECTORAL LAW.

This campaign poster shows the theme of Jackson's presidential campaign. His supporters claimed that if Jackson were elected, government would finally be in the hands of ordinary people, not just the rich and well-born.

"a worthless scoundrel" and insulted his wife, Rachel. Enraged, Jackson challenged Dickinson to a duel (fight) with pistols, even though the slave trader was said to be the best shot in Tennessee. At that time, duels were accepted as a way of settling disputes between gentlemen.

Dickinson shot first, hitting Jackson in the chest. Jackson stiffened, raised his pistol, and fired a single shot. Dickinson fell dead to the ground.

"My God," a friend exclaimed on spotting Jackson's wound. "He missed your heart only by an inch." In fact, Dickinson's bullet was lodged so close to Jackson's heart that doctors were not able to remove it. "I would have hit him," replied Jackson, "if he'd shot me through the brain!"

The People's Choice   Jackson entered politics in Tennessee, serving in both the House and Senate. But he did not become widely known until the Battle of New Orleans during the War of 1812. His glorious defense of the city made "Old Hickory" a national hero.

In 1824, the hero of New Orleans ran for president against three other candidates—Henry Clay, William Crawford, and John Quincy Adams. Jackson won the most popular votes, and the most electoral votes as well. But he did not have enough electoral votes for a majority. When no candidate has an electoral majority, the House of Representatives chooses a president from the three leading candidates.

Clay, who had come in fourth, urged his supporters in the House to back Adams. That support gave Adams enough votes to become president. Adams then chose Clay to be his secretary of state.

Bringing Clay into Adams' cabinet made sense, because the two men shared many of the same goals. Jackson's supporters, however, accused Adams and Clay of making a "corrupt bargain" to rob their hero of his rightful election. And they promised revenge in 1828.

Jackson's supporters used the time between elections to build a new political organization that came to be called the Democratic Party, the name it still wears today. This new party, they promised, would represent ordinary farmers, workers, and the poor, not the rich and well-born who had taken control of the Republican Party.

Jackson's supporters worked feverishly to reach the nation's new voters. Besides hurling insults at Adams, they organized huge parades, picnics, and rallies. At these events, supporters sang "The Hunters of Kentucky"—the nation's first campaign song—and cheered for Old Hickory. They wore Jackson badges, carried hickory sticks, and chanted catchy campaign slogans like "Adams can write, but Jackson can fight."

The result was a great victory for Jackson. But it was also a victory for the idea that the common people should control their government. This idea became known as Jacksonian Democracy.

14.4 Jackson's Approach to Governing

Jackson approached governing much as he had approached leading an army. He listened to others, but then he did exactly what he thought was right.

The Kitchen Cabinet Unlike earlier presidents, Jackson did not rely on his cabinet for advice. He made most of his decisions with the help of trusted friends and political supporters. These advisors were said to meet with him in the White House kitchen. For this reason, they were known as the "kitchen cabinet."

The rich and well-born looked at the "kitchen cabinet" with deep suspicion. In their eyes, the men around the president were not the proper sort to be running the country. One congressman accused Amos Kendall, Jackson's closest advisor, of being "the President's…lying machine!" Jackson ignored such charges and continued to turn for advice to men he trusted.

The Spoils System Jackson's critics were even more upset by his decision to replace many Republican officeholders with loyal Democrats. Most of these **civil servants** viewed their posts as lifetime jobs. Jackson disagreed. Rotating people in office was more democratic than lifetime service, he said, because it gave more people a chance to serve their government. After a few years in office, civil servants should "go back to making a living as other people do."

Jackson's opponents called the practice of rewarding political supporters with jobs the **spoils system**. This term came from the saying that "to the victor belong the spoils [prizes] of war." They also exaggerated the number of Republicans removed from office. Only about 10 percent of all civil servants were replaced, and many who were dismissed from their jobs deserved to be. One was an official who had stolen $10,000 from the Treasury. When he begged Jackson to let him stay in office, the president replied, "Sir, I would turn out my own father under the same circumstances."

But Jackson could put patriotism above party loyalty. One dismissed postmaster started to undress to show the president his wounds from the Revolutionary War. Jackson snapped, "Put your coat on at once, sir!" The next day, the postmaster got his job back.

civil servants: employees of the government

spoils system: the practice of rewarding political supporters with government jobs

In this cartoon, titled "Office Hunters for the Year 1834," Andrew Jackson is a puppet master. He is pulling strings attached to people who want to be appointed to public offices. What is the cartoonist's opinion of Jackson?

The Granger Collection, New York

Andrew Jackson and the Growth of American Democracy **193**

tariff: a tax imposed by the government on goods imported from another country

secede: to withdraw from an organization or alliance; in this case, to withdraw from the United States

14.5 The Nullification Crisis

Jackson's approach to governing was tested by an issue that threatened to break up the United States. In 1828, Congress passed a law raising **tariffs,** or taxes, on imported goods such as cloth and glass. The idea was to encourage the growth of manufacturing. Higher tariffs meant higher prices for imported factory goods. American manufacturers could then outsell their foreign competitors.

Northern states, humming with new factories, favored the new tariff law. But southerners called it the Tariff of Abominations (horrors).

Southerners opposed tariffs for several reasons. Tariffs raised the prices they paid for factory goods. High tariffs also discouraged trade among nations. Since much of the South's cotton was exported to other countries, planters worried that tariffs would hurt cotton sales.

In this cartoon, John C. Calhoun is the figure at the top of the staircase. Calhoun, who believed that states have the right to nullify, or reject, federal laws, is reaching toward a crown. The crown is a symbol of his desire for power. Andrew Jackson is pulling on the coattails of a Calhoun supporter. He wants to prevent Calhoun from trampling on the Constitution and destroying the Union.

Many southerners also believed that a law passed to favor one group—in this case, northern manufacturers—was unconstitutional. Based on this belief, John C. Calhoun, Jackson's vice president, called on southern states to declare the tariff "null and void," or illegal and not to be honored.

Jackson understood southerners' concerns. In 1832, he signed a new law that lowered tariffs—but not enough to satisfy the most extreme supporters of states' rights in South Carolina. Led by Calhoun, they boldly proclaimed South Carolina's right to nullify, or reject, both the 1828 and 1832 tariff laws. Such an action was called *nullification.* South Carolinians even threatened to **secede**—withdraw their state from the United States—if the national government tried to enforce the tariff laws.

Jackson was outraged. "If one drop of blood be shed there in defiance of the laws of the United States," he raged, "I will hang the first man of them I can get my hands on from the first tree I can find." He called on Congress to pass the Force Bill, which allowed him to use the federal army to collect tariffs if needed. At the same time, Congress passed a compromise bill that lowered tariffs still further.

Faced with such firm opposition, South Carolina backed down and the nullification crisis ended. However, the tensions between the North and the South would increase in the years ahead.

14.6 Jackson Battles the Bank of the United States

Jackson saw himself as the defender of the people, and never more so than in his battle with the Bank of the United States. The Bank was a private business that had been chartered by Congress for 20 years in 1816. The federal government owned one fifth of the Bank and deposited its money there.

Jackson distrusted the Bank and its president, Nicholas Biddle. Biddle was everything that Jackson was not—a wealthy, well-born, highly educated, widely traveled, well-mannered lawyer, politician, and banker. Still, Jackson might have waited to slay "the monster," as he called it, until the Bank's charter came up for renewal in 1836. But Henry Clay forced the issue.

Clay, who planned to run for president against Jackson in 1832, pushed a bill through Congress that renewed the Bank's charter four years early. Clay figured that if Jackson signed the bill, he would lose votes from farmers who shared his dislike of banks. But if Jackson vetoed the bill, he would lose votes from business-people who depended on the Bank for loans. What Clay forgot was that there were many more poor farmers to cast votes than there were bankers, merchants, and manufacturers.

The president vetoed the recharter bill. In his veto message, he called the Bank an unconstitutional monopoly and said that it existed mainly to make the rich richer. The voters seemed to agree. Jackson was reelected by a large majority.

Rather than let the Bank die when its charter ran out, Jackson decided to hasten its end by starving it to death. In 1833, he ordered the secretary of the treasury to remove all federal deposits from the Bank. These funds were then deposited in state banks. Jackson's enemies called these banks "pet banks" because they were run by the president's supporters.

Delegations of businessmen came to Washington to beg Jackson not to kill the Bank. Jackson responded bluntly, "It is folly to talk to me thus." He would rather suffer tortures, he said, than see "the monster" rechartered. Slaying the Bank, Jackson believed, was a victory for democracy—and for the common people—who were its greatest strength.

Andrew Jackson, on the left, is attacking the many-headed Bank of the United States with a veto stick. Nicholas Biddle is in the center wearing a top hat. The many heads represent the 24 state directors of the Bank. Vice President Van Buren is choking Massachusetts and Delaware.

14.7 Jackson's Indian Policy

By the time Jackson became president, only 125,000 Native Americans still lived east of the Mississippi River. Warfare and disease had greatly reduced the number of Indians in the East. Others had sold their lands and moved across the Mississippi. One of Jackson's goals was to remove the remaining Indians to a new Indian Territory in the West.

Most of the eastern Indians lived in the South. They belonged to five groups, called *tribes* by whites: the Creek, Cherokee, Chickasaw, Choctaw, and Seminole. Hoping to remain in their homelands, these Indians had adopted many white ways. Most had given up hunting to become farmers. Many had learned to read and write. The Cherokee even had their own written language, a newspaper, and a constitution modeled on the U.S. Constitution. Whites called these Indians the "Five Civilized Tribes."

While the Five Civilized Tribes may have hoped to live in peace with their neighbors, whites did not share this goal. As the cotton kingdom spread westward, wealthy planters and poor settlers alike looked greedily at Indian homelands. The Indians, they decided, had to go.

Sequoyah, pictured above, was a Cherokee Indian who developed an 86-letter alphabet for the Cherokee language. The alphabet contained both Roman letters and symbols that Sequoyah created. In spite of the fact that these Native Americans developed what many whites considered an advanced civilization, wealthy planters and poor settlers were still determined to force them out and seize their lands.

The Indian Removal Act In 1830, urged on by President Jackson, Congress passed the Indian Removal Act. This law allowed the president to make treaties in which Native Americans in the East traded their lands for new territory on the Great Plains. The president wrote this letter to the Creeks, hoping to persuade them to move willingly:

Friends and brothers, listen. Where you now are, you and my white children are too near to each other to live in harmony and peace…. Beyond the great river Mississippi…your father has provided a country large enough for all of you, and he advises you to remove to it. There your white brothers will not trouble you…and you can live upon it as long as the grass grows or the water runs, in peace and plenty. The land beyond the Mississippi belongs to the President and no one else, and he will give it to you forever.

Some groups agreed to move west voluntarily. Others resisted, usually with tragic results. This was true of the Sac and Fox of Illinois. Led by a chief named Black Hawk, the Sac and Fox fought removal for two years. Black Hawk's War ended in 1832 with the slaughter of most of his warriors. As he was taken off in chains, the chief told his captors:

"Black Hawk is an Indian. He has done nothing for which an Indian ought to be ashamed. He has fought for his countrymen, the squaws [women] and papooses [young children], against white men

The Granger Collection, New York

who came, year after year, to cheat them of and take away their land.
You know the cause of our making war. It is known to all white men.
They ought to be ashamed of it."

The Trail of Tears Many whites were ashamed. Washington was flooded with protests over the treatment of Indians. Still the work of removal continued. Thousands of Creeks who refused to leave Alabama were rounded up and marched west in handcuffs. "To see the remnant of a once mighty people fettered and chained together and forced to depart from the land of their fathers," wrote an Alabama journalist, "is of itself enough to move the stoutest heart."

More than 17,000 Cherokee were dragged from their homes in Georgia and herded west by federal troops. Four thousand died during their long walk to Indian Territory. Those who survived remembered that terrible journey as their "Trail of Tears." A soldier who took part in the Cherokee removal called it "the cruelest work I ever knew."

Led by a young chief named Osceola, the Seminoles of Florida resisted removal for ten years. Their long struggle was the most costly Indian war ever fought in the United States. A number of Seminoles were finally sent to Indian Territory. But others found refuge (safety) in the Florida swamps. Their descendants still live in the state today.

When Jackson left office, he was proud of having "solved" the Indian problem for good. "I feel conscious of having done my duty to my red children," he said. But as you will learn in the next two chapters, Jackson had simply moved the conflict between Indians and whites across the mighty Mississippi.

This artist painted an unrealistic picture of the Trail of Tears. Most of the Cherokees had no horses or warm blankets. They were dragged from their homes and allowed to take only the clothes they had on. Many died as they walked barefoot for hundreds of miles.

Geography Challenge

The Indian Removals

1. From which states were Indians removed?
2. To what future state were they moved?
3. How does the size of Indian Territory compare to the size of their homelands?
4. How far were Indians forced to travel to reach Indian Territory?
5. Which Native American tribe was involved in the Trail of Tears?
6. How many other tribes were forced into Indian Territory?
7. In what direction were Indians pushed? Why were they pushed in this direction?

14.8 Chapter Summary

In this chapter, you read about the presidency of Andrew Jackson. You used character portraits to evaluate Jackson's presidency from the perspective of different groups.

First-time voters, many of them farmers and frontiersmen, flocked to the polls to help elect Andrew Jackson in 1828. Jackson's supporters celebrated his election as a victory for the "common man" over the rich, well-born, and powerful. Jackson, after all, was a self-made man who rose from poverty to become president of the United States.

As president, Jackson fought a number of battles for "the people"—and rewarded his friends and supporters at the same time. For advice, he relied on his "kitchen cabinet," rather than the official cabinet. He replaced a number of Republican civil servants with Democrats. And he waged war on the powerful Bank of the United States.

A controversy over higher tariffs led to the nullification crisis, in which South Carolinians threatened to separate from the United States. Although Jackson forced them to back down, the crisis was an early sign of developing tensions between northern and southern states.

Jackson's Indian policy was simple: move the eastern Indians across the Mississippi to make room for whites. The Indian Removal Act caused great suffering for thousands of Native Americans. Furthermore, Jackson had only moved the conflict between whites and Indians to the West, not solved it. For, as you will read in the next chapter, the West was just where many white Americans were looking for new opportunities and the chance to expand their way of life across the continent.

Andrew Jackson was America's first frontier president. He came to office with great popular support. His supporters viewed him as a president of the people. His enemies saw him as a president hoping to become a king.

How do these people feel about settlers moving west?

Why is this man going west?

Manifest Destiny and the Growing Nation

15.1 Introduction

A century and a half ago, the words **"Manifest Destiny"** inspired vast hopes and dreams among Americans. They led to a war with Mexico. And they changed the map of the United States.

The phrase *manifest destiny* means "obvious fate." It was coined in 1845 by John O'Sullivan, a New York newspaperman. O'Sullivan wrote that it was America's "manifest destiny to overspread and to possess the whole of the continent." Looking at the land beyond the Rocky Mountains, he argued that "the God of nature and nations has marked it for our own."

The fact that Great Britain claimed part of this land—a huge territory known as Oregon—made no difference to O'Sullivan. After all, the United States had stood up to Britain in the War of 1812 and survived.

Nor was O'Sullivan impressed by Mexico's claims to much of the West. Like many Americans, he believed that America had a duty to extend the blessings of democracy to new lands and peoples. It was God's plan, he wrote, for Americans to expand their "great experiment with liberty."

When Americans began their "great experiment" in 1776, the idea that the United States might one day spread across the continent seemed an impossible dream. By 1848, however, the dream was a reality. In this chapter, you will learn how the United States tripled its size in a little more than a single lifetime.

As America grew, it became far more diverse. Its new territories were home to many native peoples, as well as settlers from France, Spain, Mexico, and other countries. America's growth would have a major impact on the people who were already living in the West.

Manifest Destiny took many forms. America grew through treaties, through settlement, and through war. As you read this chapter, think about the way each new territory was acquired. Was O'Sullivan right that this expansion was a matter of destiny? Or was it a matter of diplomacy and sometimes dishonorable dealings? Could Americans have made different decisions along the way?

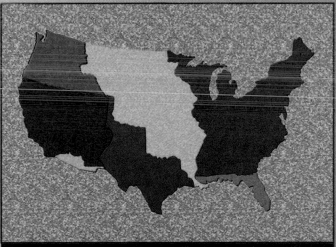

Graphic Organizer: Map of Territorial Acquisitions
You will use this map of America's acquisitions to study how and why the United States expanded across the continent.

15.2 The Louisiana Purchase

America's first opportunity for expansion during the early nineteenth century involved the vast territory to the west of the Mississippi River, then known as Louisiana. The United States wanted the port city of New Orleans, near the mouth of the Mississippi River. By 1800, thousands of farmers were settling the land to the west of the Appalachian Mountains. To get their crops to market, they floated them down the Mississippi to New Orleans. There they loaded the crops onto ships bound for Europe or for cities on the East Coast.

The farmers depended on being able to move their crops freely along this route. "The Mississippi," wrote James Madison, "is to them everything. It is the Hudson, the Delaware, the Potomac, and all the navigable rivers of the Atlantic States formed into one stream."

THE LOUISIANA PURCHASE.
MESSRS. MONROE AND LIVINGSTONE COMPLETING NEGOTIATIONS WITH TALLYRAND. APRIL 30. 1803

American diplomats (standing) work out the final details of the Louisiana Purchase with Tallyrand, the French foreign minister.

Louisiana Across the Mississippi lay the unexplored territory of Louisiana. This immense region stretched from Canada south to Texas. From the Mississippi, it reached west all the way to the Rocky Mountains. First claimed by France, Louisiana was given to Spain after the French and Indian War. In 1800, the French ruler Napoleon Bonaparte convinced Spain to return Louisiana to France.

Napoleon had plans for Louisiana. He hoped to settle the territory with thousands of French farmers. These farmers would raise food for slaves who toiled on France's sugar plantations in the Caribbean.

Napoleon's plans alarmed frontier farmers. New Orleans was part of Louisiana. If Napoleon closed the port to American goods, farmers would have no way to get their crops to market.

"A Noble Bargain" President Thomas Jefferson understood the concerns of American farmers. So, in 1803, he sent James Monroe to France with an offer to buy New Orleans for $7.5 million. By the time Monroe reached France, Napoleon had changed his plans. A few years earlier, a slave named Toussaint L'Ouverture had led a slave revolt in the French Caribbean colony known today as Haiti. The former slaves defeated the French troops who tried to take back the colony. As a result, Napoleon no longer needed Louisiana.

In addition, France and Britain were on the brink of war. Napoleon knew that he might lose Louisiana to the British. Rather than lose

Louisiana, it made sense to sell it to the United States.

Napoleon's offer to sell all of Louisiana stunned James Monroe. Instead of a city, suddenly the United States had the opportunity to buy an area as big as itself!

It didn't take long for Monroe to agree. On April 30, 1803, he signed a treaty giving Louisiana to the United States in exchange for $15 million. Said the French foreign minister, "You have made a noble bargain for yourselves, and I suppose you will make the most of it."

The Purchase Debate   To most Americans, the Louisiana Purchase looked like the greatest land deal in history. The new territory would double the country's size at a bargain price of just 2 to 3 cents an acre!

Still, not everyone approved. Some people worried that such a large country would be impossible to govern. Politicians in the East fretted that they would lose power. Sooner or later, they warned, Louisiana would be carved into enough new states to outvote the eastern states in Congress.

Others fussed about the $15 million price tag. "We are to give money of which we have too little," wrote a Boston critic, "for land of which we already have too much."

Opponents also accused Jefferson of "tearing the Constitution to tatters." They said that the Constitution made no provision for purchasing foreign territory.

Jefferson was troubled by the argument that the purchase was unconstitutional. Still, he believed that it was better to stretch the Constitution than to lose a historic opportunity.

Late in 1803, the Senate voted to ratify the Louisiana Purchase treaty. Frontier farmers cheered the news. "You have secured to us the free navigation of the Mississippi," a grateful westerner wrote Jefferson. "You have procured an immense and fertile country: and all these great blessings are obtained without war and bloodshed."

In this painting, the American flag is raised in New Orleans as the French flag is taken down. The ceremony marked the official transfer of the Louisiana Territory in 1803.

The Granger Collection, New York

Manifest Destiny and the Growing Nation   **203**

15.3 Florida

Having acquired Louisiana through **diplomacy,** President Jefferson turned next to Florida. Spain had colonized this sunny peninsula in the late 1500s. By the 1800s, Florida had a diverse population of Seminole Indians, Spanish colonists, English traders, and runaway slaves. In 1804, Jefferson sent two diplomats to Spain to buy Florida. Spain's answer was "no deal."

Many white Americans in the Southeast wanted the United States to take over Florida. Slave owners in Georgia were angry because slaves sometimes ran away to Florida. (Some of the runaways were accepted and welcomed by the Seminole Indians.) In addition, white landowners in Georgia were upset by Seminole raids on their lands.

Over the next few years, Spain's control of Florida weakened. The Spanish government could do nothing to stop the raids on farms in Georgia by Seminoles and ex-slaves.

BILLY BOWLEGS. CHOCOTE TUSTENUGGEE. ABEAM. JOHN JUMPER. PASATCHEE EMANTHLA. SARPARKEE YOHOLA.
BILLY BOWLEGS AND CHIEFS OF THE SEMINOLE INDIANS.

Escaped slaves were accepted into Seminole Indian communities, and often intermarried. Here we see Chief Abraham, a Seminole leader of both African and Seminole heritage.

diplomacy: The art of conducting negotiations with other countries. People who engage in diplomacy are called *diplomats*.

Andrew Jackson Invades Florida   In 1818, President James Monroe sent Andrew Jackson—the hero of the Battle of New Orleans—to Georgia with orders to end the raids. Jackson was told that he could chase raiding Seminoles into Florida. But he did not have authority to invade the Spanish colony.

Despite his orders, Jackson marched into Florida with a force of 1,700 troops. Over the next few weeks, he captured nearly every military post in the colony. He arrested, tried, and executed two British subjects for stirring up Indian attacks. He also replaced the Spanish governor with an American. Later Jackson said that he was sorry that he didn't execute the governor as well. Spain demanded that Jackson be called back to Washington and punished for his illegal invasion.

"Govern or Get Out"   Fearing war, Monroe asked his cabinet for advice. All but one of his cabinet members advised him to remove Jackson and apologize to Spain. The exception was Secretary of State John Quincy Adams. Rather than apologize, Adams convinced Monroe to send a blunt message to Spain. The message was, either govern Florida properly or get out.

Equally fearful of war, Spain decided to get out. In 1819, the Spanish government agreed to yield Florida to the United States. In exchange, the United States agreed to pay off $5 million in settlers' claims against Spain. The United States also agreed to honor Spain's long-time claim to Texas.

Not all Americans were happy about leaving Spain in charge of Texas. One newspaper declared that Texas was "worth ten Floridas." Even so, the Senate ratified the Florida treaty two days after it was signed.

15.4 Texas

There was a reason many Americans felt that Texas was so valuable. Much of this region was well suited for growing cotton, the South's most valuable cash crop, and many southerners hoped that one day it would become part of the United States.

Americans Come to Texas   The Texas tale begins with Moses Austin, a banker and businessman who dreamed of starting an American colony in Spanish Texas. In 1821, Spanish officials granted Austin a huge tract of land. When Moses died suddenly that year, his son Stephen took over his father's dream.

Stephen arrived in Texas just as Mexico declared its independence from Spain. Now Texas was a part of Mexico. Mexican officials agreed to let Austin start his colony—under certain conditions. Austin had to choose only moral and hardworking settlers. The settlers had to promise to become Mexican citizens and to join the Catholic Church.

Austin agreed to the Mexican terms. By 1827, he had attracted 297 families—soon known as the "Old Three Hundred"— to Texas.

Rising Tensions   The success of Austin's colony started a rush of settlers to Texas. By 1830, there were about 25,000 Americans in Texas, compared to 4,000 Tejanos, or Texans of Mexican descent. Soon tensions between the two groups began to rise.

The Americans had several complaints. They were used to governing themselves, and they resented taking orders from Mexican officials. They were unhappy that all official documents had to be in Spanish, a language most of them were unwilling to learn. In addition, many were slaveholders who were upset when Mexico outlawed slavery in 1829.

The Tejanos had their own complaints. They were unhappy that many American settlers had come to Texas illegally. Worse, most of these new immigrants showed little respect for Mexican culture and had no intention of becoming citizens.

The Mexican government responded by closing Texas to further American immigration. The government sent troops to Texas to assert its authority and enforce the immigration laws.

The Texans Rebel   Americans in Texas resented these actions. Hotheads, led by a young lawyer named William Travis, began calling for revolution. Cooler heads, led by Stephen Austin, asked the Mexican government to reopen Texas to immigration and to make it a separate Mexican state. That way, Texans could run their own affairs.

Stephen Austin made his father's dream a reality when he founded a colony in Texas in 1822. In this painting, we see a young and charismatic Austin talking with a group of Anglo American settlers about the rules Mexico required them to live by.

In 1833, Austin traveled to Mexico and presented the Texans' demands to the new head of the Mexican government, General Antonio López de Santa Anna. The general was a power-hungry dictator who once boasted, "If I were God, I would wish to be more." Rather than bargain with Austin, Santa Anna tossed him in jail for promoting rebellion.

Soon after Austin was released in 1835, Texans rose up in revolt. Determined to crush the rebels, Santa Anna marched north with approximately 6,000 troops.

The Alamo   In late February 1836, a large part of Santa Anna's army reached San Antonio, Texas. The town was defended by about 180 Texan volunteers, including eight Tejanos. The Texans had taken over an old mission known as the Alamo. Among them was Davy Crockett, a famous frontiersman and former congressman from Tennessee. Sharing command with William Travis was James Bowie, a well-known Texas "freedom fighter."

The Alamo's defenders watched as General Santa Anna raised a black flag that meant "Expect no mercy." The general demanded that the Texans surrender. Travis answered with a cannon shot.

Slowly, Santa Anna's troops began surrounding the Alamo. The Texans were outnumbered by at least ten to one, but only one man fled.

Fewer than 200 Texans fought 4,000 Mexican troops at the Alamo. When the battle was over, they were all dead— including James Bowie and the fabled frontiersman Davy Crocket.

Meanwhile, Travis sent messengers to other towns in Texas, pleading for reinforcements and vowing not to abandon the Alamo. "Victory or death!" he proclaimed. But reinforcements never came.

For 12 days, the Mexicans pounded the Alamo with cannonballs. Then, at the first light of dawn on March 6, Santa Anna gave the order to storm the fort. Desperately, the Texans tried to stave off the attackers with a hailstorm of rifle fire.

For 90 minutes the battle raged. Then it was all over. By day's end, every one of the Alamo's defenders was dead. By Santa Anna's order, those who had survived the battle were executed on the spot.

Santa Anna described the fight for the Alamo as "but a small affair." But his decision to kill every man at the Alamo filled Texans with rage. It was a rage that cried out for revenge.

Texas Wins Its Independence   Sam Houston, the commander of the Texas revolutionary army, understood Texans' rage. But as Santa Anna pushed on, Houston's only hope was to retreat eastward. By luring Santa Anna deeper into Texas, he hoped to make it harder for the general to supply his army and keep it battle-ready.

Houston's strategy wasn't popular, but it worked brilliantly. In April, Santa Anna caught up with Houston near the San Jacinto River. Expecting the Texans to attack at dawn, the general kept his troops awake all night. When no attack came, the weary Mexicans relaxed. Santa Anna went to his tent to take a nap.

Collection of the Star of the Republic Museum, Washington, Texas

The flag of the Lone Star Republic. Sam Houston was elected the first president of the independent country of Texas in 1836. In 1845, Texas was admitted to the United States. Today, Texas is known as the Lone Star State. This is the only known official Lone Star flag of the Republic of Texas of the period 1836-1846.

Late that afternoon, Houston's troops staged a surprise attack. Yelling "Remember the Alamo!" the Texans overran the Mexican camp. Santa Anna fled, but he was captured the next day. In exchange for his freedom, he ordered all his remaining troops out of Texas. Texans had won their independence. Still, Mexico did not fully accept the loss of Texas.

To Annex Texas or Not?   Now an independent country, Texas became known as the Lone Star Republic because of the single star on its flag. But most Texans were Americans who wanted Texas to become part of the United States.

Despite their wishes, Texas remained independent for ten years. People in the United States were divided over whether to **annex** Texas. Southerners were eager to add another slave state. Northerners who opposed slavery wanted to keep Texas out.

Others feared that annexation would lead to war with Mexico. The 1844 presidential campaign was influenced by the question of whether to expand U.S. territory. One of the candidates, Henry Clay, warned, "Annexation and war with Mexico are identical." His opponent, James K. Polk, however, was a strong believer in Manifest Destiny. He was eager to acquire Texas. After Polk was elected, Congress voted to annex Texas. In 1845, Texas was admitted as the 28th state.

> **annex:** To add a territory to a country. Such an addition is called an *annexation.*

Manifest Destiny and the Growing Nation   **207**

In the 1800s, wagon trains like the one depicted in this William Henry Jackson painting transported thousands of American families from established eastern settlements to the rugged West. This wagon train is winding its way across Nebraska toward Oregon Country.

15.5 Oregon Country

Far to the northwest of Texas lay Oregon Country. This enormous, tree-covered wilderness stretched from the Rocky Mountains to the Pacific Ocean. To the north, Oregon was bounded by Russian Alaska. To the south, it was bordered by Spanish California and New Mexico.

In 1819, Oregon was claimed by four nations—Russia, Spain, Great Britain, and the United States. Spain was the first to drop out of the scramble. As part of the treaty to purchase Florida, Spain gave up its claim to Oregon. A few years later, Russia also dropped out. By 1825, Russia agreed to limit its claim to the territory that lay north of the 54°40′ parallel of latitude. Today that line marks the southern border of Alaska.

That left Britain and the United States. For the time being, the two nations agreed to a peaceful "joint occupation" of Oregon.

Discovering Oregon America's claim to Oregon was based on the Lewis and Clark expedition. Between 1804 and 1806, Meriwether Lewis and William Clark had led a small band of explorers to the Oregon coast. You will read more about their epic adventure in the next chapter.

Lewis thought that many more Americans would follow the path blazed by the expedition. "In the course of 10 or 12 years," he predicted in 1806, "a tour across the continent by this route will be undertaken with as little concern as a voyage across the Atlantic."

That was wishful thinking. The route that Lewis and Clark had followed was far too rugged for ordinary travelers. There had to be a better way.

In 1824, a young fur trapper named Jedediah Smith found that better way. Smith discovered a passage through the Rocky Mountains called

South Pass. Unlike the high, steep passes used by Lewis and Clark, South Pass was low and flat enough for wagons to use in crossing the Rockies. Now the way was open for settlers to seek their fortunes in Oregon.

converts: people who accept a new religion

Oregon Fever The first American settlers to travel through South Pass to Oregon were missionaries. These earnest preachers made few **converts** among Oregon's Indians. However, their glowing reports of Oregon's fertile soil and towering forests soon attracted more settlers.

These early settlers wrote letters home describing Oregon as a "pioneer's paradise." The weather was always sunny, they claimed. Disease was unknown. Trees grew as thick as hairs on a dog's back. And farms were free for the taking. One joker even claimed that "pigs are running about under the great acorn trees, round and fat, and already cooked, with knives and forks sticking in them so you can cut off a slice whenever you are hungry."

These reports inspired other settlers who were looking for a fresh start. In 1843, about 1,000 pioneers packed their belongings into covered wagons and headed for Oregon. A year later, nearly twice as many people made the long journey across the plains and mountains. "The Oregon Fever has broke out," stated a Boston newspaper, "and is now raging."

All of Oregon or Half? Along with Texas, "Oregon fever" also played a role in the 1844 presidential campaign. Polk won the election with stirring slogans such as "All of Oregon or none!" and "Fifty-four forty or fight!" Polk promised that he would not rest until the United States had annexed all of Oregon Country.

But Polk didn't want Oregon enough to risk starting a war with Britain. Instead, he agreed to a compromise treaty that divided Oregon roughly in half at the 49th parallel. That line now marks the western border between the United States and Canada.

The Senate debate over the Oregon treaty was fierce. Senators from the South and the East strongly favored the treaty. They saw no reason to go to war over "worse than useless territory on the coast of the Pacific." Senators from the West opposed the treaty. They wanted to hold out for all of Oregon. On June 18, 1846, the Senate ratified the compromise treaty by a vote of 41 to 14.

Polk got neither "fifty-four forty" nor a fight. What he got was even better: a diplomatic settlement that both the United States and Great Britain could accept without spilling a drop of blood.

Settlers who braved the 2,000 mile trek from Independence, Missouri to Oregon Country were rewarded by fertile land in the Willamette Valley.

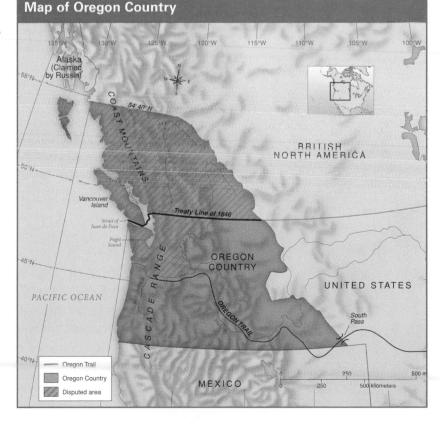

Map of Oregon Country

Oregon Trail
Oregon Country
Disputed area

Volunteers from Exeter, New Hampshire, line up as they leave New England to fight in the war against Mexico.

15.6 War with Mexico

You might think that Texas and Oregon were quite enough new territory for any president. But not for Polk. This humorless, hardworking president had one great goal. He wanted to expand the United States as far as he could.

Polk's gaze fell next on the huge areas known as California and New Mexico. He was determined to have them both—by purchase if possible, by force if necessary.

These areas were first colonized by Spain, but they became Mexican territories when Mexico won its independence in 1821. Both were thinly settled, and the Mexican government had long neglected them. That was reason enough for Polk to hope that they might be for sale. He sent a representative to Mexico to try to buy the territories. But Mexican officials refused even to see him.

War Breaks Out in Texas When Congress voted to annex Texas, relations between the United States and Mexico turned sour. To Mexico, the annexation of Texas was an act of war. To make matters worse, Texas and Mexico could not agree on a border. Texas claimed the Rio Grande as its border on the south and the west. Mexico wanted the border to be the Nueces River, about 150 miles northeast of the Rio Grande.

On April 25, 1846, Mexican soldiers fired on American troops who were patrolling along the Rio Grande. Sixteen Americans were killed or wounded. This was just the excuse for war that Polk had been waiting for. Mexico, he charged, "has invaded our territory and shed American blood on American soil." Two days after Polk's speech, Congress declared war on Mexico.

To Mexico, the truth was just the opposite. Mexican president Mariano Paredes declared that a greedy people "have thrown themselves on our territory.... The time has come to fight."

The Fall of New Mexico and California A few months later, General Stephen Kearny led the Army of the West out of Kansas. His orders were to occupy New Mexico and then continue west to California.

Mexican opposition melted away in front of Kearny's army. The Americans took control of New Mexico without firing a shot. "General Kearny," a pleased Polk wrote in his diary, "has thus far performed his duties well."

Meanwhile, a group of Americans led by the explorer John C. Frémont launched a rebellion against Mexican rule in California. The Americans

The Granger Collection, New York

arrested and jailed General Mariano Guadalupe Vallejo, the Mexican commander of Northern California. Then they raised a crude flag showing a grizzly bear sketched in blackberry juice. California, they declared, was now the Bear Flag Republic.

When Kearny reached California, he joined forces with the rebels. Within weeks, all of California was under American control.

The United States Invades Mexico   The conquest of Mexico itself was far more difficult. American troops under Zachary Taylor battled their way south from Texas. Taylor was a no-nonsense general who was known fondly as "Old Rough and Ready" because of his backwoods clothes. After 6,000 troops took the Mexican city of Monterrey, an old enemy stopped them. General Santa Anna had marched north to meet Taylor with an army of 20,000 Mexican troops.

In February 1847, the two forces met near a ranch called Buena Vista. After two days of hard fighting, Santa Anna reported that "both armies have been cut to pieces." Rather than lose his remaining forces, Santa Anna retreated south. The war in northern Mexico was over.

A month later, American forces led by General Winfield Scott landed at Veracruz in southern Mexico. Scott was a stickler for discipline and loved fancy uniforms. These traits earned him the nickname "Old Fuss and Feathers." For the next six months, his troops fought their way to Mexico City, the capital of Mexico.

Outside the capital, the Americans met fierce resistance at the castle of Chapultepec. About 1,000 Mexican soldiers and 100 young military cadets

In this painting by Hal Stone, we see the American cavalry overwhelming the enemy in the Battle of Resaca de la Palma, Texas, in May 1846.

fought bravely to defend the fortress. Six of the cadets chose to die fighting rather than surrender. To this day, the boys who died that day are honored in Mexico as *Los Niños Héroes*—the heroic children.

Despite such determined resistance, Scott's army captured Mexico City in September 1847. Watching from a distance, a Mexican officer muttered darkly, "God is a Yankee."

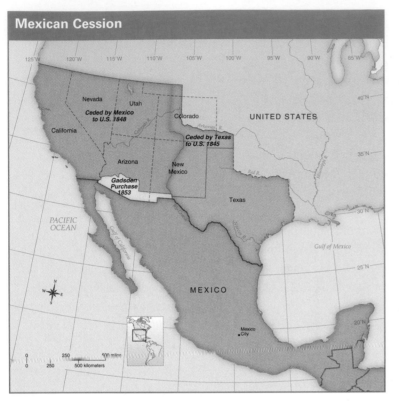

Mexican Cession

As this map shows, Manifest Destiny was accomplished by the 1850s. The country stretched from the Atlantic to the Pacific, and the present outline of the United States was complete.

The Treaty of Guadalupe Hidalgo Early in 1848, Mexico and the United States signed the Treaty of Guadalupe Hidalgo. Mexico agreed to give up Texas and a vast region known as the Mexican Cession. (A *cession* is something that is given up.) This area included the present-day states of California, Nevada, Utah, Arizona, and New Mexico, as well as parts of Colorado and Wyoming. By this agreement, Mexico gave up half of all its territory.

In return, the United States agreed to pay Mexico $15 million. It also promised to protect the 80,000 Mexicans living in Texas and in the Mexican Cession.

In Washington, a few senators spoke up to oppose the treaty. Some of them argued that the United States had no right to any Mexican territory other than Texas. They believed that the Mexican War had been unjust and that the treaty was even more so. New Mexico and California together, they said, were "not worth a dollar" and should be returned to Mexico.

Other senators opposed the treaty because they wanted even more land. They wanted the Mexican Cession to include a large part of northern Mexico as well.

To most senators, however, the Mexican Cession was a Manifest Destiny dream come true. The Senate ratified the treaty by a vote of 38 to 14.

"From Sea to Shining Sea" A few years later, the United States acquired still more land from Mexico. In 1853, James Gadsden arranged the purchase of a strip of land just south of the Mexican Cession for $10 million. Railroad builders wanted this land because it was relatively flat and could serve as a good railroad route. With the acquisition of this land, known as the Gadsden Purchase, the nation stretched "from sea to shining sea."

Most Americans were pleased with the new outlines of their country. Still, not everyone rejoiced in this expansion. Until the Mexican War, many people had believed that the United States was too good a nation to bully or invade its weaker neighbors. Now they knew that such behavior was the dark side of Manifest Destiny.

15.7 Chapter Summary

In this chapter, you read about how Americans extended their nation to the west and the south. You used a map of America's acquisitions to study how and why the United States expanded into these territories.

In the 1800s, many Americans believed that they had both the right and the duty (an idea called *Manifest Destiny*) to spread their way of life across the continent.

America's first great expansion was the Louisiana Purchase. Next, Florida was added to the United States through a treaty with Spain. A treaty with Great Britain added Oregon Country.

Americans in Texas rebelled against the Mexican government there and created the Lone Star Republic. Ten years later, the United States annexed Texas.

In 1846, the United States went to war with Mexico and acquired California and New Mexico as part of the Mexican Cession. Later, the Gadsden Purchase completed the outline of the contiguous United States.

America's expansion across the continent was now complete. Yet much of the West was only thinly settled. In the next chapter, you will learn about the people who moved into this vast area.

As the 19th century progressed, more and more settlers were lured to the West by hopes of free land and an independent and prosperous life.

Emigrants Crossing the Plains by Albert Bierstadt. Oil on canvas, 1867. 72.19/National Cowboy Hall of Fame, Oklahoma City

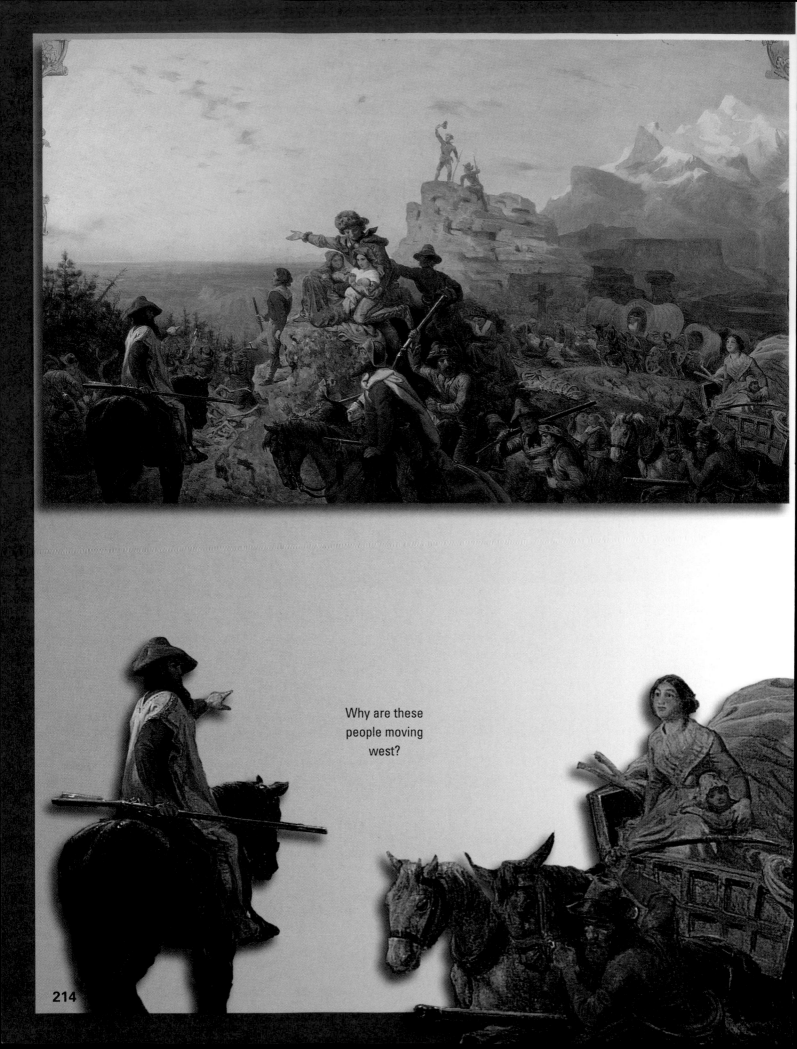

Why are these
people moving
west?

Life in the West

16.1 Introduction

The vast region that stretches from the Mississippi River to the Pacific Ocean and from Canada to Mexico is one of the most extraordinary landscapes on earth. Today, tourists come from all over to see its towering mountains, deep canyons, painted deserts, and fertile plains.

To the Spanish priests and soldiers who rode into this region from Mexico, it was the North. To French and British fur trappers who wandered into it from Canada, it was the South. To Chinese treasure seekers who sailed to it from across the Pacific, it was the East. And to the native peoples who had always lived here, it was home.

The name that stuck, however, was the one used by settlers from across the Mississippi. To Americans, this great expanse of grasslands, mountains, and deserts was the West.

For all its beauty, the West was a challenging environment. Look at the names settlers gave to its features. Where else can you find a confusion of mountains called the Crazies, a scorching desert named Death Valley, a blood-red canyon called Flaming Gorge, or a raging river known as the River of No Return?

Despite its daunting challenges, the West was never empty. Perhaps as many as 3 million Native Americans lived there before Europeans arrived. These first westerners were far more diverse in language and culture than the Europeans who claimed their land.

In the last chapter, you read about how the United States acquired this vast territory. For Americans, the West became the land of opportunity, a place where people could get a new start in life. Newspaperman Horace Greeley expressed this idea when he wrote, "If you have no family or friends to aid you, and no prospect [opportunity] opened to you...turn your face to the great West, and there build up a home and fortune."

In this chapter, you will learn about eight groups of people who turned their faces to the West in the first half of the 1800s. You will find out why they came, what hardships they faced, and what legacy they left.

Graphic Organizer: Illustration
You will use this illustration to learn about the people who settled the West.

16.2 The Explorers

In the early 1800s, a number of expeditions set out from the United States to explore the West. The most famous was the Lewis and Clark expedition, a pet project of President Thomas Jefferson.

The public purpose of the expedition was to make friendly contact with Indian groups that might be interested in trade. Its secret purpose was to find the "Northwest Passage," a water route across North America that explorers had been seeking ever since Columbus bumped into America. With the purchase of Louisiana from France in 1803, the expedition gained a third purpose—finding out just what the United States had bought.

Up the Missouri River   In May 1804, the 45-member expedition left St. Louis, Missouri, in three boats. The group was led by Jefferson's private secretary, Meriwether Lewis, and his friend William Clark. Its members included soldiers, frontiersmen, and Clark's slave York.

It was hard going from the first day. Rowing upstream against the Missouri River's strong current left the explorers' hands blistered and their muscles sore. Hungry mosquitoes feasted on sunburned faces.

By summer, the explorers had reached Indian country. Most groups welcomed the strangers, and York fascinated the Indians. They had never seen a black man before. Again and again, wrote Clark in his journal, York allowed his skin to be rubbed with a wet finger to prove "that he was not a painted white man."

The explorers made camp for the winter near a Mandan village in what is now North Dakota. There, a French fur trapper joined them along with his sixteen-year-old wife, a Shoshone woman named Sacagawea, and their infant son. As a girl, Sacagawea had been kidnapped from her people by another group. Lewis and Clark hoped she would translate for them when they reached Shoshone country.

To the Pacific and Back   In the spring of 1805, the explorers set out once more. As they moved up the Missouri, their progress was slowed by rapids and waterfalls. When they hauled their boats by land around these obstacles, the thorns of the prickly-pear cactus pierced their feet. Meanwhile, grizzly bears raided their camps, and game became scarce.

By late summer, the explorers could see the Rocky Mountains looming ahead. To cross the mountains before the first snows of winter closed the high passes, they would have to find horses—and soon.

Fortunately, the expedition had reached the land of Sacagawea's child-

William Clark (above) and Meriwether Lewis (right), two former soldiers, led an expedition to explore the newly acquired Louisiana Territory.

hood. One day a group of Indians approached. To Sacagawea's great joy, they proved to be Shoshone. As Clark described the scene, "A woman made her way through the crowd toward Sacagawea and recognizing each other, they embraced with the most tender affection." Learning that her brother was now a Shoshone chief, Sacagawea persuaded him to provide the explorers with the horses they desperately needed.

The explorers made it over the Rockies, but they were more dead than alive. The Nez Percé, an Indian people living in the Pacific Northwest, saved them from starvation. A grateful Lewis wrote in his journal that the Nez Percé "are the most hospitable, honest and sincere [people] that we have met with on our voyage."

As winter closed in, the explorers reached their final destination, the Pacific Ocean. Clark marked the event by carving on a tree, "William Clark December 3rd 1805 By Land from the U. States."

The Explorers' Legacy   After a wet and hungry winter in Oregon, the explorers headed homeward. In September 1806, two years and four months after setting out, they returned to St. Louis. Lewis dashed off a letter to Jefferson that read, "It is with pleasure that I announce to you the safe arrival of myself and party…with our papers and baggage. In obedience to our orders, we have penetrated the continent of North America to the Pacific Ocean."

Lewis and Clark had done far more than merely "penetrate the continent." They had not found the Northwest Passage, for it did not exist. But they had traveled some 8,000 miles. They had mapped a route to the Pacific. They had established good relations with western Indian peoples. Most of all, their "papers and baggage" contained priceless information about the lands that would soon beckon others—and about the peoples who called the West their home.

This painting shows members of the Lewis and Clark expedition at Three Forks, Montana. The woman is Sacagawea. To her right are Meriwether Lewis, William Clark, and Clark's slave, York.

Geography Challenge

Lewis and Clark Expedition

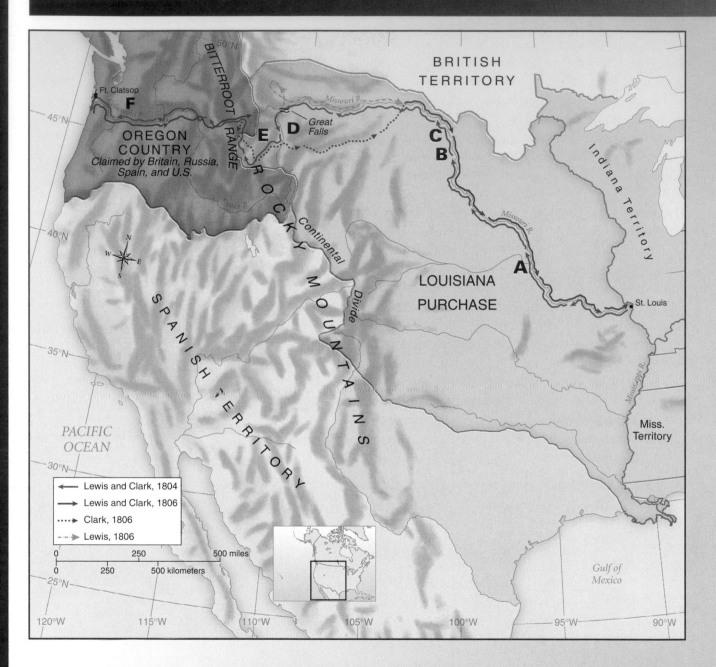

1. What details do you see on this map?

2. What specific geographic features did Lewis and Clark encounter?

3. What challenges might these features have created for them?

4. What other challenges might Lewis and Clark have faced on their expedition?

Image A: August 3, 1804. Excerpts from William Clark's journal: "chiefs," "long speech," "wishes of our government," "trading," and "a canister of (gun) powder."

Image B: November 3, 1804. Excerpts from William Clark's journal: "plenty of timber," "building," "our camp," and "we received a visit from Kagohami."

Image C: March 9, 1805. Excerpts from William Clark's journal: "grand chief of the Minnetarees," "surprised," "examined him closely," and "wash off paint."

Image D: August 6, 1805. Excerpts from Meriwether Lewis's journal: "rapid current," "baggage wet," "several articles lost," and "thrown out of one of the canoes."

Image E: August 17, 1805. Excerpts from William Clark's journal: "companions in childhood," "embraced with the most tender affection," "conference," and "interpret."

Image F: November 3, 1805. Excerpts from Joseph Whitehouse's journal: "fog so thick…we cannot see," "met several Indians in a canoe," "they signed to us," and "two hundred miles…to the ocean."

The Granger Collection, New York
Thomas Gilcrease Institute
The Granger Collection, New York

mission: A place established by missionaries for their work. A typical California mission included such things as a church, a residence, workshops, and large areas of land for raising crops.

rancho: A grant of land made by the Mexican government. Most ranchos were used for raising cattle and crops.

16.3 The Californios

If Lewis and Clark had turned south from Oregon after reaching the Pacific, they would have found Spain's best-kept secret, a sun-drenched land called California.

The California Missions   In 1769, a Spanish missionary named Junipero Serra led soldiers and priests north from Mexico to California. Serra's goal was to convert the California Indians to Christianity. To do this, he began a chain of **missions** that eventually stretched from San Diego to just north of San Francisco. Each mission controlled a huge area of land, as well as the Indians who worked it.

Settlers followed the missionaries to California. "There was never a more peaceful or happy people on the face of the earth than the Spanish, Mexican and Indian population of…California," wrote Guadelupe Vallejo. "We were the pioneers of the Pacific coast, building pueblos [towns] and missions while George Washington was carrying on the war of the Revolution."

Although the missionaries meant well, the missions were deadly to native Californians. Indians were sometimes treated harshly, and thousands died of diseases brought to California by the newcomers.

When Mexico won its independence in 1821, California came under Mexican rule. In 1833, the Mexican government closed the missions and opened mission lands to settlement. Half of this land was supposed to go to Indians. Most of it, however, went to soldiers and settlers. The typical Spanish-speaking Californian, or *Californio,* was granted a **rancho** of 50,000 acres or more.

The prosperity and pride of the Californios is evident in this painting, *Hacendado y Su Mayordomo,* meaning "The Landowner and His Foreman."

Life on the Ranchos   Life on the ranchos combined hard work and the occasional *fiesta,* or social gathering. Most families lived in simple adobe houses with dirt floors. The Californios produced almost everything they needed at home. Indian servants did much of the work.

The ranchos were so huge that neighbors lived at least a day's journey apart. As a result, strangers were always welcome for the news they brought of the outside world. During weddings and fiestas, Californios celebrated with singing, dancing, and brilliant displays of horsemanship.

In the 1830s, cattle ranching became California's most important industry. Cattle provided hides and tallow (beef fat) to trade for imported goods brought by ship. An American sailor named Richard Henry Dana described the goods his trading ship carried to California:

"We had...teas, coffee, sugars, spices, raisins, molasses, hard-ware, crockery-ware, tin-ware, cutlery, clothing of all kinds, boots and shoes ...shawls, scarfs, necklaces, jewelry... furniture...and in fact everything than can be imagined, from Chinese fire-works to English cart-wheels."

Because California was so far from the capital in Mexico City, the territory was neglected by the Mexican government. Soldiers were not paid, and they took what they needed to survive from the people they were supposed to protect. Officials sent to govern California were often unskilled and sometimes dishonest.

The Californios' Legacy　In 1846, the United States captured California as part of the war with Mexico. Before long, Californios were a minority in California.

Still, the Californios left a lasting mark. California is full of Spanish place names such as San Diego, Los Angeles, and San Francisco. The Californios also introduced many of California's famous crops, such as grapes, olives, and citrus fruits. Most of all, they opened California to the world. As you will see, the world soon rushed in.

16.4 The Mountain Men

The Lewis and Clark expedition stirred new interest in an old industry, the fur trade. Inspired by the explorers' reports of finding beaver in the Rockies, a Spanish trader named Manuel Lisa followed their route west. In 1807, Lisa led 42 trappers up the Missouri River. The next year, he took 350 trappers into the Rockies. For the next 30 years, trappers crisscrossed the West in search of valuable furs.

Mountain men, like this one pictured in a Frederick Remington painting, were rugged individualists. They often wore shirts and trousers made from animal hides and had hair that hung to their shoulders.

The Trapper's Life　The trappers, who were also called *mountain men,* lived hard and usually died young. During the spring and fall, they set their traps in icy streams. In July, they traveled to trading posts to swap furs for supplies or gathered for an annual "rendezvous," or get-together. Here is how writer Washington Irving described one rendezvous:

This, then, is the trapper's holiday.... [The men] engaged in contests of skill at running, jumping, wrestling, shooting with the rifle, and running horses.... They drank together, they sang, they laughed, they whooped; they tried to outbrag and outlie each other in stories of their adventures and achievements. Here were the free trappers in all their glory.

The Granger Collection, New York

In their search for furs, mountain men established new routes to Oregon and California.

The rendezvous may have been fun, but the trappers' lives were filled with hazards. Trappers were attacked by fur thieves, Indians, wolves, and bears. Mountain man Hugh Glass was mauled by a mother bear that threw chunks of his flesh to her hungry cubs before friends rescued him.

Accidents were common, too. A single misplaced step on a mountain, or a misjudged river rapid, often meant sudden death. Disease also took a heavy toll. When one man asked for news about a party of trappers, he learned that "some had died by lingering diseases, and others by the fatal [rifle] ball or arrow." Out of 116 men, he wrote, "there were not more than sixteen alive."

Freedom and Adventure   Trappers braved this dangerous way of life because of its freedom and adventure. A good example is Jim Beckwourth, a slave who fled Virginia to become a fur trapper. While hunting beaver in the Rockies, Beckwourth was captured by Crow Indians. According to Beckwourth, an old woman identified him as her long-lost son, and he was adopted into the tribe. "What could I do?" he wrote later. "Even if I should deny my Crow origin, they would not believe me."

Beckwourth lived with the Crow for six years and became a chief. By the time he left the tribe in the 1830s, the fur trade was in decline. Like other mountain men, however, Beckwourth continued his adventurous life as an explorer, army scout, and trader. In 1850, he discovered the lowest pass across the Sierra Nevada mountain range, known today as Beckwourth Pass.

The Mountain Men's Legacy   In their search for furs, the mountain men explored most of the West. The routes they pioneered across mountains and deserts became the Oregon and California Trails. Their trading posts turned into supply stations for settlers moving west along those trails.

A surprising number of mountain men left another kind of legacy as well—personal journals. Their stories still have the power to make us laugh and cry—and to wonder how they lived long enough to tell their tales.

16.5 The Missionaries

Ever since Lewis and Clark appeared among them, the Nez Percé had been friendly toward Americans. In 1831, three Nez Percé traveled to St. Louis to learn more about the white man's ways. There, the Nez Percé asked if someone would come west to teach their people the secrets of the "Black Book," or Bible.

Several missionaries answered that call. The best known were Marcus and Narcissa Whitman and Henry and Eliza Spalding. In 1836, the two couples traveled west from St. Louis along the **Oregon Trail**.

It was a difficult journey. Narcissa described the Rockies as "the most terrible mountains for steepness." Still, the missionaries arrived safely in Oregon, proving that women could endure the journey west.

A Difficult Start   On reaching Oregon, the group split up. The Spaldings went to work with the Nez Percé. The Whitmans worked among a neighboring group, the Cayuse. Neither couple knew very much about the people they hoped to convert. The result was a difficult start.

After three years the Spaldings finally made their first converts. In 1839, Henry baptized two Nez Percé chiefs. A year later, one of the chiefs had his infant son baptized as well. The child would grow up to be the leader best known as Chief Joseph. You will meet him again later in this book.

The Whitmans were less successful. The Cayuse were far more interested in the whites' weapons and tools than in their religion. The couple also offended the Cayuse. They refused to pay for the land they took for their mission or to offer visitors gifts, as was the Indians' custom. Not a single Cayuse converted to the new faith.

A Pioneer's Paradise   Marcus Whitman was far more successful at converting Americans to the belief that Oregon was a pioneer's paradise. "It does not concern me so much what is to become of any particular set of Indians," he wrote. "Our greatest work is…to aid the white settlement of this country and help to found its religious institutions."

In 1842, Marcus traveled east on horseback. Along the way, he urged Americans to settle in Oregon. On his return, he guided a large group of settlers along the Oregon Trail. More settlers soon followed. "The poor Indians are amazed at the overwhelming number of Americans coming into the country," observed Narcissa. "They seem not to know what to make of it."

Oregon Trail: an overland route that stretched about 2,000 miles from Independence, Missouri, to the Columbia River in Oregon

In 1836, Marcus and Narcissa Whitman married and set out for Oregon to establish a mission. Here they are seen offering prayers for a safe journey.

In 1847, measles came west with settlers and swept through the Whitman mission. Marcus treated the sick as best he could. The Cayuse noticed that whites usually recovered, while their own people were dying. Rumors spread that Whitman was giving deadly pills to Indians. Angry warriors attacked the mission, killing both Marcus and Narcissa.

The Missionaries' Legacy   Like the Spanish priests in California, American preachers in Oregon hoped that their legacy would be large numbers of Christian Indians. In fact, relatively few Indians became Christians. Many, however, died of the diseases that came west with the missionaries.

The missionaries' true legacy was to open the West to settlement. In California, Oregon, and other territories, settlers followed in the footsteps of western missionaries.

The Whitmans were killed by angry Indian warriors who blamed them for a deadly outbreak of measles.

16.6 The Pioneer Women

On a July afternoon in 1905, a crowd gathered at the Lewis and Clark Exposition in Portland, Oregon. They had come to dedicate a statue of Sacagawea, the first woman to journey across the continent.

Cheers rang out as the flag draped over the statue was pulled away. There she stood, a beautiful young woman carrying a baby on her back, her arm pointing the way forever west. The sign beneath the statue read, "In memory of Sacagawea and in honor of the pioneer mothers of Oregon." At that moment, Sacagawea represented the courage and strength of all the pioneer women who followed the missionaries west.

On the Trail   Between 1840 and 1869, about 350,000 people traveled west in covered wagons. Most of the women who made that journey were wives and mothers. But some were single women seeking **homesteads,** husbands, or other new opportunities.

The pioneers met in the spring near Independence, Missouri. Traveling alone was far too dangerous, so pioneers formed columns of wagons called *wagon trains*. Before setting out, members of a wagon train agreed on rules and elected leaders. They knew that they had to cooperate with one another in order to survive the trip west.

The journey lasted four to six months and covered about 2,000 miles. Wagon space was so limited that women were forced to leave most of the comforts of home behind. The few treasures they managed to fit in often had to be tossed out when the way became steep. The Oregon Trail was littered with furniture, china, books, and other cherished objects.

Women were expected to do the work they had done back home, but while traveling 15 to 20 miles a day. They cooked, washed clothes, and took care of the children. Meals on wheels were simple. "About the only

homestead: a plot of land where pioneers could build a home, farm, or ranch

The Granger Collection, New York

change we have from bread and bacon," wrote Helen Carpenter, "is to bacon and bread."

The daily drudgery wore many women down. Lavinia Porter recalled, "I would make a brave effort to be cheerful and patient until the camp work was done. Then starting out ahead of the team and my men folks, when I thought I had gone beyond hearing distance, I would throw myself down on the unfriendly desert and give way like a child to sob and tears."

Trail Hazards The death toll on the trail was high. Disease was the worst killer. Accidents were also common. People drowned in river crossings. Children fell from wagons and were crushed under the wheels.

Indian attacks were rare. At first, many Native Americans saw the settlers' westward movement as an opportunity. They earned money as guides or by selling supplies to the pioneers. The Sac and Pawnee collected tolls from wagons crossing their land. Some Indians even began thinking of moving eastward. Surely, they thought, the East must be empty now that "the whole white village" was moving west!

By the end of the journey, each woman had a story to tell. Some had seen buffalo stampedes and prairie fires on the Great Plains. Some had almost frozen to death in the mountains or died of thirst in the deserts. But most survived to build new lives in the West.

The Pioneer Women's Legacy The journey west changed pioneer women. The hardships of the trail brought out strengths and abilities they did not know they possessed. "I felt a secret joy," declared one Oregon pioneer, "in being able to have the power that sets things going."

Pioneers who wished to go west met in Independence, Missouri, in the spring. There they formed wagon trains before setting out on the trail.

The Granger Collection, New York

And women did set things going. Wherever they settled, schools, churches, libraries, literary societies, and charitable groups soon blossomed. One of the first colleges on the Pacific Coast was founded by sixty-six-year-old Tabitha Brown, who arrived in Oregon in 1846 with six cents to her name. Mother Joseph, a nun from Canada, designed and built the Northwest's first schools and hospitals.

Pioneer women also used their power to win a right long denied them in the East—the right to vote. By 1900, women were voting in four western states. Nowhere else in the United States did women enjoy the freedom and sense of equality of the western pioneers. This was perhaps the greatest legacy of the pioneer women.

Although pioneer women had to travel 15 to 20 miles a day, they were still expected to take care of household chores when the wagon train stopped for the night.

16.7 The Mormons

In 1846, a wagon train of pioneers headed west in search of a new home. Looking down on the shining surface of Great Salt Lake in what is now Utah, their leader, Brigham Young, declared, "This is the place!"

It was not a promising spot. One pioneer described the valley as a "broad and barren plain…blistering in the rays of the midsummer sun." A woman wrote, "Weak and weary as I am, I would rather go a thousand miles further than remain." But that was one of the valley's attractions. No one else wanted the place that Brigham Young claimed for his followers, the Mormons.

Mormons: Members of the Church of Jesus Christ of Latter-Day Saints. *Latter-Day* means "modern," while *saints* are people who dedicate their lives to following God's teachings.

A Persecuted Group   The Mormons were members of the Church of Jesus Christ of Latter-Day Saints. This new church was founded in New York by Joseph Smith in 1830. Smith taught that he had received a sacred book, *The Book of Mormon*, from an angel. He believed that it was his task to create a community of believers who would serve God faithfully.

Smith's followers lived in close communities, working hard and sharing their goods. Yet wherever they settled—first New York, then Ohio, Missouri, and Illinois—they were persecuted by their neighbors.

Many people were offended by the Mormons' teachings, especially their acceptance of polygamy—the practice of having more than one wife. Others resented the Mormons' rapidly growing power and wealth. In 1844, resentment turned to violence when a mob in Illinois killed Joseph Smith.

After Smith's murder, Brigham Young took over as leader of the Mormons. Young decided to move his community to Utah. There, the Mormons might be left alone to follow their faith in peace.

West to Utah   Young turned out to be a practical as well as pious leader. "Prayer is good," he said, "but when baked potatoes and pudding are needed, prayer will not supply their place."

Young carefully planned every detail of the trek to Utah. The pioneers he led west stopped along the way to build shelters and plant crops for those who would follow.

Even with all this planning, the journey was difficult. "We soon thought it unusual," wrote one Mormon, "to leave a campground without burying one or more persons."

When he arrived at Great Salt Lake, Young laid out his first settlement, Salt Lake City. By the time he died in 1877, Utah had 125,000 Mormons living in 500 settlements.

To survive in this dry country, Mormons had to learn new ways to farm. They built dams, canals, and irrigation ditches to carry precious water from mountain streams to their farms in the valley. With this water, they made the desert bloom.

The Mormons' Legacy   The Mormons were the first Americans to settle the Great Basin. They pioneered the farming methods adopted by later settlers of this dry region. They also helped settlers make their way west. Salt Lake City quickly became an important stop for travelers in need of food and supplies.

To the Mormons, however, their greatest legacy was the faith they planted so firmly in the Utah desert. From its center in Salt Lake City, the Mormon church has grown into a worldwide religion with more than 7 million members.

When Mormons were unable to purchase wagons or oxen for the journey to Utah, they pulled their belongings in handcarts.

16.8 The Forty-Niners

In 1848, carpenter James Marshall was building a sawmill on the American River in northern California. Suddenly, he spotted something shining in the water. "I reached my hand down and picked it up," he wrote later. "It made my heart thump, for I felt certain it was gold."

When word of Marshall's discovery leaked out, people across California dropped everything to race to the goldfields. "All were off to the mines," wrote a minister, "some on horses, some on carts, and some on crutches."

The World Rushes In　By 1849, tens of thousands of gold seekers from around the world had joined the California gold rush. About two thirds of these **forty-niners** were Americans. The rest came from Mexico, South America, Europe, Australia, and even China.

The forty-niners' first challenge was simply getting to California. From China and Australia, they had to brave the rough crossing of the Pacific Ocean. From the East, many traveled by ship to Panama in Central America, crossed through dangerous jungles to the Pacific side, and boarded ships north to San Francisco. Others made the difficult journey overland.

Most forty-niners were young, and almost all were men. When Luzena Wilson arrived in Sacramento with her family, a miner offered her $5 for her biscuits just to have "bread made by a woman." When she hesitated, he doubled his offer. "Women were scarce in those days," she wrote. "I lived six months in Sacramento and saw only two."

The search for gold was difficult. Miners spent long days searching through the mud and stones of freezing streams for this precious metal.

Life in the Mining Camps Wherever gold was spotted, mining camps with names like Mad Mule Gulch and You Bet popped up overnight. At Coyote Diggings, Luzena found "a row of canvas tents." A few months later, "there were two thousand men…and the streets were lined with drinking saloons and gambling tables." Merchants made fortunes selling eggs for $6 a dozen and flour for $400 a barrel.

With no police to keep order, the camps were rough places. Miners frequently fought over the boundaries of their claims, and they took it on themselves to punish crimes. "In the short space of twenty-four hours," wrote Louise Clappe, "we have had murders, fearful accidents, bloody deaths, a mob, whippings, a hanging, an attempt at suicide, and a fatal duel."

Digging for gold was hard and tedious work. The miners spent long days digging up mud, dirt, and stones while standing knee-deep in icy streams. All too soon, the easy-to-find gold was gone. "The day of quick fortune-making is over," wrote a miner in 1851. "There are thousands of men now in California who would gladly go home if they had the money."

Miners shoveled gravel into a narrow box called a *sluice*. The water running through washed away the lighter particles, and the gold remained.

The Forty-Niners' Legacy By 1852, the gold rush was over. While it lasted, about 250,000 people flooded into California. For California's Indians, the legacy of this invasion was dreadful. Between 1848 and 1870, warfare and disease reduced their number from about 150,000 to just 30,000. In addition, many Californios lost their land to the newcomers.

The forty-niners also left a prosperous legacy. By 1850, California had enough people to become the first state in the far west. These new Californians helped to transform the Golden State into a diverse land of economic opportunity.

16.9 The Chinese

Gam Saan—"Gold Mountain"—was what people in China called California in 1848. To poor and hungry Chinese peasants, Gam Saan sounded like paradise. There, they were told, "You will have great pay, large houses, and food and clothing of the finest description…. Money is in great plenty."

By 1852, more than 20,000 Chinese had ventured across the Pacific to California. That year, one of every ten Californians was Chinese.

An Uncertain Welcome At first the Chinese were welcome. Lai Chun-Chuen, an early immigrant, observed that they "were received like guests" and "greeted with favor." In 1852, the governor of California praised Chinese immigrants as "one of the most worthy classes of our newly adopted citizens."

As gold mining became more difficult, however, attitudes toward immigrants began to change. A miner from Chile complained, "The Yankee regarded every man but…an American as an interloper [intruder] who had no right to come to California and pick up the gold." The Chinese, too, came under attack.

American miners called on the government to drive foreigners out of the goldfields. In 1852, the state legislature passed a law requiring foreign miners to pay a monthly fee for a license to mine. As the tax collectors arrived in the camps, most of the foreigners left. One traveler saw them "scattered along the roads in every direction," like refugees fleeing an invading army.

Thousands of Chinese left their homeland and flocked to the California goldfields. Most failed to strike it rich. However, many settled in California's Central Valley, where their knowledge of farming helped the area develop.

The Chinese Stay The Chinese, however, paid the tax and stayed on. When the miners' tax failed to drive off the Chinese, Americans tried to bully them into leaving. Whites hacked off the long *queues,* or braids, worn by Chinese men. They burned the shacks of Chinese miners. Beatings followed burnings.

Discouraged Chinese immigrants left the mines to open restaurants, laundries, and stores in California's growing cities. "The best eating houses in San Francisco," one miner wrote, were those opened by the Chinese. So many Chinese settled in San Francisco that local newspapers called their neighborhood Chinatown. Today, Chinatown remains the oldest and largest Chinese community in the United States.

Other Chinese put their farming skills to work in California's fertile Central Valley. They drained swamps and dug irrigation ditches to water arid fields. In time, they would help transform California into America's fruit basket and salad bowl.

The Legacy of the Chinese Immigrants Most of the Chinese who came to California in search of gold hoped to return to China as rich men. A few did just that. Most, however, stayed on in America. Despite continued prejudice against them, their hard work, energy, and skills greatly benefited California and other western states. "In mining, farming, in factories and in the labor generally of California," observed a writer in 1876, "the employment of the Chinese has been found most desirable."

The Chinese not only helped to build the West, but they also made it a more interesting place to live. Wherever they settled, Chinese immigrants brought with them the arts, tastes, scents, and sounds of one of the world's oldest and richest cultures.

16.10 Chapter Summary

In the 1800s, the West became a magnet for people seeking adventure and opportunity. In this chapter, you learned about the people who settled the West. You used an illustration of a western town to study eight groups of settlers and their contributions to the West.

The Lewis and Clark expedition went west to find the Northwest Passage and to establish friendly relations with the native peoples. By mapping and collecting information about the West, the expedition helped prepare the way for future settlement.

In California, Spanish-speaking settlers followed in the footsteps of missionaries. The Californios' way of life centered on the rancho and the raising of cattle.

Valuable beaver furs—and a life of freedom and adventure—attracted fur trappers to the West. Many of these hardy "mountain men" stayed on as scouts, guides, and traders.

Missionaries traveled to Oregon and other western territories in hopes of converting Indians to Christianity. Although they made few converts, the missionaries attracted other settlers to the West.

Many women pioneers sought new opportunities in the West. Besides working to establish homes and farms, women brought education and culture to new settlements.

Mormon pioneers traveled to Utah in search of religious freedom. The Mormons built cities and towns, and they introduced new methods of farming to the dry plains.

Gold seekers from all over the world rushed to California in 1849. Few became rich, but many stayed to help build the economy of the new state.

The gold rush attracted thousands of Chinese immigrants to California. Although they often had to fight prejudice, most of them remained in the United States, working as laborers and starting new businesses and farms.

Many settlers who moved west built small towns. Some became huge cities. This painting shows an already sprawling Los Angeles, California, in the early 1800s.

Why does this man need a burro?

What do these packs contain?

How is this man helping the other man?

Mexicano Contributions to the Southwest

17.1 Introduction

When the United States annexed the Southwest after the war with Mexico, it acquired people as well as land. Nearly 80,000 *Mexicanos,* or Mexican citizens, lived in the territories given up by Mexico in the Treaty of Guadalupe Hidalgo. Some moved to Mexico after the war. But most remained in the Southwest and became citizens of the United States.

The treaty with Mexico promised Mexican Americans full citizenship rights, the right to keep their property, and the right to use their language. These promises were not kept. Many of the Anglo Americans who settled the Southwest looked down on Mexicanos.

Armed with the belief that they were a superior people, white settlers pushed Mexicanos off their land. They made it illegal for Mexicano children to speak Spanish in schools. They found ways to keep Mexicanos from exercising their right to vote.

Mexicanos protested each of these assaults on their rights. But the government did little to protect them. "The language now spoken in our country, the laws which govern us, the faces which we encounter daily are those of the masters of the land," wrote Mariano Vallejo in California. "He wishes his own well-being and not ours."

Even though the newcomers had little respect for the culture of Mexican Americans, they freely adopted much that was useful from the Mexican **heritage**. Spanish words such as *barbecue, chocolate, tornado,* and *corral* became part of their language. Across the Southwest, Americans used Spanish names for mountains, rivers, and cities. Whites also adopted Mexican foods, laws, technology, and architecture. In this chapter, you will learn about these and other contributions that Mexicanos made to American life.

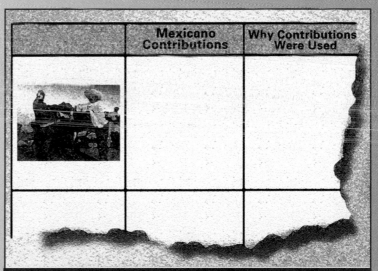

	Mexicano Contributions	Why Contributions Were Used

Graphic Organizer: Matrix
You will use this matrix to learn about Mexicano contributions to the Southwest.

tradition: a belief, custom, or way of doing something that has existed for a long time

17.2 Mexicano Mining Contributions

Mining in the West developed in three waves—gold, silver, and copper. Each wave depended on the contribution of Mexican miners. Mexicanos came to the Southwest with a rich mining **tradition**. They knew where to look for precious metals and how to get them out of the ground.

Gold Mining The Americans who rushed to California in 1849 had many skills. But they knew nothing about mining. Mexicanos introduced them to the *batea,* or gold pan. Miners scooped up mud from streambeds with the batea. Then they swished it around to wash away the lightweight sand. The heavier flakes of gold sank to the bottom of the pan.

Mexicanos also brought the riffle box to the goldfields. The bottom of this long box was crossed with pieces of wood called *riffles*. As mud washed through the box, the heavy gold sank and was trapped behind the riffles. The riffle box was used extensively by both American and Chinese miners.

Before long, miners discovered that the gold they were picking up in streams came from veins of quartz rock in the Sierra Nevada. Quartz mining was a mystery to Americans, but it was familiar to Mexicanos. Mexicanos taught other miners how to dig the quartz out of mountains. They also showed miners how to use a simple *arrastra,* or grinding mill, to crush the rock so they could easily remove the gold.

Shown below is an arrastra, or grinding mill. A horse moved a round stone to crush gold-bearing rocks from which miners could remove the precious metal.

Silver and Copper Mining A Mexican miner sparked the West's first big silver strike. In 1859, a prospector named Henry Comstock was looking for gold in Nevada. Much to his annoyance, his gold was mixed with a lot of worthless "blue stuff." One day, a Mexicano miner looked at the blue stuff and started shouting, *"Mucha plata! Mucha plata!"* ("Much silver!") In its first 20 years, the Comstock lode yielded over $300 million in silver and gold.

Mexicanos discovered copper in the Southwest in the early 1800s. When Americans began to mine copper in Arizona, they turned to Mexican miners for help. By 1940, Arizona mines had produced $3 billion worth of copper—copper that carried electricity and telephone calls to millions of homes across America.

17.3 Cattle Ranching

Cattle ranching in the West was built upon traditions brought north from Mexico. Spanish colonists imported the first cattle to the Americas. The animals adapted well to the dry conditions of Mexico and the American Southwest. In time, millions of Spanish cattle ran wild in Texas and California.

Spanish cattle were thin, wiry creatures with long, wide-spreading horns. They moved quickly and were dangerous. *Californios* (Mexicanos in California) often found themselves dodging behind trees or diving into ditches to escape the charge of an angry longhorn.

With cattle so abundant, Californios and *Tejanos* (Mexicanos in Texas) found ranching to be a good business. So did the Americans who learned the cattle business from Mexican *rancheros,* or ranchers.

The Rancho   Western cattle ranching was nothing like dairy farming in the East. Dairy farms in the East were small family businesses that produced mostly milk, butter, and cheese. Compared to these farms, western ranchos were huge. In the arid Southwest, large grants of land were needed to provide enough food and water for cattle herds. Instead of dairy products, the main products of ranchos were meat, hides, and tallow.

Ranch life followed traditions that had been developed in Spain and perfected in Mexico. Rancheros spent most of their day on horseback, overseeing their land and herds. Caring for the cattle was the work of hired *vaqueros,* or cowboys.

The Roundup   Among the vaqueros' most important jobs were the *rodeo,* or roundup, and branding (using a hot iron to burn a mark into the hide of cattle). Branding was essential because herds belonging to different owners mixed together on unfenced grasslands. To avoid conflicts, every owner had to mark his cattle with a distinctive brand.

During the rodeo, vaqueros drove unbranded calves to a roundup area. There, the calves were branded with the brand their mothers bore.

As Americans took up ranching, they adopted the rancheros' practice of branding cattle. Along with cowboys and the roundup, cattle brands are still part of ranch life in the West.

During the rodeo, or roundup, vaqueros drove unmarked cattle to special roundup areas. There the animals were branded with a rancho's distinctive identification mark. Such a practice was necessary because cattle belonging to different owners grazed together on the same open range.

adapt: to change in order to survive in a new or different environment or situation

17.4 The Cowboy

Hollywood movies make it seem that nothing is more American than the western cowboy. Cowboys, however, learned their job from the Mexican vaquero. Across the Southwest, vaqueros were admired for their skill at riding, roping, and handling cattle. American cowboys adopted the vaqueros' clothes and gear, and much of their language.

Cowboy Clothes and Gear   From head to toe, cowboys dressed in clothing borrowed from the vaqueros. For example, the cowboys' "ten-gallon hats," which shaded their eyes and sometimes served as a water pail or a pillow, came from the vaqueros' wide-brimmed *sombreros*. The leather chaps that protected the cowboys' legs from cacti and sagebrush were modeled on the vaqueros' *chaparreras*. The high-heeled, pointed-toe boots that slipped so easily into the cowboys' stirrups were based on the vaqueros' *botas*. Even the *poncho* that protected cowboys from cold and rain was borrowed from the vaqueros.

Mexicanos also invented the western (or cowboy) saddle, with its useful horn. The saddles brought to America from Europe did not have horns. When a vaquero on a European saddle roped a steer, he had to tie his rope to the horse's tail to keep it anchored. This method was hard on both the horse and the rider. By adding a horn to the saddle, vaqueros made their job easier—and their horses' job as well.

Cowboys borrowed another essential piece of gear from the vaqueros— *la riata* (the lariat). Vaqueros were masters of the art of throwing a 60-foot rope long distances with amazing accuracy. This skill was especially useful for roping calves during a roundup. In a remarkable display of roping skill, a vaquero named José Romero once roped a full-grown eagle right out of the sky!

From his hat to his boots, the American cowboy copied the dress of the Mexican vaquero. Each item of the vaquero's clothing helped him with his work. His sombrero shaded him from the sun. His neckerchief, when worn over his mouth, protected him from dust. His high-heeled, pointed boots kept him secure in the stirrups of his saddle.

Cowboy Lingo
American cowboys borrowed or adapted many ranching words from the vaqueros as well. The terms *bronco, stampede, corral, lasso, burro, buckaroo,* and *vamoose* all come from Spanish-Mexican words. So do *mesa, canyon, mesquite, chaparral,* and other terms used to describe the Southwestern landscape. The cowboy slang word for jail, *hoosegow,* came from the Spanish *juzgado.* And of course, the terms *ranch* and *rancher* came from *rancho* and *ranchero.*

17.5 Sheep Raising

In New Mexico, the most important industry was sheep raising. From the founding of the province up to the Mexican Cession, sheep fed, clothed, and supported Spanish and Mexican settlers.

The Spanish brought a long tradition of sheep raising to the Americas. Two kinds of sheep were raised in Spain—the beautiful *merinos* with their fine wool, and the ugly *churros* with their coarse wool. The Spanish brought the scrawny churro to New Mexico, and for good reason. This tough little sheep knew how to survive in a dry environment like that of the Southwest.

The Spanish Sheep-Raising System When Americans came to New Mexico, they did not think of sheep raising as a business. In the East, a farmer might raise a few sheep as a sideline, but not large herds. Once they saw the Spanish sheep-raising system in New Mexico, however, some Americans changed their minds.

Under the Spanish system, sheep raising was a big, well-organized business. The Spanish governor of New Mexico, for example, once owned 2 million sheep and employed 2,700 workers.

At the top of this business stood the *patron*, or owner of the herds. Below him were several layers of managers. These supervisors and

Sheep raising was the most important industry in New Mexico when the area belonged to Mexico. An owner of a sheep ranch might have over a million sheep.

range bosses spent their days on horseback, checking range conditions and the health of the sheep.

The lowest-level worker was the *pastor*, or herder. Each pastor was responsible for 1,500 to 2,000 sheep. A pastor stayed with his flock night and day, slowly guiding it from place to place so that the sheep could graze as they moved. During spring lambing season, the pastor assisted with difficult births, cared for orphaned lambs, and helped the newborns survive. One pastor described this busy time as a "month-long hell of worry and toil."

Americans Adopt the Spanish System Americans soon adopted the Spanish system as their own. Large-scale sheep raising spread from New Mexico across the Southwest. In California, the churro was crossed with the merino to produce a sheep with far better wool. As a result, between 1862 and 1880, U.S. wool production soared from 5 million to 22 million pounds a year.

irrigation: a system for bringing water to farmland by artificial means, such as using a dam to trap water and ditches to channel it to fields

17.6 Irrigated Farming

Americans coming to the Southwest knew as little about irrigated farming as they did about mining, cattle ranching, and sheep raising. In the East, enough rain fell year-round to water a farmer's crops. **Irrigation** was unnecessary and unknown. But in the Southwest, where six months could go by with no rain, irrigation was essential.

Mexican settlers in the Southwest brought with them irrigation techniques that had been developed centuries earlier in Spain and North Africa. They borrowed other techniques from the Pueblo Indians of New Mexico. When settlers first arrived, the Pueblos were irrigating between 15,000 and 25,000 acres of crop land in the arid Rio Grande Valley.

The Mexican System of Irrigation   Bringing water to fields involved an enormous amount of work. First, farmers had to redirect water from local streams to their fields. They began by building a dam of rocks, earth, and brush across the stream. The water that backed up behind the dam was brought to the fields by irrigation ditches.

To keep from wasting this precious water, Mexicanos carefully leveled their fields. Then they divided the fields into squares. Each square was marked off by a wall of earth high enough to hold in water. When one square had been soaked with water, farmers made a hole in its wall. The water then flowed to the next square. The farmers continued in this way until the entire field was soaked. This method of irrigation was known as "the Mexican system."

America's Fruit Basket   Using crops introduced by Mexicanos and the Mexican system of irrigation, American settlers turned the Southwest into America's fruit basket. Among the many fruits brought by Mexicanos to the Southwest were grapes, dates, olives, apples, walnuts, pears, plums, peaches, apricots, and quinces. Mexicano settlers also brought the first citrus fruits—lemons, limes, and oranges—to the region. Many of these fruits were unknown in the East, where the climate was too cold for them to grow. But they thrived in sunny Arizona and California. With the help of Mexicano farmworkers, American farmers transformed dry deserts into irrigated fruit orchards and citrus groves.

The Mexicanos introduced a system of irrigation that allowed settlers in the Southwest to turn deserts into productive, fertile fields.

17.7 Mexican Food

In 1835, William Heath Davis became one of the first Americans to settle in California. There he got his first taste of Mexican food. Davis later wrote of the Californios:

> *Their tables were frugally [simply] furnished, the food clean and inviting, consisting mainly of good beef broiled on an iron rod, or steaks with onions, also mutton [sheep], chicken, eggs.... The bread was tortillas; sometimes made with yeast. Beans were a staple dish.... Their meat stews were excellent when not too highly seasoned with red pepper.*

Davis may not have known it, but the food he was enjoying in California brought together the best of two worlds.

Corn, a food of the native Indians, was a staple in the Mexicano diet. Here, a Mexicano woman is grinding corn that she will use to make a flat cornbread called *tortillas*.

A Food Revolution   The conquest of Mexico in 1521 began one of the great food revolutions in history. The Spanish came to Mexico in search of gold, but the greatest treasures they found were Indian foods unknown in Europe. These "New World" foods included corn, tomatoes, chocolate, peanuts, vanilla, beans, squash, avocados, coconuts, sunflower seeds, and chili peppers.

The Spanish shipped these new foods back to Spain. From there they spread throughout Europe, greatly expanding people's food choices.

In turn, the Spanish brought the foods of the "Old World" to Mexico. They introduced meats such as pork, beef, lamb, chicken, and goat. They brought nuts and grains such as almonds, walnuts, rice, wheat, and barley. They planted fruits and vegetables such as apples, oranges, grapes, olives, lettuce, carrots, sugarcane, and potatoes (which they discovered in Peru). And they introduced herbs and spices such as cinnamon, parsley, coriander, oregano, and black pepper.

A New Style of Cooking   Mexican cooks combined these Old and New World foods to create a rich and flavorful style of cooking that was neither Indian nor Spanish. It was distinctly Mexican.

As Americans settled the Southwest, they were introduced to Mexican food. Many of them liked the new tastes, and they borrowed recipes from Mexicano cooks. In Texas, the mingling of Mexican and American dishes resulted in a style of cooking known as "Tex-Mex." And across America, a spicy stew of beef and beans known simply as "chili" became as American as apple pie.

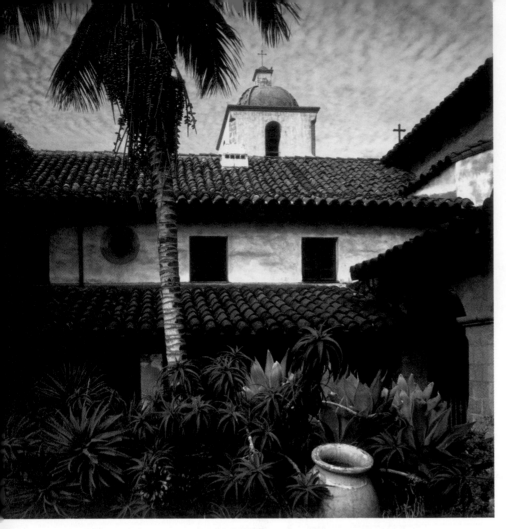

Courtyards, rounded arches, thick adobe walls, and red tile roofs are characteristics of Spanish-style architecture.

17.8 Spanish-style Architecture

Throughout the Southwest, the Mexicano contribution to architecture is easy to see. Many buildings can be found with the thick walls, red tile roofs, rounded arches, and courtyards that are typical of Spanish architecture.

Spanish architecture took root in Mexico during the colonial period. Mexican settlers brought their knowledge of this tradition to the Southwest. Their missions, homes, and other structures were simple and attractive. And they were ideally suited to the hot, dry climate of the Southwest.

Adobe Buildings   Since wood was sparse in the Southwest, Mexicanos used adobe bricks as their main building material. *Adobe* is a mixture of earth, grass, and water that is shaped into bricks and baked in the sun. Mexicanos covered their adobe homes with colorful red clay tiles. Besides being attractive and fireproof, a tile roof kept the adobe walls from being washed away during heavy rains.

Many adobe buildings featured patios and verandas. A *patio* is a roofless inner courtyard, often located at the center of a home. A *veranda* is a roofed porch or balcony extending along the outside of a building. Patios and verandas allowed Mexicanos to spend much of their time outdoors while still protected from the hot sun and dry desert winds.

Newcomers Adopt the Spanish Style   Americans moving to the Southwest quickly saw the advantages of building with adobe. Because of their thick walls, adobe structures stayed cooler in summer and warmer in winter than the wood buildings that Americans from the East were used to. Adobe structures could also be easily constructed from locally available materials.

American settlers used adobe to build not only homes, but also courthouses, trading posts, post offices, and other buildings. Later, builders adapted Spanish architecture to new materials such as concrete and stucco. By the 1930s, nearly a million Spanish-style homes had been built in California. "Who would live in a structure of wood and brick if they could get a palace of mud?" wrote an admiring easterner. "The adobes to me [make] the most picturesque and comfortable [homes]…and harmonize… with the whole nature of the landscape."

17.9 Mexican Laws

Two very different legal traditions came together in the Southwest. The American legal tradition was based on English law. The Mexicano legal tradition was rooted in Spanish law. Both traditions would shape laws in the West. But Mexicano law was particularly important in three areas—mining law, water law, and community property law.

Mining Law   Before the discovery of gold in California, there was so little mining in the United States that Americans had no mining law. Once in the goldfields, the forty-niners desperately needed rules to keep order. With the help of Mexicano miners, Americans developed a "law of the mines" based on Mexican mining law. California miners later carried this law of the mines to other parts of the Southwest.

Water Law   The water law brought west by Americans worked well enough in the East, where rainfall was abundant. Under American law, water flowing across a field or farm belonged to the owner of that land. Landowners could use their water in whatever ways they wanted.

This principle did not work well in the West, where water was scarce and precious. Disputes over who controlled streams led to endless legal conflicts and even water wars.

To end these conflicts, settlers wrote new laws based on Mexican "pueblo law." Pueblo law said that water was too valuable to be owned or controlled by any one person. Instead, water belonged to an entire community and should be used for the benefit of all.

Community Property Law   For women, the most important legal principle borrowed from Mexican law was the idea of community property. In eastern states, married women had few property rights. Any property acquired by a married couple—such as a home, farm, or business—belonged solely to the husband.

In contrast, Mexican law said that all property acquired during a marriage was "community property." If a couple separated, half of that property belonged to the wife, half to the husband.

American settlers liked the idea of sharing the gains of marriage between husband and wife. Today, Texas, California, New Mexico, Arizona, Idaho, Nevada, Washington, Wisconsin, and Louisiana are all community property states.

The Mexicano legal principle of community property gave women property rights they did not have under British law. According to the Mexican principle, women were entitled to half of all property acquired during a marriage.

17.10 Mexicano Entertainments

The Californios, observed William Heath Davis, "were about the happiest and most contented people I ever saw." Californios worked hard. But they also knew how to entertain themselves with music, dance, and *fiestas* (celebrations). Americans settling the Southwest shared in these entertainments.

The Granger Collection, New York

In the picture above, the couple is performing the fandango. During this popular Mexican dance, the man and the woman play castanets, which are small pieces of wood held in the palm of the hand and clicked together.

Music and Dancing   Mexicano music greatly influenced country and western music in the Southwest. The most important contribution was the *corrido,* or folk ballad. A corrido is a dramatic story sung to the accompaniment of guitars. The subjects of corridos ranged from exciting tales of heroes and bandits to sad songs of love and betrayal.

American settlers greatly admired the color and energy of traditional Mexicano dance. Dancing was an important part of any Mexicano fiesta. Favorite dances included the *jota*, the *fandango*, and *la bamba*. The last of these, the bamba, was danced by a young woman balancing a full glass of water on her head. Generations of schoolchildren learned another popular dance, the *jarabe tapatío*, or "Mexican hat dance," as part of their southwestern cultural heritage.

Fiestas and Rodeos   Throughout the year, Mexicanos held a variety of religious fiestas. One of the most important honored Our Lady of Guadalupe, the patron saint of Mexico. In San Antonio, Texas, Tejanos marked this day (December 12) with an elaborate procession to the cathedral. After attending church services, the Tejanos danced all night long in their homes.

Today, the most widely celebrated Mexicano holiday is *El Cinco de Mayo* (the Fifth of May). This holiday commemorates an important victory in Mexico's fight for independence from French rule in 1862. Cinco de Mayo fiestas bring together Mexican and non-Mexican Americans to enjoy Mexicano music, dance, and food.

For millions of Americans, rodeo is an exciting professional sport. Rodeo's roots go back to cattle roundups on Mexicano ranchos. During these get-togethers, Mexicano cowboys competed with each other in events such as calf roping, bull riding, and bronco busting. American cowboys joined in these contests, and soon rodeos became annual events in western cities. To its many fans, the rodeo, with its mixed Mexicano and American heritage, represents the best of the West.

17.11 Chapter Summary

In this chapter, you learned about Mexicano contributions to the culture of the Southwest. You used a matrix to organize your information. Movies and television often portray the settling of the West as a story of white pioneers taming the wilderness. As you have seen, the story is not that simple. Long before whites arrived, Mexicanos had learned to survive and even thrive in the harsh landscape of the Southwest. Although often mistreated by pioneers from the East, their knowledge would prove to be more valuable than gold to the newcomers.

American settlers learned about mining, cattle ranching, cowboy life, and sheep raising from Mexicanos. They adopted irrigation techniques that had been pioneered by Mexicanos and by Pueblo Indians. They learned to appreciate Mexicano food. They borrowed the Mexicanos' architectural styles and laws. And they learned to enjoy Mexicano entertainments.

Today, Mexicano culture survives in such American adaptations as the organization of ranches, Spanish-style homes, popular foods, and legal traditions regarding water and community property. The American language is enriched by Spanish and Mexican words like *patio, rodeo,* and *poncho.* From San Francisco to San Antonio, hundreds of place names in the West and Southwest echo the Spanish-Mexican heritage. Millions of Americans celebrate the Mexican holiday Cinco de Mayo. It is hard to imagine what the United States would be like without this rich legacy.

Mexicano contributions played a central role in turning the Southwestern United States into a unique, prosperous section of the country.

LUCRETIA MOTT.

ELIZABETH CADY STANTON.

LUCY STONE.

JULIA WARD HOWE.

SUSAN B. ANTHONY.

MRS. MARTHA C. WRIGHT.
First President N. Y. State Suffrage
Association, Elected 1860.

MRS. JEAN BROOKS GREENLEAF.
Fourth President N. Y. State Suffrage
Assn. Served 6 years, 1890-96.

REV. ANNA H. SHAW.

MRS. ELIZABETH BOYNTON HAR-
BERT.

Rev. Anna H. Shaw

A. D. R.
© 1887
AC 6294/A00.3

DOROTHEA LYNDE DIX.

This page, from a scrapbook kept by
Mary S. Anthony, pictures women who
led various reform movements.

18

An Era of Reform

18.1 Introduction

In 1851, a group of people gathered in a church to discuss the rights of women. A tall African American woman made her way through the crowd and sat down. Her name was Sojourner Truth. Back when she was a slave, she had learned to pay careful attention to white people. Now she listened as whites discussed whether women should have the same rights as men.

Sojourner heard one minister after another explain that women didn't need more rights because they weren't smart or strong enough to do much besides raise children. Women, they argued, needed help from men. One man summed it up by saying, "Women are weak."

With that, the former slave had heard enough. She rose slowly to her stately height of six feet and walked to the pulpit. The room grew quiet as everyone waited for her to speak.

"The man over there says women need to be helped into carriages and lifted over ditches and over puddles, and have the best places everywhere," she began. "Nobody helped me into carriages or over puddles, or gives me the best place."

Her voice rose to a thunderous pitch. "And ain't I a woman? Look at my arm! I have plowed and planted and gathered into barns, and no man could head [outdo] me—and ain't I a woman? I could work as much and eat as much as a man—when I could get it—and bear the lash as well! I have borne thirteen children, and seen most of 'em sold into slavery, and when I cried out with my mother's grief, none but Jesus heard me—and ain't I a woman?"

When she finished, people applauded. Some cried. One witness said, "She had taken us up in her strong arms and carried us safely."

As a woman and a former slave, Sojourner Truth represented two of the great reform movements in America in the 1800s. Between about 1820 and 1850, American **reformers** devoted themselves to such causes as ending slavery, promoting women's rights, and improving education. As you will read in this chapter, women like Sojourner Truth not only participated in these movements, but emerged as powerful leaders.

Graphic Organizer: Illustration
You will use this illustration to learn about the Era of Reform.

18.2 Planting the Seeds of Reform

It was fitting that the meeting attended by Sojourner Truth took place in a church. Many of the impulses to reform American society began with new religious movements.

Second Great Awakening: A revival of religious feeling and belief in the 1820s and 1830s. The First Great Awakening swept through the American colonies in the 1700s.

The Second Great Awakening   One such movement was the **Second Great Awakening** of the 1820s and 1830s. Day after day, people gathered in big white tents to hear a message of hope. "Repent and you shall be saved," preachers cried. Their listeners prayed, shouted, and sang hymns. Sometimes they cried for hours or fell down in frenzies.

Like the First Great Awakening during colonial days, this religious movement fired people's emotions and inspired them to become better Christians. But it also offered something new. In the past, most Christian ministers had said that people didn't control their own fates. God had already decided who would be saved and who would suffer eternal punishment. Therefore, there was little reason to perform good deeds like helping the poor.

In the early 1800s, however, preachers told their flocks that everyone could gain forgiveness for their sins. And one way to be saved was to do good works. Christians, they said, could build "heaven on Earth."

Preachers at religious meetings, such as the one pictured below, proclaimed that people could earn salvation by doing good works. This message encouraged many people to work to improve society.

The Granger Collection, New York

This optimistic message attracted enthusiastic followers throughout the West and North. The movement inspired many women to become preachers and missionaries. And it gave men and women alike a reason to work for the improvement of society.

Optimistic Ideas   Other optimistic, nonreligious ideas also inspired Americans during this time. Writers urged people to follow their own hearts to improve their lives. One of the most famous was Henry David Thoreau. "If a man does not keep pace with his companions," wrote Thoreau, "perhaps it is because he hears a different drummer. Let him step to the music he hears."

To many people, the election of Andrew Jackson as president in 1828 was proof that individuals could change society for the better. Born in a backwoods settlement, Jackson had never attended college. Yet he had achieved fame as a soldier and Indian fighter, and eventually became president. His supporters rejoiced that ordinary people could participate in democracy and even rise to positions of leadership.

18.3 Reforming the Treatment of Prisoners and the Mentally Ill

One day in 1841, a Boston woman named Dorothea Dix agreed to teach Sunday school at a jail. Dix believed that she was simply doing her Christian duty. She didn't plan on starting a reform movement. But what she witnessed that day changed her life forever.

Observing Horrors   Dix was horrified by what she found. Many inmates were bound in chains and locked in cages. Children who had been accused of minor thefts were jailed with adult criminals. Were conditions this bad everywhere? she wondered.

To find out, Dix visited hundreds of jails and prisons throughout Massachusetts. She also visited debtors' prisons, or jails for people who owed money. At about this time, more than 75,000 Americans were in debtors' prisons. Most of them owed less than 20 dollars. While they were locked up, they could not earn money to repay their debts. As a result, they remained imprisoned for years.

The Plight of the Mentally Ill   What shocked Dix most of all was the way mentally ill people were treated. Most people who were judged "insane" were locked away in dirty, crowded prison cells. If they misbehaved, they were whipped. Dix and other reformers believed that insanity should be treated as a disease, not a crime.

Horrified by what she saw during a visit to a local jail, Dorothea Dix worked tirelessly to improve conditions for prisoners and the mentally ill.

The Granger Collection, New York

Before the reforms brought about by Dorothea Dix's work, many people were put in prison simply because they owed money. Most of them owed less than 20 dollars.

Massachusetts did have one hospital for the mentally ill, called an *asylum*. Sending the mentally ill there was much better than putting them in prison. They needed treatment and care, not punishment. But only the wealthy could afford to send a family member to the asylum. Even so, it was filled to overflowing. The state needed more mental hospitals.

Dix believed that such conditions existed mostly because people didn't know about them. For two years, she quietly gathered firsthand information about the horrors she had seen. Then she prepared a detailed report for the Massachusetts state legislature. "I come as the advocate of helpless, forgotten, insane, and idiotic men and women," she said. "I proceed, gentlemen, to briefly call your attention to the present state of insane persons, confined in cages, closets, cellars, stalls, pens! Chained, naked, beaten with rods, and lashed into obedience."

Establishing Better Conditions

Shocked by Dix's report, the lawmakers ordered thousands of copies to be printed and distributed. They also voted to create public asylums for the mentally ill.

Inspired by her success in Massachusetts, Dix visited prisons in other states as well. After she prepared reports demanding justice for the mentally ill, those states also created special mental hospitals.

Dix continued working on behalf of prisoners and the mentally ill for the rest of her life. By the time she died in 1887, state governments no longer put debtors in prison. Most had created special justice systems for children in trouble. And many had outlawed cruel punishments, such as branding people with hot irons.

Dix demonstrated that reformers, including women, could lead society to make significant changes. But to do so they needed courage, dedication, and a willingness to speak out in public against injustices.

18.4 Improving Education

A second reform movement that won support in the 1800s was the effort to make education available to more children. The man who led this movement was Horace Mann, "the father of American public schools."

public schools: schools that are paid for by taxes and managed by local government for the benefit of the general public

The Need for Public Schools   As a boy in Massachusetts in the early 1800s, Horace Mann attended school only ten weeks a year. The rest of the time, he had to work on the family farm.

Mann was lucky to have even this limited chance to attend school. In Massachusetts, Puritans had established town schools. Few other areas had **public schools**—schools paid for by taxes. Wealthy parents sent their children to private school or hired tutors at home. On the frontier, 60 children might attend a part-time, one-room school. Their teachers had limited education and received little pay. Most children simply did not go to school at all.

In the cities, some poor children stole, destroyed property, and set fires. Reformers believed that education would help these children escape poverty and become good citizens. Influenced by its big cities, New York set up public elementary schools in every town as early as the 1820s.

Meanwhile, in Massachusetts, Horace Mann became the state's supervisor of education. In towns and villages, he spoke out on the need for public schools. "Our means of education," he stated, "are the grand machinery by which the 'raw material' of human nature can be worked up into inventors and discoverers, into skilled artisans and scientific farmers."

Citizens in Massachusetts responded to Mann's message. They voted to pay taxes to build better schools, to pay teachers higher salaries, and to establish special training schools for teachers.

An Unfinished Reform   By 1850, many states in the North and West used Mann's ideas. Soon most white children, especially boys, attended free public schools.

But America still did not offer education to everyone. Most high schools and colleges did not admit girls. States as far north as Illinois passed laws to keep African

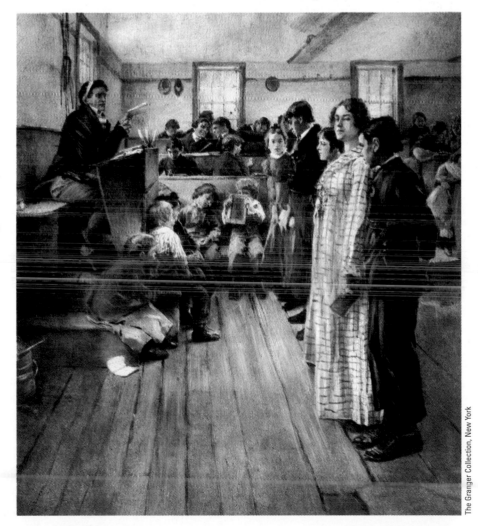

Prior to the reforms in public education led by Horace Mann, most children did not attend school. Those that did usually had to suffer overcrowded classrooms, like the one shown below, and poorly trained teachers.

The Granger Collection, New York

Americans out of public schools. When towns did allow African Americans to attend school, most made them go to separate schools that received less money. In the South, few girls and no African Americans could attend public schools.

Education for girls and women did make some progress. In 1837, Ohio's Oberlin College became the first college to admit women as well as men. When states started the first public universities in the 1860s, most accepted female students.

African Americans, however, had few options. When Prudence Crandall admitted an African American girl to her girls' school in Connecticut, white parents took their children out of the school. Crandall responded by having all African American students. Enraged, white people threw stones at the school and had Crandall jailed. After two years, she was forced to close her school.

Horace Mann realized that much more needed to be done to increase educational opportunity for women and African Americans. He became the first president of a new college for men and women, Antioch College in Ohio. There, he urged his students to become involved in improving society. "Be ashamed to die," he told them, "until you have won some victory for humanity."

Sojourner Truth, a former slave, gave speeches throughout the North against slavery and, later, in favor of women's rights.

18.5 Fighting Slavery

In 1835, a poster appeared on walls throughout Washington, D.C. The poster showed two drawings. One drawing, labeled "The Land of the Free," showed the founding fathers reading the Declaration of Independence. The other, labeled "The Home of the Oppressed," showed slaves trudging past the Capitol building, the home of Congress. The poster posed a challenging question: How could America, the "land of the free," still allow slavery? By the 1830s, growing numbers of people were asking this question. They were called **abolitionists**.

The Struggle Begins   Some Americans had opposed slavery even in Revolutionary War times. Quakers stopped owning slaves in 1776. By 1792, every state as far south as Virginia had anti-slavery societies.

Once the slave trade ended in 1808, northern shipping communities had no more interest in slaves. Still, northern factory owners liked the cheap cotton that the South provided. Although slavery ended in the North by the early 1800s, many northerners still accepted southern slavery.

Unlike their neighbors, abolitionists wanted to end slavery. But they did not always agree about how to do it. Radicals tried to inspire slaves to rise up in revolt. Others wanted to find a peaceful way to end slavery immediately. Moderates wanted to give slaveholders time to develop farming methods that didn't rely on slave labor.

From the early days, both blacks and whites worked in the abolition movement, sometimes together, sometimes separately. Black activists often maintained their independence. One African American journalist wrote, "As long as we let them think and act for us…they will outwardly treat us as men, while in their hearts they still hold us as slaves."

In 1831, a deeply religious white man, William Lloyd Garrison, started a fiery abolitionist newspaper, the *Liberator*. Braving the disapproval of many northerners, Garrison demanded the immediate freeing of all slaves. "I will be as harsh as truth," he wrote. "I will not retreat a single inch—and I will be heard." Angry pro-slavery groups destroyed Garrison's printing press and burned his house.

Frederick Douglass Speaks Out   One day, Garrison heard an escaped slave, Frederick Douglass, speaking to a meeting of abolitionists. Over six feet tall, Douglass spoke with a voice like thunder. When he described the cruel treatment of slave children, people cried. When he made fun of ministers who told slaves to love slavery, people laughed. When he finished, Garrison jumped up and cried, "Shall such a man be held a slave in a Christian land?" The crowd called out, "No! No! No!"

Frederick Douglass quickly became a leader in the abolitionist movement. His autobiography (the story of his life) became an instant bestseller. A brilliant, independent thinker, Douglass eventually started his own newspaper, *North Star*. Its motto read, "Right is of no sex— Truth is of no color—God is the father of us all, and we are all Brethren."

Women Get Involved   Many women were inspired by the religious reform movement to become involved in the fight against slavery. Like other abolitionists, they sometimes faced violence. When a young woman named Angelina Grimke spoke against slavery, an anti-abolition mob threw stones. When she kept speaking, they burned the building.

Angelina and her sister Sarah had been raised in a South Carolina slave-holding family. After traveling North and becoming Quakers, they saw slavery in a new way. The two sisters began speaking out about the poverty and pain of slavery. At first they spoke only to other women, but soon they were speaking to large groups of men and women throughout the North. The Grimkes led the way for other women to speak in public.

Some abolitionists, like Sojourner Truth, were former slaves. Truth had always been strongly spiritual and had preached throughout the North at religious meetings and on street corners. But when she met Douglass and Garrison, their enthusiasm inspired her to speak out about slavery. An outstanding speaker, Truth argued that God would end slavery peacefully.

Abolitionists were a minority, even in the North. But their efforts, and the violence directed against them, helped change northerners' attitudes toward slavery. In addition, the anti-slavery fight helped pave the way for the next great reform movement, the struggle for women's rights.

Wilson Chinn, a branded slave from Louisiana, poses with the irons used to chain him.

Courtesy, Museum of Fine Arts, Boston. Reproduced with permission. © 2000, Museum of Fine Arts Boston. All Rights Reserved.

In this painting, women are represented in traditional ways—shy, in the background, or serving men. During the Era of Reform, many women began to work to change and expand the way women were viewed.

18.6 Equal Rights for Women

Women abolitionists were in a strange position. They were trying to convince lawmakers to make slavery illegal, yet they themselves could not vote or hold office. They worked to raise money for the movement, yet their own money and property were controlled by their fathers and husbands. They spoke out against slave beatings, yet their husbands could discipline them whenever they wanted.

Even wealthy women like the Grimke sisters started to see that women and slaves had much in common. "What then can woman do for the slave," asked Angelina, "when she herself is under the feet of man and shamed into silence?"

The Struggle Begins   The organized movement for women's rights was sparked by the friendship between Lucretia Mott and Elizabeth Cady Stanton. The two women met in 1840 at the World Anti-Slavery Convention in London. When they arrived, they were outraged to discover that women were not allowed to speak at the meeting. The men who ran the convention even made women sit in the balcony, behind a curtain!

The men's decision may have backfired, because it was in the balcony that Mott and Stanton met. At first glance, the two women seemed quite different. Mott was 47 years old, the mother of four children, and an active reformer. Inspired by the Grimke sisters and her own Quaker faith, she had preached against slavery in both white and black churches. She had also helped Prudence Crandall try to recruit students for a school for black girls.

Stanton was 25 years old and newly married. She had never spoken in public. As a young girl, she had overheard women beg her father, a judge, to protect them from husbands who had beaten them. He had to tell them that there was no law against it. Later, she attended Troy Female Seminary, the nation's first high school for girls. She knew from her studies in history that America did not treat women fairly. When she met Lucretia Mott in London, she readily agreed that something had to be done about the injustices suffered by women.

Unequal Treatment of Women   Even a fine education like Stanton's did not assure women equal treatment. When Lucy Stone graduated from Oberlin College, the faculty invited her to write a speech. But a man would have to give the speech, since the school would not allow women to speak in public! Stone refused. After graduation, she spoke out for women's rights. Because women could not vote, she refused to pay property taxes. "Woman suffer taxation," she said, "and yet have no representation."

Stone's sister-in-law, Elizabeth Blackwell, wanted to be a doctor. She knew mathematics, science, and history. She had even been tutored by a helpful doctor. Yet she was rejected by 29 medical schools before one finally accepted her. She graduated at the top of her class, becoming the country's first female doctor. Still, no hospitals or doctors would agree to work with her.

To overcome such barriers, women would have to work together. By the time Elizabeth Cady Stanton and Lucretia Mott left London, they had decided "to hold a convention…and form a society to advocate the rights of women."

Declaration of Sentiments: A formal statement of injustices suffered by women, written by the organizers of the Seneca Falls Convention. *Sentiments* means "beliefs" or "convictions."

Elizabeth Cady Stanton was one of the organizers of the Seneca Falls Convention. The image below shows her reading the Declaration of Sentiments to the participants at the convention.

18.7 The Seneca Falls Convention and the Declaration of Sentiments

Eight years passed before Stanton and Mott met again. Over afternoon tea at the home of Mott's sister, they decided to send a notice to the local newspaper announcing a women's convention in Seneca Falls, New York. The organized movement for women's rights was about to begin.

The Declaration of Sentiments   On July 19, 1848, almost 300 people, including 40 men, arrived for the Seneca Falls Convention. Many were abolitionists, Quakers, or other reformers. Some were local housewives, farmers, and factory workers.

The convention organizers modeled their proposal for women's rights, the **Declaration of Sentiments,** on the Declaration of Independence. "We hold these truths to be self-evident," the document began, "that all men and women are created equal."

Just as the Declaration of Independence listed King George's acts of tyranny over the colonists, the new declaration listed acts of tyranny by men over women. Man did not let woman vote. He did not give her property rights, even to her own wages. He did not allow her to practice professions like medicine and law.

Stanton's presentation of the declaration at the convention was her first speech. A few other women also summoned the courage to speak. One of them, Charlotte Woodward, was a 19-year-old factory worker. "Every fiber of my being," she said, "rebelled [against] all the hours that I sat and sewed gloves for a miserable pittance which, after it was earned, could never be mine."

Debate about the Right to Vote The convention passed resolutions in favor of correcting these injustices. Then Stanton proposed that women demand the right to vote. For many, this step was too big. Even Mott cried, "Thou will make us ridiculous! We must go slowly."

At this point, Stanton received powerful support from another participant at the convention, Frederick Douglass. Everyone who believed that black men should have the right to vote, Douglass argued, must also favor giving black women the right to vote. And that meant all women should have this precious right. Inspired by Douglass's speech, the convention voted narrowly to approve this last resolution.

Elizabeth Cady Stanton (above) and Elizabeth Blackwell (below) were two leaders in the early struggle for women's rights.

The Legacy of Seneca Falls The Seneca Falls Convention helped to create an organized campaign for women's rights. Sojourner Truth, who would later mesmerize an audience by asking defiantly, "Ain't I a woman?" became an active campaigner in the movement.

Elizabeth Cady Stanton didn't like speaking at conventions, but she could write moving speeches. Fortunately, she made friends with Susan B. Anthony, a refomer with a flair for public speaking.

While Stanton stayed in Seneca Falls to raise her children, Anthony traveled from town to town, speaking for women's rights. Of their life-long teamwork, Stanton said, "I forged the thunderbolts, she fired them."

Slowly, reformers for women's rights made progress. New York gave women control over their property and wages. Massachusetts and Indiana passed more liberal divorce laws. Elizabeth Blackwell started her own hospital, including a medical school to train other female doctors.

Other reforms would take decades to become reality. Of all the women who signed the declaration at Seneca Falls, just one would live to vote for president legally—Charlotte Woodward.

18.8 Chapter Summary

In this chapter, you read about the reform movements that swept through the United States between about 1820 and 1850. You used an illustration of a protest march to learn about these reforms.

Many reformers were inspired by the Second Great Awakening, which taught Christians to perform good works in order to be saved. Other reformers were inspired by writers, such as Henry David Thoreau, and by the spirit of participation created by Andrew Jackson's presidency.

Dorothea Dix was a pioneer in the movement to reform the treatment of prisoners and the mentally ill. The movement to make education freely available to all was led by Horace Mann.

Women played a key role in the movement to abolish slavery. Former slaves, like Frederick Douglass and Sojourner Truth, added powerful voices to the movement.

The fight to end slavery helped spark the struggle for women's rights. The organized movement for women's rights began with the Seneca Falls Convention and its Declaration of Sentiments.

In the next chapter, you will learn that the reformers' efforts to improve the lives of slaves were unsuccessful.

In 1998, Hilary Rodham Clinton spoke at the 150th anniversary of the Seneca Falls Convention. In her speech, she said, "Much of who women are…today can be traced to the courage, vision, and dedication of the pioneers who came together at Seneca Falls. Now it is our responsibility to finish the work they began."

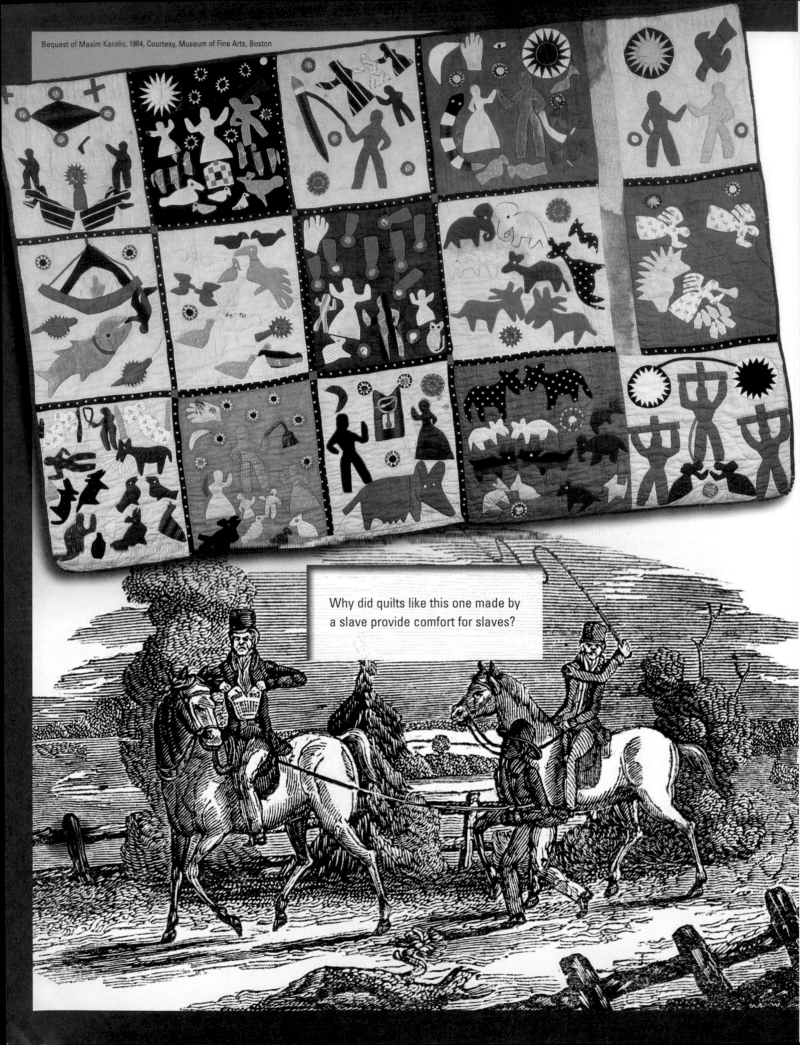

Bequest of Maxim Karolic, 1964, Courtesy, Museum of Fine Arts, Boston

Why did quilts like this one made by a slave provide comfort for slaves?

African Americans at Mid-Century

19.1 Introduction

By 1850, the population of the United States had grown to just over 23 million. This figure included 3.6 million African Americans. The great majority of African Americans lived in slavery. Harriet Powers, the woman who created the quilt you see here, was one of them.

Like many slaves, Harriet Powers grew up hearing Bible stories. In her quilts, Powers used animals and figures from Africa and America to illustrate those stories, along with scenes from her life. Hidden in her images were messages of hope and freedom for slaves.

Not all African Americans were slaves. By mid-century, there were about half a million free blacks as well. Many were former slaves who had escaped to freedom.

Whether African Americans lived in slavery or freedom, **racism** shaped their lives. Everywhere, whites looked down on blacks. Whites ignored the great contributions African Americans made to American life. They thought of the United States as "their country." Such racist thinking prompted African American scholar and reformer W. E. B. Du Bois to ask:

Your country? How came it to be yours? Before the Pilgrims landed we were here. Here we brought you our three gifts and mingled them with yours; a gift of story and song, soft, stirring melody in an...unmelodious land; the gift of sweat and brawn [physical strength] to beat back the wilderness...and lay the foundations of this vast economic empire...the third, a gift of the Spirit.

In this chapter, you will explore the experience of African Americans at mid-century. As you read, you will learn more about the gifts that African Americans brought to America.

Graphic Organizer: Story Quilt
You will use a story quilt to learn about the life of African Americans in the nineteenth century.

The Granger Collection, New York

Free African Americans usually held low-paying jobs. The barber pictured above is one example.

19.2 North and South, Slave and Free

The experiences of African Americans at mid-century depended on where they lived and whether they lived in slavery or freedom. Former slave Frederick Douglass toured the North talking to white audiences about slavery. To him, the biggest difference between slaves and free blacks was their legal status. Free blacks had some rights by law. Slaves did not.

Slaves' Legal Status

Douglass reminded his listeners that the law defined slaves as property, not human beings. Legally, slaveholders could do almost anything with their human property. They could buy and sell slaves. They could leave slaves to their children or heirs. They could give slaves away to settle a bet. But in many states, they could not set slaves free.

"The law gives the master absolute power over the slave," said Douglass. "He may work him, flog him, hire him out, sell him, and, in certain contingencies [circumstances], kill him."

As property, slaves had none of the rights that free people took for granted. "In law, the slave has no wife, no children, no country, no home," Douglass told his listeners. "He can own nothing, possess nothing, acquire nothing."

Rural and Urban Slaves   Most slaves worked on farms and plantations across the South. By 1860, there were also about 70,000 urban slaves living in towns and cities. Most were "hired out," or sent to work in factories, mills, or workshops. The wages they earned belonged to their owners. Often urban slaves were allowed to "live out" on their own, rather than under the watchful eyes of their owners. Because of such freedom, observed Douglass, "A city slave is almost a freeman compared to a slave on a plantation."

Free Blacks in the South   About half of all free African Americans lived in the South. Most worked as laborers, craftspeople, or household servants in towns and cities.

White southerners viewed free blacks as a dangerous group that had to be controlled. "The superior condition of the free persons of color," explained South Carolina slaveholders, "excites discontent among our slaves."

Free blacks were forbidden to own guns. They could not travel freely from town to town or state to state. Blacks were not allowed to work at certain jobs. Such restrictions led Douglass to conclude that, "No colored man is really free in a slaveholding state."

Free Blacks in the North   African Americans in the North lived freer lives. But nowhere were they treated as equal to whites. In many states, African Americans were denied the right to vote. Blacks experienced **discrimination,** or unequal treatment, everywhere they turned. A New Yorker observed that:

> *Even the noblest black is denied that which is free to the vilest [worst] white. The omnibus, the [railroad] car, the ballot-box, the jury box, the halls of legislation, the army, the public lands, the school, the church, the lecture room, the social circle, the [restaurant] table, are all either absolutely or virtually denied to him.*

Black children were often denied entry into public schools. Those states that did educate black children set up separate schools for that purpose. Such policies of **segregation** separated blacks from whites in nearly all public places.

African Americans had trouble finding good jobs. In the 1850s, some 87 percent of free blacks in New York held low-paying jobs. "Why should I strive hard?" asked one young African American. "What are my prospects? To what shall I turn my hand? Shall I be a mechanic? No one will employ me; white boys won't work with me."

Frederick Douglass discovered how deeply rooted this racism was when he tried to join a church in New Bedford, Massachusetts. "I was not allowed a seat in the body of the house on account of my color," Douglass wrote. "I tried all the other churches in New Bedford with the same result."

In 1853, free blacks formed the National Council of Colored People to protest such treatment. The "prejudice and persecution [experienced by] free colored people," declared the council, "would humble the proudest, crush the energies of the strongest, and retard the progress of the swiftest." That they had not been humbled or crushed was evidence of both the courage and the spirit of African Americans.

discrimination: unequal treatment based on a person's race, gender, religion, place of birth, or other arbitrary characteristic

segregation: the social separation of groups of people, especially by race

The Granger Collection, New York

Lemuel Haynes, shown here preaching from a pulpit, fought at Lexington during the Revolutionary War. He was the first African American minister of a white congregation.

19.3 The Economics of Slavery

As you read in Chapter 13, only wealthier planters could afford to buy slaves. The great majority of white southerners did not own slaves. Why, then, did the South remain so loyal to slavery? Part of the answer lies in the growth of the southern economy after the invention of the cotton gin in 1793.

The cotton gin made cotton a hugely profitable cash crop in the South. In 1790, the South produced just 3,000 bales of cotton. By the 1850s, production had soared to more than 4 million bales a year. Cotton brought new wealth to the South. Robert Fogel, a historian who has studied the economics of slavery, wrote:

If we treat the North and South as separate nations, the South would stand as the fourth most prosperous nation of the world in 1860…more prosperous than France, Germany, Denmark, or any of the countries in Europe except England.

Whether they owned slaves or not, white southerners understood that their economy depended on cotton. They also knew that cotton planters depended on slave labor to grow their profitable crop. They dreamed that someday they would

Cotton was the South's most valuable export. Most southerners knew that their economy depended upon slave labor to grow and harvest this crop.

be able to buy slaves and join the powerful planter class. It mattered little to them that owning slaves became less and less likely as the demand for, and the price of, slaves rose.

High prices were both good and bad for the men and women trapped in slavery. As prices went up, slaves became more valuable to their owners. This may have encouraged slaveholders to take better care of their workers. At the same time, the rising value of their slaves made slaveholders less willing to listen to talk of ending slavery. In their eyes, freeing their slaves could only mean one thing—complete and utter financial ruin.

Geography Challenge

The Slave System, 1801 to 1860

1. What does this map show?

2. How did the size of the area where cotton was grown change between 1801 and 1860?

3. Did the production of cotton increase or decrease between 1801 and 1860? What effect do you think this had on the use of slavery?

4. What invention accounts for the changes you can see on this map?

5. How might these changes have affected slaves? How might these changes have affected the economy of the South? Were these changes good or bad? Why do you think so?

19.4 Working Conditions of Slaves

Slaves worked on farms of various sizes. On small farms, owners and slaves worked side by side in the fields. On large plantations, planters hired overseers to supervise their slaves. Overseers were paid to "care for nothing but to make a large crop." To do this, they tried to get the most work possible out of slaves' tired bodies.

About three quarters of rural slaves were field hands who toiled from dawn to dark tending crops. An English visitor described a field hand's day:

He is called up in the morning at day break, and is seldom allowed enough time to swallow three mouthfuls of hominy [boiled corn], or hoecake [cornbread], but is immediately driven out to the field to hard labor.... About noon...he eats his dinner, and he is seldom allowed an hour for that purpose.... Then they return to severe labor, which continues until dusk.

Even then, a slave's workday was not finished. After dark, there was still water to carry, wood to split, pigs to feed, corn to shuck, cotton to clean, and other chores to be done. One slave recalled:

Slaves who worked as field hands labored from dawn to well into the night. If they failed to pick their usual amount, they were beaten.

"I never knowed what it was to rest. I jes work all the time from morning late at night. I had to do everything.... Work in the field, chop wood, hoe corn, 'till sometime I feels like my back surely break."

Not all slaves worked in the fields. Some were skilled seamstresses, carpenters, or blacksmiths. Others worked in the master's house as cooks or servants. When asked about her work, a house slave replied:

"What kind of work I did? Most everything, chile [child]. I cooked, then I was house maid, and I raised I don't know how many children.... I was always good when it come to the sick, so that was mostly my job."

No matter how hard they worked, slaves could not look forward to an easier life. Most began work at the age of six and continued until they died. As one old man put it, "Slave young, slave long."

19.5 Living Conditions of Slaves

Most masters viewed their slaves as they did their land—things to be "worn out, not improved." They provided only what was needed to keep their slaves healthy enough to work. Slaves lived crowded together in rough cabins. One recalled that:

> "We lodged in log huts, and on bare ground. Wooden floors were an unknown luxury. In a single room were huddled, like cattle, ten or a dozen persons, men, women, and children…. We had neither bedsteads, nor furniture of any description. Our beds were collections of straw and old rags, thrown down in the corners."

Slaves seldom went hungry. "Not to give a slave enough to eat," reported Frederick Douglass, "is regarded as…meanness [stinginess] even among slaveholders." Once a week, slaves received a ration of cornmeal, bacon, and molasses. Many kept gardens or hunted and fished to vary their diets. The owner described here fed his slaves well:

> Marse [master] Alec had plenty for his slaves to eat. There was meat, bread, collard greens, snap beans, 'taters, peas, all sorts of dried fruit, and just lots of milk and butter.

Slaves wore clothing made of coarse homespun linen or rough "Negro cloth." Northern textile mills made this cloth especially for slave clothes. Frederick Douglass reported that a field hand received a yearly allowance of "two coarse linen shirts, one pair of linen trousers…one jacket, one pair of trousers for winter, made of coarse negro cloth, one pair of stockings, and one pair of shoes." The shoes usually fit so badly that slaves preferred going barefoot much of the time. Children too young to work received "two coarse linen shirts per year. When these failed them, they went naked until the next allowance-day."

While slaves were poorly housed and clothed compared to most white southerners, they were more likely to receive medical care. Slaveholders often hired doctors to treat sick or injured slaves. Given doctors' limited medical knowledge, this care probably did little to improve the health of slaves.

Most slave cabins consisted of a single room where the entire family lived. They had a fireplace for cooking and heat. The windows usually had no glass.

19.6 Controlling Slaves

Slavery was a system of forced labor. To make this system work, slaveholders had to keep their slaves firmly under control. Some slaveholders used harsh punishments—beating, whipping, branding, and other forms of torture—to maintain that control. But punishments often backfired on slaveholders. A slave who had been badly whipped might not be able to work for some time. Harsh punishments were also likely to make slaves feel more resentful and rebellious.

Slaveholders preferred to control their workforce by making slaves feel totally dependent on their masters. Owners encouraged such dependence by treating their slaves like grown-up children. They also kept their workers as ignorant as possible about the world beyond the plantation. Frederick Douglass's master said that a slave "should know nothing but to obey his master—to do as it is told to do."

Slaves who failed to learn this lesson were sometimes sent to slave-breakers. Such men were experts at turning independent, spirited African Americans into humble, obedient slaves. When he was 16, Douglass was sent to a slavebreaker named Edward Covey.

Covey's method consisted of equal parts violence, fear, and overwork. Soon after Douglass arrived on Covey's farm, he received his first whipping. After that, he was beaten so often that "aching bones and a sore back were my constant companions."

Covey's ability to instill fear in his slaves was as effective as his whippings. They never knew when he might be watching them. "He would creep and crawl in ditches and gullies," Douglass recalled, to spy on his workers. Finally, Covey worked his slaves beyond endurance. Wrote Douglass:

"We worked in all weathers. It was never too hot or too cold; it could never rain, blow, hail, or snow too hard for us to work in the field. …The longest days were too short for him, and the shortest nights too long for him. I was somewhat unmanageable when I first got there, but a few months of this discipline tamed me…. I was broken in body, soul, and spirit…. The dark night of slavery closed in upon me."

AM I NOT A MAN AND A BROTHER?

Beating, or whipping, was slave owners' most common way of controlling their workers. However, most slave owners avoided savage beatings because injured slaves could not work, and lash marks reduced their resale value.

19.7 Resistance to Slavery

Despite the efforts of slaveholders to crush their spirits, slaves found countless ways to resist slavery. As former slave Harriet Jacobs wrote after escaping to freedom, "My master had power and law on his side. I had a determined will. There is power in each."

Day-to-Day Resistance   For most slaves, resistance took the form of quiet acts of rebellion. Field hands pulled down fences, broke tools, and worked so sloppily that they damaged crops. House slaves sneaked food out of the master's kitchen.

Slaves pretended to be dumb, clumsy, sick, or insane to escape work. One slave avoided working for years by claiming to be nearly blind, only to regain his sight once freed.

Resistance turned deadly when house servants slipped poison into the master's food. So many slaves set fire to their owners' homes and barns that the American Fire Insurance Company refused to insure property in the South.

Open Defiance   Quiet resistance sometimes flared into open defiance. When pushed too hard, slaves refused to work, rejected orders, or struck back violently. Owners often described slaves who reacted in this way as "insolent" [disrespectful] or "unmanageable."

Frederick Douglass reached his breaking point one day when the slave-breaker Covey began to beat him for no particular reason. Rather than take the blows, as he had so many times before, Douglass fought back. He wrestled Covey to the ground, holding him "so firmly by the throat that his blood followed my nails." For Douglass, this moment was "the turning point in my career as a slave."

The bloodiest slave uprising in the South was organized by Nat Turner, a black preacher, in 1831. This wood engraving, entitled *Nat Turner and His Contederates in Conference,* shows Turner leaning on a pole, speaking to his companions.

The Granger Collection, New York

> *"My long-crushed spirit rose, cowardice departed, bold defiance took its place; and I now resolved that, however long I might remain a slave in form, the day had passed when I could be a slave in fact. I did not hesitate to let it be known of me, that the white man who expected to succeed in whipping, must also succeed in killing me."*

Covey knew this and never laid a hand on Douglass again.

Slaves used many methods to try to escape bondage. Henry Brown, pictured above, shipped himself to freedom in a crate.

Running Away Some slaves tried to escape by running away to freedom in the North. The risks of escape were enormous. Most slaves knew little about the world beyond their owner's farm. Slaveholders hired professional slave catchers and their packs of howling bloodhounds to hunt down runaway slaves. If caught, a runaway risked being mauled by dogs, brutally whipped, or even killed.

In spite of the dangers, slaves found many ways to escape bondage. Some walked to freedom in the North, hiding by day and traveling at night when they could follow the North Star. Others traveled north by boat or train, using forged identity cards and clever disguises to get past watchful slave patrols. A few runaways mailed themselves to freedom in boxes or coffins.

Trying to escape, wrote Douglass, "was like one going to war without weapons—ten chances of defeat to one of victory." Still, he and countless other slaves took the risk. As one former slave explained:

> *"So galling was our bondage, that to escape from it, we suffered the loss of all things, and braved every peril, and endured every hardship. Some of us left parents, some wives, some children. Some of us were wounded with guns and dogs, as we fled. Some of us secreted ourselves in suffocating holds of ships. Nothing was so dreadful to us as slavery."*

Rebellion At times, resistance erupted into violent rebellion. Slave revolts occurred in cities, on plantations, and even on ships at sea. Fear of slave uprisings haunted slaveholders. "I have known times here when not a single planter had a calm night's rest," wrote a visitor to the South. "They never lie down to sleep without…loaded pistols at their sides."

In 1831, a slave named Nat Turner led a bloody uprising in Virginia. Armed with axes and guns, Turner and his followers set out to kill every white person they could find. Before their reign of terror ended two days later, at least 57 people had been hacked to death.

Nat Turner's rebellion panicked white southerners. In response, southern states passed strict slave codes that tightened owners' control of their slaves and provided for harsher punishment of slaves by authorities. As one frightened Virginian remarked, "A Nat Turner might be in any family."

19.8 Slave Families and Communities

Slavery made community and family life difficult. Legally, slave families did not exist. No southern state recognized slave marriages. Legal control of slave children rested not with their parents, but with their masters. Owners could break up slave families at any time by selling a father, a mother, or a child to someone else. Along with being whipped, slaves most feared being sold away from their loved ones.

Most slaves grew up in families headed by a father and mother. Unable to marry legally, slaves created their own weddings that often involved the tradition of jumping over a broomstick. One recalled that:

> The preacher would say to the man, "Do you take this woman to be your wife?" He says, "Yes." "Well, jump the broom." After he jumped, the preacher would say the same to the woman. When she jumped, the preacher said, "I pronounce you man and wife."

Caring for children was never easy. Frederick Douglass's mother "snatched a few moments for our care in the early morning before her work began, and at night after the day's work was done." Still, parents found time to teach their children the lessons they would need to survive.

Silence around whites was one such lesson. Elijah Marrs recalled that "Mothers were necessarily compelled to be severe on their children to keep them from talking too much." Obedience was another lesson. William Webb's mother taught him "not to rebel against the men who were treating me like some dumb brute, making me work and refusing to let me learn."

Parents also taught their children other essential lessons about caring, kindness, pride, and hope. They taught them to respect themselves and other members of the slave community, especially older slaves. "There is not to be found, among any people," wrote Douglass, "a more rigid enforcement of the law of respect to elders."

These were the lessons that helped slaves, under the most difficult conditions, to create loving families and close communities. In doing so, they met the most basic of human needs—the need for a place to feel loved, respected, and safe.

This photograph shows five generations of a slave family on a plantation in South Carolina. Enslaved African Americans often found it difficult to keep their families together because Southern laws did not recognize slave marriages or families, and owners could split up families as they wished.

Kitchen Ball at White Sulphur Springs, Virginia 1838 by Christian Mayr, North Carolina Museum of Art, Raleigh, Purchased with funds fron the State of North Carolina

This painting, entitled *Kitchen Ball at White Sulpher Springs*, shows slaves enjoying the precious free time they were given on Saturday nights and Sundays. Dancing, singing, and telling tales allowed slaves to temporarily forget their harsh conditions.

19.9 Leisure Time Activities

Come day,
Go day,
God send Sunday.

These simple words capture the weariness of slaves. They toiled all week in fields that seemed to stretch "from one end of the earth to the other." But, on Saturday night and Sunday, their time was their own.

Saturday nights were a time for social events, like corn-husking or pea-shelling parties, that combined work and fun. One slave recalled:

"I've seen many a corn huskin' at ole Major's farm when the corn would be piled as high as the house. Two sets of men would start huskin' from opposite sides of the heap. It would keep one man busy just getting the husks out of the way, and the corn would be thrown over the husker's head and filling the air like birds. The women usually had a quilting at those times, so they were pert and happy."

A quilting bee was one of the rare times when slave women could gather to work and talk. In those few precious hours, they were free to express themselves with needle and cloth. The quilts they created were not only beautiful, but very much needed as bedding for their families. Looking at a sunburst quilt she had sewn, one women exclaimed, "It's poetry, ain't it?"

When the sewing was done, men joined the party for a "quilting feast" and dancing. Slaves made music out of almost anything. "Stretch cowhides over cheese-boxes and you had tambourines," one former slave recalled. "Saw bones from a cow, knock them together and call it a drum. Or use broom straw on fiddle-strings and you had your entire band."

Sunday was a day for religion and recreation. Slaves spent their Sundays going to church, eating, hunting, fishing, dancing, singing, gambling, telling tales, naming babies, playing games, drinking whiskey, and visiting with friends. In New Orleans, hundreds of slaves gathered on Sunday afternoons in a public space known as "Congo Square" to dance, sing, and talk. All of these activities helped African Americans forget the sorrows of slavery.

19.10 Slave Churches

Many slaveholders encouraged their slaves to attend church on Sunday. Some read the Bible to their workers and prayed with them. Owners and white ministers preached the same message: "If you disobey your earthly master, you offend your heavenly Master."

Not surprisingly, this was not a popular lesson among slaves. "Dat ole white preacher just was telling us slaves to be good to our marsters," recalled Cornelius Garner. "We ain't kerr'd a bit 'bout dat stuff he was telling us 'cause we wanted to sing, pray, and serve God in our own way."

Instead, slaves created their own "invisible church" that brought together African roots and American needs. This invisible church met in slave quarters or secret forest clearings known as "hush arbors." One slave reported that:

> "When [slaves] go round singing, 'Steal Away to Jesus' that mean there going to be a religious meeting that night. The masters...didn't like them religious meetings, so us naturally slips off at night, down in the bottoms or somewheres. Sometimes us sing and pray all night."

Rather than teach about obedience, black preachers told the story of Moses leading his people out of slavery in Egypt. Black worshipers sang spirituals that expressed their desire for freedom and faith in a better world to come. A black preacher wrote that:

> The singing was accompanied by a certain ecstasy of motion, clapping of hands, tossing of heads, which would continue without cessation [stopping] about half an hour.... The old house partook of their ecstasy; it rang with their jubilant shouts, and shook in all its joints.

Whites sometimes criticized the "enthusiasm" of black worshipers, saying they lacked true religious feeling. Many slaves, however, believed that it was their masters who lacked such feeling. "You see," explained one man, "religion needs a little motion—specially if you gwine [going to] feel de spirit."

Religion helped slaves bear their suffering and still find joy in life. In their prayers and spirituals, they gave voice to their deepest longings, their greatest sorrows, and their highest hopes.

Biblical stories were frequently illustrated on quilts made by slaves.

The Granger Collection, New York

19.11 African American Culture

Africans arrived in the United States speaking many languages and following many cultural traditions. To survive, they had to learn a new language—English—and adopt a new way of life. Yet they did not forget their African roots. Across the South, slaves combined their old traditions and new realities to create a distinctive African American culture.

You can see this combining of cultures in Harriet Powers' story quilt. In square after square, Powers used African and American animals to illustrate Bible stories that she learned as a slave on a Georgia plantation. The doves in her quilt are symbols of a slave's yearning

This watercolor, entitled *The Old Plantation*, shows one aspect of the rich culture slaves developed in spite of the bondage they endured. Slave dances, songs, quilts, and folk stories all reflected a combination of slaves' old African traditions and the new life they faced in America.

for freedom. As one spiritual said with sad longing, "Had I the wings of a dove, I'd fly away and be at rest."

You can also hear this combining of cultures in the songs and spirituals sung by slaves. These songs throb with the rhythms and harmonies of Africa. But they speak about the realities of slavery. Slaves sang about faith, love, work, and the kindness and cruelty of masters. They also expressed their **oppression,** as in this song recorded by Frederick Douglass:

> We raise the wheat, dey gib [they give] us the corn;
> We bake the bread, dey gib us the cruss;
> We sif the meal, dey gib us the huss;
> We peel the meat, dey gib us the skin;
> And dat's the way dey takes us in.

oppression: the feeling of being weighed down or held back by severe and unfair force

Slave dances were based on African traditions as well. Dancing helped slaves to escape their cares, express their feelings, and refresh their spirits. According to one former slave, good dancers "could play a tune with their feet, dancing largely to an inward music, a music that was felt, but not heard."

African legends and folktales survived in the stories and jokes told by slaves. For example, Br'er Rabbit, the sly hero of many slave tales, was based on the African trickster Shulo the Hare. In these stories, the small but clever brother rabbit always managed to outwit larger, but duller, brother bear or brother fox—just as slaves hoped to outwit their more powerful masters.

19.12 Chapter Summary

In this chapter, you learned what life was like for African Americans during the nineteenth century. You looked at a story quilt made by a slave that gave you clues, or messages, about slavery.

African Americans had a great impact on the development of American life. The economy of the South was built on the labor of African American slaves. Some African Americans lived in freedom in both the North and South, but nowhere could they escape racism and discrimination.

Those who lived in slavery worked endlessly, either in the fields or as servants in the master's house. Most lived in simple, dirt-floor cabins with only straw and rags for beds. Many slaves lived in daily fear of harsh punishments. Their biggest fear was the threat of family members being sold to other farms. Many slaves learned to rebel in small ways. They might break a tool on purpose or pretend to be lame or blind. Some slaves fought back openly when the oppression became too much to bear. At great risk, many tried to run away. Some slaveholders would rather kill runaways than allow them to escape.

Slaves were encouraged to attend church, and Sunday was a day of rest for everyone. Slaves spent Saturday nights at social events and worshiped in their own secret churches on Sundays. They prayed and sang spirituals to help themselves find joy and hope in their hard lives.

In the next chapter, you will read about how different views on slavery in the North and the South threatened to divide the nation.

These cards show scenes of slavery in the United States, including abolition.

IN THE COTTON FIELD. THE CHRISTMAS WEEK. THE SALE. THE PARTING "Buy us too."

THE LASH. BLOW FOR BLOW. IN THE SWAMP. FREE!

"STAND UP A MAN!" "MAKE WAY FOR LIBERTY!" VICTORY! "HE DIED FOR ME!"

How did the people in the South and North respond to the news of civil war?

A Dividing Nation

20.1 Introduction

In 1860, after one of the strangest elections in the nation's history, a tall, plain-spoken Illinois lawyer named Abraham Lincoln was elected president. On learning of his victory, Lincoln said to the reporters covering the campaign, "Well, boys, your troubles are over. Mine have just begun."

Within a few weeks, it became clear just how heavy those troubles would be. By the time Lincoln took office, the nation had split apart over the issue of slavery and was preparing for war. The survival of the United States of America, and the fate of four million slaves, rested in Lincoln's large, strong hands.

The troubles Lincoln faced were not new. The issue dividing the nation could be traced back to 1619, when the first slave ship arrived in Virginia. Since that time, slavery had ended in half of the United States. The question was, could the nation continue half-slave and half-free?

For decades, Americans tried to avoid that troubling question. Many hoped that slavery would simply die out on its own. Instead, slavery began to expand into new territories, and the question could no longer be ignored.

Between 1820 and 1860, Americans tried to fashion several compromises on the issue of slavery. Each compromise, however, created new problems and new divisions.

Lincoln understood why. Slavery was not simply a political issue to be worked out through compromise. It was a deeply moral issue. As Lincoln wrote in a letter to a friend, "If slavery is not wrong, nothing is wrong."

In this chapter, you will learn how Americans tried to keep the United States united despite their deep divisions over slavery. And you will find out how they finally answered that most troubling question: Could a nation born in freedom endure half-slave and half-free?

Graphic Organizer: Visual Metaphor
You will use a visual metaphor of an unraveling flag to understand the compromises and decisions made to preserve the Union.

the Union: The United States as one country, united under a single government. During the Civil War, "the Union" came to mean the government and armies of the North.

20.2 Confronting the Issue of Slavery

A traveler, heading west across the Appalachians after the War of 1812, wrote, "Old America seems to be breaking up and moving westward." It was true. By 1819, restless settlers had formed seven new states west of the Appalachians.

Congress had established a process for forming new states in the Northwest Ordinance of 1787. Besides outlining the steps leading to statehood, this law also banned slavery north of the Ohio River. As a result, the three western states that were formed north of the river—Ohio, Indiana, and Illinois—were free states. The four states that were formed south of the Ohio River—Kentucky, Tennessee, Louisiana, and Mississippi—all permitted slavery.

In 1819, Alabama and Missouri applied to Congress for statehood as slave states. No one in Congress questioned admitting Alabama as a slave state. Alabama was located far south of the Ohio River, and was surrounded by other slave states.

Congress had another reason for admitting Alabama with no debate. For years there had been an unspoken agreement in Congress to keep the number of slave states and free states equal. The admission of Illinois as a free state in 1818 had upset this balance. By accepting Alabama with slavery, Congress was able to restore the balance between slave and free states. Missouri, however, was another matter.

In 1819, the number of slave states and free states stood at 11 apiece. This balance was threatened when Missouri applied for statehood as a slave state.

Slave States	Free States
Georgia	Pennsylvania
South Carolina	New Jersey
North Carolina	New York
Virginia	Connecticut
Maryland	Rhode Island
Delaware	Massachusetts
Kentucky (1792)	New Hampshire
Tennessee (1796)	Vermont (1791)
Louisiana (1812)	Ohio (1803)
Mississippi (1817)	Indiana (1816)
Alabama (1819)	Illinois (1818)

◻ Original 13 States
◼ States Entering the Union, 1791–1819

Questions about Missouri Some northerners in Congress questioned whether Missouri should also be admitted as a slave state. Most of Missouri, they observed, lay north of the point where the Ohio River flows into the Mississippi. On the eastern side of the Mississippi, slavery was banned north of that point. Shouldn't the same ban also be applied west of the Mississippi?

This question led to another one. If Missouri was allowed to enter the Union as a slave state, some asked, what would keep slavery from spreading across all of the Louisiana Territory? The vision of a block of new slave states stretching from the Mississippi to the Rocky Mountains was enough to give some northerners nightmares.

The Tallmadge Amendment When the bill to make Missouri a state came before Congress, Representative James Tallmadge of New York decided to keep that nightmare from coming true. Tallmadge proposed an amendment to the statehood bill. The amendment said that Missouri could join the Union, but only as a free state.

Southerners in Congress greeted Tallmadge's amendment with a roar of protest. What right, they asked, did Congress have to decide whether a new state should be slave or free? That decision, they said, belonged to the people of each state, not Congress.

A Deadlocked Congress   Southerners' protests were based on their fear that if Congress was allowed to end slavery in Missouri, it might try to end slavery elsewhere. The North already had more votes in the House of Representatives than the South. Only in the Senate did the two sections have equal voting power. As long as the number of free states and slave states remained equal, southern senators could defeat any attempt to interfere with slavery. But if Missouri entered the Union as a free state, the South would lose its power to block anti-slavery bills in the Senate. If that happened, southerners warned, it would be a disaster for the South.

In the North, the Tallmadge Amendment awakened strong feelings against slavery. Many towns sent petitions, or formal written requests, to Congress, condemning slavery as immoral and unconstitutional. The petitions called on Congress to stop the spread of this evil. Arguing in favor of the amendment, New Hampshire representative Arthur Livermore spoke for many northerners when he said:

> An opportunity is now presented to prevent the growth of a sin which sits heavy on the soul of every one of us. By embracing this opportunity, we may retrieve the national character and, in some degree our own. But if we suffer [allow] it to pass…let us at least be consistent, and declare that our Constitution was made to impose slavery, and not to establish liberty.

The House voted to approve the Tallmadge Amendment. In the Senate, however, southerners were able to defeat it. The two houses were now deadlocked over the issue of slavery in Missouri. They would remain so as the 1819 session of Congress drew to a close.

An auctioneer holds a baby during a slave auction, while the child's mother begs not to be separated from her child. Scenes like this fueled the moral outrage many felt toward slavery.

The Granger Collection, New York

20.3 The Missouri Compromise

secession: the act of withdrawing from an organization or alliance, such as the withdrawal of the southern states from the Union

When Congress returned to Washington in 1820, it took up the question of Missouri statehood once again. By then, the situation had changed, for Maine was now asking to enter the Union as a free state.

For weeks, Congress struggled to find a way out of its deadlock over Missouri. As the debate dragged on and tempers wore thin, southerners began using such dreaded words as **"secession"** and "civil war."

"If you persist," Thomas Cobb of Georgia warned supporters of the amendment, "the Union will be dissolved. You have kindled a fire which only a sea of blood can extinguish."

"If disunion must take place, let it be so!" thundered Tallmadge in reply. "If civil war must come, I can only say, let it come."

A Compromise Is Reached Rather than risk the breakup of the Union, Congress finally agreed to a compromise crafted by Representative Henry Clay of Kentucky. The compromise admitted Missouri to the Union as a slave state and Maine as a free state. In this way, it maintained the balance of power between slave and free states.

At the same time, Congress drew an imaginary line across the Louisiana Territory at latitude 36°30'. North of this line, slavery was to be banned forever, except in Missouri. South of the line, slaveholding was permitted.

As a result of the Missouri Compromise, Missouri entered the Union as a slave state, while Maine entered as a free state. In addition, a line was drawn at the 36°30' parallel, below which slavery would be allowed. Above this line, slavery was prohibited.

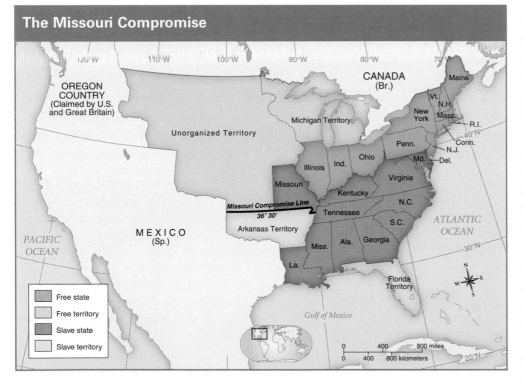

The Missouri Compromise

Free state
Free territory
Slave state
Slave territory

Reactions to the Compromise The Missouri Compromise kept the Union together. But it pleased no one. In the North, Congressmen who voted to accept Missouri as a slave state were called traitors. In the South, slaveholders deeply resented the ban on slavery in part of the Louisiana Territory.

Meanwhile, as Secretary of State John Quincy Adams recognized, the compromise had not settled the future of slavery in the United States as a whole. "I have favored this Missouri compromise, believing it to be all that could be effected [accomplished] under the present Constitution, and from extreme unwillingness to put the Union at hazard [risk]," wrote Adams in his diary. "If the Union must be dissolved, slavery is precisely the question on which it ought to break. For the present, however, the contest is laid asleep."

20.4 The Missouri Compromise Unravels

As John Quincy Adams predicted, the slavery issue was laid to rest, at least for a time. During the 1820s, most Americans paid little attention to the fate of slaves. But beneath that silence, a powerful force was building—a great revival of religious faith and fervor. This movement pushed the issue of slavery into the open again.

As you read in Chapter 18, the leaders of the Second Great Awakening promised that God would grant salvation to those who dedicated their lives to the Lord's work. And for some Americans, the Lord's work was the abolition of slavery.

Slavery in Washington, D.C. During the 1830s, abolitionists flooded the nation's capital with anti-slavery petitions. Congress, they were told, had no power to interfere with slavery in the states. Then what about the District of Columbia? asked the abolitionists. Surely Congress had the power to ban slavery in the nation's capital.

Rather than face that question, Congress voted in 1836 to table all anti-slavery petitions. To *table* means to set something aside indefinitely. This meant that Congress would neither read nor act upon the petitions. Outraged abolitionists called this action the "gag rule," because it gagged (silenced) all debate over slavery in Congress.

Abolitionists, however, were far from silenced. They continued to attack slavery in books, in newspapers, and at public meetings.

Southern Fears White southerners deeply resented the abolitionists' attacks as an assault on their way of life. The more abolitionists denounced slavery, the more fiercely slaveholders defended it.

Resentment turned to fear in 1831, when Nat Turner and six fellow slaves launched a slave rebellion. Although the uprising was crushed, southern states adopted strict new laws to control the movement of slaves. Many states also tried to keep abolitionist writings from reaching slaves. Mississippi even offered a reward of $5,000 for the arrest and conviction of any person "who shall utter, publish, or circulate" abolitionist ideas.

The horrors of slavery were detailed in many northern newspapers and periodicals such as this one.

fugitive: a person who flees or tries to escape (for example, from slavery)

Fugitive Slaves Nat Turner's rebellion was the last large-scale slave revolt. But individual slaves continued to rebel by running away to freedom in the North. These **fugitives** from slavery were often helped in their escape by sympathetic people in the North.

To slaveholders, these northerners were no better than bank robbers. A good slave was a valuable piece of property. Every time a slave escaped, it was like seeing five acres of land vanish into thin air. Slaveholders demanded that Congress pass a fugitive slave law to help them recapture their property.

Nat Turner, pictured above, led the last major slave uprising in the United States. Following the Turner revolt, southerners tightened restrictions on slaves.

Slavery in the Territories The gag rule kept the slavery issue out of Congress for ten years. Then, in 1846, President James Polk sent a bill to Congress asking for funds for the war with Mexico. Pennsylvania representative David Wilmot added an amendment to the bill known as the Wilmot Proviso. (A *proviso* is a condition added to an agreement.) Wilmot's proviso stated that "neither slavery nor involuntary servitude shall ever exist" in any part of the territory that might be acquired from Mexico.

Southerners in Congress strongly opposed Wilmot's amendment. Congress had no right, they maintained, to decide where slaveholders could take their property. The Wilmot Proviso passed the House, but it was rejected by the Senate.

Statehood for California For the next three years, Congress debated what to do about slavery in the territory gained from Mexico. Southerners wanted all of the Mexican Cession open to slavery. Northerners wanted all of it closed.

As a compromise, southerners proposed a bill that would extend the Missouri Compromise line all the way to the Pacific. Slavery would be banned north of that line and allowed south of it. Northerners in Congress rejected this proposal.

Then, late in 1849, California applied for admission to the Union as a free state. Northerners in Congress welcomed California with open arms. Southerners, however, rejected California's request. Making California a free state, they warned, would upset the equal balance between slave and free states. The result would be to make the slave states "a fixed, dreary, hopeless minority."

The year ended with Congress deadlocked over California's request for statehood. Once again, resentful southerners spoke openly of withdrawing from the Union. And once again, angry northerners denounced slavery as "a crime against humanity…a great evil."

20.5 The Compromise of 1850

On January 21, 1850, Henry Clay, now a senator from Kentucky, trudged through a Washington snowstorm to pay an unexpected call on Senator Daniel Webster of Massachusetts. Clay, the creator of the Missouri Compromise, had come up with a plan to end the deadlock over California. But to get his plan through Congress, Clay needed Webster's support.

Something for Everyone   Clay's new compromise had something to please just about everyone. It began by admitting California to the Union as a free state. That would please the North. Meanwhile, New Mexico and Utah would be organized as territories open to slavery, which would please the South.

In addition, Clay's plan ended the slave trade in Washington, D.C. Although slaveholders in Washington would be able to keep their slaves, human beings would no longer be bought and sold in the nation's capital. Clay and Webster agreed that this compromise would win support from abolitionists without threatening the rights of slaveholders.

Finally, Clay's plan called for passage of a strong fugitive slave law. Slaveholders had long wanted such a law, which would make it easier to find and reclaim their runaway slaves.

The Compromise Is Accepted   Hoping that Clay's compromise would end the crisis, Webster agreed to help push it through Congress. But despite his support, Congress debated Clay's proposals for nine frustrating months. As tempers frayed, southerners talked of simply leaving the Union peacefully.

Webster dismissed such talk as foolish. "Secession! Peaceable secession!" he exclaimed. "Your eyes and mine are never destined to see that miracle…. I see it as plainly as I see the sun in heaven—I see that secession must produce such a war as I will not describe."

A war over slavery? That was something few Americans wanted to face. In September 1850, Congress finally adopted Clay's plan.

Most Americans were happy to see the crisis end. Some southerners, however, remained wary of the Compromise of 1850. A North Carolina newspaper warned the North to "let this question of Slavery alone, take it out and keep it out of Congress; and respect and enforce the Fugitive Slave Law as it stands. *If not, we leave you!*"

The Compromise of 1850 admitted California as a free state and allowed the southwestern territories to be set up with no restriction on slavery.

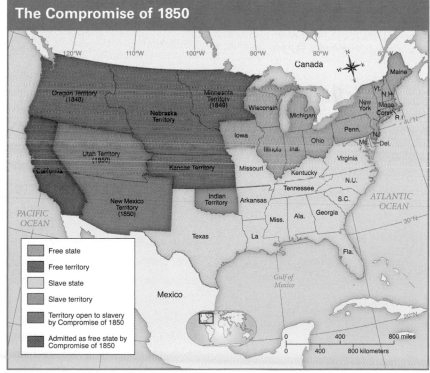

The Compromise of 1850

Free state
Free territory
Slave state
Slave territory
Territory open to slavery by Compromise of 1850
Admitted as free state by Compromise of 1850

20.6 The Compromise Satisfies No One

Clay and Webster hoped that the Compromise of 1850 would quiet the slavery controversy for years to come. In fact, it satisfied almost no one. Instead of quieting down, the debate grew louder each year.

The Granger Collection, New York

In this painting, a group of fugitive slaves are helped as they make their escape from bondage. The assistance northerners gave to escaped slaves caused hard feelings among southern slaveholders.

The Fugitive Slave Law

Both sides were unhappy with the Fugitive Slave Law, though for different reasons. Northerners did not want to enforce the law. Southerners felt the law did not do enough to ensure the return of their escaped property.

Under the Fugitive Slave Law, any person arrested as a runaway slave had almost no legal rights. Many runaways fled to Canada rather than risk being caught and sent back to their masters. Others decided to stand and fight. Reverend Jarmain Loguen, a former slave living in New York, said boldly, "I don't respect this law—I don't fear it—I won't obey it...I will not live like a slave, and if force is employed to reenslave me, I shall make preparations to meet the crisis as becomes a man."

The Fugitive Slave Law also said that any person who helped a slave escape, or even refused to aid slave catchers, could be jailed. This provision, complained New England poet Ralph Waldo Emerson, made "slave catchers of us all."

Opposition to the law was widespread in the North. When slave catchers came to Boston, they were hounded by crowds of angry citizens shouting, "Slave hunters—there go the slave hunters." After a few days of this treatment, most slave catchers decided to leave.

Notherners' refusal to support the law infuriated slaveholders. It also made enforcement of the law almost impossible. Of the tens of thousands of fugitives living in the North during the 1850s, only 299 were captured and returned to their owners.

Harriet Stowe's Vision

On a wintry Sunday morning in 1851, Harriet Beecher Stowe was sitting in church when a horrifying vision played across her eyes. Stowe raced home and scribbled down what she had seen. Then she gathered her children around her and read what she had written.

Her vision began with a saintly slave known as Uncle Tom and his cruel master, Simon Legree. In a furious rage, Legree had the old slave whipped to death. Just before Uncle Tom's soul slipped out of his bloodied body, he opened his eyes and whispered to Legree, "Ye poor miserable critter! There ain't no more ye can do. I forgive ye, with all my soul!"

When she had finished reading, Stowe's son cried out, "Oh Mama! Slavery is the cruelest thing in the world."

Uncle Tom's Cabin   The scene of the old slave's death became part of a much longer story entitled *Uncle Tom's Cabin*. The story was first published in installments in an abolitionist newspaper. In one issue, readers shared the pain of Uncle Tom's first owner, a kind slaveholder named Colonel Shelby. Unable to pay his debts, Shelby was forced to sell Uncle Tom away from his family. The cruelty of this action drove Shelby's wife to cry out, "This is God's curse on slavery! I was a fool to think I could make anything good out of such a deadly evil."

In a later issue, terrified readers held their breath as the beautiful slave Eliza chose to risk death rather than be sold away from her young son. Chased by slave hunters and their dogs, Eliza dashed to freedom across the ice-choked Ohio River, clutching her child in her arms.

Later still, Stowe's readers found themselves weeping as Uncle Tom met his death at the hands of Simon Legree. By this time, most of them agreed with Stowe's son that slavery was the cruelest thing in the world.

In 1852, *Uncle Tom's Cabin* was published as a novel. Plays based on the book toured the country, thrilling audiences with Eliza's dramatic escape to freedom. No other work had ever aroused such powerful emotions about slavery. In the South, the novel and its author were scorned and cursed. In the North, *Uncle Tom's Cabin* turned millions of people against slavery.

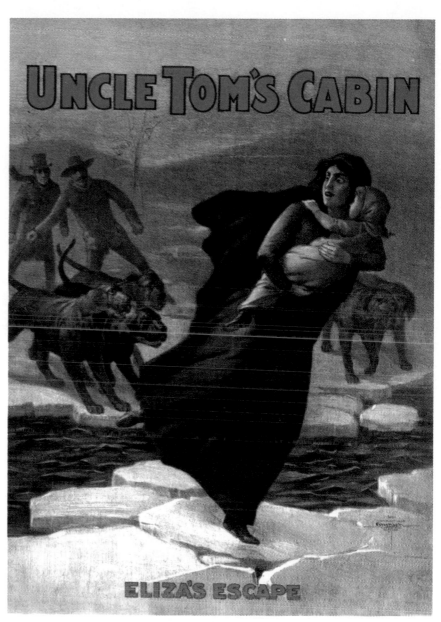

ELIZA'S ESCAPE

Perhaps no other novel in American history has had the political impact of *Uncle Tom's Cabin*. Upon meeting author Harriet Beecher Stowe, Abraham Lincoln said, "So you're the little woman who wrote the book that made this great war."

The Kansas-Nebraska Act   Early in 1854, Senator Stephen A. Douglas of Illinois introduced a bill in Congress that would have far-reaching consequences. Douglas had no intention of opening up another painful debate on slavery. He simply wanted to get a railroad built to California. This was more likely to happen, he thought, if Congress organized the Great Plains into the Nebraska Territory and opened it to settlers. Because this territory lay north of the Missouri Compromise line, his bill said nothing about slavery.

The Kansas-Nebraska Act

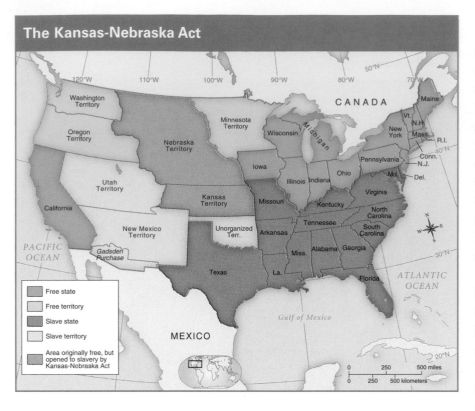

The Kansas-Nebraska Act outraged northerners because it violated the Missouri Compromise.

Southerners in Congress agreed to support Douglas's bill if he made a few changes. His final bill created two new territories, Kansas and Nebraska. It also scrapped the Missouri Compromise by leaving it up to the settlers themselves to decide what to do about slavery in the two territories. In other words, the bill opened the territories to slavery, provided voters approved. Douglas called this policy "popular sovereignty," or rule by the people.

Douglas's Kansas-Nebraska Act hit the North like a thunderbolt. Once again, northerners were haunted by nightmare visions of slavery marching across the plains. Douglas tried to calm their fears by saying that the climates of Kansas and Nebraska were not suited to slave labor. But when northerners studied maps, they were not so sure. Newspaper editor Horace Greeley charged in the *New York Tribune:*

The pretense of Douglas & Co. that not even Kansas is to be made a slave state by his bill is a gag [joke]. Ask any Missourian what he thinks about it. The Kansas Territory…is bounded in its entire length by Missouri, with a whole tier of slave counties leaning against it. Won't be a slave state!…Gentlemen! Don't lie any more!

Bloodshed in Kansas After the Kansas-Nebraska Act was passed, settlers poured into Kansas. Most were peaceful farmers looking for fertile soil. Some settlers, however, moved to Kansas either to support or to oppose slavery. In the South, towns took up collections to send their young men to Kansas. In the North, abolitionists raised money to send weapons to anti-slavery settlers. Before long, Kansas had two competing governments, one for slavery and one against it.

The struggle over slavery soon turned violent. On May 21, 1856, pro-slavery settlers and "border ruffians" from Missouri invaded Lawrence, Kansas, the home of the anti-slavery government. The invaders burned a hotel, looted several homes, and tossed the presses of two abolitionist newspapers into the Kaw River. As the invaders left Lawrence, one of them boasted, "Gentlemen, this is the happiest day of my life."

The raid on Lawrence provoked a wave of outrage in the North. Money was quickly raised to replace the destroyed presses. And more "free-soilers," as the anti-slavery settlers were called, prepared to move to Kansas.

Meanwhile, a fiery abolitionist named John Brown plotted his own revenge. Two days after the Lawrence raid, Brown and seven followers, including four of Brown's sons and his son-in-law, invaded the pro-slavery town of Pottawatomie. There they dragged five men they suspected of supporting slavery from their homes and hacked them to death with swords.

Violence in Congress   The violence in Kansas greatly disturbed Senator Charles Sumner of Massachusetts. To Sumner, it was proof of what he had long suspected—that Senator Stephen Douglas had plotted with southerners to make Kansas a slave state.

In 1856, Sumner voiced his suspicions in a passionate speech entitled "The Crime against Kansas." Using harsh, shocking language, Sumner described the "crime against Kansas" as a violent assault on an innocent territory, "compelling it to the hateful embrace of slavery." He dismissed Douglas as "a noisome [offensive], squat, and nameless animal." Sumner also heaped abuse on many southerners, including the distinguished Senator Andrew P. Butler of South Carolina.

Just what Sumner hoped to accomplish was not clear. However, copies of his speech were quickly printed up for distribution in the North. After reading it, New England poet Henry Wadsworth Longfellow congratulated Sumner on the "brave and noble speech you made, never to die out in the memories of men."

Certainly it was not about to die out in the memories of enraged southerners. Two days after the speech, Senator Butler's nephew, South Carolina representative Preston Brooks, attacked Sumner in the Senate, beating him with his cane until it broke in half. By the time other senators could pull Brooks away, Sumner had collapsed, unconscious and bloody.

Reactions to the attack on Sumner showed how badly divided the country had become. Many southerners applauded Brooks for defending the honor of his family and the South. From across the South, supporters sent Brooks new canes to replace the one he had broken on Sumner's head.

Pro-slavery men from Missouri on their way to Lawrence, the "Free Soil" capital of Kansas. These "border ruffians" used violence and threats to frighten anti-slavery citizens.

The Granger Collection, New York

Most northerners viewed the beating as another example of southern brutality. In their eyes, Brooks was no better than the pro-slavery bullies who had attacked the good people of Lawrence. One Connecticut student was so upset that she wrote to Sumner about going to war. "I don't think it is of very much use to stay any longer in the high school," she wrote. "The boys would be better learning to hold muskets, and the girls to make bullets."

The *Dred Scott* Case   In 1857, the slavery controversy shifted from the bloodied floor of Congress to the Supreme Court. The Court was about to decide a case concerning a Missouri slave named Dred Scott. Years earlier, Scott had traveled with his owner to Wisconsin, where slavery was banned by the Missouri Compromise. Upon his return to Missouri, Scott went to court to win his freedom. He argued that his stay in Wisconsin had made him a free man.

There were nine justices on the Supreme Court in 1857. Five of them, including Chief Justice Roger Taney, were from the South. Four were from the North. The justices had two key questions to decide. First, as a slave, was Dred Scott a citizen who had the right to bring a case before a federal court? Second, did his time in Wisconsin make him a free man?

Taney, however, hoped to use the *Scott* case to settle the slavery controversy once and for all. And so he asked the Court to consider two more questions: Did Congress have the power to make any laws at all concerning slavery in the territories? And, if so, was the Missouri Compromise a constitutional use of that power?

Preston Brooks savagely beats Charles Sumner on the U.S. Senate floor. It took Sumner three and a half years to recover from the beating.

The Granger Collection, New York

20.7 The *Dred Scott* Decision

On March 6, 1857, Chief Justice Roger Taney prepared to deliver the most important decision of his career. Nearly 80 years old, the chief justice had long been opposed to slavery. As a young Maryland lawyer, he had publicly declared that "slavery is a blot upon our national character and every lover of freedom confidently hopes that it will be…wiped away."

True to his words, Taney had gone on to free his own slaves. Many observers wondered whether he and his fellow justices would now free Dred Scott as well.

Dred Scott's struggle for freedom hastened the beginning of the Civil War and, in the end, led to freedom for all slaves.

Two Judicial Bombshells   The chief justice began by reviewing the facts of Dred Scott's case. Then he dropped the first of two judicial bombshells. By a vote of five to four, the Court had decided that Scott could not sue for his freedom in a federal court because he was not a citizen. Nor, said Taney, could Scott become a citizen. No African American, whether slave or free, was an American citizen—or could ever become one.

Next, Taney dropped bombshell number two. The Court had also rejected Scott's argument that his stay in Wisconsin had made him a free man. The reason was simple. The Missouri Compromise was unconstitutional.

Taney's argument went something like this. Slaves are property. The Fifth Amendment to the Constitution says that property cannot be taken from people without due process of law—that is, a proper court hearing. Banning slavery in a territory, Taney reasoned, is the same as taking property away from slaveholders who would like to bring their slaves into that territory. And that is unconstitutional. Rather than banning slavery, Congress has a constitutional responsibility to protect the property rights of slaveholders in a territory.

The *Dred Scott* decision delighted slaveholders. They hoped that, at long last, the issue of slavery in the territories had been settled—and in their favor.

Many northerners, however, were stunned and enraged by the Court's ruling. The *New York Tribune* called the decision a "wicked and false judgment." Another New York newspaper expressed outrage in its bold headlines:

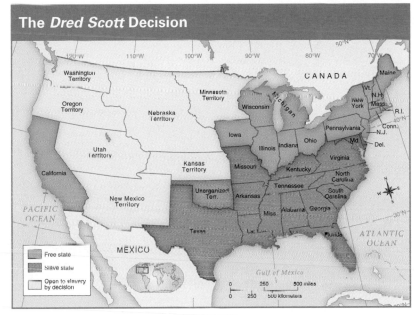

The *Dred Scott* Decision

[Map captions:] Free state · Slave state · Open to slavery by decision

As a result of the *Dred Scott* decision, slavery was allowed in all territories.

The Decision of the Supreme Court

Is the Moral Assassination of a Race

and Cannot Be Obeyed!

20.8 From Compromise to Crisis

During the controversy over the Kansas-Nebraska Act, anti-slavery activists formed a new political organization called the Republican Party. The Republicans were united by their beliefs that "no man can own another man…that slavery must be prohibited in the territories…that all new states must be free states…that the rights of our colored citizen…must be protected."

In 1858, Republicans in Illinois nominated Abraham Lincoln to run for the Senate. In his speech accepting this honor, Lincoln pointed out that all attempts to reach compromise on the slavery issue had failed. Quoting from the Bible, he warned, "A house divided against itself cannot stand." Lincoln went on: "I believe this government cannot endure, permanently half-slave and half-free. I do not expect the Union to be dissolved—I do not expect the house to fall—but I do expect it will cease to be divided. It will become all one thing, or all the other."

Abraham Lincoln addresses an audience during one of the famous Lincoln-Douglas debates. Stephen Douglas is directly behind Lincoln on the platform.

ILLINOIS BORN UNDER THE ORDINANCE OF '87

"WESTWARD THE STAR OF EMPIRE TAKES ITS WAY: THE GIRLS LINK ON TO LINCOLN, THEIR MOTHERS WERE FOR CLAY."

ABE THE GIANT-KILLER

THE LITTLE GIANT CHAWING UP OLD ABE

The Lincoln-Douglas Debates

Lincoln's opponent in the Senate race was Senator Stephen Douglas. The Illinois senator saw no reason why the nation could not go on half-slave and half-free. When Lincoln challenged him to debate the slavery issue, Douglas agreed.

During the debates, Douglas argued that the *Dred Scott* decision had put the slavery issue to rest. Lincoln disagreed. In his eyes, slavery was a moral, not a legal, issue. He declared, "The real issue in this controversy—the one pressing on every mind—is the sentiment of one class [group] that looks upon the institution of slavery as a wrong, and of the other class that does not look upon it as a wrong."

Lincoln lost the election. But he was not discouraged. In a letter to a friend, he wrote, "The fight must go on. The cause of civil liberty must not be surrendered at the end of one or even one hundred defeats."

John Brown's Raid   While Lincoln fought to stop the spread of slavery through politics, John Brown adopted a more extreme approach. Rather than wait for Congress to act, Brown planned to seize the federal arsenal (a place

The Granger Collection, New York

where weapons and ammunition are stored) at Harpers Ferry, Virginia. He wanted to use the weapons to arm slaves for a rebellion that would destroy slavery forever.

It was an insane scheme. All of Brown's men were killed or captured during the raid on the arsenal. Brown himself was convicted of treason and sentenced to die. On the day of his hanging, he left a note that read, "I John Brown am now quite certain that the crimes of this guilty land will never be purged away but with blood."

Such words filled white southerners with fear. If a slave rebellion did begin, it was their blood that would be spilled. The fact that many northerners viewed Brown as a hero, rather than a lunatic, also left white southerners uneasy.

The Election of 1860   The 1860 presidential race showed just how divided the nation had become. While the Republicans were united behind Lincoln, the Democrats had split between northern and southern factions. Northern Democrats nominated Stephen Douglas. Southern Democrats supported John C. Breckinridge of Kentucky. The election became even more confusing when a group called the Constitutional Union Party nominated John Bell of Tennessee.

With his opposition divided three ways, Lincoln sailed to victory. But it was a strange sort of victory. Lincoln won with just 40 percent of the votes, all of them cast in the North. In ten southern states, he was not even on the ballot.

For white southerners, the election had an unmistakable message. The South was now a minority section. It no longer had the power to shape national events or policies. Sooner or later, southerners feared, Congress would try to abolish slavery. And that, wrote a South Carolina newspaper, would mean "the loss of liberty, property, home, country—everything that makes life worth living."

In the weeks following the election, talk of secession filled the air. Alarmed senators formed a committee to search for yet another compromise that might hold the nation together. They knew that finding one would not be easy. Still, they had to do something to stop the rush toward disunion and disaster.

John Brown was a hero to anti-slavery northerners and a villain to the slaveholding South.

The Granger Collection, New York

The opening shots of the Civil War were fired at Fort Sumter on April 12, 1861. No one was killed in the 33-hour bombardment. It was a bloodless opening to the bloodiest war in American history.

20.9 Secession

The Senate committee held its first meeting on December 20, 1860. Just as the senators began their work, events in two distant cities dashed their hopes for a settlement.

In Springfield, Illinois, a reporter called on president-elect Abraham Lincoln. When asked whether he could support a compromise on slavery, Lincoln's answer was clear. He would not interfere with slavery in the South. And he would support enforcement of the Fugitive Slave Law. But Lincoln drew the line at letting slavery extend into the territories. On this question, he declared, "Let there be no compromise."

In Charleston, South Carolina, delegates attending a state convention voted that same day to leave the Union. The city went wild. Church bells rang. Huge crowds filled the streets, roaring their approval. A South Carolina newspaper boldly proclaimed, "THE UNION IS DISSOLVED!" Six more states soon followed South Carolina's lead.

Civil War On March 4, 1861, Lincoln became president of the not-so-United States. In his inaugural address, Lincoln stated his belief that secession was both wrong and unconstitutional. He then appealed to the rebellious states to return in peace. "In your hands, my dissatisfied fellow countrymen, and not in mine," he said, "is the momentous issue of civil war."

A month later, hotheads in Charleston, South Carolina, forced the issue. On April 12, they opened fire on Fort Sumter, a federal fort in Charleston Harbor. After 33 hours of heavy shelling, the defenders of the fort hauled down the Stars and Stripes and replaced it with the white flag of surrender.

The news that rebels had fired on the American flag unleashed a wave of patriotic fury in the North. All the doubts that people had about using force to save the Union vanished. A New York newspaper reported excitedly, "There is no more thought of bribing or coaxing the traitors who have dared to aim their cannon balls at the flag of the Union.... Fort Sumter is temporarily lost, but the country is saved."

The time for compromise was over. The issues that had divided the nation for so many years would now be decided by war.

20.10 Chapter Summary

In this chapter, you learned how a series of compromises failed to keep the United States from splitting in two over the issue of slavery. You used the metaphor of an unraveling flag that was later mended to understand the compromises and decisions that were made to preserve the Union. In 1820, the Missouri Compromise resolved the first great crisis over slavery by admitting Missouri to the Union as a slave state and Maine as a free state. The compromise also drew a line across the Louisiana Territory. In the future, slavery would be permitted only south of that line.

The furor over slavery in new territories erupted again after the war with Mexico. The Compromise of 1850 admitted California as a free state while leaving the territories of New Mexico and Utah open to slavery. In addition, the compromise ended the slave trade in Washington, D.C., and included a fugitive slave law.

Once again, compromise failed. Northerners refused to honor the Fugitive Slave Law. Attitudes on both sides were hardened further by Harriet Beecher Stowe's powerful novel *Uncle Tom's Cabin,* the Kansas-Nebraska Act, and the Supreme Court's decision on the *Dred Scott* case.

In Illinois, the issue of slavery was the focus of well-publicized debates between Abraham Lincoln and Stephen Douglas. Tempers—and fears—rose even higher after John Brown's raid on Harpers Ferry.

For many southerners, Lincoln's election as president in 1860 was the last straw. Led by South Carolina, several southern states left the Union. When southerners fired on Fort Sumter, in Charleston Harbor, the time for compromise had passed. The nation was poised on the brink of war.

This broadside, printed in December 1860, boldly announces the secession of South Carolina from the Union.

The Granger Collection, New York

How do you think people's attitudes toward the Civil War changed from the beginning of the war, pictured above, to later in the war, shown at the left?

21

The Civil War

21.1 Introduction

The cannon shells bursting over Fort Sumter ended months of confusion. The nation was at war. The time had come to choose sides. For most whites in the South, the choice was clear. Early in 1861, representatives from six of the seven states that had seceded from the Union met to form a new nation called the Confederate States of America. Southerners believed that just as the states had once voluntarily joined the Union, they could voluntarily leave it now. The men who fought for the **Confederacy** were proud defenders of "Southern Rights" and "Southern Independence."

For many northerners, the choice was just as clear. "There can be no neutrals in this war," declared Stephen Douglas after Fort Sumter, "only patriots—and traitors." Most northerners viewed the secession of southern states as traitorous acts of rebellion against the United States. They marched off to war eager to defend "Our Union! Our Constitution! and Our Flag!"

Choosing sides was harder for the eight slave states located between the Confederacy and the free states. Four of these "border states"— Virginia, Arkansas, Tennessee, and North Carolina—joined the Confederacy. The western counties of Virginia, however, remained loyal to the Union. Rather than fight for the South, they broke away to form a new state called West Virginia. The other four border states—Delaware, Maryland, Kentucky, and Missouri— remained in the Union, although many of their citizens fought for the South.

As Americans took sides, they began to see why a **civil war**—a conflict between two peoples in one country—is the most painful kind of war. This conflict divided not only states, but also families and friends. In this chapter, you will learn how this "brothers' war" turned into the most destructive of all American wars. As you read, put yourself in the shoes of the men and women who were part of this long and tragic struggle.

Graphic Organizer: Annotated Illustration
You will use this illustration of a soldier's haversack to understand the events and effects of the Civil War.

The Granger Collection, New York

This iron- and wireworks in Massachusetts was just one of many northern factories. Ninety percent of the nation's manufacturing was in the North.

21.2 Preparing for War

President Lincoln's response to the attack on Fort Sumter was quick and clear. He called for 75,000 volunteers to come forward to preserve the Union. At the same time, Jefferson Davis, the newly elected president of the Confederacy, called for volunteers to defend the South.

Both sides looked forward to a quick victory. "I cannot imagine that the South has resources for a long war or even a short one," said a Philadelphia lawyer. Southerners, on the other hand, believed they could easily whip any army Lincoln sent south. A North Carolina journalist boasted:

> The army of the South will be composed of the best material that ever yet made up an army; while that of Lincoln will be gathered from the sewers of the cities…who will serve for pay and will run away as soon as danger threatens.

Strengths and Weaknesses of the North The North began the war with impressive strengths. It had a population of about 22 million people, compared to 9 million in the South. About 90 percent of the nation's manufacturing was in the North. The North also had more farms to provide food for Union troops.

For the first time in warfare, railroads were important for providing transportation. The North had about 21,000 miles of railroad track, compared to 9,000 in the South. The northern lines allowed movement to all parts of the country, including battle sites in the South. Most of the nation's banks and wealth in gold were in the North as well.

The greatest weakness of the North was its military leadership. At the start of the war, about one third of the nation's military officers resigned and returned to their homes in the South. Of those officers who remained in the North, many were too old to command a battlefield. During much of the war, Lincoln searched for effective military leaders who could lead the Union to victory.

Strengths and Weaknesses of the South   When the war began, southerners also had reasons to be confident of victory. Unlike Union forces, southerners would be fighting a defensive war in their own territory. To win the war, the North would have to invade the South. Union troops would have to subdue people who were defending what they believed to be their liberty, honor, and traditions. The South, in contrast, could win simply by defending its territory until the North grew tired of fighting and decided to leave the Confederacy alone.

The South's great strength was its military leadership. Most of America's best military officers were southerners who chose to fight for the Confederacy. This was not an easy decision for many of them. Colonel Robert E. Lee, for example, was opposed to slavery and secession. But he decided that he could not fight against his native Virginia. Lee resigned from the U.S. Army to become the commander-in-chief of the Confederate forces.

The South's main weakness was an economy that could not support a long war. It had few factories to produce guns and other military supplies. As long as southerners could trade cotton for weapons and supplies from Europe, this was not a problem. But when Union ships blockaded southern ports and cut off this trade, Confederate armies faced severe shortages.

The Confederacy also faced serious transportation problems. The South lacked the railroad network needed to haul goods over long distances. Most rail lines were short and went only to seaport towns. Supplies had to be carried by wagon from the railroad to the troops. And as the war dragged on, horses and mules to draw these wagons were in short supply.

Money might have helped solve these problems. But most wealth in the South was invested in land and slaves. The Confederate government printed paper money to finance the war effort. But as these paper dollars flooded the South, their value quickly dropped.

Abraham Lincoln versus Jefferson Davis   The North's greatest advantage was its newly elected president, Abraham Lincoln. Through even the darkest days of the war, Lincoln never wavered from his goal of preserving the Union. Confederate president Jefferson Davis was equally devoted to the secessionist cause. But he was never able to form a strong, single nation out of 11 strongly independent states.

Abraham Lincoln was born in Kentucky on February 12, 1809. His family was poor, and his mother died while he was a young child. All in

Abraham Lincoln led the country during the Civil War. His devotion to the Union, patience, tolerance, and a sense of humor enabled the nation to survive this bloody conflict.

Jefferson Davis, trained at West Point, had little experience as a politician. When he was elected president of the Confederacy, he faced the difficult task of forming a new nation and preparing for war.

all, Lincoln figured that his schooling "did not amount to a year." It was enough, however, to excite a craving for knowledge. He read everything he could lay his hands on. "My best friend," he said, "is the man who'll get me a book I ain't read."

When Lincoln was 21, his family moved to Illinois. During the next few years, he held whatever jobs he could find—store clerk, rail-splitter, surveyor, postmaster. In the evenings, he read law books and eventually became a lawyer. Later, Lincoln served as a captain in the Black Hawk War. This was the only military experience Lincoln had before becoming president.

At six feet four inches tall, Lincoln towered above most other men. His dark, sunken eyes gave him a sad but kind appearance. In this case, looks did not lie. Lincoln was patient, thoughtful, and tolerant of others. He also possessed a good sense of humor. At moments of failure and frustration during the war, this sense of humor saved him from despair. "I laugh," he once said, "because if I didn't I would weep."

Like Lincoln, Jefferson Davis was born in Kentucky in a log cabin. He grew up on a small plantation in Mississippi. As a young man, he attended the military academy at West Point, New York. He then served as commander of the Mississippi Rifles in the Mexican War. Later that same year, he was selected to fill a term as U.S. senator from Mississippi.

Standing nearly six feet, Davis was a lean, intense person. Given his military experience, he had hoped to be chosen to command the armies of the Confederacy. Instead, he was elected president of the Confederate States. While Davis accepted this responsibility, he really did not enjoy politics. As Davis's wife said of her husband, "He did not know the arts of a politician and would not practice them if he understood."

Geography Challenge
The Civil War 1861–1865

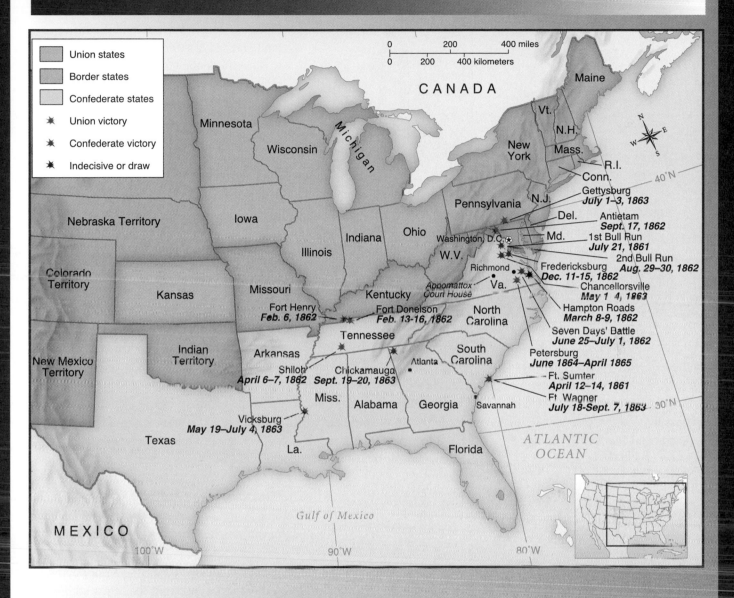

Legend:
- Union states
- Border states
- Confederate states
- ✹ Union victory
- ✹ Confederate victory
- ✹ Indecisive or draw

0   200   400 miles
0   200   400 kilometers

CANADA

Maine
Vt.
N.H.
New York
Mass.
R.I.
Conn.
40°N
Minnesota
Wisconsin
Michigan
Pennsylvania
N.J.
Del.
Gettysburg
July 1–3, 1863
Antietam
Sept. 17, 1862
Nebraska Territory
Iowa
Indiana
Ohio
Washington, D.C. ✪
Md.
1st Bull Run
July 21, 1861
Illinois
W.V.
2nd Bull Run
Aug. 29–30, 1862
Richmond
Va.
Fredericksburg
Dec. 11–15, 1862
Chancellorsville
May 1–4, 1863
Colorado Territory
Kansas
Missouri
Kentucky
Appomattox Court House
Hampton Roads
March 8–9, 1862
Fort Henry
Feb. 6, 1862
Fort Donelson
Feb. 13–16, 1862
North Carolina
Seven Days' Battle
June 25–July 1, 1862
New Mexico Territory
Indian Territory
Arkansas
Tennessee
South Carolina
Petersburg
June 1864–April 1865
Shiloh
April 6–7, 1862
Chickamauga
Sept. 19–20, 1863
Atlanta
Ft. Sumter
April 12–14, 1861
Ft. Wagner
July 18–Sept. 7, 1863
Miss.
Alabama
Georgia
Savannah
Vicksburg
May 19–July 4, 1863
Texas
La.
Florida
30°N
ATLANTIC OCEAN
MEXICO
100°W
90°W
Gulf of Mexico
80°W

1. Identify four interesting details on this map.

2. Where did most battles take place: in Union states, in Confederate states, or in border states?

3. In the early part of the war (1861–1862), which side won more battles? Why do you think this side was more successful?

4. In the later part of the war (1863–1865), which side won more battles? Why do you think this side was more successful?

21.3 Bull Run: A Great Awakening

In the spring of 1861, President Lincoln and General Winfield Scott planned the Union's war strategy. Step one was to surround the South by land and sea to cut off its trade. Step two was to divide the Confederacy into sections so that one rebel region could not help another. Step three was to capture Richmond, Virginia, the capital of the Confederacy, and destroy the rebel government. Journalists called this strategy the "Anaconda Plan" because it resembled the crushing death grip of an anaconda snake.

Rose Greenhow's Dilemma   Most northerners, however, believed that the war could be won with a single Union assault on Richmond. In 1861, thousands of volunteers poured into Washington, D.C., shouting, "On to Richmond!" These eager troops were watched carefully by an attractive young widow and Washington social leader named Rose O'Neal Greenhow.

Greenhow was a strong supporter of the southern cause. She used her friendship with government officials to learn just when and how the Union planned to attack Richmond. Her problem was to find some way to deliver this information to Confederate leaders without being discovered.

Rose Greenhow is shown here with her daughter. During her Washington parties, she collected valuable information about Union plans to attack Richmond. She passed this information on to Confederate leaders through coded messages such as the one below.

The Battle of Bull Run   On a hot July morning, long lines of soldiers marched out of Washington heading for Richmond. Their voices could be heard singing and cheering across the countryside. Parties of politicians and society folks followed the army, adding to the excitement. They had come along to see the end of the rebellion.

The troops would not have been so cheerful had they known what was waiting for them at Manassas, a small town on the way to Richmond. Rose Greenhow had managed to warn southern military leaders of Union plans. She had smuggled a coded note to them in the curls of a young girl. Southern troops were waiting for the Union forces as they approached Manassas. The two armies met at a creek known as Bull Run.

At first, Union victory looked certain. But Confederate general Thomas Jackson and his regiment of Virginians refused to give way. "Look," shouted South Carolina general Bernard Bee to his men, "there is Jackson with his Virginians, standing like a stone wall." Thus inspired by "Stonewall" Jackson's example, the rebel lines held firm until reinforcements arrived. Late that afternoon, Jackson urged his men to "yell like furies" as they charged the Union forces. The sound and fury of this charge unnerved the green (inexperienced) Union troops, who fled in panic back to Washington.

The Battle of Bull Run was a smashing victory for the South. For the North, it was a shocking blow. Lincoln and his generals now realized that ending the rebellion would not be easy. It was time to prepare for a long war.

During the Civil War, many women went to work in factories such as this munitions plant. They replaced men who were in the army.

Women Support the War   Over the next year, both the North and the South worked to build and train large armies. As men went off to war, women took their places on the home front. Wives and mothers supported their families by running farms and businesses. Many women went to work for the first time in factories. Others found jobs as nurses, teachers, or government workers.

Women also served the military forces on both sides as messengers, guides, scouts, smugglers, soldiers, and spies. Rose Greenhow was arrested for spying shortly after the Battle of Bull Run. Although she was kept under guard in her Washington home, she continued to smuggle military secrets to the Confederates. The following year, Greenhow was allowed to move to the South, where President Jefferson Davis welcomed her as a hero.

Women also volunteered to help tend sick and wounded soldiers. Dorothea Dix was already well known for her efforts to improve the treatment of the mentally ill. She was appointed director of the Union army's nursing service. Dix insisted that all female nurses be over 30 years old, plain in appearance, physically strong, and willing to do unpleasant work. Her rules were so strict that she was known as "Dragon Dix."

While most nurses worked in military hospitals, Clara Barton followed Union armies into battle, tending troops where they fell. Later generations would remember Barton as the founder of the American Red Cross. To the soldiers she cared for during the war, she was "the angel of the battlefield."

For 12 hours, Confederate and Union forces fought at Antietam in what was the bloodiest day of the Civil War. Some of the 2,770 Confederate soldiers who died during this battle are shown in this photograph.

21.4 Antietam: A Bloody Affair

The Battle of Bull Run ended northerners' hopes for a quick victory. In the months that followed that sobering defeat, the Union began to put the Anaconda Plan into effect.

The Union Blockade In 1861, the Union navy launched its blockade of southern ports. By the end of the year, most southern ports were closed to foreign ships. As the blockade shut down its ports, the Confederacy asked Britain for help in protecting its ships. The British, however, refused this request. As a result, the South could not export its cotton to Europe, nor could it import needed supplies.

Dividing the Confederacy Early in 1862, Union forces moved to divide the Confederacy by gaining control of the Mississippi River. In April, Union admiral David Farragut led 46 Union ships up the Mississippi River to New Orleans. This was the largest American fleet ever assembled. In the face of such overwhelming force, the city surrendered without firing a shot.

Meanwhile, Union forces headed by General Ulysses S. Grant began moving south toward the Mississippi from Illinois. In 1862, Grant won a series of victories that put Kentucky and much of Tennessee under Union control. A general of remarkable determination, Grant refused to accept any battle outcome other than unconditional (total) surrender. For this reason, U.S. Grant was known to his men as "Unconditional Surrender" Grant.

Attacking Richmond That same year, Union general George McClellan sent 100,000 men by ship to capture Richmond. Again, a Union victory seemed certain. But despite being outnumbered, Confederate forces stopped the Union attack in a series of well-fought battles. Once more, Richmond was saved.

The Battle of Antietam At this point, General Robert E. Lee, the commander of the Confederate forces, did the unexpected. He sent his troops across the Potomac River into Maryland, a slave state that remained in the Union. Lee hoped that this show of strength might persuade Maryland to join the Confederacy. He also hoped that a Confederate victory on Union soil would convince European nations to support the South.

On a crisp September day in 1862, Confederate and Union armies met near the little town of Sharpsburg along Antietam Creek. All day long,

McClellan's troops pounded Lee's badly outnumbered forces. The following day, Lee pulled back to Virginia.

McClellan claimed Antietam as a Union victory. But many who fought there saw the battle as "a defeat for both armies." Of the 75,000 Union troops who fought at Antietam, about 2,100 were killed. Another 10,300 were wounded or missing. Of the 52,000 Confederates who fought at Antietam, about 2,770 lost their lives, while 11,000 were wounded or missing. In that single day of fighting, more Americans were killed than in the War of 1812 and the Mexican War combined. The Battle of Antietam was the bloodiest day of the war.

The New Realities of War   The horrifying death toll at Antietam reflected the new realities of warfare. In past wars, battles had been won in hand-to-hand combat using bayonets. During the Civil War, improved weapons made killing at a distance much easier. Rifles, which replaced muskets, were accurate over long distances. Improved cannons and artillery also made it easier for armies to rain down death on forces some distance away. As a result, armies could meet, fight, bleed, and part without either side winning a clear victory.

Unfortunately, medical care was not as advanced as weaponry. Civil War doctors had no understanding of the causes of infections. Surgeons operated in dirty hospital tents with basic instruments. Few bothered to wash their hands between patients. As a result, infections spread rapidly from patient to patient. The hospital death rate was so awful that soldiers often refused medical care. An injured Ohio soldier wrote that he chose to return to battle rather than see a doctor, "thinking that I had better die by rebel bullets than Union Quackery [unskilled medical care]."

As staggering as the battle death tolls were, far more soldiers died of diseases than wounds. Unsanitary (unclean) conditions in army camps were so bad that about three men died of typhoid, pneumonia, and other diseases for every one who died in battle. As one soldier observed, "these big battles [are] not as bad as the fever."

Medical care was shockingly poor during the Civil War. Surgeries were performed without anesthetics. Thousands of soldiers died from infections or disease. Nevertheless, nurses performed heroically as they cared for the sick and wounded.

In this illustration, slaves are pictured waiting for the Emancipation Proclamation. While the proclamation had little immediate effect, it meant the Union was now fighting to end slavery.

emancipation: the act of freeing people from slavery

draft: a system for requiring citizens to join their country's armed forces

21.5 Gettysburg: A Turning Point

While neither side won the battle of Antietam, it was enough of a victory for Lincoln to take his first steps toward ending slavery. When the Civil War began, Lincoln had resisted pleas from abolitionists to make **emancipation,** or the freeing of slaves, a reason for fighting the Confederacy. He himself opposed slavery. But the purpose of the war, he said, "is to save the Union, and is not either to save or destroy slavery."

The Emancipation Proclamation   As the war dragged on, Lincoln changed his mind. Declaring an end to slavery, he realized, would discourage Europeans who opposed slavery from assisting the Confederacy. Freeing slaves could also deprive the Confederacy of a large part of its workforce.

On January 1, 1863, President Lincoln issued the Emancipation Proclamation. The proclamation, or formal order, declared slaves in all Confederate states to be free. This announcement had little immediate effect on slavery. The Confederate states simply ignored the document. Slaves living in states loyal to the Union were not affected by the proclamation.

Still, the Emancipation Proclamation changed the war from a fight to save the Union into a crusade for freedom. "The time came," Lincoln said later, "when I felt that slavery must die [so] that the nation might live."

The Draft   Meanwhile, both the North and the South had run out of volunteers to fill their armies. In 1862, the Confederacy passed the nation's first **draft** law. This law said that all white men aged 18 to 35 could be called for three years of military service. A year later, the North passed a similar law that drafted men aged 20 to 45.

Under both laws, a drafted man could avoid the army by paying a substitute to take his place. This provision led to charges that the conflict was "a rich man's war and a poor man's fight."

The Battle of Gettysburg   The need to pass draft laws was a sign that both sides were getting tired of war. Still, in the summer of 1863, Lee felt confident enough to risk another invasion of the North. He hoped to capture a northern city and help convince the weary North to seek peace.

Union and Confederate troops met on July 1, 1863, west of Gettysburg, Pennsylvania. The Union troops, about 90,000 strong, were led by newly appointed General George C. Meade. After a brief skirmish, they occupied four miles of high ground along an area known as Cemetery Ridge. About a mile to the west, some 75,000 Confederate troops gathered behind Seminary Ridge.

The following day, the Confederates attempted to find weak spots in the Union position. But the Union lines held firm. On the third day, Lee ordered an all-out attack on the center of the Union line. Cannons filled the air with smoke and thunder. George Pickett led 15,000 Confederate soldiers in a charge across the low ground separating the two forces.

Pickett's charge marked the northernmost point reached by southern troops during the war. But as the rebels pressed forward, Union gunners opened great holes in their advancing lines. Those brave men who managed to make their way to Cemetery Ridge were struck down by Union troops in hand-to-hand combat.

The losses at Gettysburg were staggering. More than 17,500 Union soldiers and 23,000 Confederate troops were killed or wounded in three days of battle. Lee, who lost about a third of his army, withdrew to Virginia. From this point on, he would only wage a defensive war on southern soil.

Opposition on the Union Home Front
Despite the victory at Gettysburg, Lincoln faced a number of problems on the home front. One was opposition to the war itself. A group of northern Democrats were far more interested in restoring peace than in saving the Union or ending slavery. Republicans called these Democrats "Copperheads" after a poisonous snake with that name.

Other northerners opposed the war because they were sympathetic to the Confederate cause. When a pro-slavery mob attacked Union soldiers marching through Maryland, Lincoln sent in troops to keep order. He also used his constitutional power to suspend, or temporarily discontinue, the right of **habeas corpus**. During the national emergency, citizens no longer had the right to a trial before being jailed. People who were suspected of disloyalty were jailed without trial.

Draft Riots
The Union draft law was passed just two months after Lincoln issued the Emancipation Proclamation. It also created opposition to the war. Some northerners resented being forced to fight to end slavery. Others protested that the new law "converts the Republic into one grand military dictatorship."

When the federal government began calling up men in July 1863, a riot broke out in New York City. For four days, crowds of angry white New

habeas corpus: a written order from a court that gives a person the right to a trial before being jailed

On July 3, 1863, General George Pickett led 15,000 Confederate troops in a charge against the Union lines. Row after row of Confederate soldiers fell under a rain of bullets until they finally retreated.

During the draft riots, white workers attacked free blacks. The whites feared African Americans would take their jobs and resented being forced to fight a war to end slavery. Almost 100 African Americans died during the four days of riots.

Yorkers burned draft offices and battled police. But their special targets were African Americans. Almost 100 black New Yorkers died as mobs attacked black boardinghouses, a black church, and a black orphanage. The rioting finally stopped when troops fresh from Gettysburg restored order.

Lincoln's Gettysburg Address Four months after the draft riots, President Lincoln traveled to Gettysburg. Thousands of the men who died there had been buried in a new cemetery overlooking the battlefield. Lincoln was among those invited to speak at the dedication of this new burial ground.

After an hour-long talk by another speaker, Lincoln rose and spoke a few words. Many of the 15,000 people gathered on Cemetery Ridge could not hear what he had to say. But the nation would never forget Lincoln's Gettysburg Address.

The president reminded his audience that the war was testing whether a nation "conceived in liberty, and dedicated to the proposition that all men are created equal…can long endure." He spoke of those who had died defending that ideal.

"The world will little note, nor long remember what we say here," he said, "but it can never forget what they did here." Finally, the president called on Americans to remain

> *dedicated to the great task remaining before us—that from these honored dead we take increased devotion to that cause for which they gave the last full measure of devotion—that we here highly resolve that these dead shall not have died in vain— that this nation, under God, shall have a new birth of freedom—and that government of the people, by the people, for the people, shall not perish from the earth.*

21.6 Vicksburg: A Besieged City

The Civil War was a war of many firsts for both sides. It was the first American war to use railroads to move troops and to keep them supplied. It was the first war in which telegraphs were used to communicate with distant armies. It was the first conflict to be recorded in photographs. It was also the first to see combat between armor-plated steamships.

The *Merrimac* and the *Monitor*   Early in the war, Union forces withdrew from the navy yard in Norfolk, Virginia. They left behind a warship named the *Merrimac*. The Confederacy began the war with no navy. They covered the wooden *Merrimac* with iron plates and added a powerful ram to its prow.

In response, the U.S. Navy built its own ironclad ship. Completed in less than 100 days, the *Monitor* had a flat deck and two heavy guns in a revolving turret. It was said to resemble a "cheese box on a raft."

In March 1862, the *Merrimac*, which the Confederates had renamed the *Virginia*, steamed into Chesapeake Bay. With cannonballs harmlessly bouncing off its sides, the iron monster destroyed three wooden ships and threatened the entire blockade fleet.

The next morning, the *Virginia* was met by the *Monitor*. The two ironclads exchanged shots for four hours before withdrawing. Neither could claim victory, and neither was harmed.

The battle of the *Merrimac* and the *Monitor* proved that "wooden vessels cannot contend with iron-clad ones." After that, both sides added ironclads to their navies. But the South was never able to build enough ships to threaten the Union blockade of southern harbors.

Control of the Mississippi   Ironclads were also part of the Union's campaign to divide the South by taking control of the Mississippi River. After seizing New Orleans in 1862, Admiral Farragut moved up the Mississippi to capture Baton Rouge and Natchez. At the same time, other Union ships gained control of Memphis, Tennessee.

The Union now controlled both ends of the Mississippi. The South could no longer move men or material up and down the river. But neither could the North as long as the Confederates continued to control one key location—Vicksburg, Mississippi.

The Granger Collection, New York

In 1862, the *Monitor* and the *Merrimac*, two ironclad ships, fought to a standstill. Nevertheless, the battle between the two signaled the end of wooden warships.

The Granger Collection, New York

For more than a month, Union forces bombarded Vicksburg with an average of 2,800 shells a day. Forced to eat horses, mules, dogs, and rats, the defenders finally surrendered.

Vicksburg The town of Vicksburg was located on a bluff above a hairpin turn in the Mississippi River. The city was easy to defend and difficult to capture. Whoever held Vicksburg could, with a few well-placed cannons, control movement on the Mississippi. But even Farragut had to admit that ships "cannot crawl up hills 300 feet high." An army would be needed to take Vicksburg.

In May 1863, General Grant battled his way to Vicksburg with the needed army. For six weeks, Union gunboats shelled the city from the river while Grant's army bombarded it from land. Slowly but surely, the Union troops burrowed toward the city in trenches and tunnels.

As shells pounded the city, people in Vicksburg dug caves into the hillsides for protection. To survive, they ate horses, mules, and bread made of corn and dried peas. "It had the properties of India rubber," said one Confederate soldier, "and was worse than leather to digest."

Low on food and supplies, Vicksburg surrendered on July 4, 1863. The Mississippi was a Union waterway, and the Confederacy was divided.

Problems on the Confederate Home Front As the war raged on, life in the South became grim. Because of the blockade, imported goods disappeared from stores. What few items were available were extremely expensive.

Unable to sell their tobacco and cotton, farmers planted food crops instead. Still, the South was often hungry. Invading Union armies destroyed crops. They also cut rail lines, making it difficult to move food and supplies to southern cities and army camps.

As clothing wore out, southerners made do with patches and rough, homespun cloth. At the beginning of the war, Mary Boykin Chesnut had written in her journal of well-dressed Confederate troops. By 1863, she was writing of soldiers dressed in "rags and tags."

By 1864, southern troops were receiving letters like this one: "We haven't got nothing in the house to eat but a little bit o' meal. I don't want to you to stop fighting them Yankees…but try and get off and come home and fix us all up some." Many soldiers found it hard to resist such pleas, even if going home meant deserting their units.

21.7 Fort Wagner: African Americans Join the War

Early in the war, abolitionists had urged Congress to recruit African Americans for the army. But at first, most northerners regarded the conflict as "a white man's war." Congress finally opened the door to black recruits in 1862. About 186,000 African Americans, many of them former slaves, enlisted in the Union army. Another 30,000 African Americans joined the Union navy.

The Massachusetts 54th Regiment   Massachusetts was one of the first states to organize black regiments. The most famous was the 54th Massachusetts Infantry, commanded by Colonel Robert Gould Shaw. Two of the 54th Infantry's 1,000 soldiers were sons of Frederick Douglass.

The men of the Massachusetts 54th were paid less than white soldiers. When the black soldiers learned this, they protested the unequal treatment by refusing to accept any pay at all. In a letter to Lincoln, Corporal James Henry Gooding asked, "Are we soldiers or are we laborers?…We have done a soldier's duty. Why can't we have a soldier's pay?" At Lincoln's urging, Congress finally granted black soldiers equal pay.

After three months of training, the Massachusetts 54th was sent to South Carolina to take part in an attack on Fort Wagner. As they prepared for battle, the men of the 54th faced the usual worries of untested troops. But they also faced the added fear that if captured, they might be sold into slavery.

African Americans at War   The assault on Fort Wagner was an impossible mission. To reach the fort, troops had to cross 200 yards of open, sandy beach. Rifle and cannon fire poured down on them. After losing nearly half of their men, the survivors of the 54th regiment pulled back. But their bravery won them widespread respect.

During the war, 166 African American regiments fought nearly 500 battles. Black soldiers often received little training, poor equipment, and less pay than white soldiers. They also risked death or enslavement if captured. Still, African Americans fought with great courage to save the Union and to end slavery forever.

African American soldiers demonstrated their courage during their attack on Fort Wagner. The 54th Massachusetts Infantry charged across 200 yards of open beach in their effort to reach the fort. The regiment withdrew after almost half of their men were lost.

In 1864, Lincoln gave command of all Union forces to Ulysses S. Grant. Grant believed in using his larger army to wear down the enemy regardless of the casualties that his own forces suffered.

21.8 Appomattox: Total War Brings an End

During the first years of the war, Lincoln had searched for a commander who was willing to fight the Confederates. None of his commanders caused him more frustration than George McClellan. After the failure of the Union army at the Battle of Bull Run, General McClellan continued to train his force, but refused to risk them in battle. When his patience had reached its limits, Lincoln wrote the following letter:

My dear McClellan:

If you are not using the army,
I should like to borrow
it for a while.

Yours respectfully,
A. Lincoln

Grant Takes Charge   The president finally found the leader he needed in General Grant. Grant's views on war were quite straightforward: "The art of war is simple enough. Find out where your enemy is. Get at him as soon as you can. Strike him as hard and as often as you can, and keep moving on."

Using this strategy, Grant mapped out a plan for ending the war. He would lead a large force against Lee to capture Richmond. At the same time, General William Tecumseh Sherman would lead a second army into Georgia to take Atlanta.

On to Richmond   In May 1864, Grant invaded Virginia with a force of more than 100,000 men. They met Lee's army of 60,000 in a dense forest known as "The Wilderness." In two days of fierce fighting, Grant lost 18,000 men. Despite these heavy losses, Grant would not retreat. "I propose to fight it out along this line," he said, "if it takes all summer." He followed Lee's army to Cold Harbor, where he lost 7,000 men in 15 minutes of fighting.

By the time the two forces reached Petersburg, a railroad center 20 miles south of Richmond, Grant's losses almost equaled Lee's entire army. But he was able to reinforce his army with fresh troops. Lee, who had also suffered heavy losses, could not.

Total War   Grant believed in total war—war on the enemy's will to fight and its ability to support an army. With his army tied down in northern Virginia, Grant ordered General Philip Sheridan to wage total war in Virginia's grain-rich Shenandoah Valley. "Let that valley be so left that crows flying over it will have to carry their rations long with them," ordered Grant.

In May 1864, General Sherman left Tennessee for Georgia with orders to inflict "all the damage you can against their war resources." In September, he reached Atlanta, the South's most important rail and manufacturing center. His army set the city ablaze.

The Reelection of Lincoln Any hope of victory for the South lay in the defeat of President Lincoln in the election of 1864. The northern Democrats nominated General George McClellan to run against Lincoln. Knowing that the North was weary of war, McClellan urged an immediate end to the conflict.

During most of the campaign, Lincoln doubted he would be reelected. Grant seemed stuck in northern Virginia. The large numbers of casualties suffered by his forces appalled many voters. Worse yet, there was no end to the conflict in sight.

Luckily for Lincoln, Sheridan's destruction of the Shenandoah Valley and Sherman's capture of Atlanta came just in time to rescue his campaign. These victories changed northern views of Lincoln and his prospects for ending the war. Lincoln was reelected in November 1864 and inaugurated the following March.

Sherman's March through Georgia After burning Atlanta, Sherman marched his army toward Savannah, promising to "make Georgia howl." His purpose was to destroy the last untouched supply base for the Confederacy.

During Sherman's march through Georgia, his troops destroyed everything they found of value. Fields were trampled or burned. Houses were ransacked (robbed). Hay and food supplies were burned. Roads were lined with dead horses, hogs, and cattle that his troops could not eat or carry away. Everything useful in a 60-mile-wide path was destroyed.

In December 1864, Sherman captured Savannah, Georgia. From there, he turned north and destroyed all opposition in the Carolinas. Marching 425 miles in 50 days, he reached Raleigh, North Carolina, by March 1865. There he waited for Grant's final attack on Richmond.

The End at Appomattox For nine months, Grant's forces battered Lee's army at Petersburg, the gateway to Richmond. On April 1, 1865, the Union forces finally broke through Confederate lines to capture the city. Two days later, Union troops marched into Richmond.

General Sherman, a believer in total war, cut a path of destruction through Georgia. The photograph below shows the burned ruins of Atlanta.

General Lee surrendered to General Grant at Appomattox Courthouse in Virginia. Grant was generous to Lee's soldiers, sending food to the troops and allowing them to keep their horses and mules.

Grant's soldiers moved quickly to surround Lee's army. Lee told his officers, "There is nothing left for me to do but go and see General Grant, and I would rather die a thousand deaths."

A Noble Surrender   On April 9, 1865, General Lee, in full dress uniform, arrived at Wilmer McLean's house in the village of Appomattox Courthouse. He was there to surrender his army to General Grant. The Union general met him in a mud-splattered and crumpled uniform.

Grant's terms of surrender were generous. Confederate soldiers were to be allowed to go home if they promised to fight no longer. They could take with them their own horses and mules, which they would need for spring plowing. Officers could keep their swords and weapons. Grant also ordered that food be sent to Lee's half-starved men. Lee accepted the terms.

As Lee returned to his headquarters, Union troops began to shoot their guns and cheer wildly. Grant told them to stop celebrating. "The war is over," he said, "the rebels are our countrymen again."

The Costs of War   The bloodiest war in the nation's history had ended at last. The Union had been saved and slavery abolished—but at horrifying costs. Billions of dollars had been spent on the conflict. Almost every family had lost a member, a relative, or a friend. More than 620,000 Union and Confederate soldiers lay dead in their graves. Thousands more came home missing an arm or a leg. In addition, the South had been devastated.

For President Lincoln, the end of the war was a happy day. "Thank god I have lived to see this," he said. "I have been living a nightmare for four years, and now the nightmare is over."

21.9 Chapter Summary

In this chapter, you read about the Civil War between the Union and the Confederacy. You used an annotated illustration of a soldier's haversack to help you understand the events and effects of the Civil War.

Both sides had advantages and disadvantages going into the war. The North had a larger population and more factories and railroads than the South, but it lacked strong military leadership. The South had serious economic problems, but it had capable generals and the advantage of fighting a defensive war.

New weapons and military tactics allowed soldiers to kill from greater distances. They also caused horrifying numbers of deaths and casualties. Unfortunately, medical knowledge was not as advanced as the weapons of war. Infection and disease spread rapidly through field hospital tents. More soldiers died of diseases than wounds, by a ratio of three to one.

After the Battle of Antietam, President Lincoln decided to issue his Emancipation Proclamation, freeing all slaves in the Confederacy. The proclamation helped to make the war a fight to end slavery.

As the war dragged on, both the Union and the Confederacy had to pass draft laws to gather more troops. Everyone wanted the war to be over. The defeat of Lee at Gettysburg ended the South's last attempt to invade the North. It proved to be a turning point.

President Lincoln finally found the leader he'd been looking for in General Grant. Grant began waging total war on the Confederacy. Union soldiers marched through the South, burning fields and houses and terrifying all those in their path.

When the Union army surrounded Confederate troops at Appomattox Courthouse, General Lee was forced to surrender. Grant was generous to the southern troops. He fed them and sent them home to rebuild their lives.

The rebellion had ended. The time had come to rebuild. In the next chapter, you will read about how the country tried to become whole again.

This painting, *End of the Rebellion in the United States,* 1865, celebrates the conclusion of the Civil War and the preservation of the Union.

The Granger Collection, New York

What is this man doing?

How are the lives of these former slaves different now?

The Reconstruction Era

22.1 Introduction

By the end of the Civil War, Americans longed for peace. But what kind of peace? One that punished the South for its rebellion? A peace that helped rebuild the devastated region? A peace that helped the four million African Americans freed from slavery become full and equal citizens? In his second inaugural address, delivered in 1865, President Abraham Lincoln spoke of a healing peace.

> *With malice [hatred] toward none, with charity for all, with firmness in the right as God gives us to see the right, let us strive on to finish the work we are in, to bind up the nation's wounds, to care for him who shall have borne the battle and for his widow and orphan, to do all which may achieve and cherish [hold dear] a just and lasting peace.*

The nation would never know how Lincoln planned to achieve such a peace. On April 14, 1865, just five days after the war ended, the president was assassinated (murdered) while attending a play at Ford's Theater in Washington, D.C. His murderer was an actor named John Wilkes Booth. Booth thought that killing Lincoln would somehow save the Confederacy.

With Lincoln dead, the task of healing the nation's wounds fell to Vice President Andrew Johnson. **Reconstruction,** or rebuilding the South and bringing the southern states back into the Union, would not be easy. For while the nation was united again, Americans remained deeply divided.

As you read about how Reconstruction was carried out, think about Lincoln's dream of "a just and lasting peace." Did the end of the war and of slavery lead to a peace based on liberty and justice for all? Or was Reconstruction just the first stage in a long and difficult struggle for equal rights for all Americans?

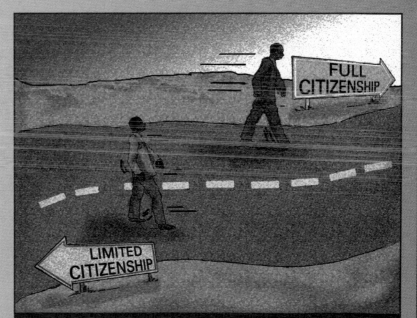

Graphic Organizer: Visual Metaphor
You will use this visual metaphor of a road to understand African Americans' struggle to gain full rights as citizens during Reconstruction.

freedmen: African Americans who had been set free from slavery

During Reconstruction, former slaves were granted the right to marry and live with family members from whom they had been separated. Forms, such as this one, allowed freedmen to keep a record of their marriage and family.

22.2 Presidential Reconstruction

In May 1865, President Andrew Johnson announced his Reconstruction plan. A former Confederate state could rejoin the Union once it had written a new state constitution, elected a new state government, repealed its act of secession, canceled its war debts, and ratified the Thirteenth Amendment, which abolished slavery.

Republicans in Congress suggested that southern states should also be required to give freed slaves the right to vote. Johnson, a southerner from Tennessee, disagreed. "White men alone," he said, "must manage the South."

By the fall of 1865, every southern state had met the president's requirements, and the Thirteenth Amendment became part of the Constitution. Presidential Reconstruction had begun.

The End of Slavery   While new governments were being formed across the South, **freedmen,** as former slaves were called, were testing the meaning of freedom. For some, freedom meant choosing a new name for a new life. For others, it meant getting married and knowing that the marriage was not only legal, but could last "until death do us part." Still others used their freedom to reunite scattered families.

Freedom brought problems as well as opportunities. Many freedmen began their new lives with nothing. Some were helped by their former masters. Others were left to fend for themselves. "The Yankee freed you," said one angry planter to his former slaves. "Now let the Yankee feed you."

The Freedmen's Bureau   Before the war ended, Congress established the Freedmen's Bureau to assist former slaves. The bureau provided food and medical care to both blacks and whites in the South. It also built schools for freedmen who were desperate to get an education. Booker T. Washington, who learned to read in such a school, later wrote:

It was a whole race trying to go to school. Few were too young, and none to old, to make the attempt to learn. As fast as teachers could be secured, not only were day-schools filled, but night-schools as well.

Forty Acres and a Mule Along with education, freedmen were desperate for land to farm so that they could support themselves. During the war, Congressman Thaddeus Stevens called on Congress to break up the South's large plantations and give every freed slave "forty acres and a mule" as payment for years of unpaid labor. "We have turned, or are about to turn, loose four million slaves without a hut to shelter them or a cent in their pockets," argued Stevens. "If we do not furnish them with homesteads…we had better left them in bondage."

Congress, however, did not support Stevens' plan. Most lawmakers argued that taking planters' land without paying for it would be a violation of the Constitution, which protects people's property rights.

The Black Codes As new state governments took power in the South, Stevens and others in Congress were alarmed to see that they were headed by the same people who had led the South before the war—wealthy white planters. Once in office, these leaders began passing laws known as *black codes* to control their former slaves.

The black codes served three purposes. The first was to spell out the rights of freedmen. Generally, they were given the right to marry, to own property, to work for wages, and to sue in court. But other rights of citizenship (civil rights) were denied them. Blacks, for example, could not vote or serve on juries in the South.

The second purpose of the black codes was to help planters find workers to replace their slaves. The codes required freedmen to work. Those without jobs could be arrested and hired out to planters. The codes also limited freedmen to farmwork or jobs requiring few skills. African Americans could not enter many trades or start businesses.

The third purpose of the black codes was to keep freedmen at the bottom of the social order in the South. Most codes called for the segregation of blacks and whites in public places. Black children were not allowed to attend public schools. A Louisiana lawmaker defended this ban by saying that it made no sense to spend tax money to educate "any but the superior race of man—the White race."

This political cartoon shows President Andrew Johnson using his veto to try to do away with the Freedmen's Bureau.

The Granger Collection, New York

22.3 Congressional Reconstruction

As 1865 came to a close, President Johnson announced that Reconstruction was over. The southern states were ready to rejoin the Union. Republican leaders in Congress did not agree. These lawmakers believed that the South would not be reconstructed until freedmen were granted full rights of citizenship.

The following year, Congress enacted two bills designed to help freedmen. The first extended the life of the Freedmen's Bureau. The second was the **Civil Rights** Act of 1866. It struck at the black codes by declaring freedmen to be full citizens with the same rights as whites. Johnson declared both bills unconstitutional and vetoed them. An angry Congress overrode his vetoes.

civil rights: the rights that the Constitution entitles all people to as citizens, especially equal treatment under the law

The Fourteenth Amendment To further protect the rights of African Americans, Congress approved the Fourteenth Amendment. This amendment declared former slaves to be citizens with full civil rights. "No state," it said, "shall…deny to any person…the equal protection of the laws." This meant that state governments could not treat some citizens as less equal than others.

President Johnson opposed the Fourteenth Amendment and called on voters to throw Republican lawmakers out of office. Instead, Republican candidates won a two-thirds majority in both houses of Congress in the 1866 election. From that point on, Congress controlled Reconstruction.

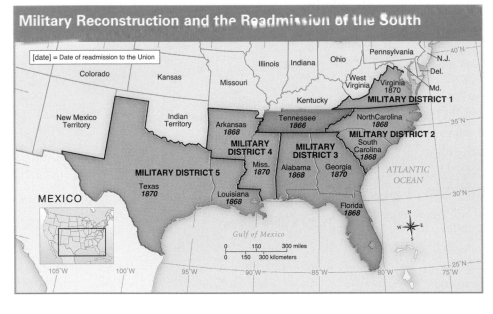

Military Reconstruction and the Readmission of the South

[date] = Date of readmission to the Union

Radical Republicans in Congress reorganized the South into the five military districts shown on this map.

Military Reconstruction Act Early in 1867, the new Congress passed its own Military Reconstruction Act. Once again, it did so over Johnson's veto. This plan divided the South into five military districts, each governed by a general who was backed by federal troops. The state governments set up under Johnson's Reconstruction plan were declared illegal. New governments were to be formed by southerners loyal to the United States—both black and white. Southerners who had supported the Confederacy were denied the right to vote.

Lawmakers also passed two acts designed to reduce Johnson's power to interfere with Congressional Reconstruction. The Command of the Army Act limited his power over the army. The Tenure of Office Act barred him from firing certain federal officials without the Senate's consent. President Johnson blasted both laws as unconstitutional. Then, to prove his point, he fired one of the officials protected under the Tenure of Office Act.

The Impeachment of Johnson   The House of Representatives responded to Johnson's challenge by voting to impeach the president. Besides violating the Tenure of Office Act, Johnson was charged with bringing "the high office of the President of the United States into contempt, ridicule, and disgrace, to the scandal of all good citizens."

During his trial in the Senate, the president's lawyers argued that Johnson's only "crime" had been to oppose Congress. If he were removed from office for that reason, they warned, "no future President will be safe who happens to differ with a majority of the House and Senate."

Two thirds of the Senate had to find the president guilty in order to remove him from office. Despite very heavy pressure to convict him, 7 Republicans and 12 Democrats voted "not guilty." Johnson escaped removal from office by one vote, but his power was broken.

Sharecropping   While Congress and the president battled over Reconstruction, African Americans in the South struggled to build new lives. Most former slaves desperately wanted land to farm but had no money to buy it. Meanwhile, their former owners desperately needed workers to farm their land but had no money to pay them. Out of the needs of both groups came a farming system called *sharecropping*.

Planters who turned to sharecropping divided their land into small plots. They rented these plots to individual tenant farmers (farmers who pay rent for the land they work). A few tenants paid the rent for their plots in cash. But most paid their rent by giving the landowner a share— usually a third or a half—of the crops they raised on their plots.

Sharecropping looked promising to freedmen at first. They liked being independent farmers

who worked for themselves. In time, they hoped to earn enough money to buy a farm of their own.

However, most sharecroppers had to borrow money from planters to buy the food, seeds, tools, and supplies they needed to survive until havest-time. Few ever earned enough from their crops to pay back what they owed. Rather than leading to independence, sharecropping usually led to a lifetime of poverty and debt.

Sharecroppers, such as these shown growing cotton, rented their land from plantation owners. In exchange, most paid one third to one half of their crops back to the landowners.

This poster celebrated the passage of the Fifteenth Amendment, which said that a citizen's right to vote could not be denied on account of race, color, or previous condition of servitude. The poster includes pictures of students, soldiers, preachers, teachers, and statesmen.

scalawags: white southerners who supported the federal government after the Civil War

carpetbaggers: northerners who went to the South after the Civil War to gain money and political power

22.4 Southern Reconstruction

The U.S. Army returned to the South in 1867. The first thing it did was begin to register voters. Because Congress had banned former Confederates from voting, the right to vote in the South was limited to three groups—freedmen, white southerners who had opposed the war, and northerners who had moved south after the war.

The South's New Voters   African Americans made up the South's largest group of new voters. Most black voters joined the Republican Party—the party of Lincoln and emancipation.

White southerners who had not supported secession were the next largest group. Many were poor farmers who had never voted before. In their eyes, the Democratic Party was the party of wealthy planters and secession. As a result, they also supported the Republican Party. Southern Democrats were appalled. They saw any white man who voted Republican as a traitor to the South. Democrats scorned such people as **scalawags,** or worthless scoundrels.

The last group of new voters were northerners who had moved south after the war. Yankee-hating southerners called the newcomers **carpetbaggers** after a type of handbag used by many travelers. They saw carpetbaggers as fortune hunters who had come south "to fatten on our misfortunes."

The 1868 Election   These new voters cast their first ballots in the 1868 presidential election. The Republican candidate was former Union general Ulysses S. Grant. Grant supported Reconstruction and promised to protect the rights of African Americans in the South. His Democratic opponent, Horatio Seymour, promised to end Reconstruction and return the South to its traditional leaders—white Democrats.

Seymour won a majority of white votes. Grant, however, was elected with the help of half a million black votes. The election's lesson to Republicans was that if they wanted to keep control of the White House and Congress, they needed African American votes.

The Fifteenth Amendment   In 1869, at President Grant's urging, Congress passed the Fifteenth Amendment. This amendment said that a citizen's right to vote "shall not be denied...on account of race, color, or previous condition of servitude." Its purpose was to protect the right of African American men to vote.

With the passage of this amendment, most abolitionists felt their work was done. The American Anti-Slavery Society declared the Fifteenth Amendment to be "the capstone and completion of our movement; the fulfillment of our pledge to the Negro race; since it secures to them equal political rights with the white race."

New State Constitutions   When the army finished registering voters, southern Reconstruction got underway. Across the South, delegates were elected to constitutional conventions. About a fourth of those elected were African Americans.

The conventions met and wrote new constitutions for their states. These constitutions were the most progressive, or advanced, in the nation. They guaranteed the right to vote to every adult male, regardless of race. They ended imprisonment for debt. They also called for the establishment of the first public schools in the South. The Georgia constitution stated that these schools should be "forever free to all the children of the state."

New State Governments

Elections were then held to fill state offices. To the dismay of southern Democrats, a majority of those elected were Republicans. About a fifth were African Americans.

The South's new state governments quickly ratified the Fourteenth and Fifteenth Amendments. By 1870, every southern state had finished this final step of Reconstruction and rejoined the Union.

Next, southern governments turned to the task of rebuilding. Work was begun on damaged roads, bridges, and railroads. Schools and hospitals were built. To pay for these projects, state legislatures raised taxes. Between 1860 and 1870, taxes in the South increased by up to 400 percent.

HON. ROBERT B. ELLIOTT, of South Carolina.

African Americans in Office   About a fifth of the South's new officeholders were African Americans. Blacks served in every southern legislature and held high offices in three states. Twenty-two African Americans represented their states in Congress—20 in the House, and 2 in the Senate. After watching these representatives, many of whom had been born slaves, Pennsylvania Congressman James G. Blaine observed:

This painting, by Robert Elliot, shows an African American congressman arguing for civil rights. During Reconstruction, many African Americans were elected to the House of Representatives and the Senate.

The colored men who took their seats in both the Senate and House did not appear ignorant or helpless. They were as a rule studious, earnest, ambitious men, whose public conduct...would be honorable to any race.

The Grange Collection, New York

22.5 The End of Reconstruction

Most whites in the South bitterly resented the southern Reconstruction governments. They hated the fact that these governments had been "forced" on them by the Yankees.

Many taxpayers also blamed their soaring tax bills on corruption (misuse of public office for personal gain) by the South's new leaders. One outraged Democrat called Republican rule in the South the "most stupendous system of organized robbery in history." While some southern officeholders did line their pockets with public funds, most, whether black or white, were honest, capable leaders. Still, when taxes increased, so too did opposition to the new state governments.

But what bothered southerners most about their Reconstruction governments was seeing former slaves voting and holding public offices. Across the South, Democrats vowed to regain power and return their states to "white man's rule."

Ku Klux Klan members, shown above, were determined to prevent African Americans from participating in politics. Using threats, beatings, and even murder, the Klan eventually reestablished white Democratic rule in the South.

White Terrorism   At first, Democrats tried to win black voters away from the Republican Party. When that failed, they tried using legal tricks to keep blacks from voting or taking office. In Georgia, for example, the legislature refused to seat elected black lawmakers until forced to by the state supreme court. When legal tricks failed, whites turned to terrorism, or violence.

Throughout the South, whites formed secret societies to drive African Americans out of political life. The most infamous of these groups was the Ku Klux Klan. Dressed in long, hooded robes and armed with guns and swords, Klansmen did their work at night. They started by threatening black voters and officeholders. African Americans who did not heed their threats were beaten, tarred and feathered, and even murdered.

The Enforcement Acts   In 1870 and 1871, Congress passed three laws to combat terrorism against African Americans. Known as the Enforcement Acts, these laws made it illegal to prevent another person from voting by bribery, force, or scare tactics.

President Grant sent troops into the South to enforce these acts. Hundreds of people were arrested for their terrorist activities. Those who were brought to trial, however, were seldom convicted. Few witnesses and jurors wanted to risk the Klan's revenge by speaking out against one of its members.

The Amnesty Act of 1872   By this time, however, most northerners were losing interest in Reconstruction and the plight of the freedmen. It was time, many people said, to "let the South alone." One sign of this changing attitude was the passage of the Amnesty Act of 1872. (*Amnesty* means forgiveness for past offenses.) This law allowed most former Confederates to vote once again.

The effects of the Amnesty Act were quickly seen. By 1876, Democrats had regained control of all but three states in the South. Republicans clung to power in South Carolina, Louisiana, and Florida, but only with the help of federal troops.

The Disputed Election of 1876   In 1876, Americans went to the polls to choose a new president. The Democrats nominated New York governor Samuel J. Tilden as their candidate. Rutherford B. Hayes was the Republican nominee. When the votes were tallied, Tilden won a majority of popular votes and 184 electoral votes, just one short of the 185 needed for election. Hayes received 165 electoral votes. Twenty electoral votes from four states were in dispute.

Congress, which was controlled by Republicans, appointed a commission to decide who should get the disputed votes. The commission awarded all 20 to Hayes, giving him exactly the 185 electoral votes he needed to win. Outraged Democrats in Congress threatened to block the election of anyone. Inauguration day drew near with no president in sight.

The Compromise of 1877   At the last moment, the two parties agreed to compromise. Democrats allow Hayes to become president. In return, Hayes agreed to give southern states "the right to control their own affairs."

Once in office, President Hayes withdrew all remaining federal troops from the South. After that, Democrats quickly took control of the last southern states. "This is a white man's country," boasted South Carolina senator Ben Tillman, "and white men must govern it."

Most white southerners cheered the end of Reconstruction. But for freedmen, the return of the South to "white man's rule" was a giant step backward. "The whole South—every state in the South," observed a Louisiana freedmen, "has got into the hands of the very men that held us as slaves."

Thomas Nast's political cartoon "Is This a Republican Form of Government?" condemns northern indifference to the violence that African Americans had to endure as Reconstruction ended.

The Granger Collection, New York

22.6 Reconstruction Reversed

With Reconstruction over, southern leaders talked of building a "New South" humming with mills, factories, and cities. Between 1880 and 1900, the number of textile mills in the South grew rapidly. Birmingham, Alabama, became a major iron-making center. Still, most southerners, black and white, remained trapped in an "Old South" of poverty.

Losing Ground in Education   During Reconstruction, freedmen had pinned their hopes for a better life on education provided by the South's first public schools. When southern Democrats regained control of states, however, they cut spending on education. "Free schools are not a necessity," explained the governor of Virginia. Schools, he said, "are a luxury…to be paid for, like any other luxury, by the people who wish their benefits."

As public funding dried up, many schools closed. Those that stayed open often charged fees. By the 1880s, only about half of all black children in the South attended school.

This painting shows a new South rising from the ashes of the Civil War. Although southern leaders hoped this would be the future of the South, most whites and African Americans continued to live in poverty.

Losing Voting Rights   Southern Democrats also reversed the political gains made by freedmen after the war. Many southern states passed laws requiring citizens who wanted to vote to pay a poll tax. The tax was set high enough that voting, like education, became a luxury that many black southerners could not afford.

Some southern states also required citizens to pass a literacy test to show that they could read before allowing them to vote. These tests were rigged (set up) to fail any African American, regardless of his education.

In theory, these laws applied equally to blacks and whites and, for that reason, did not violate the Fifteenth Amendment. In practice, however, whites were excused from paying poll taxes or taking literacy tests by a "grandfather clause" in the laws. This clause said the taxes and tests did not apply to any man whose father or grandfather could vote on January 1, 1867. Since no blacks could vote on that date, the grandfather clause applied only to whites.

African Americans protested that these laws denied them their Constitutional right to vote. The Supreme Court, however, ruled that the new voting laws did not violate the Fifteenth Amendment because they did not deny anyone the right to vote on the basis of race.

Drawing a "Color Line" During Reconstruction, most southern states had outlawed segregation in public places. When Democrats returned to power, they reversed these laws and drew a "color line" between blacks and whites in public life. Whites called the new segregation acts **Jim Crow laws**.

Not all white southerners supported segregation. When a Jim Crow law was proposed in South Carolina, the Charleston *News and Courier* tried to show how silly it was by taking segregation to ridiculous extremes.

> If there must be Jim Crow cars on railroads, there should be Jim Crow cars on the street railways. Also on all passenger boats.... There should be Jim Crow waiting saloons [waiting rooms] at all stations, and Jim Crow eating houses.... There should be Jim Crow sections of the jury box, and a separate Jim Crow...witness stand in every court—and a Jim Crow Bible for colored witnesses to kiss.

Instead of being a joke, as intended, most of these "silly" suggestions soon became laws.

Plessy v. Ferguson African Americans argued that segregation laws violated the Fourteenth Amendment's guarantee of "equal protection of the laws." Homer Plessy, who was arrested for refusing to obey a Jim Crow law, took his protest all the way to the Supreme Court. His case is known as *Plessy v. Ferguson.*

In 1896, the majority of Supreme Court justices ruled that segregation laws did not violate the Fourteenth Amendment as long as the facilities available to both races were roughly equal. Justice John Marshall Harlan, a former slaveholder, disagreed. "Our Constitution is color blind," he wrote, "and neither knows nor tolerates classes among citizens."

After the Supreme Court's decision in *Plessy v. Ferguson,* more Jim Crow laws were passed. Blacks and whites attended separate schools, played in separate parks, and sat in separate sections in theaters. But despite the Court's ruling that these separate facilities must be equal, those set aside for African Americans were almost always inferior to facilities labeled "whites only."

Jim Crow laws: Laws enforcing segregation of blacks and whites in the South after the Civil War. "Jim Crow" was a black character from an entertainer's act in the mid-1800s.

In the cartoon below, Thomas Nast attacks the Ku Klux Klan and other white supremacist groups. According to this cartoon, what did supremacist groups do to African Americans? What does the label "Worse Than Slavery" mean?

The Granger Collection, New York

22.7 Responding to Segregation

African Americans responded to segregation in many ways. The boldest protested openly. Doing so, however, was dangerous. Blacks who spoke out risked being attacked by white mobs. Some were even lynched, or murdered (often by hanging), for speaking out against "white rule." During the 1890s, there was an African American lynched somewhere in the United States almost every day.

African Americans responded to the segregation that accompanied the end of Reconstruction with various self-help programs. This photograph shows medical students in 1900 at Howard University, an institution in Washington, D.C., that is devoted to educating African Americans.

Migration Thousands of African Americans responded to segregation by leaving the South. A few chose to return to Africa. In 1878, some 200 southern blacks declared that "the colored man had no home in America." They chartered a ship and sailed to Liberia, a nation founded by freed American slaves on the coast of West Africa. Most, however, chose to stay in the United States. "We are not Africans now," wrote one freedman, "but colored Americans."

Many blacks migrated from the South to cities in the North. There they competed for jobs with recent immigrants from Europe. Others headed to the West where they found work as cowboys and Indian fighters.

Benjamin "Pap" Singleton and Henry Adams organized the migration of thousands of black families to Kansas in the "Exodus of 1879." The "exodusters," as the migrants were known, faced many hardships on their journey west. Bands of armed whites patrolled roads in Kansas in an effort to drive the migrants away. Still, the exodusters pushed on, saying, "We had rather suffer and be free."

Self-Help Most African Americans, however, remained in the South. They worked hard in families, churches, and communities to improve their lives. While most blacks farmed for a living, a growing number started their own businesses. Between 1865 and 1903, the number of black-owned businesses in the South soared from about 2,000 to 25,000.

Families, churches, and communities also banded together to build schools and colleges for black children across the South. Because of these efforts, literacy among American Americans rose rapidly. When slavery ended in 1865, only 5 percent of African Americans could read. By 1900, more than 50 percent could read and write.

22.8 Chapter Summary

In this chapter, you learned about the events of Reconstruction in the South after the Civil War. You used a visual metaphor to understand African Americans' struggle to achieve full rights as citizens during the five phases of Reconstruction.

In the first phase, the Thirteenth Amendment became part of the Constitution, and slavery became illegal. However, freedmen still could not vote and were allowed to work only at unskilled jobs. African Americans were kept separate from whites in public. Black children could not attend public schools.

Congressional Reconstruction was an attempt to give African Americans all the rights of citizens. The Fourteenth Amendment granted full citizenship to all people born in the United States.

Congress sent federal troops back to the South to begin Southern Reconstruction. The Fifteenth Amendment guaranteed the right to vote to eligible citizens of all races. Many African Americans were elected to state government offices during this third phase of Reconstruction.

During the fourth phase of Reconstruction, President Hayes withdrew federal troops from the South. Throughout the South, the men who had held African Americans in slavery before the war were again in charge of their lives and livelihoods.

During the final stage of Reconstruction, southern state governments began reversing the gains that African Americans had made. Education and the right to vote in the South became luxuries that only white southerners could afford. Jim Crow laws quickly reestablished segregation.

African Americans were free to leave the South, and many did. They migrated to the North and the West, or returned to Africa. But most remained in the South, where they formed communities to help themselves build better lives.

In the next chapter, you will read about the tensions that arose as Americans settled the West.

This Thomas Nast cartoon celebrates the Civil Rights Bill of 1875. This bill and other Reconstruction legislation tried to give full citizenship rights to African Americans.

The Granger Collection, New York

Why is this soldier fighting on foot?

What country's army does this soldier belong to?

What group does this soldier belong to? Why is he fighting?

The Granger Collection, New York

Tensions in the West

23.1 Introduction

In the spring of 1889, two women arrived at the Nez Percé reserva-tion in Lapwai, Idaho. One of them, Jane Gay, had nursed soldiers during the Civil War. The other, Alice Fletcher, had been a leader in the growing movement for women's rights. Now a new cause had brought these women west. They wanted to improve the lives of Native Americans.

Gay and Fletcher were just two of the thousands of Americans who moved west after the Civil War. As you read in the last chapter, during this period politicians in the East were arguing over Reconstruction. Mean-while, railroad builders, miners, ranchers, and farmers continued to push westward. In this chapter, you will read about how the settlers' dreams of freedom and opportunity clashed with the dreams of the Native Americans who already lived in the West.

The conflict between settlers and Indians was not just a fight over land. It was a conflict between two very different cultures and ways of seeing the world.

Jane Gay and Alice Fletcher discovered these deep differences soon after they arrived at Lapwai. Like other Indians, the Nez Percé had already been forced onto reservations to make way for new set-tlers. Now Fletcher told the Indians that the government wanted to divide the Lapwai Reservation into farm plots. Each family would receive one plot. Then the Nez Percé could live like other Americans.

The Indians listened in stony silence. Settlers might think of owning a plot of land as a way to be free. But to a Nez Percé, being tied to one spot of earth would be like being in jail.

Finally, one man spoke. "We do not cut up our land in little pieces," the Indian said. "We have not told you to do it. We are content to be as we are."

The Indian's words show why tensions were bound to develop between settlers and Native Americans. As you read about the Nez Percé and other Indian groups, you will see how the progress of the settlers meant the end of the Indians' ways of life.

Graphic Organizer: Annotated Illustration
You will use an annotated illustration of a buffalo hide to record information about four groups of settlers and their impact on native peoples.

23.2 The Nez Percé

For centuries, the Nez Percé freely roamed the lush mountains and valleys where Oregon, Washington, and Idaho come together today. Their name, which means "pierced nose" in French, was given to them by French explorers. The French had confused the Nez Percé with other Indians who decorated their noses with pieces of shell. In reality, the Nez Percé did not usually pierce their noses or wear nose ornaments.

When horses arrived in the Northwest in the 1700s, the Nez Percé became expert riders and horse breeders. They developed their own special breed known as the Appaloosa. These beautiful, spotted horses were fast, strong, and brave. The Nez Percé trained them to ride into stampeding buffalo herds and single out one animal for the kill.

The Nez Percé treasured their homeland and way of life. But in the years after the Civil War, more and more strangers arrived from the East to settle in the Pacific Northwest. The world of the Nez Percé would never be the same.

Friendship with Whites For decades the Nez Percé were among the friendliest of all western Indians toward whites. In 1805, they saved Lewis and Clark and their expedition from starvation. They were also friendly with the first trappers, traders, and missionaries who came to the Northwest. The Nez Percé had never killed a white person.

The friendship was finally broken by Americans' hunger for land and riches. In the 1860s, miners swarmed over Nez Percé land, looking for gold. Settlers followed. Some Nez Percé bands signed treaties in which they agreed to give up their land and move to the Lapwai Reservation in Idaho. Other bands refused to sign any treaty.

One of these "no treaty" bands lived in the Wallowa Valley of eastern Oregon. It was led by a man whose Indian name meant "Thunder Rolling in the Mountains." The newcomers called him Chief Joseph. In 1877, representatives of the United States government presented Chief Joseph with a terrible choice. You can give up your land peacefully and move to Lapwai, they told him, or else army troops will come and force you out.

Fearing a war he could not win, Chief Joseph agreed to move. "I would give up my country," he said, "rather than have

Hurricane Creek runs majestically through the Wallowa Valley, home to the Nez Percé Indians. In the background is Chief Joseph Mountain.

the blood of white men upon the hands of my people."

Blood Is Shed That summer, 700 Nez Percé left the Wallowa Valley, their hearts filled with bitterness. One night, a group of angry young warriors slipped out of camp and murdered several whites. Chief Joseph knew that the killings would bring soldiers to punish his people. For the first time, the Nez Percé would be at war with whites.

The soldiers came. Still hoping to avoid war, Indians carrying the white flag of peace came forward to talk. Foolishly, the troops opened fire anyway. Minutes later, 34 soldiers were dead. "I have been in lots of scrapes," reported a survivor, "but I never went up against anything like the Nez Percé in all my life."

The Flight to Canada In desperation, the Nez Percé headed for the one place where they might still live free—Canada. For the next three months, Chief Joseph led the U.S. Army on a chase of more than 1,000 miles through rugged mountain country. Although greatly outnumbered, his warriors won several battles.

The chase ended less than 40 miles from the Canadian border. Forced to surrender, Chief Joseph spoke his heart in these words:

Chief Joseph was a great leader among the Nez Percé. He promised his dying father that he would not sell or give away his people's land. Tragically, white settlers and government troops drove the Nez Percé from their homes in the 1870s. Chief Joseph died of a "broken heart" on a remote Indian reservation in 1904.

> *"I am tired of fighting. Our chiefs are killed.... The old men are all dead.... It is cold and we have no blankets. The little children are freezing to death. My people, some of them, have run away to the hills, and have no blankets, no food; no one knows where they are.... Hear me, my chiefs. I am tired; my heart is sick and sad. From where the sun now stands I will fight no more forever."*

After their surrender, Chief Joseph and his followers were sent to a barren reservation in Oklahoma. There they began to fall sick and die. Soon they had a cemetery just for babies, with more than a hundred graves.

Chief Joseph begged the government to allow his people to join the rest of the Nez Percé in Lapwai. Although some did go to Lapwai, others, including Chief Joseph, were sent to the Coleville Reservation in Washington. They never went back to their homeland. When the chief died in 1904, the doctor listed the cause of death as "a broken heart."

homesteader: a farmer who is given a plot of public land (called a *homestead*) in return for cultivating it

transcontinental railroad: a railroad that crosses a continent (*trans* means "across")

23.3 New Interest in the West

Settlers had been gradually forcing Native Americans from their land ever since the first colonists arrived in North America. Still, by the start of the Civil War, the West was populated mostly by roaming Indians and huge herds of buffalo. Then, in 1861 and 1862, Congress passed two laws that stirred new interest in the West—the Homestead Act and the Pacific Railroad Act.

The Homestead Act   The Homestead Act offered farmers 160 acres of public land in the West for free. All the farmer, or **homesteader,** had to do was clear the land and farm it for five years. At the end of that time, the homesteader was given ownership of the land.

The impact of the new law was enormous. Year after year, the promise of free land drew hopeful homesteaders west. Between 1860 and 1910, the number of farms in the United States tripled from 2 million to more than 6 million.

The Pacific Railroad Act   The Pacific Railroad Act called for the building of a **transcontinental railroad** to link the Atlantic and Pacific coasts. This huge construction project was given to two railroad companies, the Union Pacific and the Central Pacific.

To help the companies pay for the project, Congress gave them sections of free land for every mile of track they laid. Later, the railroads could sell this land to settlers. The government also loaned the two companies more than 60 million dollars.

As settlers moved west, they seized more and more land from the Native Americans who lived and hunted there. Below we see a Native American village near Fort Laramie, in what is now Wyoming.

The Pacific Railroad Act kicked off the greatest period of railroad construction in the nation's history. In 1860, there were 30,000 miles of track in the United States, mostly in the Northeast. By 1900, the country had 200,000 miles of track, much of it in the West.

Railroads opened the West to a flood of new settlers. The newcomers included farmers and ranchers, prospectors and preachers, schemers and dreamers, and more than a few crooks. But most were ordinary folk who dreamed of a new start. For them, the West was a place where a lot of hard work and a little luck could make their dreams come true.

23.4 The Railroad Builders

The Granger Collection, New York

The plan for building a transcontinental railroad looked simple enough on paper. The Union Pacific would start in Nebraska and build tracks westward across the Great Plains and the Rocky Mountains. Meanwhile, the Central Pacific would start in California and lay tracks eastward across the Sierra Nevada mountains and the Great Basin. The two lines would meet somewhere in between the starting points. The company that laid the most track would get more land, more loans, and more profits.

Laying track was hard work. First the surveyors studied the land and chose the route for the tracks. They were followed by the graders, who prepared the land. Armed with picks and shovels, the graders cut through hills and filled up valleys to make the route as level as possible.

Chinese laborers were recruited to do the backbreaking work required to lay rails across the Sierra Nevada mountains. They were paid one dollar a day for their labor.

Next came the tracklayers. They put down wooden ties and hauled in heavy iron rails. One rail weighed 700 pounds, and there were 400 rails in each mile of track. Last came the spikers. The spikers nailed the rails to the ties with spikes—ten spikes per rail, three hammer blows for every spike.

The Union Pacific Builds West   The Union Pacific got off to a slow start. Then, in 1866, a former Civil War general named Grenville Dodge took charge of construction. Dodge had built railroads before the war, and, as a military officer, he knew how to lead men. Now he commanded an army of 10,000 workers. Most of them were Irish immigrants who were fleeing the slums of eastern cities. They were joined by other immigrants, ex-soldiers, Mexicans, and freed slaves. All were young men who needed jobs and craved adventure. Most of all, they hoped to start new lives in the open spaces of the West.

Native Americans depended heavily on the buffalo for food, shelter, and clothing. As the railroad moved west, bored passengers and hunters shot buffalo out the windows of trains. Between 1872 and 1874, nine million buffalo were killed. By 1900, there were fewer than 50 buffalo left in the United States.

By 1867, Dodge's crews were laying as much as seven miles of track a day across the plains. The workers lived in tent cities that followed the tracks west. These portable towns were tough, often dangerous places. A reporter wrote, "Not a day passes but a dead body is found somewhere in the vicinity with pockets rifled of their contents."

For the Plains Indians, the railroad was an invasion of their homeland. They watched in anger as millions of buffalo were slaughtered, destroying their main source of food. Warriors attacked the work crews and derailed supply trains by prying up sections of track. Grenville Dodge demanded military help, and soon he had 5,000 troops guarding his crews as they inched their way west.

The Central Pacific Builds East   In California, the Central Pacific Railroad faced different problems. Soon after the company began laying track, many of the workers dashed off to newly discovered silver mines in Nevada. Construction practically stopped.

In desperation, Charles Crocker, the head of construction, hired 50 Chinese workers. He doubted that the Chinese were big enough to do heavy construction. On average, they weighed just 110 pounds. But the Chinese surprised him. They could do as much work in a day as any other crew, and often more.

Crocker was so impressed that he sent agents to China to hire more Chinese workers. The agents were lucky. War and unrest had driven millions of Chinese into poverty and debt. Young men jumped at the chance of going to America to build a railroad. Most of them planned to save their money and return to China as wealthy men.

More than 12,000 Chinese laborers worked for the Central Pacific. They cleared trees, shoveled dirt, blasted tunnels, and laid tracks. At least 1,000 Chinese workers lost their lives in explosions, snow slides, and other accidents. Despite these losses, the workers managed to lay up to ten miles of track in a day.

The Two Lines Meet   On May 10, 1869, the two lines met at Promontory Point, Utah. A golden spike was driven in to complete the 1,800 miles of track. In time, a network of railroads would bring new settlers, encourage construction of towns and cities, and allow mail and supplies to be shipped clear across the country.

The Chinese workers, who had contributed so much to building the railroad, were not acknowledged at the celebration. Their reward for years of hard work was to lose their jobs. A few of them fulfilled their dream of returning to China. But most stayed on in America, helping to build new farms and businesses across the West.

23.5 The Miners

A second group of pioneers—the miners—dreamed of striking it rich. The discovery of gold in California in 1848 set off a great treasure hunt in the mountains and deserts of the West. By 1874, gold or silver had been found in California, Oregon, Washington, Nevada, Montana, Colorado, Arizona, and New Mexico.

Boomtowns and Ghost Towns   Mining in the West followed a predictable pattern. First came the discovery of gold or silver. Soon fortune seekers from around the world flocked to the site. Almost overnight, mining camps mushroomed into fast-growing settlements called *boomtowns*.

The discovery of gold or silver often resulted in instant "boomtowns" throughout the West. Pictured here is Leadville, Colorado, in the 1870s. After mining was finished, ghost towns quickly replaced the boomtowns.

Heavy machinery, used to remove gold and silver buried deep in rocks, badly damaged the land.

Newspaper reporter J. Ross Browne described the birth of one such town, Gila City, in present-day Arizona:

> *Enterprising men hurried to the spot with barrels of whiskey and billiard tables.... Traders crowded in with wagons of pork and beans. Gamblers came with cards.... There was everything in Gila City within a few months but a church and a jail.*

These instant towns had no government, no law, and little order. Robbery and murder were common. Honest miners fought back by forming "vigilance committees" to control crime. The members of these committees, called *vigilantes,* handed out quick justice. A suspected murderer might be arrested, tried, convicted, and hanged all in the same day. If asked about their methods, the vigilantes pointed out that there were no courts or jails nearby. And no miner had time to waste guarding criminals.

When the easy-to-find gold or silver was gone, most miners moved on. Just seven years after its birth, Gila City was a ghost town. All that remained, wrote Browne, were "three chimneys and a coyote."

Mining Changes the West In many ways, mining was destructive. It damaged the land and displaced many Native Americans. But most Americans saw mining as a source of wealth and opportunity. Some boomtowns, like Reno and Denver, survived to become prosperous cities. Mining also opened up the West's mountains and deserts to other settlers. Some were businesspeople who invested in the heavy equipment needed to extract hard-to-find ore from western mountains. Others were farmers and ranchers. These were the people who would turn lonely territories into new western states.

23.6 Ranchers and Cowboys

A third group of settlers in the West consisted of ranchers and the cowboys who tended their herds of cattle. At the end of the Civil War, millions of longhorn cattle roamed the plains of Texas. The longhorns got their name from their impressive horns, which could measure more than seven feet from tip to tip. The market for all this beef was the crowded cities of the East. Cattle worth 3 dollars a head in Texas might be sold for 50 dollars in New York or Chicago. The problem was how to transport the cattle to the cities. This challenge was complicated by the presence of angry Indians and stampeding buffalo herds.

The Extermination of the Buffalo   The railroads made the ranchers' task much easier. As the railroads moved onto the Great Plains, buffalo hunters followed. The hunters killed huge numbers of buffalo for their hides and bones, which were shipped by rail for sale in the East.

The Plains Indians depended on the buffalo for food. They were horrified by the slaughter. So were some other Americans. In 1874, Congress passed a bill outlawing the killing of more buffalo than could be used for food. But President Grant refused to sign the bill into law. General Philip Sheridan supported Grant's decision. "You ought to give each hunter a medal," he said. "Let them kill, skin and sell until the buffalo are exterminated [wiped out]. Then your prairies can be covered with cattle and the cowboy."

By 1880, the buffalo had all but vanished. With their food gone, the Plains Indians had little choice but to move to reservations. The plains were now open to ranchers and their cattle.

The "Long Drive"   The railroads also solved the cattlemen's transportation problem. In 1867, Joseph McCoy built a stockyard next to the railroad in Abilene, Kansas. A *stockyard* is a large holding pen where cattle are kept temporarily. That summer, cowboys herded a few thousand cattle from Texas to the Abilene stockyard, in what they called the "long drive." There the cattle were loaded into boxcars and shipped east. Over the next 20 years, cowboys drove more than 5 million cattle to Abilene and other "cow towns" beside the rails.

Being a cowboy was dangerous and low-paying work. Still, life on the trail attracted many young adventurers. Most were Texans. About a third were of Mexican or African American heritage. Rarely, however, were black cowboys promoted to trail boss. Jim Perry, for example, was an expert rider, roper, and trail cook. He once said, "If it weren't for my damned old black face, I'd have been a boss long ago."

During the long drive, cowboys worked 17 hours a day, seven days a week, for three to four months. Much of the work was boring—except for moments of terror when a herd stampeded. By the time they reached the end of the trail, most cowboys were ready for rowdy fun, including drinking, gambling, and brawling. That made the cow towns wild, noisy, and often dangerous places.

The most notorious cow town was Dodge City in Kansas. An eastern

Cowboys, like Isom Dart, pictured below, moved out west to herd cattle. Many cowboys dreamed of getting their own herd and making their fortune in the rapidly growing cattle empire.

The Granger Collection, New York

The Granger Collection, New York

Dodge City, Kansas, shown above, was a wild cow town. When cowboys reached the end of the drive, they were ready for fun.

newspaper described it as "a wicked little town." Between 1872 and 1878, 64 victims of gunfights were buried on the hill above the town. Later, several graves were dug up to make way for a new school. The gravediggers turned up a fine collection of skeletons, most still wearing their cowboy boots. To this day, the Dodge City cemetery is known as Boot Hill.

The End of the "Long Drive"   After growing rapidly for 20 years, the cattle industry collapsed in 1887. The winter of 1886–1887 was the worst that anyone could remember. January was so cold that one cowboy described his life as "hell without the heat." Whole herds of cattle froze to death. Ranchers called that terrible winter the "Great Die-Up." Many of them lost everything. The survivors reduced their herds and fenced their grazing lands. They built barns and raised hay so that they could shelter and feed their animals in winter. The days of the long drive were over. Wild cow towns became civilized ranching centers. Adventuresome cowboys settled down to work as ranch hands.

The cattlemen's glory years faded into the past. Still, they had much to be proud of. They had opened the Great Plains to settlement. And they had created an industry that remains an important part of life in the West today.

23.7 The Homesteaders

Farmers followed the ranchers onto the Great Plains. For half a century, the plains had been viewed as too dry for farming. Mapmakers labeled the area the "Great American Desert." Then in the 1870s, a few homesteaders plowed and planted the grassland. They were lucky. These were years of plentiful rain, and their fields yielded fine crops.

The western railroads and land dealers made the most of this good luck. Maybe the plains used to be too dry for farming, they said, but not any more. Some even said that rain had followed the rails west. "The increase of railroads," wrote a Colorado journalist, "has the…effect of producing more showers." Others gave farming the credit for the wet years, claiming that "rain follows the plow."

The Homesteaders Arrive   Rain might not follow the rails or the plow, but a rush of new settlers did. By 1900, some 500,000 homesteaders had moved onto the Great Plains. Many were farm families from the East who were lured west by the promise of free or cheap land. Some were former slaves looking for a new start in freedom. Tens of thousands of European immigrants also settled the plains. While most of them were seeking land, one group, Russian Mennonites, came looking for religious freedom.

Farming the Dry Plains   The homesteaders faced huge challenges as they struggled to turn grasslands into grain fields. Rain was unreliable. Some years their crops withered under the hot prairie sun. Other years clouds of locusts, or large grasshoppers, swept across the plains, eating everything in their path. In addition, the plains had few trees, so there was little wood for homes.

Over time, the homesteaders solved these problems. Instead of using wood, they built houses out of chunks of sod (mats of soil held together by grassy roots). They used windmills to pump water from deep in the ground. They learned how to plow deeply to reach moist soil. The Mennonites introduced a type of winter wheat that thrived on the plains. With hard work and the right crop, homesteaders made the Great Plains the most productive wheat-growing region in the world.

The plains greeted newcomers with miles and miles of treeless grassland. Since lumber was expensive or unavailable, farmers built homes out of sod, or mats of soil. Sod houses proved to be cool in the summer and warm in the winter.

Geography Challenge
Land Losses of Native Americans

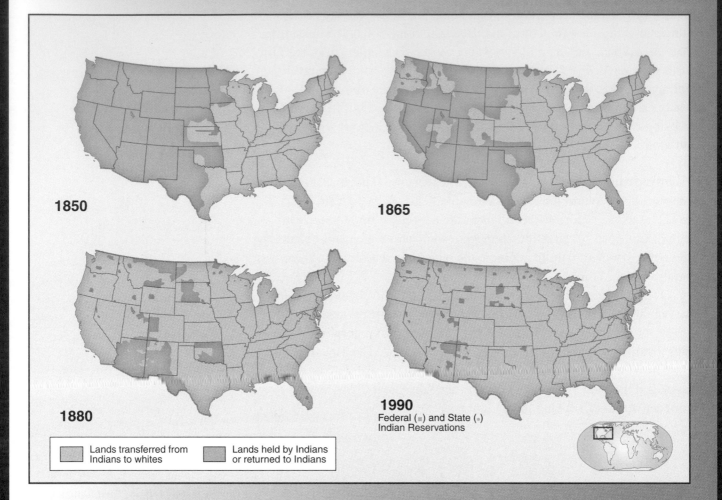

1850

1865

1880

1990
Federal (■) and State (•)
Indian Reservations

Lands transferred from Indians to whites	Lands held by Indians or returned to Indians

1. Identify at least four interesting details on these maps.

2. Approximately what percentage of the land in the continental United States was held by Native Americans in 1850? 1865? 1880? 1990?

3. What are some of the reasons Native Americans lost so much land between 1850 and 1990?

4. How did you think Native Americans responded to this loss of land?

23.8 War on the Plains

In 1874, a long column of soldiers marched into the Black Hills of the Dakota Territory. The troops were led by a famous Indian fighter named George Custer. Officially, Custer was looking for a place to build a fort. Unofficially, he had heard rumors that the Black Hills were filled with gold. And he meant to find it.

The Black Hills were sacred to the Sioux Indians, and the United States had signed a treaty that set this region aside as the Sioux homeland. But once Custer's men found traces of gold, the treaty meant little. The Sioux would just have to get out of the way.

It was a familiar scene. During the 1860s, a number of small wars had raged across the West as Native Americans tried to save their homelands. In the 1870s, the wars on the plains would settle the issue once and for all.

Reservation Life   In 1867, Congress tried to separate Indians and settlers by forcing the Indians onto reservations. In exchange for their land, the Native Americans were promised food, farm tools, and schools where their children would learn to "live like whites."

The nomadic Plains peoples hated the idea of being penned up on a reservation. A Sioux chief named Sitting Bull spoke for many Indians when he said:

> "I will remain what I am until I die, a hunter, and when there are no buffalo or other game I will send my children to hunt and live on prairie mice, for when an Indian is shut in one place, his body becomes weak."

Despite Sitting Bull's words, the buffalo were disappearing, and most Plains Indians had little choice but to move to reservations. Once they did, however, the promised food often failed to arrive. Sometimes dishonest Indian agents sold it to settlers instead. Often the food was spoiled by the time it reached the Indians.

Hungry and unhappy with reservation life, many warriors left the reservations to look for game or to attack settlers. When they did, they were hunted down by army troops.

General George Crook sympathized with the Indians. "I do not wonder that when these Indians see their wives and children starving they go to war," he wrote. "And then we are sent out to kill. It is an outrage."

Sitting Bull's Indian name was Tatanka-Iyotanka. This Sioux chief resisted white settlement with passion and courage. Nevertheless, his leadership was not enough to stop the tide of newcomers.

The Granger Collection, New York

This artist's depiction of Custer's Last Stand, or the Battle of the Little Big Horn, shows Sioux warriors overwhelming Custer's troops. Custer himself was killed by a gunshot to the head. The battle lasted only half an hour.

The Battle of the Little Big Horn The most famous battle in this long struggle was the Battle of the Little Big Horn, which was fought near the Little Big Horn River in present-day Montana. The battle soon came to be known by another name—Custer's Last Stand.

The trouble began when Custer's men found gold in the Black Hills. Within months, 15,000 gold-hungry whites were swarming over Sioux land. Rather than remove the miners, the government demanded that the Sioux sell the Black Hills. The Sioux refused. "I never want to leave this country," a leader named Wolf Necklace told the government agents. "All my relatives are lying here in the ground, and when I fall to pieces I am going to fall to pieces here."

The army was ordered to force the Indians out. In June 1876, army scouts reported that several thousand Sioux and Cheyenne were camped beside the Little Big Horn River. Custer was ordered to locate the camp and then wait for reinforcements.

Once Custer spotted the Indian camp, however, he decided to attack at once. The attack ended in disaster. Custer split up his troops, and the group that he led suddenly found itself surrounded by angry warriors. A warrior named Low Dog remembered:

"I called to my men, 'This is a good day to die. Follow me.' We massed our men, and that no man should fall back, every man whipped another man's horse and we rushed right upon them."

The battle, said another warrior, lasted no longer than a hungry man needs to eat his dinner. In those few minutes, Custer and all his men—about 260 soldiers—were killed.

Custer's Last Stand proved to be the Indians' last stand as well. Over the next few months, the army tracked down the Sioux and Cheyenne and forced them onto reservations. Ignoring earlier treaties, Congress took the Black Hills and another 40 million acres of land away from the Sioux. Never again would Indians roam freely across the Great Plains.

23.9 Chapter Summary

In this chapter, you read about the tensions that developed between settlers and Native Americans in the West after the Civil War. You used an illustration of a buffalo hide to record information about four groups of settlers and their impact on the West's native peoples.

As settlers moved west, Native Americans were pushed off their lands and onto reservations. When Indians like the Nez Percé resisted, soldiers were sent to move them by force.

During the Civil War, the Homestead Act and the Pacific Railway Act aroused new interest in the West. The completion of the first trans-continental railroad in 1869 opened the West to a flood of new settlers.

Much of the West was first explored by miners seeking gold and silver. The railroads helped ranchers and cowboys introduce large-scale cattle ranching to the Great Plains. Homesteaders turned the Great Plains into the most productive wheat-producing region in the world.

The wars between settlers, soldiers, and Plains Indians came to a head in the Battle of the Little Big Horn. The Indians won the battle, but soon afterward the Sioux and Cheyenne were forced onto reservations.

The settling of the West helped to make the United States one of the world's largest and wealthiest countries. In the next chapter, you will learn how the rise of big business created new opportunities and problems for workers, immigrants, and politicians from east to west.

Settlers rush to claim land in the Oklahoma Territory in 1893.

The Granger Collection, New York

What do you think this man's job is?

How do you think this woman feels about her job?

24

The Rise of Industry

24.1 Introduction

The tragedy started late in the afternoon on March 25, 1911. The quitting bell had just sounded in New York City's Triangle Shirtwaist Factory. Nearly 500 employees, most of them young immigrant women, headed toward the exit. It was Saturday, and they were looking forward to a day off with family and friends.

One woman sniffed the air. Something was burning! Another spotted flames leaping out of a pile of cloth scraps. Before she could react, the wooden table above the fabric was ablaze. From there the flames jumped to the paper fabric patterns hanging above the table. Flaming bits of paper and fabric whirled around the room, setting other tables on fire.

The room filled with smoke, and the air became so hot that it burst the windows. Fresh air poured into the room, sending the flames even higher. Fingers of the blaze started to scorch workers' clothing and hair.

"I heard somebody cry, 'Fire!' I left everything and ran for the door," recalled one woman. "The door was locked and immediately there was a great jam of girls before it." She could see at once that, "If we couldn't get out, we would all be roasted alive."

Such factories and their dangers were a relatively new part of life in the United States. You read in Chapter 13 how the Industrial Revolution began. After the Civil War, new inventions and business methods allowed Americans to create industry on a much larger scale than ever before. Unfortunately, this industrial progress brought not only economic benefits, but also tragedies to the United States. The nation's new mills and factories produced a wondrous assortment of goods that made life better for many. But the people who were employed in these new industries often lived and worked in the most miserable, even dangerous, conditions.

In this chapter, you will read the rest of the story of the Triangle Shirtwaist Factory fire. You will also read how, by 1900, the United States became the world's leading industrial nation.

Graphic Organizer: Illustration
You will use this illustration to learn more about the expansion of industry and the effects of this expansion on workers.

industrialization: the birth and growth of businesses that make and distribute products through the use of machinery

24.2 Improved Technology

By the 1860s, many of the factors necessary for the rapid **industrialization** of the United States were already in place. Machines had taken over much of the work once done by hand. Work had moved from homes to factories. Railroads had begun to connect customers and manufacturers with an efficient transportation system.

After the Civil War, new inventions and improved technology prompted the growth of new industries. Some of these innovations, or new ideas, helped businesses to grow and become more efficient. Others made daily life easier for many Americans.

The Granger Collection, New York

Sparks fly in a steel-manufacturing plant as molten metal meets cold air in the Kelly-Bessemer process. The process cleaned the steel of impurities.

The Age of Steel Before the Civil War, the nation's railroads ran on iron rails that wore out quickly. Railroad owners knew that rails made of steel—a mixture of iron, carbon, and sometimes other metals—were stronger and would last longer. Steel, however, was difficult and costly to make.

In 1872, a Scottish immigrant named Andrew Carnegie went to England to study a less expensive method of making steel, invented by Henry Bessemer. Carnegie owned a company that made iron bridges for railroads. But he knew that his bridges would be better if made out of steel. Carnegie was so impressed by the Bessemer process that he brought it back to the United States. "The day of iron has passed," he announced. "Steel is king!"

Carnegie was right. Within a decade, steel was replacing iron in rails, locomotives, and bridges. Other industries also took advantage of less expensive steel. Steel nails, needles, and knives became common household items.

Many steel companies competed fiercely to supply steel for such products. To remain the leader, Carnegie hired scientists to improve the quality of his company's steel. He employed good managers to make his steel mills run efficiently. His recipe for success was, "Adopt every improvement, have the best machinery, and know the most."

To keep costs low, Carnegie set out to control every step in the steel-making process. He purchased iron mines to supply his ore, coal fields to fire his furnaces, and railroads to ship his finished steel to customers.

To reduce his competition, Carnegie also bought up several rival steel companies. He then combined them all to form the giant Carnegie Steel Company. By 1900, Carnegie Steel produced a quarter of the nation's steel.

Electric Power   During this era, inventor Thomas Edison helped to transform electricity from a scientific curiosity into a practical source of light and power. In 1876, Edison opened an "invention factory" in New Jersey. With a team of workers, he set out to create a "minor" invention every few days and a "big thing every six months or so."

Edison succeeded brilliantly. His workshop turned out the first practical electric lightbulb, the phonograph, the motion picture projector, and many other inventions.

In 1882, Edison built the first electrical power station and distribution system in New York City. His team invented everything the system required, including generators, regulators, meters, switches, light sockets, fuse boxes, and underground electric cables. When he finally turned the generator on, electricity began to flow to homes, stores, and factories. The age of electricity had begun.

By 1900, some 25 million lightbulbs were glowing across the country. In many factories, electric motors were replacing waterwheels and steam engines as sources of power. New electric-powered devices, such as washing machines and vacuum cleaners, were making housework easier.

The Collection of the New-York Historical Society, negative number 2946

Electric lines form a criss-crossed canopy over this city street. Thomas Edison's invention of the lightbulb in the 1880s spurred tremendous growth in the electric industry.

The Telephone   The telephone was invented by a Scottish immigrant named Alexander Graham Bell. In 1876, as he was getting ready to test his "talking machine," Bell spilled acid on himself. "Watson, come here, I want you," he commanded his assistant. Watson, who was in another room, heard every word over a telephone.

Bell's invention worked. It worked so well that, by 1915, Americans were communicating with one another over nine million telephones. All these telephones made American industry more efficient and competitive. They allowed suppliers, producers, sellers, and customers to communicate quickly and easily.

New Production Methods   New methods of organizing work were also making business more efficient. Factory owners adopted Eli Whitney's idea of assembling a wide variety of products from interchangeable parts. They also used the assembly line. In a shoe factory, for example, one worker operated a heel-cutting machine. Another operated a sole-cutting machine. Another made shoelaces. Still other workers assembled, labeled, and packaged the shoes.

With this assembly-line process, workers produced more goods per day at less cost. As prices dropped, more Americans could afford to buy manufactured products. More customers meant more factories. By 1900, almost four times as many Americans worked in factories as had a generation earlier.

The Triangle Factory

The Triangle Shirtwaist Factory was just one of many new businesses that took advantage of improved technology to mass-produce a quality product at a good price. The Triangle Factory specialized in a style of women's blouse known as a *shirtwaist*. A shirtwaist had puffy sleeves, a neat collar, front buttons, and a snug waist. Women liked shirtwaists so much that by 1909, New York City had more than 500 factories that made only such blouses.

Sam Bernstein, the production manager at the Triangle Shirtwaist Factory, loved watching his workers use up-to-date tools and production methods. Each person at the cutting tables had a special steel knife. This knife could slice through many layers of fabric at a time, cutting dozens of sleeves, then fronts, then backs. That was the way to get things done in a modern factory!

From the next floor of the building, Bernstein could hear the whirring of 240 sewing machines. The machines were neatly laid out in 16 tightly packed rows. Flexible belts connected each machine to a rotating axle running down each row just above the floor. This axle, which was spun by an electric motor, delivered power to each machine. The machines clattered loudly as women sewed the pieces of shirtwaists together.

Piles of finished blouses were then lifted to the floor above by electric freight elevators. There, two rows of workers gave the shirtwaists a final pressing. Finally, shipping clerks packed the shirtwaists into boxes for shipment.

Usually, the factory almost ran itself. But if a problem occurred, the company's switchboard operator could reach Bernstein by telephone on any of the three floors of the factory.

Sewing machines, shirtmakers, bobbins, and piles of cloth crowd this factory. Imagine working here in the heat of summer.

24.3 The Rise of Big Business

When Carnegie opened his first factory in 1865, most businesses were still owned by one person or a few partners. Because the owners' funds were limited, businesses were small. Owners knew their employees and often treated them like family.

Growth of Corporations A partnership might work well for a garment, or clothing, factory. But big businesses, such as railroads, needed much more capital—money to start a business—than a few partners could provide. To raise larger sums, entrepreneurs—people who start new businesses—set up **corporations**. A corporation is a business that is owned by many investors, or people who help pay its initial expenses.

A corporation raises funds by selling stock, or shares in a business. The investors who buy the stock are known as *stockholders*. In return for their investment, stockholders hope to receive dividends, or a share of the corporation's profits.

The money invested by the stockholders is used to build the business. To make sure their money is used properly, stockholders elect a board of directors. The people on the board of directors oversee the running of the corporation.

After the Civil War, corporations attracted large amounts of money from investors. By the 1880s, thousand of corporations were doing business across the United States.

Rockefeller's Oil Trust A giant in the oil business, John D. Rockefeller introduced another form of business organization known as the **trust**. A trust is a group of corporations run by a single board of directors.

Rockefeller invested in his first oil refinery in 1862, at the age of 23. At that time, petroleum, or oil found underground, was just becoming a valuable resource. Oil refineries purify petroleum into fuel oil. During the nineteenth century, oil was used to light homes, cook food, and run engines and generators.

Before long, many small refineries were competing fiercely in the oil business. The amount of oil produced by these firms rose and fell wildly, along with prices. Rockefeller saw this as wasteful and inefficient. To reduce competition, he did everything he could to drive his rivals out of business. Those companies he could not destroy, he bought.

Like Carnegie, Rockefeller took control of every step of his business. He bought oil fields along with railroads, pipelines, and ships to move his oil. He built his own warehouses and even made his own oil barrels for storing oil products. By 1880, Rockefeller controlled 95 percent of the nation's oil refining.

To manage his many businesses, Rockefeller combined them into the Standard Oil Trust. The trust made the oil industry more efficient than ever before. But, as a **monopoly**, it had the power to control oil prices. This worried people who depended on oil in their homes and businesses.

Following Rockefeller's example, entrepreneurs created trusts in other businesses such as railroads, meatpacking, sugar, whiskey, and tobacco.

corporation: a business that is owned by many investors

trust: a group of corporations that unite in order to reduce competition and control prices in a business or an industry

monopoly: a company that controls all production and sales of a particular product or service

J. P. Morgan, pictured above, was to banking and finance what Carnegie and Rockefeller were to steel and oil. In 1901, Morgan used his financial resources to buy Carnegie's steel company. Morgan founded U.S. Steel, America's first billion-dollar corporation.

The "people's entrance" to the United States Senate is "closed" in this turn-of-the-century cartoon. According to the cartoonist, the Senate was controlled by business trusts, depicted here as giant, bloated moneybags.

The business leaders who controlled these huge trusts became fabulously wealthy. Because most had made their fortunes by crushing their competitors, critics called them "robber barons."

The Evils of Trusts   The growth of trusts alarmed many Americans. They saw these monopolies as a threat to the free-enterprise system. This system depends on free competition among businesses to provide the public quality products at fair prices. A monopoly, people argued, has little reason to improve its products or to keep prices low because it has no competition.

People also worried about the influence of trusts on the political process. Wealthy entrepreneurs, they complained, were using their enormous wealth to buy elections and corrupt public officials. As the *Chicago Tribune* warned, "liberty and monopoly cannot live together."

The Triangle Factory

The Triangle Shirtwaist Factory would never be the size of U.S. Steel or Standard Oil. However, it was the largest shirtwaist factory in the country. The two men who owned the factory, Max Blanck and Isaac Harris, were known in the garment industry as "the shirtwaist kings."

The owners worked well together. While Max Blanck entertained buyers from stores to convince them to carry Triangle products, Isaac Harris ran the factory. Harris kept up with garment production, machinery maintenance, and work flow. He did not, however, try to keep up with his workforce. The factory had too many workers for him to get to know them all personally.

The shirtwaist business made Blanck and Harris very wealthy. They drove fancy cars and enjoyed comforts that their workers could only dream about. Both had worked hard in a competitive business and probably felt that they had earned their success.

24.4 The Growth of Cities

Industrialization brought with it **urbanization,** or city growth. Most of the nation's new industries were located in cities. Immigrants and rural Americans flocked to these industrial centers looking for jobs. Chicago, for example, more than tripled its population between 1880 and 1900.

urbanization: the growth of cities

Urban Tenements   As cities swelled with workers, demand for cheap housing exploded. To meet this demand, developers threw up cheap apartment buildings called *tenements*. One person described tenements as "great prison-like structures of brick, with narrow doors and windows, cramped passages and steep, rickety stairs." By 1900, about two thirds of New Yorkers lived in such buildings.

A poor family might occupy just one or two rooms in a tenement, usually with no heat or water. Friends or family often took in newcomers who arrived in cities without money for rent. As a result, tenement neighborhoods were some of the most heavily populated areas on Earth.

Tenements were unclean and even dangerous places to live. Only a few rooms had windows to provide light and fresh air. The rest were dark and airless. In some tenements, the only source of water was a single faucet in a courtyard. Many lacked sewer services. In such conditions, diseases such as typhoid and cholera spread quickly, killing infants and young children. Fire was another constant worry.

Cities Expand Upward   As cities expanded, urban land costs shot up. In New York, land that had sold for $80 in 1804 was selling for $8,000 by 1880. Such prices inspired builders to construct more building space on less land by going upward. Using lightweight steel beams to support walls and ceilings, builders constructed skyscrapers that rose ten or more stories into the air. Electric elevators whisked people and freight effortlessly from floor to floor.

Businesspeople rented space in city skyscrapers for their offices and factories. Factory owners preferred the top floors. Rents were cheaper higher up, and the natural light was better, saving owners money on electric lighting. The cost of insurance was low as well because steel buildings were thought to be fireproof. By the early 1900s, more than half of New York City's workers labored above the seventh floor.

City Excitement   For all their problems, cities were also exciting places to live. City stores were filled with products never seen on a farm. City dwellers enjoyed all sorts of entertainment from operas and art museums to dance halls and sporting events. When writer Hamlin

A family in a New York City tenement in the early 1900s. Cramped, dirty, dark, and crowded, tenements spread disease and misery among their inhabitants.

Garland came to Chicago with his brother, he found that, "Everything interested us.... Nothing was commonplace; nothing was ugly to us."

The Triangle Factory

Blanck and Harris located their thriving shirtwaist business on the top three floors of the ten-story Asch Building in New York City. They chose this space partly because of the morning sunlight that streamed in through its large windows. Their landlord, Joseph Asch, boasted that when construction was completed in 1901, "the architects claimed my building was ahead of any other building of its kind which had previously been constructed."

It may have been ahead of other buildings, but the Asch Building was not perfect. It had only two staircases, even though the city building code required three. The city had agreed to count the building's fire escape as the third staircase. But the fire escape ended at the second floor. Nor was the Asch Building well designed for evacuation during an emergency. Its staircases were narrow. Instead of opening outward to let people escape easily, the building's doors opened inward. Despite scares from several small fires in the building, Asch had not bothered to fix these problems.

The ten-story Asch Building in New York City had only two staircases, even though the city required at least three for safety reasons.

The Triangle Factory's workforce was made up mainly of young immigrant women, most of them Italians and Jews from Eastern Europe. Even if they had been aware of these safely problems, they would have hesitated to demand improvements for fear of being fired. Often their jobs provided their family's only income.

Like most factory workers, Triangle employees could only afford housing in crowded slums. "I lived in a two-room tenement with my mother and two sisters and the bedroom had no windows," recalled one employee. "There was nothing to look forward to."

Geography Challenge
United States Industries in 1890

1. Identify at least four interesting details on this map.

2. What two cities were the centers of steel production?

3. How many U.S. Steel factories were located in Cleveland? In Pittsburg? How many independent factories were located in these two cities?

4. What do you believe were some of the effects of U.S. Steel's monopoly over steel production in these two cities?

A young girl stands between looms in a textile factory. At the turn of the century, millions of children worked long hours in mines, mills, and factories.

24.5 Working Conditions

Working conditions in most industries were appalling. Gone were the days when business owners knew and cared about the people who worked for them. Men like Carnegie and Rockefeller knew little about their workers.

Working Families   Gone too were the days when factory workers could expect decent pay. With so many people looking for jobs, business owners could pay low wages. Many wages were so low that men could not support their families. To get by, wives and children had to work as well, usually at even lower wages.

Most factory women earned about $1 to $3 per day. If business was slow, wages dropped. A boss might not pay a new worker anything until she had learned her job. Then he would charge her for the sewing machine she worked on. If a worker complained, she could easily be replaced with a new one, perhaps for less money.

Millions of young children worked in mines, mills, and factories. A newspaper reported that young boys hired by coal miners to separate lumps of coal from rocks, "go to work…at seven o'clock in the morning and work till it is too dark to see any longer. For this they get $1 to $3 a week." They also got curved spines from bending over piles of coal all day.

Inside Factories   Mills and factories were hot in summer and cold in winter. To keep costs low, owners crowded workers together.

Of all working dangers, fire claimed the most lives. In New York, tall buildings often lacked fire escapes. New York City's fire chief wanted buildings to have fire escapes and sprinkler systems that could put out fires quickly. But factory owners objected to such added expenses.

New York City did require that factory doors "open outwardly" and "shall not be locked" so workers might escape quickly in case of fire. The law was not enforced, however. In 1910, some 94 percent of all factory doors in the city opened inward instead of outward.

The Triangle Factory

Saturday was payday at the Triangle Shirtwaist Factory. Most workers earned only $9 per week, with the most experienced making up to $12. The younger workers, some only 13 years old, earned just $6 per week for sewing on buttons all day. The very youngest earned even less. Worker Pauline Newman recalled:

> *"We were young, eight, nine, ten years old.... The hours were from 7:30 in the morning to 6:30 at night when it wasn't busy. When the [busy] season was on we worked until 9 o'clock. No overtime pay, not even supper money.... My wages were $1.50 for a seven-day week."*

Of course, these pay rates were what workers earned before deductions. The company charged its employees for the thread and electricity they used, for the chairs they sat on, and even for using Triangle's coat lockers.

Everybody was expected to work at least 59 hours a week. This included every Saturday, plus occasional Sundays. To keep workers from claiming overtime pay, the managers sometimes set the clock back. To keep workers from being "interrupted," the heavy steel doors to the hall and stairs remained locked until closing time.

To make sure workers didn't steal any shirtwaists, fabric, or lace, the factory built a narrow corridor leading to the elevators. Every day at quitting time, employees filed through this corridor one at a time so that a watchman could inspect each woman's handbag.

Working at Triangle was unhealthy, uncomfortable, and unsafe. Managers seldom let workers leave the factory floor to use the toilet or drink from the dirty tap in the hallway. In the crowded sewing room, women could barely squeeze by each other's machines. The wooden chairs behind the machines often lacked backs to support the sewers while they worked. When all the machines were in use, the noise could be deafening.

Fire hazards abounded. Even though the city prohibited smoking, the factory rarely enforced that rule. Workers stuffed leftover fabric into wooden bins where it sat for months just waiting for a misplaced spark to set it ablaze. The Asch Building's only fire protection was a few hundred pails of water scattered throughout its ten floors.

An inspector points to a bolted door in the Triangle Shirtwaist Factory. The inspection came too late for the women who lost their lives in the fire. Tragically, the factory owners had locked the door to keep workers on the job.

trade unions: early labor
organizations that brought
together workers in the same
trade, or job, to fight for better
wages and working conditions

24.6 Labor Unions

As a teenager, Rose Schneiderman found work in a cap factory. After three years, she later wrote, "it began to dawn on me that we girls needed an organization. We were helpless; no one girl dared stand up for anything alone."

Workers like Rose Schneiderman had been forming unions since the 1830s. These early labor organizations were **trade unions**. They organized workers in the same trade, or job, to fight for better wages and working conditions. Sometimes these unions went out on strike, refusing to work until their employers agreed to meet their demands.

Knights of Labor   In 1869, Uriah Stephens organized a new union known as the Knights of Labor. Stephens hoped to unite "men and women of every craft, creed, and color" into "one common brotherhood." The Knights led several successful strikes against telegraph and railroad companies. With such victories, the union grew to over 700,000 members.

In 1886, nearly 200,000 workers went on strike nationwide to demand an eight-hour workday. During a rally at Haymarket Square in Chicago, someone threw a bomb at police. The police shot back, injuring many workers. Four workers were sentenced to death for the bombing, even though no evidence tied them to the bomb.

Fearing more violence, employers fired anyone associated with the Knights. Membership dropped quickly, and the organization faded away.

American Federation of Labor   As the Knights declined, a group of local trade unions formed the American Federation of Labor (AFL). Instead of strikes, the AFL used collective bargaining to reach its goals. In collective bargaining, union representatives meet with employers to try to reach agreement on such issues as wages.

Despite the AFL's peaceful approach, many employers made their

Strikes often pitted the police against labor organizers. This image shows a policeman being shot on Haymarket Square in Chicago during a strike of the Knights of Labor in 1886. A short time later, a dynamite bomb killed or injured several dozen persons, including police.

The Granger Collection, New York

workers sign pledges not to join unions. They also fired union members and exchanged lists of such "troublemakers" with other employers.

The Homestead Strike   Some bosses used force to defeat unions. When workers struck at a Carnegie steel plant in Homestead, Pennsylvania, Henry Clay Frick, Carnegie's partner, refused to talk about their demands. Instead Frick made plans to reopen his plant with non-union workers. To protect these strikebreakers, he hired 300 armed guards.

When the guards arrived in Homestead, they faced an angry crowd of strikers. A battle broke out in which both guards and strikers died. Still Frick went ahead with his plan. When the Homestead plant reopened with strikebreakers, the union collapsed in defeat.

Women Organize   Such tactics kept many women from joining unions, but not Rose Schneiderman. Upset by pay cuts, Schneiderman organized the women in her factory as part of the National Board of United Cloth Hat and Cap Makers. Soon after she joined the union, she wrote,

> "A strike was declared in five of the biggest factories. There are 30 factories in the city. About 100 girls went out. The result was a victory, which netted us—I mean the girls—$2 increase in our wages on the average…. But all was not lovely by any means, for the bosses were not at all pleased with their beating and had deter- mined to fight us again."

The largest women's union was the International Ladies' Garment Workers' Union (ILGWU), which represented women in clothing factories. In 1909, thou- sands of New York City garment workers walked off their jobs to protest poor working conditions and low pay. As the strike grew, so did public sympathy for the young women. The newspapers called this movement "The Uprising of the 20,000."

The strike ended months later when employers agreed to a shorter workweek and better pay. They also ended fees for the use of factory equipment. The employers refused, however, to meet the workers' demands for safety improvements. Most garment factories remained unsafe.

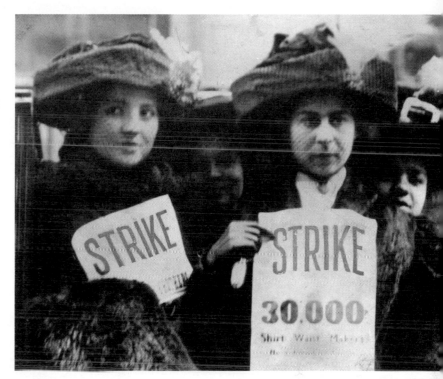

Shirtwaist workers display strike leaflets for a newspaper photographer. Strikers wanted shorter hours, higher pay, and safer working conditions.

The Triangle Factory
About 5,000 workers from the Triangle Shirtwaist Factory were part of the ILGWU strike of 1909. Their demands included unlocked doors during working hours and safer fire escapes in the Asch Building.

Rather than meet those demands, Blanck and Harris responded by locking the strikers out of the factory and advertising for replacements. "If the union had won, we would have been safe," said striker Rose Safran. "But the bosses defeated us and we didn't get the open doors or the better fire escapes." Because of that defeat, 146 workers would die needlessly.

The cause of the fire that swept through the Triangle Shirtwaist Factory in 1911 was never known. But suddenly people on the eighth floor began to cry, "Fire!" Within minutes, the entire floor was a "mass of flames." Escaping workers rushed to the stairs or pushed their way into the two small elevators. The stairs, however, were soon ablaze, and the elevators stopped running.

On the tenth floor, Mary Alter was warned of the fire by telephone. Harris and Bernstein led everyone out onto the roof. People from neighboring buildings stretched ladders between the rooftops to help the workers on the roof escape.

Workers on the ninth floor had no warning. The fire just appeared. Some women died immediately. Firemen later found them as "skeletons bending over sewing machines." Those who had time to escape found themselves trapped by the locked factory door. In desperation, they rushed to the windows and began to jump.

The crowd that gathered outside the Asch Building watched in horror as girls began to fall out of the sky—"fire streaming back from their hair and dresses." Their bodies hit the pavement with sickening thuds.

Firefighters arrived quickly, but had trouble bringing their equipment close to the building because of the bodies on the pavement. Not that it mattered. There was little the firemen could do. Their ladders were not tall enough to reach beyond the sixth floor. Their safety nets were just as useless. The workers fell with such force, said one fireman, that they "went right through the life nets."

At the public funeral for the Triangle victims, garment workers marched under a banner proclaiming, "We demand fire protection." As she marched, Rose Schneiderman glanced up at the buildings lining the funeral procession. "There they were. Girls right at the top of hundreds of Buildings, looking down on us," she recalled. "The structures were no different from the Asch Building…many were in a far worse condition."

Mourners stand shoulder to shoulder in the rain to honor the women who died in the Triangle Shirtwaist Factory fire. One hundred forty-six girls and women were killed or fell to their deaths in the preventable tragedy.

Honoring the Triangle Victims

24.7 Chapter Summary

In this chapter, you read about the rapid industrialization of the United States and how this progress influenced the way average people earned their livings. You also read an account of an infamous event in history—the Triangle Shirtwaist Factory fire. You used an illustration to learn about the expansion of industry and the effects of this expansion on workers.

New inventions and ideas made it possible for businesses to grow in size and efficiency. While these innovations allowed more Americans to afford manufactured items, there was a hidden price to pay. With the rise of big business through corporations, trusts, and monopolies, the wealthy got wealthier and the poor got poorer.

As cities grew, factories rose ten or more stories above the ground, and people from all over came looking for jobs. People lived in crowded, unclean, and dangerous tenement buildings. Men, women, and children worked long hours for low wages in crowded, unsafe factories. Doors were kept locked, and workers could not leave their stations without permission. Most worked in miserable conditions.

Workers didn't dare speak up for fear of losing their jobs. By joining trade unions, they could fight as a group for better wages and working conditions. When organized workers went on strike, factory owners often responded with violence or by simply hiring other workers. Unfortunately, it took the horrors of the Triangle Factory fire to make the dangers of factory life real to the American public.

In the next chapter, you will read about how the many immigrants that worked in these factories viewed their lives in America.

This cartoon shows the women of the Triangle Shirtwaist Factory desperately trying to open one of the few exit doors. A man dressed in a suit decorated with dollar signs holds the door closed. The cartoonist believes that the women died because of the greed of factory owners.

What does this statue symbolize?

What might these people be thinking?

The Great Wave of Immigration

25.1 Introduction

As the steamship full of immigrants approached New York City, 17-year-old Emma and her sister scrambled to the ship's crowded deck. Emma recalled:

"Helena and I stood pressed to each other, enraptured by the sight of the harbor and the Statue of Liberty suddenly emerging from the mist. Ah, there she was, the symbol of hope, of freedom, of opportunity. She held her torch high to light the way to the free country, the asylum [place of safety] for the oppressed of all lands. We, too, Helena and I, would find a place in the generous heart of America."

When Emma Goldman arrived from eastern Europe in 1886, the Statue of Liberty was brand new. Over the next few decades, more immigrants than ever before would enter the United States. Millions of new arrivals would gaze on the great statue and feel the same hope and excitement that Emma did.

During the 40 years from 1880 to 1920, "push" and "pull" factors combined to propel a huge wave of immigrants to the United States. Poverty, political violence, and religious persecution pushed millions out of their homelands to seek safety elsewhere. Others felt the pull of economic opportunities in the United States.

In the 1880s, many newcomers came seeking farmland in the American West. By 1900, most land that could be farmed had been claimed. After that, immigrants usually settled in the nation's growing cities, where they found jobs in rapidly expanding industries.

In this chapter, you will meet various immigrant groups from around the world. You'll share their experiences of journeying to this country and beginning a new life. You will also find out how Americans' attitudes toward immigration changed by the 1920s. Never again would the United States hold open its doors so wide to people from other lands.

Graphic Organizer: Illustration
You will use an illustration to record information about four different immigrant groups.

The Granger Collection, New York

refugees: people who flee their homes or countries because of war, persecution, or other causes

25.2 Immigration from around the Globe

In the early 1880s, a young American Jew named Emma Lazarus visited a boatload of Jewish immigrants who had just arrived in New York City. These Jews were **refugees** fleeing a religious massacre in Russia. Inspired by their suffering, Lazarus wrote a poem in which the Statue of Liberty welcomes immigrants. The poem begins:

Give me your tired, your poor,
Your huddled masses yearning to breathe free.

Today, Emma Lazarus's words are inscribed on a plaque at the base of the famous statue.

In the 1880s, patterns of immigration changed. People from Europe and Asia flocked to the United States in search of a better life.

"The Huddled Masses" By the time Lazarus wrote her poem, improvements in transportation were making it easier to reach the United States. Oceangoing steamships made voyages faster, safer, and less expensive. Once immigrants arrived at port cities, railroads made it easier for them to travel inland to new farmland or to jobs in distant industrial cities and towns.

Between 1880 and 1920, more than 23 million immigrants arrived in the United States. This vast number of newcomers changed the nation. By 1920, more than one third of the nation's population had been born in another country. In many major cities, over two thirds of residents were foreign-born or the children of immigrants.

New Immigration Patterns Before the 1880s, most immigrants to the United States came from northern Europe, particularly Ireland and Germany. But by 1890, most immigrants were coming from countries in southern Europe, such as Greece and Italy, and from eastern European nations, such as Russia and Poland.

Immigration from other parts of the world increased as well. Chinese immigrants had been coming to the United States since the California gold rush in 1849. After 1880, they were joined by immigrants from other parts of Asia, including Japan, the Philippines, India, and Korea. Newcomers also crossed into the United States from Canada and Mexico.

Compared with earlier arrivals, fewer of these new immigrants spoke English, and they tended to be poorer and less well educated. The newcomers also included large numbers of Jews, Catholics, Greek and Russian Orthodox, Buddhists, and Confucianists, all of whom increased the country's religious diversity. Many Americans, even earlier immigrants themselves, wondered how these arrivals would affect the country.

Geography Challenge
Immigration to the United States, 1820–1990

1. Identify at least four interesting details on this map.

2. What do the arrows on the map indicate?

3. Between 1820 and 1990, where did the greatest number of immigrants come from? Where did the least number of immigrants come from? How do you know?

4. Which of the arrows on the map shows where your family or ancestors came from?

5. What are or were some of the effects on the United States of the immigration patterns shown on this map?

25.3 Italian Immigrants

When Pascal D'Angelo heard that his father was leaving their poor Italian village to work overseas, he was angry. "America was stealing my father from me," he later said. His mother tried to soothe him, saying that soon Papa would return, "laden with riches." But Pascal begged his father to take him along. His father agreed, and the two of them boarded a steamship bound for the United States.

From Italy to America Like millions of other Italians, Pascal and his father came to America to escape poverty. In the late 1800s, much of Italy, and especially mountainous southern Italy, could not support the country's rapidly growing population. Farmers struggled to eke out a living on worn-out, eroded land where crops too often failed. There were few factories to provide other jobs.

Poor immigrants like Pascal and his father usually made the ocean passage in "steerage." Steerage was a deck, deep in the ship, that was reserved for the passengers who paid the lowest fares. These passengers were given narrow beds in crowded compartments that smelled of spoiled food, human waste, and sweating people who had nowhere to bathe.

Steerage passengers were allowed on deck only once a day. The rest of the time, they tried to amuse themselves by playing games, singing, and making music with accordions, mandolins, and other instruments.

After almost two weeks, the weary travelers arrived at the immigration station on Ellis Island in New York Harbor. There they had to pass medical examinations and answer questions about how they planned to support themselves in the United States. People who did not pass these inspections could be sent home, even if other family members were allowed to enter. So many families were forced to separate that Italians started calling Ellis Island "The Island of Tears."

Millions of Italians, anxious to escape the poverty of their homeland, journeyed by ship to America. During the long voyage, they endured crowded, smelly conditions and poor food.

Starting a New Life   Judged healthy and ready to work, Pascal and his father entered New York City. A fellow Italian, a work agent called a *padrone,* helped them to find jobs building roads. Padrones helped many Italian immigrants get unskilled construction work building sewers, subways, and roads, cleaning streets, and laying bricks for new **tenement buildings**.

Nearly half of all Italian immigrants returned to Italy. Most were young men who earned some money in construction or agriculture and then went back home when their jobs ended for the winter. When several co-workers died in a work accident, Pascal's father decided to return to Italy as well. "We are not better off than when we started," he said.

Pascal, however, decided to stay in his new country. He settled in a poor Italian neighborhood in New York, one of the many "Little Italys" that sprang up in American cities. These mostly Italian neighborhoods bulged with residents who could afford only the cheapest tenement housing. Crowded together in tiny apartments, most families had no privacy. The difficulties of their new life led some immigrants to depression and despair.

Fortunately, Italian neighborhoods also offered opportunities for fun. Most Italians were Catholics who celebrated saints' days as they had in Italy. They strung colored lights, flags, and streamers along the shops and streets. Children dashed among booths that offered food and games. Fireworks, music, and dancing reminded everyone of life back home.

Above everything else, Italians valued family closeness. Some Italian parents didn't send their children to school because they feared that learning English would distance their children from the family. Besides, a child in school wasn't earning money to help the family.

tenement buildings: crowded and usually run-down buildings with many small, cheap apartments

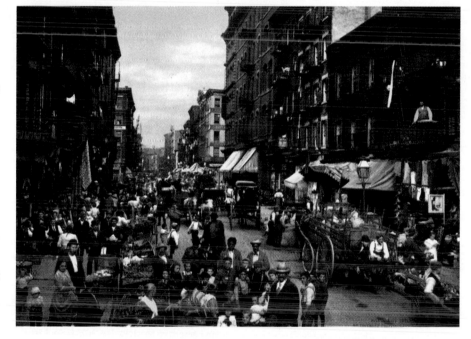

Italian immigrants often moved to "Little Italys" such as Mulberry Street in New York City, shown in the photograph. Here, rents were cheap and living conditions crowded.

As a result, many immigrant children never learned the skills they needed for better jobs.

Because many Italian newcomers were poor and uneducated, Americans tended to look down on them. When a few Italians turned to crime and became notorious gangsters, some people started thinking of all Italians as criminals. As a group, however, Italian immigrants were generally more law-abiding than average Americans.

Some Americans feared that this huge wave of immigrants from Italy would always be poor and illiterate. Pascal D'Angelo was one of many who proved them wrong. After arriving in America, Pascal bought himself a dictionary and learned to read and write English. In time, he became a well-known poet whose work was published in national magazines.

25.4 Jewish Immigrants from Eastern Europe

Maryusha Antonovksy was no more. In her place stood Mary Antin, the same immigrant Jewish girl but with a new, "American," name. Mary had also bought "real American machine-made garments" to replace her "hateful" homemade European-style clothes. "I long to forget," she said. "It is painful to be conscious of two worlds."

Fleeing Persecution Mary Antin's first world had been a Jewish village in Russia. For centuries, Russians had resented Jews, who dressed, worshiped, and ate differently from their Christian neighbors. By the 1800s, Russia had hundreds of anti-Jewish laws. Jews could live only in certain areas. They couldn't live in big cities or own land.

In 1881, assassins killed the Russian monarch Czar Alexander II. Nervous government leaders blamed Jews for his murder, even though the assassin wasn't Jewish. Angry Russians raged through Jewish villages, burning, looting, and killing. These attacks, called **pogroms,** happened repeatedly for more than 30 years.

Many Jews fled these terrors, hoping to find refuge in America. Between 1881 and 1924, some 2.4 million Jews came to the United States from Russia and other countries in eastern Europe. Mary Antin's father was one of them.

Mary's father left for America in 1891, hoping to earn enough money to send for his family. In his first letter home, Mary sensed "an elation [joy], a hint of triumph…. My father was inspired by a vision. He saw something—he promised us something. It was this 'America.'"

When Antin sent a steamship ticket for his family to join him, the people in Mary's village gathered, filled with longing. "They wanted to handle the ticket," Mary remembered, "and mother must read them what is written on it."

After long rides in overcrowded trains and weeks of delay, Mary's family finally boarded a ship in Hamburg, Germany. Although richer immigrants enjoyed comfortable cabins, the Antins were crowded together with hundreds of other passengers deep down in the ship. Seasick at first, they frequently came up on deck for fresh air, where "sailors and girls had a good many dances."

When immigrants arrived at Ellis Island, they faced the dreaded medical inspection. Those judged to be in poor health had to stay on Ellis Island until they were well. Those who never improved were sent home.

pogroms: Organized and often violent persecutions of minority groups. The word *pogrom* comes from Russian words meaning "like thunder."

Like most European immigrants, the Antins entered the United States via New York Harbor. Wealthier passengers in first-class and second-class cabins were questioned briefly before being admitted to their new country. But the majority of arrivals were taken on crowded barges to the immigration station on Ellis Island. Often they had to wait for hours while inspectors and doctors examined each person. Fortunately, most new arrivals spent less than a day on the island before proceeding to shore and the beginning of their new life in America.

Jewish Life in America   From Ellis Island, Jews headed for New York City's Lower East Side neighborhood. There they established shops, newspapers, religious schools, and synagogues (community centers and places of worship). The Lower East Side became the most densely populated neighborhood in the city. People lived packed into cheap tenements, often sleeping three or four to a room.

Some Jews worked as street vendors, using a pushcart to sell everything from coal to second-hand clothes. Pushcart vendors saved their money to buy horse-drawn carts and then little stores. Although most Jews were poor, they arrived in America with a wide range of skills. Jews worked as cobblers, butchers, carpenters, and watchmakers. Almost half found jobs in the city's garment factories.

Jewish immigrants did whatever they could to keep their children in school. In Europe, Jews had honored educated people, but schooling had cost money. As a result, many Jews had never learned to read and write. In America, Mary Antin wrote, "Education was free.... It was the one thing that [my father] was able to promise us when he sent for us: surer, safer than bread or shelter."

Immigrants were often forced to take jobs in sweatshops, such as the one shown here, where most of the work was done by women and children. Workers were usually paid 25 to 40 cents a day.

Parents who made a little money often sent their sons, and sometimes their daughters, to the city's inexpensive public colleges. By 1910, more Jewish youths over 16 were still in school than were young people of any other ethnic group.

Like other immigrant groups, Jews faced prejudice and discrimination. Most private schools and clubs refused to accept Jews. Hospitals would not hire Jewish doctors; the New York Bar Association would not admit Jews (as lawyers). Many ads for jobs stated simply, "Christians only."

Still, eastern European Jews were grateful to be in their new country. One immigrant recalled, "There were markets groaning with food and clothes.... There was no military on horseback and no whips."

25.5 Chinese Immigrants

As you read in earlier chapters, the first Chinese immigrants came to the United States to seek gold in California. Later, many helped to build the first transcontinental railroad. Some of these immigrants returned to China with money they had made in America. Their good fortune inspired Lee Chew to leave his poor village for the United States in 1882.

Traveling to California Lee paid 50 dollars for a bunk on a crowded steamship making the month-long voyage to San Francisco. On the ship, he got his first taste of foreign food and marveled at machinery he had never seen before. "The engines that moved the ship were wonderful monsters," he wrote, "strong enough to lift mountains."

Lee arrived just in time. In the United States, anti-Chinese sentiment (feeling) had been building ever since whites had pushed Chinese off their mining claims. As the number of Chinese immigrants increased, labor leaders warned of hordes of Chinese workers who would work for less pay than whites and take away their jobs. In 1882, Congress passed an Exclusion Act that banned Chinese laborers from immigrating to the United States. The law also denied Chinese immigrants the right to become citizens.

As a result of the Chinese Exclusion Act, Chinese immigration slowed to almost nothing. Then, in 1906, an earthquake and fire destroyed much of San Francisco, including most birth records. Suddenly, many Chinese men could claim to be native-born citizens. As citizens, they were allowed to bring their wives and children to the United States.

Chinese claiming American birth started arranging for people in China to immigrate to the United States as their relatives. On the long ship voyage, the newcomers studied hundreds of pages describing their "families." When they reached San Francisco Bay, they threw the papers overboard.

These "paper relatives" landed at Angel Island in San Francisco Bay. Government immigration officials "locked us up like criminals in compartments like the cages in zoos," said one Chinese immigrant. Chinese usually remained on the island for three to four weeks, but sometimes they spent months or even years there. To pass the time, they carved poems on the wooden walls with silverware smuggled from the dining halls. One wrote,

"Why do I have to sit in jail? It is only because my country is weak and my family is poor. My parents wait at the door in vain for news. My wife and child wrap themselves in their quilt, sighing with loneliness."

Chinese immigrants were sometimes detained for several months on Angel Island before they were allowed to enter the United States. In their crowded barracks, some carved poems on the wooden walls, expressing despair over their condition.

Before being allowed to leave the island, each immigrant faced detailed questioning by suspicious officials. "How many steps are there in your house?" "Where do you sleep in your house?" "Who lives next door?" Then they asked a "family" witness from San Francisco the same questions. If the answers didn't match, officials could deport the newcomer. Nearly one in ten Chinese who came to America was sent back to China.

Chinese Life in the United States   When Lee Chew arrived, he worked first as a servant, and then set up his own laundry. Many Chinese started laundries because, as Lee explained, "It requires little capital [money] and is one of the few opportunities that are open. Men of other nationalities who are jealous of the Chinese…have shut him out of working on farms or in factories or building railroads."

Like Lee, most Chinese settled in city neighborhoods like San Francisco's bustling Chinatown. Here, they could find work at Chinese laundries, restaurants, and stores. Chinese newspapers, herbal medicines, foods, and festivals provided comfort and support.

For many years, most Chinese immigrants were men. In 1900, only about 1 in 20 Chinese on the United States mainland was female. With so few women and families, the Chinese population in America began to decline. In 1880, about 105,000 Chinese lived in the United States. By 1920, just 61,600 remained.

Gradually, more women and children arrived, especially in San Francisco. Housing was closed to Chinese in most areas, so Chinatown became more and more crowded.

For white Americans, Chinatown became a tourist attraction, a "mysterious" place to see "strange faces" and eat new foods. To most Chinese immigrants, however, Chinatown was home.

Chinese immigrants settled in Chinatowns like this one in San Francisco. There they preserved the culture they had left behind.

By 1900, railroad lines linked the United States and Mexico. Trains provided convenient transportation for Mexicans, who were free to enter the United States without passports.

passport: a document issued by a citizen's home government that identifies a person and permits him or her to travel to other countries

25.6 Mexican Immigrants

Soldiers were shooting all around. A flying bullet almost hit him. That was when Pablo Mares decided he had to get out of Mexico. "I had to come to the United States," he said later, "because it was impossible to live down there with so many revolutions."

Mares had been caught in the middle of a bloody civil war. The conflict began when Mexico's president allowed wealthy landowners to take over the lands of 6 million Indians and 8 million poor farmers. In 1910, landless farmers rebelled, breaking up large landholdings and giving the land to poor families. In response, soldiers attacked villages, killing thousands of peasants.

Crossing the Border   The Mexican Revolution dragged on for ten terrible years. Between 1910 and 1920, about 500,000 Mexicans entered the United States. They entered freely, without **passports** or money.

Many Mexicans walked hundreds of miles to reach the border, carrying all they owned on their backs. In just one day, a Texas reporter saw "hundreds of Mexicans, all journeying northward on foot, on burroback and in primitive two-wheel carts." Others traveled north by rail. By 1900, railroad lines connected American and Mexican cities. Railroads provided both transportation and jobs for Mexican immigrants. One Mexican newspaper reported, "There is not a day in which passenger trains do not leave for the border, full of Mexican men who are going in gangs to work on railroad lines in the United States."

Mexicans in America   Many American employers welcomed the Mexicans. Expanding railroads and large-scale farms and ranches in the Southwest depended on laborers who were willing to work hard for little pay. After Congress banned Chinese immigration in 1882, these employers looked to Mexico for new workers. "Where I came from," said one Mexican construction worker, "I used to work ten hours for $1.25.... Then I came here and they paid $1.25 for eight hours—it was good."

Some Mexican immigrants found jobs with railroads, mines, factories, and canneries. But most found work in agriculture. Mexican farmworkers moved from region to region, harvesting crops as they ripened. They picked oranges in southern California, almonds in central California, and then apples in Oregon. They harvested cotton in Texas and Arizona, and then moved on to sugar beets in Colorado.

Farmwork paid very little. One Texas farmer said, "I was paying Pancho and his whole family 60 cents a day.... He worked from sun to sun." Children worked in the fields beside their parents to help support their families. Few of these children had a chance to attend school.

Farmworkers often lived in camps that they built near the fields. "Shelters were made of almost every conceivable thing—burlap, canvas, palm branches," said one visitor. Some farms and ranches provided housing for their workers. Either way, these temporary homes usually lacked running water and basic sanitation.

After harvest season, farmworkers sometimes moved to nearby towns. *Barrios,* or Mexican neighborhoods, sprang up on the edges of cities near such farming areas as Los Angeles, California, and San Antonio, Texas. Food stands and grocery stores in the barrio offered familiar tastes and smells. Residents helped each other take care of the sick and find jobs. On Mexican religious holidays, Catholic churches held special ceremonies. On those days, the barrio was filled with singing, dancing, and fireworks.

Many Mexican immigrants originally planned to return to Mexico once the revolution was over. Whites who believed that Mexicans were taking their jobs encouraged such returns. One wrote, "I wish the Mexicans could be put back in their country."

Mexicans who remained in the United States often faced strong prejudice. Compared to whites, they earned very low wages, and they had little say in their working conditions. In schools, white children were sometimes taught to "boss" their Mexican classmates, as they were expected to do when they grew up.

Despite these problems, many Mexican immigrants chose to stay. Like Isidro Osorio, a farm and railroad worker, they hoped for a better future in their new homeland. "I have worked very hard to earn my $4.00 a day," reported Osorio. "That is why I want to give a little schooling to my children so that they won't stay like I am."

Some Mexicans, such as those in this photograph, found jobs in mines. Most, however, were employed as agricultural workers.

Immigrants like the Chinese man in the cartoon above often faced discrimination and lack of acceptance in their new country.

quota: a limit based on numbers or proportions—for example, the proportion of a country's population allowed to immigrate to the United States

visas: government documents that allow people from other nations to enter the country for a limited period of time

25.7 Closing the Immigration Door

In 1920, a mob stormed through the Italian neighborhood of West Frankfort, a small Illinois town. The crowd was frustrated by a mining strike and angered by bank robberies that Italian criminals were rumored to have committed. For three days, mobs beat up Italian immigrants and burned their homes. This attack reflected a surge of anti-immigrant feeling in the United States that peaked around this time.

The Tide Turns against Immigrants

The United States has always been a nation of immigrants, yet each new group has suffered discrimination. Earlier arrivals have generally looked down on the newcomers who came after them. Descendants of German Jews who had arrived before the Civil War, for example, considered themselves superior to recently arrived Jews from eastern Europe. Similarly, old Californio families held themselves above recent arrivals from Mexico.

Native-born Americans blamed immigrants for everything from slums and crime to hard times. "Unless something is done," warned the head of the government's immigration service, "the mighty tide of immigration… will soon poison or at least pollute the very fountainhead of American life and progress."

Restricting Immigration   Something was done. As you read, in 1882 Congress banned further immigration by Chinese laborers. In 1907, Japanese immigrants were also forbidden entry to the United States. In 1917, Congress required immigrants to prove that they could read and write before allowing them into the United States.

To further limit immigration, Congress established a **quota** system in 1921 and refined it in 1924. Under this system, only 150,000 Europeans were allowed to enter the United States each year. Quotas limited immigration from any one country to 2 percent of the number of people from that country who lived in the United States in 1890. Most eastern and southern Europeans had arrived after that year. As a result, more than 80 percent of the 150,000 quota spaces were reserved for northern Europeans, primarily immigrants from Great Britain.

The new laws did not limit Mexican immigration. However, Mexicans now needed passports and **visas** to enter the United States. For the first time, America was closing its doors.

25.8 Chapter Summary

In this chapter, you read about the great wave of immigration to the United States between 1880 and 1920. You used an illustration to learn about four of the groups that immigrated, their journey to America, and their life once they arrived.

Immigrants were drawn to the United States by the "push" of hard times in their home countries and the "pull" of new opportunities. Some were escaping from poverty. Others were fleeing wars or persecution. The promise of freedom and opportunity in America were powerful magnets for people who hoped for a better life.

Each group of immigrants faced its own challenges in journeying to America. Once they arrived, most had to pass inspection at immigration stations like those on Ellis Island in New York Harbor and Angel Island in San Francisco Bay. There they could be denied entry and sent home.

The immigrants who were allowed to enter the country often faced prejudice and discrimination. In cities, they crowded into their own neighborhoods and worked at lower-paying jobs. In the West and the Southwest, Mexican farmworkers labored long hours in the fields and followed the crops from region to region.

In the 1920s, anti-immigrant feeling led Congress to limit the number of people who would be allowed into the United States. These immigration-restriction laws brought an end to the great wave of immigration. But by then, the United States had become a far more diverse country. Only time would tell whether Americans would embrace this diversity and extend the promise of equal opportunity to all the nation's people.

The great wave of immigration during the late 19th century created a nation of rich, diverse cultures. People from many backgrounds came together and became Americans. In this photograph, a mix of immigrants are in class together learning English.

What does the scientist think he will find as he tests the milk and the sugar?

26

The Progressive Era

26.1 Introduction

"The men who start the great new movements in the world are enthusiasts," said Sam McClure at his college graduation, "whose eyes are fixed upon the end they wish to bring about."

Some of his fellow students may have brushed off McClure's words as mere speech making. They shouldn't have. This immigrant from Ireland was serious about starting "great new movements." And he had just the enthusiasm to do it. But how?

McClure's answer was to start a journal called *McClure's Magazine*. McClure prided himself on knowing what people wanted to read about. "If I like a thing," he said, "then I know that millions will like it."

In 1900, McClure decided that Americans wanted to know the truth about trusts, those giant business monopolies that worked to reduce competition. He hired a reporter named Ida Tarbell to write a history of one of the biggest trusts—John D. Rockfeller's Standard Oil. McClure ran Tarbell's report as a serial, printing one part at a time in issue after issue. The report told about unfair pricing putting Standard Oil's competitors out of business. McClure's popularity soared.

McClure began hiring more journalists to uncover the truth about other evils in America. Some people called his journalists *muckrakers* because they spent so much effort stirring up dirt and filth. Writers like Tarbell adopted this name with pride.

McClure and his muckrakers were part of a larger reform effort known as the **Progressive movement.** Looking back at the century just ended, Progressives could see great progress. Slavery had ended. The United States had become an industrial giant. Still, huge problems remained to be solved.

As you will read in this chapter, the Progressives didn't work as one group. While some fought railroad monopolies, others marched with child factory workers. As some worked for equal rights for African Americans, others struggled to protect forests. But whatever their cause, you will find that the Progressives had one thing in common. They believed that ordinary people could start "great new movements" that would improve American life.

Graphic Organizer: Panel of Historical Figures
You will use this panel to help you understand the views and work of social leaders during this time.

The Granger Collection, New York

Andrew Carnegie made a huge fortune in the steel industry. When he retired, he began to give away most of his money. Here we see him carrying libraries like gifts, symbolizing the libraries he gave to thousands of communities.

26.2 Andrew Carnegie and John D. Rockefeller: Captains of Industry

When business leaders like Andrew Carnegie and John D. Rockefeller looked at the United States in 1900, they saw progress everywhere. Railroads linked towns and cities across the nation. The increased ease of delivering goods by rail had nourished countless new industries, including their own. Both men were proud to be "captains of industry," leading the way in this growth. "Mere money-making has never been my goal," wrote Rockefeller. "I had an ambition to build."

Industry Brings Progress   New industries meant more jobs for a growing nation. With immigrants pouring into the country, the population of the United States tripled between 1850 and 1900. Every new factory or mill created jobs for the newcomers. Carnegie Steel alone employed more than 20,000 workers, many of them immigrants.

The nation's new industries turned out a wealth of new products at prices ordinary Americans could afford. "The home of the laboring man in our day boasts luxuries which even in the palaces of monarchs as recent as Queen Elizabeth were unknown," wrote Carnegie. "What were luxuries for some," he noted, "are now necessities for all."

The Benefits of Bigness   What made such progress possible? The growth of big business, answered the captains of industry! Only big business enterprises could deliver quality goods at prices everyone could afford. As Carnegie explained in an article defending big business to its critics:

> [The] cheapness [of goods] is in proportion to the scale of production.... The larger the scale of operation the cheaper the product.... Instead of attempting to restrict [bigness], we should hail every increase as something to be gained, not for the few rich, but for the millions of poor.

Bigness, in Carnegie's view, was the inevitable result of competition. When many small companies compete in the same industry, some are more likely to do well than others. Those that are run most efficiently will thrive from competition and grow larger. Those that are not well run will perish. "The law of competition," Carnegie argued, "may be sometimes hard for the individual, [but] it is best for the race, because it ensures the survival of the fittest in every department."

When Carnegie wrote about "the survival of the fittest" in business, he was borrowing an idea from the British naturalist Charles Darwin. Darwin had observed that, in nature, animals and plants compete for food and living space. Those that are best adapted to their environments are the most likely to survive. This idea was popularized as "survival of the fittest."

It did not take long for people to apply Darwin's idea to human society. The result was a theory known as **Social Darwinism**. According to this theory, people and societies compete for survival just as plants and animals do. The most fit—men like Rockefeller and Carnegie—become wealthy and successful. The least fit struggle just to survive.

Giving Away Wealth   In 1901, Carnegie sold his steel company for $250 million. Then he retired to devote his life to philanthropy, or generosity to charities. Rich people, he believed, have a responsibility to use their wealth to help others. "The man who dies rich," he wrote, "dies disgraced."

Carnegie used his wealth to build concert halls, universities, and hospitals. But most of all, he loved building libraries. A library, he said, "outranks any other one thing that a community can do to benefit its people." Before 1880, few Americans had access to free public libraries. Just one generation later, 35 million people a day were using libraries that Carnegie had helped to build.

Rockefeller was so impressed that he wrote to Carnegie:

> *"I would that more men of wealth were doing as you are doing with your money but, be assured, your example will bear fruits, and the time will come when men of wealth will more generally be willing to use it for the good of others."*

Rockefeller used his fortune to fund universities, medical research, the arts, and education for all. Before his death, he founded four charitable organizations. One of these was the Rockefeller Foundation, to which he contributed about $182 million. The foundation's goal was to promote "the well-being of mankind throughout the world."

Social Darwinism: the idea that people and societies compete for survival, with the fit becoming wealthy and successful while the weak struggle to survive

John D. Rockefeller's Standard Oil Company controlled 90% of the oil refined in the United States at the turn of the century. His business methods were deemed ruthless by his critics and brilliant by his supporters.

regulation: the enforcement of laws that control conduct or practices; government regulations control the way goods, food, and drugs are produced and sold to the public

26.3 Theodore Roosevelt: Trust-Busting President

Not everyone admired big business the way Rockefeller and Carnegie did. Many thought big businesses took unfair advantage of workers and consumers. In 1890, Congress passed the Sherman Antitrust Act to outlaw any form of business monopoly. The law was so vague and big business so powerful, however, that for years the law was not enforced. The Sherman Antitrust Act got its first real test only after Theodore Roosevelt became president in 1901.

Breaking a Railroad Trust   Roosevelt came into the White House with a reputation as a reformer. As president, he attacked business monopolies with great energy. "We do not want to destroy corporations," he assured the public, "but we do wish to make them [serve] the public good."

Roosevelt's first target was a railroad monopoly called the Northern Securities Company. This company controlled nearly every rail line between Chicago and the Pacific Northwest. Roosevelt had the Justice Department sue Northern Securities for violating the Sherman Antitrust Act. The justices of the Supreme Court ordered the monopoly to be broken up into smaller railroad companies.

Trust-Busting Expands   Just after Roosevelt filed suit against Northern Securities, *McClure's Magazine* began publishing Ida Tarbell's history of the Standard Oil Trust. In her report, Tarbell documented how Rockefeller had driven his competitors out of business. She told about secret deals he had made with railroads to ship his oil at lower prices than other oil companies paid. She explained how Rockefeller had cut his oil prices below what the oil cost to produce. This attracted customers away from other oil companies. After his competitors went out of business, he raised prices again.

A shocked public demanded action. Roosevelt filed suit against not only Standard Oil, but against 44 other trusts as well. In 1911, Standard Oil was "busted"—broken up into five major oil companies and several smaller ones.

Roosevelt thought government **regulation,** or enforcement of laws, was a good long-term solution to bad business behavior. "The great development of industrialism," he said, "means that there must be an increase in the supervision exercised by the Government over business enterprise."

"Trust-busting" Teddy Roosevelt is shown here vigorously shaking the railroad trust. Roosevelt tried to break up monopolistic trusts in order to make American business fair for all.

The Granger Collection, New York

26.4 Robert La Follette: Fighter for Political Reform

In 1890, Robert La Follette of Wisconsin ran for reelection to Congress and lost. Still a young man, he returned to his work as a laywer. Then something happened. Senator Philetus Sawyer, a powerful Republican Party boss, offered La Follette a bribe to "fix" a court case. Sawyer thought that he could pay La Follette to guarantee that he would win the case. An insulted La Follette reported the bribery attempt to the newspapers.

An equally insulted Sawyer decided to crush La Follette. But "Battling Bob" was not an easy man to put down. Sawyer had made him so mad that La Follette decided to run for governor of Wisconsin. As governor, he could put the party bosses out of business.

In Wisconsin and other states, political machines, or groups run by party bosses, controlled local and state governments. To make sure that their candidates were elected, corrupt bosses were known to bribe voters and "stuff" ballot boxes with fake votes.

Party bosses controlled the American political system through a corrupt system of bribery. Reformers like Robert La Follette sought to take power out of the hands of the bosses and return it to the people.

Thus, the bosses, not the people, chose each party's candidates for office. The candidates, men like lumber millionaire Sawyer, usually represented powerful business interests. Without the party's support, upstart reformers like La Follette had little chance of reaching voters. La Follette was defeated twice by Wisconsin's powerful Republican "machine," but finally won election as governor in 1900.

Once elected, La Follette pushed reforms that put the people in charge of politics. Wisconsin became the first state to adopt the direct primary. This election system allowed party members, not bosses, to chose party candidates. By 1916, over half the states had adopted the "Wisconsin Idea." With the people choosing their leaders in primary elections, reform governors swept into office across the nation.

Oregon introduced three other reforms that put political power into the hands of the people. The *initiative* allowed citizens to enact laws by a popular vote. The *referendum* allowed voters to overturn an existing law. The *recall* allowed voters to remove an elected official from office.

What all these reforms had in common, wrote La Follette, was a belief that each state could become a place where "the opportunities of all its people are more equal… [and] human life is safer and sweeter."

26.5 Mother Jones: Champion of Workers' Rights

In 1903, labor leader Mary Harris Jones—known as Mother Jones—went to Pennsylvania to support a strike by 75,000 textile workers. About 10,000 of the strikers were children. Jones wrote of these young workers:

> *Every day little children came into Union Headquarters, some with their hands off, some with the thumb missing, some with their fingers off at the knuckle. They were stooped little things, round shouldered and skinny. Many of them were not over ten years of age.*

Child Labor Laws   The situation Mother Jones found in Pennsylvania was not unusual. In the early 1900s, more than 1 million children under the age of 16 worked in mines and factories for up to 13 hours a day. To publicize their plight, Jones led a "March of the Mill Children" from Pennsylvania all the way to Oyster Bay, New York, to petition President Roosevelt to support child labor laws.

The children's march prompted stories and photographs of child workers in newspapers and magazines. Across the country, reformers demanded an end to child labor. Employers claimed that abolishing child labor would produce "a nation of sissies." But, by 1909, 43 states had passed laws that outlawed the hiring of children.

Improving Working Conditions   Progressive reformers also worked to improve the lives of adult workers. In 1903, for example, Oregon passed a law that limited women workers to a ten-hour workday. Maryland set up a program to assist workers who had been injured on the job.

New York responded to the tragic 1911 Triangle Shirtwaist Factory fire by setting up a state committee to investigate conditions in factories. Based on the committee's work, the state legislature passed 56 worker-protection laws. Many of these laws called for improvements in factory safety. One permitted women workers to take pregnancy leaves. (A *leave* is time away from work.) Another required employers to provide garment workers with chairs that had backs, rather than simple stools.

Mother Jones saw progress for the worker in such reforms. "Slowly his hours are shortened, giving him leisure to read and to think," she wrote. "Slowly the cause of his children becomes the cause of all."

At the turn of the century, school-age children worked long hours for meager wages in America's mines and factories.

26.6 John Muir: Protector of the Environment

John Muir was so clever with machines that he might have been a great inventor. Then, one day, a file slipped from his hand and hit him in the eye. This accident sent Muir's life down a different path. After recovering from his injury, Muir decided to spend his life roaming wild places. "I might have been a millionaire," he said. "I chose to become a tramp."

Muir found his wilderness home in Yosemite Valley, a place of great natural beauty in California's Sierra Nevada mountains. "God seems to be doing his best here," he wrote of Yosemite.

Humans, in contrast, seemed to be doing their worst. Loggers were felling Yosemite's ancient redwood trees. Herds of sheep were stripping its meadows and hillsides bare. "To let sheep trample so divinely fine a place seems barbarous!" wrote Muir.

Yosemite was not the only wild place threatened by human activity. Rapid growth had brought massive environmental changes. Loggers were felling the nation's forests at an alarming rate. Miners were scarring mountains and polluting rivers. Many species of birds and animals were near extinction or already lost forever.

Muir believed that wonders like Yosemite should be preserved in their natural state. To gain support for his views, he started publishing articles urging the passage of laws to protect wilderness. "It took more than three thousand years to make some of the trees…waving and singing in the mighty forests of the Sierra," he told his readers. Such wonders were too precious to destroy. By 1890, Muir's writings had attracted enough public support to convince Congress to create Yosemite National Park.

Muir found an ally in President Theodore Roosevelt. While Roosevelt was in office, he increased the amount of land set aside as national forest from 47 million to 195 million acres. He also doubled the number of national parks. To Muir's delight, the president also prohibited logging and ranching in Yosemite and other national parks.

"Wilderness is a necessity," said Muir. "Mountain parks and reservations are useful not only as fountains of timber and irrigating rivers, but as fountains of life."

Theodore Roosevelt and John Muir are pictured high on a cliff in Yosemite National Park. Muir (on the right) founded the Sierra Club, an organization committed to the preservation of the environment.

In 1917, the NAACP, which W.E.B. Du Bois helped form, organized this silent protest parade against lynching.

26.7 W. E. B. Du Bois: Spokesman for Equal Rights

In 1897, a black sociologist named W. E. B. Du Bois joined the faculty of Atlanta University. His plan was to study social problems "in the light of the best scientific research."

Everywhere he looked, Du Bois saw the terrible effects of racism on African Americans. In the South, Jim Crow laws segregated schools, trains, parks, and other public places. These laws also banned blacks from voting in most states. Blacks in the North were not legally segregated, but they still faced discrimination, particularly in housing and jobs.

African Americans who fought these injustices risked being lynched, or brutally attacked and killed. Between 1892 and 1903, almost 3,000 African Americans were lynched across the South. "One could not be a calm, cool, and detached scientist," Du Bois found, "while Negroes were lynched, murdered, and starved."

Du Bois wanted to do something, but what? Booker T. Washington, the best-known black leader of that time, advised African Americans to make the best of segregation. Washington was a former slave who had founded Tuskegee Institute, a vocational school for blacks. He believed that job skills for African Americans would lead to economic progress and eventual acceptance. "The wisest among my race understand that the agitation of questions of social equality is the extremest folly," he said.

Du Bois could not accept such thinking. In 1905, he gathered influential African Americans at Niagara Falls to push directly for voting rights. He wanted to see an end to discrimination, or unfair treatment based on race. "We want the Constitution of the country enforced," they declared. "We are men! We will be treated as men."

This group, known as the Niagara Movement, continued to meet each year. In 1909, they joined a group of white reformers who were also dissatisfied with Booker T. Washington's cautious approach. Together, they formed the National Association for the Advancement of Colored People (NAACP). The new organization pledged to work for equal rights and opportunities for all African Americans. By 1920, the NAACP had over 90,000 members. Their goal was to make 11 million African Americans "physically free from peonage [servitude], mentally free from ignorance, politically free from disenfranchisement [denial of rights], and socially free from insult."

26.8 Upton Sinclair: Truth Writer

When Upton Sinclair wrote a novel about the horrors of slavery, few people bought it. Then a publisher asked if Sinclair would write a book about factory workers who were treated like slaves. Sinclair jumped at the chance. Workers at a Chicago meatpacking plant had just been brutally defeated in a labor dispute. Sinclair would write about them.

Meatpacking Horrors   In 1900, Chicago was the home of the nation's biggest meatpacking companies. Disguised as a worker, Sinclair spent seven weeks in the slaughterhouses. There he observed how cattle and hogs became steaks and sausages. He observed employees with missing thumbs, and fingers eaten away by acid. He heard stories of deadly falls into cooking vats.

Based on his research, Sinclair wrote a tragic story of poor immigrants trapped in poverty by greedy meatpackers. In his novel *The Jungle,* he described the horrors of the meatpacking plants in great detail. He told of sick animals being processed into food. He described sausage made from old, rotten meat mixed with everything from sawdust to rodents. "Rats were nuisances," he wrote, "and the packers would put poisoned bread out for them; they would die, and then rats, bread, and meat would go into the hoppers together."

The Jungle became America's biggest bestseller since *Uncle Tom's Cabin.* But readers were more upset about the contents of their sausage than the treatment of the "wage slaves." "I aimed at the public's heart," said Sinclair, "and by accident I hit it in the stomach."

Safer Food and Drugs   After reading *The Jungle,* President Roosevelt ordered an investigation of the meatpacking industry. When his investigators confirmed that conditions were as bad as Sinclair had claimed, Congress passed the Meat Inspection Act. This set health standards for meatpacking and ordered federal inspection of meat.

Other muckrakers revealed similar problems in the food-canning and drug industries. Congress passed the Pure Food and Drug Act. This law requires manufacturers to use safe ingredients in their products and to advertise them truthfully. Future decades would bring more laws protecting American consumers.

Upton Sinclair shocked readers with his description of conditions inside meatpacking plants such as this one. The unsanitary conditions prompted the government to begin meat inspections.

suffrage: the right to vote

26.9 Alice Paul: Heroine of Women's Rights

By 1900, women had won their fight for **suffrage,** or the right to vote, in four western states. Elsewhere, the drive for voting rights seemed stalled. The Progressive movement, however, breathed new life into the campaign begun at Seneca Falls in 1848. Many Progressives believed that their reforms would be adopted more quickly if women had the right to vote.

A New Suffrage Movement   In 1916, a young reformer named Alice Paul formed what came to be known as the National Woman's Party. Older women's groups had worked to win the right to vote state by state. Paul and her supporters were determined to win the vote by a constitutional amendment.

To build momentum for a suffrage amendment, Paul organized a parade in Washington, D.C. More than 5,000 women marched amidst jeers and insults from onlookers. Newspapers applauded the courage of the "suffragettes," as the activists came to be known.

Women across the country made banners, marched, and banded together to demand the right to vote.

Passing the Nineteenth Amendment   By 1918, women could vote in 12 states, but they had made little progress on the suffrage amendment. The Woman's Party began holding silent vigils outside the White House. The protesters held banners that read, "Mr. President, What Will You Do for Woman Suffrage?" and "How Long Must Women Wait for Liberty?"

Police arrested 200 women for blocking the sidewalk. While in jail, Paul and her supporters went on a hunger strike. When the jailers tried to force-feed them, the public became enraged. The women were released to a hero's welcome.

Less than two months later, a suffrage amendment was approved by the House of Representatives by just one vote more than the two-thirds majority required. The amendment had been introduced by Jeanette Rankin of Montana, the first woman elected to Congress. Senate approval took another 18 months. The states finally ratified the Nineteenth Amendment on August 26, 1920. That year, women across the country voted in their first national election.

Paul went on to draft another amendment guaranteeing equal rights to women. "I never doubted that equal rights was the right direction," she said, even though the amendment was never ratified. "Most reforms, most problems are complicated. But to me there is nothing complicated about ordinary equality."

26.10 Chapter Summary

In this chapter, you learned about the Progressive movement of the early twentieth century. You used a panel of historical figures to help understand the views and work of social leaders during this time.

Men of industry, such as Rockefeller and Carnegie, believed that all of America had benefited from the advances achieved during the industrial age. They saw a country that was growing in wealth. They saw luxuries in the home that were unthinkable a century before. But not everyone in America agreed with them. Some people began to see problems in American society that resulted from industrialization. They began to investigate and draw attention to such issues as child labor, fair business practices, and equal rights. These "Progressives" came from many different backgrounds and fought for different causes, such as the rights of workers, women, African Americans, and consumers. They all worked to improve American society.

Progressives understood that many industrial advances were good for the country. However, they also understood that ordinary citizens needed to be protected from abuse by big businesses. They used newspapers, magazines, and books to inform the public about what was really going on in the marketplace. Their goal was to control the negative effects of the industrial age through government regulation.

By the early twentieth century, the work of Progressives gave hope for a better future for millions of Americans. In the next chapter, you will read about how America's successes helped the country to become a powerful world leader.

The Progressive Era was characterized by a spirit of reform. Americans faced a host of serious problems and tried to correct them. Did they succeed, or are some of the problems still evident today?

How would you describe the expression on the eagle's face?

Why is the American flag placed here?

27

The Granger Collection, New York

America Becomes a World Power

27.1 Introduction

William McKinley owed Theodore Roosevelt a big favor. Roosevelt had just helped him get elected president. The fiery Roosevelt had spoken all over America in 1896, promoting McKinley's support of business and industry. With energy and inspiration, he attacked the supporters of McKinley's opponent, like farmers and workers who felt left out of industry's great profits. These opponents, Roosevelt cried, planned nothing less than "revolution."

Now Roosevelt wanted McKinley to appoint him to be assistant secretary of the navy. McKinley, who favored peace, feared that Roosevelt was too warlike. Still, he gave Roosevelt the job. As he took office, Roosevelt said, "No triumph of peace is quite so great as the supreme triumphs of war.... It is through strife, or the readiness for strife, that a nation must win greatness."

Some newspapers called Roosevelt patriotic. Others worried that he would push the country into war. Americans had mixed feelings about getting involved in international affairs. Expanding across the continent had given America enough territory to move into for decades. Recovery from the Civil War, followed by industrial expansion, had also given Americans plenty to focus on at home.

Now, the West was more settled, and the United States had become an industrial and agricultural leader. To keep the economy growing, business leaders wanted overseas markets. Seeing European countries controlling foreign lands, they didn't want to be left out. The national pride that had inspired Manifest Destiny was calling for new challenges.

Roosevelt agreed. He allied himself with American **expansionists**—people who wanted to extend the nation's power within the Western Hemisphere and around the world. In this chapter, you will learn how the expansionists achieved their goals. As it flexed its muscles overseas, the United States acquired new territories and became a world power. Before long, it would be drawn into a global war—and a difficult struggle to restore the peace.

Graphic Organizer: Front Page Headline
You will use this front page headline to summarize key information about U.S. foreign policy from the late 1800s to 1920.

imperialism: the policy of extending a nation's power by gaining political and economic control over other countries

27.2 America Stretches Its Wings

In 1867, Secretary of State William Seward arranged for the United States to purchase Alaska from Russia. At the time, few people thought that acquiring this vast wilderness was a good idea. Even at a price of just two cents an acre, many labeled the deal "Seward's Folly."

But the "arctic wasteland" turned out to have thick forests, plentiful fish and wildlife, and mild coastal climates. Eventually settlers would discover gold, copper, coal, and other minerals there. With such potential treasures at stake, expansionists felt that America should gain control over other areas of the world as well.

The Granger Collection, New York

In this political cartoon, Secretary of State William Seward is pictured pulling a wheelbarrow containing a useless block of ice. President Andrew Johnson is pushing the wheelbarrow. What do you think this cartoonist thought about the purchase of Alaska?

Rise of Expansionism Some Americans objected to expansionism, saying that it was contrary to American values. Taking over other lands, declared former senator Carl Schurz, would mean that "our old democratic principle that governments derive their just powers from the consent of the people will have to go overboard."

Others warned that such takeovers would cause revolutions abroad. Some raised racist objections, arguing that nonwhites in other countries could never learn American values.

William Jennings Bryan, who had run for president against McKinley, believed that the United States could be powerful without taking over other lands. He said that America "has exerted upon the human race an influence more potent than all the other nations of the earth combined, and it has exerted that influence without the use of the sword or Gatling [machine] gun."

By the 1890s, however, American business leaders were eager to dig mines and establish plantations in new places. Others wanted new markets for finished products. European countries had long ago taken up **imperialism,** building empires by taking control of the governments and economies of other countries. American expansionists wanted to follow their example. Senator Henry Cabot Lodge declared, "Commerce follows the flag.... As one of the great nations of the world, the United States must not fall out of the line of march."

Expansion in Asia and the Pacific America's foreign expansionism started with measures to protect profitable overseas trading. In Asia, several European countries had made efforts to control trade with China. The

United States announced that American companies would trade anywhere in China they wanted. The government also established trade treaties with Japan.

To reach such Asian ports, ships crossing the Pacific needed to be able to stop at strategically located islands for fuel and food. To keep European countries from claiming all these places for themselves, the United States occupied the Midway Islands, which were located in the Pacific between California and Asia.

Annexing Hawaii

Closer to California lay a larger, more fertile group of islands that Americans found even more attractive—Hawaii. Americans had first come to these islands in the 1820s as missionaries. Their goal was to convert the native Hawaiians to Christianity. The Hawaiians, whose ancestors had come from the South Pacific, had lived on these islands for more than a thousand years. They were ruled by their own kings and queens.

In 1835, a Boston merchant established a large sugar plantation in Hawaii. Before long, American-owned sugar and

Queen Liliuokalani, the last reigning monarch of Hawaii, insisted that native Hawaiians should control the islands. American planters, fearing they would lose their land, organized a revolt that dethroned her.

pineapple plantations dotted the islands. The planters brought laborers to Hawaii from China and Japan to work in their vast fields. Under pressure from the planters, the Hawaiians agreed in 1887 to let the United States establish a naval base at Pearl Harbor, on the island of Oahu. The planters also persuaded Congress to allow Hawaiian sugar to be imported into the United States without paying any tariff (import tax).

U.S. sugar growers objected that the law now favored Hawaiian sugar over domestically grown sugar. They convinced Congress to give a bonus to growers in the United States. Hawaiian planters wanted that bonus, too. So they asked the United States to annex Hawaii.

Meanwhile, native Hawaiians increasingly resented being pushed around by Americans. When Queen Liliuokalani took the throne in 1891, people rallied around her call of "Hawaii for Hawaiians." Americans in Hawaii feared that they would lose their land. With help from U.S. marines, planters forced Queen Liliuokalani to give up her throne and established a new government for the islands.

Despite the planters' wishes, President Grover Cleveland refused to support the annexation of Hawaii. Cleveland, who opposed imperialism, said that Hawaii should be ruled by Hawaiians. But in 1898, under President McKinley, the United States did annex Hawaii.

The Granger Collection, New York

When an explosion sunk the battleship *Maine* and killed 200 men, Americans immediately accused Spain of causing the tragedy, and demanded war. In 1976, Admiral H. G. Rickover, acting for the U.S. Navy, presented evidence that the explosion was probably caused by spontaneous combustion in one of the coal containers.

yellow journalism: the practice of publishing sensational and often exaggerated news stories in order to attract readers

27.3 "A Splendid Little War"

Americans also established huge sugar plantations on the Caribbean island of Cuba, only 90 miles from Florida. Like nearby Puerto Rico, Cuba was still a Spanish colony.

By the 1890s, American expansionists wanted to annex both of these islands. To support their ambitions, they argued that it was time for the United States to enforce the Monroe Doctrine. No European country, they said, should control territory in the Western Hemisphere.

Cubans Struggle for Independence

The Cubans themselves had staged an unsuccessful revolt against Spain in 1868. In 1895, under the inspiring leadership of José Martí, Cubans again tried to win their independence.

To crush this movement, the Spanish herded men, women, and children into "reconcentration camps." Forced to live without beds, toilets, medical care, or much food, tens of thousands died.

American newspapers jumped at the chance to report stories of Cuban suffering. Competing fiercely for customers, some newspapers resorted to **yellow journalism,** offering sensational and shocking reports. Some of these stories were based on rumors and untruths. One said that a Spanish general was "feeding prisoners to sharks."

As sympathy for Cubans grew, more and more Americans were willing to go to war for Cuba. To help Americans in Cuba in case of trouble, President McKinley sent the new battleship *Maine* to the island's capital city, Havana.

The Spanish-American War   Trouble soon erupted in Havana. On February 15, 1898, an explosion shook the *Maine,* sinking the battleship and killing 260 American sailors. No one knew whether the explosion was caused by an accident or a mine (bomb). But many Americans were quick to blame Spain. Said Theodore Roosevelt, "The *Maine* was sunk by an act of dirty treachery on the part of the Spaniards!"

Young men rushed to join the army, raising the battle cry "Remember the *Maine*!" Senators shouted "Free Cuba!" Hoping to avoid war, McKinley offered to work out a solution between the Spanish and the Cubans. But the Spanish did not respond.

Faced with newspapers and members of Congress calling him a coward, McKinley asked Congress to declare war. Congress quickly agreed, and on

April 19 voted to go to war with Spain to free Cuba. At the same time, Congress approved a resolution stating that the United States intended "to leave the government and control of the Island [Cuba] to its people."

The American army quickly grew from 30,000 to over 274,000 men. Roosevelt resigned from his position as assistant secretary of the navy and put together his own regiment. A mixture of powerful, wealthy men and seasoned ranch hands, it came to be called the Rough Riders.

After long preparations, the Rough Riders and 17,000 other Americans arrived in Cuba. Seeing that Cuban fighters lacked the strength or the weapons to force the Spanish out of fortified cities and harbors, Roosevelt and his Rough Riders decided to capture Santiago, a major city. To do this, they had to capture nearby San Juan Hill, from which Spanish forces were able to defend the city.

The attacking force included the Rough Riders and African American troops from several regiments. Up the hill they charged, braving Spanish fire. "They walked to greet death at every step, many of them, as they advanced, sinking suddenly or pitching forward…but others waded on… creeping higher and higher up the hill," wrote an American reporter. "It was a miracle of self-sacrifice, a triumph of bull-dog courage."

The Americans captured San Juan Hill. Realizing that Santiago was lost, the Spanish tried to save their ships, sending them steaming out of the harbor. But Americans sank or captured every ship. The Spanish soon surrendered.

The Spanish-American War lasted just four months. Only 345 Americans died in combat, although 5,500 died of disease. Many Americans agreed with Secretary of State John Hay that it had been "a splendid little war."

In the peace treaty with Spain, Cuba gained its independence, while Puerto Rico came under American rule. The United States agreed to remove all of its troops from Cuba. However, Cuba was forced to agree that American troops could return if necessary to preserve law and order as well as defend the island's independence. The United States was also allowed to keep naval bases in Cuba. Despite a revolution that forced American businesses out of Cuba in the 1950s, the naval bases still remain today.

The African American 10th Calvary provided strong support to Theodore Roosevelt's Rough Riders as they charged up San Juan Hill. The capture of the hill allowed American guns to bombard Santiago Harbor. When the Spanish fleet attempted to escape, it was complete destroyed, and Spain sued for peace.

The Granger Collection, New York

27.4 The Philippines

After the *Maine* exploded in Cuba, Assistant Naval Secretary Theodore Roosevelt sent a telegram to the head of America's Pacific fleet, Admiral George Dewey. "In the event of declaration of war," the telegram ordered, "[begin] offensive operations in Philippine Islands."

Battle at Manila Bay The Philippines provided Spain's main base in the Pacific. The islands' people, called Filipinos, had tried many times to throw off Spanish colonial rule. In 1898 they were trying again. Led by General Emilio Aguinaldo, they had begun attacking the Spanish army and government officials. Now their struggle was about to become part of the war between the United States and Spain.

Dewey's fleet arrived in Manila, the Philippine capital, just five days after war with Spain was declared. At dawn on May 1, American battleships faced Spanish gunships. As naval bands struck up "The Star Spangled Banner," sailors stood on deck and saluted the flag. These men were about to engage in the first battle of the Spanish-American War.

By 11 A.M., the entire Spanish fleet was burning, sunk, or sinking. Spain's old wooden ships were no match for the modern steel American ships with well-trained crews. Only one American had died in the battle.

General Emilio Aguinaldo believed that the United States would help the Philippines gain independence from Spain. When the United States annexed the Philippines, he fought for Filipino freedom.

Defeating the Spanish Dewey blockaded Manila's port until American troops could arrive to take the city. Filipino fighters, allied with Dewey, surrounded Manila. The Filipinos believed that the coming Americans would help them gain independence. While they waited, Aguinaldo issued the Philippine Declaration of Independence, formed a national government, and designed a national flag.

Once U.S. reinforcements showed up, the Spanish agreed to "lose" a fake battle in order to surrender to the Americans. They didn't want to give themselves up to the Filipinos, who resented Spanish rule so intensely.

Fighting the Filipinos In a treaty negotiated after the surrender, the United States "bought" the Philippines from Spain for $20 million. Then, in 1899, Congress voted to annex the Philippines.

Aguinaldo's government felt betrayed. Angrily, the Filipino leader called for "war without quarter to the false Americans who have deceived us! Either independence or death!"

For three years, over 80,000 Filipino fighters fought off better-trained and better-armed American troops. Soldiers on both sides tortured prisoners. Americans became increasingly cruel, harming civilians and destroying villages.

Some Americans protested that denying independence to the Philippines violated American ideals. Carl Schurz was a leader among these anti-imperialists. Said Schurz, "We shall, for the first time since the abolition of slavery, again have two kinds of Americans: first-class Americans, who have the privilege of taking part in government, and second-class Americans, who are to be ruled by the first-class Americans."

But expansionists won the day. Senator Henry Cabot Lodge argued that "Manila with its magnificent bay…will keep us open to the markets of China." President McKinley himself believed that the Philippines could become "a land of plenty… a people redeemed from savage and indolent [lazy] habits…set…in the pathway of the world's best civilization."

More than 20,000 Filipinos and about 4,000 Americans died in the struggle. When the revolt was finally put down, the Americans set up a nonmilitary government to "prepare Filipinos for independence." Americans built roads, hospitals, and schools. But the United States did not grant the Philippines independence until 1947.

The Granger Collection, New York

A long war between the United States and the Filipinos who resisted U.S. control resulted in heavy casualties. More than 20,000 Filipinos were killed before the Philippines became independent in 1947.

27.5 Panama and the Canal

By 1901, America's favorite hero from the Spanish-American War, Theodore Roosevelt, had become vice president. "We stand on the threshold of a new century," Roosevelt declared. "Is America a weakling, to shrink from the work of the great powers? No. The young giant of the West stands on a continent and clasps the crest of an ocean in either hand."

Dreaming of a Canal   Roosevelt wanted to join those two oceans with a canal. If ships could move quickly between the Atlantic and the Pacific, the navy would be better able to defend America's new territories. And businesses would gain from lower shipping costs.

In September 1901, President McKinley was shot and killed by an assassin, and Roosevelt became president. In his first speech to Congress, Roosevelt argued for the canal. "No single great material work which remains to be undertaken on this continent is of such consequence to the American people," he told the nation.

Congress soon approved funding. In 1903, Roosevelt offered Colombia $10 million for land in their province of Panama, the narrowest part of Central America. The Colombian senate refused, feeling that the United States was trying to take a weaker country's valuable resources.

Furious, Roosevelt sent an American warship to Panama. Roosevelt knew that Panamanians wanted independence. The day after the ship arrived, a revolution started in Panama. With American marines keeping Colombian soldiers from reaching Panama's harbors, the rebels quickly won.

The new country of Panama agreed to accept $10 million in exchange for giving the United States control over a "canal zone" ten miles wide. Some American senators and newspapers, and countries all over the world, objected to America's "gunboat diplomacy." But most of the public supported the president. He was living out his personal motto, "Speak softly and carry a big stick."

The Culebra Cut, shown here, was one of the engineering miracles that allowed engineers to complete the Panama Canal in ten years. Millions of pounds of dynamite blasted apart the mountain. The earth was then used to construct dams to form lakes.

Building "The Big Ditch"

Construction on the canal began in 1904. Workers faced terrible conditions. "We had to bathe, wash our clothes in the same river; drink the same river water and cook with it," said one. A year later, three quarters of American workers had quit the project.

The majority of employees were workers from the West Indies who couldn't afford to go home. To prevent deadly yellow fever and malaria, crews worked to eliminate the mosquitoes that carried these diseases. They drained ditches, spread oil on swamps, and screened doors and windows. Within two years, canal workers were no longer dying from these diseases.

A new chief engineer improved housing and strictly organized the huge project. Using dynamite and huge steam shovels, men made a wide, deep cut through Panama's mountains. The excavated dirt was moved by railroad car to lower elevations. Here workers created earthen dams to form three giant lakes. Engineers supervised the construction of locks, a type of gate that would allow water levels to be raised and lowered along the canal.

By the time the 51-mile-long canal opened in 1914, Roosevelt had left office. His influence in the Panamanian revolution continued to be controversial. Roosevelt himself admitted, "I took the Canal Zone." In 1921, Congress apologized to Colombia and gave it $25 million. But anti-American feelings remained high in Latin America, and Panamanians increasingly resented American control of the Canal Zone. In 2000, the United States returned the zone to Panama.

Geography Challenge

U.S. Expansion around the World, 1867–1903

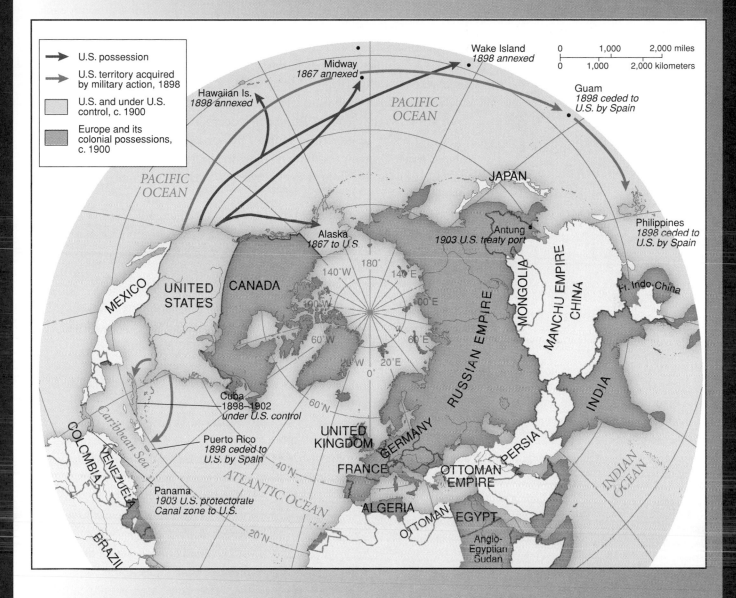

Legend:
- → U.S. possession
- → U.S. territory acquired by military action, 1898
- U.S. and under U.S. control, c. 1900
- Europe and its colonial possessions, c. 1900

Scale: 0 — 1,000 — 2,000 miles / 0 — 1,000 — 2,000 kilometers

Map labels:
- Wake Island, *1898 annexed*
- Midway, *1867 annexed*
- Hawaiian Is., *1898 annexed*
- PACIFIC OCEAN
- Guam, *1898 ceded to U.S. by Spain*
- Philippines, *1898 ceded to U.S. by Spain*
- JAPAN
- Alaska, *1867 to U.S.*
- Antung, *1903 U.S. treaty port*
- Fr. Indo-China
- MONGOLIA
- MANCHU EMPIRE
- CHINA
- INDIA
- RUSSIAN EMPIRE
- MEXICO
- UNITED STATES
- CANADA
- PACIFIC OCEAN
- Cuba, *1898–1902 under U.S. control*
- Puerto Rico, *1898 ceded to U.S. by Spain*
- Panama, *1903 U.S. protectorate Canal zone to U.S.*
- Caribbean Sea
- COLOMBIA
- VENEZUELA
- BRAZIL
- ATLANTIC OCEAN
- UNITED KINGDOM
- GERMANY
- FRANCE
- OTTOMAN EMPIRE
- PERSIA
- ALGERIA
- OTTOMAN
- EGYPT
- Anglo-Egyptian Sudan
- INDIAN OCEAN

nationalism: devotion to a national or ethnic identity, including the desire for independence from rule by foreign countries

militarism: a policy of glorifying military power and military ideas and values

27.6 The Outbreak of World War I

By the time the first ship sailed through the Panama Canal, the world's attention was not on Panama, but on far-off Europe. In August 1914, German troops poured across Belgium, on their way to try to conquer France. Europe was at war.

Tensions in Europe   European countries had long competed with each other for colonies, trade, and territory. By the early 1900s, **nationalism** was complicating these rivalries. Austria-Hungry had built an empire by taking over smaller countries in the part of eastern Europe known as the Balkans. Nationalism inspired in the Balkan people a burning desire to be independent of Austrian rule.

In this tense atmosphere, European leaders looked for safety in **militarism,** a policy of glorifying military power and military ideas and values. When Germany built up its navy to challenge Britain's fleet, Britain constructed more battleships. As Germany's army grew, France built up its own army.

European countries also looked for safety in alliances. In secret treaties, Germany and Austria-Hungary agreed to help each other in case of attack. Britain, Russia, and France made similar agreements. Europe was dividing into armed camps.

Assassination Leads to War   An outburst of nationalism lit the fuse of war. On June 28, 1914, the heir to the Austro-Hungarian throne, Archduke Franz Ferdinand, was visiting the city of Sarajevo in the province of Bosnia. Many Bosnians were Serbs who wanted to be part of nearby Serbia. A Serbian nationalist jumped out of a crowd and fatally shot the archduke and his wife.

Outraged, Austria-Hungary accused Serbia of having a hand in the assassinations and pressured Serbia to give up most of its independence. When the Serbs refused, Austria-Hungary declared war. The Russians stepped in to defend the Serbs. The Germans came to the aid of Austria-Hungary by declaring war on Russia. Russia's ally, France, began to prepare for war.

Eventually, more than a dozen countries took sides in the "Great War." (Decades later, people called the conflict World War I.) Austria-Hungary and Germany headed the Central Powers. France, Russia, and Britain led the Allied Powers.

Like most Americans, President Woodrow Wilson wanted to stay out of the war. Declaring that the United States would remain neutral, Wilson begged citizens to be "impartial in thought as well as deed."

The Archduke Franz Ferdinand and his wife are shown here shortly before they were assassinated by a Serbian nationalist. The assassination triggered World War I.

27.7 A New Kind of Warfare

By September 1914, six million soldiers were on the march across Europe. On Germany's Eastern Front, German troops fought Russians. On the Western Front, German forces advanced quickly before being stopped by French and British troops at the Marne River, about 40 miles outside Paris.

With neither army able to advance, both sides dug long, narrow ditches called *trenches* to protect their soldiers. A new kind of warfare was beginning.

Trench Warfare   For the next three years, the war in the west was fought from two parallel lines of trenches. Men ate, slept, fought, and died in these miserable ditches. Eventually, the lines of trenches stretched for 600 miles across France.

Each side protected its front trench with barbed wire and booby traps. Between the opposing trenches lay a deadly "no-man's land." Attacking soldiers came under intense fire from the men in the trenches. Thousands upon thousands of soldiers died trying to advance their line of trenches a few yards.

The trenches were wretched places, infested with rats, lice, and disease. "We are not leading the life of men at all," wrote an American who had volunteered to fight with the British forces, "but that of animals, living in holes in the ground, and only showing outside to fight and to feed."

New Weapons   New weapons added to the horror of trench warfare. "We never got anywhere near the Germans," one English corporal remembered. "The machine-guns were just mowing the top of the trenches." These new machine guns fired hundreds of bullets a minute. By the end of 1914, the French had lost 300,000 men. Germany lost more than 130,000 soldiers in a single battle.

The next spring, a green cloud floated over the Allied lines. Soldiers gasped and died, their throats and noses burning. The Germans had invented poison gas. Soon both sides were using chemical weapons.

The armies' new technology and strategies were effective for defense, but not for decisive attack. At one point, the British tried for six months to

During World War I, a new kind of war called *trench warfare* began. Hundreds of miles of trenches, like this trench for British soldiers, provided protection for infantrymen and allowed supplies and reinforcements to be safely delivered to the front.

The Granger Collection, New York

advance their lines. They gained only five miles, and lost 420,000 men. "The deadlock here is permanent," wrote an American volunteer.

War at Sea To supply soldiers in the trenches with food, ammunition, and other supplies, the warring nations bought goods from neutral countries. Each side tried to cut off the flow of supplies to its enemy.

Most trade, especially with the United States, was by sea. Britain had the world's greatest fleet and numerous ocean ports. Germany had a strong navy, but its only access to the ocean was through the North Sea. To close

The American public was furious when a U-boat sank the *Lusitania,* which the Germans suspected of carrying weapons to the Allies. Germany apologized and promised to stop sinking passenger ships without warning. However, Germany broke its promise and continued its attacks.

German ports, Britain mined the North Sea. This blockade stopped most of the neutral shipping and kept the German fleet bottled up in harbors for most of the war.

Unable to use its surface ships, the German navy tried to blockade Britain using submarines, called *U-boats* (for "underwater boats"). Fearing that the British would try to disguise their ships as neutrals, Germany announced that it might sink vessels flying the flags of neutral countries. Because submarines on the surface were easy targets for enemy fire, German submarines began sinking vessels on sight, instead of rising to the surface to give warning, as was traditional.

Germany Sinks the *Lusitania* The German embassy in the United States placed newspaper ads warning passengers not to sail to Britain, and specifically not to take the *Lusitania,* a British luxury liner. On May 7, 1915, six days after leaving New York, the *Lusitania* neared the coast of Ireland. Suddenly a ship's lookout shouted, "Torpedo coming on the starboard side!" Within moments, the ship exploded and quickly sank, killing 1,198 people, including 128 Americans.

Americans were outraged. One newspaper called the German attack "wholesale murder." When President Wilson protested, Germany said that the *Lusitania* had been carrying arms. Still, Germany apologized and offered to pay for damages. Hoping to keep the United States out of the war, Germany also promised not to attack merchant and passenger ships without warning in the future.

Protected by this promise, U.S. manufacturers increased their trade with the Allies. Trade with Allied countries swelled to $3.2 billion in 1916, while trade with the Central Powers dropped to $1 million. Americans weren't fighting in the war, but they had definitely taken sides.

27.8 To Make the World Safe for Democracy

After the sinking of the *Lusitania,* Wilson decided that the United States needed to prepare in case war became necessary. He worked with Congress to get money to improve the army and navy. Still, neither Wilson nor the country wanted war. In 1916, Wilson won reelection under the slogan, "He Kept Us out of War."

Wilson also tried to start peace talks. But European leaders, having lost so many soldiers, rejected Wilson's call for "peace without victory."

America Enters the War The Germans soon risked war with the United States again. Even though U-boats were sinking 50 to 100 British merchant ships per month, enough were getting through to keep the Allies going. Desperate to prevent an Allied victory, the Germans decided to cut off British supplies before their own ran out. In February 1917, Germany resumed sinking merchant ships from other countries without warning.

In March, U-boats torpedoed three U.S. merchant ships, killing many Americans. In fact, these ships had been carrying weapons to the Allies. The Germans knew that this attack might bring the United States into the war, but they hoped to win before America was ready to fight.

It was a fatal mistake. Addressing a special session of Congress, Wilson urged a declaration of war. America would fight alongside the Allies, he said, not just to protect neutral shipping, but because "the world must be made safe for democracy."

Congress greeted Wilson's speech with applause. Later, Wilson reflected, "My message today was a message of death for our young men. How strange it seems to applaud that."

In the photograph below, Woodrow Wilson appears before Congress to ask for a declaration of war against Germany. Although Wilson tried to avoid war, continued U-boat attacks on merchant ships gave him no choice.

To recruit the necessary men for an army to send to Europe, the United States resorted to the draft. All men between the ages of 18 and 45 had to register. Within a few months, the army grew from 200,000 men to over 4 million.

Americans Prepare to Fight On April 6, 1917, Congress declared war. The Allies rejoiced, hoping for American supplies—and soldiers. Allied ships were sinking faster than they could be replaced. To get U.S. supplies delivered safely, convoys of American warships starting escorting cargo vessels, protecting them from attack. American destroyers also helped the British navy assault U-boats. These strategies dramatically reduced shipping losses.

When the United States entered the war, it had only 200,000 soldiers, and most of those had limited training. Congress quickly authorized a national draft. Soon, 3 million men were drafted. Another 2 million volunteered.

Fighting and Winning American troops who sailed overseas were called the American Expeditionary Force (AEF). As they began arriving in Europe in June 1917, AEF soldiers soon learned from the Allies about trench warfare. The American commander, General John J. Pershing, hated these terrible conditions for soldiers. He also realized that trench warfare wasn't winning the war. He worked on a plan for driving the Germans out of the trenches and forcing them to retreat into open country.

Meanwhile, Russia had dropped out of the war. With millions of soldiers dead and starvation spreading across the country, Russians had revolted against their ruler, the czar. Russia's new government made peace with the Germans. This enabled Germany to bring soldiers back from the east, swelling their western forces to 3,500,000 men.

The German forces rushed to capture Paris before large numbers of Americans could arrive from overseas. They pushed quickly through the village of Chateau-Thierry and a nearby forest called Belleau Wood. They were within 50 miles of Paris when Americans reinforced the exhausted French. Gradually, American machine guns and artillery enabled the Allies to push the Germans back.

By the summer of 1918, more than a million Americans were in Europe. Pershing set his Allied offensive into motion. His plan took advantage of several offensive capabilities that had been developed during the war. Tanks could advance through trenches. Airplanes could deliver machine-gun fire and drop bombs. Carefully coordinating huge numbers of soldiers, tanks, airplanes, and artillery, the Allies forced the weakened Germans back to their own border.

To avoid the invasion of their own country, German leaders agreed to an armistice, or cease-fire. On November 11, 1918, for the first time in four years, the guns were silenced.

The costs of the war horrified the world. More than 9 million people had died. Entering the war late, the United States lost 116,000 lives. Throughout the warring nations, people mourned the loss of so many of their young men.

27.9 The Struggle for Peace

Less than two months after the fighting ended in Europe, President Wilson traveled to Paris to take part in peace talks. He was cheered by huge crowds. The United States had saved the French from endless war. And many Europeans welcomed Wilson's eagerness to prevent future wars.

Fourteen Points for World Peace

Months earlier, Wilson had presented to Congress a 14-point proposal for a postwar agreement. The first five points aimed to prevent conflict. Nations were asked to avoid secret treaties, to practice free trade, and to reduce their weapon supplies. Wilson asked that new borders be drawn based on self-determination, or the will of the people in each area.

Points 6 through 13 described new boundaries for many European countries. Finally, the ambitious fourteenth point called for nations to join a general association of countries to protect each other's independence. With this League of Nations, Wilson believed, the world could achieve a lasting peace.

Germany had surrendered with the expectation that Wilson's 14 points would be the basis for a fair and just peace. But after years of fighting and dreadful losses, some Allied leaders weren't satisfied with a just peace.

This painting shows the signing of the peace treaty that ended World War I at the Hall of Mirrors in Versailles. The treaty treated Germany harshly and planted the seeds of hatred that would lead to World War II.

The Treaty of Versailles On January 18, 1919, delegates from dozens of countries assembled at a gorgeous French palace outside Paris called Versailles. In addition to Wilson, three Allied leaders dominated the treaty talks. They were David Lloyd George of England, Georges Clemenceau of France, and Vittorio Orlando of Italy.

The German representatives were not allowed to speak. This was a clue to the Allies' anger and their determination to punish Germany and remove it as a future threat. They created a treaty that forced Germany to disband almost all of its armed forces, give up its colonies, and surrender territory in Europe. In addition, they called on Germany to pay **reparations,** or money to make up for damages and war deaths. The amount of these reparations was later set at $33 billion.

President Wilson opposed such harsh treatment of Germany. However, he eventually accepted the Allied leaders' demands for punishment in order to win their support for his Fourteen Points.

The Allies rejected some of Wilson's points, including freedom of the seas. But the peace conference did create new national boundaries in

reparations: debts imposed on a defeated nation to pay for the harm done during a war

Europe based on self-determination. Most important to Wilson, the Treaty of Versailles established a League of Nations. Wilson thought that this agreement would make the peace treaty successful. The League of Nations, he believed, could fix any problems created by the treaty.

Struggling for Senate Ratification Wilson needed the approval of two thirds of the U.S. Senate to ratify the peace treaty. He quickly ran into opposition, especially to the League of Nations. Some senators worried that other countries would force American soldiers to fight in international conflicts. They argued that only Congress had the Consitutional power to send Americans to war.

Woodrow Wilson toured the country seeking public support for the League of Nations, which was opposed by Congress. On his tour, he suffered from a massive stroke. He was unable to continue his fight with Congress, and the Senate refused to approve the Treaty of Versailles.

Many didn't want the United States involved in messy European problems anyway.

The struggle over the treaty became a fight between political parties. Republicans had a majority in the Senate. They felt that Wilson, a Democrat, had made his Fourteen Points a political issue by not appointing any Republicans to his negotiating team.

Anxious to increase public support for the League of Nations, Wilson undertook an intense speaking tour. In 22 days, he toured 29 cities, speaking up to four times a day, with hardly any rest. Finally, he collapsed with severe headaches. He rushed back to Washington, D.C., where he suffered a massive stroke.

Recovering slowly, Wilson was less willing or able to compromise with opposition senators. In March 1920, the Senate rejected the Treaty of Versailles.

The Legacy of Versailles Once again, America was heading toward isolationism. When the League of Nations opened in Geneva, Switzerland, the United States did not participate.

In later years, the League of Nations did settle a few small border disputes. But when big crises developed in Europe, the League lacked the power that Wilson hoped it would have.

In Germany, the Treaty of Versailles left a bitter legacy. Germans felt betrayed by the treaty—especially a former corporal named Adolf Hitler, who had been temporarily blinded by gas during the war. At a rally in 1922, Hitler shouted, "It cannot be that two million Germans should have fallen in vain.... No, we do not pardon, we demand—revenge!"

27.10 Chapter Summary

In this chapter, you read about American expansionism and the nation's involvement in World War I. You used a front-page headline to summarize key information about U.S. foreign policy from the late 1800s to 1920.

America's first great expansion after the Civil War was the purchase of Alaska. The United States also expanded westward by taking over the Midway Islands in the Pacific and annexing Hawaii.

As a result of the Spanish-American War, the United States gained two new possessions—Puerto Rico and the Philippines. Although the United States did not take over Cuba, it did keep the right to send troops to the island and to maintain naval bases there.

In Central America, the United States encouraged revolution in Panama, and then purchased a strip of land from the new country in order to build the Panama Canal. The United States maintained its control over the Canal Zone for the rest of the twentieth century.

Does this political cartoon support or oppose U.S. expansion?

By the time World War I broke out, the United States was becoming a world power. America remained neutral until late in the war, and then entered the conflict on the side of the Allied Powers. President Wilson described the war as a fight to make the world safe for democracy.

Americans helped to win the war, but Wilson was unable to get all of his peace plan adopted. The U.S. Senate refused to ratify the peace treaty, preventing the United States from joining the League of Nations. In Europe, the harsh terms imposed by the victorious Allies caused great bitterness in Germany.

As the United States turned back toward isolationism, Europe was once again at peace. But that peace would prove to be very fragile.

399

WORLD'S HIGHEST STANDARD OF LIVING

There's no way like the American Way

General Outdoor Adv Co

Why is this sign out of place?

28

The Roaring Twenties and the Great Depression

28.1 Introduction

In April 1933, classrooms in Chicago, Illinois, were about to shut down. Teachers had received little or no pay for months because schools had run out of money. So had just about everybody, it seemed. Children came to school hungry, so teachers found bread to give them. Some pupils couldn't afford shoes to protect their feet in the freezing weather, so teachers somehow came up with shoes.

Outraged, thousands of teachers charged into City Hall, demanding to be paid. Outside, students and parents marched with signs supporting the teachers. Protesters poured into banks, demanding that the banks lend the city enough money to pay teachers. In a few minutes, police arrived. Soon, one newspaper reported, "unpaid policemen were cracking their clubs against the heads of unpaid schoolteachers."

The scene in Chicago reflected the hard times that had overtaken the entire country. Governments couldn't pay their employees, and companies couldn't pay their workers. Everywhere, people were losing their farms and homes. The country was in the grip of a deep **depression**—a severe downturn in business activity.

The depression was all the more shocking because the 1920s had been a prosperous time for many Americans. World War I had brought a lot of new business to American industries. After the war, the good times continued as factories shifted from wartime production to consumer goods.

Yet by 1932, many businesses had failed. One in four workers didn't have a job, and for many families, the future looked bleak. A teacher recalled of the depression, "I thought it was going to be forever and ever. That people would always live in fear of losing their jobs. You know, fear."

In this chapter, you will learn how the nation's fortunes changed so drastically. You will also learn about the steps taken by an optimistic president to try to rescue Americans from the hardships of the depression.

Graphic Organizer: Sensory Figures
You will use a series of sensory figures to learn about the experiences of the 1920s and 1930s.

Young women called *flappers* cut their hair short, wore short, loose dresses, and enjoyed the excitement of the Roaring Twenties.

28.2 The Roaring Twenties

During the 1920s, a glance down Main Street in most American towns revealed a sight that was new in the United States: cars. For the first time, many Americans could afford to buy an automobile. Cars moved faster than the horse-drawn buggies they replaced. In fact, just about everything was moving faster, from assembly lines to music and dancing. Values were changing rapidly, too. Many people were eager for a little fun, and "modern women" stepped out of their traditional roles. This exciting decade became known as the Roaring Twenties.

Modern Life Begins   When World War I ended, Americans looked forward to better times ahead. Factories, no longer turning out supplies for war, responded by producing **consumer goods** that made life easier and more comfortable. Electricity was now supplied to many towns, making electric appliances both practical and desirable. Americans quickly shifted from iceboxes to refrigerators, and from carpet sweepers to electric vacuum cleaners.

Automobiles also changed American life. People who owned cars could travel farther to work. To escape crowding, many moved to suburbs that were springing up around major cities.

consumer goods: products intended for personal use by consumers, such as cars, refrigerators, and vacuum cleaners

Modern Women   With housework becoming easier, more women than ever went to work outside of the home. By the end of the decade, women made up more than a quarter of the workforce. Women also gained political power. In 1920, the passage of the Nineteenth Amendment guaranteed women's right to vote in national and state elections.

Women's new sense of freedom was reflected in changes in fashion. Young women who called themselves *flappers* cut their hair short and wore makeup. They traded their mothers' long, heavy skirts for short, thin dresses that barely reached their knees. These "modern women" wanted to have as much fun as men—smoking, drinking, and riding in automobiles.

Prosperous Times   For many Americans, these changes took place at a time of growing prosperity. By the middle of the decade, the country had the highest standard of living the world had ever known.

Living standards were rising because manufacturing was becoming more efficient. In 1914, for example, Henry Ford introduced a moving assembly line into his car factories. This revolutionary new method drastically cut the time needed to assemble cars. Such changes increased workers' productivity, or the amount of goods they could produce at a given cost. As a result, companies could sell their products at lower prices while raising workers' wages—and still make more money.

Each new industry sparked others. The rise of the automobile industry, for instance, increased the demand for steel for car bodies, rubber for tires, and oil refineries to make gasoline.

People flocked to the famous Harlem nightclub, the Cotton Club, to hear Duke Ellington and his band play jazz.

To encourage consumers to buy goods, stores started offering **credit**. Customers could take home a product after paying just a part of the purchase price in cash. Then they made monthly payments until the item was paid for. By 1929, three of every four cars were bought on credit. So were half of all major appliances such as washing machines and radios.

The Stock Market Booms As you learned in Chapter 24, companies raise money by selling stock, or shares in the ownership of the company. When many people want to invest in a company, the price of its shares goes up. When few people want to buy, the price goes down. Such price shifts make investing risky, because people can't be sure what the value of their stocks will be in the future.

During the 1920s, Americans were very optimistic about business, and those with money to spare invested heavily in the stock market. One millionaire remarked, "Taxi drivers told you what to buy. The shoeshine boy could give you a summary of the day's financial news." As President Calvin Coolidge said, "The business of America is business."

As stock prices soared, eager investors began using "margin buying" to purchase stocks. This meant that buyers paid just part of the price of the stock and borrowed the rest through their stockbrokers. The stockbrokers, in turn, often borrowed money from banks. Everybody involved was betting that stock prices would go up. Later, investors hoped to sell their stock at a higher price, which would give them the cash to repay the borrowed money and still make a profit. But if stock prices fell, investors could be stuck with huge debts.

As the stock market boomed, few worried about prices going down. In just three weeks in 1928, shares of Radio Corporation of America (RCA) rose from $95 to $178. Shares of General Electric tripled in value in 18 months. Happy investors imagined that stock prices would continue going up indefinitely.

credit: an arrangement in which a seller trusts a buyer to repay part of an item's purchase price over time

Prohibition: The outlawing of the making, selling, and transporting of alcoholic beverages under the Eighteenth Amendment. The amendment was repealed in 1933.

Fun Times   With their pockets full of money, many Americans enjoyed life as never before. They went to clubs to dance and to listen to jazz, a new musical style in which musicians improvise, making up music as they play. Young people loved this fresh style of music.

Part of the attraction of going to many clubs was the opportunity to drink illegal alcohol. In 1919, anti-alcohol reformers had succeeded in passing the Eighteenth Amendment, which prohibited (outlawed) the making, selling, and transporting of alcoholic beverages. This attempt to eliminate alcohol consumption was called **Prohibition**.

In response to Prohibition, bars and liquor stores closed. At the same time, thousands of illegal clubs called *speakeasies* sprang up to sell illegal alcohol. In many large cities, police often looked the other way as people went on buying and drinking alcohol. Making and selling alcohol became big business for people operating outside the law.

Over 40,000 Ku Klux Klan members marched through the streets of Washington, D.C., in 1925. Because of their large numbers, many members felt safe enough to discard the masks they traditionally wore to hide their identities.

The Dark Side of the 1920s

The Roaring Twenties also had a dark side. Many Americans were left out of the new prosperity, including many farmers and poor whites, Hispanics, and African Americans. In addition, some Americans became victims of intolerance.

After World War I, a new Ku Klux Klan emerged. The revived Klan used both political power and mob violence to lash out against African Americans, immigrants, Catholics, Jews, and anyone else it regarded as an enemy. Although its power had faded by 1930, during the 1920s the Klan spread terror through many communities, especially in the South.

Other Americans supported less violent forms of intolerance. As you read in Chapter 25, during the 1920s Congress limited immigration to the United States, especially from countries in Asia.

Still, most Americans looked forward to even better times. On taking office in 1929, President Herbert Hoover proclaimed, "We in America today are nearer to the final triumph over poverty than ever before in the history of any land."

28.3 The Economy Sinks into Depression

In September 1929, investors celebrated as stock prices hit an all-time high. Suddenly, the bubble burst. Stock prices began to tumble, and some investors who had bought their stocks "on margin" sold their shares to pay off losses. As a result, prices dropped even further. The stage was set for disaster.

A large crowd surrounded this bank in 1929, desperate to withdraw their money before the bank failed.

The Stock Market Crash   On Thursday, October 24, the opening bell sounded at the New York Stock Exchange in New York City. Almost at once, stockbrokers were trying to sell tens of thousands of shares. No one was buying. Prices began falling faster and faster.

Investors panicked. Their money was locked up in stocks that were suddenly worth less and less. When brokers demanded cash from investors to pay off their margin debts, many investors sold still more stocks to raise the money. With more sellers than buyers in the market, prices went even lower. People's "paper wealth" was disappearing.

Brokers screamed out their orders to sell shares. They pushed each other out of the way, losing glasses and shoes in the chaos. One newspaper journalist wrote, "I heard it—and I can still hear it...the sound of running feet, the sound of fear."

Over the next few days, sellers continued to outnumber buyers. The following Tuesday, investors filled the streets around the Stock Exchange. Grim, curious, and noisy, they waited. The opening bell sounded. Within minutes, the bottom fell out of the market. As people tried to dump their stocks, prices fell more and more steeply. Before the day was over, many stocks were worthless. The market had collapsed. The terrifying day became known as Black Tuesday. It was, said the *New York Times,* "the most disastrous day in the stock market's history."

BANK FAILURES

The Depression Begins The crash of the stock market was a dramatic sign that America's good times had come to a sudden end. By the time the stock market stabilized a bit in November, businesses and investors had lost over $30 billion, an amount equal to the total cost of World War I. Newspapers told of ruined investors leaping to their deaths off skyscraper ledges. In Kansas City, a man with big stock losses called out, "Tell the boys I can't pay them what I owe them," and shot himself.

The stock market crash affected millions of Americans, some right away, some over the years to come. Many banks had invested heavily in the stock market, or loaned money on margin. After the crash, they didn't have enough money to pay depositors—people who kept their money in the bank.

On October 7, 1931, President Hoover announced a plan to end the crisis of bank failures. Examine the graph above. Do you think Hoover's plan was a success?

They went bankrupt, or closed down without paying off debts. Depositors lost their life savings.

Even healthy banks suffered as panicky depositors withdrew their money. When banks ran out of cash, they closed their doors. In 1930, more than 1,000 banks went out of business.

Businesses lost their deposits when banks closed. Others found banks no longer willing or able to make loans. Without funds to help them through rough times, thousands of businesses failed.

Banks that served farmers were also closing down. These banks had been in trouble beginning in the 1920s as many farmers went deeply into debt and could not repay their loans.

The stock market crash and the problems of farmers were two of the many reasons the economy sank into a depression. Another problem was that millions of families had been left out of the prosperity of the 1920s. They didn't have the money to buy the products that factories were turning out. Still another problem was that banks had loaned huge sums of money to foreign nations that could not afford to repay those debts. These and other factors combined to plunge the economy into depression.

Losing Jobs and Homes   By 1933, about 85,000 businesses had failed. Many more were barely surviving. Businesses that did stay open needed fewer employees. At Ford Motor Company, employment dropped from 128,000 to 37,000, while "hundreds of half-finished automobile bodies gathered dust."

Even people with jobs were earning less. Secretaries who once received $40 per week settled for $10. Many cities couldn't afford to pay their employees. As fewer people were able to afford consumer goods, factories fired their workers. By 1933, over 12 million Americans had lost their jobs.

When workers couldn't find jobs, they spent their savings and then sold what they owned. Finally, they had no way to pay their bills. By the beginning of 1933, almost 1,000 families per day were losing their homes. For the first time, homelessness became a major problem in America.

"All of a sudden we had to move," remembered one child. "My father lost his job and we moved into a double garage." Homeless families often built shacks out of scraps of wood, tin, and tar paper. Little "towns" of such shelters grew up around cities and were called "Hoovervilles," after President Hoover. As the economy collapsed further, some people simply slept under newspapers on the streets.

Unable even to buy groceries, families scrounged for food in garbage cans and alleys. One boy said, "Every now and then my brother or Dad would find some sort of odd little something. Then…we'd go wild over food. We'd eat until we were sick."

Under such stresses, families started breaking up. Jobless young people sometimes hopped onto freight trains to other cities and begged for food. Some families placed their children in orphanages—homes for children without parents—to keep them from starving.

Hoover Tries to Respond   Americans had suffered through depressions before. But in the past, these downturns in the economy had lasted

Homeless people built towns of shacks made from tarpaper, cardboard, and scrap material. These towns were called "Hoovervilles" as a criticism of President Hoover, whom many blamed for the depression.

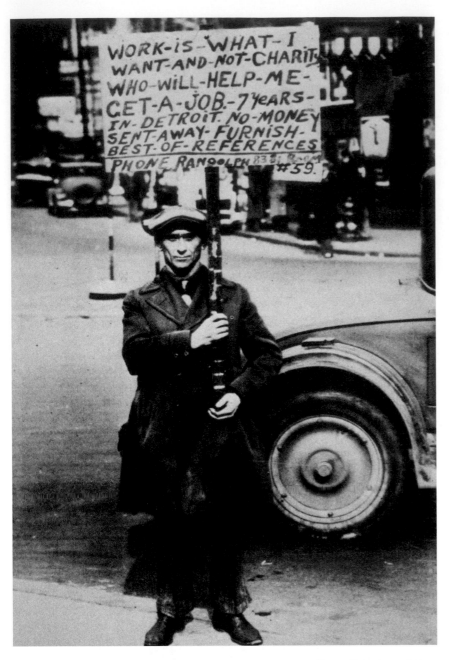

Unemployment soared in spite of President Hoover's efforts to end the depression with increased spending on public works.

only a few months before business picked up again. By the end of 1930, it was clear to President Hoover that this depression was not going to cure itself.

At Hoover's request, Congress increased spending on public works, government-sponsored projects such as highways and dams. The federal government also made loans to banks and railroads to get the economy moving again. "Prosperity is just around the corner," Hoover told the nation.

Hoover was wrong. This downturn was so deep and lasted so long that people called it the "Great Depression." When Hoover's efforts to end the depression failed, Americans began looking for a new leader. They wanted a president who was willing to do whatever it took to turn the country around.

28.4 The New Deal

As the 1932 election drew near, the Republicans nominated Hoover to run for a second term. The Democrats chose the governor of New York, Franklin Delano Roosevelt, as their candidate.

To many, Hoover seemed cold and helpless in the face of the country's misery. Even though Roosevelt came from a wealthy family, he seemed to care about ordinary citizens. And his beaming smile radiated confidence and optimism.

In accepting his party's nomination, Roosevelt pledged "a new deal for the American people." Just what he meant wasn't clear, but people liked his warmth and energy. Roosevelt related the country's hardships to his own experiences when he became paralyzed by polio at the age of 39. "Once I spent two years lying in bed," he said, "trying to move my big toe. That was the hardest job I ever had to do. After that, anything else was easy." Roosevelt won the election by a landslide.

The First Hundred Days "This nation asks for action, and action now," Roosevelt boldly proclaimed at his inauguration. "The only thing we have to fear is fear itself."

Roosevelt began his energetic presidency by targeting the bank crisis. More than 9,000 banks had already failed, and panicked depositors were withdrawing their money from those that still survived. Roosevelt quickly closed all banks for four days. He promised that government officials would inspect bank records, allowing only banks with sufficient funds to open again.

To help Americans understand this drastic step, Roosevelt addressed the nation by radio. More than 60 million Americans listened as their president spoke to them in ordinary words, as if sitting with them around a living-room fireplace. "I can assure you that it is safer to keep your money in a reopened bank than under a mattress," he said.

When banks reopened, more people put money in than took money out. Pleased, Roosevelt continued to use "fireside chats" to explain his programs to the public.

During Roosevelt's first hundred days in office, he pushed Congress to deal quickly with the nation's problems. In that short time, Congress passed 15 major bills, a record for that number of days. This legislation, along with laws passed later on, established programs with three goals: immediate relief for the needy, economic recovery, and reform intended to keep such problems from developing in the future. Together these programs became known as the **New Deal**.

Relief for the Needy   Several New Deal measures were designed to help the 13 million Americans who were unemployed. The Federal Emergency Relief Act (FERA), for example, gave money to states to help them provide food and assistance to the needy. Some business leaders objected to this use of government money, saying that in the long run it would be better to help businesses provide more jobs. A member of

> **New Deal:** the set of programs adopted under the Roosevelt administration to combat the Great Depression of the 1930s

To ease the suffering of the hungry, President Roosevelt established the Federal Emergency Relief Act, which gave money to states to provide food for the hungry.

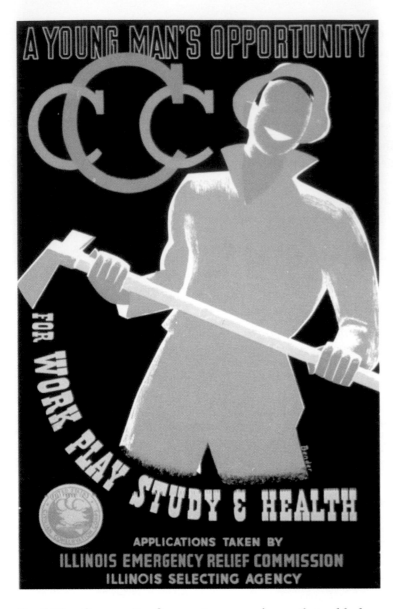

A YOUNG MAN'S OPPORTUNITY

CCC

FOR WORK PLAY STUDY & HEALTH

APPLICATIONS TAKEN BY
ILLINOIS EMERGENCY RELIEF COMMISSION
ILLINOIS SELECTING AGENCY

The Civilian Conservation Corps put more than 2.5 million young men to work on environmental projects. CCC workers earned only $1 a day, but were provided with meals and camp lodging.

pension: a sum of money paid to a retired person, usually on a monthly basis

Roosevelt's staff responded, "People don't eat in the long run. They have to eat every day."

Other New Deal relief programs offered paychecks in exchange for useful public work, such as building bridges, lighthouses, schools, and sewer systems. One observer said of the workers in such programs, "For many, many of them it was the first money they'd seen in months. They took it with wide grins and made beelines for the grocery stores."

The Civilian Conservation Corps (CCC) paid young men of all backgrounds to work on environmental improvement projects like replanting forests, draining swamps, and fighting fires. "I really enjoyed it," said one man. "I had three wonderful square meals a day.... You learned that everybody here was equal."

One of the bigger relief programs, the Works Progress Administration (WPA), created over 8 million jobs. WPA employees built 120,000 public buildings and half a million miles of roads. WPA artists painted murals on public buildings that can still be seen today. As FDR remarked, such jobs preserved "not only the bodies of the unemployed...but also their self-respect, their self-confidence, courage, and determination."

One of the most lasting parts of the New Deal was the Social Security Act, which was passed by Congress in 1935. To help older people in need, this law provided a small amount of money each month to elderly people who were extremely poor. To help the elderly of the future, the law established a national **pension** for most retired workers, to be paid for by taxes on workers and employers. Dependent children and handicapped persons could also get aid. In addition, states received funds to aid people who were temporarily unemployed.

Economic Recovery   Ending the Great Depression required more than just giving people money from the government, even for useful projects. The New Deal had to make America's economy strong again, so that businesses and farms could succeed on their own.

Early in the New Deal, Congress established the National Recovery Administration (NRA). To spur increased production, the agency let competing companies work together to set prices, maximum working hours, and minimum wages. The NRA also guaranteed workers the right to join unions and to bargain for contracts.

Federal funding of huge construction projects like dams and bridges also helped to rebuild businesses and provide jobs. Builders who received government contracts hired workers, and the projects also increased jobs in major industries like lumber, steel, and cement.

One major project, the Tennessee Valley Authority (TVA), was headed by the government rather than by private business. This ambitious program was created to supply electric power at reasonable rates and, at the same time, to show that even the poorest regions of America could recover from the depression. All along the Tennessee River, the federal government built dams and waterways, eliminating disastrous flooding and harnessing water power to produce electricity. As electricity was brought to the valley for the first time, industry was encouraged to move in. The TVA also encouraged farmers to adopt better farming techniques. While much of the region remained poor, the TVA did improve the lives of thousands of people.

Agricultural Recovery   Other recovery efforts focused on agriculture. In the early years of the depression, farmers produced more food than people could buy. As a result, farm prices fell to the point that it did not pay farmers to harvest their crops or bring their livestock to market. With no money coming in, many farmers couldn't earn enough to pay their debts and feed their families. One third of them lost their farms.

In response to this problem, Congress created the Agricultural Adjustment Administration (AAA) in 1933. This agency paid farmers to plant less land and raise fewer animals. Many Americans resented paying farmers to grow less food while people were hungry. But within a year, farm prices did start to rise. Later, the government bought excess food instead, storing it to sell when prices got higher.

New Dealers also sought solutions to the serious problem of soil erosion. During the 1930s, a combination of poor farming practices and years of low rainfall on the Great Plains created a new terror—howling dust storms. During these "black blizzards," sand and dust covered everything

This photograph shows a dust storm enveloping Baca County, Colorado, in the 1930s. Winds skimmed the precious top soil of the Great Plains and sent it swirling into the air.

and even made breathing difficult. One observer wrote, "There were no fields, only sand drifting into mounds…. In the farmyard, fences, machinery, and trees were gone, buried."

By 1938, some 10 million acres in the "Dust Bowl" had lost five or more inches of topsoil. With their farms destroyed, nearly 3.5 million people left the Great Plains. Some moved to nearby states. Others pushed west, seeking better futures in California and the Pacific Northwest.

To save the country's farms, FDR established the Soil Conservation Service (SCS). This agency planted belts of trees to break up the winds and hold down soil. One such belt, 100 miles wide, stretched from Texas to North Dakota. SCS also taught farmers how to avoid erosion and keep the soil in place for future generations.

Roosevelt's New Deal programs had three goals: relief, reform, and recovery. Which of the agencies or programs below still exist(s) today?

New Deal Programs

Relief

Federal Emergency Relief Administration (FERA)	Provided funds to organizations and state and local governments offering direct relief to the needy
Works Progress Administration (WPA)	Provided jobs for the unemployed, often building public works projects
Social Security	Provided aid to elderly, and, through the states, to individuals temporarily unemployed
Civilian Conservation Corps (CCC)	Employed young men to work on environmental projects in exchange for food, lodging, and a small salary

Recovery

Agricultural Adjustment Administration (AAA)	Raised agricultural prices by paying farmers to reduce the amount of crops and animals sold on the market
National Recovery Administration (NRA)	Created labor and industry standards to help revive American industry
Tennessee Valley Authority (TVA)	Developed electricity and other resources in the impoverished Tennessee River Valley

Reform

Federal Deposit Insurance Corporation (FDIC)	Guaranteed (insured) bank deposits to help people regain confidence that their money was safe in banks

Banking Reform Relief and recovery were intended to help the nation escape from the depths of the depression. But New Dealers also wanted reforms that would prevent such a depression from happening again.

A major target of reform was the banking industry. Congress quickly passed Roosevelt's plan to protect America from banking problems. It established the Federal Deposit Insurance Corporation (FDIC) to insure depositors' bank accounts. It also made bankers avoid investments that were too risky. Together with Roosevelt's bank inspections, these actions helped calm people's fears about the banking industry.

28.5 Impact of the New Deal

In 1936, Roosevelt ran for a second term as president. Despite the fact that the depression still continued, he was reelected by an even larger majority than in 1932.

By this time, most of his recovery and relief programs were in place. And the New Deal was being attacked both by people who thought the government should do even more, and by those who wanted the government to do (and spend) less.

Still, the New Deal had a significant impact on the United States. In the short run, Roosevelt's programs helped many Americans survive the darkest days of the Great Depression. In the long run, the New Deal left a lasting mark on American society and government.

FDR began many new programs (represented above by the medicine bottles on Uncle Sam's table) to help the nation out of the depression. How many programs can you identify in the cartoon?

Impact on the Poor and Unemployed All over the country, New Deal construction projects put the unemployed to work. As a result, America had better roads, bridges, dams, schools, and other public buildings. These projects not only put money in people's pockets, but also raised their spirits. As one Tennessee worker said, "I'm proud that I worked on that Crossville dam. I wasn't afraid to tackle anything after that."

The New Deal also introduced "safety nets" for many of the nation's needy. Social Security and unemployment insurance still exist today, providing a major source of income for retired workers and the unemployed. In later years, other welfare, training, and assistance programs were established as Americans began to accept the idea that government had a responsibility to aid those in need.

Still, neither the New Deal nor the programs that followed ended poverty in America. And the New Deal did little to solve problems of discrimination against African Americans and other minorities.

Impact on Workers and Business Legal problems slowed some efforts to assist workers and business. The Supreme Court declared the National Recovery Administration (NRA) unconstitutional, saying that it supported business monopolies.

In response, Congress passed the National Labor Relations Act in 1935. This act gave workers the right to join unions and to bargain with employers for improved wages and working conditions. It also created the National Labor Relations Board (NLRB) to settle disputes between employers and workers. Supported by this legislation, union membership grew rapidly. The NLRB still exists today.

Another lasting effect of the New Deal was that the government became more involved in regulating the stock market and the banking industry. The Federal Deposit Insurance Corporation (FDIC) still protects bank depositors by insuring bank accounts. Laws limit margin buying, and other rules forbid banks from taking risks in the stock market with depositors' funds.

Impact on Farmers and Rural Americans   By raising crop prices and providing farmers with low-interest loans, New Deal programs helped farmers keep their farms. But not every New Deal farm program was a complete success. When the government paid farmers to plant less, they didn't need as much hired help. As a result, many farmworkers lost their jobs. Some farmers also cut production by turning sharecroppers off their rented land.

Another New Deal agency, the Rural Electrification Administration (REA), helped improve life on the farm. The REA made loans to help bring electricity to rural areas. When this program was begun in 1935, only one farm in ten had electricity. Within 20 years, nine out of ten farms were electrified.

The New Deal changed American attitudes toward the role of government. Many people came to believe that the government has a responsibility to help those in need.

"Yes, You Remembered Me"

Impact on Government   By 1939, most New Deal programs had come to an end. But FDR's ambitious response to the Great Depression had permanently changed both the size and the role of the national government. In 1931, the federal government had 580,000 employees. By 1941, 1.3 million people were government employees.

Before the Great Depression, most Americans probably agreed with Thomas Jefferson that the best government was that which governs least. Roosevelt disagreed. He strongly believed that one of government's most important duties was to care for citizens who could not provide for themselves. "That responsibility," he delcared, "is recognized by every civilized nation."

In the coming years, Americans would continue to debate how far the government should go in meeting this responsibility, and how it should go about it. But by the end of the 1930s, most Americans were prepared to accept that government did have a responsibility to lend a helping hand to those in need.

As the 1940s began, the depression still lingered. It would finally be brought to an end by a new and even greater crisis. America was about to go to war.

28.6 Chapter Summary

In this chapter, you read about the Great Depression that followed the prosperity of the Roaring Twenties, and President Franklin Roosevelt's efforts to respond to this economic crisis. You used sensory figures to express the social and economic climate of the era.

For many Americans, the Roaring Twenties were a time of new prosperity and rapidly changing values. The soaring stock market reflected a "get rich quick" spirit and the belief that good times were here to stay.

The stock market crash of 1929 was a dramatic sign that all was not well with the economy. The crash was followed by a deep depression. As banks and other businesses failed, millions of Americans lost their jobs and even their homes. Drought in farming states contributed to the nation's misery.

Franklin Roosevelt's New Deal responded to the crisis with a series of ambitious government programs. These programs focused on providing immediate relief, encouraging economic recovery, and fostering reform. Most New Deal programs ended in the 1930s, but a few, such as Social Security, continue today.

The New Deal helped millions of Americans survive the Great Depression. It also permanently changed the role of the federal government. Americans were persuaded that the government had a responsibility to help people who could not help themselves. They also accepted an increase in government regulation of some parts of the economy. As a result, the federal government became larger than ever before.

But even greater challenges lay ahead. As you will read in the next chapter, Americans were about to confront their responsibility to people and places far from home.

This mural shows many of the accomplishments of the National Youth Administration. Government support of the arts allowed for the creation of many lasting works of arts such as this.

29

World War II

29.1 Introduction

Late one night in 1939, men in Polish army uniforms burst into a German customs office and radio station in Poland. When they left, bullet-ridden German bodies lay everywhere. The next day, September 1, German leaders cried for revenge. They ordered one million soldiers to invade Poland.

The men wearing Polish army uniforms were actually German secret police. The bodies they left behind were German prisoners they had already killed. The whole incident was a trick to give Germany an excuse to invade Poland.

For years, the world had watched and worried as Adolf Hitler and his Nazi Party gained power in Germany. Hitler, who ruled Germany as a **dictator,** dreamed of creating a new empire with vast "living space" for the German people. To create this empire, Hitler built the world's most powerful military force. Before attacking Poland, he had already made Austria and Czechoslovakia part of Germany.

Empire builders were also in power in Italy and Japan. In 1936, Italy's dictator, Benito Mussolini, had taken over the African country of Ethiopia. In Japan, military leaders were plotting to conquer all of East Asia. In 1940, Germany, Italy, and Japan formed a military and economic alliance. They called themselves the Axis Powers.

After declaring war on Poland, Germany sent tanks sweeping across the country. The German forces quickly overpowered Polish soldiers in light tanks and on horseback. German planes bombed cities, factories, and even schools. Within weeks, Poland was conquered. Outraged by Hitler's aggression, Britain and France declared war on Germany.

As you will read in this chapter, the war that began in Europe became a worldwide conflict that touched all Americans. Despite its tradition of isolationism, the United States would soon be leading the struggle to save the world from the dark dreams of dictators.

Graphic Organizer: Illustration
You will use this illustration to learn about the experiences of different groups during World War II.

29.2 The United States Gets Involved

At first, the Axis Powers seemed unstoppable. By the end of 1941, Japanese forces had conquered much of East Asia. Germany and Italy controlled most of Europe and North Africa. Britain and the Soviet Union stood alone in Europe against the dictators.

America Helps Out   President Franklin Roosevelt knew that Americans were not yet ready to abandon isolationism and join the war. But he was able to persuade Congress to sell, lend, or lease war supplies to "any nation whose defense is vital to the United States."

At the same time, Roosevelt prepared for war. He got funding from Congress for ships and planes, and started the first peacetime draft.

On December 7, 1941, the Japanese launched a surprise attack against the U.S. Pacific fleet at Pearl Harbor. In the photograph, the ammunition on the U.S. destroyer *Shaw* explodes during the attack.

Japan Attacks Pearl Harbor

While the war in Europe grabbed headlines, tensions were also rising between the United States and Japan. In 1941, Japan invaded Indochina (now Vietnam and Cambodia). The United States protested by halting trade with Japan. This trade embargo cut Japan off from the one thing its leaders could not live without—oil for their war machine. They could get oil by seizing the Dutch East Indies (now Indonesia). But the United States and its navy stood in their way.

Sunday, December 7, 1941, dawned cloudy at Pearl Harbor, Hawaii, the home of the U.S. Navy's Pacific fleet. Aboard the battleship *Oklahoma,* servicemen were eating breakfast when loudspeakers blared out, "Real planes, real bombs; this is no drill!"

Japanese bombers roared out of the clouds, raining bombs on the naval base.

The *Oklahoma* sank almost immediately. All 415 men aboard were drowned. Nearby, the battleship *Arizona* caught fire and disappeared beneath the waves, taking 1,000 men with her. In two hours, the Japanese had sunk or damaged 19 ships and 149 planes, almost half the navy's fleet. More than 2,400 Americans were killed.

The next day, Roosevelt spoke to a shocked nation. "Yesterday," he began, "December 7, 1941—a date which will live in infamy [evil fame]—the United States of America was suddenly and deliberately attacked by naval and air forces of the Empire of Japan." Within an hour, Congress declared war on Japan. In turn, the Axis Powers declared war on the United States.

America was finished with isolationism. It was time to fight.

29.3 The War in Europe

America did not face the Axis Powers alone. Together with Britain and the Soviet Union, the United States led a group of 48 countries known as the Allies. Believing that Germany posed a bigger threat to the world than Japan, the Allies concentrated first on the war in Europe.

North Africa and Italy When the United States entered the war, the Allied Powers were not strong enough to attack Germany directly. Instead, they began their campaign in North Africa, where the German defenses were weaker.

In November 1942, more than 100,000 Allied troops landed in North Africa. Their mission was to capture Germany's Afrika Korps, led by General Edwin Rommel, the legendary "Desert Fox." After months of fierce desert fighting, the Afrika Korps surrendered in May 1943.

From North Africa, the Allies crossed the Mediterranean to attack Italy. The Italian island of Sicily fell quickly. But conquering the mountainous Italian peninsula proved to be far more difficult. Even after the Italians surrendered, German troops stubbornly defended Italy. It took the Allies almost two years to drive the Germans off Italian soil.

The Battle of Stalingrad Meanwhile, Hitler had attacked the Soviet Union. Advancing rapidly, German troops reached the industrial city of Stalingrad in the summer of 1942. Over the next few months, the Germans bombed Stalingrad into a blackened wasteland. Still, the Russians held on. As the brutal Russian winter set in, the German army attacking the city was surrounded by Soviet troops and forced to surrender.

The bloody defense of Stalingrad cost the Soviets 1,250,000 soldiers and civilians—more than all the American casualties in the entire war. However, the victory marked a turning point. After Stalingrad, the Russian army stopped retreating and began to advance on Germany.

D-Day While the Soviet Union prepared to attack Germany from the east, its allies readied an invasion from the west. **D-day,** or invasion day, came on June 6, 1944. Early that morning, 176,000 troops, 4,000 landing craft, 600 warships, and 11,000 planes left England for the beaches of Normandy, on the coast of German-occupied France.

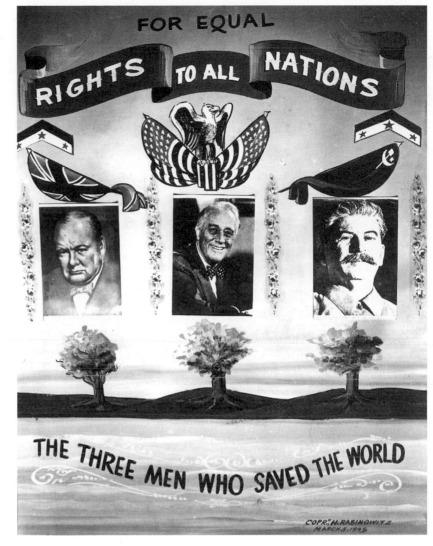

The major leaders of the Allied Powers are shown in this poster. From left to right, they are Winston Churchill of Great Britain, Franklin Roosevelt of the United States, and Joseph Stalin of the Soviet Union.

D-day: a day specified for launching an operation, such as the Allied invasion of Normandy

World War II **419**

General Dwight D. Eisenhower is shown here preparing his troops for the D-day invasion in which 176,000 British and American troops landed on the coast of German-occupied France.

the Holocaust: the mass murder of European Jews and other victims by Adolf Hitler and his followers

The D-day invasion was the largest combined land-sea-air operation in history. It began with a massive air and sea bombardment of German positions on the Normandy coast. Even with this support, troops landing on the beaches were met by murderous fire from the cliffs above. "It seemed we had entered hell itself," an American recalled. "The whole beach was a great burning fury. All around were burning vehicles, puffed-up bodies.... The water was burning."

Despite heavy losses, the troops took the Normandy beaches. Within two weeks, the Allies landed a million soldiers in France and began to move inland.

German Concentration Camps

By 1945, the Allies were closing in on Germany. While marching across Poland toward the German capital of Berlin, Soviet troops came upon a German concentration camp. There they found a thousand people so weak and sick that they seemed like "living corpses." They also found the world's largest crematorium (a furnace for burning dead bodies). "This is not a concentration camp," reported a stunned Soviet. "It is a gigantic murder plant."

He was right. Long before invading Poland, Hitler and his followers had declared war against Jews and other groups, including Gypsies and Poles. They viewed these groups as inferior to the German "master race." Wherever German troops went, these "inferior" people were rounded up and sent to prison camps. The lucky ones were forced to work as slaves. The rest were murdered.

This massive program of systematic murder came to be called **the Holocaust**. Across Europe, 11 million people perished in the Holocaust, more than half of them Jews.

As the Allies pushed toward Berlin from the west, they found more death camps, each more horrifying than the last. One American wrote home to his wife, "For the first time I truly realized the evil of Hitler and why this war had to be waged."

V-E Day By April 30, 1945, Hitler knew the war was lost. To escape the "disgrace" of surrender, the German dictator committed suicide in his Berlin headquarters. A week later, Germany surrendered to the Allies.

Throughout the Allied countries, people celebrated V-E Day (Victory in Europe Day). But the struggle was only half over. On the other side of the world, the Pacific war still raged.

Geography Challenge
The War in Europe

Map legend:
- Axis Powers before World War II
- Extent of Axis control early Nov. 1942
- Allies
- Neutral nations
- ← Allied troop movements

ICELAND

0 200 400 miles
0 200 400 kilometers

NORWAY

SWEDEN

FINLAND

Volga R.

North Sea

Baltic Sea

Moscow

DENMARK

Sept 1944

IRELAND

GREAT BRITAIN

Pas de Calais

NETH.

Berlin captured May 2, 1945

East Prussia (Ger.)

SOVIET UNION

London

July 1944

ATLANTIC OCEAN

Normandy D Day June 6, 1944

Paris liberated Aug. 25, 1944

BEL.

Rhine R.

Apr. 1945

Elbe R.

Oder R.

Warsaw

Mar. 1944

Aug. 1943

Stalingrad Aug. 21, 1942– Jan. 31, 1943

GERMANY

Czechoslovakia

POLAND

Aug. 1944

Ukraine

FRANCE

SWITZ.

Danube R.

Austria

HUNGARY

ROMANIA

VICHY FRANCE (Occupied Nov. 1942)

Aug. 1944

YUGOSLAVIA

Black Sea

CAUC

PORTUGAL

ITALY

Dec. 1944

BULGARIA

SPAIN

Rome liberated June 4, 1944

ALBANIA (It.)

TURKEY

GREECE

Nov. 1942

Tunis occupied May, 12 1943

July 1943

Sicily

SYRIA

Casablanca

LEBANON

MOROCCO

TUNISIA

Mediterranean Sea

PALESTINE (Br.)

Alexandria

Suez Canal

SAUDI ARABIA

FRENCH NORTH AFRICA

Nov. 1942

El-Alamein Oct. 23–Nov. 5, 1942

ALGERIA

LIBYA (It.)

EGYPT

29.4 The War in the Pacific

The United States did not wait until V-E Day to move against Japan. But while the Americans rebuilt their Pacific fleet, Japan quickly expanded its Asian empire. By the spring of 1942, Japanese forces controlled an area covering almost a seventh of the earth.

The Battle of Midway   In May 1942, a huge Japanese invasion fleet headed for Midway Island in the Pacific. From that point, Japanese forces could easily invade Hawaii.

Although outnumbered, U.S. bombers attacked the Japanese fleet again and again. By the end of the Battle of Midway, Japan had lost four irreplaceable aircraft carriers and 322 planes. Never again would Japan directly threaten the United States. The tide of battle in the Pacific had turned.

Island Hopping   After Midway, the Allies began the task of driving the Japanese off hundreds of islands scattered over thousands of miles of ocean. Rather than attack every Japanese stronghold, the Allies adopted a strategy known as "island hopping."

Following this strategy, Allied troops seized islands that were less well defended. Then they used these islands as bases from which to attack Japanese ships supplying nearby islands. As a result, reported a Japanese officer, "Our strong points were gradually starved out."

While the strategy worked, few islands fell easily. Japanese soldiers viewed surrender as deeply shameful, and they offered fierce resistance. One U.S. marine observed, "You don't really comprehend it until you get out there and fight people who are faced with an absolutely hopeless situation and will not give up."

Crewmen abandon the USS *Lexington,* which is beginning to sink after having been hit by Japanese bombs and torpedoes. The *Lexington* was sent to protect Australia and New Zealand from Japanese invasion.

Okinawa, the Final Stepping Stone By V-E Day, the Japanese navy and air force had been largely destroyed. Only one obstacle stood in the way of a final Allied assault on Japan—the island of Okinawa.

As the Allies prepared to invade Okinawa, Japanese pilots flew planes filled with explosives into American warships to blow them up. The men flying these suicide missions were called *kamikaze* pilots. (Kamikaze, which means "divine wind," was the name given to a legendary storm that saved Japan from invasion by sea in 1281.)

Kamikaze attacks killed 5,000 American seamen. Another 40,000 Americans were killed or injured in ground fighting. The Japanese lost more than 100,000 men. But finally Okinawa was taken.

When American soldiers landed on Iwo Jima, they faced fierce opposition from the Japanese, who believed in fighting to the death. Almost 7,000 Americans died during the battle over this small island.

The Atomic Bomb President Roosevelt did not live to see this hard-won victory. On April 12, 1945, he died from a stroke. Vice President Harry S. Truman became the nation's new president.

A few days later, Truman was handed a memo that began, "Within four months we shall in all probability have completed the most terrible weapon ever known in human history." This was the first Truman had heard of the Manhattan Project and the **atomic bomb**.

The Manhattan Project was a secret program dedicated to building an atomic weapon. When the first bomb was successfully tested in July 1945, Truman faced a terrible choice. He could order an invasion of Japan, which might cost a million American lives. Or he could use this frightening new weapon.

atomic bomb: an immensely powerful weapon whose violent energy comes from splitting the atom (the basic unit of matter)

V-J Day Truman did not hesitate. "I regarded the bomb as a military weapon and never had any doubt that it should be used," he wrote of his decision. Japan was warned that it faced "prompt and utter destruction" unless it surrendered at once. No surrender came.

On August 6, 1945, a lone American plane dropped an atomic bomb on the Japanese city of Hiroshima. A blinding flash filled the sky. The explosion that followed killed 100,000 people, most in mere moments. "I felt I had lost all the bones in my body," recalled a survivor. "I saw a beautiful blue sky and a dead city."

A stunned Japan did not surrender. Three days later, a second atomic bomb exploded over the city of Nagasaki, killing an estimated 70,000 people. "I cannot bear to see my innocent people suffer any longer," said Japanese emperor Hirohito. He announced Japan's surrender.

On August 15, 1945, Americans celebrated V-J Day (Victory in Japan Day). After signing the surrender treaty, American general Douglas MacArthur announced, "A great victory has been won. The skies no longer rain death—the seas bear only commerce—men everywhere walk upright in the sunlight. The entire world is quietly at peace."

Geography Challenge

The War in the Pacific

29.5 American Servicemen

The day after the attack on Pearl Harbor, thousands of Americans signed up to fight. Over 5 million people volunteered for the military during World War II. Another 10 million were drafted.

Becoming a GI   The military mixed Americans together as never before. Northerners and southerners, city dwellers and farmers, Protestants, Catholics, and Jews—all trained together. After three months of basic training, they were battle-ready GIs. The term *GI*—meaning "Government Issue"—was stamped on government-issued uniforms and supplies. But soon the troops were applying it to themselves.

Military life began at training camps, where raw recruits were turned into fighting teams. Officers expected obedience to every order. Recruits exercised, drilled, and crawled through the mud with heavy equipment as machine guns fired overhead. After basic training, fewer than half the troops were sent overseas to fight. The rest worked on military bases in the United States in a wide variety of jobs.

This poster, one of many directed at civilians, urged people to avoid unnecessary train travel, so that servicemen could easily visit their homes before being sent overseas.

Life in Combat   All soldiers griped about the military. But combat soldiers had the most to complain about. They griped about their rations of dried and canned food. They complained about having no beds, toilet paper, or showers. They grumbled about endless marching, about digging trenches, about cold nights and hot days.

Combat was deafening and terrifying. "The ground all around us shook with gigantic explosions," said one soldier. "Each man is isolated from everyone else. Death is immediately in front of him. He only knows that his legs and arms are still there and that he has not been hit yet. In the next instant he might."

Yet even when overwhelmed by fear, most GIs did the job they were trained to do. Where did ordinary men find such courage? When asked, they answered that they were motivated by patriotism and by the desire to help their buddies.

More than 292,000 Americans died in World War II battles. Those who survived were proud of their military service. "You felt you were doing something worthwhile," said a GI who was part of the D-day invasion. "I always felt lucky to have been part of it."

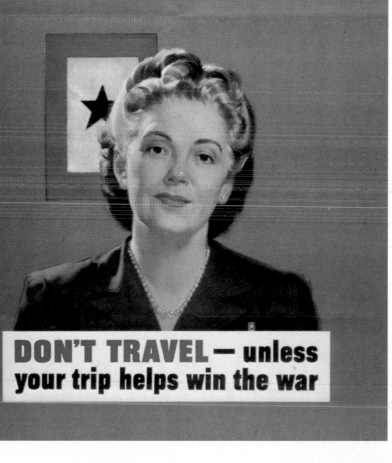

"Won't you give my boy a chance to get home?"

DON'T TRAVEL—unless your trip helps win the war

29.6 Wartime Government

When World War II began, the American economy was focused on producing consumer goods. The head of the German air force joked that "Americans can't build planes—only electric iceboxes and razor blades." It probably shocked Germany to see how quickly the American government transformed the United States into the "arsenal of democracy."

American factories, guided by the War Production Board, turned out an avalanche of weapons for World War II. Thousands of tanks, aircraft, and ships, like those shown below, rolled off American assembly lines.

Increasing Production A month after Pearl Harbor, President Roosevelt set up the War Production Board. This agency's job was to transform American factories into machines for making the necessities of war. The Board banned the production of nonessential civilian goods, from cars to coat hangers. Automakers began manufacturing tanks, jeeps, and trucks. Shirtmakers went to work making mosquito nets.

The War Production Board also organized nationwide drives to collect scrap iron, tin cans, paper, rags, and cooking fat for recycling into war goods. Children took part by searching through their homes, vacant lots, and back alleys for useful scrap. During a paper drive in Chicago, schoolchildren collected 36 million pounds of paper in just a few months.

To prevent worker strikes that might shut down essential wartime production, the government also established the War Labor Board. The Board worked with unions and workers to settle labor issues without disrupting production.

Americans took pride in aiding the war effort. In 1939, U.S. aircraft companies turned out only 6,000 planes. By 1944, they were producing 96,000 planes a year. Shipbuilders cut the time needed to make military cargo vessels, known as Liberty ships, from 8 months to 22 days. Within two years of Pearl Harbor, U.S. factories were producing more military equipment than all of the Axis countries combined.

bond: A government certificate that pays interest. Selling bonds is a way for the government to raise money temporarily for some public purpose.

Supporting the War Effort Huge amounts of money were needed to fight the war. To raise these funds, the government borrowed from banks, businesses, and individuals. Millions of Americans bought war **bonds** as a way of lending the government money for the war.

To keep spirits high, the government established an Office of War Information. This office provided upbeat stories and photographs to newspapers, magazines, and radio stations. Government officials read news stories before they were published. Often they cut out reports of setbacks and tragedies to keep them from reaching the public.

29.7 Wartime Consumers

As factories and farms focused on military needs, consumers were hit by shortages of almost everything. While some complained, most Americans encouraged each other to "use it up, wear it out, make it do, or do without."

Price Controls and Rationing Expanding war production created millions of new jobs, ending the depression. With more money flowing into workers' pockets, the government feared **inflation,** which would cause a rapid rise in the price of scarce consumer goods. It established the Office of Price Administration (OPA) to control the prices of most goods.

The OPA also set up a rationing system. *Rationing* means limiting the amount of scarce items that any one individual can buy. Each person received ration coupons labeled for specific items. Anybody who wanted to buy a rationed item, such as shoes or gas, had to provide the proper coupons along with the money.

Every meal reminded Americans of the war. Meat, sugar, and coffee were tightly rationed. Most people understood why. Meat was needed to feed soldiers. Sugarcane was better used for making gunpowder than sugar cubes. And importing coffee from Latin America required ships that were better used to support troops overseas.

Homemakers planned their meals around substitutes. "I remember thinking a can of corned beef was just marvelous," recalled one housewife. "We ate a lot of Spam."

Victory Gardens and Pocketless Pants To supplement their food rations, Americans planted "victory gardens" in backyards and playgrounds. By 1943, 20 million gardens were producing a third of all the vegetables eaten in the United States.

Wartime shortages changed what was available to Americans to buy. With steel needed for weapons, stores didn't have lawn mowers, bicycles, or even hairpins. With cloth needed for uniforms, the War Production Board ordered that women's skirts be made without pleats and men's trousers be made without pockets and cuffs.

In 1943, the government hired a Harvard professor to find out how Americans were reacting to rationing. "The good temper and common sense of most people under restrictions and vexations [annoyances] was really impressive," he reported. "My own observation is that most people are behaving like patriotic citizens."

When voluntary efforts to reduce consumption of certain foods such as meat proved inadequate, the government rationed these items. Consumers received ration books with coupons that were needed, in addition to money, to purchase a product.

inflation: An increase in the amount of money in circulation, compared to the goods available for purchase. Inflation reduces the value of money and causes prices to rise.

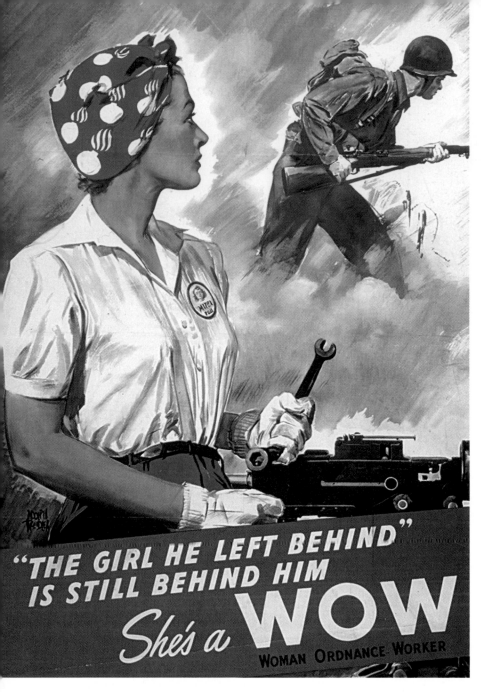

During World War II, more than 6 million women joined the workforce as mechanics, electricians, welders, and machinists. Half had never earned a wage before.

29.8 Women at War

As men went into military service, business owners worried that the nation would not have enough workers to meet its military and industrial needs. They were wrong. By 1944, nearly 18 million workers were laboring in war industries, three times as many as in 1941. More than 6 million of these workers were women.

Women on the Job   At first, war industries were reluctant to hire women. Employers feared that women weren't strong enough for factory work. But once women showed they could use a riveting gun as well as a man, employers couldn't hire enough of them. Women worked as welders, electricians, and machinists. They became police officers, doctors, taxi drivers, and railroad workers. But no matter how well they worked, women were paid only about 60 percent as much as men doing the same jobs.

New work also posed new difficulties. Women in industry were often criticized as being "unfeminine," especially those whose jobs required them to wear pants.

Despite the challenges and lower pay, women valued their new opportunities. "Those years changed our lives," recalled one woman. "All of a sudden I was making money. I was head of a household and it made a different person of me."

Most women wanted to keep their jobs after the war was over. "I like my work so much that they'll have to fire me before I leave," said one electrical worker. As it turned out, many women were fired at war's end to make way for returning men.

Women in the Military   Women also took on new jobs in the military. Until World War II, the military had accepted women only as nurses. Under the slogan "Free a Man to Fight," women were now recruited into the armed forces to take on a variety of noncombat assignments.

More than 200,000 women played vital roles in the armed services as radio operators, armed guards, translators, codebreakers, and mechanics. Women served as test pilots and flight instructors. More than 200 women, mostly nurses, died in the line of duty during the war.

29.9 Japanese Americans

On December 7, 1941, an angry white neighbor came to the home of a Japanese American family. "You…started the war," the neighbor yelled. "You bombed Pearl Harbor!" Of course, Japanese Americans had nothing to do with starting the war. But after the Japanese attack on Pearl Harbor, a cloud of suspicion settled on these loyal citizens.

internment camps: places where people are forcibly confined

Internment Camps   Japanese immigrants to the United States had already endured decades of racial prejudice. After Pearl Harbor, politicians, military leaders, and opinion makers warned that Japanese Americans might be secretly working to help Japan attack the West Coast. The *Los Angeles Times* warned, "A Japanese American, born of Japanese parents, grows up to be a Japanese, not an American."

In response to these fears, President Roosevelt ordered the removal of people of Japanese ancestry from the West Coast. About 120,000 Japanese Americans were forced to leave their homes and businesses and move to distant internment camps. There they would remain for three long years, even though not one Japanese American was ever accused of spying or treason.

Most of the hastily constructed camps were located in bleak deserts. Families were crowded together in flimsy housing with no running water. Barbed wire and armed guards surrounded each camp. One resident recalled, "We struggled with the heat, the sandstorms, the scorpions, the rattlesnakes, the confusion, the overcrowded barracks, and the lack of privacy."

Overcoming Injustice   Despite the injustice suffered by their families, many young men in the camps volunteered for military service. In the Pacific, Japanese Americans worked as interpreters. In Europe, the Japanese American 442nd Regiment earned more medals than any other army brigade in U.S. history. President Truman welcomed the brigade when they returned home. "You fought not only the enemy," the president said. "You fought prejudice—and you won."

After the war, many Japanese Americans did not fight for justice for those who had been imprisoned. In 1988, Congress passed legislation that gave $20,000 to every Japanese American who had been interned (confined) in the camps. With each check came a written apology from President George Bush for "the serious injustices that were done to Japanese Americans during World War II."

As part of a war emergency measure, 120,000 Japanese Americans were placed in internment camps during World War II. In 1988, Congress apologized and gave $20,000 to each Japanese American who had been subjected to this injustice.

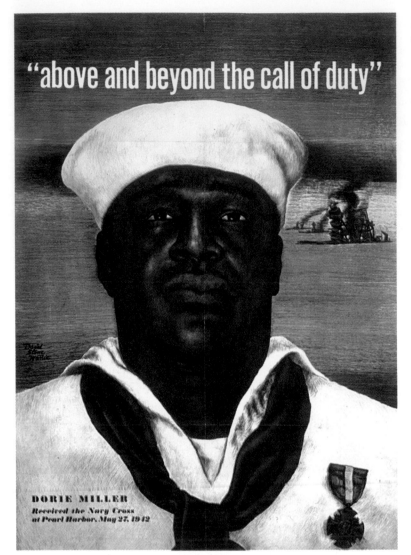

"above and beyond the call of duty"

DORIE MILLER
*Received the Navy Cross
at Pearl Harbor, May 27, 1942*

This poster honors Dorie Miller, an African American sailor who received the Navy Cross for heroism. Although they faced segregation and discrimination, African Americans served with distinction in all branches of the armed forces.

29.10 African Americans

When Japanese bombs hit the battleship *West Virginia* at Pearl Harbor, an African American kitchen worker named Dorie Miller grabbed an anti-aircraft machine gun and started shooting. Miller, who had never been trained to fire a weapon, shot down four Japanese planes. Later, he was praised as a hero.

Miller had no weapons training because the military limited black soldiers and sailors to unskilled support jobs. As a result, African Americans in the armed forces faced what some called the "Double Victory" campaign. They were fighting dictatorship overseas as well as discrimination at home.

African American Servicemen Almost 900,000 African Americans served in the military during the war. Trained in segregated camps, they were assigned to noncombat jobs such as driving trucks and cooking.

Under great pressure from civil rights organizations, the military changed its policy. African Americans began to serve in every kind of combat, from fighter pilots to tank operators to sailors. Although still in segregated units, by the end of the war blacks served alongside whites on Navy ships.

Many black units distinguished themselves in combat. The 92nd Infantry Division, nicknamed the "Buffaloes," won more than 200 medals for courage under fire. The 99th Pursuit Squadron, better known as the Tuskegee Flyers, was decorated for its daring aerial combat against the German air force.

Progress at Home As factories geared up for war production, many would not hire African Americans. "Negroes will be considered only as janitors," announced North American Aviation. "It is not company policy to employ them as mechanics and aircraft workers."

To protest such discrimination, the nation's leading black labor leader, A. Phillip Randolph, called for a march on Washington, D.C. President Roosevelt responded by issuing an order calling on employers and labor unions to end "discrimination because of race, creed, color, or national origin" in defense industries.

By 1944, some 2 million African Americans were working in defense plants across the nation. "The war made me live better," said one black woman. "My sister always said that Hitler was the one that got us out of the white folks' kitchen."

29.11 Mexican Americans

Sergeant José López was called a "one-man army." In one battle, he single-handedly held off dozens of attacking Germans so that his company could retreat to safety. For his courage, he received the nation's highest military decoration, the Congressional Medal of Honor.

Mexican American Servicemen   More than 500,000 Latinos, most of them Mexican Americans, served in the military during World War II. Unlike African Americans, they did not fight in segregated units. But they did meet with prejudice. "I'll never forget the first time I heard [a racial insult]," one Mexican American soldier recalled. "It really hurt me." Still, military service had its rewards. A California solider remembered:

> *"I view the service and World War II, for me and many others, as the event that opened new doors. I, like so many of the Hispanic people, was from a farm family. When I went into the Air Corps and I found that I could compete with Anglo people effectively, even those with a couple years of college, at some point along the way I realized I didn't have to go back to the farm."*

Shown in this photograph is the arrest of Mexican Americans dressed in zoot suits. "Zoot suiters" were also the focus of a 1943 riot in Los Angeles, where Mexican Americans were attacked by white soldiers and sailors.

Braceros and Zoot Suits   To help American farmers grow more food, the United States began the Bracero Program (after *brazo,* the Spanish word for *arm*). Under this program, large numbers of Mexican farmworkers were brought into the United States to pick crops. Farmers liked hiring braceros because they were cheap labor. One farmworker complained, "Many times, we worked twelve hours a day but we never got paid for more than eight."

Many Mexican Americans moved to cities to take jobs in defense industries. They found housing in poor, mostly Mexican neighborhoods called *barrios*. In the barrios, young Mexican Americans developed a style of dress called the "zoot suit" that featured a long jacket and baggy trousers.

Influenced by generations of prejudice, whites associated youths in zoot suits with gang violence and crime. In June 1943, hundreds of white soldiers and sailors roamed through Los Angeles attacking zoot suiters. The violence quickly escalated to race riots that spread from Los Angeles to other cities.

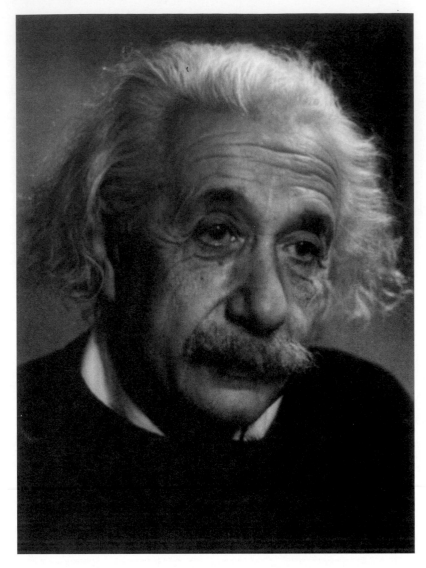

29.12 Jewish Americans

When Hitler took power in 1933, the United States was home to 4.5 million Jews. Some were recent immigrants. Others were members of families who had come to America in colonial times. But all lived under the shadow of **anti-Semitism,** or prejudice against Jews. While this prejudice worried American Jews, they were far more concerned about the fate of Jews in Europe.

Jewish Refugees   Hitler and his Nazi Party had gained power by blaming Germany's problems on its Jews. After taking power, Hitler ordered Jews to be removed from government jobs. They were stripped of their civil rights and forced to wear a yellow star on their clothing to mark them as Jews.

Every year, tens of thousands of Jews fled Germany. But few countries would accept them. Between 1933 and 1941, the United States admitted only 100,000 Jewish refugees. Despite the persecution of Jews in Europe, the government refused to relax its strict immigration limits. Widespread anti-Semitism played a part in this decision. In addition, many Americans worried that accepting more refugees would mean added

Albert Einstein was one of the 100,000 Jewish refugees from Nazi persecution allowed to enter the United States. This brilliant nuclear physicist urged President Roosevelt to begin the top-secret American atomic bomb project.

competition for jobs that were already scarce due to the depression.

Many Jewish Americans protested the government's reluctance to help Jewish refugees. In 1942, when Americans began to hear stories about German death camps, 400 Jewish rabbis marched in Washington, D.C., "to protest the silence of the world when an entire people is being murdered."

In 1944, President Roosevelt finally created the War Refugee Board. In just a few months, the board rescued 200,000 Jews from the Nazis. But this effort came too late to help the vast majority of Europe's Jews.

Jewish American Servicemen   More than 550,000 Jews served in the military during World War II, a greater proportion than among Americans overall. By the end of the war, Jewish war heroes had received 52,000 decorations.

Jewish soldiers had even more reason than others to be horrified at what they found in Hitler's death camps. "Some cried," wrote an officer, "while others raged." A rabbi who served with the army said grimly, "If my own father had not caught the boat [out of Europe] in time, I would have been there."

anti-Semitism: Prejudice against Jews. The term comes from *Semite,* a word for ancient peoples of the Middle East, including the ancestors of modern Jews.

29.13 Chapter Summary

In this chapter, you read about World War II and how it affected people in the United States. You used an illustration to understand the experience of different American groups during World War II. World War II began in Europe and grew until it engulfed the globe. All Americans were touched in some way by the war.

The Japanese attack on Pearl Harbor brought the United States decisively into the war. The conflict centered on two areas—Europe and the Pacific. In Europe, the Allies attacked Germany from three directions before finally winning victory on V-E Day. Only after defeating Germany did the Allies discover the extent of the Holocaust, Germany's systematic murder of millions of Jews and other peoples. In the Pacific, Allied forces battled the Japanese on many small islands before dropping the atomic bombs that destroyed Hiroshima and Nagasaki and forced Japan to surrender, ending the war.

Fighting the war required a unified effort. Millions of Americans served in the armed forces. The government created new agencies to manage production and to control the flow of war information. American consumers contributed to the war effort by coping creatively with rationing and food shortages. Women replaced men in vital occupations and served in noncombat roles in the armed forces.

For Japanese Americans on the West Coast, the war was a painful time of unjust confinement in internment camps. African Americans and Mexican Americans also coped with prejudice even as they contributed to the war effort. Jewish Americans witnessed how anti-Semitism and a fear of refugees kept the United States from responding sooner to the plight of European Jews. Although fighting the war helped to unify the nation, the experiences of these groups reveal some of the divisions that still exist in American society.

On August 15, 1945, Americans celebrated V-J Day, Victory in Japan Day, which ended World War II.

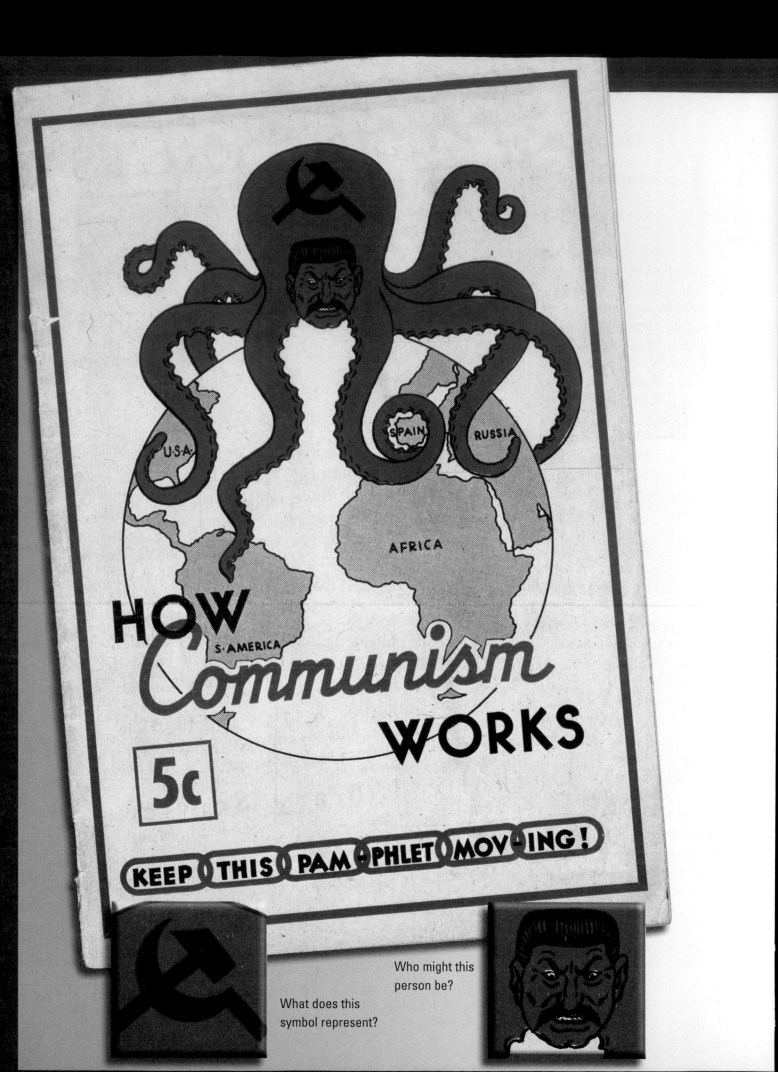

HOW *Communism* WORKS

5c

KEEP THIS PAM-PHLET MOV-ING!

What does this symbol represent?

Who might this person be?

The Cold War

30.1 Introduction

Even before World War II came to an end, the Allies were preparing for peace. In April 1945, delegates from 50 nations met in San Francisco to establish a new organization called the United Nations (UN). The UN was founded to preserve world peace by promoting international cooperation.

A generation earlier, the United States had refused to participate in the League of Nations after World War I. This time, America's response was quite different. The United States not only joined the UN, but also gave it a home. Since 1952, the UN's headquarters has been located in New York City.

Hopes for a more peaceful world, however, faded quickly as the United States and the Soviet Union emerged from World War II as bitter rivals. This rivalry led to the Cold War, an intense competition for global power and influence that lasted more than 40 years.

The Cold War began in 1945 as the dictator of the Soviet Union, Josef Stalin, seized control of several eastern European nations. The people in these nations were denied the freedom to choose their own governments, to travel, and even to speak freely.

Stalin's takeover of these countries alarmed leaders in the United States and Western Europe. Former British prime minister Winston Churchill warned that "an iron curtain has descended across the continent." In the view of western democracies, that iron curtain divided the free world of the West from the Soviet-dominated world of the East.

In this chapter, you will learn why and how the United States and the Soviet Union waged their cold war without ever fighting each other directly. As you read, think about how the Cold War resembled a game—a deadly game that threatened to destroy the world.

Graphic Organizer: Visual Metaphor
You will use this metaphor of a game of tag to understand the power struggle between the United States and the Soviet Union.

bipolar: organized around two opposite extremes

capitalism: an economic system based on private ownership of farms and businesses

communism: an economic system based on the idea that farms and businesses should be owned in common by the workers who do the labor

Josef Stalin planned to increase factory and farm production through total government control. He brutally persecuted anyone who disagreed with his policies.

30.2 Choosing Sides: A Bipolar World

After World War II, the once-mighty nations of Japan, Germany, and Great Britain lay in ruins. Only two nations came out of the war strong enough to dominate world affairs. These "superpowers" were the United States and the Soviet Union. The ideals and ambitions of the two superpowers were as opposite as the north and south poles. Their rivalry created a **bipolar** world—a world deeply divided into two warring camps.

The Soviet Union   The Soviet Union was born out of the Russian Revolution of 1917. That year, revolutionaries known as Bolsheviks overthrew the Russian government and later killed Russia's royal family.

The Bolsheviks were inspired by the writings of a German philosopher named Karl Marx. In his *Communist Manifesto,* written in 1848, Marx called on the workers of the world to unite and overthrow the capitalist economic system. Under **capitalism,** farms and businesses are privately owned by individuals with money, or capital. According to Marx, wealthy capitalists take advantage of the labor of workers to enrich themselves.

Marx claimed that the future belonged to an economic system he called **communism.** Under communism, workers would own all farms and businesses and run them for the benefit of everyone. The result, Marx predicted, would be a workers' paradise.

The Bolsheviks called the ruling councils of workers "soviets." But in the new Soviet Union, power was concentrated in the central government rather than in committees of workers.

When Josef Stalin took over the government in the 1920s, he was determined to transform the Soviet Union from a backward rural nation into a modern industrial giant. Stalin stamped out all individual ownership of farms and businesses. The government took over all economic planning. The Soviet people were forced to work for government-run farms and factories.

To protect his power, Stalin turned the Soviet Union into a vast police state. No one was safe from the prying eyes and ears of Stalin's spies and secret police. "Enemies of the people"—those suspected of opposing Stalin—were ruthlessly eliminated. During the 1930s, between 3 and 8 million people were executed in the Soviet Union. Millions more were imprisoned in labor camps. Instead of a workers' paradise, the Soviet Union became a brutal dictatorship.

Containing Communism   Most
Americans were appalled by what was
happening in the Soviet Union. They saw
communism as a cruel system that took
away people's property and denied them
such basic rights as freedom of speech and
religion. Even worse, the Soviet government was doing all it could to spread
communism to other countries. Americans
saw Stalin's takeover of Eastern Europe as
proof that he intended to convert the
whole world to communism.

President Truman responded to this
threat with a foreign policy known as
containment. The goal of this policy
was to keep communism from spreading
any further by containing, or limiting, it
to the countries where it had already taken
hold.

Truman first turned his attention to
Europe, where World War II had left many
people homeless and hungry. George
Marshall, Truman's secretary of state,
developed a plan to help Europe recover
from the war. Under the Marshall Plan, the
United States sent vast amounts of money
to 16 nations in Europe for rebuilding
cities, railroads, factories, and electric systems. As life in these countries improved,
the appeal of communism weakened. Both
Americans and Europeans hailed the
Marshall Plan as a success.

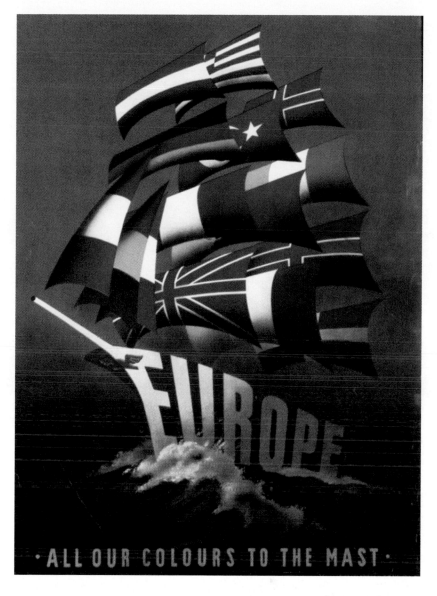

This Dutch poster celebrates the
Marshall Plan. Under the plan, the
United States gave financial aid to war-
torn countries of western Europe.

The effort to contain communism suffered a major setback in 1949,
when Mao Zedong's communist revolutionaries seized control of China,
the world's most populous nation. With the success of this revolution,
nearly a billion people came under communist rule.

The Third World   The Cold War created a new set of divisions in the
world. The United States and its democratic, industrialized allies came to
be known as "First World" nations. The Soviet Union and its communist
allies were seen as a "Second World."

There was also a "Third World" of poorer, less-developed nations in
Latin America, Africa, and Asia. Many of these countries had only recently
gained their independence from colonial rulers.

Both the United States and the Soviet Union tried to convince these
nations to join their "team" in the Cold War. But many Third World countries, such as India, remained **non-aligned nations**—countries that
refused to line up with either side.

containment: the U.S. policy
of fighting the spread of communism by limiting it to countries
where it already existed

non-aligned nations: countries that refused to side with
either the United States or the
Soviet Union during the Cold
War

Children cheer as an American plane brings them food and supplies during the Berlin Airlift. When the Soviet Union closed all land access to West Berlin, the Allies decided to supply the city through the air rather than give in to Stalin's demand that they leave West Berlin. At one time during the airlift, a supply plane landed every minute.

30.3 Forming Teams: Cold War Alliances

The Cold War saw powerful new alliances led by the United States and the Soviet Union. These alliances came about as a result of the first great confrontation of the Cold War—the Berlin blockade.

A Divided City When Germany surrendered in 1945, it was divided in two. Soviet troops occupied East Germany, while American, British, and French forces controlled West Germany. The capital city of Berlin, located in East Germany, was also split into western and eastern parts.

The Soviets set up a communist government in East Germany and demanded that the Allies leave West Berlin. When the Allies refused to budge, Stalin ordered a blockade of Berlin in 1948. Hoping to starve the Allies out of the city, Stalin closed all roads and railroads leading to West Berlin. He also cut electrical power to West Berlin.

The Allies faced a tough choice. They did not want to give in to Stalin and abandon West Berlin. But they feared that efforts to break through the blockade on land might lead to war. Instead, American and British planes began to airlift food, clothing, medicine, and fuel into West Berlin.

At first people worried that the Soviets would try to end the airlift by shooting down the Allies' planes. But the Soviets also wanted to avoid war. Stalin bided his time, hoping that the Allies could not afford to continue flying in supplies for 2 million people.

For ten long months, the airlift continued. Finally, the Soviets gave up and removed the blockade. The lights went back on in Berlin.

Berlin continued to be a potential flashpoint throughout much of the Cold War. In 1961, East Germany and the Soviet Union tried to stem the tide of East Germans fleeing to West Berlin by putting up a wall between the two parts of the city. On the eastern side of the Berlin Wall, armed guards stood ready to shoot anyone trying to escape to freedom in West Berlin. For the next 30 years, the Berlin Wall served as a grim symbol of a divided Europe.

NATO: The Western Alliance   The Berlin blockade convinced the United States and its allies to form a more permanent alliance for their mutual protection. In April 1949, ten Western European countries, the United States, and Canada formed the North Atlantic Treaty Organization (NATO). An attack upon any NATO country, they agreed, would be treated as an attack against them all.

Ratification of the NATO treaty was a big step for the United States. For the first time in its history, the United States had gone against George Washington's warning to "steer clear of permanent alliances with any portion of the foreign world." With the creation of NATO, American aid to Europe began to shift from economic assistance to military assistance.

The Warsaw Pact: The Eastern Alliance   Despite the failure of the Berlin blockade, the Soviets still hoped to unite Berlin—and Germany— under a communist government. Twice in the twentieth century, German armies had invaded Russia. Soviet leaders believed that the best way to prevent future invasions was to gain firm control over all of Germany.

The Soviets' hopes for a united, communist Germany soon began to fade. In 1949, West Germany became an independent nation with a democratic government. Six years later, West Germany was allowed to join NATO and rebuild its military.

The prospect of West Germany building a new army pushed the Soviets to create their own military alliance in 1955. The Warsaw Pact (named after the capital of Poland) called for military cooperation among the Soviet Union, Albania, Bulgaria, Czechoslovakia, Hungary, Poland, Rumania, and East Germany. If any one of these nations was attacked, the others promised to come to its defense. As part of this agreement, Soviet troops were stationed throughout Eastern Europe.

With the establishment of NATO and the Warsaw Pact, Europe had been divided into two opposing teams. The alliances made members of each team feel more secure. At the same time, the alliance system increased the risk that a dispute between two small nations could trigger a third world war—a war fought with terrifying new weapons.

Delegates from 12 nations meet to sign the treaty creating the North Atlantic Treaty Organization. Under this agreement, an attack on one nation would be considered an attack upon them all.

30.4 The Nuclear Arms Race

When the United States dropped atomic bombs on Japan in 1945, a frightening new age began—the Atomic Age. Four years later—aided by spies who had worked on America's secret atomic bomb project—the Soviet Union successfully tested its own bomb.

Soon, both sides were developing nuclear weapons—even more powerful versions of the atomic bomb. Suddenly, the world was faced with the threat of unthinkable destruction if a war broke out between the superpowers. It was this threat that made the Cold War so terrifying. What if the war turned hot?

What message is this political cartoon trying to make regarding the arms race?

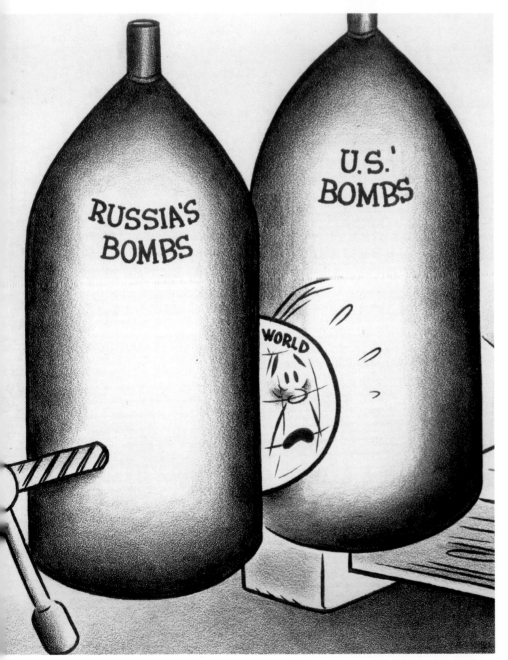

McCarthyism The Soviet Union's successful atomic bomb test fueled fears that communist spies were everywhere in the United States. Senator Joseph McCarthy took advantage of those fears to launch a well-publicized campaign to uncover suspected communists. Without any real evidence, McCarthy accused many people of being communists and working for the Soviet Union. Those who questioned McCarthy or his charges were branded "communist sympathizers." The senator's practice of publicly accusing people of being disloyal with little or no evidence became known as "McCarthyism."

During McCarthy's spy hunt, many Americans lost their jobs and reputations after being accused of being communists. McCarthy finally lost public support for his crusade in 1954, when he made false charges against the U.S. Army on television. But those who had been hurt by McCarthyism were among the casualties of the Cold War.

The Arms Race Begins While McCarthy was busy hunting for communists, President Truman announced plans to develop a hydrogen bomb. This was a nuclear weapon that would be hundreds of times more powerful than the bomb that had destroyed Hiroshima in 1945.

Year	1946	1950	1956	1960	1970	1980	1988
Total U.S. and Soviet nuclear warheads	9	400	2,207	3,471	7,176	18,088	23,444

The Soviets set to work to match this goal. The result was a nuclear **arms race,** a competition to develop and manufacture ever more powerful and destructive weapons.

By 1953, both superpowers had tested their first hydrogen bombs. Both nations also began work on long-range missiles that could carry nuclear weapons to any point on Earth. By 1960, both superpowers could launch nuclear missiles at each other from the land, air, and sea.

Mutual Assured Destruction   When John F. Kennedy became president in 1961, it was clear that neither side could win the arms race. By then, each superpower had enough nuclear weapons to destroy the other many times over. In the face of this overwhelming threat, the United States adopted a military policy known as Mutual Assured Destruction (MAD).

MAD was based on the belief that Soviet leaders would not order a nuclear attack on the United States if doing so meant the certain destruction of their own country. The way to ensure such destruction was to build so many missiles that they could not all be wiped out by a surprise Soviet attack. The surviving missiles would then destroy the Soviet Union. As one writer summed up MAD, "Whoever shoots first, dies second."

Anti-nuclear Protests   The nuclear arms race inspired "ban the bomb" protests in both the United States and Europe. Most protesters were deeply concerned that the effects of a nuclear war could destroy all life on Earth. Many were also upset by the huge amounts of money being spent on the arms race. As President Eisenhower once noted, "Every gun that is made, every warship launched is a theft from those who hunger and are not fed, from those who are cold and are not clothed."

Early in the arms race, protesters also focused on the problem of fallout—radioactive dust from the explosion of nuclear weapons that is potentially harmful to living things. As testing increased, scientists began to detect radioactive material in drinking water, in crops, and in the bones of children. Demands that the superpowers stop testing weapons grew louder year by year.

Towards Arms Control   In 1963, the superpowers took their first step toward controlling the arms race when they signed the Limited Test Ban Treaty. This agreement banned nuclear testing in the air, the ocean, and outer space. Underground tests were still permitted. Kennedy called the treaty "an important first step—a step toward reason—a step away from war." But despite this step, both sides continued to spend vast sums of money developing new weapons.

During the Cold War, the United States and the Soviet Union rushed to build nuclear weapons. Even though the Cold War ended, it was estimated that there were 35,000 nuclear warheads still in existence in 2000. A single megaton warhead can kill 220,000 people and injure 420,000.

arms race: a competition to develop and manufacture more and more powerful weapons

30.5 The Cold War Heats Up

As the superpowers armed themselves with nuclear weapons, war between them became something neither side could hope to win. Instead of confronting each other directly, they competed in **proxy wars**. A proxy war was a conflict between nations, or within a single country, in which the superpowers backed opposite sides without fighting each other directly. The superpowers supplied advisors, weapons, and sometimes troops to their "proxies," or substitutes. Most of these proxy wars took place in small nations in Asia, Africa, and Latin America.

The Korean War The first major proxy war erupted in Korea in 1950. At the end of World War II, the Korean Peninsula was occupied by both American and Soviet troops. Unable to agree on what kind of government the Korean people should have, the superpowers divided the country. The Soviets installed a communist government in North Korea, while in South Korea the Americans encouraged a government that favored capitalism.

In 1950, North Korean troops armed with Soviet tanks and weapons overran most of South Korea. Their goal was to unite the country under a communist government. President Truman ordered the U.S. military to support South Korea. The United Nations also took action by calling on member nations to assist South Korea. In all, 15 nations sent more than half a million troops to Korea. More than 90 percent of the UN forces were American.

The UN forces pushed the communist invaders back into North Korea almost as far as its border with China. At that point, 300,000 Chinese soldiers poured into North Korea and drove the UN troops back into South Korea. Fearing that the struggle in Korea could widen into a world war, Truman pushed for a peace settlement.

The agreement ending the Korean War left Korea divided as it had been before the war. Americans were pleased that communism had been contained in North Korea without starting a third world war. But the costs of containment were high. About 54,000 Americans died in a war that cost the nation over $20 billion. More than a million Koreans also lost their lives.

When the North Korean communists, aided by the Soviet Union, invaded South Korea, the United States sent troops to aid the South Koreans. After more than three years of fighting, a truce ended the war with the Korean Peninsula still divided. The war cost over 54,000 American lives.

proxy wars: wars in which the superpowers backed different sides that acted as substitutes (proxies) for the superpowers themselves

Communism Comes to Cuba The United States and the Soviet Union nearly came into direct conflict over Cuba. As you read in Chapter 27, the United States first became involved in Cuban affairs during the Spanish-American War of 1898. Even after Cuba gained its independence, the United States maintained a naval base on the island. Americans also invested heavily in Cuba. By 1956, Americans owned 90 percent of Cuba's mining wealth and 40 percent of its sugar crop. U.S. influence was so great that the American ambassador was reported to be "the second most important man in Cuba, sometimes more important than the [Cuban] president."

In 1959, rebels led by Fidel Castro took control of the island and promised "to revolutionize Cuba from the ground up." President Eisenhower tried to maintain friendly relations with the new Cuban government. But when Castro declared himself a communist and seized control of American-owned farms and businesses, Eisenhower broke off relations with Cuba.

The president also allowed the Central Intelligence Agency (CIA) to begin training Cuban exiles living in the United States for an invasion of Cuba. The CIA hoped that the invasion would trigger a massive revolt against Castro.

Soon after taking office in 1961, President John F. Kennedy approved the CIA's invasion plan. On April 17, about 1,400 Cuban exiles landed on a Cuban beach in the Bay of Pigs. Nothing went as planned. The Cuban people did not rise up in revolt, and the invaders were quickly killed or captured.

One observer commented that the bungled invasion made Americans "look like fools to our friends, rascals to our enemies, and incompetents to the rest." An embarrassed President Kennedy promised that one day the invaders' flag would fly over a "free Cuba."

The Cuban Missile Crisis Cuban president Fiedel Castro had a powerful ally in Nikita Khrushchev, the leader of the Soviet Union. Khrushchev sent Soviet advisors and weapons to Cuba, including nuclear missiles.

In October 1962, U.S. spy planes photographed secret missile bases built by the Soviets in Cuba. Missiles launched from these bases could reach U.S. cities in a matter of minutes.

President Kennedy met this challenge head-on. He demanded that the Soviets remove their missile bases in Cuba. He also declared that the United States would consider any missile attack from Cuba as an attack by the Soviet Union.

At first, the United States supported Fidel Castro when he took control of Cuba. After he announced he was establishing a communist government and began receiving aid from the Soviet Union, however, the United States broke off relations.

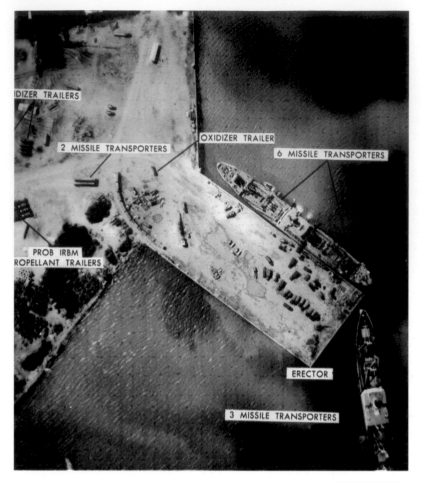

IDIZER TRAILERS

2 MISSILE TRANSPORTERS

OXIDIZER TRAILER

6 MISSILE TRANSPORTERS

PROB IRBM
PROPELLANT TRAILERS

ERECTOR

3 MISSILE TRANSPORTERS

This intelligence photograph proved that the Soviet Union had given Cuba nuclear missiles that could reach the United States in minutes. President Kennedy insisted the Soviets remove the weapons. For six days, the world moved dangerously close to nuclear war. Then, the Soviet Union agreed to Kennedy's demand.

Next, Kennedy ordered a naval blockade of Cuba to prevent Soviet ships from delivering any more missiles to the island. Finally, he ordered the U.S. military to prepare for an invasion of Cuba to remove the missile bases by force if necessary.

For the next six days, tensions mounted unbearably as Soviet ships, which were thought to be carrying more missiles, steamed toward Cuba. "We were on the edge of the precipice [cliff] of nuclear war," Khrushchev later said of that terrifying week. "Both sides were ready to go."

To the relief of the entire world, the Soviet ships stopped when they reached the U.S. blockade. "We're eyeball to eyeball," observed Dean Rusk, Kennedy's secretary of state, "and I think the other fellow just blinked." The Cuban missile crisis ended when Khrushchev agreed to remove the missile bases in exchange for Kennedy's promise not to invade Cuba.

Containment in Southeast Asia   Half a world away from Cuba, a new communist threat appeared in the southeast Asian country of Vietnam. Once a French colony, Vietnam won its independence from France in 1954.

As part of Vietnam's independence agreement, elections were to be held in 1956 to determine who would rule the new country. The most likely winner of the elections would have been Ho Chi Minh, the leader of Vietnam's independence movement and a supporter of communism. The elections, however, were never held.

Backed by a few hundred military advisors from the United States, anticommunist leaders took control of the southern half of Vietnam. By the time Kennedy took office, communist rebels backed by North Vietnam were waging a guerilla war against the South Vietnamese government. The rebels, known as the Viet Cong, attacked suddenly and then faded away.

"The Free World," President Kennedy declared, "must increasingly protect against and oppose communist subversive [rebellious] activity . . . in Southeast Asia." To back up his words, Kennedy increased the number of U.S. military advisors in South Vietnam to more than 16,000.

Johnson Sends More Troops   Lyndon Johnson, who became president after Kennedy was assassinated in 1963, was faced with the problem of how far to go in supporting the government of South Vietnam. Many argued that, in the end, South Vietnam would have to win its own fight. But Johnson decided that the United States could not afford a communist overthrow of the South Vietnamese government.

Johnson used reports of a North Vietnamese attack on an American destroyer to win approval of a Congressional resolution that, he argued, authorized him to increase the American military presence in Vietnam. By the end of 1965, there were 180,000 U.S. troops in Vietnam. Two years later, the number had increased to 500,000. The United States was involved in a full-scale war.

Despite this massive buildup of troops, the war did not go well for South Vietnam and its American ally. U.S. soldiers were often unable to tell friends from enemies. Sometimes they burned entire villages in their search for Viet Cong rebels. After shelling one village, an officer explained, "It became necessary to destroy the town in order to save it." Many Americans protested the Vietnam War, calling it unfair, destructive, and unwinnable.

Nixon Ends the War   Johnson's successor, President Richard Nixon, promised to get the United States out of Vietnam. He carried out part of this promise by bringing all but 150,000 troops home by 1972.

At the same time, Nixon secretly expanded the war into the neighboring countries of Laos and Cambodia. In 1971 alone, the U.S. dropped 800,000 tons of bombs on Vietnam and the other southeast Asian countries. When the air raids became public, massive protests erupted throughout the United States.

A peace agreement was finally worked out in January 1973. In April, the final American troops withdrew. In 1975, North Vietnamese troops reunified Vietnam under a communist government.

For both the United States and Vietnam, the human costs of this long war were huge. More than 58,000 Americans died in the conflict. Hundreds of thousands more came home wounded, disabled, or suffering from emotional and mental problems. In Vietnam, up to 2 million people died, while millions more were wounded and left homeless.

For the United States, perhaps the greatest cost was a loss of faith in the nation's leaders. For the first time in its history, the United States had lost a war. While people argued over the cause of this defeat, the Vietnam War left many wondering if containment was worth so many lives and a deeply divided nation.

The Vietnam Veterans Memorial, designed by Maya Yang Lin, honors the more than 58,000 Americans who died in the Vietnam War. Their names, inscribed in black granite, serve as a reminder of the terrible cost of trying to contain communism.

Geography Challenge
The Cold War

1. Identify four details about this map.

2. Where did Cold War conflicts occur?

3. What areas were free of Cold War conflicts?

4. In what part of the world did the United States have the most influence?

5. In what part of the world did the Soviet Union have the most influence?

PACIFIC OCEAN

ATLANTIC OCEAN

N W E S

A The Korean War 1950–1953

B Communist revolution in China 1949

C The Vietnam War 1964–1975

D Communist revolution in Cambodia 1975

E Soviet invasion of Afghanistan 1979

F U.S.-supported coup in Iran 1953

G French and British attack Suez Canal in Egypt 1956

H Arab-Israeli conflicts: 1948, 1956, 1967, 1973, 1982

I Angola turns communist 1975

J Communist coup in Zaire (Congo) 1963

K Soviets support Mozambique 1977–1991

L Communist coup in Ethiopia 1974

M U.S.-supported coup in Chile 1973

N U.S. invasion of Grenada 1983

O Communist revolution in Cuba 1959
U.S.-supported invasion fails 1961
Cuban missile crisis 1962

P U.S.-supported coup in Guatemala 1954

Q Communist revolution in Nicaragua 1979
U.S. supports rebels 1981–1989

R Large U.S. military aid to Honduras 1981–

S Large U.S. military aid to El Salvador 1981–

T Soviets stop uprising in Hungary 1956

U Soviets stop uprising in Czechoslovakia 1968

V Berlin blockade and airlift 1948–49, Berlin Wall 1961

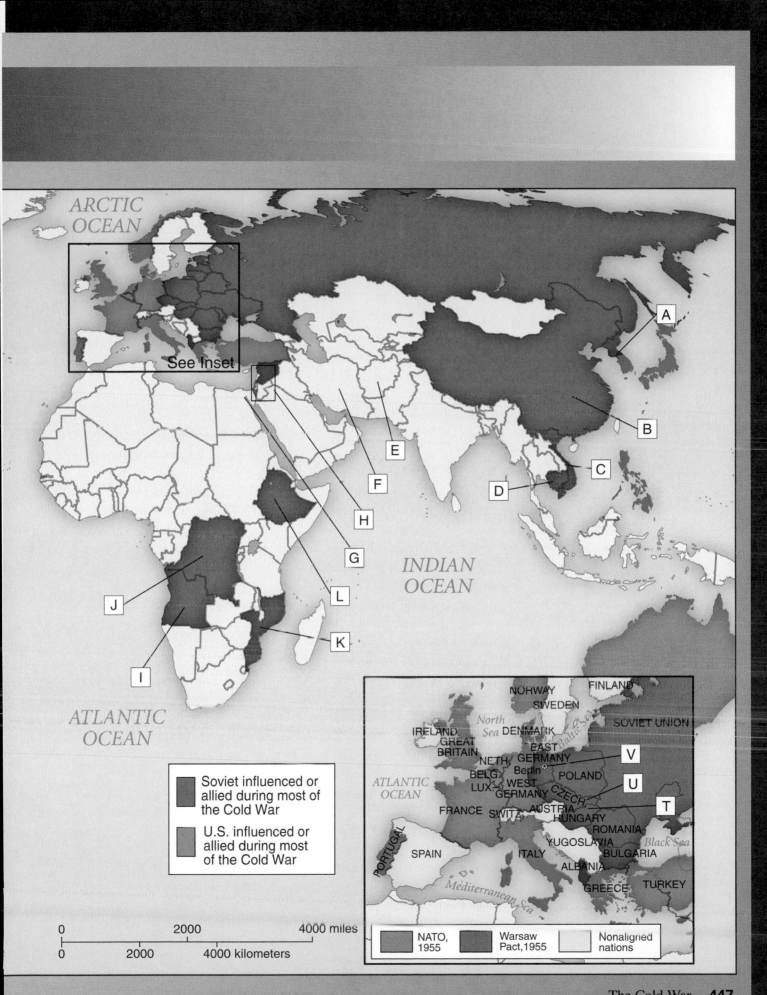

ARCTIC OCEAN

See Inset

ATLANTIC OCEAN

INDIAN OCEAN

A

B

C

D

E

F

G

H

I

J

K

L

Soviet influenced or allied during most of the Cold War

U.S. influenced or allied during most of the Cold War

| 0 | 2000 | 4000 miles |
| 0 | 2000 | 4000 kilometers |

NORWAY

FINLAND

SWEDEN

North Sea

IRELAND

DENMARK

SOVIET UNION

GREAT BRITAIN

Baltic Sea

EAST GERMANY

NETH.

V

ATLANTIC OCEAN

Berlin

POLAND

BELG.

WEST GERMANY

U

LUX.

CZECH.

T

FRANCE

SWITZ.

AUSTRIA

HUNGARY

ROMANIA

PORTUGAL

YUGOSLAVIA

Black Sea

SPAIN

ITALY

BULGARIA

ALBANIA

TURKEY

GREECE

Mediterranean Sea

| NATO, 1955 | Warsaw Pact, 1955 | Nonaligned nations |

30.6 The End of the Cold War

President Ronald Reagan, who took office in 1981, had no doubts about fighting communism. Reagan publicly denounced the Soviet Union as an "evil empire" and greatly increased military spending. In his second term, however, Reagan's attitude toward the Soviet Union softened. The reason was a new leader in the Soviet Union named Mikhail Gorbachev.

Armed with chisels and sledgehammers, Germans destroyed the Berlin wall, a powerful reminder of the communist dictatorship in East Germany. Soon after, other countries overthrew their communist governments, and the Soviet Union did not interfere.

A New Soviet Leader

When Gorbachev took office in 1985, the Soviet economy was not working well. Heavy military spending had kept the nation from meeting the human needs of the Soviet people. Farms and factories owned by the government were inefficient and unproductive.

Gorbachev came into power hoping to reform the communist system and make it work better. He began a policy of *glasnost* (openness), which led to increased freedom of the press, speech, and religion. He started an economic program called *perestroika* (restructuring) that was supposed to improve the economy. And he reduced the size and power of the Soviet military.

Reagan and Gorbachev met twice to discuss ways to end the arms race. For the first time ever, both sides agreed to reduce the number of their nuclear weapons.

Communism Collapses Gorbachev's policies gave hope to reformers throughout Eastern Europe. In August 1989, Poland freely elected a non-communist government. In November, bulldozers tore down the Berlin Wall. As one country after another overthrew its communist government, Gorbachev told his people, "We have no right…to interfere."

Then the uprisings against communism spread to the Soviet Union itself. In August 1991, a second Russian Revolution took place as supporters of democracy, led by Boris Yeltsin, seized power. One of Yeltsin's first official acts was to ban communists from power.

With the end of communist rule, 9 of the 15 republics that had made up the Soviet Union declared their independence. The remaining republics formed a new nation called the Russian Federation. In December, a Russian official announced that "the Soviet Union has ceased to exist."

After more than 40 years, the Cold War was over. Americans rejoiced that the free world had won. Still, communism survives in such countries as China, Vietnam, North Korea, and Cuba.

30.7 Chapter Summary

In this chapter, you read about the conflict known as the Cold War. You used the metaphor of a game of tag to understand the power struggle between the United States and the Soviet Union as each tried to dominate global politics.

The Cold War was a struggle between two superpowers and two very different ways of life, communism and capitalism. Under President Truman, the United States adopted a policy of trying to contain communism.

The rivalry between the superpowers created a bipolar world in which many nations took the side of either the United States or the Soviet Union. Many Third World countries, however, remained non-aligned nations.

The first confrontation of the Cold War took place in Berlin. As a result of the Berlin blockade, the United States joined with western democracies to form a new alliance, NATO. The Soviet Union responded by joining with eastern European countries in the Warsaw Pact.

Both the United States and the Soviet Union engaged in a costly and frightening arms race. The United States hoped to prevent a nuclear war through the strategy of Mutual Assured Destruction.

With neither side wanting a nuclear war, the superpowers struggled for influence through proxy wars. In Korea and Vietnam, tens of thousands of Americans died in efforts to contain the spread of communism. In Cuba, the Soviet Union supported Fidel Castro and installed nuclear missile bases. The resulting crisis brought the superpowers to the brink of war.

The Cold War ended with the collapse of communism in Eastern Europe and in the Soviet Union. The United States and the free world had won the struggle, but only at great cost.

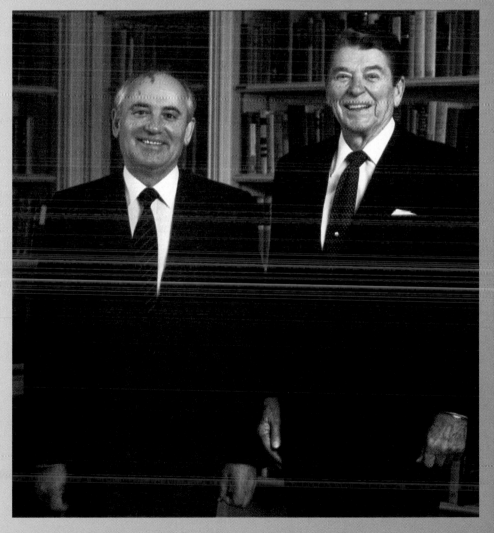

Friendly meetings between Mikhail Gorbachev and Ronald Reagan helped ease the tensions of the Cold War. Eventually, Gorbachev's policies led to the collapse of the Soviet Union and the end of the Cold War.

Why are these people carrying an American flag?
What might these people be protesting?

31

The Civil Rights Movement

31.1 Introduction

When he was 14 years old, Martin Luther King, Jr. entered a speech contest on the theme "The Negro and the Constitution." The contest was held in Dublin, Georgia, a long bus ride from King's home in Atlanta. King made the trip with his teacher, Mrs. Bradley, who beamed with pride when he won first prize. As the two headed for home, their happy mood was spoiled. King later recalled:

"Mrs. Bradley and I were on a bus returning to Atlanta, and at a small town along the way, some white passengers boarded the bus, and the white driver ordered us to give the whites our seats. We didn't move quickly enough to suit him, so he began cursing us.... I intended to stay right in that seat, but Mrs. Bradley finally urged me up, saying we had to obey the law. And so we stood in the aisle for the ninety miles to Atlanta. That night will never leave my memory. It was the angriest I have ever been in my life."

King was far from alone. Across the South, African Americans seethed at the insults and injustices heaped on them by whites. "Lord, child!" observed a Mississippi woman to African American journalist Louis Lomax. "We colored people ain't nothing but a bundle of resentments and sufferings going somewhere to explode."

In this chapter, you will read how African Americans used this anger to fuel a powerful new movement for civil rights in the 1950s and 1960s. The goal of the Civil Rights movement was to end segregation and secure equal rights for all Americans, no matter what their race or color. As you read, try to put yourself in the place of those who took part in this movement. Try to feel their anger and share their hope for a more just society.

Graphic Organizer: Annotated Illustration
You will use this illustration of a protest sign to learn about the Civil Rights movement.

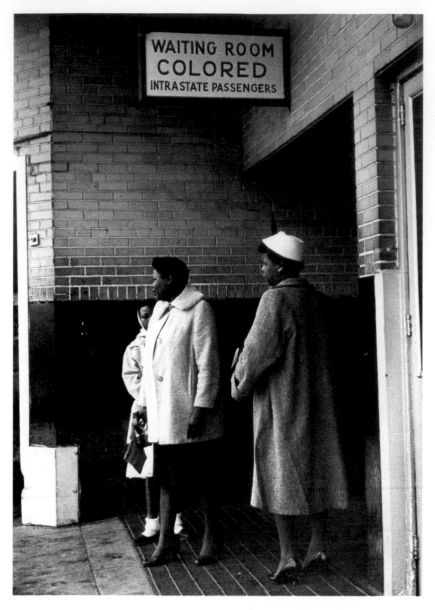

31.2 Discrimination against African Americans

In the 1950s, African Americans faced discrimination and prejudice everywhere in the United States. But discrimination was especially harsh in the South, where laws and customs enforced segregation of blacks and whites.

In Mississippi, for example, a law banned people of different races from sharing taxicabs. Throughout the South, African Americans were forced to use separate entrances to buildings, separate elevators and stairways, separate drinking fountains, and separate restrooms. They were forced to live in separate neighborhoods and attend separate schools.

Public transportation was often where segregation was most obvious and humiliating. Blacks could not sit in the same train car with white people. On buses, they had to give up their seats to whites and stand or sit in the back.

Like most black children, Martin Luther King, Jr. learned about discrimination early. One day when he went to a friend's house to play, he was told not to come again because "they were white and I was colored." Later, King described how he ran home in tears and asked his mother to explain.

Before the Civil Rights movement, African Americans were forced to use separate and unequal waiting rooms, drinking fountains, restrooms, and other facilities.

"My mother took me on her lap and began by telling me about slavery and how it had ended with the Civil War. She tried to explain the divided system of the South—the segregated schools, restaurants, theaters, housing; the white and colored signs on drinking fountains, waiting rooms, lavatories—as a social condition rather than a natural order. Then she said the words that almost every Negro hears before he can yet understand the injustice that makes them necessary: 'You are as good as anyone.'"

Many hesitated to speak out against discrimination for fear of being beaten, or worse. There were few places where blacks felt safe, outside their homes and churches. It was there that black children learned how to survive in a confusing world. "On the one hand, my mother taught me that I should feel a sense of somebodiness," recalled King. "On the other hand, I had to go out and face the system, which stared me in the face every day, saying, 'You are less than. You are not equal to.'"

31.3 The Supreme Court Ends School Segregation

The Fourteenth Amendment to the Constitution guarantees all American citizens "equal protection of the laws." However, in 1896, the Supreme Court ruled in *Plessy v. Ferguson* that segregation laws did not violate the Fourteenth Amendment as long as the facilities made available to both races were roughly equal.

Separate but Not Equal In reality, separate facilities for African Americans were seldom equal to those available to whites. School buildings for African Americans were often old and dingy. Classrooms were overcrowded. Students had few, if any, textbooks, maps, or library materials. In South Carolina's Clarendon County, for example, every white student had a desk. Two of the African American schools in the county, on the other hand, had no desks at all.

Throughout the 1940s and early 1950s, southern universities and colleges routinely turned away African Americans. When black students did gain admission, they found themselves victims of rigid rules that segregated college campuses. For example, G. W. McLaurin, an African American who was preparing to be a teacher, was admitted to the University of Oklahoma. McLaurin was assigned a separate table in the library and in the cafeteria. He wasn't allowed to sit in the same classroom as white students. Instead, he had to strain to hear his professors' lectures from an empty classroom next door.

In 1896, the Supreme Court declared that separate but equal facilities were constitutional. Based on that decision, the South segregated its public schools. The African Americans in this photograph are protesting this practice because their children usually received a vastly inferior education.

Brown v. Board of Education

In 1953, there were 21 states with segregated schools. The National Association for the Advancement of Colored People (NAACP), which you read about in Chapter 26, led the legal fight against this practice.

The NAACP brought a number of cases to court that challenged school segregation laws. In Topeka, Kansas, Reverend Oliver Brown sued the state for the right to send his daughter to a white neighborhood school rather than a black school much farther away. In South Carolina, African American parents sued the Clarendon County school board for equal funding for white and black students. In Farmville, Virginia, black students at Moton High School went to court to protest the overcrowded conditions at their school.

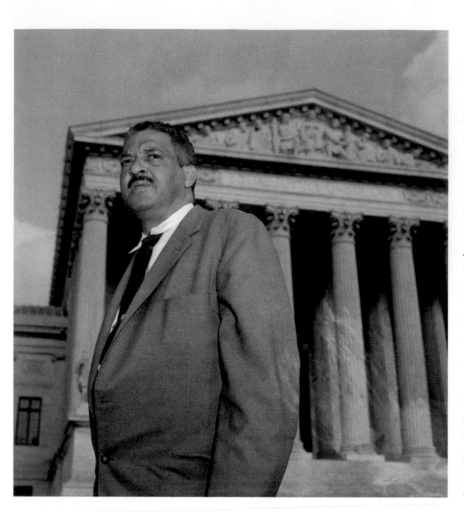

Thurgood Marshall, the first African American Supreme Court justice, presented the NAACP's side in the landmark case *Brown v. Board of Education*. In a unanimous decision, the Court ruled that segregated schools were inherently unequal and unconstitutional.

These three cases, plus two more from Delaware and Washington, D.C., found their way to the U.S. Supreme Court. There they were joined together as one case under the name *Brown v. Board of Education*.

Lawyers from the NAACP argued the case before the Supreme Court. They were led by Thurgood Marshall, who would later become the nation's first African American Supreme Court justice. Marshall had already won 13 of the 15 cases he had taken to the Supreme Court for the NAACP. John W. Davis represented the states. Davis had argued more cases before the Supreme Court than any other lawyer at that time.

In his argument before the Supreme Court, Marshall said that segregated schools could never be "equal." The simple act of separating people, he argued, suggested that one group was seen as better than the other.

Davis responded that education was a local issue. Each state, he said, should be allowed to decide for itself whether to segregate its schools. The Constitution did not prevent the separation of blacks and whites, as long as the states provided equal facilities for each group.

The federal government came into the case on the side of the black parents. Secretary of State Dean Acheson asked the Court to consider the impact of racial discrimination on the country's efforts to lead the free world in the Cold War era.

> *The continuation of racial discrimination in the United States remains a source of constant embarrassment to this government in the day-to-day conduct of its foreign relations.... It jeopardizes [threatens]...our moral leadership of the free and democratic nations of the world.*

On May 17, 1954, the Supreme Court announced its decision. "We conclude, unanimously," the Court declared, "that in the field of public education...'separate but equal' has no place. Separate educational facilities are inherently [by nature] unequal." A year later, the Court ordered an end to school segregation "with all deliberate speed." These historic decisions brought an end to legal segregation in schools and inspired new attacks on discrimination in other areas.

31.4 The Montgomery Bus Boycott

On December 1, 1955, a 43-year-old seamstress named Rosa Parks got on a city bus in Montgomery, Alabama. She was on her way home from work. Parks made her way to a seat in the first row of the black section of the bus. It was a law in Montgomery that the first ten rows of seats were reserved for white people. African Americans had to sit in the back, even if no one else was on the bus.

As the bus traveled its route and more people got on, Parks paid no attention. She just wanted to get home and put her feet up. Eventually, all the seats in the first ten rows were full, and one white man was left standing. The bus driver ordered the African Americans sitting in the eleventh row to move so that the white man could sit down. Only one seat was needed, but all the African Americans in that row were told to move.

Rosa Parks refused to give up her seat. She was tired, and she was fed up with being pushed around. The driver stopped the bus and called the police, who arrested Parks and took her to jail. E. D. Nixon, a former president of the local NAACP chapter, posted bail money for her release. Parks's trial was set for the following Monday.

In many southern states, buses were segregated. Whites sat in the front, while African Americans sat in the back and were required to give up their seats to whites when asked.

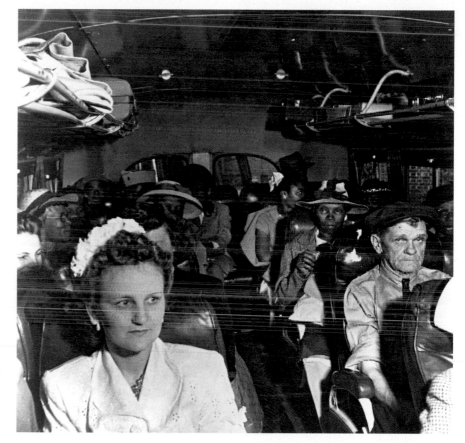

"Stay off the Buses" Rosa Parks was a well-respected member of Montgomery's black community. She had served as a secretary for the Montgomery NAACP for 12 years. Word of her arrest spread like wildfire through black neighborhoods.

That night, a group of black women led by English professor Jo Ann Robinson met and put out a call for action. They stayed up all night printing flyers that called on African Americans to boycott the buses the following Monday. "Another Negro woman has been arrested and thrown into jail because she refused to get up out of her seat and give it to a white person," they began. "The next time it may be you, or you, or you." African American ministers promoted the bus boycott in their Sunday sermons.

On Monday, the buses that rolled through black neighborhoods were empty. Some 17,000 black riders had found some other way to get to work. That evening, a meeting was held in an African American church. The crowd decided to continue the boycott until the city agreed to seat bus riders on a "first come, first served basis" and to hire black bus drivers. The Civil Rights movement had begun.

Martin Luther King, Jr. That night, a young minister named Martin Luther King, Jr. was chosen to lead the bus boycott. King knew that the boycott would be a struggle for most black workers, who relied on buses to get to work. Some formed carpools. Others rode mules. Those who couldn't find rides walked each day to their jobs. No matter how far the distance or how tired their feet, they stayed off the buses for month after month. "I'm not walking for myself," said one elderly woman. "I'm walking for my children and my grandchildren."

While studying to be a minister, King had come to believe in the power of nonviolent protest to end injustice. "The only weapon that we have," he said as the boycott began, "is the weapon of protest." His commitment to nonviolence was tested when he was

Rosa Parks, who refused to give up her seat to a white man on a segregated bus, is shown being fingerprinted after her arrest. Her protest against this unfair treatment sparked the Montgomery bus boycott. Ultimately, the Supreme Court declared segregated buses unconstitutional.

arrested and hauled to jail, and again when his house was bombed. Still, King continued to urge his followers to follow the path of peace.

"This is not a war between the white and the Negro but a conflict between justice and injustice. If we are arrested every day, if we are exploited every day, if we are trampled over every day, don't ever let anyone pull you so low as to hate them. We must use the weapon of love."

More than a year after Rosa Parks' arrest, the Supreme Court ruled that Alabama's state and local laws requiring segregated buses violated the Constitution. The bus boycott was finally over. Looking back on the year, King reflected that "we have discovered a new and powerful weapon— non-violent resistance." Soon, this powerful weapon would be put to use across the South.

integration: the blending of all people as equals; the opposite of segregation

31.5 Nonviolent Protests

Despite the Supreme Court ruling calling for schools to be desegregated with "all deliberate speed," progress was painfully slow. African Americans continued to attend separate schools in most of the South.

Resistance to school desegregation was led by white business leaders who organized White Citizens Councils. These groups used their economic power to fight the **integration** of schools in their communities. Blacks who were active in the fight against segregation lost their jobs and had trouble finding new ones.

Crisis in Little Rock In 1957, a federal judge ordered public schools in Little Rock, Arkansas, to begin desegregation. Alabama's governor, Orval Faubus, vowed to resist the order. When nine African American students tried to enter all-white Central High School in the state capital of Little Rock, Faubus called in troops from the Alabama National Guard to block their way. The troops were backed by an angry mob of whites. One white woman spat on the black students. Others screamed racial insults.

Day after day, the black students tried to enter the school without success. And day after day the mob grew larger and meaner. After two weeks of this, President Eisenhower sent federal troops to Little Rock to protect the African American students. "Mob rule cannot be allowed to override the decisions of our courts," he said. For the first time in 81 years, a president was sending troops to the South to protect the rights of black citizens.

Protected by armed soldiers, army jeeps, and helicopters, the nine African American students, who came to be known as the "Little Rock Nine," finally walked in the front door of Central High School. The first battle was won, but these nine students would face displays of hatred at school every day. Melba Patillo remembered white students stepping on the heels of her shoes until her ankles bled. But she held her head high. "When a passerby…lashed out at me using nasty words," she wrote, "I began to see that to allow their words to pierce my soul was to do exactly what they wanted."

Sit-in Following King's call for nonviolent resistance to segregation, African American students began protesting discrimination in shops, restaurants, and public facilities. The new wave of protests began in 1960,

In Little Rock, Arkansas, nine African American students attempted to enroll in an all-white high school. They were met by an angry mob of whites who threatened to lynch them.

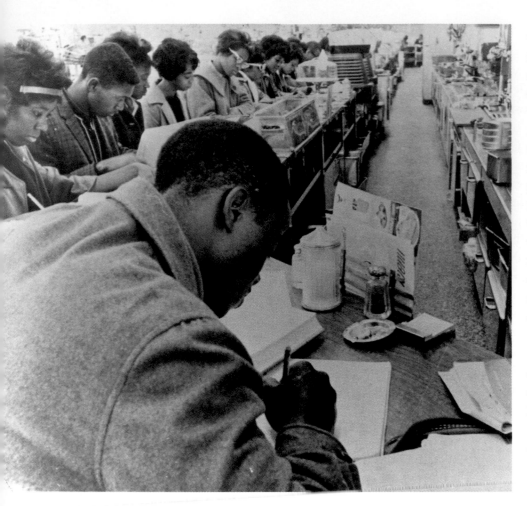

Students organized sit-ins at lunch counters and other facilities in an effort to end segregation. They were told to react nonviolently to any attacks by whites. Often, hostile crowds would mock the protesters and dump food on them.

when four black college students in Greensboro, North Carolina, sat down at the whites-only lunch counter in the downtown Woolworth store. The African American waitress at the counter told them, "Fellows like you make our race look bad," and refused to serve them. The four freshmen sat there all afternoon until closing time. As they left, they promised to return the next morning to continue their "sit-down protest." The next day, 19 students joined the **sit-in**. The day after that, the number swelled to 85.

Sit-in protesters quickly developed a list of dos and don'ts. "Do show yourself friendly on the counter at all times. Do sit straight and always face the counter," the list read. "Don't strike back, or curse back, if attacked. Don't laugh. Don't hold conversations. Don't block entrances." Most importantly, the protesters refused to move until they were either served or arrested and dragged away.

Soon students were staging sit-ins across the South. White students sometimes joined African Americans in these protests. From lunch counters, the protests spread to segregated stores, supermarkets, libraries, and public swimming pools. At a lunch counter in a Mississippi bus station, one student reported the following scene:

> *"The station operator told the Negroes seated at the counter to get out. A [white man] grabbed a cup of coffee and struck one of us...sharply at the base of the skull with the cup, spilling coffee over him.... About a dozen whites...pushed us around and over counters and tables and kicked us through the door."*

sit-in: a form of peaceful protest in which people occupied seats in a segregated facility

Sit-in protesters remained nonviolent even when they had ketchup and mustard dumped on their heads or were hauled off to jail. Sheer stubbornness sometimes won out as the protesters gripped the edge of a lunch counter with their hands and arms, determined not to let go.

Eventually, the sit-ins hit businesspeople where it hurt the most—in their wallets. Faced with a choice between losing business or making peace with African Americans by treating them the same as whites, most chose peace and profits.

31.6 Filling the Jails in Birmingham

In the summer of 1962, the Civil Rights movement focused its attention on the city of Birmingham, Alabama. The city had been defying new desegregation laws. "Whites only" signs remained on drinking fountains and restrooms. Public parks, playgrounds, swimming pools, and golf courses were closed in order to keep blacks and whites separate. King later called Birmingham "probably the most thoroughly segregated city in the United States."

Birmingham's African American citizens marched and held sit-ins to protest their unequal treatment. Store owners agreed to paint over their "whites only" signs. But the city's racist chief of police, Bull Connor, threatened to throw the store owners in jail. It was time to bring the Civil Rights movement to Birmingham.

King was well aware that Bull Connor was a bigoted bully who would do anything to keep African Americans "in their place." King and his supporters counted on Connor to respond to their peaceful demonstrations with brutality. News coverage of Connor's bullying tactics would show all of America the ugly face of southern racism.

Letter from a Birmingham Jail   A few days after King joined the marches in Birmingham, Connor arrested him for "parading without a permit." King spent eight days in jail, three of them in solitary confinement. While he was there, he wrote a letter explaining the goals of the Civil Rights movement. He wrote the letter on toilet paper and in the margins of a newspaper with a pen smuggled in by a friend. In response to accusations that the protests created tension between the races, King wrote:

Police in Birmingham, Alabama, used high-pressure hoses on protesters. Television cameras broadcast these cruel scenes and prompted sympathy for the movement around the country.

Racial hatred continued in Birmingham, Alabama, even after segregation ended. In 1963, a bomb exploded outside the Sixteenth Street Baptist Church, killing four African American girls attending Sunday school. The funeral of one of the young victims is shown above.

"We who engage in nonviolent direct action are not the creators of tension. We merely bring to the surface the hidden tension that is already alive. We bring it out in the open, where it can be seen and dealt with."

The Children's Marches   When King was released from jail, he found fewer and fewer people willing to risk arrest. So many were already in jail. Who was left to do anything about it? Without people willing to march and protest and fill the jails, the movement would slow down.

To keep the movement alive, thousands of children, some as young as six and seven, hit the streets. They had been taught the rules of nonviolent protest and ways to reduce the chances of being hurt. But few were prepared for what was about to happen.

The first day, Connor arrested almost a thousand children. On the second day, a thousand African Americans gathered at the Sixteenth Street Baptist Church. Connor blocked them in and turned high-pressure fire hoses on them. The force of the water tore bark off trees and threw children and adults to the ground, ripping off their clothes and leaving them bloody. Police swung nightsticks at people's heads and released attack dogs into the crowd.

With his jails full, Connor continued to use fire hoses and police dogs on protesters for the next four days. There was chaos in the streets. Businesspeople watched with alarm. No one was doing any shopping in downtown Birmingham. "There were Negroes on the sidewalks, in the streets, standing, sitting in the aisles of downtown stores. There were square blocks of Negroes, a veritable sea of black faces," recalled one observer. "Downtown Birmingham echoed to the strains of the freedom songs."

Americans watched in horror as the violence unfolded on television. Newspaper photographs showed snarling police dogs lunging at men and women. On May 12, President Kennedy ordered 3,000 army troops to Birmingham to restore peace.

As a result, Birmingham merchants took down their signs from drinking fountains, restrooms, and lunch counters. The city's mayor grudgingly reopened the public library, golf courses, parks, and schools to all of the city's residents.

Birmingham had achieved desegregation, but racial hatred lingered. On a Sunday morning in September 1963, a bomb exploded at King's old headquarters, the Sixteenth Street Baptist Church. Four black girls were killed. "My God," a woman exclaimed as she stood in the street, tears streaming down her face. "We're not even safe in church!"

31.7 The March on Washington and Civil Rights Laws

The violence of the police in Birmingham outraged most Americans. In response, President John F. Kennedy called racial equality a "moral issue" and asked Congress to pass a strong civil rights law.

When Congress dragged its feet on the bill, Civil Rights leaders planned a "march for freedom" in Washington, D.C. The marchers would demand passage of the civil rights bill, integration of schools, an end to job discrimination, and a program of job training.

On August 28, 1963, a quarter of a million people massed near the Lincoln Memorial. From the steps of the memorial, movie stars and singers entertained the festive crowd. Preachers and politicians rose to speak. The last speaker of the day was Martin Luther King, Jr.

"I Have a Dream" King had a speech prepared, but he put it aside when a shout encouraged him to "Tell about the dream!" King's deep and musical voice rang out as he spoke from the heart.

Civil rights leader Dr. Martin Luther King, Jr. was a believer in nonviolent protest. During the March on Washington, he delivered his famous "I Have a Dream" speech.

"I have a dream that one day on the red hills of Georgia the sons of former slaves and the sons of former slaveowners will be able to sit down together at the table of brotherhood.... I have a dream that my four little children will one day live in a nation where they will not be judged by the color of their skin but by the content of their character. ...When we let freedom ring, when we let it ring from...every state and every city, we will be able to speed up that day when all of God's children, black men and white men, Jews and Gentiles, Protestants and Catholics, will be able to join hands and sing in the words of the old Negro spiritual, 'Free at last! Free at last! Thank God almighty, we are free at last!'"

The Civil Rights Laws of 1964 and 1965 Three months after the March on Washington, President Kennedy was gunned down by an assassin in Dallas, Texas. Vice

President Lyndon B. Johnson of Texas became the nation's new leader. Despite fears that a southerner would not support civil rights, Johnson persuaded Congress to pass the strongest civil rights law in the nation's history.

The Civil Rights Act of 1964 outlawed segregation in public facilities. It also banned discrimination in employment based on a person's race, gender, religion, or nationality.

The following year, Congress passed the Voting Rights Act. Among other provisions, this law outlawed so-called "literacy tests." Whites in the South had used these tests to prevent blacks from voting by asking them questions that even the best-educated citizens couldn't answer. In addition, President Johnson sent federal examiners to seven southern states to register black voters.

A Shift in Goals Despite the passage of these important civil rights laws, the struggle for equal opportunity was far from won. In the North, African Americans had been able to vote and to eat at lunch counters for years. But unemployment among blacks was twice as high as among whites. "The black cat in Harlem [had] been riding the bus for fifty years," said one New Yorker. "What he didn't have was the fare."

After 1965, King switched his attention to the economic and social barriers that kept African Americans from enjoying full equality. He launched a new movement designed to bring whites and blacks together in a Poor People's Campaign. The campaign's goal was an "economic bill of rights" that would guarantee all Americans decent housing, a good education, and a job.

The new campaign was just taking shape when, on April 4, 1968, King was shot to death in Memphis, Tennessee. A white man named James Earl Ray was arrested and convicted for his murder.

King's accomplishments were enormous. Under his leadership, the Civil Rights movement had ended the rule of fear in the South. Segregation had been outlawed. Laws now protected African Americans' right to vote. Across America, King had also opened the eyes of farmworkers, women, and Native Americans to the possibility of overcoming the injustices in their lives.

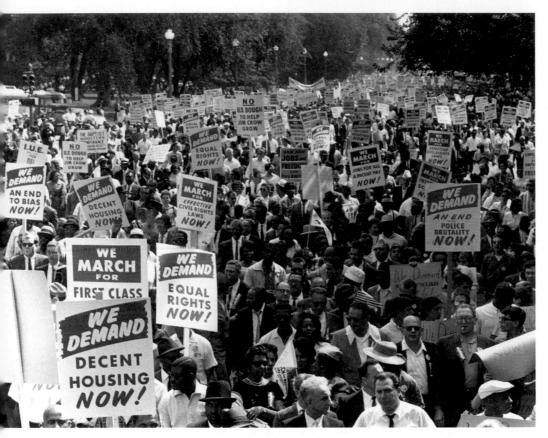

More than 200,000 people participated in the March on Washington in 1963 to show their support for the Civil Rights movement. "Jobs and Freedom" was their slogan.

31.8 Black Power

By the time King died, many African Americans had lost faith in his vision of a society in which the color of a person's skin didn't matter. Angry young blacks looked instead to new leaders who talked about black pride and black power.

Groups that rejected all things white and talked of building a separate black nation gained many followers, especially in northern cities. The most powerful of these black power groups was the Nation of Islam, whose members called themselves Black Muslims. The Nation of Islam turned white racism on its head by declaring that black people were superior to whites and preaching hostility, not peace, among races.

Malcolm X, a prominent militant leader of the African American community, condemned the nonviolent programs of other Civil Rights leaders. He taught that equality would come only when African Americans built their own businesses and defended themselves against injustice.

Malcolm X   In the 1960s, Malcolm X was the Nation of Islam's most effective leader. Malcolm X was born Malcolm Little in Omaha, Nebraska. A difficult childhood led to a life of crime, reform school, and, finally, prison. During his years in prison, Malcolm met Black Muslim preachers who introduced him to the teachings of the Nation of Islam. From them he learned that white people were his enemies and the cause of everything bad in his life. He left prison determined to save other African Americans from the "white devils."

When he joined the Nation of Islam, Malcolm Little changed his name to Malcolm X. Before long, he was one of the group's most powerful speakers. Malcolm urged blacks to be proud of their blackness and their African roots. He told them to see themselves with their "own eyes, not the white man's." He said that blacks would never gain respect by depending on whites for jobs and protection. It was time for blacks to build their own businesses, to learn to defend themselves, and to seize their freedom "by any means necessary."

In 1964, Malcolm left the Nation of Islam. By then, he had softened his attacks on whites. "I haven't changed. I just see things on a broader scale," he told a reporter. "If you attack [a man] because he is white, you give him no out. He can't stop being white." When asked if he still believed in a separate black nation, he replied, "No, I believe in a society in which people can live like human beings on the basis of equality."

The following year, Malcolm X was assassinated by members of the Nation of Islam. But death did not silence his voice. His life story, *The Autobiography of Malcolm X,* continued to inspire black activists.

Black Power   Many of these younger reformers were more interested in black power than civil rights. "We been saying freedom for six years and we ain't got nothing," complained Stokely Carmichael, leader of the Student Nonviolent Coordinating Committee (SNCC). "What we gonna start saying now is Black Power!"

To some, this slogan meant revolution against white-controlled society. For others, it meant focusing on building black-owned businesses and black-controlled communities. For still others, black power simply meant taking pride in being black.

This new pride was expressed in many ways. Young African Americans wore Afro hairstyles and African-inspired clothing. Blacks of all ages enjoyed black soul food and the music of African American artists. African American students and professors started black studies programs in colleges and universities. Above all, black power meant a new appreciation of African American's culture and identity. As soul singer James Brown told concert audiences, "Say it loud—I'm black and I'm proud!"

The music of James Brown, the "god-father of soul," is enjoyed by African Americans and whites alike. His work led to an appreciation of African American culture and identity.

A Lasting Legacy   The Civil Rights and black power movements did not eliminate racism and discrimination from American life. But they did bring about important changes. In addition to ending laws that supported discrimination and segregation, these movements brought African Americans back into politics. After the passage of the Voting Rights Act, voter-registration drives were held across the South. These drives brought thousands of African Americans to the voting booth for the first time. The number of blacks elected to public office soared.

The success of these movements also inspired women, Native Americans, Mexican Americans, and others to demand equal rights for themselves. No one would have been more pleased by this legacy than Martin Luther King, Jr. "Injustice anywhere is a threat to justice everywhere," he once said. "Whatever affects one directly affects all indirectly."

31.9 Chapter Summary

In this chapter, you read about the Civil Rights movement and African Americans' struggle for social and economic equality. You used an illustration of a protest sign to learn about the Civil Rights movement.

The Civil Rights movement began as a fight against segregation in the South. The movement gained force when the Supreme Court ruled against "separate but equal" schools in 1954.

In the 1950s and 1960s, African Americans and their supporters directly confronted segregation. Among the key events during this time were the Montgomery bus boycott, the integration of schools in Little Rock, and the lunch counter sit-ins staged by black students.

Martin Luther King, Jr. gained sympathy and support for the movement through nonviolent protest. The conscience of the nation was aroused by the brutality of police in Birmingham and by King's eloquent speech during the massive March on Washington. Under President Johnson, Congress passed sweeping civil rights laws. These laws banned many types of discrimination and protected African Americans' voting rights.

During the 1960s, black leaders like Malcolm X urged a more radical response to racial injustice. Malcolm encouraged black pride and spoke out for a separate black nation. Although Malcolm eventually softened his attitudes toward whites, many African Americans continued to be inspired by calls for black power and for taking pride in their African heritage.

The Civil Rights movement had a lasting effect on American society. In the next chapter, you will read about other changes that have helped to shape the country you know today.

Dr. Martin Luther King, Jr. and Malcolm X were prominent leaders of the Civil Rights movement. While Dr. King preached nonviolence, Malcolm X emphasized the importance of African American self-reliance.

465

During what decade do you think each of these three images was taken?

32

Contemporary American Society

32.1 Introduction

The year 1946 was one second old when Kathleen Casey was born to the wife of a navy machinist in Philadelphia. Seconds later, the wife of an army trombone player gave birth to Mark Bejcek in Chicago. Of course, babies are born in the United States every day. But these two births were special. They marked the beginning of the greatest population boom in American history.

This **baby boom** caught most Americans by surprise. For more than a century, the nation's birth rate—the number of new babies born in proportion to the size of the population—had been falling. Suddenly, there were babies everywhere. In 1954, the number of births topped 4 million for the first time. There were now more new babies each year than the entire population of the United States in 1790.

The baby boom lasted about 20 years. Then, almost as suddenly as it began, the boom ended. By 1967, the birth rate had dropped to the lowest level in the nation's history.

About 79 million Americans were born during the baby boom. Over the past five decades, this army of baby boomers has been called many things. In the 1950s, the first boomers to hit their teens became the "rock and roll generation." By the mid-1960s, young boomers were the "love generation." In the 1970s, the next wave of boomers became the "me generation." In the 1980s, young-adult boomers were labeled "yuppies," short for "young urban professionals."

Labels such as these can be misleading, because they never fit everyone. In addition, history doesn't always divide neatly into decades. Still, the names given to baby boomers reflect some of the important changes that took place in the United States over the past 50 years. In this chapter, you will read about how these changes shaped the lives of baby boomers and their children—and the world you know today.

Graphic Organizer: Time Capsule
You will use a time capsule to organize artifacts representing the decades from the 1950s through the 1990s.

Large tracts of suburban homes provided affordable housing during the 1950s. Houses sold for as little as $7,900. Freeways linked these areas to nearby cities.

32.2 The 1950s: Growth and Prosperity

The first baby boomers came into the world at a good time. For large numbers of Americans, the 1950s were a time of prosperity and progress.

Good Times For many businesses and industries, the baby boom was an economic boom as well. Demand for housing soared as millions of young couples looked for homes for their growing families. Developers kept up with the demand by building large tracts of affordable houses in suburbs outside major cities.

Congress helped many families buy their first home by passing a law known as the GI Bill. This law provided veterans with inexpensive home loans. It also gave veterans help with tuition if they chose to attend college.

The baby boom was good for other businesses as well. Factories worked overtime to produce everything from cars to diapers to washing machines. New fast-food restaurants like McDonald's provided young families with inexpensive and convenient meals.

For many Americans, only two shadows fell over these happy times. The first was the Cold War and the never-ending fear of a nuclear attack by the Soviet Union. The second was the growing conflict over the demand of African Americans for equal rights and social justice. You read about both of these problems in earlier chapters. The first wave of baby boomers would struggle with issues of peace and equal rights when they reached young adulthood in the 1960s.

Traditional Families Most baby boomers grew up in traditional families. Fathers left home each day to support their families. Mothers stayed home to keep house and take care of their children. One popular book advised women, "The family is the center of your living."

Stay-at-home moms often did volunteer work in their communities. Women who worked outside the home were usually limited to traditionally female jobs, such as nursing, teaching, or working as secretaries and clerks.

Automobile Culture For families living in the suburbs, the automobile quickly became a necessity. Many suburban homes had two cars parked in their driveways. Men used one to drive to work in the city. Women used the other to do their shopping and take their children from place to place.

Cars made people more mobile, and thriving businesses needed to ship goods by truck. As a result, the country badly needed more highways. To meet this need, in 1956 Congress passed the Interstate Highway Act. This ambitious law called for the construction of 41,000 miles of highways. The project took more than 25 years to complete and cost over $100 billion.

The new interstate highways changed the look of the country forever. Restaurants and motels popped up to feed and house travelers. Businesses, shopping centers, and new towns also grew up along interstate highways.

As people spent more and more time in their cars, businesses began offering drive-in services. Drive-in banks, restaurants, and theaters allowed people to do their banking, eat meals, and watch movies without leaving their cars. At drive-in restaurants, a server, often on roller skates, took orders and then brought the food to the car. At drive-in theaters, viewers parked their cars in front of a huge screen and hooked a speaker onto the car window to hear the movie.

Television and Rock and Roll   The baby boomers were the first generation to grow up with a new form of news and entertainment—television. The first practical television system began operating in the 1940s, but television sets did not become affordable until the 1950s. The new technology soon swept the nation. By 1955, about 67 percent of American families owned television sets.

Besides providing fun and entertainment, television allowed Americans to see the world in a new way. For the first time, people could see film of happenings thousands of miles away within just a few hours of the event. The world suddenly seemed much smaller, and events in distant places became more important.

Although radio stations were threatened by the popularity of TV, many stations thrived by offering baby boomers a new form of popular music. In 1951, a radio disc jockey in Cleveland, Ohio, began playing African American rhythm and blues music that he called "rock and roll." Teenagers loved the new sound. "Rock" became the music that the baby boomer generation adopted as its own.

Although television was developed in the 1930s, it did not become popular until the 1950s. By 1955, two thirds of American families owned television sets, which they watched four to five hours a day.

counterculture: a way of life that runs counter to (against) society's traditional culture

32.3 The 1960s: Social Change and Unrest

By the time the first baby boomers graduated from high school in 1964, the good times of the 1950s were giving way to a decade of social change and unrest. During the 1960s, the country divided bitterly over war in Vietnam and issues of social injustice. Violence was in the air, from race riots in big cities to the shocking assassinations of President John F. Kennedy, his brother Robert, Martin Luther King, Jr., and Malcolm X. Baby boomers were caught up in these dramatic tensions just as they were beginning to question their parents' traditional values.

The Counterculture As a group, the boomers who reached young adulthood in the 1960s were very idealistic. Seeing injustice and violence in the world, they openly challenged their society's values and sources of authority.

Many of these young people rejected the pursuit of money and possessions. Calling themselves "hippies," they began "dropping out" of school, jobs, and suburban life. Journalists described the hippie movement as a **counterculture**.

Hippies dreamed of starting a new era of peace, love, and freedom. They let their hair grow long and dressed in jeans, beads, and tie-dyed T-shirts. Many experimented with drugs. Some banded together in communes, groups of people who work together and share everything.

One of the counterculture's favorite expressions was "Do your own thing." Doing your own thing meant doing what was right for you, not what others wanted you to do. Looking back on this time, a *Newsweek* journalist wrote:

President John F. Kennedy promoted a spirit of optimism and idealism in his inauguration speech. His assassination prevented him from realizing his goal of creating a society of equal rights and opportunities for all citizens.

> *The most critical lesson of the 1960s was that it's OK to "do your own thing."… It is OK to be black, OK to be female, OK to be Christian or Jew—which is no small gain for the nation and its increasingly diverse population.*

The Anti-war Movement As you read in Chapter 30, in 1964 the United States began sending troops to Vietnam to combat the spread of communism. As the war effort grew, hundreds of thousands of young people were sent to fight in Southeast Asia. Meanwhile, many of those who remained behind began to vigorously protest the war.

Anti-war protests took many forms. On college campuses, students organized so-called "teach-ins" in which speakers questioned the government's account of events in Vietnam. In major cities, young people organized huge anti-war marches and noisy street demonstrations. When the government began drafting young men to fight in Vietnam, protesters burned their draft cards. Thousands of young men tried to "dodge" the draft by moving to Canada or Mexico.

Television also turned many people against the war. For the first time, news broadcasts brought the horrors of war into Americans' living rooms. Some viewers were so shocked by what they saw that they, too, joined the anti-war movement.

feminists: people who are actively concerned with achieving social, political, and economic equality for women

The Women's Movement   The anti-war movement was just one of many protest movements that rocked the nation during the 1960s. As you read in Chapter 31, the Civil Rights movement inspired other groups to rise up and speak out, including Mexican Americans, Native Americans, and others. The largest of the new protest movements, however, was the women's movement.

One woman in particular helped to inspire this movement. In 1963, Betty Friedan published a best-selling book called *The Feminine Mystique*. Friedan attacked the picture of happy homemakers shown on television and in women's magazines. Although many women felt great satisfaction in running a home and caring for a family, others wanted more choices. Friedan urged women to "break out of the housewife trap and truly find fulfillment…by fulfilling their own unique possibilities as human beings."

Encouraged by Friedan, women across the country began coming together to work for change. Some groups focused on ending discrimination against women in the workplace. Others were more interested in education, child care, or women's health issues. Women who supported these causes called themselves **feminists**.

In 1966, the National Organization for Women (NOW) was formed "to take action to bring American women into full participation in…American society." With Betty Friedan as its president, NOW launched an ambitious campaign to fight discrimination against women in many areas of life. Between 1966 and 1968, NOW's membership soared from about 300 to 175,000.

In the 1960s, women began to demand change. They called for an end to discrimination in the workplace, where their pay averaged only three-quarters that of men and where opportunities for advancement were limited. They also focused on women's issues, such as education and childcare.

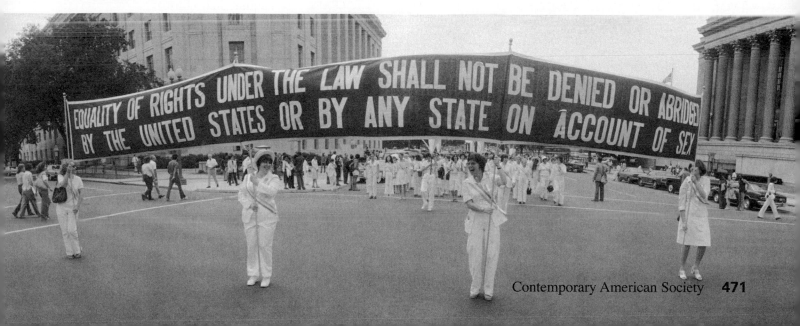

environmentalists: people who are actively concerned with protecting the environment

32.4 The 1970s: A Time of Distrust

By the 1970s, the oldest of the baby boomers were raising their own families, and the counterculture began to fade. Younger boomers seemed to turn away from social causes, becoming the "me generation." Still, much of the idealism of the 1960s lived on—and so did distrust of government.

The Environmental Movement   During the 1970s, a new cause attracted millions of Americans: protecting the environment. Factories, cars, and power plants were spewing poisons into the air. City sewage, factory wastes, and chemicals used in farming were flowing into streams, killing fish and wildlife.

On April 22, 1970, **environmentalists** organized the first Earth Day to encourage people to learn more about the environment. Later that year, Congress responded to public pressure by creating the Environmental Protection Agency (EPA) to help clean up the nation's air, soil, and water.

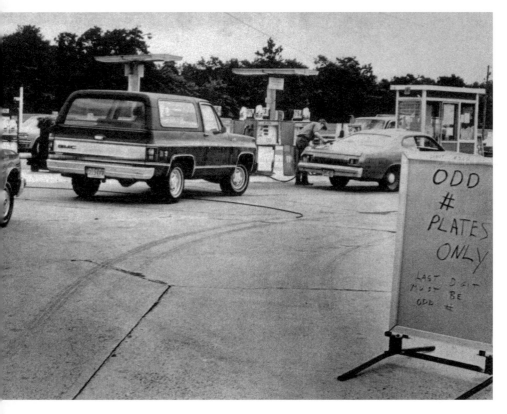

In 1973, Middle East nations stopped sending oil to the United States, resulting in an energy crisis. Motorists faced long lines at service stations and could buy gas only on alternate days.

Energy Crisis   A second problem that grabbed the nation's attention during the 1970s was the energy crisis. By the 1960s, American consumers depended on oil imported from other countries to heat their homes and fuel their cars. Most of these oil-producing countries were in the Middle East.

In 1973, a war in the Middle East caused suppliers to stop exporting oil to the United States. Suddenly, Americans faced an "energy crisis." Gas shortages forced drivers to spend hours waiting in line at gas stations. Homeowners worried about the rising cost of heating their houses.

The crisis ended in 1974, when Middle East nations resumed supplying oil to the U.S. However, Americans remained concerned about their dependence on foreign oil and the need to conserve energy.

Growing Distrust of Government   Distrust of government leaders, which had begun with the anti-war movement, grew stronger during the 1970s. One reason for this growing distrust was President Richard Nixon's policy in Vietnam. Nixon was elected in 1968 on the promise that he would quickly end the Vietnam War. Instead, the fighting dragged on. Still trying to win a "peace with honor," Nixon ordered the bombing of the enemy's supply lines in Cambodia.

...from Herblock: A Cartoonist's Life (Times Books, 1998)

In May 1970, students at Kent State University in Ohio gathered to protest Nixon's expansion of the war into Cambodia. Ohio's governor called on the National Guard to restore order. The Guard arrived on campus wearing gas masks and carrying loaded rifles.

The next day, guardsmen fired into a crowd of students in a parking lot. Fifteen students were injured, and four were killed.

President Nixon blamed the protesters for the deadly incident. "This should remind us," the president said, "that when dissent turns to violence, it invites tragedy." But many Americans, horrified by the killing of unarmed students, put the blame on government.

The Watergate Scandal

Distrust in the nation's government reached a peak during a strange series of events known as the Watergate scandal. The scandal began in the presidential election year of 1972. In June, five men were arrested after breaking into Democratic Party headquarters at the Watergate Hotel in Washington, D.C. The burglars were trying to steal documents and plant electronic equipment that would allow them to listen to private telephone conversations.

At first, the break-in seemed like a minor story. Then the news media learned that the Watergate burglars worked for the Committee to Re-Elect the President, President Nixon's campaign organization. Worse, people with important White House jobs had arranged for the burglars to be paid to keep silent.

Led by two reporters for the *Washington Post,* journalists started to uncover evidence of widespread wrongdoing among people who worked for Nixon or his campaign organization. Congressional committees began holding hearings. A special prosecutor was appointed to investigate the scandal that everyone now called "Watergate."

In 1973, a Senate committee learned that President Nixon regularly taped conversations in the Oval Office. The special prosecutor immediately demanded the audiotapes for his investigation. Eventually, the Supreme Court ordered a defiant Nixon to surrender them.

The tapes proved that Nixon himself had been deeply involved in trying to stop investigations into Watergate. When a committee of the House of Representatives recommended impeachment, Nixon resigned from office rather than face a possible trial in the Senate.

The Watergate scandal left many Americans deeply disillusioned. When a 1974 poll asked people how much faith they had in the executive branch of government, 43 percent answered "Hardly any."

President Richard Nixon taped most conversations he held in his office. When the tapes became public, it was obvious that Nixon had tried to cover up the investigation into the break-in at the Democratic Party headquarters. As a result of this scandal, Nixon became the first U.S. president to resign from office.

32.5 The 1980s: A Return to Optimism

When Ronald Reagan ran for president in 1980, the majority of baby boomers were old enough to vote. By this time, the energy crisis, the Watergate scandal, and a sharp downturn in the economy had left many Americans deeply pessimistic about the future.

In the face of this gloom, Reagan, a former actor and governor of California, was optimistic and hopeful. "There is nothing wrong with America," he said, "that—together—we can't fix." Voters agreed. In 1981, Reagan took office as president declaring that it was "morning in America."

Ronald Reagan was elected president in 1980. To combat the slow growth in the economy, he introduced a program called "Reaganomics." Under this program, large tax breaks were given to businesses and the wealthy so that they could invest in businesses. These businesses would, in turn, create new jobs.

Reaganomics Reagan believed that the best way to get the economy moving again was to lower taxes on the wealthy and on businesses. This policy, he argued, would encourage people to invest more money in businesses. As businesses expanded, new jobs would be created for working people. In this way, prosperity would "trickle down" from the wealthiest Americans to the poorest. This economic policy came to be known as "Reaganomics."

In 1981, Congress passed the largest income tax cut in the nation's history. At Reagan's urging, Congress also relaxed many government regulations that limited what businesses could do. As a result of these changes, business boomed and new jobs were created.

Critics of Reaganomics, however, pointed out that not all Americans were benefiting from the boom. When Congress cut taxes, it also cut spending on many programs that helped the poor, such as food stamps and free school meals. In addition, unemployment remained high among African Americans, Latinos, and unskilled workers.

A New Wave of Immigration Optimism about the future helped fuel a new wave of immigration into the United States during the 1980s. More than 7 million newcomers entered the United States, more than in any other decade since 1910.

In 1965, Congress ended the immigration quotas that it had passed back in 1924. This action made it easier for non-Europeans to enter the country. The result was a dramatic increase in immigrants from Latin America, Asia, and the Caribbean.

The most popular destination of these new immigrants was California. A student who came to California from Mexico in the 1980s observed:

"I was surprised when I arrived to see so many kinds of people—Black people, Asians. I found people from Korea and Cambodia and Mexico. In California I found not just America, I found the world."

Social Problems Despite the optimism of the 1980s, the nation faced serious social problems. With cutbacks in social programs, homeless people began appearing on city streets. The gap between the wealthiest and poorest Americans seemed to be widening. Rising crime rates made people fearful of strangers. In 1983, a presidential commission reported that American schools were failing at their job of educating all students.

Another serious issue was drug abuse. In 1980, only 10 cities reported serious problems with gangs selling crack cocaine and other illegal drugs. By 1990, more than 125 cities had serious problems with drug abuse and crime stemming from the illegal drug trade.

The Reagan administration responded to the rise in drug abuse by declaring a "war on drugs." New laws stiffened penalties for people caught with illegal drugs. The armed forces were used to patrol the nation's borders to reduce the smuggling of illegal drugs into the United States. As the war on drugs continued into the 1990s, more and more people were jailed for selling or possessing illegal drugs. Many Americans questioned whether harsher penalties were helping to reduce drug abuse.

Another troubling issue was the appearance of a frightening new disease called **AIDS** (acquired immune deficiency syndrome). AIDS is caused by a virus known as HIV, which attacks the body's ability to fight off disease. The HIV virus is spread through contact with bodily fluids such as blood. By 1995, more than 270,00 Americans had died of AIDS. An estimated 1 million more were infected with HIV.

As more information about AIDS became available, Americans organized to raise money for research and treatment. In 1988, a huge quilt honoring AIDS victims toured the nation. By 2000, the AIDS Memorial Quilt had more than 44,000 panels, each one honoring the life of a loved one lost to this terrible disease.

AIDS: a disease marked by a weakening of the body's immune system, or its ability to fight off life-threatening illnesses

The AIDS quilt was first displayed on Capitol Mall in 1987. At that time, it had 1,920 panels. By 2000, the quilt had grown to more than 44,000 panels. Each panel honors the life of an AIDS victim.

32.6 The 1990s: The Information Age

When the first baby boomers entered the workforce in the 1960s, a majority of American workers had jobs that involved manual labor. Whether working on farms, in factories, in mines, or in the transportation industry, most workers either made or moved things. By 1990, however, only one worker in five was a maker or mover of goods.

While manual labor jobs were disappearing, jobs for "knowledge workers" exploded. *Knowledge workers* are workers who use information and ideas to create or do something of value. Such workers include engineers, computer programmers, lawyers, artists, and managers, among many others. Looking at this change, economists declared that America had entered a new information age. In the information age, brain power was quickly replacing muscle power as the nation's most valuable human resource.

Tomahawk missiles, fired from ships 500 miles away, bombarded Baghdad, Iraq, during the Persian Gulf War. This became America's first "high-tech" war as the nation relied upon computer-guided bombs and missiles rather than troops.

The Computer Revolution   The explosion of jobs for knowledge workers was fueled by the computer revolution. This revolution began with the development of the first computers after World War II. These early computers, called *mainframes*, filled entire rooms and cost as much as battleships. Only large businesses, government agencies, and universities could afford such massive machines.

In the early 1980s, improvements in computer technology led to the introduction of personal computers (PCs). Compared to mainframes, PCs were small, cheap, and easy to use. These small but powerful computers made computing available to ordinary people. In addition, even smaller computers were built into products ranging from sports watches to automobile engines.

By the 1990s, it was hard to imagine life without computers in the United States. Computer-guided robots were replacing human workers in factories. Bank customers were doing their banking at automated teller machines (ATMs). For many families, computers were also becoming an important source of information and entertainment. By 1999, PCs could be found in at least half of the homes in America.

High-Tech Warfare   The computer revolution also changed warfare in the 1990s. In the past, wars were fought mainly by troops and pilots who operated their own weapons by hand. High-technology ("high-tech") warfare relied much more on computer-guided missiles and bombs. These "smart" weapons were designed to find and destroy specific enemy targets with great accuracy.

The nation's first high-tech war—the Persian Gulf War—was triggered by Saddam Hussein, the president of the Middle East nation of Iraq. In 1990, Hussein ordered his army to invade Iraq's neighbor, oil-rich Kuwait. The Iraqi invaders looted Kuwait and then moved on toward Saudi Arabia and its oil fields.

With support from the United Nations, U.S. president George Bush launched Operation Desert Storm against Iraq in 1991. The war began with massive high-tech air attacks on Iraqi military targets. It ended six weeks later when UN troops from 28 nations successfully liberated Kuwait. By using high-tech weapons, the American-led UN forces had won a swift victory while suffering fewer than 400 casualties.

The Internet   In 1991, most people around the world followed the Persian Gulf War on television. Today, they would have another place to follow war reports—the **Internet**.

The Internet was created in the 1960s as a network that used telephone lines to link distant computers, allowing them to share information. Until the 1990s, this network was used mostly by scientists and other skilled computer users.

The Internet changed radically with the introduction of the World Wide Web in 1989. The Web made it much easier to share information—including pictures, video, and sound—over the Internet. Using a computer program called a *Web browser*, average computer users could readily find information published by organizations and individuals around the world. By the end of the decade, there were more than a billion pages of information on the Web. In addition, the Internet allowed people to shop, play games, retrieve music, and communicate almost instantly using e-mail, or electronic messages.

In 1992, Bill Clinton became the first baby boomer to be elected president. Clinton was quick to see the value of making the vast information on the Internet available to students in schools. In 1996, he set a national goal of installing computers in every classroom and wiring those computers to the Internet. "That's how we must prepare our children for the 21st century," President Clinton declared, "with the full promise of the Information Age at their fingertips."

Internet: a network that allows computers in locations around the world to share information

With cellular phones and handheld computers, communication and information are immediately available. It is because of devices such as these that the 1990s have been called the Information Age.

32.7 A New Frontier

In 1969, the United States landed the first men on the moon. Neil Armstrong stepped onto the surface first and was joined 19 minutes later by Buzz Aldrin, shown above.

As you read at the start of this chapter, looking at history in ten-year chunks has its limitations. Many important developments take place over much longer spans of time. A good example is a story that is still unfolding: humankind's movement into space.

For baby boomers, space became America's new frontier. The exploration of this frontier began in the 1950s as the United States and the Soviet Union raced to launch rockets and, eventually, human astronauts into space. In 1961, President John F. Kennedy challenged the National Aeronautics and Space Administration (NASA) to "put a man on the moon" within ten years.

Kennedy's goal was fulfilled in 1969, when three astronauts rode a spacecraft to the moon. Millions of Americans watched on television as Neil Armstrong became the first person in history to step onto another world. Said Armstrong, "That's one small step for man, one giant leap for mankind."

In the 1970s, NASA began development of the space shuttle. This reusable spacecraft takes off like a rocket and lands like an airplane. The first space shuttle, *Columbia,* lifted off in 1981. More shuttle missions followed in the 1980s and 1990s as NASA carried out space-based research projects. Meanwhile, unmanned probes began to explore the mysteries of Earth's neighbors in space, including the sun, planets, asteroids, and comets.

In 1998, space shuttle astronauts began assembling an International Space Station in Earth's orbit. The space station has been designed and built by 16 nations, led by the United States. It is designed to be a long-term laboratory for scientists carrying out research on both Earth and space.

In November 2000, the first space station crew—an American and two Russian astronauts—moved into their new quarters. "It's a great moment," said James Van Laak, the manager of space station operations. Van Laak went on:

> *"Hopefully, from this point on we'll never have a period where humans are not living in space…. We'll learn to conquer low-Earth orbit, how to keep people alive for years at a time and move on to the moon and on to Mars and who knows where we can go from there."*

32.8 Chapter Summary

In this chapter, you read about the key events of the last 50 years that have helped shape American society as you know it today. You used a time capsule to organize artifacts and icons that symbolize the decades from the 1950s through the 1990s.

The baby boomers born from 1946 to 1967 have lived through eventful decades that brought many changes to American life. While many Americans remember the 1950s as a period of traditional values and good times, the 1960s brought new tensions and social unrest. Members of the counterculture rejected the traditional values of their parents. Many boomers were active in such protest movements as the anti-war movement and the women's movement.

The 1970s were marked by increasing concern over the environment, an energy crisis, and growing distrust in government. As the 1980s began, President Ronald Reagan tried to restore American optimism and spur economic growth. But the nation continued to be concerned about such social problems as homelessness, drug abuse, and the spread of AIDS. Meanwhile, new immigrants from Asia, Latin America, and the Caribbean added to America's diversity.

By the 1990s, America had entered the information age. Computers changed the nature of jobs, enabled high-tech warfare, and allowed people around the world to share information over the Internet.

Developments in history often unfold over many decades. A good example is America's exploration of space. The United States began its space program in the midst of the Cold War of the 1950s. By the end of the 1990s, America was cooperating with other nations, including Russia, to explore humankind's new frontier.

In the decades following World War II, the United States assumed the role of a world leader. It is the responsibility of the nation's next generation to preserve the accomplishments of the past and guide the nation in the 21st century.

The Declaration of Independence

In Congress, July 4, 1776
The unanimous Declaration of the
thirteen United States of America

Preamble (Introduction)

The Preamble explains why the Declaration was written. The Declaration is a statement to the world that explains why the colonies believe they should be independent.

Statement of Human Rights

This section boldly states that all people have rights that no government can take away. Three of these rights are life, liberty, and the pursuit of happiness. If a government does not respect these rights, the people have the right to change the government. By his actions, the king has failed to respect the colonists' rights.

Statement of Charges against the King

This section lists more than 20 ways that the king has violated the colonists' rights. By interfering with laws, the king has taken away the colonists' right to govern themselves. Some of his laws have prevented the colonists from pursuing happiness in their own way. And by sending soldiers to fight the colonists, he has even threatened their right to life.

When in the Course of human events it becomes necessary for one people to dissolve the political bands which have connected them with another and to assume among the powers of the earth, the separate and equal station to which the Laws of Nature and of Nature's God entitle them, a decent respect to the opinions of mankind requires that they should declare the causes which impel them to the separation.

We hold these truths to be self-evident, that all men are created equal, that they are endowed by their Creator with certain unalienable Rights, that among these are Life, Liberty and the pursuit of Happiness. —That to secure these rights, Governments are instituted among Men, deriving their just powers from the consent of the governed, — That whenever any Form of Government becomes destructive of these ends, it is the Right of the People to alter or to abolish it, and to institute new Government, laying its foundation on such principles and organizing its powers in such form, as to them shall seem most likely to effect their Safety and Happiness. Prudence, indeed, will dictate that Governments long established should not be changed for light and transient causes; and accordingly all experience hath shewn that mankind are more disposed to suffer, while evils are sufferable than to right themselves by abolishing the forms to which they are accustomed. But when a long train of abuses and usurpations, pursuing invariably the same Object evinces a design to reduce them under absolute Despotism, it is their right, it is their duty, to throw off such Government, and to provide new Guards for their future security. —Such has been the patient sufferance of these Colonies; and such is now the necessity which constrains them to alter their former Systems of Government. The history of the present King of Great Britain is a history of repeated injuries and usurpations, all having in direct object the establishment of an absolute Tyranny over these States. To prove this, let Facts be submitted to a candid world:

He has refused his Assent to Laws, the most wholesome and necessary for the public good.

He has forbidden his Governors to pass Laws of immediate and pressing importance, unless suspended in their operation till his Assent should be obtained; and when so suspended, he has utterly neglected to attend to them.

He has refused to pass other Laws for the accommodation of large districts of people, unless those people would relinquish the right of Representation in the Legislature, a right inestimable to them and formidable to tyrants only.

He has called together legislative bodies at places unusual, uncomfortable, and distant from the depository of their Public Records, for the sole purpose of fatiguing them into compliance with his measures.

He has dissolved Representative Houses repeatedly, for opposing with manly firmness his invasions on the rights of the people.

He has refused for a long time, after such dissolutions, to cause others to be elected, whereby the Legislative Powers, incapable of Annihilation, have returned to the People at large for their exercise; the State remaining in the mean time exposed to all the dangers of invasion from without, and convulsions within.

He has endeavoured to prevent the population of these States; for that purpose obstructing the Laws for Naturalization of Foreigners; refusing to pass others to encourage their migrations hither, and raising the conditions of new Appropriations of Lands.

He has obstructed the Administration of Justice by refusing his Assent to Laws for establishing Judiciary Powers.

He has made Judges dependent on his Will alone for the tenure of their offices, and the amount an payment of their salaries.

He has erected a multitude of New Offices, and sent hither swarms of Officers to harass our people and eat out their substance.

He has kept among us, in times of peace, Standing Armies without the Consent of our legislatures.

He has affected to render the Military independent of and superior to the Civil Power.

He has combined with others to subject us to a jurisdiction foreign to our constitution, and unacknowledged by our laws; giving his Assent to their Acts of pretended Legislation:

For quartering large bodies of armed troops among us:

For protecting them, by a mock Trial from punishment for any Murders which they should commit on the Inhabitants of these States:

For cutting off our Trade with all parts of the world:

For imposing Taxes on us without our Consent:

For depriving us in many cases, of the benefit of Trial by Jury:

For transporting us beyond Seas to be tried for pretended offences:

For abolishing the free System of English Laws in a neighbouring Province, establishing therein an Arbitrary government, and enlarging its Boundaries so as to render it at once an example and fit instrument for introducing the same absolute rule into these Colonies:

For taking away our Charters, abolishing our most valuable Laws and altering fundamentally the Forms of our Governments:

For suspending our own Legislatures, and declaring themselves invested with power to legislate for us in all cases whatsoever.

He has abdicated Government here, by declaring us out of his Protection and waging War against us.

He has plundered our seas, ravaged our Coasts burnt our towns, and destroyed the lives of our people.

He is at this time transporting large Armies of foreign Mercenaries to compleat the works of death, desolation, and tyranny, already begun with circumstances of Cruelty & Perfidy scarcely paralleled in the most barbarous ages, and totally unworthy the Head of a civilized nation.

He has constrained our fellow Citizens taken Captive on the high Seas to bear Arms against their Country, to become the executioners of their friends and Brethren, or to fall themselves by their Hands

He has excited domestic insurrections amongst us, and has endeavoured to bring on the inhabitants of our frontiers, the merciless Indian Savages whose known rule of warfare, is an undistinguished destruction of all ages, sexes and conditions.

The Government's Failure to Answer the Colonists' Complaints

This section states that the colonists have tried many times to solve their problems with Britain peacefully. Both the king and the British government have failed to answer their complaints. For this reason, the colonists have no choice except to break away from Britain.

Statement of Independence

This section declares the colonies' independence. The writers of the Declaration emphasize that they are acting as the representatives of the people. As the Preamble stated, it is the people who have the right to form a new government. The colonies are now separate countries that have all the powers and rights of other nations.

In every stage of these Oppressions We have Petitioned for Redress in the most humble terms: Our repeated Petitions have been answered only by repeated injury. A Prince, whose character is thus marked by every act which may define a Tyrant, is unfit to be the ruler of a free people.

Nor have We been wanting in attentions to our British brethren. We have warned them from time to time of attempts by their legislature to extend an unwarrantable jurisdiction over us. We have reminded them of the circumstances of our emigration and settlement here. We have appealed to their native justice and magnanimity, and we have conjured them by the ties of our common kindred. to disavow these usurpations, which would inevitably interrupt our connections and correspondence. They too have been deaf to the voice of justice and of consanguinity. We must, therefore, acquiesce in the necessity, which denounces our Separation, and hold them, as we hold the rest of mankind, Enemies in War, in Peace Friends.

We, therefore, the Representatives of the United States of America, in General Congress, Assembled, appealing to the Supreme Judge of the world for the rectitude of our intentions, do, in the Name, and by Authority of the good People of these Colonies, solemnly publish and declare, That these United Colonies are, and of Right ought to be Free and Independent States, that they are Absolved from all Allegiance to the British Crown, and that all political connection between them and the State of Great Britain, is and ought to be totally dissolved; and that as Free and Independent States, they have full Power to levy War, conclude Peace contract Alliances, establish Commerce, and to do all other Acts and Things which Independent States may of right do. — And for the support of this Declaration, with a firm reliance on the protection of Divine Providence, we mutually pledge to each other our Lives, our Fortunes and our sacred Honor.

The foregoing Declaration was, by order of Congress, engrossed, and signed by the following members:

New Hampshire:
Josiah Bartlett, William Whipple, Matthew Thornton

Massachusetts:
John Hancock, Samuel Adams, John Adams, Robert Treat Paine, Elbridge Gerry

Rhode Island:
Stephen Hopkins, William Ellery

Connecticut:
Roger Sherman, Samuel Huntington, William Williams, Oliver Wolcott

New York:
William Floyd, Philip Livingston, Francis Lewis, Lewis Morris

New Jersey:
Richard Stockton, John Witherspoon, Francis Hopkinson, John Hart, Abraham Clark

Pennsylvania:
Robert Morris, Benjamin Rush, Benjamin Franklin, John Morton, George Clymer, James Smith, George Taylor, James Wilson, George Ross
Delaware:
Caesar Rodney, George Read, Thomas McKean

Maryland:
Samuel Chase, William Paca, Thomas Stone, Charles Carroll of Carrollton

Virginia:
George Wythe, Richard Henry Lee, Thomas Jefferson, Benjamin Harrison, Thomas Nelson, Jr., Francis Lightfoot Lee, Carter Braxton

North Carolina:
William Hooper, Joseph Hewes, John Penn

South Carolina:
Edward Rutledge, Thomas Heyward, Jr., Thomas Lynch, Jr., Arthur Middleton

Georgia:
Button Gwinnett, Lyman Hall, George Walton

The Constitution of the United States

Preamble

The Preamble says that the Constitution receives its authority from the people of the United States. The people agree to form a government to protect their rights and provide for safety and order.

Article I: The Legislative Branch

The government's lawmaking branch is Congress, made up of a Senate and a House of Representatives. The comments below point out some of the specific powers of this branch.

Representation in the House: In the House, the number of representatives for each state depends on the number of people who live in the state.

Checks and balances: Impeachment. Only the House has the power to impeach federal officials.

Representation in the Senate: Each state is represented by two senators.

We the People of the United States, in Order to form a more perfect Union, establish Justice, insure domestic Tranquility, provide for the common defence, promote the general Welfare, and secure the Blessings of Liberty to ourselves and our Posterity, do ordain and establish this Constitution for the United States of America.

ARTICLE I

Section 1. All legislative Powers herein granted shall be vested in a Congress of the United States, which shall consist of a Senate and House of Representatives.

Section 2. The House of Representatives shall be composed of Members chosen every second Year by the People of the several States, and the Electors in each State shall have the Qualifications requisite for Electors of the most numerous Branch of the State Legislature.

No Person shall be a Representative who shall not have attained to the Age of twenty five Years, and been seven Years a Citizen of the United States, and who shall not, when elected, be an Inhabitant of that State in which he shall be chosen.

[Representatives and direct Taxes[1] shall be apportioned among the several States which may be included within this Union, according to their respective Numbers, which shall be determined by adding to the whole Number of free Persons, including those bound to Service for a Term of Years, and excluding Indians not taxed, three fifths of all other Persons.][2] The actual Enumeration shall be made within three Years after the first Meeting of the Congress of the United States, and within every subsequent Term of ten Years, in such Manner as they shall by Law direct. The number of Representatives shall not exceed one for every thirty Thousand, but each State shall have at Least one Representative; and until such enumeration shall be made, the State of New Hampshire shall be entitled to choose three, Massachusetts eight, Rhode-Island and Providence Plantations one, Connecticut five, New York six, New Jersey four, Pennsylvania eight, Delaware one, Maryland six, Virginia ten, North Carolina five, South Carolina five, and Georgia three.

When vacancies happen in the Representation from any State, the Executive Authority thereof shall issue Writs of Election to fill such Vacancies.

The House of Representatives shall choose their Speaker and other Officers; and shall have the sole Power of Impeachment.

Section 3. The Senate of the United States shall be composed of two Senators from each State, [chosen by the Legislature thereof,][3] for six Years; and each Senator shall have one Vote.

Immediately after they shall be assembled in Consequence of the first Election, they shall be divided as equally as may be into three Classes. The Seats of the Senators of the first Class shall be vacated at the Expiration of the second Year, of the second Class at the Expiration of the fourth Year, and of the third Class at the Expiration of the sixth Year, so that one third may be chosen every second Year; [and if Vacancies

---

1. Changed by the Sixteenth Amendment
2. Changed by Section 2 of the Fourteenth Amendment
3. Changed by the Seventeenth Amendment

happen by Resignation, or otherwise, during the Recess of the Legislature of any State, the Executive thereof may make temporary Appointments until the next Meeting of the Legislature, which shall then fill such Vacancies.][4]

No Person shall be a Senator who shall not have attained to the Age of thirty Years, and been nine Years a Citizen of the United States, and who shall not, when elected, be an Inhabitant of that State for which he shall be chosen.

The Vice President of the United States shall be President of the Senate, but shall have no Vote, unless they be equally divided.

The Senate shall choose their other Officers, and also a President pro tempore, in the Absence of the Vice President, or when he shall exercise the Office of President of the United States.

The Senate shall have the sole Power to try all Impeachments. When sitting for that Purpose, they shall be on Oath or Affirmation. When the President of the United States is tried, the Chief Justice shall preside: And no Person shall be convicted without the Concurrence of two thirds of the Members present.

Judgment in Cases of Impeachment shall not extend further than to removal from Office, and disqualification to hold and enjoy any Office of honor, Trust or Profit under the United States: but the Party convicted shall nevertheless be liable and subject to Indictment, Trial, Judgment and Punishment, according to Law.

Section 4. The Times, Places and Manner of holding Elections for Senators and Representatives, shall be prescribed in each State by the Legislature thereof; but the Congress may at any time by Law make or alter such Regulations, except as to the Places of choosing Senators.

The Congress shall assemble at least once in every Year, and such Meeting shall be [on the first Monday in December,][5] unless they shall by Law appoint a different Day.

Section 5. Each House shall be the Judge of the Elections, Returns and Qualifications of its own Members, and a Majority of each shall constitute a Quorum to do Business, but a smaller Number may adjourn from day to day, and may be authorized to compel the Attendance of absent Members, in such Manner, and under such Penalties as each House may provide.

Each House may determine the Rules of its Proceedings, punish its Members for disorderly Behaviour, and, with the Concurrence of two thirds, expel a Member.

Each House shall keep a Journal of its Proceedings, and from time to time publish the same, excepting such Parts as may in their Judgment require Secrecy; and the Yeas and Nays of the Members of either House on any question shall, at the Desire of one fifth of those Present, be entered on the Journal.

Neither House, during the Session of Congress, shall, without the Consent of the other, adjourn for more than three days, nor to any other Place than that in which the two Houses shall be sitting.

Section 6. The Senators and Representatives shall receive a Compensation for their Services, to be ascertained by law, and paid out of the Treasury of the United States. They shall in all Cases, except Treason, Felony and Breach of the Peace, be privileged from Arrest during their Attendance at the Session of their respective Houses, and in going to and returning from the same; and for any Speech or Debate in either House, they shall not be questioned in any other Place.

Checks and balances: Impeachment. Only the Senate has the power to put impeached officials on trial.

4. Changed by the Seventeenth Amendment
5. Changed by Section 2 of the Twentieth Amendment

No Senator or Representative shall, during the Time for which he was elected, be appointed to any civil Office under the Authority of the United States, which shall have been created, or the Emoluments whereof shall have been encreased during such time; and no Person holding any Office under the United States, shall be a Member of either House during his Continuance in Office.

Section 7. All Bills for raising Revenue shall originate in the House of Representatives; but the Senate may propose or concur with Amendments as on other Bills.

Proposing laws: Either house of Congress can propose and vote on new laws. Only the House can propose new taxes.

Every Bill which shall have passed the House of Representatives and the Senate, shall, before it becomes a Law, be presented to the President of the United States; If he approve he shall sign it, but if not he shall return it, with his Objections to that House in which it shall have originated, who shall enter the Objections at large on their Journal, and proceed to reconsider it. If after such Reconsideration two thirds of that House shall agree to pass the Bill, it shall be sent, together with the Objections, to the other House, by which it shall likewise be reconsidered, and if approved by two thirds of that House, it shall become a Law. But in all such Cases the Votes of both Houses shall be determined by Yeas and Nays, and the Names of the Persons voting for and against the Bill shall be entered on the Journal of each House respectively. If any Bill shall not be returned by the President within ten Days (Sundays excepted) after it shall have been presented to him, the Same shall be a Law, in like Manner as if he had signed it, unless the Congress by their Adjournment prevent its Return, in which Case it shall not be a Law.

Checks and balances: Overriding the president's veto. Bills passed by Congress become laws when the president signs them. If the president vetoes (rejects) a bill, Congress can overrule the president's veto by a two-thirds vote of both houses.

Every Order, Resolution, or Vote to which the Concurrence of the Senate and House of Representatives may be necessary (except on a question of Adjournment) shall be presented to the President of the United States, and before the Same shall take Effect, shall be approved by him, or being disapproved by him, shall be repassed by two thirds of the Senate and House of Representatives, according to the Rules and Limitations prescribed in the Case of a Bill

Section 8. The Congress shall have Power To lay and collect Taxes, Duties, Imposts and Excises, to pay the Debts and provide for the common Defence and general Welfare of the United States; but all Duties, Imposts and Excises shall be uniform throughout the United States

Creating and collecting taxes: Congress has the power to create and collect taxes.

To borrow Money on the credit of the United States;

To regulate Commerce with foreign Nations, and among the several States, and with the Indian Tribes;

To establish an uniform Rule of Naturalization, and uniform Laws on the subject of Bankruptcies throughout the United States;

To coin Money, regulate the Value thereof, and of foreign Coin, and fix the Standard of Weights and Measures;

Creating a system of money: Congress has the power to create a national currency (system of money).

To provide for the Punishment of counterfeiting the Securities and current Coin of the United States;

To establish Post Offices and post Roads;

To promote the Progress of Science and useful Arts, by securing for limited Times to Authors and Inventors the exclusive Right to their respective Writings and Discoveries;

Creating federal courts: Congress has the power to create new federal courts.

To constitute Tribunals inferior to the supreme Court;

To define and punish Piracies and Felonies committed on the high Seas, and Offenses against the Law of Nations;

To declare War, grant Letters of Marque and Reprisal, and make Rules concerning Captures on land and Water;

Declaring war: Only Congress can declare war on another country.

To raise and support Armies, but no Appropriation of Money to that Use shall be for a longer Term than two Years;

To provide and maintain a Navy;

Creating and paying for armed forces: Congress has the power to create an army and navy, and to raise the money to pay for them.

To make Rules for the Government and Regulation of the land and naval Forces;

To provide for calling forth the Militia to execute the Laws of the Union, suppress Insurrections and repel Invasions;

To provide for organizing, arming, and disciplining, the Militia, and for governing such Part of them as may be employed in the Service of the United States, reserving to the States respectively, the Appointment of the Officers, and the Authority of training the Militia according to the discipline prescribed by Congress;

To exercise exclusive Legislation in all Cases whatsoever, over such District (not exceeding ten Miles square) as may, by Cession of particular States, and the Acceptance of Congress, become the Seat of the Government of the United States, and to exercise like Authority over all Places purchased by the Consent of the Legislature of the State in which the Same shall be, for the Erection of Forts, Magazines, Arsenals, dock-Yards and other needful Buildings;—And

To make all Laws which shall be necessary and proper for carrying into Execution the foregoing Powers, and all other Powers vested by this Constitution in the Government of the United States, or in any Department or Officer thereof.

Making other laws: Congress has the power to make all laws that are needed to carry out the government's powers under the Constitution.

Section 9. The Migration or Importation of such Persons as any of the States now existing shall think proper to admit, shall not be prohibited by the Congress prior to the Year one thousand eight hundred and eight, but a Tax or duty may be imposed on such Importation, not exceeding ten dollars for each Person.

The Privilege of the Writ of Habeas Corpus shall not be suspended, unless when in Cases of Rebellion or Invasion the public Safety may require it.

No Bill of Attainder or ex post facto Law shall be passed.

No Capitation, or other direct, Tax shall be laid, unless in Proportion to the Census or Enumeration herein before directed to be taken.[6]

No Tax or Duty shall be laid on Articles exported from any State.

No Preference shall be given by any Regulation of Commerce or Revenue to the Ports of one State over those of another: nor shall Vessels bound to, or from, one State, be obliged to enter, clear, or pay Duties in another.

No Money shall be drawn from the Treasury, but in Consequence of Appropriations made by Law; and a regular Statement and Account of the Receipts and Expenditures of all public Money shall be published from time to time.

No Title of Nobility shall be granted by the United States: And no Person holding any Office of Profit or Trust under them, shall, without the Consent of the Congress, accept of any present, Emolument, Office, or Title, of any kind whatever, from any King, Prince, or foreign State.

6. See Sixteenth Amendment

Section 10. No State shall enter into any Treaty, Alliance, or Confederation; grant Letters of Marque and Reprisal; coin Money; emit Bills of Credit; make any Thing but gold and silver Coin a Tender in Payment of Debts; pass any Bill of Attainder, ex post facto Law, or Law impairing the Obligation of Contracts, or grant any Title of Nobility;

No State shall, without the Consent of the Congress, lay any Imposts or Duties on Imports or Exports, except what may be absolutely necessary for executing it's inspection Laws: and the net Produce of all Duties and Imposts, laid by any State on Imports or Exports, shall be for the Use of the Treasury of the United States; and all such Laws shall be subject to the Revision and Controul of the Congress.

No State shall, without the Consent of Congress, lay any Duty of Tonnage, keep Troops, or Ships of War in time of Peace, enter into any Agreement or Compact with another State, or with a foreign Power, or engage in War, unless actually invaded, or in such imminent Danger as will not admit of delay.

Article II: The Executive Branch

The head of the executive branch is the president. The comments below point out some of the specific powers of this branch.

ARTICLE II

Section 1. The executive Power shall be vested in a President of the United States of America. He shall hold his Office during the Term of four Years, and, together with the Vice President, chosen for the same Term, be elected, as follows:

Each State shall appoint, in such Manner as the Legislature thereof may direct, a Number of Electors, equal to the whole Number of Senators and Representatives to which the State may be entitled in the Congress: but no Senator or Representative, or Person holding an Office of Trust or Profit under the United States, shall be appointed an Elector.

[The Electors shall meet in their respective States, and vote by Ballot for two Persons, of whom one at least shall not be an Inhabitant of the same State with themselves. And they shall make a List of all the Persons voted for, and of the Number of Votes for each; which List they shall sign and certify, and transmit sealed to the Seat of the Government of the United States, directed to the President of the Senate. The President of the Senate shall, in the Presence of the Senate and House of Representatives, open all the Certificates, and the Votes shall then be counted. The Person having the greatest Number of Votes shall be the President, if such Number be a Majority of the whole Number of Electors appointed; and if there be more than one who have such Majority, and have an equal Number of Votes, then the House of Representatives shall immediately choose by Ballot one of them for President; and if no Person have a Majority, then from the five highest on the List the said House shall in like Manner choose the President. But in choosing the President, the Votes shall be taken by States, the Representation from each State having one Vote; A quorum for this Purpose shall consist of a Member or Members from two thirds of the States, and a Majority of all the States shall be necessary to a Choice. In every Case, after the Choice of the President, the Person having the greatest Number of Votes of the Electors shall be the Vice President. But if there should remain two or more who have equal Votes, the Senate shall choose from them by Ballot the Vice President.][7]

The Congress may determine the Time of choosing the Electors, and the Day on which they shall give their Votes; which Day shall be the same throughout the United States.

No Person except a natural born Citizen, or a Citizen of the United States, at the time of the Adoption of this Constitution, shall be eligible to the Office of President; neither shall any person be eligible to that Office who shall not have attained to the Age of thirty five Years, and been fourteen Years a Resident within the United States.

7. Changed by the Twelfth Amendment

[In Case of the Removal of the President from Office, or of his Death, Resignation, or Inability to discharge the Powers and Duties of the said Office, the Same shall devolve on the Vice President, and the Congress may be Law provide for the Case of Removal, Death, Resignation or Inability, both of the President and Vice President, declaring what Officer shall then act as President, and such Officer shall act accordingly, until the Disability be removed, or a President shall be elected.][8]

The President shall, at stated Times, receive for his Services, a Compensation, which shall neither be increased nor diminished during the Period for which he shall have been elected, and he shall not receive within that Period any other Emolument from the United States, or any of them.

Before he enter on the Execution of his Office, he shall take the following Oath or Affirmation:—"I do solemnly swear (or affirm) that I will faithfully execute the Office of President of the United States, and will to the best of my Ability, preserve, protect and defend the Constitution of the United States."

Section 2. The President shall be Commander in Chief of the Army and Navy of the United States, and of the Militia of the several States, when called into the actual Service of the United States; he may require the Opinion, in writing, of the principal Officer in each of the executive Departments, upon any Subject relating to the Duties of their respective Offices, and he shall have Power to grant Reprieves and Pardons for Offenses against the United States, except in Cases of Impeachment.

Commanding the armed forces: The president is commander-in-chief of the armed forces of the United States.
Granting pardons: The president can grant pardons for federal crimes, except in cases of impeachment.

He shall have Power, by and with the Advice and Consent of the Senate, to make Treaties, provided two thirds of the Senators present concur; and he shall nominate, and by and with the Advice and Consent of the Senate, shall appoint Ambassadors, other public Ministers and Consuls, Judges of the supreme Court, and all other Officers of the United States, whose Appointments are not herein otherwise provided for, and which shall be established by Law: but the Congress may by law vest the Appointment of such inferior Officers, as they think proper, in the President alone, in the Courts of Law, or in the Heads of Departments.

Checks and balances: Treaties and appointments. The president can sign treaties with other countries. But the Senate must approve treaties by a two-thirds vote. The president can name certain officials and federal judges, but the Senate must approve the president's choices.

The President shall have Power to fill up all Vacancies that may happen during the Recess of the Senate, by granting Commissions which shall expire at the End of their next Session.

Section 3. He shall from time to time give to the Congress Information of the State of the Union, and recommend to their Consideration such Measures as he shall judge necessary and expedient; he may, on extraordinary Occasions, convene both Houses, or either of them and in Case of Disagreement between them with Respect to the Time of Adjournment, he may adjourn them to such Time as he shall think proper; he shall receive Ambassadors and other public Ministers; he shall take Care that the Laws be faithfully executed, and shall Commission all the Officers of the United States.

Powers of leadership: The president can propose ideas for new laws and reports to Congress on the State of the Union. In emergencies, the president can call Congress into special session.

Section 4. The President, Vice President and all civil Officers of the United States, shall be removed from Office on Impeachment for, and Conviction of, Treason, Bribery, or other high Crimes and Misdemeanors.

Checks and balances: Impeachment. Presidents and federal officials can be removed from office if they misuse their powers.

ARTICLE III

Article III: The Judicial Branch
The judicial branch consists of the Supreme Court and other federal courts. The comments below point out some of the specific powers of this branch.

Section 1. The judicial Power of the United States, shall be vested in one supreme Court, and in such inferior Courts as the Congress may from time to time ordain and establish. The Judges, both of the supreme and inferior Courts, shall hold their Officer during good Behaviour, and shall at stated Times, receive for their Services, a Compensation, which shall not be diminished during their Continuance in Office.

8. Changed by the Twenty-Fifth Amendment

Checks and balances: Interpreting the Constitution. The judicial branch has the power to decide whether laws and treaties are constitutional.
Resolving disputes: Federal courts have the power to settle disputes involving the federal government, different states, or citizens of different states.

Section 2. The judicial Power shall extend to all Cases, in Law and Equity, arising under this Constitution, the Laws of the United States, and Treaties made, or which shall be made, under their Authority, —to all Cases affecting Ambassadors, other public Ministers and Consuls; —to all Cases of admiralty and maritime Jurisdiction, —to Controversies to which the United States shall be a Party; —to Controversies between two or more States, —[between a State and Citizens of another State;][9] between Citizens of different States, —between Citizens of the same State claiming Lands under Grants of different States, [and between a State or the Citizens thereof, and foreign States, Citizens or Subjects.][10]

In all Cases affecting Ambassadors, other public Ministers and Consuls, and those in which a State shall be Party, the supreme Court shall have original Jurisdiction. In all the other Cases before mentioned, the supreme Court shall have appellate Jurisdiction, both as to Law and Fact, with such Exceptions, and under such Regulations as the Congress shall make.

The Trial of all Crimes, except in Cases of Impeachment; shall be by Jury, and such Trial shall be held in the State where the said Crimes shall have been committed but when not committed within any State, the Trial shall be at such Place or Places as the Congress may by Law have directed.

Section 3. Treason against the United States, shall consist only in levying War against them, or in adhering to their Enemies, giving them Aid and Comfort. No Person shall be convicted of Treason unless on the Testimony of two Witnesses to the same overt Act, or on Confession in open Court.

The Congress shall have Power to declare the Punishment of Treason, but no Attainder of Treason shall work Corruption of Blood, or Forfeiture except during the Life of the Person attainted.

Article IV: Relations between the States

This article says that each state must honor the laws and authority of other states, as well as the rights of their citizens. The article also describes how new states can be added to the Union.

ARTICLE IV

Section 1. Full Faith and Credit shall be given in each State to the public Acts, Records, and judicial Proceedings of every other State; And the Congress may by general Laws prescribe the Manner in which such Acts, Records and Proceedings shall be proved, and the Effect thereof.

Section 2. The Citizens of each State shall be entitled to all Privileges and Immunities of Citizens in the several States.

A Person charged in any State with Treason, Felony, or other Crime, who shall flee from Justice, and be found in another State, shall on Demand of the executive Authority of the State from which he fled, be delivered up, to be removed to the State having Jurisdiction of the Crime.

[No Person held to Service or Labour in one State, under the Laws thereof, escaping into another, shall, in Consequence of any Law or Regulation therein, be discharged from such Service or Labour, but shall be delivered up on Claim of the party to whom such Service or Labour may be due.][11]

Section 3. New States may be admitted by the Congress into this Union; but no new State shall be formed or erected within the Jurisdiction of any other State; nor any State be formed by the Junction of two or more States, or Parts of States, without the Consent of the Legislatures of the States concerned as well as of the Congress.

9. Changed by the Eleventh Amendment
10. Changed by the Eleventh Amendment
11. Changed by the Thirteenth Amendment

The Congress shall have power to dispose of and make all needful Rules and Regulations respecting the Territory or other Property belonging to the United States; and nothing in this Constitution shall be construed as to Prejudice any Claims of the United States, or of any particular State.

Section 4. The United States shall guarantee to every State in this Union a Republican Form of Government, and shall protect each of them against Invasion; and on Application of the Legislature, or of the Executive (when the Legislature cannot be convened) against domestic Violence.

ARTICLE V

The Congress, whenever two thirds of both houses shall deem it necessary, shall propose Amendments to this Constitution, or, on the Application of the Legislatures of two thirds of the several States, shall call a Convention for proposing Amendments, which in either Case, shall be valid to all Intents and Purposes, as Part of this Constitution, when ratified by the Legislatures of three fourths of the several States, or by Conventions in three fourths thereof, as the one or the other Mode of Ratification may be proposed by the Congress; Provided that no Amendment which may be made prior to the Year One thousand eight hundred and eight shall in any Manner affect the first and fourth Clauses in the Ninth Section of the first Article; and that no State, without its Consent, shall be deprived of its equal Suffrage in the Senate.

ARTICLE VI

All Debts contracted and Engagements entered into, before the Adoption of this Constitution, shall be as valid against the United States under this Constitution, as under the Confederation.

This Constitution, and the Laws of the United States which shall be made in Pursuance thereof; and all Treaties made, or which shall be made, under the Authority of the United States, shall be the supreme Law of the Land; and the Judges in every State shall be bound thereby, any Thing in the Constitution or Laws of any State to the Contrary notwithstanding.

The Senators and Representatives before mentioned, and the Members of the several State Legislatures, and all executive and judicial Officers, both of the United States and of the several States, shall be bound by Oath or Affirmation, to support this Constitution; but no religious Test shall ever be required as a Qualification to any Office or public Trust under the United States.

ARTICLE VII

The Ratification of the Conventions of nine States, shall be sufficient for the Establishment of this Constitution between the States so ratifying the Same.

Done in Convention by the Unanimous Consent of the States present the Seventeenth Day of September in the Year of our Lord one thousand seven hundred and Eighty seven and of the Independence of the United States of America the Twelfth In Witness whereof We have hereunto subscribed our Names.

Article V: Amending the Constitution
This article describes how the Constitution can be amended, or changed. Amendments must be ratified (approved) by three fourths of the states.

Article VI: The Constitution as the Supreme Law of the Land
This article makes the Constitution the supreme (highest) law of the nation. No federal or state law can contradict the Constitution.

Article VII: Ratifying the Constitution
This article says that the Constitution must be ratified (approved) by 9 of the original 13 states.

The Bill of Rights and Later Amendments

Original Ten Amendments: The Bill of Rights
Passed by Congress September 25, 1789.
Ratified December 15, 1791.

Congress cannot make laws that violate Americans' basic freedoms, including freedom of speech, religion, and the press. Citizens have the right to gather peacefully and to ask the government to correct wrongs.

AMENDMENT 1
BASIC FREEDOMS
Congress shall make no law respecting an establishment of religion, or prohibiting the free exercise thereof; or abridging the freedom of speech, or of the press, or the right of the people peaceably to assemble, and to petition the Government for a redress of grievances.

Citizens have the right to own and carry weapons for use in state militias.

AMENDMENT 2
RIGHT TO BEAR ARMS
A well regulated Militia, being necessary to the security of a free State, the right of the people to keep and bear Arms, shall not be infringed.

In peacetime, the government cannot force citizens to let soldiers stay in their homes.

AMENDMENT 3
QUARTERING OF SOLDIERS
No Soldier shall, in time of peace be quartered in any house, without the consent of the Owner, nor in time of war, but in a manner to be prescribed by law.

Government officials cannot search citizens or their property, or seize their belongings, without good reason. Normally, searches and seizures require a warrant approved by a judge.

AMENDMENT 4
SEARCH AND ARREST
The right of the people to be secure in their persons, houses, papers, and effects, against unreasonable searches and seizures, shall not be violated, and no Warrants shall issue, but upon probable cause, supported by Oath or affirmation, and particularly describing the place to be searched, and the persons or things to be seized.

Citizens who are accused of crimes have certain basic rights. They cannot be tried twice for the same crime, or be forced to testify against themselves. They cannot be jailed or lose their property except through proper legal actions.

AMENDMENT 5
RIGHTS IN CRIMINAL CASES
No person shall be held to answer for a capital, or otherwise infamous crime, unless on a presentment or indictment of a Grand Jury, except in cases arising in the land or naval forces, or in the Militia, when in actual service in time of War or public danger; nor shall any person be subject for the same offence to be twice put in jeopardy of life or limb, nor shall be compelled in any criminal case to be a witness against himself, nor be deprived of life, liberty, or property, without due process of law; nor shall private property be taken for public use, without just compensation.

Citizens who are accused of crimes have the right to a trial by jury that is fair and public. They have the right to question witnesses, and they have the right to a lawyer.

AMENDMENT 6
RIGHT TO A FAIR TRIAL
In all criminal prosecutions, the accused shall enjoy the right to a speedy and public trial, by an impartial jury of the State and district wherein the crime shall have been committed; which district shall have been previously ascertained by law, and to be informed of the nature and cause of the accusation; to be confronted with the witnesses against him; to have compulsory process for obtaining witnesses in his favor, and to have the assistance of counsel for his defence.

Citizens have the right to demand a jury trial to settle disputes over things of value.

AMENDMENT 7
RIGHTS IN CIVIL CASES
In Suits at common law, where the value in controversy shall exceed twenty dollars, the right of trial by jury shall be preserved, and no fact tried by a jury shall be otherwise re-examined in any Court of the United States, than according to the rules of the common law.

AMENDMENT 8
BAIL, FINES, PUNISHMENT
Excessive bail shall not be required, nor excessive fines imposed, nor cruel and unusual punishments inflicted.

Bail and fines that are set by a court must be reasonable. Punishments for crimes cannot be cruel or unusual.

AMENDMENT 9
RIGHTS RETAINED BY THE PEOPLE
The enumeration in the Constitution of certain rights shall not be construed to deny or disparage others retained by the people.

The government must respect all the rights of Americans, including rights that are not listed in the Constitution.

AMENDMENT 10
STATES' RIGHTS
The powers not delegated to the United States by the Constitution, nor prohibited by it to the States, are reserved to the States respectively, or to the people.

The states and the people keep any powers that the Constitution does not specifically give to the federal government.

Later Amendments

AMENDMENT 11
LAWSUITS AGAINST STATES
The Judicial power of the United States shall not be construed to extend to any suit in law or equity, commenced or prosecuted against one of the United States by Citizens of another State, or by Citizens or Subjects of any Foreign State.

People cannot sue a state in federal court if they are citizens of a different state, or of a foreign country.

Ratified February 7, 1795.

AMENDMENT 12
PRESIDENTIAL ELECTIONS
The Electors shall meet in their respective states, and vote by ballot for President and Vice-President, one of whom, at least, shall not be an inhabitant of the same state with themselves; they shall name in their ballots the person voted for as President, and in distinct ballots the person voted for as Vice-President, and they shall make distinct lists of all persons voted for as President, and of all persons voted for as Vice-President, and of the number of votes for each, which lists they shall sign and certify, and transmit sealed to the seat of the government of the United States, directed to the President of the Senate;—The President of the Senate shall, in the presence of the Senate and House of Representatives, open all the certificates and the votes shall then be counted;—The person having the greatest number of votes for President, shall be the President, if such number be a majority of the whole number of Electors appointed; and if no person have such majority, then from the persons having the highest numbers not exceeding three on the list of those voted for as President, the House of Representatives shall choose immediately, by ballot, the President. But in choosing the President, the votes shall be taken by states, the representation from each state having one vote; a quorum for this purpose shall consist of a member or members from two-thirds of the states, and a majority of all the states shall be necessary to a choice. [And if the House of Representatives shall not choose a President whenever the right of choice shall devolve upon them, before the fourth day of March next following, then the Vice-President shall act as President, as in the case of the death or other constitutional disability of the President.][12] The person having the greatest number of votes as Vice-President, shall be the Vice-President, if such number be a majority of the whole number of Electors appointed, and if no person have a majority, then from the two highest numbers on the list, the Senate shall choose the Vice-President; a quorum for the purpose shall consist of two thirds of the whole number of Senators, and a majority of the whole number shall be necessary to a choice. But no person constitutionally ineligible to the office of President shall be eligible to that of Vice-President of the United States.

The vice president will be elected separately from the president. In the original Constitution, the candidate who finished second in the voting for president automatically became vice president. Under that system, the president and vice president were likely to be political enemies. The 12th Amendment allows the same political party to win the elections for both president and vice president.

Ratified June 15, 1804.

[12]Superseded by Section 3 of the Twentieth Amendment

No person in the United States can be kept as a slave. No person can be forced to work for someone else, except as a legal punishment for a crime.

All Americans, including former slaves, have the right to be treated as citizens. For example, states must respect the constitutional rights of all citizens. States must give all their citizens equal protection in their laws. In addition, they cannot deny the right of eligible men to vote in federal elections. If they do, they will lose some of their representatives in Congress.
The 14th Amendment also deals with other questions that arose because of the Civil War. For instance, it prevents people who have rebelled against the United States from being elected to office. It also says that the federal government is not responsible for Confederate debts.

AMENDMENT 13
END OF SLAVERY
Section 1. Neither slavery nor involuntary servitude, except as a punishment for crime whereof the party shall have been duly convicted, shall exist within the United States, or any place subject to their jurisdiction.

Section 2. Congress shall have power to enforce these article by appropriate legislation.

Ratified December 6, 1865.

AMENDMENT 14
CIVIL RIGHTS
Section 1. All persons born or naturalized in the United States and subject to the jurisdiction thereof, are citizens of the United States and of the State wherein they reside. No State shall make or enforce any law which shall abridge the privileges or immunities of citizens of the United States; nor shall any State deprive any person of life, liberty, or property, without due process of law; nor deny to any person within its jurisdiction the equal protection of the laws.

Section 2. Representatives shall be apportioned among the several States according to their respective numbers, counting the whole number of persons in each State, excluding Indians not taxed. But when the right to vote at any election for the choice of electors for President and Vice President of the United States, Representatives in Congress, the Executive and Judicial officers of a State, or the members of the Legislature thereof, is denied to any of the male inhabitants of such State, being twenty-one years of age, and citizens of the United States, or in any way abridged, except for participation in rebellion, or other crime, the basis of representation therein shall be reduced in the proportion which the number of such male citizens shall bear to the whole number of male citizens twenty-one years of age in such State.

Section 3. No person shall be a Senator or Representative in Congress, or elector of President and Vice President, or hold any office, civil or military, under the United States, or under any State, who, having previously taken an oath, as a member of Congress, or as an officer of the United States, or as a member of any State legislature, or as an executive or judicial officer of any State, to support the Constitution of the United States, shall have engaged in insurrection or rebellion against the same, or given aid or comfort to the enemies thereof. But Congress may by a vote of two thirds of each House, remove such disability.

Section 4. The validity of the public debt of the United States, authorized by law, including debts incurred for payment of pensions and bounties for services in suppressing insurrection or rebellion, shall not be questioned. But neither the United States nor any State shall assume or pay any debt or obligation incurred in aid of insurrection or rebellion against the United States, or any claim for the loss or emancipation of any slave; but all such debts, obligations and claims shall be held illegal and void.

Section 5. The Congress shall have power to enforce, by appropriate legislation, the provisions of this article.

Ratified July 9, 1868

AMENDMENT 15
VOTING RIGHTS
Section 1. The right of citizens of the United States to vote shall not be denied or abridged by the United States or by any State on account of race, color, or previous condition of servitude.

States cannot deny anyone the right to vote because of the person's race or color, or because the person used to be a slave.

Section 2. The Congress shall have power to enforce this article by appropriate legislation.

Ratified February 3, 1870.

AMENDMENT 16
INCOME TAXES

The Congress shall have power to lay and collect taxes on incomes, from whatever source derived, without apportionment among the several States, and without regard to any census or enumeration.

Ratified February 3, 1913.

Congress has the power to collect taxes from individual citizens based on their income (wealth).

AMENDMENT 17
SENATORIAL ELECTIONS

The Senate of the United States shall be composed of two senators from each State, elected by the people thereof, for six years; and each Senator shall have one vote. The electors in each State shall have the qualifications requisite for electors of the most numerous branch of the State legislature.

When vacancies happen in the representation of any State in the Senate, the executive authority of such State shall issue writs of election to fill such vacancies: Provided, That the legislature of any State may empower the executive thereof to make temporary appointments until the people fill the vacancies by election as the legislature may direct.

This amendment shall not be so construed as to affect the election or term of any Senator chosen before it becomes valid as part of the Constitution.

Ratified April 8, 1913.

Members of the Senate will be elected directly by voters. Previously, senators were elected by state legislatures.

AMENDMENT 18
PROHIBITION OF LIQUOR

Section 1. After one year from the ratification of this article, the manufacture, sale, or transportation of intoxicating liquors within, the importation thereof into, or the exportation thereof from the United States and all territory subject to the jurisdiction thereof for beverage purposes is hereby prohibited.

Section 2. The Congress and the several States shall have concurrent power to enforce this article by appropriate legislation.

Section 3. This article shall be inoperative unless it shall have been ratified as an amendment to the Constitution by the legislatures of the several States, as provided in the Constitution, within seven years from the date of the submission hereof to the States by the Congress.

Ratified January 16, 1919. Repealed by the Twenty-First, December 5, 1933

This amendment outlawed the making and selling of liquor (alcohol) in the United States. The 21st Amendment removed this amendment from the Constitution.

AMENDMENT 19
WOMEN'S SUFFRAGE

The right of citizens of the United States to vote shall not be denied or abridged by the United States or by any States on account of sex.

Congress shall have power to enforce this article by appropriate legislation.

Ratified August 18, 1920.

Neither the federal government nor the states can deny people the right to vote because of their sex. This amendment guaranteed the right of women to vote.

This amendment changes the dates when elected federal officials began serving their terms. It also deals with special situations, such as the death of a president-elect before the start of the president's term in office.

AMENDMENT 20
TERMS OF OFFICE

Section 1. The terms of the President and Vice President shall end at noon the 20th day of January, and the terms of Senators and Representatives at noon on the 3d day of January, of the years in which such terms would have ended if this article had not been ratified; and the terms of their successors shall then begin.

Section 2. The Congress shall assemble at least once in every year, and such meeting shall begin at noon on the 3d day of January, unless they shall by law appoint a different day.

Section 3. If, at the time fixed for the beginning of the term of the President, the President elect shall have died, the Vice President elect shall become President. If a President shall not have been chosen before the time fixed for the beginning of his term, or if the President elect shall have failed to qualify, then the Vice President elect shall act as President until a President shall have qualified; and the Congress may by law provide for the case wherein neither a President elect nor a Vice President elect shall have qualified, declaring who shall then act as President, or the manner in which one who is to act shall be selected, and such person shall act accordingly until a President or Vice President shall have qualified.

Section 4. The Congress may by law provide for the case of the death of any of the persons from whom the House of Representatives may choose a President whenever the right of choice shall have devolved upon them, and for the case of the death of any of the persons from whom the Senate may choose a Vice President whenever the right of choice shall have devolved upon them.

Section 5. Sections 1 and 2 shall take effect on the 15th day of October following the ratification of this article.

Section 6. This article shall be inoperative unless it shall have been ratified as an amendment to the Constitution by the legislatures of three fourths of the several States within seven years from the date of its submission.

Ratified January 23, 1933.

The 18th Amendment is repealed (removed from the Constitution).

AMENDMENT 21
REPEAL OF PROHIBITION

Section 1. The eighteenth article of amendment to the Constitution of the United States is hereby repealed.

Section 2. The transportation or importation into any State, Territory, or possession of the United States for delivery or use therein of intoxicating liquors, in violation of the laws thereof, is hereby prohibited.

Section 3. The article shall be inoperative unless it shall have been ratified as an amendment to the Constitution by conventions in the several States, as provided in the Constitution, within seven years from the date of the submission hereof to the States by the Congress.

Ratified December 5, 1933.

AMENDMENT 22
TERM LIMITS FOR THE PRESIDENCY

Presidents cannot serve more than two full terms in office.

Section 1. No person shall be elected to the office of the President more than twice, and no person who has held the office of President, or acted as President, for more than two years of a term to which some other person was elected President shall be elected to the office of the President more than once. But this Article shall not apply to any person holding the office of President when this Article was proposed by the Congress, and shall not prevent any person who may be holding the office of President, or acting as President, during the term within which this Article becomes operative from holding the office of President or acting as President during the remainder of such term.

Section 2. This article shall be inoperative unless it shall have been ratified as an amendment to the Constitution by the legislatures of three fourths of the several States within seven years from the date of its submission to the States by the Congress.

Ratified February 27, 1951.

AMENDMENT 23
WASHINGTON, D.C., SUFFRAGE
Section 1. The District constituting the seat of government of the United States shall appoint in such manner as the Congress may direct:

A number of electors of President and Vice President equal to the whole number of Senators and Representatives in Congress to which the District would be entitled if it were a state, but in no event more than the least populous State; they shall be in addition to those appointed by the States, but they shall be considered, for the purposes of the election of President and Vice President, to be electors appointed by a State; and they shall meet in the District and perform such duties as provided by the twelfth article of amendment.

Section 2. The Congress shall have power to enforce this article by appropriate legislation.

Ratified March 29, 1961.

AMENDMENT 24
ABOLITION OF POLL TAXES
Section 1. The right of citizens of the United States to vote in any primary or other election for President or Vice President, for electors for President or Vice President, or for Senator or Representative in Congress, shall not be denied or abridged by the United States or any State by reason of failure to pay any poll tax or other tax.

Section 2. The Congress shall have power to enforce this article by appropriate legislation.

Ratified January 23, 1964.

AMENDMENT 25
PRESIDENTIAL SUCCESSION
Section 1. In case of the removal of the President from office or of his death or resignation, the Vice President shall become President.

Section 2. Whenever there is a vacancy in the office of the Vice President, the President shall nominate a Vice President who shall take office upon confirmation by a majority vote of both Houses of Congress.

Section 3. Whenever the President transmits to the President pro tempore of the Senate and the Speaker of the House of Representatives his written declaration that he is unable to discharge the powers and duties of his office, and until he transmits to them a written declaration to the contrary, such powers and duties shall be discharged by the Vice President as Acting President.

This amendment gives the District of Columbia the right to participate in electing the president and vice-president. The District of Columbia is the nation's capital and is not part of any state.

No state can deny someone the right to vote because the person failed to pay a special voting tax. Before this amendment, some states used a tax to prevent African Americans from voting.

This amendment deals with situations in which the president dies or is unable to carry out his or her duties. It spells out when the vice president should act for the president or take over as president. It also says how a new vice president should be elected if the vice president dies or leaves office between elections.

Section 4. Whenever the Vice President and a majority of either the principal officers of the executive departments or of such other body as Congress may by law provide, transmit to the President pro tempore of the Senate and the Speaker of the House of Representatives their written declaration that the President is unable to discharge the powers and duties of his office, the Vice President shall immediately assume the powers and duties of the office as Acting President.

Thereafter, when the President transmits to the President pro tempore of the Senate and the Speaker of the House of Representatives his written declaration that no inability exists, he shall resume the powers and duties of his office unless the Vice President and a majority of either the principal officers of the executive department or of such other body as Congress may by law provide, transmit within four days to the President pro tempore of the Senate and the Speaker of the House of Representatives their written declaration that the President is unable to discharge the powers and duties of his office. Thereupon Congress shall decide the issue, assembling within forty-eight hours for that purpose if not in session. If the Congress, within twenty-one days after receipt of the latter written declaration, or, if Congress is not in session, within twenty-one days after Congress is required to assemble, determines by two-thirds vote of both Houses that the President is unable to discharge the powers and duties of his office, the Vice President shall continue to discharge the same as Acting President; otherwise, the President shall resume the powers and duties of his office.

Ratified February 10, 1967.

AMENDMENT 26
18-YEAR-OLD SUFFRAGE

The federal government and the states cannot deny citizens who are 18 years and older the right to vote.

Section 1. The right of citizens of the United States, who are eighteen years of age or older, to vote shall not be denied or abridged by the United States or by any State on account of age.

Section 2. The Congress shall have power to enforce this article by appropriate legislation.

Ratified June 30, 1971.

AMENDMENT 27
CONGRESSIONAL PAY RAISES

Congress cannot change the pay of senators and representatives who are serving in that session of Congress. Changes in pay will take effect only after the next election for the House of Representatives.

No law, varying the compensation for the services of the Senators and Representatives, shall take effect, until an election of Representatives shall have intervened.

Ratified May 7, 1992

Presidents of the United States

1.	George Washington	1789-1797	(no party)
2.	John Adams	1797-1801	(Federalist)
3.	Thomas Jefferson	1801-1809	(Democratic-Republican)
4.	James Madison	1809-1817	(Democratic-Republican)
5.	James Monroe	1817-1825	(Democratic-Republican)
6.	John Quincy Adams	1825-1829	(Democratic-Republican)
7.	Andrew Jackson	1829-1837	(Democrat)
8.	Martin Van Buren	1837-1841	(Democrat)
9.	William Henry Harrison	1841	(Whig)
10.	John Tyler	1841-1845	(Whig)
11.	James Knox Polk	1845-1849	(Democrat)
12.	Zachary Taylor	1849-1850	(Whig)
13.	Millard Fillmore	1850-1853	(Whig)
14.	Franklin Pierce	1853-1857	(Democrat)
15.	James Buchanan	1857-1861	(Democrat)
16.	Abraham Lincoln	1861-1865	(Republican)
17.	Andrew Johnson	1865-1869	(Democrat/National Union)
18.	Ulysses Simpson Grant	1869-1877	(Republican)
19.	Rutherford Birchard Hayes	1877-1881	(Republican)
20.	James Abram Garfield	1881	(Republican)
21.	Chester Alan Arthur	1881-1885	(Republican)
22.	Grover Cleveland	1885-1889	(Democrat)
23.	Benjamin Harrison	1889-1893	(Republican)
24.	Grover Cleveland	1893-1897	(Democrat)
25.	William McKinley	1897-1901	(Republican)
26.	Theodore Roosevelt	1901-1909	(Republican)
27.	William Howard Taft	1909-1913	(Republican)
28.	Woodrow Wilson	1913-1921	(Democrat)
29.	Warren Gamaliel Harding	1921-1923	(Republican)
30.	Calvin Coolidge	1923-1929	(Republican)
31.	Herbert Clark Hoover	1929-1933	(Republican)
32.	Franklin Delano Roosevelt	1933-1945	(Democrat)
33.	Harry S Truman	1945-1953	(Democrat)
34.	Dwight David Eisenhower	1953-1961	(Republican)
35.	John Fitzgerald Kennedy	1961-1963	(Democrat)
36.	Lyndon Baines Johnson	1963-1969	(Democrat)
37.	Richard Milhous Nixon	1969-1974	(Republican)
38.	Gerald Rudolph Ford, Jr.	1974-1977	(Republican)
39.	James Earl Carter	1977-1981	(Democrat)
40.	Ronald Wilson Reagan	1981-1989	(Republican)
41.	George Herbert Walker Bush	1989-1993	(Republican)
42.	William Jefferson Clinton	1993-2001	(Democrat)
43.	George Walker Bush	2001-	(Republican)

The Pledge of Allegiance

I pledge allegiance to the Flag
of the United States of America,
and to the Republic
for which it stands,
one Nation under God, indivisible,
with liberty and justice for all.

The Star-Spangled Banner

September 20, 1814
By Francis Scott Key

Oh, say can you see, by the dawn's early light,
What so proudly we hailed at the twilight's last gleaming?
Whose broad stripes and bright stars, through the perilous fight,
O'er the ramparts we watched, were so gallantly streaming?
And the rockets' red glare, the bombs bursting in air,
Gave proof through the night that our flag was still there.
O say, does that star-spangled banner yet wave
O'er the land of the free and the home of the brave?

On the shore, dimly seen through the mists of the deep,
Where the foe's haughty host in dread silence reposes,
What is that which the breeze, o'er the towering steep,
As it fitfully blows, now conceals, now discloses?
Now it catches the gleam of the morning's first beam,
In full glory reflected now shines on the stream:
'Tis the star-spangled banner! O long may it wave
O'er the land of the free and the home of the brave.

And where is that band who so vauntingly swore
That the havoc of war and the battle's confusion
A home and a country should leave us no more?
Their blood has wiped out their foul footstep's pollution.
No refuge could save the hireling and slave
From the terror of flight, or the gloom of the grave:
And the star-spangled banner in triumph doth wave
O'er the land of the free and the home of the brave.

Oh! thus be it ever, when freemen shall stand
Between their loved homes and the war's desolation!
Blest with victory and peace, may the heaven-rescued land
Praise the Power that hath made and preserved us a nation.
Then conquer we must, for our cause it is just,
And this be our motto: "In God is our trust."
And the star-spangled banner forever shall wave
O'er the land of the free and the home of the brave!

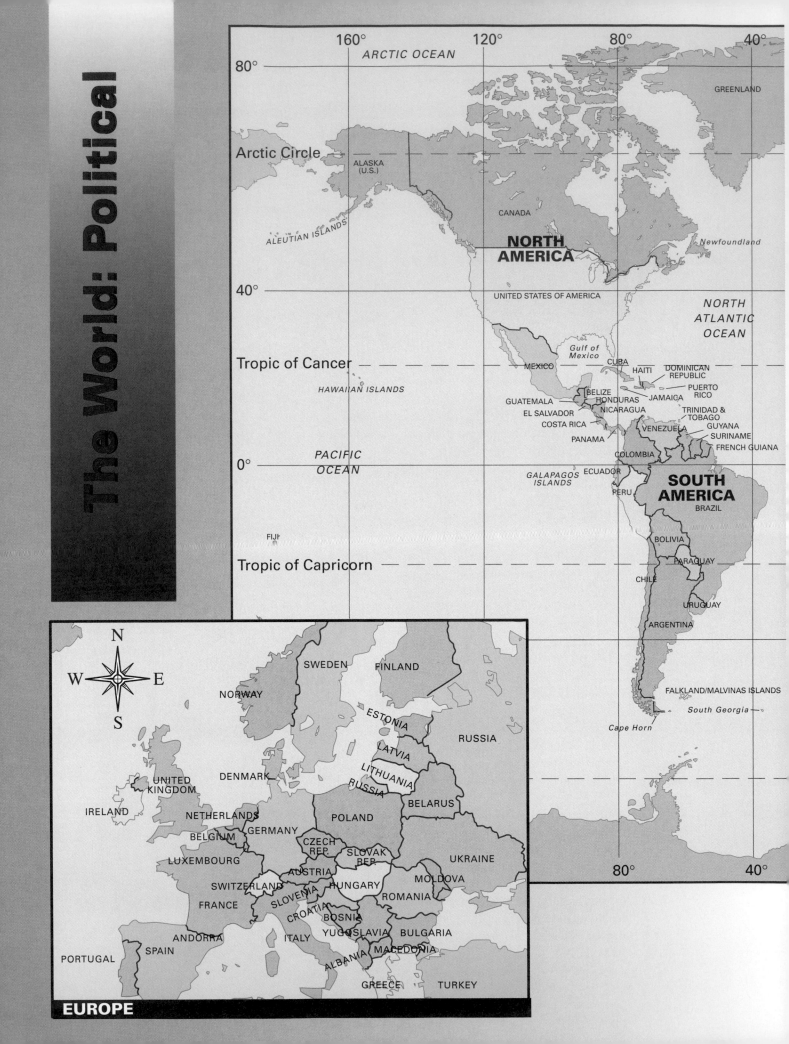

The World: Political

ARCTIC OCEAN

80°

Arctic Circle

GREENLAND

ALASKA
(U.S.)

ALEUTIAN ISLANDS

CANADA

**NORTH
AMERICA**

Newfoundland

40°

UNITED STATES OF AMERICA

NORTH
ATLANTIC
OCEAN

Tropic of Cancer

Gulf of
Mexico

MEXICO

CUBA

HAITI

DOMINICAN
REPUBLIC

PUERTO
RICO

HAWAIIAN ISLANDS

BELIZE

GUATEMALA

HONDURAS

JAMAICA

EL SALVADOR

NICARAGUA

TRINIDAD &
TOBAGO

COSTA RICA

VENEZUELA

GUYANA

SURINAME

PANAMA

FRENCH GUIANA

COLOMBIA

0°

PACIFIC
OCEAN

GALAPAGOS
ISLANDS

ECUADOR

PERU

**SOUTH
AMERICA**

BRAZIL

FIJI

BOLIVIA

PARAGUAY

Tropic of Capricorn

CHILE

URUGUAY

ARGENTINA

FALKLAND/MALVINAS ISLANDS

South Georgia

Cape Horn

80°

40°

EUROPE

N
W E
S

SWEDEN

FINLAND

NORWAY

ESTONIA

RUSSIA

LATVIA

LITHUANIA

DENMARK

RUSSIA

BELARUS

UNITED
KINGDOM

IRELAND

NETHERLANDS

POLAND

BELGIUM

GERMANY

CZECH
REP.

LUXEMBOURG

SLOVAK
REP.

UKRAINE

AUSTRIA

MOLDOVA

SWITZERLAND

HUNGARY

SLOVENIA

ROMANIA

FRANCE

CROATIA

BOSNIA

ANDORRA

ITALY

YUGOSLAVIA

BULGARIA

PORTUGAL

SPAIN

MACEDONIA

ALBANIA

GREECE

TURKEY

160°

120°

80°

40°

ARCTIC OCEAN

SVALBARD
ZEMLYA FRANTSA IOSIFA
SEVERNAYA ZEMLYA
ARCTIC OCEAN

0°   40°   80°   120°   160°

80°

Novaya Zemlya

ICELAND   Arctic Circle

Area of Inset

EUROPE   RUSSIA   ASIA

ALEUTIAN ISLANDS

KAZAKHSTAN

MONGOLIA

GEORGIA   40°
UZBEKISTAN   KYRGYZSTAN
ARMENIA   AZERBAIJAN   NORTH
TURKMENISTAN   TAJIKISTAN   KOREA
CYPRUS SYRIA   SOUTH   JAPAN
TUNISIA   LEBANON   AFGHANISTAN   KOREA
MOROCCO   ISRAEL IRAQ   IRAN   CHINA
CANARY   JORDAN
ISLANDS   ALGERIA   LIBYA   SAUDI   QATAR   PAKISTAN   NEPAL BHUTAN   Tropic of Cancer
WESTERN   EGYPT   ARABIA   U.A.E.   BANGLADESH   BURMA   PACIFIC
SAHARA   INDIA   TAIWAN   OCEAN
MAURITANIA   AFRICA   ERITREA   OMAN   LAOS
MALI   YEMEN   THAILAND   VIETNAM
SENEGAL   NIGER   CHAD   SUDAN   DJIBOUTI   CAMBODIA   PHILIPPINES
BURKINA   SRI
GUINEA   FASO   NIGERIA   CENTRAL   ETHIOPIA   LANKA   BRUNEI
SIERRA   IVORY   AFRICAN REPUBLIC   MALAYSIA
LEONE   COAST   CAMEROON   UGANDA   SOMALIA   0°
LIBERIA   GABON CONGO RWANDA   KENYA   EAST INDIES   MELANESIA
GHANA   REPUBLIC BURUNDI   PAPUA
GUINEA-BISSAU   TOGO   OF CONGO   TANZANIA   SINGAPORE   INDONESIA   NEW   SOLOMON
GAMBIA   BENIN   GUINEA ISLANDS
EQUATORIAL
GUINEA   ANGOLA   INDIAN
SOUTH   ZAMBIA   MALAWI   OCEAN
ATLANTIC   NAMIBIA ZIMBABWE MOZAMBIQUE   Coral Sea   VANUATU   FIJI
OCEAN   BOTSWANA   MADAGASCAR   MAURITIUS
                                    RÉUNION   AUSTRALIA   Tropic of Capricorn
                    SOUTH   SWAZILAND   AUSTRALIA
                    AFRICA LESOTHO

North I.
NEW
ZEALAND   40°
South I.

0   2000   4000 miles (at equator)

0   2000   4000   6000 kilometres (at equator)

Gall Projection

Antarctic Circle

ANTARCTICA

0°   40°   80°   120°   160°

The World: Physical

ARCTIC OCEAN

80°

160°   120°   80°   40°

Chukchi
Sea

Beaufort
Sea

Baffin
Bay

Arctic Circle

Mt. McKinley
20,320 ft.
(6,194 m)

Bering Sea

Gulf of
Alaska

Mt. Logan
19,524 ft.
(5,591 m)

Yukon

Mackenzie

Hudson
Bay

NORTH
AMERICA

Newfoundland

ALEUTIAN ISLANDS

Columbia

ROCKY MOUNTAINS

Missouri

Great Lakes

GREAT PLAINS

Mississippi

APPALACHIAN MTS.

40°

Mt. Whitney
14,494 ft.
(4,418 m)

Colorado

Rio Grande

Gulf of
Mexico

NORTH
ATLANTIC
OCEAN

Tropic of Cancer

HAWAIIAN ISLANDS

Citlaltepetl
18,701 ft.
(5,700 m)

YUCATAN
PENINSULA

WEST INDIES

Caribbean Sea

PACIFIC
OCEAN

0°

Orinoco

Guiana
Highlands

GALAPAGOS
ISLANDS

AMAZON   Amazon

BASIN

SOUTH
AMERICA

ANDES MOUNTAINS

São Francisco

Tropic of Capricorn

Brazilian
Highlands

Paraná

Mt. Aconcagua
22,831 ft.
(6,959 m)

40°

North I.

South I.

South Georgia

Cape Horn

Antarctic Circle

160°   120°   80°   40°

Lambert's equal-area projection

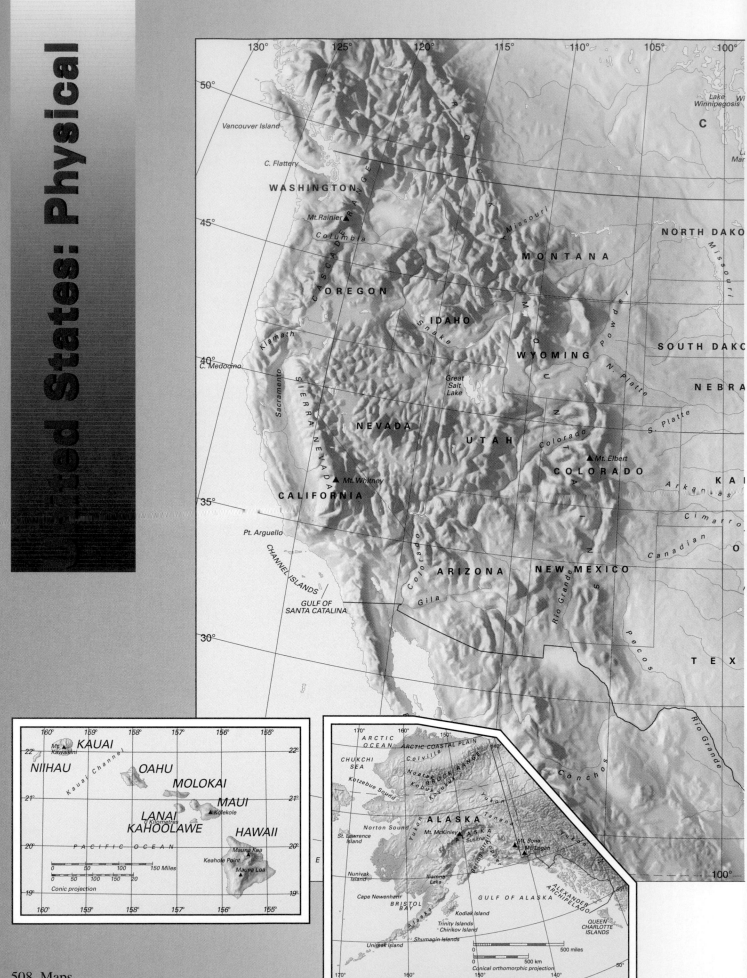

United States: Physical

508 Maps

A

abolitionists: people who favored abolition, the ending of slavery

adapt: to change in order to survive in a new or different environment or situation

AIDS: a disease marked by a weakening of the body's immune system, or its ability to fight off life-threatening illnesses

aliens: people who have come from other countries and are not yet citizens

ally: a nation that joins another nation in some common effort, such as winning a war

amendment: a change to the constitution

annex: To add a territory to a country. Such an addition is called an *annexation*.

anti-Semitism: Prejudice against Jews. The term comes from *Semite,* a word for ancient peoples of the Middle East, including the ancestors of modern Jews.

arms race: a competition to develop and manufacture more and more powerful weapons

arsenal: a place where weapons and ammunition are stored

Articles of Confederation: The first written plan of government for the United States. A "confederation" is an association of states who cooperate for common purpose.

assembly: an elected group of lawmakers

atomic bomb: an immensely powerful weapon whose violent energy comes from splitting the atom (the basic unit of matter)

B

baby boom: a large increase in the number of babies born in proportion to the size of a population

bicameral: Having two lawmaking parts. *Bicameral* comes from Latin words meaning "two rooms."

bill: a proposed law

Bill of Rights: a formal listing of the basic rights of citizens

bipolar: organized around two opposite extremes

bond: A government certificate that pays interest. Selling bonds is a way for the government to raise money temporarily for some public purpose.

boycott: To refuse to buy one or more goods from a certain source. An organized refusal by many people is also called a boycott.

C

capitalism: an economic system based on private ownership of farms and businesses

carpetbaggers: northerners who went to the South after the Civil War to gain money and political power

cash crops: crops, such as tobacco, sugar, and cotton, raised in large quantities in order to be sold for profit

checks and balances: the system that allows each branch of government to limit the powers of the other branches

civil rights: the rights that the Constitution entitles all people to as citizens, especially equal treatment under the law

civil servants: employees of the government

civil war: a war fought between the people of a single country

class: A part of society defined by such qualities as wealth, occupation, and inherited titles or honors. A society may have an upper class, a middle class, and a lower class.

Cold War: the global struggle for power and influence between the United States and the Soviet Union that followed World War II

colony: a new settlement or territory established and governed by a country in another land

communism: an economic system based on the idea that farms and businesses should be owned in common by the workers who do the labor

compromise: an agreement in which both sides in a dispute agree to give up something they want in order to achieve a settlement

Confederacy: the independent country declared by 11 southern states, who called themselves the Confederate States of America

conquistadors: Spanish soldier-explorers, especially those who conquered the native peoples of Mexico and Peru

constitution: a written plan that provides the basic framework of a government

consumer goods: products intended for personal use by consumers, such as cars, refrigerators, and vacuum cleaners

containment: the U.S. policy of fighting the spread of communism by limiting it to countries where it already existed

converts: people who accept a new religion

corporation: a business that is owned by many investors

cotton gin: a hand-operated machine that cleans seeds and other unwanted material from cotton

counterculture: a way of life that runs counter to (against) society's traditional culture

credit: an arrangement in which a seller trusts a buyer to repay part of an item's purchase price over time

cultural region: an area in which a group of people share a similar culture and language

culture: a people's way of life, including beliefs, customs, food, dwellings, and clothing

D

D-day: a day specified for launching an operation, such as the Allied invasion of Normandy

Declaration of Sentiments: A formal statement of injustices suffered by women, written by the organizers of the Seneca Falls convention. *Sentiments* means "beliefs" or "convictions."

defendants: people who are required to defend themselves in a legal action; an example is an accused person who is put on trial for a crime

democratic: Ruled by the people. In a democracy, citizens elect representatives to make and carry out laws.

depression: a period of low economic activity and high unemployment

dictator: a ruler who has absolute power

diplomacy: The art of conducting negotiations with other countries. People who engage in diplomacy are called *diplomats*.

discrimination: unequal treatment based on a person's race, gender, religion, place of birth, or other arbitrary characteristic

doctrine: a statement of official government policy, especially in foreign affairs

draft: a system for requiring citizens to join their country's armed forces

E

Electoral College: The group established by the Constitution to elect the president and vice president. Voters in each state choose their electors.

emancipation: the act of freeing people from slavery

embargo: a government order that stops merchant ships from leaving or entering a country's ports

environment: all of the physical surroundings in a place, including land, water, animals, plants, and climate

environmentalists: people who are actively concerned with protecting the environment

executive branch: the part of government that "executes" (carries out) the laws

expansionists: Americans who favored extending the United States' power by taking control of new territories

F

federalism: the constitutional system that shares power between the national and state governments

feminists: people who are actively concerned with achieving social, political, and economic equality for women

First Great Awakening: a revival of religious feeling and belief in the American colonies that began in the 1730s

foreign policy: guidelines for how a country handles political and economic interactions with other countries

forty-niners: the people (almost all young men) who joined the rush for gold in California in 1849

freedmen: African Americans who had been set free from slavery

fugitive: a person who flees or tries to escape (for example, from slavery)

G

guerrillas: soldiers who operate on their own and are not part of a regular army

H

habeas corpus: a written order from a court that gives a person the right to a trial before being jailed

heritage: the traditional beliefs, values, and customs of a family or country

Holocaust: the mass murder of European Jews and other victims by Adolf Hitler and his followers

homestead: a plot of land where pioneers could build a home, farm, or ranch

homesteader: a farmer who is given a plot of public land (called a *homestead*) in return for cultivating it

I

immigrant: A person who moves from one country to live in another. Such a movement is called *immigration*.

impeach: to formally accuse an official of a crime related to official duties

imperialism: the policy of extending a nation's power by gaining political and economic control over other countries

inauguration: a formal ceremony to mark the beginning of something, such as a president's term of office

indentured servant: A person who signed an indenture, or an agreement to work for a master for a period of years. Indentured servants were not free until they completed their term of service.

independence: freedom from control by another government or country

Industrial Revolution: The dramatic change in economies brought about by the use of machines to do work formerly done by hand. The Industrial Revolution began in England in the late 1700s and spread to America and the rest of Europe.

industrialization: the birth and growth of businesses that make and distribute products through the use of machinery

inflation: An increase in the amount of money in circulation, compared to the goods available for purchase. Inflation reduces the value of money and causes prices to rise.

integration: the blending of all people as equals; the opposite of segregation

Internet: a network that allows computers in locations around the world to share information

internment camps: places where people are forcibly confined

irrigation: a system for bringing water to farmland by artificial means, such as using a dam to trap water and ditches to channel it to fields

isolationism: a policy of avoiding political or military agreements with other countries; first established by George Washington

J

Jim Crow laws: Laws enforcing segregation of blacks and whites in the South after the Civil War. "Jim Crow" was a black character in an entertainer's act in the mid-1800s.

judicial branch: the part of government, consisting of the Supreme Court and lower federal courts, that interprets the laws

L

legislative branch: The lawmaking part of government, called the *legislature*. To *legislate* is to make a law.

Loyalists: American colonists who were loyal to the British government

M

Manifest Destiny: the belief that it was America's right and duty to spread across the North American continent

mercenaries: professional soldiers who fight for anyone who will pay them

migrate: To move from one place and establish a home in a new place. A move of a large number of people is called a *migration,* and the people are called *migrants*. Some animals are also said to migrate, usually with the seasons.

militarism: a policy of glorifying military power and military ideas and values

militia: a small army made up of ordinary citizens who are available to fight in an emergency

mission: A place established by missionaries for their work. A typical California mission included such things as a church, a residence, workshops, and large areas of land for raising crops.

missionaries: people who travel to a territory or community in order to make converts to their religion

monopoly: a company that controls all production and sales of a particular product or service

Mormons: Members of the Church of Jesus Christ of Latter-Day Saints. "Latter-day" means "modern," while "saints" are people who dedicate their lives to following God's teachings.

N

nationalism: devotion to a national or ethnic identity, including the desire for independence from rule by foreign countries

natural resources: useful materials found in nature, including water, vegetation, animals, and minerals

neutrality: a policy of not choosing sides in a war or dispute between other countries

New Deal: the set of programs adopted under the Roosevelt administration to combat the Great Depression of the 1930s

New World: The European name for the Americas. These continents were a "new" world for the Europeans, but not for the native peoples who lived there.

non-aligned nations: countries that refused to side with either the United States or the Soviet Union during the Cold War

nullify: To refuse to recognize a federal law. This action by a state is called *nullification*.

O

oppression: the feeling of being weighed down or held back by severe and unfair forces

Oregon Trail: an overland route that stretched about 2,000 miles from Independence, Missouri, to the Columbia River in Oregon

P

Parliament: the lawmaking body of England, consisting of representatives from throughout the kingdom

party: an organized political group

passport: a document issued by a citizen's home government that identifies a person and permits him or her to travel to other countries

Patriots: American colonists who believed that the colonies had the right to govern themselves

pension: a sum of money paid to a retired person, usually on a monthly basis

petition (noun): a formal, written request

petition (verb): to make a formal demand or request

plantation: a large area of privately owned land where crops were grown through the labor of workers, usually slaves, who lived on the land

pogroms: Organized and often violent persecutions of minority groups. The word *pogrom* comes from Russian words meaning "like thunder."

popular sovereignty: the idea that the authority of government comes from the people

Progressive movement: a political reform effort of the early 1900s that focused on improving American life by fighting for such causes as equal rights, better working conditions, and protection of wilderness areas

Prohibition: A ban on the production, sale, and transport of alcoholic beverages under the Eighteenth Amendment. The amendment was repealed in 1933.

proxy wars: wars in which the superpowers backed different sides that acted as substitutes (proxies) for the superpowers themselves

public schools: schools that are paid for by taxes and managed by local government for the benefit of the general public

Puritans: People who wanted to "purify" the English Church. Puritans wanted to simplify the Church's ceremonies and its ranks of authority.

Q

quota: a limit based on numbers or proportions—for example, the proportion of a country's population allowed to immigrate to the United States

R

racism: prejudice based on race

rancho: A grant of land made by the Mexican government. Most ranchos were used for raising cattle and crops.

ratify: To formally approve a plan or an agreement. The process of approval is called *ratification*.

Reconstruction: the period after the Civil War when the federal government ruled the southern states in order to rebuild them and allow them back into the Union

reformers: people who work to correct failings or injustices

refugees: people who flee their homes or countries because of war, persecution, or other causes

regulation: the enforcement of laws that control conduct or practices; government regulations control the way goods, food, and drugs are produced and sold to the public

reparations: debts imposed on a defeated nation to pay for the harm done during a war

repeal: to take back, or to cancel, a law

republic: a country governed by elected representatives

reservation: An area of land set aside ("reserved") by the government for Native Americans. Reservations generally were on poor land that settlers didn't want.

Revolutionary War: The struggle of the former British colonies in America to gain their independence from Britain. Also called the War for Independence or the American Revolution.

rights: powers or privileges that belong to people as citizens and that cannot or should not be taken away by the government

S

scalawags: white southerners who supported the federal government after the Civil War

secede: to withdraw from an organization or alliance; in this case, to withdraw from the United States

secession: the act of withdrawing from an organization or alliance, such as the withdrawal of the southern states from the Union

Second Great Awakening: A revival of religious feeling and belief in the 1820s and 1830s. The First Great Awakening swept through the American colonies in the 1700s.

secretary of state: The head of the State Department, who oversees matters relating to foreign countries. The secretary of state is an important member of the president's cabinet.

sedition: the crime of encouraging rebellion against the government

segregation: the social separation of groups of people, especially by race

self-incrimination: the act of giving testimony that can be used against oneself

self-made: achieving wealth or influence through one's own effort rather than being born to a privileged family

sit-in: a form of peaceful protest in which people occupied seats in a segregated facility

slavery: The treatment of people as property for the purpose of forcing them to do labor. People who are denied freedom in this way are called *slaves* and are said to be *enslaved*.

slave trade: the business of capturing, transporting, and selling people as slaves

Social Darwinism: the idea that people and societies compete for survival, with the fit becoming wealthy and successful while the weak struggle to survive

spoils system: the practice of rewarding political supporters with government jobs

states' rights: All rights kept by the states under the Constitution. Supporters of states' rights sometimes argued that states were not obliged to honor federal laws that they believed violated the Constitution.

strategy: An overall plan (for example, for winning a war). Specific ways of carrying out a strategy are called *tactics*.

suffrage: the right to vote

T

tariff: a tax imposed by the government on goods imported from another country

tenement buildings: crowded and usually run-down buildings with many small, cheap apartments

territory: A region designated by Congress and organized under a governor. A territory may apply to become a state when it has a large enough population.

trade unions: early labor organizations that brought together workers in the same trade, or job, to fight for better wages and working conditions

tradition: a belief, custom, or way of doing something that has existed for a long time

traitor: person guilty of the crime of treason, or disloyalty to the government

transcontinental railroad: a railroad that crosses a continent (*trans* means "across")

trappers: adventurers who capture and kill animals, such as beavers, for their fur

treaty: a formal agreement between nations

trust: a group of corporations that unite in order to reduce competition and control prices in a business or industry

tyranny: The unjust use of government power. A ruler who uses power in this way is called a *tyrant*.

the Union: The United States as one country, united under a single government. During the Civil War, "the Union" came to mean the government and armies of the North.

U

urbanization: the growth of cities

V

veto: To reject a proposed law, or a bill. Only the president can veto bills.

visas: government documents that allow people from other nations to enter the country for a limited period of time

W

warrant: an order from a judge that authorizes police or other officials to take a certain action, such as searching someone's property

well-born: born to an upper-class (wealthy, respected) family

Y

yellow journalism: the practice of publishing sensational and often exaggerated news stories in order to attract readers

Index

Teal words are defined in the Glossary; page numbers in italics indicate word definitions; an "m" following a page number indicates a map.

Abenaki

Bering Strait

Acknowledgments

Table of Contents
vi, Petroleum Museum/Abell-Hanger Foundation; vi, Massachusetts Historical Society; vi, The Granger Collection, New York; vi, Corbis; vii, Library of Congress; vii, The Granger Collection, New York; vii, The Granger Collection, New York; vii, The Granger Collection, New York; vii, Randy Well/Stone; viii, Library of Congress; viii, The Granger Collection, New York; viii, Library of Congress; viii, Library of Congress; ix, The Granger Collection, New York; ix, Library of Congress; ix, Detail from *Westward the Course of Empire Takes its Way* 1861 by Emanuel G. Leutze/National Museum of American Art, Washington DC/Art Resource, NY; ix, Arizona Historical Society, Tuscon; x, Library of Congress; x, Detail from *Harriet Powers Quilt*/National Museum of American History/Smithsonian Institution; x, Library of Congress; x, Medford Historical Society Collection/Corbis; x, The Granger Collection, New York; x, The Granger Collection, New York; xi, UNITE Archives, Kheel Center Cornell University, Ithaca NY; xi, The Granger Collection, New York; xi, Corbis; xii, The Granger Collection, New York; xii, Corbis; xii, Library of Congress; xii, Library of Congress; xiii, Matt Herron/Take Sk; xiii, Library of Congress; xiii, Library of Congress; xiii, Charles Gupton/The Sk Market;

Chapter 1
xiv, Petroleum Museum/Abell-Hanger Foundation; 03,Corbis; 06, *She Walks With Spirits* by Merlin Little Thunder/Oklahoma Indian Art Gallery; 07, Thomas Kitchin/Tom Stack & Associates; 08, Dennis Flaherty/Photo Researchers Inc.; 09, © David Muench 2000; 10, © David Jensen 2000; 11, © David Muench 2000; 2, Dale O'Dell/The Stock Market; 13, © David Muench 2000; 14, Adam Jones/Photo Researchers Inc.; 15, Library of Congress

Chapter 2
16, Corbis; 18, Library of Congress; 19, The Granger Collection, New York 20, The Granger Collection, New York; 22, The Granger Collection, New York; 23, Corbis; 24, Mission at San Carlos del Rio Carmelo by Oriana Day/The Fine Arts Museum of San Francisco, Gift of Eleanor Martin, 37566; 25, New York Public Library, Rare Book Division; 26, Library of Congress; 27, The Granger Collection, New York; 28, The Granger Collection, New York; 29, National Portrait Gallery, Smithsonian Institution/Art Resource; 30, The Granger Collection, New York; 31, The Granger Collection, New York; 33, The Granger Collection, New York

Chapter 3
34, The Granger Collection, New York; 34, Tockwotton From Fort Hill, by Kinsley Gladding/ Oil on canvas, Rhode Island Historical Society (RHIx4111); 34, The Granger Collection, New York; 37, Library of Congress; 38, Tim Wright/Corbis; 39, North Wind Pictures; 40, North Wind Pictures; 41, Corbis; 42, North Wind Pictures; 43, The Granger Collection, New York; 44, The Granger Collection, New York; 45, The Granger Collection, New York; 46, The Granger Collection, New York; 47, Bettmann/Corbis

Chapter 4
48, Massachusetts Historical Society; 50, Library of Congress; 51, North Wind Pictures; 52, The Granger Collection, New York; 53, The Granger Collection, New York; 54, Corbis; 55, The Granger Collection, New York; 56, Library of Congress; 57, The Granger Collection, New York; 58, North Wind Pictures; 59, The Granger Collection, New York; 59, Library of Congress; 60, The Granger Collection, New York; 61, The Granger Collection, New York

Chapter 5
62, Library of Congress; 64, Corbis; 65, The Granger Collection, New York; 67, Massachusetts Historical Society; 67, North Wind Pictures; 68, H. F. du Pont Winterthur Museum; 69, Library of Congress; 70, Library of Congress; 71, The Granger Collection, New York; 72, Library of Congress; 73, Corbis; 74-75, The Connecticut Historical Society, Hartford, Connecticut; 76, The Connecticut Historical Society, Hartford, Connecticut; 76, Photri Inc.; 77, The Granger Collection, New York

Chapter 6
78, The Granger Collection, New York; 80, The Granger Collection, New York; 81, Library of Congress; 82, Library of Congress; 83, Library of Congress; 85, Library of Congress

Chapter 7
86, The Granger Collection, New York; 86, Library of Congress; 88, Archive Photos/Hulton Getty Picture Library; 89, The Granger Collection, New York; 90, Archive Photos/Hulton Getty Picture Library; 91, The Connecticut Historical Society, Hartford, Connecticut; 92, Library of Congress; 93, The Granger Collection, New York; 94, The Granger Collection, New York; 95, The Granger Collection, New York; 96, The Granger Collection, New York; 97, The Granger Collection, New York; 100, Winterthur Museum; 101, The Granger Collection, New York

Chapter 8
102, The Granger Collection, New York; 104, The Granger Collection, New York; 105, The Granger Collection, New York; 106, The Granger Collection, New York; 107, Library of Congress; 108, The Granger Collection, New York; 108, The Granger Collection, New York; 108, The Granger Collection, New York; 110, Library of Congress; 112, Abby Aldrich Rockefeller Fold Art Museum, Williamsburg, VA -accession number 1978.301.1; 113, *Village Tavern* (1954.13) by John Lewis Krimmel/1813-14, oil on canvas, 16 7/8 x 22 1/2 in. Toledo Museum of Art, Purchased with funds from the Florence Scott Libbey Bequest in Memory of her Father, Maurice A. Scott; 114, U. S. Senate Legislative Collections; 115, Library of Congress; 116, Library of Congress; 117, Independence National Historical Park

Chapter 9
118, Randy Well/Stone; 118, Peter Gridley/FPG; 118, Bob Burch/Bruce Coleman Inc.; 120, The Library Company of Philadelphia; 121, Terry Ashe/Liaison; 122-123, Sipa Press; 125, Brad Markel/Liaison; 126, Randy Well/Stone; 126, Peter Gridley/FPG; 126, Bob Burch/Bruce Coleman Inc.; 128, Library of Congress; 129, The Granger Collection, New York

Chapter 10
130, Library of Congress; 132, Library of Congress; 133, Ted Streshinsky/Photo 20-20; 134, AP/Wide World Photos; 135, AP/Wide World Photos; 136, The Granger Collection, New York; 137, Rob Crandall/Rainbow; 138, Corbis; 139, John Neubauer/Rainbow; 140, Universal Press Syndicate; 141, Kevin Fleming/Corbis

Chapter 11
142, The Granger Collection, New York; 144, Library of Congress; 145, The Granger Collection, New York; 146, The Granger Collection, New York; 147, Library of Congress; 148, Bettmann/Corbis; 149, Library of Congress; 150, Kirby Collection of Historical Paintings, Lafayette College, Easton, Pennsylvania; 151, The Granger Collection, New York; 152, The Granger Collection, New York; 153, The Granger Collection, New York; 154, The Granger Collection, New York; 155, The Granger Collection, New York; 155, The Granger Collection, New York; 156, The Granger Collection, New York; 157, Library of Congress; 157, The Granger Collection, New York

Chapter 12
158, Library of Congress; 161, Laurie Platt Winfrey Inc./Woodfin Camp and Associates; 162, The Granger Collection, New York; 163, The Granger Collection, New York; 165, The New-York Historical Society; 166, The Granger Collection, New York; 167, Library of Congress; 168, The Granger Collection, New York; 169, Swalkwijk/Art Resource, New York; 170, The Granger Collection, New York; 171, The Henry Francis du Pont Winterthur Museum

Chapter 13
172, Library of Congress; 172, The Granger Collection, New York; 174, Stephen J. Krasemann/DRK Photo; 175, Stephen G. Maka/DRK Photo; 176, The Granger Collection, New York; 177, Corbis; 178-179, Corbis; 180, Museum of Art, Rhode Island School of Design/Mary B. Jackson Fund; 181, Library of Congress; 184, The Granger Collection, New York; 185, The Granger Collection, New York; 186, The Granger Collection, New York; 187, The Granger Collection, New York

Chapter 14
188, The Granger Collection, New York, 190, Library of Congress; 191, George Lepp/Corbis; 192, Library of Congress; 192, The New-York Historical Society; 193, The Granger Collection; New York; 194, Unknown/Check book; 195, Library of Congress; 196, Library of Congress; 197, The Granger Collection, New York; 199, Library of Congress

Chapter 15
200, Library of Congress; 202, Library of Congress; 203, The Granger Collection, New York; 204, Corbis; 205, Texas State Library; 206, Friends of the Governor's Mansion, Austin; 207, Collection of the Star of the Republic Museum, Washington, Texas; 208, Scotts Bluff National Monument; 210, Amon Carter Museum, Fort Worth, Texas; 211, The Granger Collection, New York; 213, National Cowboy Hall of Fame

Chapter 16
214, *Westward the Course of Empire Takes its Way 1861* by Emanuel G. Leutze/National Museum of American Art, Washington, DC/Art Resource, NY; 216, Independence National Historical Park Collection; 216, Independence National Historical Park Collection; 217, Montana Historical Society/Photo by Don Beatty; 220, Seaver Center for Western History Research/Natural History Museum of Los Angeles County; 221, The Granger Collection, New York; 222, *Trappers at Fault - Looking for the Trail.* By Arthur Fitzwilliam Tait, The Anschutz Collection; 223, Corbis; 224, Oregon Historical Society; 224, Oregon Historical Society; 225, The Granger Collection, New York; 226, The Granger Collection, New York; 227, *Handcart Pioneers, 1900* by C. C. A. Christensen/Museum of Church History and Art; 228, *Miners in the Sierras* by Charles Christian

Nahl/National Museum of American Art, Washington, DC/Art Resource, NY; **229**, California State Library; **230**, Corbis; **231**, Library of Congress; **219**, Library of Congress; **219**, Library of Congress; **219**, The Granger Collection, New York; **219**, Library of Congress; **219**, Thomas Gilcrease Institute; **219**, The Granger Collection, New York

Chapter 17
232, Arizona Historical Society, Tuscon; **234**, Arizona Historical Society, AHS#14546; **235**, Bancroft Library, University of California, Berkeley; **236**, *California Vaqueros* painting by James Walker/The Anschutz Collection; **237**, *Mission San Gabriel Arcangel* by Oriana Day/Fine Arts Museums of San Francisco/Gift of Eleanor Martin, DY37556; **238**, Arizona Historical Society, AHS#3767; **239**, *Mariana Coronel Grinding Corn* by A. Harmer/Seaver Center for Western History Research, Los Angeles County Museum of Natural History; **240**, David Muench Photography; **241**, Seaver Center for Western History Research, Los Angeles County Museum of Natural History; **242**, The Granger Collection, New York; **243**, Stone/Hulton Getty Collection

Chapter 18
244, Library of Congress; **246**, The Granger Collection, New York; **247**, Corbis; **248**, The Granger Collection, New York; **249**, The Granger Collection, New York; **250**, State Archives of Michigan; **251**, Library of Congress; **252**, *Pic Nick Camden Maine* by Jerome B. Thompson/Museum of Fine Arts, Boston. Gift of Maxim Karolik for the M and M Karolik Collection of Anmerican Paintings, 1815-1865.; **253**, Bettmann/Corbis; **254**, Corbis; **254**, The Schlesinger Library/Radcliffe Institute; **255**, AP/Wide World Photos; **255**, AP/Wide World Photos

Chapter 19
256, Museum of Fine Arts, Boston; **256**, Bettmann/Corbis; **258**, The Granger Collection, New York; **259**, The Granger Collection, New York; **260**, Bettmann/Corbis; **262**, Bettmann/Corbis; **263**, Library of Congress; **264**, Library of Congress; **265**, The Granger Collection, New York; **266**, The Library of Congress; **267**, Library of Congress; **268**, North Carolina Museum of Art; **269**, National Museum of American History/Smithsonian Institution; **270**, The Granger Collection, New York; **271**, Library of Congress

Chapter 20
272, Library of Congress; **272**, Bettmann/Corbis; **275**, The Granger Collection, New York; **277**, Bettmann/Corbis; **278**, Corbis; **280**, The Granger Collection, New York; **281**, Library of Congress; **283**, The Granger Collection, New York; **285**, Library of Congress; **286**, The Granger Collection, New York; **287**, Tim Wright/Corbis; **288**, The Granger Collection, New York; **289**, The Granger Collection, New York; **284**, The Granger Collection, New York

Chapter 21
290, Medford Historical Society Collection/Corbis; **290**, Corbis; **292**, The Granger Collection, New York; **293**, Library of Congress; **294**, Library of Congress; **296**, Brown Brothers; **296**, National Archives; **297**, Library of Congress; **298**, Corbis; **299**, Corbis; **300**, Library of Congress; **301**, Library of Congress; **302**, Library of Congress; **303**, The Granger Collection, New York; **304**, The Granger Collection, New York; **305**, *Attack on Battery Wagner* by Tom Lovell/The Greenwich

Workshop Press; **306**, Library of Congress; **307**, Library of Congress; **308**, Tom Lovell/National Geographic Image Collection; **309**, Library of Congress

Chapter 22
310, The Granger Collection, New York; **312**, Library of Congress; **313**, The Granger Collection, New York; **315**, Brown Brothers; **316**, Library of Congress; **317**, Archive Photos; **318**, The Granger Collection, New York; **319**, Library of Congress; **320**, The Granger Collection, New York; **321**, The Granger Collection, New York; **322**, Library of Congress; **323**, The Granger Collection, New York;

Chapter 23
324, The Granger Collection, New York; **326**, David Jensen; **327**, Bettmann/Corbis; **328**, *Fort Laramie* by A. J. Miller/ Beinecke Rare Book and Manuscript Library. Western Americana Collection, Yale University; **329**, The Granger Collection, New York; **330**, North Wind Pictures; **331**, Colorado Historical Society; **332**, Library of Congress; **333**, The Granger Collection, New York; **334**, The Granger Collection, New York; **335**, Bettmann/Corbis; **337**, Corbis; **338**, The Granger Collection, New York; **339**, The Granger Collection, New York

Chapter 24
340, UNITE Archives, Kheel Center Cornell University, Ithaca NY; **342**, The Granger Collection, New York; **343**, *Broadway and Maiden Lane*, lithograph by J. J. Fogerty/The New-York Historical Society; **344**, Library of Congress; **345**, Library of Congress; **346**, Library of Congress; **347**, Brown Brothers; **348**, Bettmann/Corbis; **350**, Library of Congress; **351**, Bettmann/Corbis; **352**, The Granger Collection, New York; **353**, Brown Brthers; **354**, UNITE Archives, Kheel Center Cornell University, Ithaca NY; **355**, UNITE Archives, Kheel Center Cornell University, Ithaca, NY

Chapter 25
356, The Granger Collection, New York; **358**, Cobris; **360**, Library of Congress; **361**, Library of Congress; **362**, Culver Pictures; **363**, Brown Brothers; **364**, Philip Gould/Corbis; **365**, Corbis; **366**, Bettmann/Corbis; **367**, Arizona Historical Society, Negative #64323; **368**, The Granger Collection, New York; **369**, Corbis

Chapter 26
370, Corbis; **372**, The Granger Collection, New York; **373**, Library of Congress; **374**, The Granger Collection, New York; **375**, Photo Courtesy of The Newberry Library, Chicago; **376**, The Library of Congress; **377**, The Library of Congress; **378**, The Library of Congress; **379**, Corbis; **380**, The Library of Congress; **381**, The Library of Congress; **381**, The Library of Congress; **381**, The Library of Congress

Chapter 27
382, The Granger Collection, New York; **384**, The Granger Collection, New York; **385**, Bettmann/Corbis; **386**, The Granger Collection, New York; **387**, The Granger Collection, New York; **388**, Brown Brothers; **389**, The Granger Collection, New York; **390**, Brown Brothers; **392**, Culver Pictures; **393**, Archive Photos/Hulton Getty Collection; **394**, The Granger Collection, New York; **395**, Library of Congress; **396**, Library of Congress; **397**, *The Signing of Peace in the Hall of Mirrors*, Versailles, 28th June, 1919 by Sir William Orpen/Imperial War Museum, London; **398**, Library of Congress; **399**, Bettmann/Corbis

Chapter 28
400, Corbis; **402**, Library of Congress; **403**, Corbis; **404**, Library of Congress; **405**, Brown Brothers; **407**, Corbis; **408**, Archive Photos; **409**, Library of Congress; **410**, Library of Congress; **411**, Corbis; **413**, Library of Congress; **414**, Libary of Congress; **415**, FDR Library Hyde Park, New York

Chapter 29
416, Library of Congress; **418**, Library of Congress; **419**, The Library of Congress; **420**, Library of Congress; **422**, UPI/Corbis; **423**, Library of Congress; **425**, National Museum of American History, Artist: Montgomery Melbourne, cat. 1984.0473.058, 22by28, SI# 97-8788; **426**, Library of Congress; **427**, Library of Congress; **428**, Library of Congress; **429**, National Archives; **430**, Library of Congress; **431**, Library of Congress; **432**, Library of Congress; **433**, Bettmann/Corbis

Chapter 30
434, Library of Congress; **436**, Bettmann/Corbis; **437**, Library of Congress; **438**, Bettmann/Corbis; **439**, Corbis; **440**, Library of Congress; **442**, Library of Congress; **443**, Corbis; **444**, AP/Wide World; **445**, Joseph Sohm-ChromoSohm Inc./Corbis **448**, Owen Franken/Corbis; **449**, Archive Photos

Chapter 31
450, Matt Herron/Take Stock; **452**, Library of Congress; **453**, National Archives; **454**, Bettmann/Corbis; **455**, New York Public Library Astor, Lenox and Tilden Foundations.; **456**, Library of Congress; **457**, New York Public Library Astor, Lenox and Tilden Foundations; **458**, New York Public Library Astor, Lenox and Tilden Foundations; **459**, Bettmann/Corbis; **460**, AP/Wide World Photos; **461**, Bettmann/Corbis; **462**, Library of Congress; **463**, Library of Congress; **464**, Neal Preston/Corbis; **465**, AP/Wide World Photos

Chapter 32
466, Library of Congress; **466**, Library of Congress; **466**, Charles Gupton/The Stock Market; **468**, Archive Photos; **469**, Library of Congress; **470**, Bettmann/Corbis; **471**, Leif Skoogfors/Corbis; **473**, Herblock Cartoon; **474**, Ronald Reagan Library/Corbis; **475**, Reuters/Giroux/Archive Photos; **476**, Corbis; **477**, Reuters/Kai Pfaffenbach/Archive Photos; **478**, NASA; **479**, Bill Losh/FPG